S0-AIG-133

Owls—they whinny down the night;
    Bats go zigzag by.
Ambushed in shadow beyond sight
    The outlaws lie.

Old gods, tamed to silence, there
    In the wet woods they lurk,
Greedy of human stuff to snare
    In nets of murk.

Look up, else your eye will drown
    In a moving sea of black;
Between the tree-tops, upside down,
    Goes the sky-track.

Look up, else your feet will stray
    Into that ambuscade
Where spider-like they trap their prey
    With webs of shade.

For though creeds whirl away in dust,
    Faith dies and men forget,
These aged gods of power and lust
    Cling to life yet—

Old gods almost dead, malign,
    Starving for unpaid dues:
Incense and fire, salt, blood and wine
    And a drumming muse,

Banished to woods and a sickly moon,
    Shrunk to mere bogey things,
Who spoke with thunder once at noon
    To prostrate kings:

With thunder from an open sky
    To warrior, virgin, priest,
Bowing in fear with a dazzled eye
    Toward the dread East—

Proud gods, humbled, sunk so low,
    Living with ghosts and ghouls,
And ghosts of ghosts and last year's snow
    And dead toadstools.

              Robert Graves, "Outlaws"

Also by Stephen Davis:

Hammer of the Gods

Walk This Way

Reggae Bloodlines

Reggae International

Bob Marley

Say Kids! What Time Is It?

Moonwalk

Fleetwood

This Wheel's on Fire

Jajouka Rolling Stone

Old gods

almost dead

The 40-Year Odyssey of the Rolling Stones

STEPHEN DAVIS

Broadway Books New York

BROADWAY

A hardcover edition of this book was published in 2001 by Broadway Books.

OLD GODS ALMOST DEAD. Copyright © 2001 by Stephen Davis. All rights reserved. No part of this book may be reproduced or transmitted in any form or by any means, electronic or mechanical, including photocopying, recording, or by any information storage and retrieval system, without written permission from the publisher. For information, address Broadway Books, a division of Random House, Inc., 1540 Broadway, New York, NY 10036.

Broadway Books titles may be purchased for business or promotional use or for special sales. For information, please write to: Special Markets Department, Random House, Inc., 1540 Broadway, New York, NY 10036.

PRINTED IN THE UNITED STATES OF AMERICA

BROADWAY BOOKS and its logo, a letter B bisected on the diagonal, are trademarks of Broadway Books, a division of Random House, Inc.

Visit our website at www.broadwaybooks.com

First trade paperback edition published 2002

Book design by Maria Carella
Background photograph of sandstone is courtesy Corbis Royalty-free Images

The Library of Congress has cataloged the hardcover edition as follows:

Davis, Stephen.
    Old gods almost dead: the 40-year odyssey of the Rolling
    Stones / Stephen Davis.—1st ed.
        p. cm.
    Includes bibliographical references.
    1. Rolling Stones. 2. Rock musicians—England—Biography.
    I. Title.
    ML421.R64 D36 2001
    782.42166'092'2—dc21
    [B]   2001035683

ISBN 0-7679-0313-7
10 9 8 7 6 5 4 3 2 1

For Stu Werbin and Bob Palmer

In memoriam

Contents

The Difference

Our source was sitting in the sun on the terrace of a café in London's Notting Hill on a recent spring afternoon. She's a sophisticated Scots pixie in her fifties, wearing her white hair cropped short and no makeup, in cool black clothes with Berber silver and coral on her wrists and ears. She worked for the Rolling Stones for years and still has their home phone numbers in her book. She knows everything and everyone—the wives, ex-wives, old ladies, kids, even the grandchildren. She knows where they buried the bodies, at least some of them.

"There is this continental divide between Mick on one side, and Keith and Ronnie on the other," she says. "And nobody—no one—can cross that invisible line and be mates with both sides. They are in separate universes. Anyone who works for the Stones and even tries... You don't get called for the next tour. You're over, baby. Dead meat. You can't imagine what that feels like. You haven't experienced rejection until you've been rejected by the Rolling Stones.

"There's an old saying among those who have known the Stones a long time. It's that Mick wants to be Keith, and they all want to be Charlie. Why Charlie? Because he's genuinely hip, he's got innate good taste, and understands restraint. Charlie kept his family together, and he never got off on the star trip that the rest of them did. He's just Charlie Watts, and when the job's over, he goes home and feeds his horses.

"But there's a wall between Mick and Keith, forty years after they started that band, and no one gets through it. Anyone who tries to bridge that gap—forget it. You don't stand a chance in hell."

Dionysus Is in the House

July 1962, London. Cross busy Oxford Street to enter the neon world of Soho, with its strip clubs, peep shows, coffee bars, Italian restaurants, and basement music clubs. The narrow streets are full of night people and tourists, garish women, touts luring people into clubs with clever cockney street raps. The smell of espresso is in the air, the smell of sex, the smell of suicide. It is a desperately lively world—the tawdry nightlife of a central London still scarred by World War II bomb damage.

Outside the Marquee, a basement club on Oxford Street, a small mob of kids can't get down the crowded stairs. Up the steps throbs some crude-sounding, powerful rock and roll music, crisp and black. Drum and bass back up a pounding boogie piano and wailing harmonica. A voice drawls Chicago blues with an American accent. It's the public debut of a new West London band who call themselves the Rollin' Stones.

Two years later, and they've spilled across the Atlantic. Five shaggy, shadowy young men stare out from the viscerally jarring sleeve of *England's Newest Hitmakers,* their first American album. Unlike the tidy and cheeky Beatles, the sullen Rolling Stones look medieval, saw-toothed and weird, like something out of time. Like characters in an old saga. And the music: the Stones play hard-hearted, funky anthems—"The Last Time," "It's All Over Now"—the polar opposites of the familiar pop love songs of the time. Mick Jagger's loose lips, indecently long hair, sharp clothes, and blatant insolence seem even more important than the music. Brian Jones's magical cathode-ray aura, his flaxen blond hair glowing like a silver crown, transfixes a generation of young romantics. The Stones come on like a working-class gang armed with black music, rebels with a cause. They stake their claim with incendiary live shows featuring a harmony of sexual panic, fighting, riots, tear gas, violent cops, fan mania, mobbed limos, and chaotic getaways. The Stones, their audience, and the cops clash in a mass, desperate embrace that is loud, edgy, and blatantly erotic. Sex and death go hand in hand. Sirens scream and the earth moves. Dionysus is in the house.

———

Of course they're not really gods, only gifted mortals upon whom modern media have conferred a kind of immortality. But the Rolling Stones story does have a pantheistic mythos to it. Their advent was uncannily prophesied by a shaman twenty years earlier and five thousand miles away. They started as a band of starving young outcasts on an improbable quest, and ended up a Plutonian offshore corporation that could generate megamillions when it mobilized for a tour. Their imagery is unforgettably Olympian: romantic heroes, senses deregulated, bathed in red-lit narcosis as they celebrated their black masses of carnal cravings and occasional human sacrifice. Rose petals flung from a wicker basket flutter down on drenched, exhausted worshipers. A priapic rock godling rides a giant throbbing phallus to climax a steamy indoor fertility rite. Twin brotherly guitarists, gaunt from constant intoxication, playing the stars from the sky like a pair of magic ravens. Tiny figures on immense, Babylonian stadium stages, magnified and projected by oracular Jumbotrons, remote as gladiators in the arena. Their lives, and deaths, echo the legends of the old gods with their operatic comings and goings, planetary mobility, and mercurial tales of love, lust, and revenge. The Rolling Stones were more than just a rock and roll band. They took the trouble to show us new worlds, and new ways of living in them as well.

———————

In 1963, John Lennon was asked how long the mighty, unstoppable Beatles would last. He answered five years. They lasted six. But the Rolling Stones plowed on, deploying a complex, improvisational mix of artistic integrity, steel-hearted careerism, bold appropriation, media manipulation, sexual tension, shameless hype, and quality aesthetics—an intuitive blend of instinct, luck, and calculation that kept them relevant, and improbably cool, through four decades of style revolutions, cultural changes, and technological advances.

Aside from the strength of their music and the hold it continues to have on two generations of fans, the most interesting aspect of the Rolling Stones has been the cross-pollinating interaction they had with almost every important artistic movement of the past forty years. There was a certain epic grandeur in how Brian Jones's early Rolling Stones led a successful crusade to inoculate America with its own neglected rhythm and blues while forcing a sclerotic and diminished England to inhale a whiff of anarchic insolence. The Stones then morphed into a soul band, introducing Motown and Memphis hits to their European audience, before they brashly crashed America in 1965 as the epitome of the flash London pop group with a string of dark, ascerbic hit records, starting with the legendary "Satisfaction." From then on, the Stones became indispensable icons of pop and intersected with, borrowed from, and reinspired some of the most important artists of the times. With the Beatles and Bob Dylan, they cornered a heroic transatlantic triad of sixties pop genius. The Stones had important links with the international Beat fathers (William Burroughs, Allen Ginsberg, Brion Gysin, Terry Southern), Andy Warhol's pop art demimonde in New York, the California music scene, and masters of avant-garde European cinema like Godard, Vadim, and Antonioni. When their music needed fresh inspiration, the Stones became adept at grabbing crucial new sounds at the moment they emerged aboveground:

Moroccan rhythms, Brazilian samba, the glam rock of David Bowie, the New Orleans funk of the Meters, Jamaican reggae, disco, punk, hip-hop, and techno. But ultimately, Sex was what the Rolling Stones were all about. Their famous logo—scarlet lips open in invitation, lolling wet tongue, smiling white teeth—advertises oral sex like it's their real trademark. And their taboo-breaking sadomasochism—in their music and presentations as well as their daily reality—drove audiences to frenzy, while their love stories—their famous golden muses and the sexual tension inside the band—captivated a loyal army of fans for decades.

———

The Stones and the other great rock bands were about climax, catharsis, narcissism, virtuosity, excess, and the transformative power of love. The Stones personified the exalted status of rock musicians as the troubadours of our age, preserving, in their often clumsy and unconscious way, the ancient popular romantic traditions of the West. The best rock concerts were the rites of crypto-religious societies that actually formed the largest mass audience in history. The amplified power of the music, its visionary themes, and its jungle rhythms opened expansive spiritual vistas for its audience far beyond the routines of everyday life. It validated the yearnings and expressed the fantasies of millions of listeners. The greatest rock stars, living in the moment of performance and on the edge of psychic derangement, rewarded in their youth beyond their wildest dreams, became their generation's Byronic exemplars of action and experience. When they flamed out and died, like Brian Jones, they were transformed into sacrificial heroes and mythologized. Their fans made their graves into shrines.

The cultural landscape that nurtured all this is now history. Rock music has become "classic rock." The pop music the Stones' own kids listen to is fragmented into digital bits of subcultural info: techno, hip-hop, remixes, deejay culture, ambient soundscaping, speed garage, multi-culti world beat, and so on. The twentieth-century rock hero is obsolete in these antiheroic times. Video killed the sheer mystique of bands that kids once had to pay to see, if only to find out what they looked like, just as the excited dash to the record store has become the downloading of a computer file. The bald turntablist replaces the longhaired rock virtuoso. The ritualistic rock concert gives way to the more democratic rave.

The Rolling Stones, at this writing, are still the reigning world champions of rock, untouchable icons of their age. Any attempt at a full biography is limited by the happy fact that their story isn't over; that the Stones might be laying waste beyond the ramparts of your town, tonight, as you read this. They will hold their heavyweight title as long as they choose, and as long as they remain in the keeping of the generation that understands their entire value, their music's deepest meanings, and the transcendental distinction of their great songs. That understanding is what this book is all about.

Something magical happens, whether in a garage or a stadium, when the drummer sits down and starts to rock the beat. It's the call of the orgy, the death of the square, the end of civilization. Primitive instincts kick in as the mating dance starts, and the tribal elders begin to initiate the young. Draw closer to the fire and listen as the story burns away the days, the years, and the decades. The oft-mocked creases and wrinkles of a veteran rocker's middle age tighten into the beauty of rebel youth. The primal Bo Diddley beat—a jungle telegram of drum and bass line—throbs in the ambient, subsonic background. And away we go, back into the past, to the dusty Delta of the Mississippi River, from where the Rolling Stones drew their original, brilliant, and enduring inspiration.

Old gods almost dead—but not just yet.

Rolling . . .

The Delta is a low, flat water world of bayous, creeks, levees, and dikes holding back the river from flooding some of the best land in the world for growing cotton and rice. The blues comes from a landscape of cotton fields, gravel roads, groves of pecan trees, kudzu vines, cane-breaks, sharecroppers' cabins, tenant farmhouses, flooded rice fields, and an immense white sky full of water and dust. When the cotton is high, it's a hundred degrees in the shade.

One hot day in July 1941, an old Ford raised a yellow cloud of dust on the gravel road leading to Sherrod's Plantation, near Clarksdale, Mississippi. A tall black farmer, twenty-six years old, named McKinley Morganfield became alarmed when the car turned off the road and headed for his cabin behind a row of trees. He worried the car contained Mississippi state revenue agents looking for the corn liquor still, hidden in a thicket nearby, that supplied a juke joint he ran on the side.

But inside the car was Alan Lomax, a young folklorist collecting field recordings from southern plantations and prison farms for the Library of Congress. Lomax had heard of Morganfield's singing fame on the streets of Clarksdale, where he was known as Muddy Waters. That afternoon, after hours gaining his trust, Lomax recorded Muddy Waters for the first time, performing Robert Johnson's "Walkin' Blues," which Lomax retitled "Country Blues No. 1."

Lomax questioned Muddy closely about Robert Johnson, the flamboyant slide guitar prodigy, who was rumored to have cut a deal with the devil at a deserted gravel crossroads, trading his immortal soul for mastery of his instrument. Johnson played on street corners in Delta market towns like Clarksdale and Helena, Arkansas, where he was discovered by a talent scout in the music store where he bought his strings. He played his rawboned country blues in backwoods juke joints, fish fries, house parties, levee camps, taverns, lumber camps. He could light a fire under dancers high on corn liquor with propulsive rhythms and a tapping foot. His own songs were a mix of psychic torment and funny imagery full of salacious metaphors for sex.

Johnson's archetypal recordings—"I Believe I'll Dust My Broom," "Stop Breakin' Down Blues," "Love in Vain," "Walkin' Blues," "I'm a Steady Rollin' Man," "Hellhound on My Trail"—became the structural template on which future musicians built the rhythm and blues, rock and roll, and eventually rock music that captured the cultural arenas of the West forty years later. Robert's uncanny guitar often sounded like two or three people playing together, and the rhythms he tapped out with his right foot anticipated the R&B band arrangement. "Bach on the bottom and Mozart on top," as Keith Richards put it.

Muddy insisted he had never actually seen Robert in person, but had been taught Robert's songs by the older bluesman Son House. Much later, Muddy did remember seeing Robert Johnson playing on a street corner in Friar's Point, Mississippi, with a big crowd around him. But, he said, "I got back into the car and left, because he was a dangerous man. He was really *using* that guitar . . . I crawled away and pulled out, because it was too heavy for me."

Before Lomax left, he also recorded Muddy singing "I Be's Troubled," the emotional ancestor to "(I Can't Get No) Satisfaction." Late in 1942, Muddy left the Delta and took the country blues off to wartime Chicago, where a mass migration of black southerners working in war industries had created a cash market for down-home musicians like himself.

But Chicago showed Muddy Waters that his country style was already old-fashioned by the time he arrived.

Blues singing had originally evolved on the plantations of the Mississippi Delta in the late nineteenth century as the secular expression of the first generation of African Americans born out of slavery, but still tied to the land in agricultural peonage. As it developed early in the twentieth century and began to be heard via recordings (called race records), blues singing—slow tempos, flattened thirds and sevenths, moaning lyrics of yearning, melancholy, and remorse—remained a vivid minority music in the American South. Sometimes blues styles surfaced into the commercial mainstream of American music as a featured style or a passing fad, but its origins and its stars were ignored by the outside media until the wartime migrations of the 1940s brought the blues onto the radio and the jukeboxes.

But the blues needed a drummer and amplifiers to be heard above the din of crowded cities. Muddy built his first Chicago band around Little Walter Jacobs and his brilliant amplified harmonica. Extremely popular on the South Side, they were recording by 1946, and soon started to work for two white Polish immigrants, Leonard and Phil Chess. The Chess brothers, who ran several bars and clubs on the South Side, built a studio in 1947 when they realized that the wildly popular black musicians they employed didn't have recording contracts.

Muddy's first record for Chess was a reworked version of "I Be's Troubled" called "I Can't Be Satisfied," paired with "I Feel Like Going Home." It was Delta blues greased with electric buzz, and an immediate smash in the summer of 1948. When Muddy added a drummer, the whole Chicago blues thing took off. The new rhythm and blues was dark, sweaty, jumped-up: the dusty mojo of the country hopped up to the violent, frantic pace of the city. The records the Chess brothers made with

Muddy and his band sold as fast as they could be pressed. By 1950, Muddy Waters was the undisputed king of the blues, and his band—Muddy on slide guitar, Jimmie Rodgers on second guitar, Otis Spann on piano, Little Walter on wailing, demonic harp, and drummer Elgin Evans—was the most popular group in Chicago.

In 1950, Muddy reached back into the Delta for an old song called "Catfish Blues." Played slow and solo on the bottom strings of his guitar, retitled "Rollin' Stone," the record eerily prophesied the future and a new blues generation, telling in a possessed, mysterious chant of "a boy child coming, gonna be a rollin' stone, gonna be a rollin' stone."

The rest is legend, as Muddy gathered the best musicians around him in the early 1950s. Junior Wells replaced Little Walter on harp. The Chess brothers' bass player and arranger Willie Dixon wrote "I'm Your Hoochie Coochie Man" for Muddy, another smash hit. Chester Burnett, known as Howlin' Wolf, arrived in Chicago from West Point, Mississippi, in 1953 and lived with Muddy, who showed him around. A huge man famous in the Delta for performing on his hands and knees, baring his teeth and howling out pure murder, Wolf soon began a rivalry with Muddy that lasted as long as both lived.

By 1955, Muddy was in his prime, full of regal authority, Cadillacs, and women. But in 1956, Elvis Presley, Little Richard, and Bill Haley took over pop music, speeding up R&B with a faster, rocking backbeat. Rock and roll damaged the market for blues records. Muddy Waters and his band still ruled in the taverns of Chicago and in the urban South, but now the Chess brothers had to find a new sound to stay in business.

The diddley-bow is an ancient Delta poverty slide guitar, a one-stringed instrument made from a two-by-four, a couple of nails, some broom wire, and a crushed snuff can. You use a nail or a bottle cap for a slide and you get this piercing African tone that can carry for a hundred yards across a cotton field.

Bo Diddley was born Otha Ellas Bates McDaniel in southwest Mississippi in 1928 and arrived in Chicago at the age of seven to live with his grandmother. When he was twelve, his sister gave him a guitar. "I'm completely self-taught and I don't play like nobody else," he says. "I was *all* rhythm, and I could drive you right out of your tree with *chords* and that fast wrist work." He grew up as a ghetto fighter and street musician in the 1940s, playing with little groups called the Hipsters and the Jive Cats. Handy with tools, he was building his own electric guitars and amplifiers as Muddy's band began taking over the professional blues scene. But "Mac" and his friends were half a generation younger; they began speeding up Muddy's rhythms, and adapted the post-bop swing of hepcats like bandleader Louis Jordan and Nat Cole. A throbbing tremolo electric guitar gave the music an exotic, primitive edge. Since drums were hard to deploy on street corners, Mac used maracas for percussion, which gave his music an irresistible African sizzle and drive.

In February 1955, he walked into the Chess studio on South Cottage Grove Avenue and tried to interest the man sitting at the counter in a demo recording of a song called "I'm a Man." But Little Walter, who was helping around the office for pocket money, told Mac to go away. As he was leaving, Phil Chess came out and said he could play the tape. Within a month, they changed Mac's name to Bo Diddley and released "I'm a Man" as a single, with "Bo Diddley" on the A side, and a new sound was born: an updated version of the shave-and-a-haircut rhythm, a grungy tremolo guitar, and the greasy buzzing of the maracas. This was early black rock and roll, and it was an instant hit on the radio. Soon every young band in America realized that the "Bo Diddley beat" could really jungle up a dance, and the rhythm just exploded. Other masterpieces followed: "Diddley Daddy," "Pretty Thing," "Who Do You Love," "Hey Bo Diddley," "Cops and Robbers," and especially "Mona," a love call to a young stripper Bo liked. Most of these were recorded later by the Rolling Stones, and Bo Diddley probably would have been their biggest influence if the Chess brothers hadn't released "Maybellene" only two months after they put out "Bo Diddley."

————

Chuck Berry was born in St. Louis in 1926, a carpenter's son, and he grew into a tall, handsome young man with a quick wit and huge hands capable of really strangling a guitar. When he was eighteen, a judge gave him ten years for a robbery spree across Missouri. Doing his time, he began to entertain the other prisoners with music, impressed the warden, and eventually got paroled.

In late 1952, Chuck met piano player Johnnie Johnson and joined his band, Sir John's Trio. Three years later, in 1955, he visited Chicago for the first time. He went to hear the greats: Howlin' Wolf, Elmore James, his hero, Muddy Waters. When Chuck pushed his way through the crowd to ask Muddy whom he should see in Chicago about cutting a record, Muddy told him about Leonard Chess.

Two weeks later, Chuck Berry walked into the Chess studio, tape reel in hand. "Leonard listened to my tape," Berry later wrote, "and when he heard one hillbilly selection I'd included called 'Ida Red' played back on the one-mike, one-track home recorder, it struck him most as being commercial. He couldn't believe that a 'hillbilly song' could be written and sung by a black guy. He said he wanted us to record that particular song, and he scheduled a recording session for May 21, 1955, promising me a contract at that time." They cut "Ida Red," but Leonard Chess told Chuck to come up with a better title. So Ida Red became a car and got her name changed to Maybelline.

"Maybelline" was a national hit record, and Chuck Berry never looked back. His humor and wit overlaid a light, swinging kind of rockabilly that teenagers liked to dance to. "Around and Around," "Reelin' and Rockin'," "Carol," "Roll Over Beethoven," "School Days," "Little Queenie": over the next five years, Chuck Berry wrote thirty-five songs that became the cornerstone of the new pop music, a huge influence on John Lennon and the Beatles, and the main inspiration of Keith Richards's drive to power up the early Stones.

The Blitzkrieg and the Blues

And the guns start to roar / From the ship to the shore /
And the bombs start to fall / As we crouch in the hall . . .

"War Baby," Mick Jagger

Adolf Hitler and Nazi Germany declared war on England in 1940 and began bombing English cities and the countryside. English children born during the war spent their earliest years stressed and sleepless because of the banshee air-raid sirens, bursting incendiary and high-explosive bombs, wailing fire engines and ambulances. Charlie Watts (born June 2, 1941), Brian Jones (February 28, 1942), Mick Jagger (July 26, 1943), and Keith Richards (December 18, 1943) heard the fuzz-toned reverb of the Luftwaffe's buzz bombs and doodlebugs, the chugging AA batteries, the wild feedback of V-1 flying bombs, and the almost silent whoosh of V-2 missiles. Overhead, the insect whines of Spitfire and Hurricane fighter planes could be heard as they dueled with Messerschmidts and the German bombers. Bill Wyman, older than the rest (born October 24, 1936), remembers hearing Winston Churchill on the radio: "Let us therefore brace ourselves to our duty, and so bear ourselves that, if the British Commonwealth and its Empire lasts for a thousand years, men will still say, 'This was their finest hour.' "

Keith's family's house in Dartford, Kent, was badly bombed. His father was wounded in Normandy later in the war. Food was scarce and heavily rationed. Meat, eggs, sugar, and fruit were rare treats, and the English people were deprived of protein in favor of those fighting in the war. The Stones and their generation were slight of stature, thanks to Hitler and his armies.

The war ended in 1945, but England was devastated, and rationing continued. Candy—sweets—didn't reappear until 1953, and children rioted when the shops finally opened. London, Liverpool, Manchester were pocked by gutted buildings and the gaping holes of bomb craters. The urban landscape was one huge building site as the poverty-stricken kingdom tried to rebuild. It's no accident that for their first promo pictures as a five-piece group, the Stones were photographed on a London bomb site, almost twenty years after the end of the war, as if they identified themselves as a new generation emerging from the rubble of the old.

Cold War. The American B-29s landing in the late 1940s were the first occupying force in Britain for a thousand years. The American servicemen brought their music with them: country music and the blues, sounds the English began to love. But the British music union was protectionist, so one didn't hear much on BBC radio. Country blues came to England in 1951 when Big Bill Broonzy arrived with a touring jazz show. Broonzy played up-tempo city blues when he performed in Chicago and New York, but in England he only did the old Delta songs he thought the British jazz audience wanted to hear.

In England, jazz still meant New Orleans band music. After the vaudeville-style English music halls faded in the 1930s, they were replaced by dance bands playing a circuit of ballrooms around the country. After the war, the American "progressive jazz" of Charlie Parker and Miles Davis had a cult associated with bohemian intellectuals, but in England, jazz meant the old New Orleans style called Dixieland in America (where it had already died out) and trad in England. Trad jazz was popularized by trumpeter Humphrey Lyttleton, an aristocrat distantly related to the queen, and then taken over by the popular Chris Barber Jazz Band and groups led by trumpeter Ken Colyer and Mr. Acker Bilk.

Then rock and roll hit England hard, when the Hollywood "juvenile delinquency" exploitation movie *Blackboard Jungle* opened in 1956 with its theme song, "Rock Around the Clock," blasted out by Bill Haley and the Comets. It was shake, rattle and roll as Haley's subsequent English tours sparked riots when teenage audiences trashed the movie theaters where Haley played. There was similar mania for other American rockers like Little Richard, Jerry Lee Lewis, Eddie Cochran, and especially the hoodlum-looking Gene Vincent and his blue suede shoes. Suddenly England had its own delinquents, tough "Teddy boys" sporting leopard-skin lapels and armed with bike chains. The Teds and their girls filled the old dance band ballrooms now. Keith Richards: "We were very conscious we were in a totally new era. Rock and roll changed the world. It reshaped the way people think. It was like A.D. and B.C., and 1956 was year one."

English rock and roll: Cliff Richard and the Shadows, Rory Storm and the Hurricanes, Johnny Kidd and the Pirates. Low-voltage R&R controlled by mobsters from the East End of London, working out of Soho, the dark and shabby (but very alive) strip-club showbiz zone south of Oxford Street in London's West End. The vivid, hustling ambience of Soho is captured in the 1959 movie *Expresso Bongo!*, in which sleazo talent agent Laurence Harvey "discovers" raw teenage talent Cliff Richard in a Soho coffee bar and makes him a star.

Another craze hit England in the mid-fifties when "skiffle" music got big. Played on washboards, banjos, and basses made out of tea chests, skiffle adapted American hillbilly jug band music with a local English spin. Breeding a few stars like Lonnie Donegan and Johnny Duncan, skiffle was easy to play and very catchy. John Lennon's earliest bands and Ray Davies's Kinks started as after-school skiffle clubs, and by the time the music faded, skiffle had made its mark as England struggled to find its own voice in the postwar world.

Bandleader Chris Barber was a jazz fan, and he liked to feature American stars in his popular trad concerts. In 1957, he began bringing over blues musicians to guest with his band: Broonzy, Sonny Terry and Brownie McGhee, Sister Rosetta Tharp. Then, in October 1958, Barber changed the history of the blues when he invited Muddy Waters to perform in Britain for the first time.

Muddy brought his piano player, Otis Spann, and they embarked on a ten-day tour with Barber's band. After Barber played Dixieland in the first half, Muddy came out with only Spann on piano. English fans came expecting down-home bluesmen in overalls and straw hats. Muddy and Otis were nattily attired in sharp-cut suits, conk hairdos, and pointed black boots. Instead of an acoustic set, they revved up with electric guitar, ferocious singing, and Spann's driving left-hand rhythms. Audiences loved it, but the critics were stunned. "Screaming Guitar and Howling Piano" read one headline. Muddy was booed in London when he plugged his guitar into a small amp. They did the hits—"Long Distance Call," "I Can't Be Satisfied"—and Muddy would perform "Rollin' Stone" alone as a country blues with its cosmic prophecy of another generation of bluesmen slouching like some rough beast toward London, waiting to be born. He didn't know it at the time, but Muddy Waters was arming the English for what would come next, as young musicians were infected with the blues. Eric Burdon, who would later star with the Animals, came to the show in Newcastle and left a budding blues singer. Among the fans mobbing the two nervous bluesmen after the concert in London were two English jazz musicians who would provide the linkup to the Stones: Cyril Davies and, more important, Alexis Korner.

————

Alexis Korner was the kind of dark, woolly-headed, Mediterranean exotic for whom there has always been a place on the minstrel fringes of England. Born in 1928 in Paris, mother Greek, father Austrian. The family moved around Europe and North Africa with the Korner family shipping business, arriving in England in 1939. Alexis was thrown out of good schools for being weird and musicianly. Made his own guitar out of plywood and a table leg. Did menial jobs for record companies and worked at the BBC. In 1949, Alexis joined Chris Barber to play banjo and guitar. He was already interested in obscure blues singers like Jimmy Yancey and Scrapper Blackwell. Korner replaced Barber's washboard-playing singer Tony Donegan (who later changed his name to Lonnie and had a hit skiffle record with "Rock Island Line"). Barber and Korner started a jazz-skiffle group within the Barber band, which lasted until Donegan came out of the army. Alexis left when Donegan returned, resolving to find some other cats with whom to play a more pure type of blues.

"By '53 or '54," Korner told the BBC, "I'd got passable enough [singing the blues] to go round working solo in clubs. My wife Bobbie tossed a coin and said, 'If it lands heads, you're freelance'...I met Cyril Davies in the London Skiffle Club above the Roundhouse [in Wardour Street, Soho], and he said, 'Look, man, I'm tired of all this skiffle shit. If I close the place down, will you come in with me and open it up as a blues club?' "

Cyril Davies was a big man, like his heroes Sonny Boy Williamson and Howlin' Wolf. He worked in a junkyard, had a gruff, no-nonsense demeanor, and blew a pretty fair blues harp for a Welshman. He'd been to Chicago, sat in with Muddy, considered himself a bluesman, the real deal. Like Korner, he was a blues evangelist. They opened the London Blues and Barrelhouse Club in the back room of a pub on Tottenham Court Road in 1957. Three people showed up the first night. It was the height of the skiffle scene—the old club had been packed with students and punters every night—and now two white guys were jamming the blues and nobody cared. But they ran the club for three years of Thursday nights, the only place in England where you could hear blues music, which a tiny community considered a soulful alternative to the bloodless version of jazz that trad represented to them.

So Korner and Davies began their work as blues catalysts. They imported American blues singers, many of whom lived with Alexis's family while they were in London and greatly appreciated the warm hospitality and respect that was on offer. Alexis's daughter was often sung to sleep by the hellacious Big Bill Broonzy.

After Muddy blew through town, his mojo working full-bore, Korner and Davies realized they had to plug in and get some serious amplifiers. It was too loud for the landlord, and the pub threw them out in 1960. No other club would even let them bring their amps inside. So they joined up with the Chris Barber Jazz Band as an internal blues duo, performing a miniset in the middle of Barber's trad/Dixieland act.

———

One night in 1961, the Barber band played a date in the old spa town of Cheltenham, in Gloucestershire, about a hundred miles from London. Alexis and "Squirrel" Davies did some Blind Boy Fuller blues during their set, which was well received by the unusually hip crowd. In the bar during the interval, the very approachable Korner was bearded by a short blond teenager who softly burbled away, almost in a whisper, that he, too, was a bluesman, from around here, living on his own now, got a couple kids already and, man, if only they could get together, he could maybe play Alexis some stuff because, actually, he wanted to get out of town and come to London and maybe get something together on his own, and . . .

Yeah, sure, all right, said Korner. Meet me in the wine bar after the gig. And the kid—Brian Jones—took his girlfriend home and ran off to get his guitar.

Old Gods Almost Dead

one:
The Rollin' Stones

The Rolling Stones, 1963.

Yes, I will be famous. No, I won't make thirty.

Brian Jones

I Will Be Famous

It would later seem ironic to many that Brian Jones, Wild Man of the Sixties, came from Cheltenham, the old Regency-era spa town in the Cotswolds whose springs had dried up long ago. Cheltenham was known for its bourgeois conformity and legions of the retired. It was a hotbed of rest. Cheltenham Ladies College was the most proper girls' school in Britain. But there was another side to Cheltenham that owed a lot to the American air bases nearby. The town had five movie theaters, ballrooms where bands played, coffee bars for hanging out. A clever boy like Brian could easily get an idea of the world waiting beyond the provincial beauty of the West Country.

Lewis Brian Hopkins-Jones was born on a winter Saturday night in 1942, during the dark days of the war. Father worked in the aircraft industry, mother played and taught the piano. Pure Welsh stock on both sides—a race of singers, musicians, poets despised by the English for being the descendants of the true Britons they displaced in Arthurian times. Brian Jones was a short, strong, charismatic blond kid who pulled one in with his soft, well-spoken voice, intelligent eyes, and blond hair, his famous tool for seduction. He could get a girl pregnant with the toss of his head.

There was something else about Brian, something dark and alluring. "Brian possessed a hidden cruelty," Mick Jagger would later say, "which in a way was very sensual."

Did well in school. High I.Q., top grades in literature, math, physics. Strong at sports: the "little Welsh bull" that Keith would later describe. Nine O-level passes by sixteen in 1958—quite respectable—but skipped school, laughed at the teachers, and was often caned. An aggressive little guy: one didn't mess with his girlfriends. Brought up in a musical family, he showed uncommonly early promise as a piano student (he was the only Stone with a proper music education), could read music, played clarinet and sax. Got a Spanish acoustic guitar for his seventeenth birthday, which he mastered within weeks. Hobbies were trainspotting and jazz records, which led to New Orleans blues singer Champion Jack Dupree's trenchant, down-home *Blues from the Gutter* album, which opened the door to the future.

Some who knew Brian Jones thought of him as two people: soft, charming, intelligent one day; a nasty little bugger the next. Sometimes both in the same day, the same hour. The Stones saw it all as they grew up with him in his twenties: the tantrums, mysterious illnesses, "absences," general bloody-mindedness.

Bill Wyman thinks Brian suffered from undiagnosed epilepsy.

Brian started playing sax in local groups when he was fourteen. The Bill Nile Jazz Band. The Cheltone Six. The Ramrods. He was the cool kid in the proper collar and tie, blowing alto saxophone and making eye contact with the girls. All he had to do was look at one hard enough, and soon she had something in the oven. Brian Jones as Bran, the Welsh fertility god, a stocky little sprite with a long green penis. The first girl to have one of his many illegitimate children was Valerie, aged fourteen. Good morning, little schoolgirl. Brian wanted an abortion, she wanted the child, which she put up for adoption at birth. Word got out, huge scandal in Cheltenham. The girl refused to see him again, and Brian's parents, socially destroyed and unable to cope, asked the seventeen-year-old father to move out of the house.

In 1959, Brian's father took him to London for a job interview with an optical firm. Brian was hired and he moved into a one-room flat. But he hated it and spent days in the music shops hunting for records by his blues heroes: Sonny Boy Williamson, T-Bone Walker, and especially Jimmy Reed, the youngest and most successful Chicago bluesman of the 1950s. He quit and went home, moving in with his friend Dick Hattrell. But Cheltenham was too hot for Brian. The parents of the girl he impregnated ran him out of town, and he set off for a tour of Scandinavian blondes with his Spanish guitar on his back. Out of money by early 1960, his brains thoroughly screwed out, he returned home again and tried to settle in. One night he went to see a band play in nearby Guildford. A young married girl, only twenty-three, caught his eye. He took her home, made love to her once, and his second child was born nine months later.

To support his blues studies, Brian got a job in a factory, which he quit after he was hurt in a car accident. His leg was injured, and a front tooth knocked out. For the rest of his life, Brian covered his mouth with his hand when he laughed. So he hung around Cheltenham's beatnik coffee bars, waiting for something to happen. He met a pretty sixteen-year-old beautician named Pat Andrews, and together they began work on Brian's child number three. He was eighteen years old, a scuffling young blues apprentice struggling to survive.

———

Chris Barber played Cheltenham in 1960, and Brian was there. Barber's blues guest that night was Sonny Boy Williamson from Helena, Arkansas, an imposing blues giant in a London-bought homburg and a two-toned gray flannel suit that he had tailored as his vision of an English gentleman. Sonny Boy blew harp with a vengeance and a bottle of bourbon in his back pocket. Brian noticed that his huge mouth was roughly callused from years of playing the harp, and that Sonny Boy sang through his harmonica, his hoarse vocal passing through the metal instrument, honing his voice like a razor so it hit the microphone with an extra metallic slash. Brian's future as a bluesman was settled that night.

He kept scuffling, working as a bus conductor in Cheltenham and other jobs. He and Hattrell moved in with some art students, and soon Pat Andrews was pregnant. Brian started seeing other girls. Their son was born in October 1961, and Brian named him Julian, after his jazz hero Julian "Cannonball" Adderley. He tried to visit Pat and the baby every day until her furious mother started beating him over the head with her umbrella when he showed up.

In December 1961, on a long English winter night just before Christmas, Chris Barber's band was playing Cheltenham Town Hall. For over a year, they'd been playing at the famous Marquee Club in Soho every week, with Alexis Korner and Cyril Davies doing electric blues between Barber's sets. Brian went with Pat and Dick and was mind-blown by the Korner-Davies blues set. He used his local musician's street cred to get backstage, and charmed Alexis into a private drink at the Patio Wine Bar across the road after he dumped Pat at home and got his guitar.

Brian connected with his future mentor in the back room. Korner knew what time it was, saw a glimmer of what was coming, gave Brian Jones his phone number and address, and invited him to London. He and Cyril were leaving Chris Barber to put their own blues band together, and maybe this kid could help.

Brian and Pat visited London in early January 1962, and Brian spent several days listening to Alexis's record collection. Rock music's equivalent of St. Paul's conversion on the road to Damascus occurred when Brian first heard Elmore James's stunning electric slide guitar version of "Dust My Broom." It was raw, soulful, and charged like a shot of battery acid. Jesus! Back in Cheltenham, Brian borrowed enough to buy a cheap electric pickup for his guitar. Unable to afford an amp, he converted a German tape recorder and ran the guitar through the speaker. He made a bottleneck slide and spent the next months obsessively listening to blues jams and learning the slide. By March, he could make his guitar whine like a tigress in heat.

That's when he saw the little ad in the London music paper *Jazz News* for Alexis Korner's new band, Blues Incorporated. "The Most Exciting Event of the Year." And it gave directions: Ealing Broadway Station. Turn left, cross the zebra (pedestrian stripes), and go down the steps between ABC Teashop and the jeweler's. Saturday at 7:30 P.M.

That morning, Brian hitched to London. It was March 17, 1962.

Charlie Boy

Alexis Korner needed a drummer to form a Chicago-style R&B group. He found one playing cool jazz in a Knightsbridge coffee-house, the Troubadour.

Charlie Watts.

His family called him Charlie Boy. He was born in 1941 in North London as the bombs were falling, the only child of a lorry driver for the railroad. The family moved to Wembley after the war, when the now-crowded London suburb was still farmland. Charlie grew to be a shy, unassuming teenager: focused, hardworking, short of stature, somewhat pampered by his parents. He lived at home until well into his twenties, and his father bought his clothes for him.

When he was ten, Charlie heard Earl Bostic's "Flamingo" on the radio, and it woke him up. The next year, he heard Chico Hamilton playing drums on Gerry Mulligan's "Walkin' Shoes" and started beating on pots and pans. His first instrument, a banjo, he bought himself at fourteen. He took it apart, converted the banjo body into a snare drum, and built a stand out of a Meccano kit (called an Erector set in the United States). In 1955, his parents bought him his first drum set for Christmas, and Charlie began playing along to jazz records. He hated rock and roll; was instead obsessed by cool jazz. He saw himself, at fifteen, as Miles Davis, standing outside the Village Vanguard in an Ivy League suit, waiting to go on with 'Trane and Philly Joe Jones.

He left school at sixteen, studied graphic design at Harrow School of Art in the late fifties, and in 1960 got a job in a London ad agency, where he learned lettering and poster design. He was making a little money, which he spent on smart clothes and Charlie Parker records.

Charlie Parker. Bird. In 1939, improvising on his alto saxophone,

Parker had fallen through the chord changes of the standard "Cherokee" and discovered bebop, the free-flowing and inspired jazz that grew into a hipster cult whose trademarks were the beret, the goatee, and the needle. Bebop was the cutting edge of music, and its players—Bird, Dizzy Gillespie, Thelonious Monk, Charles Mingus—were the artistic astronauts of the time. Charlie Watts loved Charlie Parker so much that, in 1961 at the age of twenty, he wrote a children's book called *Ode to a High-Flying Bird,* with little illustrations that told the bebop story in a sweet, innocent style.

————

Summer 1961. Charlie was playing drums with brushes behind a little Thelonious-style combo at the Troubadour when Alexis Korner came to sit in and play some blues. Korner took his little portable amp and hung it on the wall behind Charlie, who, though not particularly assertive, got up and took the amp off the wall. If it had to be amplified, it wasn't going to drown the rest of the band. Alexis liked Charlie's impeccable time and swinging approach, which recalled Papa Jo Jones of Count Basie's orchestra. Alexis asked Charlie to join the blues group he was putting together for bandleader Acker Bilk. Charlie instead went on a Danish tour with veteran bebop reedman Don Byas, a cool gig for a twenty-year-old.

Back in London, Charlie Watts met Alexis Korner again and joined the first lineup of Blues Incorporated in late January 1962.

————

But Charlie Watts was confused by Blues Incorporated. They wanted a Chicago-style backbeat, but Alexis and Cyril Davies were fighting (as they usually did) about how heavy it should be. Davies wanted a blues shuffle; Alexis wanted it to swing.

"It was an amazing band," Charlie said, "but a total cacophony of sound. On a good night, it was a cross between R&B and Charlie Mingus, which was what Alexis wanted." Korner had seen Mingus's band, the Jazz Workshop, in action in London around 1960. Mingus, protean New York jazz bassist and composer, ran his shows as rehearsals, demanding his players redo passages that he didn't like. Now Alexis Korner wanted a similar band that could develop its own audience and even a wider blues scene. The regular lineup and auxiliary musicians in the club could be joined by anyone from the audience with enough bottle to get up and wail with the best cats in London. Korner knew, from run-ins with young talent like that Brian kid in Cheltenham, that there were young blues fanatics out there, just drooling for the chance to get up and show their stuff.

Charlie Watts was bemused by the whole disorganized lot. "When I first played with Cyril Davies, I thought, 'What the fuck is happening here?' " Watts had never heard an amplified harmonica before. Everyone was coming from their own special interest in the blues. "I didn't know what the hell was going on." During the winter of 1961, Korner, Davies, and Watts jammed together, joined by other Korner recruits, as they tried to line up club dates for the new group.

But nobody wanted to hear it. The club owners felt threatened because their clientele wanted jazz, and these guys were playing the blues, considered primitive and uncool. Korner tried to book Blues Incorporated on the National Jazz Federation's circuit of clubs and was bluntly told to get lost. The excuse was "acoustic only," but this was war. If blues got big in England, the jazz clubs would go out of business. Money, jobs, and prestige were at stake, and so the jazzers tried to suppress Korner's new movement. It provoked a lot of bitterness in London over the next two years.

Finally Korner found the dank underground barroom down piss-smelling stairs under a tea shop at the end of a tube line in the western London suburb of Ealing. They set it up as a club, strung a tarp under the skylight to keep the stage from flooding when it rained, and charged five shillings membership admission. The Ealing Club could hold about two hundred.

———

March 17, 1962. Blues Incorporated made its debut with eight musicians: Korner on guitar, Davies on harp, Watts on drums, jazz guy Dick Heckstall-Smith on sax, plus bass and piano. There were two singers: Long John Baldry, a tall and blustery young blues shouter, and Art Wood, a softer vocalist in the Mose Allison style. Starting at about eight o'clock on Saturday night, they played electric blues for a small group of fans. Attracted by the *Jazz News* ad, Brian Jones showed up with his friend Paul Pond, whose blues group Brian had briefly joined in Oxford.

Brian had his guitar and asked Alexis if he could sit in with the band. "Not tonight, mate," Korner said. "Come back next week and you're on."

Brian was back the following Saturday, March 24. There had been a good review about the new blues club in that week's *Melody Maker,* and this time they got a good crowd. "Thank you very much," Korner said after finishing his version of "Hoochie Coochie Man." "Now we have a visitor who's come all the way from Cheltenham, and he's going to play some bottleneck guitar with us. Please give a warm welcome to..." Korner had forgotten the stage name Brian wanted him to say.

"Elmo Lewis," whispered Brian.

"To Elmo Lewis! Take it away, Elmo!"

And Brian ripped into the clarion riff of his hero Elmore James's take on Robert Johnson's old "Dust My Broom," and the room started rocking as Charlie Watts clicked in, and it was groove city. The humid, beer-soaked old drinking club gave off a solid juke-joint ambience, Brian looked great in his turtleneck sweater under a sports jacket, his short blond hair cut like jazz star Gerry Mulligan's, and the piercing sting of the slide guitar cut through the cigarette smoke like a rusty blade. It was that weird, slithery diddley-bow African delta sound, an echo of hypnotic country blues.

Bill Wyman: "Brian was the first person in England to play bottleneck guitar, when *nobody* knew what it was."

And watching intently, standing in the back of the crowd, were three young blues fans who had come up from Dartford, Kent, on the bus and the tube. They couldn't take their eyes off Elmo Lewis, this guitar prodigy almost exactly their own age, maybe just a year older. They had their own amateur blues band back in Dartford, these kids: Mike Jagger, Keith Richards, and Dick Taylor. They were all eighteen years old.

Mike

Dartford is an ancient town southeast of London in Kent, a rest stop on the old pilgrims' road to Canterbury. Suburban now, back then it was a sleepy mix of housing, fields, marshland, and factories.

Michael Philip Jagger, "Mike" to his mates, was born there in July 1943. His father, Basil "Joe" Jagger, was a serious, athletic northerner from a Baptist family in Yorkshire. Mike's mother, Eva Scutts, was born in Australia and came to England as a child. They married in 1940 as the Blitzkrieg was starting. Mike was the first son, joined by brother Chris four years later. Joe Jagger worked as a physical education teacher. Ambitious, he took graduate courses and became a sports professor at a teachers' college. Later Joe Jagger became the foremost British authority on American basketball and the author of a landmark textbook on teaching the sport.

In 1950, when he was seven, Mike started at nearby Wentworth Primary School. In his class was a dark, runty little boy called Ricky, who lived on the same street as the Jaggers. This was Keith Richards, a big Roy Rogers fan who knew the names of Roy's horse, dog, Jeep, etc. (Cowboys and Indians was *the* game for English boys in those postwar days when their dreams had a distinct American accent.) Mike and Keith knew each other, but weren't really friends. While Mike was outgoing and popular, Keith kept to himself and went home after school.

In 1954, the Jaggers moved to a bigger house on Denver Road in a better part of Dartford. Mike started at Dartford Grammar, the next rung up the British educational system's ladder of success. He was a good student who fit in well and excelled in sports like cross-country running and basketball. At the same time, he annoyed some of his teachers with his cruelly dead-on impersonations of their foibles.

The Jagger household was prim and very proper, kept orderly by meticulous, somewhat snobby Eva Jagger, who sold cosmetics door-to-door. Mike didn't invite his friends to the house, preferring to spend time at their houses, or to be alone. Some of the local kids thought he was a mama's boy. The focus at home was on school and especially sports. Joe Jagger took his boys "down the Valley" to see the local football team, Charlton Athletic, and its famous keeper, Sam Bartram. In 1957, when Mike was fourteen, he started appearing with his dad in the ATV television series *Seeing Sport,* which promoted activities such as rock climbing. It was the beginning of his career in showbiz, and it set him a little apart from his friends, who were nonplussed when Mike announced he had to rush off to the studio to be on the telly.

"In those slightly post-Edwardian days," Mick later told an interviewer, "everybody had to do a turn at family gatherings. You might recite poetry, and Uncle Whatever would play the piano and sing, and you all had something to do. And I was just one of those kids. You have to want some sort of approval, but it's also just the love of doing it."

Mike Jagger was into music early. The Jaggers had a radio but no record player until much later. Mike couldn't hear the American music he liked on the BBC, so like other R&B fans, he tuned in the distant signal of the American AFN (Armed Forces Network) broadcasting from Germany. The AFN played music that nobody else in Europe heard: jazz, country and western, and especially Chicago blues. It was a gold mine for a few English kids in love with American sounds and the faraway dreams they represented. Mike also picked up Americana at a summer job teaching children sports at an American air base, where a black cook was always playing R&B.

He got his first guitar at fourteen, a Spanish acoustic bought while on holiday in Spain. Already adept at singing tunes he heard on the radio, Mike started learning to play Ritchie Valens's big hit "La Bamba." A gifted mimic since he learned to talk, Mike bawled out a phonetic version of the Spanish lyric with an eye-popping intensity that scared his parents. At fifteen Mike Jagger already knew how to put a song over. Soon he was practicing his guitar in the garden shed in back of the house on Denver Road so his mother couldn't hear him. She didn't really approve.

Buddy Holly came to England that year, 1958, as pivotal a musical event as Muddy Waters's almost concurrent tour.

Holly was a gawky, goofy-looking Texan with Coke-bottle glasses, a neat little band, the Crickets, and a bag of great rock and roll songs: "That'll Be the Day," "Peggy Sue," "Maybe Baby," "Oh Boy," "Rave On." Holly's stuttering style and geeky demeanor gave immense hope to anyone, especially in England, who felt out of it and yet ready, ready, ready to rock and roll.

Mike and his friend Dick Taylor went to see Holly at a movie theater, the Woolwich Granada. Young Jagger had seen American rockers only on television shows like *Cool for Cats, Oh Boy,* and *Six Five Special,* which had introduced rockabilly stars like Eddie Cochran, Gene Vincent, and Ronnie Hawkins to England. Buddy Holly—twitching, stuttering, really intense Texas music—was Mike Jagger's first experience of living rock on the hoof.

Mike discovered Howlin' Wolf in Dick Taylor's record collection, and the two started to look for imports in the record shops along the Charing Cross Road. Mike began writing to Chess Records in Chicago to order LPs that were impossible to find in England. He got hold of a Blind Willie Johnson EP, *Dark Was the Night, Cold Was the Ground,* and wore it out. Mike and Dick and some chums in Dartford started jamming in the front room of Dick's house in Bexleyheath. Dick's mum would serve tea to the boys and giggle with Dick's sister in the kitchen as Mike Jagger belted out "La Bamba" for the umpteenth time.

They called themselves Little Boy Blue and the Blue Boys. ("Little Boy Blue" was Sonny Boy Williamson's *nom de bleus.*) Mick recalled later, "I used to do Saturday night shows with all these little groups. If I could get a show I would do it. I used to do *mad* things—get on my knees and roll on the floor—when I was fifteen, sixteen years old. And my parents were extremely disapproving of it all, because it was just not *done.* This was for very low-class people, remember. I didn't have any inhibitions. I saw Elvis and Gene Vincent and thought, 'Well, I can do this.' It's a real buzz, even in front of twenty people, to make a complete fool of yourself.

"But people seemed to like it, and it always seemed to be a success, and people were shocked. I could see it in their faces ... Yeah, I thought it was a bit wild for what was going on at the time, in these little places in the suburbs."

Mike Jagger finished Dartford Grammar in 1960 and won a grant to attend the prestigious London School of Economics, whose graduates usually went on to run the British Empire. Mike told friends he wanted to be a barrister or a journalist, maybe even a politician. During the summer, to earn money for his record addiction, he sold ice cream outside the Dartford library. Keith bought one once and they chatted briefly.

Mike started classes in September 1960, commuting by train from Dartford to LSE in Aldwych, in central London. He quickly identified the blues cultists among his fellow students and helped organize an informal club. Mike started bringing LPs from his impressive collection to school, and he was carrying a bunch of these when he was approached early one misty, gray October morning on the platform of Dartford Station by a starved-looking art student, who looked like he'd slept in his purple shirt and was carrying a guitar case. Mike knew the face: he'd been at school with him. "I always knew where he lived," Mick recalled, "because my mother would never lose contact with anybody, and she knew where they'd moved. I used to see him coming home from his school, which was less than a mile away from where we lived."

It was his new brother from the other side of the tracks, Keith Richards.

The Boy at the Top
of the Stairs

Keith's beloved grandfather, Theodore Augustus "Gus" Dupree, was a musician and bandleader descended from the Huguenots, Protestants who fled Catholic France in Elizabethan times and settled around Canterbury in Kent. Gus played some guitar, had dance bands in the area in the early 1930s, and fathered six pretty daughters. The youngest, Doris, married Bert Richards from northeast London in 1936. When the war came, she got pregnant to avoid factory work, and Keith was born in December 1943 in the same Dartford hospital where Mike Jagger had been born five months earlier.

With the Luftwaffe's bombs falling, the family was evacuated to the country while Bert was in the army. He was wounded in Normandy and after the war took a job in a factory in Hammersmith. Keith didn't see much of him and was raised an only child, doted on and coddled, in the musical world of the Dupree sisters and their dad. The Dupree girls were all talented, could play instruments, wanted to be actresses or movie stars. The family lived on Morland Avenue in Dartford and called their little boy "Ricky."

Gus Dupree played guitar, fiddle, and piano and breathed music into his grandson, especially the country and western styles of Ernest Tubb, Hank Williams, and Jimmie Rodgers. To supplement his income as a baker during the 1950s, he had a C&W group that played at American bases. Doris loved jazzy pop music, and the radio was always playing Sarah Vaughan, Ella Fitzgerald, Count Basie, Billy Eckstine, Django Reinhardt. When Keith visited his granddad's house in London, he would be drawn to Gus's guitar, which lived on top of the piano. Gus would take it out of its case, polish it with a cloth, tune it, play a little for the boy. He never offered the instrument, never pushed it on Keith, just let him be fascinated by it. Sometimes the two would visit Gus's friends in the repair shop under Ivor Marantz's music store in Charing Cross Road. Keith sat in the corner while the men repaired guitars and violins. The cozy room smelled of hot, bubbling glue, steamed wood, and tobacco, and Keith watched as they rebuilt old instruments and hung them from the ceiling to dry.

At age seven, Keith went to school. He hated it with a passion, preferring life in his mother's cheery house. He cried in the mornings, and they almost had to force him out of the house. At school, he met Mike Jagger, who remembered: "I asked him what he wanted to be when he grew up, and he said he wanted to be a cowboy like Roy Rogers, roping ponies and playing guitar."

Keith's two passions were animals and singing. By age eight, he was in the school choir, and a teacher picked him out as a natural harmonist, able to descant almost any tune by ear. At age ten, he was one of the best young choristers in London. The choir won several competitions, which is how Keith and three others—"the three biggest hoods in the school"—were picked to sing in the massed choirs at the coronation of the new English queen, Elizabeth II, at Westminster Abbey in 1953. He made several more appearances in the abbey at Christmastime, before his voice finally broke at thirteen.

In 1955, Bert Richards moved the family to the Temple Hill council estate on the other side of Dartford. It was government housing for working families, and for twelve-year-old Keith, it was rough. The older kids were Teds, Teddy boys, tough little thugs in exaggerated Edwardian costume who thought nothing of beating up weaker kids for their pocket money. It was the Teds who rioted when Bill Haley barnstormed the U.K. in '56. It was bicycle chains and razors in the ballrooms, the lead pipe down the trousers. The chicks were as tough as the cats. So Keith learned to keep his head down, watch his mouth, watch his back.

In 1956, Keith's poor grades channeled him into Dartford Technical College, where underachievers learned manual trades. He hated it and ended up having to do a year over again with younger kids, which he hated even more. But that was year one, when rock and roll hit England, and that was it for Keith's formal education. In early 1958, the family got its first record player, and for his birthday that December, Doris bought Keith his first guitar, a seven-quid Rosetti acoustic, and he started to practice almost every minute, sitting in a sonically cool place at the top of the staircase in the little council house. Keith had learned the rudiments from Gus Dupree, who had taught him to play the Spanish guitar classic "Malagueña." Now Keith hardly moved from the stairs as he laboriously taught himself guitarist Scotty Moore's bouncy riff from Elvis's "That's All Right, Mama" and the rhythmic lick from "Blue Moon of Kentucky." Scotty Moore was Keith's first mentor on the guitar via records, all the way from Sun Studios in Memphis, Tennessee.

Thrown out of school at sixteen for insolence, tight trousers, and cutting class, Keith enrolled at Sidcup Art School, where he took classes in commercial art. England's art colleges in the late 1950s were the real incubators of the rock movement. As David Bowie has said, "In Britain there was always this joke that you went to art school to learn to play blues guitar." Sidcup was full of talented kids like Keith with guitar cases slung over their shoulders. The smoky lavs were packed with teenage pickers teaching each other Woody Guthrie and Ramblin' Jack Elliott songs, trying to duplicate Leadbelly's ringing twelve-string orchestrations on cheap Spanish guitars with gut strings. The first song Keith learned to play in art school was Jack Elliott's version of "Cocaine Blues" (Keith didn't know what cocaine was). This is where Keith met Dick Taylor, who happened to be in Little Boy Blue and the Blue Boys with Mike Jagger.

Dick was another art student, more serious than Keith. They began to practice guitar together at Dick's house. Another schoolmate formed a country and western band, and Keith and Dick joined up. Keith Richards's first gig ever was at a dance in Eltham, south of London near Sidcup. The band didn't get paid, but this is where Keith started to play the easy progression that powers Hank Snow's classic country song "I'm Movin' On."

Chuck Berry got to England late, because his early records weren't released there and the movies he appeared in weren't distributed. Keith first heard him around 1959, and it was all over. "Chuck Berry was my *man*," he says. "He was really the one who made me say, as a teenager, 'Jesus Christ! I want to play guitar!' And then suddenly I had a focal point, not that I was naive enough to ever expect it to pan out. But now at least I had something to go for, some way to channel the energies you have at that age. And definitely, with rock and roll, you have to start somewhere around then."

Keith's discovery of Chuck Berry coincided with the young Richards's dreadful split with his father. Bert Richards worked in a warehouse, left home at five in the morning, and came back exhausted at seven at night to hear his boy making a racket at the top of the stairs with his guitar when he should have been doing his schoolwork. Bert hated his spotty son's art school look, the way he wore his hair long, his sullen, rebellious attitude. Mutual loathing developed, and Keith and his father stopped speaking around 1960. His parents divorced a couple years later. Despite occasional attempts to reach his dad by mail, it would be more than twenty years before Keith and his father were reconciled.

Dartford Station

Early commuter train from Dartford to Victoria Station in London, October 1960.

"So I get on the train one morning," says Keith, "and there's Mike Jagger, and under his arm he has four or five albums. I haven't seen him since the time I bought an ice cream off him, and we haven't hung around since we were five, six, ten years. We recognized each other straight off. 'Hi, man,' I say.

" 'Where ya goin'?' he says. And under his arm he's got Chuck Berry [*Rocking at the Hop*] and Little Walter, Muddy Waters [*The Best of Muddy Waters*]. I say, 'You're into Chuck Berry, man, really? That's a coincidence. I can play that shit. I didn't know you were into that.'

"He says, 'Yeah, I've even got a little band. And I got a few more albums. Been writin' away to this, uh, Chess Records in Chicago and got a mailing list thing and got it together, y'know?'

" 'Wow, man.' So I invited him up to my place for a cup of tea. He started playing me these records and I really turned on to it."

Keith was impressed. It wasn't just that Mike was carrying these records. It was more that anyone in England had them at all. Expensive imports, they had to be specially ordered. The orders were filled by Leonard Chess's own eighteen-year-old son, Marshall, who worked in the Chess stockroom in Chicago.

Keith: "Back then the long-playing record was a very small market in England. Top-of-the-line stuff . . . Flash son of a bitch, because he comes from a better side of town than me. It's the music I'm trying to listen to. I've got a few singles, but he's got the bloody albums. *One Dozen Berries*. I'm afraid he might reach the [train door] handle before I rob them off him."

Keith managed to borrow *The Best of Muddy Waters*. He abandoned his post at the top of the stairs and spent days studying the album. It changed his life.

Keith: "Just sitting in that train carriage in Dartford, it was almost like we made a deal without knowing it, like Robert Johnson at the crossroads. There was a *bond* made there that, despite everything else, goes on and on. Like a solid deal."

So Mike and Keith linked up. They both knew Dick Taylor, and in short order Keith became a Blue Boy. Dick Taylor switched from guitar to bass, and Keith played lead guitar. They spent eighteen months jamming Buddy Holly, "Sweet Little Sixteen," and "Around and Around" in Dick's front room. Dick's mum liked to watch because Mike was already doing his little moves, tossing his head, dramatizing the tunes. Mike went on summer holiday in Devon with Keith's family and delivered his first public performance during the summer of 1961 at a local pub, doing Everly Brothers songs, with Keith singing harmony and playing guitar.

Then Keith satisfied his Chuck Berry obsession by trading a bunch of records for an electric guitar: a cheap, blond, no-name, f-hole acoustic with a Japanese pickup. The amplifier was an old radio. But it worked—sometimes. The pickup would get loose. "Does anyone have a soldering gun?" Soon Keith was learning "Maybelline" and "Beautiful Delilah," songs that Berry played so easily with his huge hands.

Keith now got to work, popping speed—purple hearts, French blues, female period pills, anything—to get the stamina to practice these riffs over and over. All this went on until he and Mike heard about the new blues club in Ealing and decided to go to the club's second session on March 24, 1962.

This time, Alexis Korner let Brian Jones get up and play. Brian and Charlie Watts had just spoken to each other for the first time. Mike, Keith, and Dick were gob-smacked by the Elmo Lewis persona, glowing with the groove and blasting loud, firey guitar over Charlie Watts's solid backbeat. Mike went over and spoke with Elmo after the number and got pulled in by the soft patter, the hair, the penetrating eyes, the uncanny bluesman's cool. They talked about him all the way back to Dartford.

On April 7, Mike, Keith, and Dick were back at the Ealing Club. Alexis again brought Elmo Lewis onstage.

Keith: "Suddenly it's *Elmore James,* man, this cat . . . And it's *Brian,* man, and he's sitting on this little [stool], and he's bent over . . . *da-da-da, da-da-da* on acoustic guitar with a pickup. We thought he was just fucking incredible, so this time we both went up and spoke with him, and he told us he was forming a band. He could have easily joined Blues Incorporated, because Alexis wanted him, but he needed to have his own, and he wanted it to be his own baby."

The lads from Dartford were also impressed when Brian told them he already had his own baby—in fact, a bunch of babies—with maybe another on the way. This bloke was only twenty, but he seemed so *seasoned.*

Keith: "He was a good guitar player then. He had the touch and was just peaking. He was already out of school, he'd been fired from a bunch of jobs. He was already living on his own and told us he was trying to find a pad for his old lady and their kid. Whereas Mick and I were just kicking around in back rooms, still living at home."

At the same time, when they talked about him, they mocked Brian for his posh accent and his soft manner, which they regarded as provincial. They may have been from the suburbs, but Mike and Keith thought themselves Londoners, disdainful of anyone they considered a hick. This was when Mike (under the influence of the egalitarian, pro-Labour LSE students he admired) was beginning to be downwardly mobile into the newly chic working class, adopting a faux-cockney accent in the tones of the East End, growing his hair, changing his moniker from Mike to the more laddish Mick.

Mick Jagger.

Had a certain edge to it.

Blues Incorporated

Back in Dartford, the Blue Boys recorded a tape reel of their favorites—"Around and Around," "Bright Lights, Big City," and some others—and sent it to Alexis Korner with a worshipful letter written by Mick. Korner liked the energy, and Cyril Davies heard something in Jagger's voice, so Mick and Keith were invited to visit the Korner household. They arrived to find Brian Jones waking up from a night under the Korners' kitchen table. They listened to records—Muddy, Memphis Slim, and Robert Johnson, unknown to the boys from Kent. Next time they visited the Ealing Club, Mick got invited to jump onstage and sing Billy Boy Arnold's "Bad Boy." But there was a rush to the bar as he started to sing, and no one noticed him.

The second time he sang with Blues Incorporated, Mick brought Keith on, and they did Chuck Berry's "Around and Around" and "Beautiful Delilah" to a smattering of polite applause and then stony silence from the 120 paying members of the Ealing Club. "Good voice you got," Cyril said to Mick, not deigning to notice shy Keith. Dick Taylor, sitting in the audience, scratched his new goatee and realized *everyone* in the club hated Keith as an unwelcome intrusion of déclassé rock and roll.

And yet, even so, Mick was just . . . *glowing*. He drank a quick lager to wet his whistle and was so jazzed on the pure heat of it that he couldn't say a word, let alone worry about the negative reaction to Keith's raw chords. On the way home, they agreed to keep going.

By late April '62, Mick had become one of five rotating singers in Blues Incorporated, performing three songs a night in a cardigan sweater and a skinny black tie. He'd sing half-drunk because he was so nervous, shouting "Got My Mojo Working" with Long John Baldry and Paul Pond on either side of him. Other singers included Eric Burdon and Manfred Mann. Eric Clapton, before he owned a guitar, would show up at Ealing on Tuesday nights, ask to sing "Roll Over Beethoven" (the only song he knew), and then disappear. They called Clapton "Plimsolls" because he looked down at his sneakers when he sang.

As he gained confidence, Mick started doing his act: tossing his hair, rolling his eyes, dipping his shoulders, suggestive hand gestures, tight-assed little spins, acting out the risqué lyrics with his eyes and especially his lips. They were full-fledged, pouty, *serious* lips, and he kept licking them between verses, diminutive flicks of the tongue. All this got noticed. Cyril Davies called him "Marilyn Monroe" behind his back, and there was no doubt that at age nineteen Mick was already bringing an ironic, "camp" sensibility to his delivery of the songs.

The Ealing crowd never saw Keith without Mick. Keith was the sidekick, the interior of Mick's outgoing persona. When Mick got onstage to sing, Keith stood in the shadows, waiting for his turn. Then Mick brought Keith on to rock the house with Chuck Berry's "Around and Around," annoying Cyril Davies, who hated rock and roll. Davies refused to even speak to Keith, who didn't care because he in turn hated Blues Incorporated. To Keith, they were just a dreary bunch of middle-aged men. Keith was into the mating dance of rock and roll, not the weary fatalism of the older blues guys.

Then a serious buzz began about Mick, the new face in town. The weekly music paper *Disc*, May 19, 1962: "A nineteen-year-old Dartford rhythm and blues singer, Mick Jagger, has joined the Alexis Korner group, Blues Incorporated, and will sing with them regularly on their Saturday dates at Ealing and their Thursday sessions at the Marquee Jazz Club, London." As the Ealing Club caught on, a few trendy types began to show up, the hipper fringe of Swinging London slumming in Ealing. Alexis saw Mick going down well with the girls, so he started bringing him along to sing at the debutante parties Alexis was hired to entertain. This was Blues Incorporated as a society band, though without Charlie, who couldn't be bothered.

This was also Mick's entrée into posh society; at the deb parties, he met London's *jeunesse dorée,* young members of the aristocracy and rich families—the Honorable This, Lady Arabella That, the legendary Tara Browne, Guinnesses, Tennants, Ormsby-Gores—with whom he happily hung out ("That's where we met all our friends," he claimed years later). It was a giant step up in the stratified English class system from his roots in petit-bourgeois exurbia.

Brian Jones was also very much part of the scene at Ealing and the increasingly clamorous Thursday nights at the Marquee, where the customers had started dancing on the tables. He turned Charlie Watts on to Robert Johnson's just-released posthumous compilation album, *King of the Delta Blues Singers.* But soon Pat Andrews arrived with baby Julian in tow and sent Brian into shock by moving in with him. So Brian took a job in a department store while Pat worked in a laundry. Brian was quickly fired for stealing, and the young couple was evicted. Brian found a flat in Notting Hill Gate and another job in another store. He got fired from that, too, for stealing.

Brain was determined to have his own R&B band and kept hustling. In May 1962, he advertised for R&B musicians in *Jazz News,* rehearsals to begin in the back room of a pub in Leicester Square. One of the first to answer the ad was an older guy: a brawny, unhip, geezer-type Scot named Ian Stewart.

Stu, as he was known, was born in Scotland in 1938. The family moved to suburban London when he was a baby, and Stu grew up playing the piano in the parlor. Drafted in 1956, he was released for medical reasons and took a clerical job with a chemical company. He'd been to Ealing a couple of times, had seen Brian play, but was a bit chagrined when he showed up at the White Bear pub and found that Brian was into small group Chicago blues. Stu was a committed boogie-woogie piano scholar, who'd started out admiring white swing bands and then discovered old "barrelhouse" players Albert Ammons and Pete Johnson, whose boogie piano duets he found "very moving." Stu liked the big American R&B ensembles of the early fifties—Louis Jordan and Wynonie Harris—where the piano played eight to the bar and the saxes ruled. But Stu could see Brian's potential and stifled his disappointment when Jones kept talking about Jimmy Reed and Muddy Waters.

They began rehearsing, got thrown out of the pub after Brian was caught stealing cigarettes, then moved to the Bricklayer's Arms in Lisle Street, Soho, where golden Brian Jones and solid, true-hearted Ian Stewart became the two founding members of the Rolling Stones.

————

Alexis Korner helped Brian find players for his new band. Geoff Bradford had recorded with Alexis and also played slide guitar (better than Brian, according to Charlie). Brian Knight was a good blues singer and played the harmonica well enough to teach Brian Jones a little. But Bradford was a serious blues purist, deep into Elmore and John Lee Hooker, and didn't want to rock out. Knight quarreled with Jones over songs—Knight wanted to do country blues—and quit. Brian asked Charlie Watts to join on drums, but Charlie didn't want to turn pro. He'd turned down Korner's offers to play full-time because he didn't want to give up his job. In fact, when Blues Incorporated got really big that summer, Charlie left the group, later joining a band, Blues by Six, that didn't interfere with his work schedule. So other drummers were in and out of Brian's new band: Ginger Baker, Carlo Little, Tony Chapman, Mick Avory.

And Brian wanted Mick Jagger because the buzz was out that this weird new talent was out there, this young cat who was putting (and this was, of course, completely unspoken) a sex appeal spin on R&B, the only possible way to transcend the rigid boundaries of fandom and maybe take R&B *to the kids*. Brian knew that Jagger was the guy he wanted to be in a band with. Over a pint of ale in a pub during the interval of a Marquee gig, Brian invited Mick and (somewhat grudgingly) Keith to a rehearsal the next day.

The Rollin' Stones

Keith Richards—eighteen years old, rail-thin, in jeans, denim jacket, and purple shirt, looking like, in William Burroughs's phrase, a sheep-killing dog—slung his cheap guitar in a plastic case down Wardour Street as strippers darted past him in wigs and brassieres. Bricklayer's Arms, at the corner of Wardour and Lisle, smelled of warm ale and last night's cigarettes. Cheery old barmaid. "We're supposed to rehearse here. Would you know—?" "Second floor, luv."

Keith heard the piano by the time he hit the first landing. Beautiful rolling boogie with a touch of Crescent City stride—relaxed, soulful, totally, craftsmanly expert. Keith slipped into the room and doughty Ian Stewart was sitting at the piano, which had been pushed over by the window. He was playing whorehouse piano licks, Jelly Roll Morton and Professor Longhair, and he didn't know anyone was listening. He was staring out the window because, Keith later realized, his bicycle was chained to a post outside and he was worried someone would nick it.

Keith was impressed, *riveted*. He'd seen Stu play with Korner and pull the amateurish band together with his authority. He knew Stu didn't care shit for Chuck Berry. To hard-core blues fans like Stu, Keith was rock and roll and should have been ducking brawls on the ballroom circuit with Neil Christian and the Crusaders (whose guitarist was seventeen-year-old Jimmy Page). Keith just stood in awe and listened to the fluid pianism of this Pinetop Perkins in the body of a square-jawed Scot. Every few minutes Stu would comment on one of the strippers flashing down the street in her high heels. Finally Stu turned around, inspected Keith, and deflatingly deadpanned: "And you must be the Chuck Berry artist."

————

Rehearsals got under way. Brian Jones was in charge, the leader. Geoff Bradford, ten years older and visibly uptight, on blues guitar. Brian on guitar. Keith on rhythm guitar. Dick Taylor on bass. Stu on piano. Mick singing. Various drummers, Mick Avory a lot. They started learning Elmore James songs, dissecting Jimmy Reed masterpieces, and speeding up Chuck Berry.

Brian was encouraging to Dick Taylor, who was new on the bass, and tried to be accommodating to Mick and his mates, who wanted Chuck and Bo, though he himself was really interested in being the white Jimmy Reed. There was a little conflict and some mixed feelings, but all were impressed by Brian's brilliant musicianship, his out-of-town diligence, and his certainty that they were cool and that something was gonna happen, man.

Something had to happen, because none of them had a shilling to his name.

————

Their break came when the BBC offered Blues Incorporated a slot on its *Jazz Club* radio show on Thursday, July 12, 1962. But the BBC only had a budget to pay five musicians, and the producer didn't want Mick anyway because it was a jazz show. Since Korner couldn't make his Thursday gig at the Marquee, Harold Pendleton had to find another act. He hired Long John Baldry's group, but was persuaded by Brian to hire his new group to play between Baldry's sets. Panic set in when Brian realized they didn't have decent enough amplifiers for a paid performance, so Mick got his dad to lend them enough to rent some cheap Harmony amps, and Brian got hold of a used Harmony Stratotone electric guitar.

When Pendleton told Brian the group needed a name for the adverts, Brian came up with "the Rollin' Stones," from Muddy Waters's classic "Rollin' Stone." Stu hated the name ("It sounds like a troupe of fucking

Irish acrobats"), but it stuck. To Brian's dismay, the ad for the gig read, "Mick Jagger and the Rollin' Stones."

And so, consciously or not, the Stones anointed themselves as the anticipated messiahs of the blues—the sons, the boy-children, of Muddy Waters, agents of Mississippi Delta culture to the world. It was a prophesy they managed to fulfill, introducing blues and R&B to their huge postwar generation, and so keeping the endangered species alive.

————

The Rollin' Stones played their debut gig at the Marquee in Oxford Street on a bright London summer evening in July. Their gear was humped down the narrow stairs by Stu and Brian's friend Dick Hattrell, who acted as their unpaid roadie. The crowd was half Marquee jazz regulars and half young R&B fans glazed over from speed, cigarettes, and too much espresso. Mick, Keith, and Brian were the front line, with Stu on piano and maracas, Dick Taylor on bass, and (possibly) Mick Avory on drums. Wearing coats and ties, they lit into "Kansas City." Despair as Brian and Stu realized that the drummer was way off. But they continued for an hour of chugging, clunky, piano-driven R&B: "Honey What's Wrong," "Confessin' the Blues," "Bright Lights," "Dust My Blues," with Brian's clarion slide guitar that woke the audience up. Mick and Brian got some kids dancing. "Down the Road Apiece" injected some up-tempo Chuck Berry rocking into the set. Back to laconic Jimmy Reed blues with "I Want to Love You." "Bad Boy." "I Ain't Got You." Jimmy Reed again with "Hush Hush." Muddy's "Ride 'Em on Down." Chuck Berry's "Back in the U.S.A." "Feel Kind of Lonesome." Elmore James's "Blues Before Sunrise." "Big Boss Man." Billy Boy Arnold's "Don't Stay Out All Night." And (according to the set list jotted down by Stu in his diary along with the keys the songs were in) they finished with Jimmy Reed's "Tell Me That You Love Me" and Elmore James's "Happy Home."

They had a drink in a pub afterward and split the twenty-pound fee among them.

Charlie Watts went to see them that night. "There were a lot of people dancing," he recalled, "but the usual Marquee jazz crowd was saying, 'This is *really* terrible.' But really, they were very popular even then. The thing was, the bands that were doing that stuff—me included—were eccentric old men. Now the Stones, the front line at any rate, were young, so there was obvious appeal for the kids that wanted to dance. Alexis's band was a joke to look at, but this lot crossed the barrier. They actually looked like rock stars, I suppose, but *they could play.*"

———

They rehearsed for the rest of the summer, finding occasional substitute gigs at the Marquee. Mick Avory left and was replaced by Tony Chapman, who played in a South London rock and roll band, the Cliftons. (Some believe it was Chapman, not Avory, who played the first Stones gig at the Marquee.) The other Stones didn't like Chapman, but he kept showing up. Brian asked Charlie Watts to join, but he again declined. Satisfied with his job and his amateur Blues by Six gig, Charlie Watts was out of Brian's reach, at least financially.

In August, Mick found a cheap flat at 102 Edith Grove in the unfashionable part of Chelsea called World's End. It was a two-room dump with bare lightbulbs and a shilling-fed gas fire for heat, and for the next eight months it was Stones world headquarters. Mick and Keith both left Dartford and moved in, along with a young printer named Jimmy Phelge, who kept everyone laughing with his disgusting personal hygiene and sick, gross-out humor. Brian lived at Edith Grove but had Pat and their baby in another flat. Food and money were in extremely short supply, and that fall the little group was saved from starvation by Doris Richards, who turned up occasionally with groceries and clean laundry.

As the autumn of 1962 wore on, the Rollin' Stones picked up occasional jobs, at a parish hall in Richmond, arranged by Brian, and at the Red Lion pub in Stu's hometown, Cheam, in Surrey. Dick Taylor left the band in September to attend the Royal College of Art. For a couple of months, the bass chores were handled by various people, most often Colin Golding, who probably played around eight gigs, even more than

Dick Taylor (who went on to start the legendary R&B band Pretty Things, with fellow Sidcup student Phil May).

Gigs were hard to come by because the old jazz promoters who controlled the clubs were against playing blues. "We were a blues band that played in clubs," Mick said, *"not* a rock band that played in ballrooms. We didn't play any Eddie Cochran numbers." Brian Jones was moved to write a detailed letter to *Jazz News,* explaining that R&B was a fresh wind blowing in from Chicago that deserved a proper hearing. The jazzers thought that Alexis and the Stones were trying to kill trad, and they were right. They tried to starve the Rollin' Stones out and almost succeeded. Even Cyril Davies fired the Stones as a support band for his powerful R&B All-Stars after a bitter argument with Mick about blues singing. Sarcastic Harold Pendleton needled them constantly about their act and beatnik appearance until one night Keith grabbed his guitar by the neck and tried to smash Pendleton in the head. After that, the Stones were banned from the Marquee. Occasional gigs at Ken Colyer's Studio 51 and Giorgio Gomelsky's Piccadilly Club didn't make up for the loss of the West End's premier venue.

It was the Rollin' Stones against the music business. No young band had ever taken on the big boys before and come out with all their fingers intact.

The Luckiest Man
in the World

Now it was late autumn in England, John Keats's season of mists and mellow fruitfulness. England was about to suffer its worst winter in years.

Late 1962 was an uncertain time for the Rollin' Stones. With few gigs and no permanent rhythm section, Mick Jagger was getting a little vague. He was still doing the occasional gig and society party with Alexis. The new term at LSE had begun, and Mick's student grant was his only source of income. Brian and Keith had burned their bridges, were committed to the band and frustrated that Mick seemed to be waffling. When Brian got fired from his last job for stealing, he had to talk his way out of being arrested. Now he and Keith began to really bond, spending their days in the freezing Edith Grove flat, learning to weave their guitars in an aggressive blues phalanx. At one point, after Jagger missed some rehearsals to study for exams, Brian and Keith felt abandoned and talked about forming an Everly Brothers—style duo together. While they were plotting, Mick visited Brian's flat and made love to his girlfriend, Pat.

It was around this time that Brian really got into the harmonica, with Little Walter and Sonny Boy as his models. Soon Brian even lost interest in playing guitar, his saxophone background providing a good foundation for blowing the harp with his band in rehearsal.

Keith: "Brian and me would be home in this pad [Edith Grove] all day, trying to make one foray a day either to pick up empty beer bottles from a party or raid the local supermarket because we were so hungry. We'd try and get some eggs or potatoes or something.

"I went out one morning and came back in the evening and Brian was blowing harp! Man! He's got it *together.* He's standin' at the top of the stairs, saying, 'Listen to this: *waaaaaaaah wah, waaaaaaaaaaah wah wah wah wah, waaaaaa waaa aaa.*' All these blues notes coming out. He says, 'I've learned how to do it! I've figured it out.' And he did it in one fucking day."

———

There was shock in Edith Grove when they first heard "Love Me Do" on the radio by a new group from Liverpool called the Beatles. "Love Me Do" was a little pop blues with a harmonica solo and a touch of Buddy Holly and the Everlys. It was a bolt from the blue; the Beatles were unknown in London and only a rumor in Soho.

John Lennon, Paul McCartney, George Harrison, and their new drummer, Ringo Starr, had survived their leather-jacketed years in

Hamburg dives and were now fighting their way out of remote Liverpool, which might have been Mars as far as London was concerned. Their manager, Brian Epstein, had cleaned them up, let their hair grow, put them in modernist suits, but had been rebuffed by the big labels in London. Then he sold a demo to Parlophone, which in October 1962 released their first single, "Love Me Do," chosen (according to their biographer Philip Norman) "with difficulty from an eccentric and uncommercial repertoire."

It made Mick Jagger sick. Keith was in shock. "It was an attack from the north," he said later. "We thought we were the only guys in the world."

The Stones wanted to be the Next Big Thing, but the Beatles from uncool Liverpool had beaten them to stardom, launching the "Mersey Sound" of Liverpool groups that dominated white pop for the next two years. It took the Stones that long to catch the Beatles' wave, after which the two bands would form what Keith has called "a double act" that lasted for the rest of the sixties.

———

Brian Jones, de facto manager of the Rollin' Stones, realized he had to make something happen, so he deployed his soft-edged charm and impressive faith in his band to massage his contacts to get a record deal, the Holy Grail of bandhood.

He hustled some studio time at Curly Clayton Sound Studios in North London, and on October 27 the Rollin' Stones cut a three-song demo: Muddy's "Soon Forgotten," Jimmy Reed's "Close Together," and a new Bo Diddley number, "You Can't Judge a Book (by Looking at the Cover)." Brian sent their demo tape to an executive at EMI, one of the two major record labels (the other was Decca) in England at the time. EMI passed, and they were back where they started.

At a Wednesday night gig by a band called the Presidents (led by young musician Glyn Johns) at the Red Lion pub, drummer Tony Chapman brought along the bass player from his old band, Bill Perks, and introduced him to Ian Stewart, who was in the audience. Stu mentioned that the Stones were looking for a full-time bass and suggested Bill audition for them at their Friday rehearsal at the Wetherby Arms. Bill promised to show up.

———————

Bill Perks was older than the Stones, born to an impoverished family in Penge, a tough part of South London, in 1936. He felt the war: evacuation, his neighborhood flattened by bombs, schoolmates killed. They ate horsemeat and whale for protein when they could get it.

Willy was good at numbers and won a place at a good grammar school, where he was mocked for his cockney accent. In Penge, the kids threw bricks at him because they didn't like his school blazer and cap. He was beaten by his dad for wasting his time playing boogie-woogie piano instead of practicing classical scales. In 1953, his dad pulled him out of school two months before his last exams and put him to work in a bookmaker's shop for three pounds ten shillings a week.

Bill loved music and spent his evenings glued to the radio. His autobiography, *Stone Alone,* claims impressive sexual precocity. By 1955, he was in the Royal Air Force in Germany, where skiffle was the rage. He caught Chris Barber's band with Lonnie Donegan and picked up his first guitar. He also became friends with a fellow RAF airman, Lee Wyman, to whose last name Bill took a shine. Back home, he took a clerical job and married a local girl, Diane, who was three months gone at the time. This was 1959, and a son, Stephen, was born the following year.

Bill started playing in rock and roll bands and got involved with the Cliftons in the spring of 1962, switching to bass guitar (which he built himself) because they already had a lead. Many rehearsals, a few gigs around South London, and Bill bought a couple of amps, a Vox Phantom and an AC-30 as a spare, on the installment plan. That summer, Tony Chapman answered Brian Jones's ad for a bass player and started with the Stones. When Dick Taylor left and they couldn't find anyone good, Tony introduced Bill, which is how he found himself in a pub in Chelsea on December 7, being contemptuously snubbed by Keith and Brian. They looked like scruffy, arty-type bohemian bums to Bill, and Bill looked like a Ted to them—"a real London Ernie," as Keith put it.

Hate at first sight.

Bill: "It was snowing, there were two inches on the ground, and it was absolutely freezing. Tony and I went in his father's car to Chelsea for the audition. I brought all my stuff with me, including my spare amp, the echo unit, plus the enormous wardrobe [cabinet] I'd built, with my eighteen-inch speaker and the amplifier that ran it. They all knew who I was but no one spoke to me. Stu I'd met once before and I kind of said hello to him, but Brian and Keith were drinking at the bar and they totally ignored me for an hour and a half . . . Mick came over and said something, so I got my amp and that was a bit more interesting. We began playing 'I'm a King Bee,' the Jimmy Reed thing, and I found it easy to get into, just a simple twelve-bar riff."

Keith: "We turned up [at the rehearsal] and in walks Bill Wyman, ladies and gentlemen! Huge speaker he's got, and a spare Vox AC-30 amp, which is the biggest fuckin' amp we've ever seen in our lives. And that's *spare*! He says, 'You can put one of your guitars through there.' *Whew.* Put us up quite a few volts goin' through that thing.

"He had the bass together already, because he'd been playing in terrible, shitty rock bands for a few years. He's older than us; he knows how to play."

After they jammed for a while, Bill stood them a round of drinks and offered cigarettes. "These were jumped on," he says, "like I was offering famine relief." Still, Brian and Keith were cool, distant. Mick asked Bill if he knew any music by the Chicago bluesmen, and Bill replied that all he knew was Chuck Berry and Fats Domino. Bill said he didn't know Bo Diddley's stuff, drawing eye-rolling contempt from Brian and Keith.

But at the end of the day, they invited Bill back to their next rehearsal and somehow manipulated him into leaving his amps and gear in the front room of their lair in Edith Grove. Bill was appalled by the scene he found there—filth, old food and dirty socks strewn about, tubercular damp walls smelling of stale grease and poverty—but despite their misgivings about him, Bill Wyman was about to become a Rollin' Stone. Ian Stewart recalled, "There's a certain amount of truth in the old story about Bill being taken on because he had a few amplifiers. But remember, Bill was *very* good."

Hard-core Stones fans still call Bill the luckiest man in the world.

Swinging London

If timing is everything, the Rollin' Stones certainly picked the perfect moment. "It began in 1963," wrote Philip Larkin, quintessential poet of midcentury British angst, and by "it" Larkin meant the generational shift and daring pop experiments that made the stodgy gray kingdom blossom with art, wit, style, and hype that year. A manic new energy emerged as the generation born during the war remade British culture in its own image, an image broadcast to the wider world via music and design. "Swinging London" was the catchphrase for what happened in the capital in the early sixties. When the Stones burst out of their isolation into a rhythm and blues cult, they became among Swinging London's most famous avatars.

The only significant postwar English art movement until then had been the so-called Angry Young Men, the name loosely applied to a number of playwrights and novelists in the mid-1950s whose politically radical or anarchic work depicted existential alienation and malaise. The archetype emerged from director Tony Richardson's discovery of playwright John Osborne, whose *Look Back in Anger* pulled British theater into the twentieth century. Angry Young Men were portrayed by a new group of actors—Richard Burton, Laurence Harvey, Richard Harris, Dirk Bogarde—in a new cycle of movies that dealt with the harsh realities of postwar British life: *Room at the Top, The Loneliness of the Long Distance Runner, A Taste of Honey,* and later *The Servant.* In some ways, with their dark looks, foreign music, and threatening sexuality amid the sunny, unisex pop of early Swinging London, the Rollin' Stones might have been England's last Angry Young Men.

Angry Young heroes included fashion photographers, among the first sixties Englishmen to merge technology with style and get their work published widely. And then there were the Angry Young gangsters, tough East End hoodlums in sharp suits and flattened noses who operated in the underworld of gambling, extortion, leg-breaking and show business, owning and managing nightclubs. The masters of this world were the notorious Kray twins, Reg and Ron, whose sadistic and (closeted) homosexual crew of thugs controlled Plutonian activities in London after dark. The Krays in turn inspired a younger generation of petty criminals, drug dealers, and goons who became known as Chelsea Villains when a few were absorbed into the more upscale social order of Swinging London in the 1960s. A few of them gained fame "minding" rock stars on American tours a decade later.

By 1961, satire began to take the edge off some of the anger. *Beyond the Fringe* began as a Cambridge University student production lampooning politics and the church. It took London by storm, then Broadway. The magazine *Private Eye* skewered every target available, lowering the taste barrier and raising political consciousness. By 1963, the virus had spread to traditionally hidebound British TV when *That Was the Week That Was* began to laugh at the royal family on the BBC.

When the so-called Profumo Scandal broke in 1963, all social bets in England suddenly seemed off. The scandal involved a ring of beautiful call girls, a prominant society doctor, some titled names, London's West Indian underground, and the minister of war, John Profumo, who was caught sharing a girlfriend, Christine Keeler, with a Russian spy. Profumo resigned in the glare of publicity, and London's rarely viewed sexual underbelly was exposed to the world. Now a new group of faces— perhaps only two hundred people in all—took over a new batch of clubs and discotheques and created the inspired ambience called Swinging London.

There are several ways of looking at Swinging London, which lasted roughly from 1962 to 1965.

In one, Swinging London was a British Renaissance of pop music, pop art, fashion, design, and photography in which class barriers gave way to talent, style, and hard work. In this view, pop stars, louche young aristocrats, the fashion world, and talented art dealers created an exciting vibration that captured the speedy zeitgeist of the early sixties.

In another, Swinging London was a cynical marketing campaign that masked the loss of the British Empire to decolonization (and outright rebellion in Rhodesia) and the subsequent loss of national wealth, the rise of the welfare state, and the degradation of a once-great nation.

And then there's Ian Stewart's view of Swinging London as a load of bollocks in which no-talent bands competed with horrible "art" to outshine each other in a drugged world of cheap hustlers and incredible pretense—a soulless cavalcade of crap and wasted lives. A lot of others felt that way too, but by then London was in full swing, and the money was pouring in as the "British Invasion" stormed American teenage markets.

Swinging London preferred American pop songs and dances like the twist and so was at first ambivalent about the Beatles when they arrived in London in 1963. The Beatles felt this, famously sticking together in nightclubs for protection against snubs and put-downs. The Beatles had been transformed by manager Brian Epstein from a punkish band in black leather to a sanitized pop group in matching suits and boots. Moptop hair replaced greasy pompadours, and sometimes-cruel insolence (Lennon's spastic imitations) had turned into bluff, clever repartee. Now the Beatles were unstoppable: their second single, "Please Please Me," took the country by storm, and their personal charm captured teenage girldom. When met with resistance from the London press, Epstein hired a nineteen-year-old Soho P.R. kid named Andrew Oldham, who had started running errands for designer Mary Quant. Speed-happy Andrew got a buzz going in the papers and helped sell the Beatles to London, no mean feat.

Many other Swinging London faces would impact the Stones. The young art dealer Robert Fraser opened a gallery that brought New York's pop art stars Andy Warhol and Jim Dine to England. Antiques dealer Christopher Gibbs was making his first forays into Morocco, returning with the wild Berber fabrics and artifacts that would launch the orientalism of the era. Donald Cammell was painting brilliant portraits in his Chelsea studio, dabbling in the occult, and reading the magic-realist stories of Jorge Luis Borges, the Argentine master whose work only became available in English in 1962.

And then there was Tara Browne. By 1963, Tara was a deliciously rich and fey eighteen-year-old heir to the Guinness brewing fortune. He lived in Paris with his mother and in a castle in Ireland. When in London, he was installed in a suite at Claridge's. He got around town in a chauffeured Lincoln equipped with a rare, battery-powered singles changer that played fresh American pop hits that Tara had flown in monthly. It was Bobby Vee's "Rubber Ball" and "Take Good Care of My Baby" and the Beach Boys' "Surfin' USA" as Tara cruised the West End and Chelsea in lavender silk shirts from Paris, starting instant disco parties in train stations when he and his friends set up the little record player and danced around the photo booths. Tara was golden, aristocratic, warm, generous, beautiful, and a little crazed. If anyone typified the instinctive hedonism and expansive personality of Swinging London, it was young Tara Browne. He helped tune in the essential romantic signal of the times, and both the Beatles and the Stones loved him to death.

Pandemonium in Richmond

With Bill Perks now in the band (having adopted the Stones' daring, combed-forward hairstyle), the Rollin' Stones began to sound good. If only they could score a decent drummer . . .

Brian Jones kept hustling with jesuitical fervor. Right after the start of the new year, 1963, he wrote to the BBC asking for an audition so the Stones' "authentic Chicago rhythm and blues music" could get on the radio. Brian was tireless in looking for gigs to keep the band together. He also collected and paid out the band's money and, like any good rock and roll manager, started padding the group's expenses, stealing whatever he could. "He conned us," Wyman later said, "and we knew it." The Stones played Ealing, the Flamingo in Soho, and the Red Lion, where Charlie Watts turned up; once again Brian, Mick, and Keith begged him, without much hope, to join them. They desperately needed him. According to Keith, "The desire to get Charlie was one of the driving forces that nailed this band together. It was a conspiracy on our part. 'We've got to keep going long enough to offer Charlie Watts five pounds a week.' " Charlie liked their music and told them they needed "a fucking great drummer," but he was still working with Blues by Six and was reluctant to give up his secure job. He asked Bobbie Korner what he should do, and she told him to give the Stones a go. Charlie was tired of hauling his drum kit around on the tube anyway. Stu later recalled, "We said to Charlie, 'Look, you're in the band. That's it.' And Charlie said, 'Yeah, all right then, but I don't know what my dad's gonna say.' "

After two more gigs with drummer Tony Chapman, they fired him at the Ricky Tick in Windsor. "Sorry, man," Brian told him, "but you have to fuck off." Chapman was angry and turned to Bill, whom he had brought into the band. "Right, Bill, come on—we can start a new band." But Bill looked away and kept wiping off his bass guitar. "Sorry, Tony, but I'm happy where I am, and I think I'll stay for a while."

Charlie Watts's first show with the Rollin' Stones was at the Flamingo in Piccadilly on January 14, 1963. The band watched in near disbelief as smiling Charlie, head tilted characteristically to his right, locked into a locomotive groove with Bill that made them really cook. Stu realized the Stones now had the best young drummer in England and that this could be the making of the group.

The next night, they played the Marquee, opening for Cyril Davies's All-Stars, a powerful blues band (with future Stones sideman Nicky

Hopkins on piano). The new Stones blew Davies off the stage and into oblivion.

Charlie started hanging out in frigid Edith Grove, where the only heat came from a gas meter on the wall fed with scarce shillings. Compulsive Brian infuriated his mates by using all their hot water to constantly wash his hair (they called him "Mr. Shampoo"). Brian and Keith spent their days wrapped in blankets, trying to practice guitar with gloves on. Charlie furthered his R&B education with the records Brian played for him, hour after hour.

"By the time I joined the Stones, I was a bit used to rock and roll," Charlie recalled. "I knew most of the rock and roll guys, people like Screaming Lord Sutch [whose act lampooned class pretentions], though I'd never had any desire to *play* it myself. But by the time I joined them, I was quite used to Chuck Berry and that. It was actually sitting up endlessly with Keith and Brian, waiting for jobs to come up, just listening to Little Walter and all that, that it got really ground in."

From the beginning, Charlie changed the Stones. Before, they had basically been copying the records they liked. But on a song like Chuck Berry's "Talkin' 'Bout You," Charlie would tap out a counterrhythmic shuffle beat under the Stones. Bill would play fast eighth notes to keep up with him, and the two guitars followed them. The phrase "shuffle and eighths" soon became an in-band description of the new style they were learning to play over Charlie's more sophisticated time.

Brian, meanwhile, ordered Charlie to grow his hair longer and start combing it forward.

––––––

Early in February 1963, Brian contacted filmmaker and R&B impresario Giorgio Gomelsky, who entered the scene when he made a film of the Chris Barber band at the first Richmond Jazz Festival in 1961. Brian heard he was starting a jazz club in suburban Richmond, just southwest of London, and started to pester him.

"Giorgio," Brian would whisper, "you *must* come hear my band, best

thing in London, we're playing rhythm and blues, Chicago, you'll dig it."
Russian-born, beatnik-goateed, with instinctive cosmopolitan tastes in
music, Gomelsky came to a Stones gig at the Red Lion in early February
and was impressed with the new kick that Charlie brought into play.
But when Brian asked for Gomelsky's Sunday evening slot at his new
club, he was turned down because it had been promised to another
band . . . which never showed up.

Giorgio called Stu on Monday morning. "Tell everybody in the
band you guys are on next Sunday for a quid apiece." So on February 24,
the Rollin' Stones made their debut at Gomelsky's yet-to-be-named club
in the back room of the Station Hotel, across from the Richmond tube
stop. Playing for about thirty kids, the Stones rocked through "Talkin'
'bout You," "Mona," "Pretty Thing," and others, finishing with their new,
orgasmic Bo Diddley showstopper, "Hey Crawdaddy."

"Ah gotta line an' yew gotta pole, less go fishin' at da crawdad
hole . . ."

What Charlie Watts could do with the Bo Diddley beat can't be put
into words. Any drummer who mastered the primitive rhythm saw what
it could do to a party. Gomelsky saw what it did at the Station Hotel, with
kids jumping around and dancing, and he offered the Stones a Sunday residency. Word spread like a disease. Sixty kids showed up the following
week, and it doubled after that. You had to arrive early and queue to get in.

Sundays at the Crawdaddy, the name Gomelsky gave his club when
he saw the mayhem the Stones' "Crawdaddy" vamp caused, quickly became a tribal rite. At first, the larger crowd of kids, trying to be cool, didn't
know how to react. Then a Crawdaddy employee got up during "Mona"
and started dancing on one of the tables. The Stones loved this anarchic
move and revved up the music even higher. The room just *exploded*. It
started an audience-participation dance called the shake that became a
sweat-soaked ritual when the Stones launched into their hypnotic,
Diddley-pumping finale, throbbing with lust and hoodoo jive.

By early March, the Stones were also playing paid rehearsals on
Sunday afternoons at Ken Colyer's club, Studio 51, on Great Newport

Street in Soho, from four until six. Then they had to get across London to play in Richmond that evening. So Ian Stewart took a bonus he'd earned from his job at the chemical company and used it as a down payment on a Volkswagen bus so he could haul the amps, the drums, and the guitars over to the next gig.

———

Brian Jones was telling everyone that with Charlie Watts in the band the Stones were unstoppable. The Beatles were the biggest act in England, and Brian was anxious to get there too. The Stones needed some national exposure, so Brian kept calling and writing the BBC to get the band on the radio.

When the BBC told Brian it would be easier to get the Stones an audition if they had a new demo tape, he hustled an hour at IBC Studios in Portland Place. The sessions were set up and produced by Glyn Johns, who worked as a tape operator at IBC. On March 11, the Stones recorded straight-up readings of Bo Diddley's "Road Runner," "Crackin' Up," and "Diddley Daddy," Jimmy Reed's "Bright Lights, Big City" and "Honey What's Wrong," and Willie Dixon's "I Want to Be Loved." These tapes reveal the early Stones as a rhythm band, with Brian's Hohner Echo "Super Vamper" harp as the lead instrument. Stu's barrelhouse piano drives the music, and Brian plays the guitar solos on "Honey" and "Road Runner," currently a big Stones jam at the Crawdaddy Club.

Copies of the Stones' tape made the rounds of the record companies, all of whom passed. They wanted pop groups in suits, not an artsy R&B band.

But the Stones' reputation as a hot live band began to really build. They got more gigs and drew big crowds of younger fans—art students from the Kingston College of Art and teenagers who'd been excluded from the cultish milieu of R&B fans. One of these was Chrissie Shrimpton, the fifteen-year-old sister of supermodel Jean Shrimpton— "the Shrimp," as she was known to Swinging London. At a club in Maidenhead, a friend dared lively and precocious Chrissie to go up and kiss the Stones' sexy, big-lipped singer after the gig. Mick kissed her back and promptly asked her out. Soon Chrissie and Mick Jagger were an item.

Jean Shrimpton's boyfriend then was David Bailey, the hottest fashion photographer in London. Though he was already married, Bailey and the Shrimp were the royal couple in the hot clubs of Swinging London. Bailey recalled, "Mick and I became friends, though I think I was lacking in his eyes because I wasn't a musician; but I became his link to another world—and I knew this rude, longhaired git was on his way. By this time I was a man of the world, so when Mick wanted to go to a proper restaurant, I took him to Cassarole in the Kings Road. He slopped his food like a good lower-middle-class boy. I, being working-class, noticed bad manners more than most. To Mick's amazement I told him he had to leave a 15 percent tip. I think that was his first realization of things to come.

"[Actor] Terry Stamp had taken Jean and me to a place in the sky called the Ad Lib, a Soho penthouse converted into a discotheque with loud music, mirrored walls, and a huge window looking down on London. The clients were pop stars, young actors and actresses, artists and photographers. I took Mick, and soon, like a fifties debutante, he came out with a little help from his friends."

Doing the Crawdaddy

By April 1963, R&B was killing trad. The jazz club on Eel Pie Island in the Thames near Richmond was down to two nights a week from four. The rebels were on the outskirts and closing fast. Ground zero of the scene had moved to Richmond. Sunday night was a jungle grope lit only by a red spotlight. Half an hour of the Stones doing Bo Diddley's "Pretty Thing" turned the place into a torrid steam bath. Younger musicians—the Who, the Yardbirds, the Pretty Things, the Small Faces—

jammed into the Crawdaddy, learning the moves. The raw power of the Stones energized London for years afterward.

First Stones article, *Richmond and Twickenham Times,* April 17, 1963:

> ... Hair worn down Piltdown-style, brushed forward from the crown like the Beatles pop group—"We looked like this before they became famous" [says Brian]—the rhythm section provides a warm, steady backing for the blues of the harmonica and lead guitars.
>
> Save for the swaying forms of the group on the spotlit stage, the room is in darkness. A patch of light from the entrance doors catches the sweating dancers and those who are slumped on the floor.
>
> Outside in the bar, the long hair, suede jackets, gaucho trousers and Chelsea boots rub shoulders with the Station Hotel regulars, resulting in whispered mocking, though not unfriendly remarks about the "funny" clothes.

By mid-April, Giorgio Gomelsky thought he had a handshake deal with the Stones to manage the band, who told everyone he didn't. He started hustling for them. Hearing that the Beatles were taping "From Me to You" for the TV show *Thank Your Lucky Stars* on Sunday, April 14, he went to the studios to pitch a Beatles film to Brian Epstein, and invited the boys to come see the Stones at the Crawdaddy Club that night.

Later at the steamy club, the Stones, playing in jackets and ties, were drenched in sweat as they launched into the last twenty minutes of the night, Bo Diddley's "Mona," with the dancers packed together like goats, shaking up and down with arms pinned to their sides, since there was no room to move to the dark throb of the beat. Mick was in front, wiggling and twisting, with Brian and Keith seated on barstools on either side. Bill and Charlie were at the back, Stu playing maracas beside them. The scene was loud, raw, and raving.

Suddenly Mick and Brian noticed that a space had opened in front

of the stage and four longhaired men in long black leather coats were standing there looking at them. Bill turned to Charlie: "Shit! Them's the Beatles."
Brian was grinning madly, playing his ass off. The Beatles were checking
them out! The audience picked up on it and began to shake even harder.
Another explosive night at the Crawdaddy.

They finished the set, and John, Paul, George, and Ringo came back
to say hello. Paul was effusive. George told them they were the best new
group he'd seen. John was a little distant. He wasn't keen on Jagger's sex
appeal, thought his gyrations passé—"bullshit movement," as he put it—
something the Beatles had left behind in Hamburg. But they all got on
well, so Brian invited the Beatles back to Edith Grove.

At the Stones' flat, Brian was the deejay, playing the Stones' demo
tape and Jimmy Reed records until four in the morning (despite the hy-
peropinionated Lennon's blunt dismissal of Chicago blues). The Beatles
were charmed by Brian, a fellow provincial with a respectful attitude, and
stayed friends with him for the rest of his life. They invited the Stones to
Albert Hall a few days later, where they were playing a Pop Proms concert on Thursday night. Before the Beatles left, Brian got them to sign a
photo of themselves from a magazine, which he proudly stuck on the wall
like any fan.

Brian, Mick, and Keith cabbed to Kensington on April 18 to see the
Beatles and got in free by carrying in the gear. In the dressing room, the
Stones were astonished to see the Beatles putting on stage makeup.
(McCartney says the next time they saw the Stones perform, Mick was
made up like a tart.) When the Beatles went on, the Stones checked out
the mass Beatlemania of the young girls packed into enormous Albert
Hall—the screaming, the hysteria, the undies and the candy raining down
on the stage—and were deeply, indelibly impressed. Afterward, Brian and
Giorgio were helping to get the Beatles' gear out the stage door. Brian was
mistaken for one of the mop-tops and was mobbed: hair pulled, clothes
torn, face ripped by fingernails, deafened by screams. Brian Jones, ignored
for too long, now had his first taste of stardom. Driving him back to
Chelsea, Gomelsky noticed he seemed dazed and asked if he was all right.

"That's what I want," Brian whispered. "That's what I want."

———

Giorgio saw himself as the next Brian Epstein, who had just launched his second Liverpool band, Gerry and the Pacemakers. Epstein was building an empire, and Giorgio wanted one too. He started work on a film about the Stones, and they recorded "Pretty Thing" for the sound track. He invited Peter Jones, a respected music journalist, to come to the Crawdaddy. "The fans were going mad with excitement," Jones recalled. "During the break, Giorgio brought over Brian and Mick, introduced them as the Rolling Stones. We ate hot [meat] pies; drank a few glasses of beer. They said, 'You can see how the fans go for us down here, but we're already fed up. The clubs in London don't want to know us. The recording scene seems dead. The local papers have given us fantastic write-ups, but nobody can be bothered to even read them.' " The two Stones seemed sullen and exhausted to Jones, who promised he would spread the word about their "wild, raw-edged music."

On Tuesday, April 23, Giorgio got them to the BBC for a radio audition. Cyril Davies's rhythm section subbed for Charlie and Bill, who couldn't leave their jobs. Stu managed to get away from the chemical company because his piano was so crucial to the drive of the band.

The next night, the Rollin' Stones started playing the failing jazz club on Eel Pie Island in the Thames, a rickety old ballroom with a sprung dance floor. To get there, you paid a toll and crossed a little footbridge from the Twickenham shore. They served brown Newcastle ale, and if you were overcome by the sweat and the smoke, you could fall out on the grassy lawn outside. Eel Pie Island was where many fans saw the Stones for the first time, and it became a legendary venue for them.

———

Back at Edith Grove, alliances among the Stones shifted around like the changing spring weather. It was still cold and the walls were covered in damp. John Lennon dropped by and found Mick and Keith huddled in bed together for warmth. All they had to eat was potatoes: boiled, mashed, and fried. Brian and Keith were closely bonded, playing guitars incessantly, deconstructing R&B to build a new, more modern sound with a jagged edge of adolescent sex drive. "With gloves on, freezing my balls off, that's the closest I ever got to Brian Jones," Keith said. "We had two guitars weaving around each other. We'd play these things so much that we knew both guitar parts. So when we got to the crucial point where we got it really flash, we'd suddenly switch. The lead picks up the rhythm, and the rhythm picks up the lead. It's what Ronnie [Wood] and I call the ancient art of weaving. We still do it today. We don't even have to look at each other, almost. You can feel it. You say, 'Ah, he's gonna take off now, okay, I'll go down.' And vice versa."

Sometimes Mick Jagger picked up a guitar and tried to play along. He'd ask Brian to show him a chord or a lick, but Brian refused, insisting that Mick stick to singing.

Mick was going through an ironic "camp" period, mincing about the filthy flat in housecoat and slippers, trying to tidy up a bit. The fetid squalor and chaos of Edith Grove was getting to him. Brian was dealing with the severe stresses of his life by drinking as much brandy as he could hold. When he was really loaded, he liked to beat up his girlfriends in the front room. Brian and Keith amused themselves by blowing gobs of snot on the walls and thinking up colorful names for the disgusting blotches. With Jimmy Phelge, who walked around wearing his soiled underwear on his head, Brian and Keith worked on perfecting their most insolent face, the "nanker," pulling down their eyes while pushing up their nostrils in a cretinous mask of contempt. When Mick complained about the toxic conditions in their flat, they pulled the nanker on him. Mick was also doubtful about what he was doing, and nervous about his parents' reaction if he told them he was leaving LSE for the life of a full-time musician.

In late April 1963, music journalist Peter Jones tipped off teenage London press agent Andrew Oldham about the Rollin' Stones and insisted he visit Richmond to hear for himself. Andrew was nineteen, a hyper baby promoter with a desk in Soho and an eye to find the next Beatles.

"Well, okay," said Oldham. "I don't mind having a look at them. But you know I hear about new groups every day of the week, and I wouldn't give most of them the steam off my shit, but if you want, I might go down there and see them."

On April 28, Andrew turned up in Richmond in his peaked Bob Dylan cap and shouldered his way through the mob of mods waiting to get out of the cold drizzle. Making his way to the alley behind the club, Andrew heard some hard words and a girl shouting. As he entered the Crawdaddy Club through the back door, he passed Mick and his new girlfriend, Chrissie Shrimpton, standing in the shadows, having a blazing row.

Andrew went inside, and that was the end of the Rollin' Stones.

two:

We Want the Stones!

Membership card for the Crawdaddy Rhythm
and Blues Club signed by all five Rolling Stones,
including drummer "Charlie Boy," in July 1963.

CRAW DADDY
CRAW DADDY
CRAW DADDY
CRAW DADDY
CRAW DADDY
RHYTHM AND BLUES CLUB

GRAHAM. DAWES.
RUNNYMEDE GDNS
HITTON
Dawes.
12 May 1964

R&B was a minority thing that had to be defended

at all times. There was this kind of crusade mentality.

Mick Jagger

Messenger of the Gods

Andrew Loog Oldham stood in the back of the Crawdaddy Club as the Stones started their set. "The stuttering beat spoke of sex the instant it started a little dance in my heart." He looked at Mick Jagger, in critic George Melly's famous joke, like Sylvester looked at Tweety Pie. Andrew's destiny revealed itself as he checked out Mick's obscene lips, the future fast-forwarding in a screaming chaos of fame, money, power, sex. All those lips needed was someone who knew what to do with them.

Andrew was the one. He was mercurial Hermes, messenger of the gods. He was a cheap hustler, younger than the Stones, hipper than thou, speedier, druggier, manic-depressive. His hypersensitive antennae were perpetually scanning the horizon for the Next Big Thing and already tracking the shift toward a media-controlled pop marketplace ruled by image and hype. He immediately saw the Stones as a paradigm of his latest obsession, Anthony Burgess's just-published novel *A Clockwork Orange*, with its thuggish new language of aggro and social control. Andrew's semimystic revelation as he felt the aggressive jungle boogie of the Stones in his very bones was that this new band and its dark, marginal R&B were the antidote to the Beatles' wholesome and cheery pop image. The Stones would sell massive amounts of records and concert seats, and the seats would be sopping wet as soon as they started to play.

"Even before I got into the club," Andrew later said, "I knew this was the *one*. I stood outside and watched Mick and Chrissie Shrimpton, sister of Jean, having a fight in the alleyway. They were as attractive as each other, and I knew I was onto something."

Giorgio Gomelsky's father had died, and he was in Switzerland for the funeral. After the gig, Andrew started talking to Mick and Keith. Brian butted in, told Andrew he was the leader of the group. Andrew did his number on them, jive-talking outlandish claims about how he could make them bigger than the Beatles. He talked American slang, went on about knowing Phil Spector, legendary American producer of the Crystals and Ronettes and the first teenage millionaire in the pop world. Andrew wore eye makeup, came on very cutting, very camp, all "darling" and "my dear," and he got their total attention. He was irreverent, cynical about the record business, and they got the (erroneous) impression that Andrew loved the blues and R&B as much as they did. He told them they had to begin making records immediately and that he would style them as the anti-Beatles, looking the opposite of them. "To the extent that they looked all clean-cut and good," Keith said, "we would look scruffy and evil."

Andrew was more like them than they were, talked like them, wore the same clothes, had the same contempt for the wankers of the world. By the end of the evening, Andrew had the Stones in his pocket. They went home to Edith Grove and stayed up, almost insane with excitement, all night. Brian Jones was completely ecstatic because someone had discovered them. Giorgio Gomelsky would get the shock of his life on his return to London, but nothing mattered to Brian, who was determined to be a pop star at any price, with no apology.

Andrew Oldham's father was a Dutch airman killed in the war. Born out of wedlock in Hampstead in 1944 to a well-off English girl, Andrew spent his youth getting kicked out of good schools for blackmail, shoplifting, and wearing the wrong trousers. He started tramping the streets of Soho at fourteen, trying to live the lives portrayed by playwright Wolf Mankowitz in the stage version of *Expresso Bongo,* which his mother took him to (Paul Scofield was the pop manager played by Laurence Harvey in the later film). He was an early mod, a young English "sixties mega-spiv" with a taste for sharp clothes and American music, all flash and plastic. Tall, blond, totally rude, he talked his way into a job with

Mary Quant, working by night as a waiter at the Flamingo and even releasing a couple of singles as "Sandy Beach" before working little P.R. jobs in London. An early client was Don Arden, tough-guy promoter of rock and roll shows. Arden reportedly fired Andrew after he proudly showed reporters the razor-slashed, urine-soaked seats that fans had left behind after an Arden show. Andrew was in the studio when the Beatles made their first national TV broadcast on *Thank Your Lucky Stars* in February 1963, and was hired by Brian Epstein to do P.R. for "Please Please Me" and for his other groups. Another client was American record producer Phil Spector, inventor of the Wall of Sound, paranoid mogul of pop, "the first tycoon of teen," as Tom Wolfe called him. When Spector visited London, Andrew grooved on his wise-guy persona: the limos, bodyguards, muscle, guns, and especially the know-how. Spector told him if he ever found a band to produce, Andrew should record it himself, and only lease the tapes to a record label, retaining ownership (and control).

Andrew rented an office on Regent Street from an old-line talent agent, Eric Easton, a thirty-six-year-old former theater organist and veteran of variety shows. The next week, he took Easton to Richmond to see the Stones. They lured Brian Jones to Regent Street, where he surrendered control of his group, signing a three-year management contract on behalf of the band on May 1, 1963 (the contract gave the Stones' new management 25 percent of all earnings). At first, Easton said he wanted Jagger out of the band because he couldn't sing. Brian seemed amenable, but Andrew insisted that Jagger stay.

Brian also insisted on being secretly paid five pounds more a week than the rest of the band, because he was the leader. When Gomelsky returned to London a few days later, Brian gave him the bad news that they were movin' on.

Things started to happen fast. Andrew impulsively decided to put the Stones in uniforms like the Beatles. On Carnaby Street, he bought them black jeans, black turtlenecks, and Cuban-heeled boots. Brian hated this. Mick didn't like the tight boots and stopped wearing them in favor of his loafers.

They kept playing their regular venues, the Ricky Tick in Windsor and Eel Pie Island, and Andrew got them publicity gigs, like *News of the World*'s fun fair in Battersea Park on the south bank of the Thames on the afternoon of May 4. Pat Andrews showed up with baby Julian, and Brian proudly held the boy and took him around the fair. Afterward, Andrew took Brian aside and told him to lose the kid and the girlfriend, man, if he ever wanted to be a pop star. Pat and her son went back to Cheltenham soon after.

————

Within a week of signing the Stones, Andrew got them their dreamed-of record deal, a preposterous swindle that worked out badly for the Stones in the end.

There were only two big record companies in England, EMI and Decca. Both were subsidiaries of giant electronic corporations. EMI had the Beatles, and Decca needed the Next Big Thing. Decca executive Dick Rowe was notorious for having passed on the Beatles a year earlier. When he ran into George Harrison cojudging a talent show in Liverpool, George told him his favorite new band was playing the next night in Richmond. Rowe drove all day to be at the Crawdaddy Club in time to catch the Rollin' Stones' raucous rite of spring. He made a deal with Andrew almost on the spot. They played Rowe the IBC demos from March, Andrew acted his "little teenage tycoon shit" to the hilt, and they leveraged a desperate Decca Records into giving them a two-year deal and a 20 percent royalty.

Andrew went to Brian and crowed that he'd made Decca fucking *crawl*, baby, and that he'd managed to get the band a whopping *6 percent* royalty—better than the Beatles' (famously horrendous) contract with EMI. Andrew and Eric Easton incorporated a company called Impact Sound, which would record and own the master tapes, leasing them—Spector-like—to hapless Decca for worldwide distribution. Brian immediately signed a three-year recording contract with Impact Sound on behalf of the Rollin' Stones. Andrew didn't tell Brian that Impact Sound would retain 14 percent of the Stones' royalties.

At this point, Brian let drop that he'd already signed a contract with

IBC when they cut their earlier demo tapes. Easton gave Brian a hundred pounds, and Brian went to IBC, told them the Stones were breaking up, bought out their contract, and got the tapes back, in what Keith called "one of his fantastic get-out schemes."

When the Decca contract was finally signed, Andrew's mother, with whom he still lived, had to act as legal guardian for him, since he was nineteen years old, too young to sign the papers by himself.

Come On

On May 10, 1963, Andrew took the band into Olympic Studios, an advertising-jingle factory near Marble Arch, to record their first songs for Decca. They cut Chuck Berry's "Come On" and (after much debate) Muddy Waters's "I Want to Be Loved" and thought they were through for the day until the engineer asked the departing Andrew, who'd acted as producer, if he wanted to mix the tapes. Huh? The engineer explained that they had recorded four tracks but had to edit it down to one monaural track in order to manufacture the record. Patiently Andrew explained that he didn't know anything about recording, or even about music, and had never been in a studio before. *"You* mix them," Andrew said, "and I'll be back in the morning for the tape."

"Come On" was a Chuck Berry St. Louis rhumba, unreleased in England, that Andrew thought would be a good first single. They came up with a fast arrangement that echoed the Jamaican ska style that was sweeping England (where it was called bluebeat). Andrew: "We're all very tense [in the studio]. We all felt a bit of panic through that three-hour session. We kept rushing out to have a drink in an effort to keep the nerves down." The Stones played it fast, clocking in at under two minutes, and they hated the result. Decca hated it too and later sent the band into their West Hampstead studio to redo it with Eric Easton supervising. The band was tense—red-light fever—in Decca's stuffy studio and disliked the clean but stiff new version with its nervous rhythm and Brian's wah-wah harp. "I don't think 'Come On' was very good," Mick said later. "In fact, it was shit." He sang the two-word chorus in falsetto, a device he would use for his entire career. Decca released it as the renamed Rolling Stones' first single on June 7, 1963.

Andrew and Decca worked the record, and it eventually reached a semirespectable no. 21 on the charts, even though reviewers wrote that it sounded nothing like the Stones. The first photos of the group were shot by Gered Mankowitz (son of the author of *Expresso Bongo*) and released by Decca with the record. They showed the shaggy band slouching on a London bomb site and drew even more (sarcastic) comment than the music. The Stones refused to play "Come On" in public. Keith: "It was done just to get a record out. We never even wanted to hear it. The idea was Andrew's: get a strong single so they would let us make an album, which back then was a privilege."

The *Daily Mirror* did a positive story on the wild little scene in Richmond, and attendance at the Stones' still-small gigs started to get too big for the Station Hotel to handle. As the Stones' began their inexorable liftoff, other transitions were afoot. Andrew changed Keith's last name to Richard, because it echoed Cliff Richard. Bill Perks changed his name to Bill Wyman. Charlie, Bill, and Stu quit their day jobs that summer to devote all their time to the band. Their families thought they were crazy.

June 1963. Someone at the BBC told the Stones they were "unsuitable" for an audition. (Actually they thought Mick sounded too black, and Easton again mooted getting rid of him.) They kept playing the rickety ballroom on Eel Pie Island, alternating with blues rivals the All-Stars, featuring Long John Baldry. When Baldry wanted a break, he'd introduce the big-nosed, bouffant-haired mod Rodney Stewart in his high-heeled boots, who'd scream his head off. When the Piccadilly Jazz Club changed its name to the Scene Club, the Stones played the opening. Then the BBC started to get angry letters from Stones fans, and a BBC rep finally called Eric Easton to ask about a possible audition for the band.

Early in July, the Stones were offered their first TV slot on a summer spin-off of *Thank Your Lucky Stars.* The gig had come through Easton, who repped the show's host. Andrew sent the band to a tailor for matching jackets in houndstooth check with black velvet collars. When the finished suits arrived and the Stones showed up to try them on, there were only five suits. Andrew had told the tailor not to bother with Stu's because he was out of the band.

The crushing news was broken to Stu by Brian, who told him Andrew insisted on it. Stu was older, straighter, a big geezer type who didn't fit the image. The Rolling Stones had to be pretty, thin, longhaired boys. At a band meeting on Eel Pie Island, Andrew facetiously explained that six was too fucking many for a band anyway, since the kids could only count to five. Brian didn't like Andrew, was nervous about his obvious preference for Mick as point man and sex symbol, but went along. So did the others.

It was a big moment, the end of the R&B band called the Rollin' Stones and the beginning of the group that would rival the Beatles. Stu took being fired from the band he and Brian had founded philosophically. "I mean," he said later, "there would have been a group exactly like the Rolling Stones, and they would have been as good as the Rolling Stones, whether Brian and I existed or not."

They asked Stu to stay on as road manager, to keep playing piano at the gigs and on the records, and bighearted Stu agreed, not without some lingering bitterness. He grew to hate Brian Jones for this easy betrayal. As for Andrew Oldham, despite his admiration for Andrew's careful and brilliant handling of the group in days to come, Stu said, "I wouldn't piss on him if he were on fire."

Andrew didn't care. He *was* on fire now, his manic energy ricocheting in every direction. He was operating in a super-heated continuum of hype in a faux-gay persona modeled on the closeted homosexual style of England's most successful pop merchants: Brian Epstein, promoter Robert Stigwood, the Who's co-manager Kit Lambert. These were the guys, Pete Townshend later emphasized, who really knew how to sell boy bands to a girl audience.

Lucky Stars

Birmingham, Sunday, July 7. The Rolling Stones appeared smiling nervously on TV for the first time (*Lucky Stars Summer
Spin*), miming to a tape of "Come On" in their juvenile black-velvet-col-
lared checked suits, last on a bill with half a dozen now-forgotten acts.
Mick shook his Beatles-cut hair and twitched spastically as the studio
crew looked on in horror. Critics in the papers began to compare the
Stones unfavorably to the more charming Beatles. Words like "apes" and
"cavemen" were deployed in an ultimately successful effort to brand the
Stones as the ugly, thuggish flip side of the sunny and engaging lads from
Liverpool. Andrew thought this was brilliant and encouraged it, to the
dismay of the Stones' families.

On July 13, the Stones opened for the Hollies in one of the Stones'
first shows outside London. The north of England was a foreign country
to the London-bred Stones. Keith had never been farther north than the
north of London. The Hollies, from Manchester, were a pop group ("Bus
Stop") featuring close harmony vocals that influenced the Stones in a
more pop direction. Graham Nash and the other Hollies became close to
the Stones, and Brian, in his almost desperate run for the rainbow, suddenly wanted to emulate their lighter style. Even Stu liked them. Ex-
choirboy Keith was a good harmony singer and a plausible alternative
vocalist, unlike Brian, who had an ugly singing voice. Bill Wyman started
to sing backup vocals with Keith.

On July 21, the Stones played Studio 51 on Great Newport Street in
Soho, their first London gig since their record came out. The tiny sweat
lodge of a club was crammed with young musicians—future Small Faces,
Kinks, and Zombies; proto-Zeppelins—eager to hear the Stones, who
didn't bother to play their new record or even play to their audience.

Instead, they pumped out their lusty, rumbling R&B and impressed everyone by not smiling or "entertaining" like every other hopeful young band. The Rolling Stones just stood there and played, cool to the point of intimidation, radiating a tough, potent, and extremely influential Evil.

———————

Andrew Oldham's brilliant "styling" of the Stones began in earnest with the next round of interviews and photo sessions. In a process of spontaneous and instinctive invention relying as much on language as on a look or an attitude, he styled the Stones as sullen, inarticulate droogs. Photos displayed the group's dissolute, delinquent body language, cribbed from icons of coolness in French New Wave cinema. Interviews were deliberately monosyllabic and unhelpful. Charlie Watts was ordered to stick out his tongue at newsreel cameras. If the Beatles were a blast of oxygen into a wheezing England, the Rolling Stones would be a dopey whiff of nitrous oxide. Teen rebellion and rock and roll had gone steady since the mid-1950s, but Andrew Oldham's rethink of the Stones' image built a successful model of pouting, rudeness, and contempt since used by hundreds of bands through four decades of rock, punk, and Brit-pop.

Andrew got the Stones an endorsement deal with Vox, makers of instruments and amplifiers, and the Stones went to the Vox factory (in Dartford) to be photographed in skinny ties and leather vests. Vox gave Brian Jones the pear-shaped white guitar that he famously used for the next three years. Late in July, the Stones played a deb party for the daughter of Lord and Lady Killerman. Mick liked these affairs, but Brian hated them. He got drunk, vomited in Stu's minibus, and passed out, missing the gig entirely.

Meanwhile, the nervous brewery that owned the Station Hotel evicted the Crawdaddy Club. Gomelsky moved to the clubhouse of the Richmond Athletic Association, a bigger room where it got even crazier on Sunday nights as the Stones were finishing their sets with Chuck Berry's "Bye Bye Johnny." More girls showed up, hoisted onto their boyfriends' shoulders. More fights broke out as rabid kids pushed up to get close to the band. The Stones were getting too big for the club, and soon found themselves booked out of town on Sunday nights. Giorgio replaced them with the Yardbirds, Eric Clapton's raving R&B group, or the Detours, an early incarnation of the Who before Keith Moon joined on drums. Wistfully the Stones would find themselves headed up north on Sunday afternoons, while their friendly, familiar Crawdaddy slot (where their friends came to see them) was filled by a rival band.

———

In August, Eric Easton began booking the Stones into the circuit of ballrooms they had previously shunned. Their days as a blues band were over; now they had to come up with catchy dance numbers. Decca wanted another single right away, and Andrew was desperately trying to find the right song. "Come On" had sold forty thousand records, Eric Easton told the band as he doled out their royalties, amounting to a pathetic eighteen pounds apiece. The Beatles were writing their own hit records, but the Stones depended on covering American R&B songs unreleased in England. On August 19 in Decca's studio, they recorded the Coasters' "Poison Ivy" and the hoodoo shuffle "Fortune Teller." This second single was canceled by Decca after a few hundred copies had already been pressed. Everyone involved was frustrated that the Stones' cannedsounding versions of American records couldn't match the intense rush of their live sound.

On August 23, the Stones mimed "Come On" during their first appearance on the new pop TV show *Ready Steady Go!* on the independent ITV channel. *Ready Steady Go!,* hosted by mod fashion plate Cathy McGowan, had recently begun showcasing young English acts and visiting Motown stars lip-synching on pop art sets and scaffolds on Friday nights. Andrew had been hanging out in *RSG*'s trendy greenroom since it first went on the air, and had an easy entrée to the show. Its young director, Michael Lindsay-Hogg, was sympathetic to the Stones and took care to project the sullen, Byronic image of the band that Andrew desired. *RSG* helped make the Stones major figures in England. Their long hair and angular features were perfect for the glare and shadows of black-and-white television. The hot TV lights cast a glowing corona around Brian's golden head, and there was an inherent visual drama in the backlit faces of Mick and especially Bill Wyman, on whom the camera seemed to linger in fascination. Mick's childhood TV experience helped his natural ability to deliver a song, almost matching his intimate appeal on a club-size stage. TV brought the Stones into English living rooms and made them seem more human, more familiar. All except for Brian Jones: his watchful, serious charisma and untouchable, otherworldly mystique were only enhanced by the cathode-ray aura that seemed to radiate from his image on a television screen.

August also saw the end of the Stones' residence at 102 Edith Grove. Brian had already left to move in with the family of his new girlfriend, Linda Lawrence, a sixteen-year-old hairdressing student he'd met at the Ricky Tick in Windsor, where he liked to walk the Lawrences' pet white goat on a lead through the streets while exquisitely dressed in the latest fashion. Mick and Keith moved into a flat at 33 Mapesbury Road, West Hampstead, and were soon joined by Andrew, who turned up on their doorstep claiming that his mother had thrown him out of her house. A few weeks later, Chrissie Shrimpton moved in as well. She and Mick fought all the time about almost everything. Andrew noted how often she hit Mick with her little fists. Keith also had a new girlfriend, Linda Keith, a cool, beautiful Jewish model he'd met through Andrew's girlfriend Sheila Klein. Linda Keith was a star-quality free spirit, the first serious love of Keith's life.

Bill Wyman was living in Penge with his wife and son, but was beginning his reign as the Stones' priapic love machine by bedding every girl he could find on the road, notching the tally of deflowered virgins in his diary like a bean counter. Charlie was already involved with the slightly older art student Shirley Ann Shepherd, whom he would soon secretly marry.

The squalid flat at Edith Grove was left to Jimmy Phelge. "Lovable," Keith later said of him. "A hidden hero." A tattered Rolling Stones poster pasted to the outside wall of the house would remain for almost fifteen years.

————————

Late in August, Brian started missing gigs. He had trouble breathing, a possible asthmatic condition aggravated by constant drinking and anxiety attacks. He was still the nominal "leader" of the Stones, trying to hold his tenuous position by playing Mick and Keith off against each other, constantly whispering lies and gossip about one to the other, succeeding only in planting jealousy and confusion in his own group. Brian and Andrew were suspicious of each other and barely spoke. Andrew was only interested in pushing Mick to the fore and was also bothering Mick and Keith to start writing songs together. Brian was left out of this, couldn't come up with a simple pop melody, and he resented this, which didn't help his health problems. If he couldn't make the gig, Stu sat in on piano, if one was available.

This newly fragile Brian could barely take the long journeys in Stu's bus as it bumped along Britain's primitive roads crammed with gear, amps, and sullen, chain-smoking musicians. Crafty Bill claimed he got carsick and could only ride in the front seat next to Stu. So the others were stuffed in the back. Plus, they were always running late, and Stu would refuse to stop when they had to relieve themselves. Keith complained bitterly that he had to piss out of the VW's air vent as the Stones hurtled along on ten-hour drives to far-off gigs in deepest Wales. They ate mainly greasy eggs, chips, and sausages at truck stops, lived on restless exhaustion, could only dream of collapsing when they got home late at night. It was a way of life none of them would have traded for the world.

Mick: "It was very exciting, the whole thing. The first time we got our picture in *Record Mirror* was so exciting, you couldn't believe it . . . And then to go from the music-oriented press to the national press and national television, and everyone seeing you [on the] two television channels, and then being recognized by everyone from builders to people working in shops . . . It goes to your head—a very champagne feeling."

Wanna Be Your Man

Tuesday, September 10, 1963. Summer held on to gray London. The Profumo Scandal was raging. Red double-decker buses and black cabs choked the streets with diesel smoke. Andrew Oldham was walking along Jermyn Street, St. James, head down, wondering where the Rolling Stones' second single was coming from. The band was rehearsing in Soho. Andrew had just gotten them a spot on a package tour going out later in the month with their heroes Bo Diddley and the Everly Brothers. The Stones would get an education in classic rock and roll, but first Andrew had to find their next record and was coming up with fuck-all.

A black taxi pulled up sharply next to him. "Get in, Andy, we've got something for you."

It was half the Beatles, John and Paul, jolly and a bit tight, having had one or two at the Variety Club Awards luncheon at the Savoy. The Beatles had just appeared on the big TV variety show *Sunday Night at the London Palladium* and were certified Big Stars, currently working on their second album. Andrew jumped into the cab, speed-rapping about his single problem with the Stones until Paul helpfully mentioned, *"We've got some fresh numbers that might be right for the Stones."*

Andrew ordered the driver to take them to Studio 51 in Great Newport Street. They crashed down the steps to the basement club. "Mick!" John called. "We've got yer next fookin' record!" Handed guitars, Lennon and McCartney played them the first verse and chorus of "I Wanna Be Your Man," which they'd written for Ringo to sing.

Andrew's problem was solved. Rescued by the Beatles! Andrew told them he wanted the song, and John said, "Well, we have to finish it, then, don't we?" They sat in a corner and wrote the middle eight bars on the spot. The simple mating chant was so hot that after the Stones recorded it, the Beatles did too. Even Bob Dylan, soon to be besotted with the English bands, would cut a version.

The confidence, speed, and ease they saw in John and Paul impressed Mick and Keith. "I mean, the way they used to hustle tunes was great," Mick said. It knocked them all out.

A few days later, the Stones played a charity benefit at Albert Hall, the opening act on an interminable bill topped by the Beatles. A teen magazine had organized it, and there were a thousand girls on the street, the first time the Stones had to make a serious run for the stage door.

Early in the month, Mick dropped out of the LSE. He informed the school and told his parents. "It was very, very difficult," he recalled, "because my parents didn't want me to do it. My father was absolutely furious with me. *Anything* but this. He couldn't believe it. It was probably a stupid thing to do, but I didn't like being in college. It was a dull, boring course I was stuck on." The LSE told Mick he could come back to school anytime in the next year.

Pressured by young fans, the BBC finally relented, and the Stones recorded four songs for the *Saturday Club* radio program: "Come On," two more Chuck Berry numbers, and "I Just Want to Make Love to You." The producers asked Brian, Charlie, and Bill to remain at the studio to back up Bo Diddley, who was arriving later that afternoon to tape some songs. Brian agreed, but then disappeared, unready to meet an idol whose songs they played night after night in clubs and ballrooms (they had even recently made Diddley's witty playlet "Cops and Robbers" the centerpiece of their show). Bill Wyman and Charlie Watts did the backing, and Bo thanked and complimented them afterward.

———

By the end of September, the Rolling Stones had retired as a club act. The Crawdaddy Club residency ended on the twenty-second, and the Stones were replaced by the rip-roaring Yardbirds. Their last gig at the Ricky Tick in Windsor came two days later, and they played Eel Pie Island for the last time the next night.

On Sunday, September 29, amid the din of hundreds of screaming girls, the Stones opened the Bo Diddley/Everly Brothers tour with two shows at the New Victoria Theater in London before heading out on the road. It was the Stones' first package tour, a Don Arden Enterprises Ltd. production, a big deal. Arden was a music business heavy who made his fierce reputation by hanging Australian promoter Robert Stigwood out of his office window by his ankles, three stories above Oxford Street, after Stigwood had caused a spot of bother. Stigwood famously shat himself, and no one ever crossed Don Arden again. If you were a musician working for him and didn't show up for the gig, you might have your fingers broken.

Bo Diddley had his sister, the Duchess, and legendary maracas shaker Jerome Green ("Bring it on home, bring it to Jerome") with him. The Kentucky-bred Everly Brothers—Don and Phil—headed the bill with their classic string of hits and a sweet harmony style that was finished in the United States and fading in England. Chuck Berry, who was to have headlined, was in jail in Missouri, serving time for promoting prostitution at his nightclub in St. Louis. The Stones opened the show with a four-song set: "Come On," "Route 66," "Poison Ivy," and "Money," Barrett Strong's 1960 hit that became a big jam with every band in the world. They dropped all Bo Diddley covers in deference to the master.

The Stones started the tour in their absurd checked uniform jackets with skinny black ties, but these were quickly abandoned when Keith spilled coffee and whiskey on his jacket and Charlie "lost" his. After the first gigs, the Stones appeared in collarless white shirts and black leather vests. Most of the gigs were in movie theaters, and the cramped conditions backstage led to much jamming and socializing among the musicians. Bo Diddley was friendly and gracious toward the Stones, so Brian borrowed a set of ornate gold cuff links from a photographer and gave them to Bo as an offering from the band. Bo's act was pure gutbucket rock, with the Duchess's skintight gold-lamé catsuit providing sexy flash. Diddley and the Stones became "jug buddies," in Diddley's words, drinking wine together before going on.

Keith watched Don Everly from the wings almost every night like it was a master class. "Plenty to learn in a real short time, following those guys around," he recalled. "The Everlys came on with just their trio and themselves. Don Everly is one of the best rhythm guitar players in the world. The *killer* rhythm man, always used an open tuning. It's country shit, basically. That's why the Everly Brothers' stuff was so hard, because it was all on acoustic [guitars]." Watching Don, Keith also picked up his dramatic technique of windmilling the strings, swinging his arm in a wide circle to dramatize the chord (and Pete Townshend stole it from Keith when his band, the Detours, next played with the Stones).

On October 3, the tour did two shows at the Odeon in Southend. Keith was going home to his girlfriend afterward and was looking forward to a night of love. Exhausted by the adrenaline of playing every night, he ordered a chicken dinner delivered to the dressing room. Brian got there first and ate it.

"You *cunt,*" Keith yelled. "You et me fuckin' dinner!" He smashed Brian in the face as hard as he could. Mr. Jones appeared onstage for the second show with a massive black eye, trying to smile but looking miserable.

Things were *very* tense within the Stones. Brian was jealous of the attention Mick was getting and began to insist on singing lead on some songs. From the start, Brian had been at the front of the stage with Mick, teasing the kids and drawing his sometimes-bigger share of adulation and screams. But as Mick's confidence increased and his persona developed into the Stones' all-powerful front, Brian's instrumental work naturally cast him in a secondary role, which he deeply resented. Brian wasn't shy about acting out his anger. He got drunk, played poorly, fucked up in other ways. The other Stones resented this even more, ignored or mocked him, even began to hate him for being on a petty ego trip. His girlfriend Linda Lawrence came along on part of the tour, working as their hairdresser, and Brian had a deal with Eric Easton that had them staying in better hotels than the rest of the band. The Stones started taking big doses of speed to work and stay awake, and Brian's paranoia index went off the chart. Keith: "Brian was the only guy in the world who thought he could take on Mick as the onstage personality. [He'd say,] 'All the chicks liked me better than Mick.' And [this] went on for so long."

While they were up north, a dejected Brian told Bo Diddley he was thinking of leaving the Stones.

"They were fixing to break up," Diddley recalls, "but I told them to hang in there. They were down. They had problems in the band. I told 'em, if they abandoned what they had going, they were stupid. I told 'em: 'You gonna outlast the Beatles because you play like *black dudes.*' I got Brian off to one side and I said, 'Brian, you look like the one with the level head. Hold this group together because you guys goin' to be a *mother-fucker.* If you don't be *bigger* than the Beatles, you gonna last *longer.*'"

Two nights later, in Watford, legendary rocker Little Richard arrived, added to the tour to boost slow ticket sales. The awe factor was ratcheted way up as the Stones watched, wide-eyed, as androgynous, godlike Richard and his guitar player blasted out "Tutti Frutti" and "Good Golly Miss Molly."

Keith: "When the lights went down, before he even came onstage, he'd let the band riff on 'Lucille' for five, ten minutes. He'd come out the back, the spotlight would hit him, and the place was one solid *roar.*" Richard started at the piano, then jumped on top of it, did a lot of the shows on his knees. Some nights he stripped to his shorts while the band vamped on "Long Tall Sally." The rest of the tour sold out.

The next night, at two shows in Cardiff, Wales, the Stones added "I Wanna Be Your Man" to the show, dropping "Poison Ivy." Brian's slide guitar howled over the fast, pumping rhythm, and even Bo Diddley came to the wings and watched him, commenting he'd never heard anything like it before.

Meanwhile, Keith was coming into his own onstage. He'd raise his hand above his head just as the curtain was opening, poised to hit that first big chord. He played mostly with his back to the audience, focusing on Charlie, crouching down to blast out a key passage, all taut body language and movement, building the template for the rock guitarists who followed him.

It wasn't just a matter of style; Keith *had* to focus on Charlie because the drums were all he could hear. The screaming girls drowned out Mick and Bill. Keith started the songs, and Charlie followed him into them, so

Keith was always just slightly ahead of the beat, one of the secrets of the Rolling Stones' sound. "It was just Charlie and me," Keith said. "I developed more of the rhythm thing with the drum licks because that's really all I was playing to."

We Want the Stones!

There was a break in the tour on October 7, during which the Stones cut their next single. Stu's van had broken down on the way back to London, so the five of them piled into a black cab with their gear and rode to De Lane Lea Studio. Brian claimed he was skint—broke—so Mick paid the fare. Their manager and producer couldn't make the session. The Beatles coup had been far too exciting for high-strung Andrew, who went into a manic episode, hospitalized himself, then left for Paris to recuperate. Andrew diagnosed himself as manic-depressive and launched into epic experiments with self-medication that made him an adventure to be around. When the pressure got to be too much over the next two years, Andrew sometimes simply disappeared.

The Stones banged out "I Wanna Be Your Man" in an almost hysterical fury. The Beatles didn't bother with preambles when they wrote, so the Stones hit the first verse running. Bill Wyman played a pumping, Beatles-style bass line. Mick bawled about making an erotic connection, and the song crash-landed in a hard little rave-up. It was a brilliant performance of an aggressive, wailing pop raga. But it was Brian who set the session completely on fire. His bottleneck slide guitar burned a blue sexual fervor into the groove. "Brian *made* that record," Keith said. "No one in England had ever played that kind of guitar on a pop record."

For the flip side, they cut an instrumental titled "Stoned," stolen from the hit song "Green Onions" by Memphis soul band Booker T. and the MGs. "Stoned" had a bleary lyric drawled by Mick: "Ah'm stoned . . . outta mah mind . . . here ah go." It was a blues hymn to marijuana, one of the earliest drug references in the new music (Decca printed "Stones" as the title on the early pressings). Since the whole band wrote it, they used "Nanker Phelge" for the publishing credit, in tribute to their months perfecting the nanker at Edith Grove with Jimmy Phelge. Nanker Phelge became the publishing credit for material to which the whole band contributed, royalties shared equally among them. (Eric Easton scammed the Stones and his partner, Andrew, by assigning "Stoned" 's publishing rights to a company he secretly controlled.)

After their Liverpool show, the Stones visited the Cavern Club, ground zero of the Beatles, where they were mobbed by kids wanting autographs. In Newcastle, they visited a club after the gig and hung out with the Animals (still the Alan Price Combo at that point). In Bradford, there were squadrons of sharp-looking, pill-popping, music-digging mods on their chrome-plated Vespa and Lambretta scooters. They rushed the stage in speed-crazed mayhem during banging, frenetic "Route 66" when Jagger goofy-footed during the guitar solo and shook his bum at them.

Some nights, after the shows, the Stones would find Stu's white bus dyed red from the lipstick of girls passionately kissing the van while the Stones were playing. Eric Easton got them a new Volkswagen van, which was stripped clean of everything, including the license plate, within a few days.

The Rolling Stones' postgraduate education with the American rockers ended (badly) on November 3 with the final two London shows at the Hammersmith Odeon. The London kids were rabid for the Stones, whose new single, "I Wanna Be Your Man," released just two days earlier, was already climbing the charts. (*Disc* called the record "fuzzy . . . complete chaos.") The Stones closed with "I Wanna Be Your Man" and the audience went bonkers. When the Everlys came out, the kids started chanting "We want the Stones!" and threw debris at Don and Phil, who walked off early.

There was a farewell party backstage afterward; all the groups had been friendly and supportive of each other, and the tour ended up making money. The party continued at Mick and Keith's place, blues records and Stan Getz, bossa nova, on the turntable.

The next night, the Stones were back in the ballrooms.

There was a big fight at the hotel after a show at the Cavern Club in Liverpool. Andrew, tired of Brian's egomania and paranoia, told the rest of the band that Brian was getting more money than them. Keith: "Everybody freaked out. We just said *fuck you* to him. That was the beginning of the decline of Brian."

And that was it. Brian lost his last vestige of control over the Stones, who were disgusted with him. He started to isolate himself from the group.

Mick: "[Brian] went from being obsessive about the band, obsessive about the band's image, to being rather an outsider. He'd turn up late to recording sessions and he'd miss the odd gig every now and then. He let his health deteriorate because he drank too much and took drugs when they were new, hung out too much, stayed up too late . . . and didn't concentrate on what he was doing. He started to let his talent slide."

Back to Kingsway Studio in Holborne on November 7 to record the Stones' first EP—an "extended play" four-song album on a seven-inch disc. They cut another version of "Poison Ivy" (uptempo, Beatlesque ending), "Money," "Bye Bye Johnny" (their current show-closer) and their first attempt at a soul music cover—Arthur Alexander's "You Better Move On," with strummed acoustic guitars over Charlie's slow, sexy thump. Keith and Bill sang backup, and a new Stones sound emerged. The soul ballad became a big thing for the Stones, presenting a cool, restrained, pent-up side unseen by their fans.

On November 17 the Stones drove back to Birmingham for another shot on *Thank Your Lucky Stars*. Also on the show was the American singer Gene Pitney, "the Rockville Rocker," who was in England promoting his latest record, "24 Hours from Tulsa." Clean-cut Pitney was at first put off by the Stones' sulking demeanor and long hair, but the Stones and Pitney got along well, talked a lot of music, and Pitney asked Mick and Keith for a song after he heard them working out a new tune backstage.

The creation myth of the Jagger/Richards songwriting team is that Andrew Oldham locked them in the kitchen of their flat and told them not to come out until they had a song. Supposedly they emerged an hour later with "As Tears Go By." But as early as November 1963, they were recording "dubs" for songs at Regent Sound, a tiny demo studio on Denmark Street, London's Tin Pan Alley. Here they worked on a song for Pitney called "My Only Girl," which Pitney later recorded as "That Girl Belongs to Yesterday." (It was a hit in England and marked the debut of the Jagger/Richards team in the Top Ten.) A dozen other song demos were also recorded with Andrew, some of which were later released by obscure singers (George Bean et al.) without much impact.

December 1963. Andrew arranged for the Stones to pick up some extra cash by recording a TV commercial for Kellogg's Rice Krispies. Over a Chuck Berry vamp, with Brian wailing on harmonica, Mick sang the ad like he's selling King Biscuit Flour on KFFA in Helena, Arkansas: "Rice Krispies for you! And you! And you!" The band hated it, and they never did another commercial again.

Around this time, Linda Lawrence got pregnant. Charlie's girlfriend took her and Brian to a doctor to see about an abortion, but the doctor refused to do it when the couple said they were in love. Brian's parents didn't take it well, Andrew ranted that it was a mortal blow for the Stones, and there was a lot of upset.

The rest of 1963 was spent playing one-nighters in ballrooms and town halls all over England. And so the Rolling Stones were launched. They had mutated from an R&B band, flitting between authenticity and commercial appropriation, to a heat-seeking pop group about to reposition itself as a rock and soul band. Their anarchic manager's understanding of the power of theater and confrontation had served the Stones well. Everyone talked about them, and Brian and Mick were becoming national icons. Andrew had been right that an angry pose would be a successful marketing strategy. While Brian Epstein still worked hard to soften the Beatles' northern working-class roughness, Andrew would now spin the Stones a new image of sex and danger that turned on the bourgeoisie and the suburbanites.

The band was also playing well. Touring had sharpened them into a tight performing unit that took no prisoners, and no chances either. The Rolling Stones tended to stay within well-defined arrangements, leaving little room for jamming or improvisation. Within the group, increasingly sad and bitter tension coexisted with the heady rush of pop stardom. Even the reticent Charlie Watts, who seemed genuinely not to care about fame and fortune, was affected by it, even when he had a new suit torn to shreds and had been stabbed in the eyes by girls' fingernails during a violent mobbing outside a ballroom in Kilburn, a heavily Irish neighborhood in London.

Mick: "In England, they were very ready for another band. It was funny, because the Beatles had only been around a year. Things happened so quickly. Then there were a lot of popular bands from the north, and people are snobby in [London], so they wanted a band from the south. We were it."

Keith: "We knew we'd become successful when we did that first tour . . . I was nineteen when it started to take off, just an ordinary guy, and then, suddenly, Adonis! And you know this is so ridiculous, so insane. It was really a bugger. It makes you very cynical. But it's a hell of a thing to deal with. It took me years to get it under control."

Top of the Pops

The new English music scene blew wide open in 1964. A year earlier, five or six groups had a choice of two or three clubs in London where they could play maybe twice a week. By 1964, there were thirty full-time groups and maybe fifty semipro bands getting steady club work in the city and the provinces. Hundreds of trad jazz clubs switched to a pop or R&B policy, and the movement took off nationally, chasing the Beatles.

In January, the Stones began five months of incessant touring and television work, cementing their position as Britain's number two band. On New Year's Day, they headlined *Top of the Pops,* a new BBC television show rolled out to compete with ITV's *Ready Steady Go! Pops* was taped in a new studio converted from an old church in Manchester, so it was less chaotic than *RSG,* a live gig where the band was jostled by the kids in the studio. Miming to records became an art in itself, requiring more rehearsal and tedious blocking of camera shots.

The next day, the Stones went into Regent Sound on Denmark Street to begin work on their first album. They cut "Carol," "Route 66," and Bo Diddley's "Mona." The throbbing twin guitar attack on "Mona" was Brian's arrangement, demonstrating what Bill Wyman called "Brian's supremacy and instinctive musicianship." Keith recalled that "Diddley himself [said] that Brian was the only cat he knew who'd worked out the secret of the Bo Diddley thing." Regent Sound was only a one-room demo studio with a two-track Revox tape recorder, a speaker hung on a nail for playback, and egg boxes stuck to the walls for soundproofing. It was as primitive a studio as one could find in an industrialized country, but over the next year the Rolling Stones would cut some of their best early music there.

On January 6, they began a package tour, Group Scene '64, headlined by the Ronettes, the girl group whose big hit was "Be My Baby." There was immediate tension as Mick and Keith competed for the attention of sultry Ronnie Bennett, girlfriend and future wife of producer Phil Spector. Mick won this little battle, and Keith hung out with Ronnie's sister Estelle. One of the other acts was a new London group, the Cheynes, with drummer Mick Fleetwood.

"It was our big break," Fleetwood recalls, "and the beginning of my friendship with Brian Jones. He showed up in our dressing room, offering cigarettes around, very friendly and open, showing interest in who we were and what we were doing. Then, for some reason, he brought me into the Stones' dressing room and asked me to help him wash and dry his hair, a function I was happy to fill for a lot of that tour. Brian really knew how to bring you in, with his quiet voice that made you lean close to hear him. His hair, when reflected in the stage lights, had almost magical effect. The girls screamed to him while they played. He was mesmerizing. I was very impressed by him. We all were."

————

"I Wanna Be Your Man" was a big hit by this time, no. 12 in England. The Stones needed another single to follow it. One day at their flat on Mapesbury Road, Andrew heard Keith experimenting with the chords of Buddy Holly's "Not Fade Away," chopping at them Bo Diddley style. On January 10 at Regent Sound, the Stones began work on the record. Andrew brought in Gene Pitney to help. "I was at my hotel," Pitney recalled, "and Andrew Oldham called and said they were trying to cut 'Not Fade Away' and it wasn't making it. The Stones were fighting with each other and there was no energy. So I grabbed a couple bottles of cognac and went to the studio. I told them it was my birthday, got everyone drunk, and within a couple of hours they were playing their asses off and had 'Not Fade Away' in the can." Decca executives didn't like the results, but Andrew insisted it was a hit. "That's what we fought for when we started," Keith said, "the right to deliver the finished product in all its glory, take it or leave it."

Meanwhile, it started to get really scary on the road. The audiences were now much younger kids who went nuts when the curtain rose and they saw the Stones blasting into "Talkin' 'Bout You." From the stage, the musicians looked down and saw improbable tableaux of riot, rapture, and mania. At Glasgow on January 13, the Stones had to quit after three songs when the kids rushed the stage of the Barrowlands Ballroom in a human wave attack that trampled police trying to protect the band.

Now the group was playing seven nights a week, all over the country. Keith: "We were still sleeping in the back of this van every night because of the most hard-hearted and callous roadie I've ever encountered—Stu. From one end of England to another in Stu's VW bus with just an engine and a rear window and all the equipment, and then you fit in. The gear first, though."

Ian Stewart was less than reverential about his charges. Five minutes before the gig, he'd stick his head in the dressing room and grumble, "Come on, my little shower of shit—you're on!"

The Stones' punishing schedule was punctuated by multiple radio and TV gigs every week, and got even more hectic as 1964 progressed. Between shows with the Ronettes, the Stones continued recording their album while their EP *The Rolling Stones* climbed the charts, after Andrew got the BBC to put "You Better Move On" in the rotation with the hits of the day. The Stones would record more than fifty separate tracks during the year.

Phil Spector was in London in February to keep tabs on the Ronettes, among other things. Despite his annoyance when he found out Keith had the hots for Ronnie, Spector was persuaded by Andrew Oldham to attend the Stones all-night session at Regent Sound on February 4.

Spector was a gun-toting eccentric—slight, with a vampire's pallor—who wore intimidating shades night and day. His grandiose Wall of Sound records were "little symphonies for the kids." The Ronettes were his baby, the Crystals too. He'd cowritten "Spanish Harlem," played guitar for the Drifters' "On Broadway," and produced the Isley Brothers' epic version of "Twist and Shout." He was about to score four Top Ten records with the Righteous Brothers. Spector was a boy genius at twenty-three, the crazy spirit of American pop music moving toward pop art. It was perfect that he was on the first Stones album.

With Pitney on piano, Stu on organ, and Spector playing maracas, the Stones cut Marvin Gaye's "Can I Get a Witness," a Nanker Phelge instrumental titled "Now I've Got a Witness," and "Little By Little," a collaboration by Spector and the Stones. These were Memphis soul-style jams, continuing the Stones' transition from an R&B band to a rhythm and soul group. After midnight, Graham Nash and Allan Clarke of the Hollies showed up, and the now-drunken ensemble recorded some obscene novelties, with Mick and Phil trading vocals that parodied Andrew Oldham's flash persona and sexual appetites. Known as "Andrew's Blues" or "And Mr. Spector and Mr. Pitney Came Too," these hilarious tracks remain available only on bootleg releases.

———

The grueling schedule continued as the Stones' third
British tour began on February 8, 1964, run by Robert Stigwood. (There
was a lot of tension between Andrew Oldham and Eric Easton after
Andrew discovered that Easton had demanded kickbacks from local promoters.) The set list was "Talkin' 'Bout You," "Road Runner," "Roll Over
Beethoven," Rufus Thomas's "Walking the Dog" (which the Stones
played down and dirty), "You Better Move On," and "I Wanna Be Your
Man" for a finale, if the shows lasted that long before the livid mobs of
kids began to scare the promoters and the cops.

They did even more TV and radio, which helped reposition them
as a teen attraction. They played nightly gigs in Odeons, Gaumonts, and
Granadas all over the land and continued recording on Denmark Street.
Meanwhile, the Beatles' "Can't Buy Me Love" was a big hit single in the
wake of their February conquest of the United States, where they'd been
met by three thousand screaming girls at the airport in New York and appeared on Ed Sullivan's Sunday night TV variety program, charming the
immense American audience, opening the door for the so-called British
Invasion that followed them across the Atlantic.

In March, the Stones were interviewed by the London music paper
Melody Maker. The famous headline—WOULD YOU LET YOUR SISTER GO
WITH A ROLLING STONE?—was written by Andrew, whose confrontational
strategy separated the Stones from the mainstream and emphasized their
marginal, underdog pose. The press was happy to go along.

Early that month, Andrew gave the band a week off. Mick went to
Paris. Charlie flew to Gibraltar, where he ran into jazz bassist Charles
Mingus at the airport and asked for his autograph. Brian left Linda
Lawrence at home and took a new girlfriend, Dawn Molloy, to Scotland.
Dawn often traveled with the Stones around England after that and be-
came pregnant with Brian's child.

Later in March, the Stones went to a party in Windsor for ingenue
singer Adrienne Posta, whom Andrew was representing. In the middle of
things, Mick had a loud argument with Chrissie, whose subsequent flood

of tears caused her false eyelashes to peel off. Lots of London scene-makers were there: Paul McCartney and his girlfriend Jane Asher, her brother, singer Peter Asher, and Peter's friend John Dunbar, a dashing university student and London man-about-town. Dunbar brought along his stunning seventeen-year-old girlfriend, Marianne Faithfull.

Conversation died when Marianne walked into the room. Girls like her, Scott Fitzgerald wrote, "do all the breathing for everyone, and finally even the men have to go outside for air." She was a dreamy vision of Anglo-European drop-dead beauty: long blond hair, eyes like blue ice, a "large balcony" (as the French call big breasts), and full, inviting lips plumped like downy pillows. Marianne was also educated, well read, and highly intelligent, and her innocent gaze fell on a man like a heat wave.

Andrew was on her in a flash. She noticed he was wearing makeup and reeked of cologne. "Can she sing?" he asked not Marianne, but Dunbar, who answered yeah, man, she can sing too. Andrew turned on the charm and got her phone number. Tipsy Mick Jagger, keen to be noticed, spilled his drink down the front of her dress.

Tell Me

It was probably no accident that the appearance of Marianne Faithfull on the scene inspired Mick Jagger and Keith Richards to begin writing good songs. Young artists need muses to achieve creative goals, and Marianne was born for the role. Her mother was a war refugee with an obscure Austro-Hungarian title—Baroness Erisso—the granddaughter of Leopold von Sacher-Masoch, whose 1870 novel, *Venus in Furs,* inspired the term "masochism" for pain-is-pleasure syndrome. Marianne's mother married a British army major of Welsh extraction, Glyn Faithfull, and Marianne was born in December 1946. She was raised at her professor father's socially progressive school/commune on an old country estate, Brazier's Park, in Oxfordshire. Her parents split and she was enrolled in a

convent school to be educated by nuns. Marianne developed into a
lovely teenage actress and coffee bar folksinger. She met John Dunbar at
a Cambridge University ball, which led to her fateful discovery in
Windsor.

Andrew was frothing to get this girl into a recording studio and then
on TV. "I saw an angel with big tits and signed her" was his favorite line
on Marianne. He began pestering Mick and Keith for a song for her,
metaphorically locking them in the kitchen of the Mapesbury Road flat
until they emerged a few hours later with "As Time Goes By," which became "As Tears Go By."

Keith: "The force of Andrew's logic was already apparent to us:
you've either got to capture a songwriter or start doing it yourselves,
which was quite a shocking thought. So he put us in a room and said,
'Don't come out until you've got a song.' I don't know if he actually turned
the key or not. So Mick and I sat there staring at the tape recorder. We
smoked. [Eventually] we really had to pee. So we finally put something
together and banged on the door. Andrew got up from watching TV, we
gave him the tape and headed for the bathroom."

Marianne recorded the simple, melancholy song in her cool, vibra-
toless alto voice. Mick and Keith came to the session but didn't say a
word. The arrangement was done by Mike Leander, who had worked on
other Stones demos with Andrew. As Andrew foresaw, "As Tears Go By"
was a hit record that summer and launched Marianne's long, dangerous,
and often-brilliant career.

Mick Jagger was hanging out with David Bailey, enjoying the fast action and the girls at Bailey fashion shoots. Bailey took the scruffy singer to
a French *Vogue* job in Paris, where they were thrown out of their hotel
when a drunken party with some girls got too crazy. In the spring of 1964,
Bailey took Mick to New York with him. He brought Mick by the offices
of *Vogue,* which would run his shot of the full-lipped English singer as the
Stones were about to make their American debut. Bailey also introduced
Mick to the hip Manhattan nexus of fashion and pop art, and Mick made
a deep impression on that scene's principal avatar, the pope of pop, Andy
Warhol.

Warhol had come to New York from Pittsburgh ten years earlier and made his name as a successful commercial artist. When he arrived, the New York art world was still dominated by the abstract expressionists, a bunch of macho, brawling drunks like Willem de Kooning and Jackson Pollock. But by 1960, the New York style was turning away from introspective abstraction and embracing the stark imagery of advertising and commercial art. Pop artists like Jasper Johns and Robert Rauschenberg produced images that anyone could recognize—flags, comic strips, celebrities, Coke bottles—the stuff the abstract expressionists tried so hard to get away from. Andy Warhol's first shows of his silk-screen paintings in New York and Los Angeles in 1962 were a sensation because he played with the raw imagery of national icons and TV ads: Campbell's soup cans, Green Stamps, Elvis, Marilyn Monroe, Jackie Kennedy. "Once you 'got' Pop," Warhol wrote, "you could never see a sign the same way again. And once you thought Pop, you could never see America the same way again."

Pop artists like Warhol were a different breed. Their undeclared manifesto held that the post–abstract expressionist sensibility would be homosexual or ambivalent, not hypermasculine. This sensibility would color the Rolling Stones' own vivid streak of pop art singles beginning in 1965 and would echo down through Warhol's pet band, the Velvet Underground, and on through David Bowie in the decade to follow.

Warhol and Jagger met at the apartment of a twenty-two-year-old New York socialite, Jane Holzer. Nicky Haslam, *Vogue*'s trendy English art director, brought Warhol and invited Mick and Bailey, who were staying in Haslam's apartment. "At Jane Holzer's dinner I noticed Bailey and Mick," Warhol wrote. "They each had a distinctive way of dressing: Bailey all in black, and Mick in light-colored, unlined suits with very tight hip trousers and striped T-shirts, just regular Carnaby Street sports clothes, nothing expensive, but it was the way he put things together that was so great—this pair of shoes with that pair of pants that no one else would have thought to wear."

This was the start of a long, sometimes-fruitful, sometimes-contentious liaison between Mick and the Stones and the febrile Manhattan-chic style of Warhol and his Factory.

————

The Stones' first album, *The Rolling Stones,* came out in England in April and in the United States in May, where Decca's American subsidiary, London Records, retitled it *England's Newest Hitmakers.* The album cover photo by Nicholas Wright was dark, almost black, with the band's faces half in shadow. Long hair, longer than the Beatles', vests, jackets, and ties. There was a brief liner note—"The Rolling Stones are more than just a group, they are a way of life"—from newly re-named "Andrew Loog Oldham," whose middle name conveniently rhymed with "droog," *A Clockwork Orange*'s term for hoodlum.

The album was a blast of R&B energy, a stark alternative to the Beatles' tuneful love songs. "Not Fade Away" lifted off with Keith's acoustic chop and Brian's wailing harp. "Route 66" and "I Just Want to Make Love to You" were furious jams, the latter a sped-up Delta blues for the Atomic Age featuring Brian on harp. "Honest I Do" was a slow Jimmy Reed blues. The first side finished with two of the "filler" tracks recorded with Spector and Pitney, "Now I've Got a Witness" and "Little by Little."

"I'm a King Bee" opened the second side, driven by Bill's buzzing bass line. Brian deployed a stinging slide guitar part and some more har-monica on the fade. The momentum picked up with some sped-up Chuck Berry on "Carol" with an overdrive fueled by handclaps.

"Tell Me" was in many ways the showpiece of the album and the first Jagger/Richards song to be released by the Stones. A dark, acoustic folk rock ballad of pleading love with a soft/hard dynamic, moving from intimacy to insistence, "Tell Me" was written in the studio, one of the first seeds of the modern Stones sound. Keith played twelve-string guitar and sang harmonies into the same microphone as the twelve-string. With its off-key, echolike atmosphere, "Tell Me" was especially big in the United States when it was released as a single in May. The song conveyed an ag-gressive longing and sexual malaise ("I hear the telephone / that hasn't rung") that appealed to young men bored with soppy emotional re-sponses to unobtainable girls. "Tell Me" was described by Andrew as "a blues traveler resting his head in a commercial space." It was so unlike the surf pop and post-folk optimism prevalent on American radio in 1964 that it eclipsed even the Stones' powerhouse R&B interpretations.

England's Newest Hitmakers finished with Stu playing piano boogie and Mick the tambourine on the Motown hit "Can I Get a Witness"; Mick playing soul singer on Gene Allison's obscure "You Can Make It If You Try"; and the Stones' epochal take on Rufus Thomas's "Walking the Dog." Unlike Thomas's funny novelty tune, the Stones' version played it straight to the groin. Brian whistles and sings harmony (perhaps his only vocal on a Stones record), and the clapping dance rhythm came close to matching the infectious energy of the Stones onstage. "Walking the Dog" launched thousands of garage bands, particularly in America. Aerosmith covered the Stones' unironic version on their own first album, almost ten years later.

The Stones' first album located its audience within days of release. By the end of April, it knocked the seemingly invincible *With the Beatles* down to no. 2 on the English charts, only a week after it first appeared in the shops. In England, the album was no. 1 for twelve weeks, dethroned only by the soundtrack album of the new Beatles film, *A Hard Day's Night*. If '63 was the year of the Beatles, '64 would be the year of the Stones.

————

From April to June, the Stones stayed on the road, the gigs getting shorter and weirder as rabid young fans rioted and the cops stopped the shows.

Keith: "There was a period of six months in England where we couldn't play in ballrooms anymore because we never got through more than three songs every night. Man! Chaos. Too many kids in the places, and the girls are fainting. We'd walk into some of these places and it was like the battle of the Crimea going on: people gasping, tits hanging out, chicks choking, nurses, ambulances. We couldn't hear ourselves. It became impossible to play as a band onstage."

The English papers also began to press an offensive against
the Stones. Conservative critics were aghast at the Stones' hair and
clothes, especially Mick's preference for performing in a loose sweatshirt
and corduroy trousers. The *London Evening Standard,* March 21, 1964:
"This horrible lot have done terrible things to the music scene, set it back
about eight years. Just when we'd got our pop singers looking all
neat, tidy and cheerful, along come the Stones looking like beatniks.
They've wrecked the image of the pop singer of the Sixties . . . They're
a horrible-looking bunch, and Mick is indescribable."

Brian tried to explain: "We seem to arouse some sort of personal anxiety in people. They think we're getting away with things they never could.
It's a sort of frustration . . . A lot of men would like to wear their hair long,
but they daren't. I am one of the few people who is doing what he wants."

Stones shows were now so truncated by riots that the band was for-
getting how to play a whole set of songs. The shortest Stones show happened on April 30, 1964, in a ballroom in Birkenhead, near Liverpool.
The Stones were onstage, the curtain down, Keith's hand raised over his
head, ready to strike. The curtain went up, the band played *three bars* of
"Talkin' 'bout You," and the place erupted. The fans launched a frontal assault at the stage, the curtain was dropped, and before Mick sang a word
the show was over, the band hustled backstage, protected by a cordon of
pissed-off cops. The Rolling Stones still talk about Birkenhead, even
though a lifetime of gigs has gone by.

May 1964. "High Heel Sneakers" and "I'm All Right" aroused passions that made for the band's craziest nights. "Bye Bye Johnny" closed
the shows. Some nights Keith was pulled off the stage and had to be rescued. "I Just Want to Make Love to You" was a sensation on *Top of the
Pops.* The Stones recorded the demo for "As Tears Go By" on May 4. On
May 9 the whole band went to see Chuck Berry, released from prison and
touring England with fellow ur-rocker Carl Perkins, *auteur* of "Blue Suede
Shoes." Expecting mellow showbiz backstage bonhomie, the Stones were

disappointed and hurt when famously ill-tempered Chuck Berry snubbed them, refusing to meet his worshipful young disciples. Two weeks later Mick and Charlie encountered Berry in a hotel elevator. Chuck turned his back on them and didn't say a word.

On May 14, in Bradford, the Stones were forced to make a dash for their hotel, across the road from the hall they were playing. Mick and Keith won their race, but Bill and Charlie were forced back through the stage door by a howling mob of Bacchae. Brian was caught alone, knocked down, and the girls almost tore his clothes off before he was rescued by the cops and hustled away from the danger.

Four thousand fans, many with forged tickets, rioted outside the hall the Stones were playing in Scotland four days later. Dozens were taken to hospitals, some with serious injuries. This scene would be repeated all over England for at least another year, as the Furies began to gather wherever the Rolling Stones played their hopped-up sex machine songs.

A Sore Pimple in Omaha

The Rolling Stones followed the Beatles to America as best they could in June 1964. The Beatles had arrived in New York the previous February, three months after the Kennedy assassination, and seemed to miraculously wipe away the national shock and grief over the president's murder with their sharp looks, cheeky repartee, and bag of cheery, innocent love songs. It was almost as if the Liverpool pop quartet had responded to an occult summons to confound America's darkness and personify teenage lust on a scale as yet unimagined. Their presence in New York City inspired molten crowds of girls to ring their hotel in hysterical demonstrations of female desire that threatened to dismember the band if they were caught alone. The Beatles charmed everyone by taking this mania in stride and seeming to enjoy the moment among themselves, like a private joke.

On June 1, 1964, the Rolling Stones flew to New York to begin their chaotic first American tour, hastily organized by Eric Easton and Decca's hapless American branch, London Records. London's best-selling act was Mantovani, king of mood music, and the label was clueless when it came to marketing the hot English acts it now got from Decca. London had already botched the Stones' first U.S. single when it pressed the instrumental "Stoned" as the flip side of "Not Fade Away." The record was suppressed when the label's president objected to "Stoned," and "Not Fade Away" was reissued with "I Wanna Be Your Man."

At the airport, the Stones were greeted by five hundred excited girls and a chorus of dopey, shouted questions at a raucous press conference. "Hey! Over here! You guys wearing wigs? Do you sing like the Beatles?"

Promo men whisked them over to WINS, the big New York rock and roll station, to appear on *Murray the K's Swinging Soiree*. Murray (Kaufman), who called himself the Fifth Beatle since he'd latched onto their February tour, played "Not Fade Away" and interviewed the Stones on the air. After the show, he played them a new song by the Valentinos called "It's All Over Now" and suggested that the Stones could advance their career by covering it.

The next morning, they woke to find the Astor Hotel in Times Square teeming with a hundred girls, many armed with scissors and determined to cut a lock of long English hair. Bill was sick with the flu, it was Charlie's twenty-third birthday, and when anyone left the hotel for some sight-seeing, he was swamped by autograph-seeking teenagers.

———

Early on June 3, the Stones, joined by Andrew Oldham, flew to Los Angeles to tape their national TV debut on Dean Martin's *Hollywood Palace* variety show. (Ed Sullivan, revolted by photographs of the shaggy, loutish Stones, had turned them down flat for his more popular show.) Dean Martin was an old-style fifties crooner at the height of his career—the leader, along with his pal Frank Sinatra, of the legendary

Hollywood/Las Vegas Rat Pack that celebrated booze, broads, and gambling in song and lascivious patter. Martin's producer offered to buy the Stones uniforms and they refused. Then Martin and the Stones' new tour manager, Bob Bonis, had a loud fight backstage over how many numbers they would tape. Dino felt threatened by the Stones and went out of his way to insult them in his introduction.

"Now, something for the youngsters, five singing boys from England who've sold a lot of albeeums . . . albums [Martin was feigning being drunk]. They're called the Rolling Stones. [Aside:] I've been rolled when I was stoned myself. I don't know what they're singing about, but here they are."

The Stones appeared in dark suits and blasted into "I Just Want to Make Love to You," rocking the old Muddy Waters tune, Brian switching harmonicas for the bridge and appearing to give old Dino the finger while he was playing.

Dino came back afterward, rolling his eyes with withering sarcasm: "Aren't they great?" Audience laughter. "Y'know, these singing groups are under the impression they have long hair. Not true at all! It's an optical illusion—they just have low foreheads and high eyebrows, that's all." The next act was a trampoline acrobat. Dino: "That's the Rolling Stones' father—he's been trying to kill himself ever since!"

Backstage the band was furious, but came back and performed "Not Fade Away" and their new single, "Tell Me." Dino: "Now don't go away, folks. You wouldn't want to leave me with those Rolling Stones!" When the show was broadcast on ABC two weeks later, the Stones' segment had been cut to just sixty-five seconds of "I Just Want to Make Love to You." Furious, Mick called Eric Easton in London and yelled at him for booking them on the show.

But, "after we'd had some big records in the States," recalled Bill Wyman, "they reran the show—'And now the fabulous Rolling Stones'— with screams and cheers added in the background."

There was outrage in certain circles over Dino's rough treatment of the band. In the liner notes to his 1964 album *Another Side of Bob Dylan*, Dylan took the trouble to write, "Dean Martin should apologize t' the

Rolling Stones." It was evident to the Stones' generation that they were killing the old showbiz mentality. The Rat Pack's scummy booze culture was history, demoted from the Big Rooms and into the Lounges where they belonged. Even Frank Sinatra's career as a huge seller was almost over. The new wind from England blew the middle-aged crooners away.

A month later, at the Newport Folk Festival, Bob Dylan was jamming at his hotel, trying to match the harmonies of "Tell Me" with fellow folkie Tony Glover. Dylan was a Stones fan from early on.

The Stones spent their time in Los Angeles going to music stores, buying clothes, hanging out. (Brian Jones attracted small crowds when he visited music stores in his seersucker jacket and new wraparound shades.) At RCA Studios, they met Jack Nitzsche, Phil Spector's resident arranger and keyboard player, the key man in Spector's musical scheme, who would also become a major element in future Stones records. There were parties every night, where the Stones met the Beach Boys and some of the L.A. crowd, like promo man Sonny Bono and his girlfriend, Cher, yet to have their first folk rock hit record.

Keith: "America was a real fantasyland. It was still Walt Disney and hamburger dates and kids going steady. We watched the presidential debates [Lyndon Johnson and Barry Goldwater] and noticed that kids were more into what was going on [politically]. It was what we'd been dreaming of—better music, better cars . . . the girls were better looking, ha ha! It was like throwing a load of demons into heaven."

On June 5, the Stones played their first American gig in San Bernardino, about an hour from L.A., on a bill with the Chiffons, Bobby Goldsboro, Bobby Comstock, and Bobby Vee and his band the Shadows. Bobby Vee's band (which had once employed a young, pre-Dylan Bobby Zimmerman) included a twenty-year-old tenor saxophonist named Bobby Keys. Bobby Vee, accustomed to the scorching heat of the American Southwest in summertime, appeared onstage in cool Bermuda shorts; he was amused to see the Stones playing in their usual jeans and sweatshirts, sweltering in the blazing sun of the outdoor gigs.

At least the Stones got a warm welcome too. There were 4,500 kids at the San Bernardino show, mostly deeply tanned teenage girls in tight shorts, bare feet, bare tummies. The band played an eleven-song set, Mick dancing around the stage, shaking his ass and his four maracas, leaping into the air with his scissors kick. Girls started rushing the stage, which sent the cops into action: flying tackles, body slams, pile-ons. One girl grabbed Mick and it took three cops to get her off. Brian almost had his harp pushed down his throat. Keith: "It was a straight gas. They all know the songs and they were bopping! It was like being back home. 'Route 66' mentioned San Bernardino and everybody was into it. We went out on the road and in Omaha there'd be six hundred kids. You get deflated. That's what stopped us from turning into pop stars. Then we really had to work America and it really got the band together. We'd fallen off playing in England because nobody was listening. We'd do four numbers and be gone. Don't blink, you'll miss us."

The next day, the tour flew to Texas to play the San Antonio Teen Fair. The Stones' scruffy hair drew fire at the airport and in hotel lobbies. Crew-cut local rednecks, getting their first taste of long hair, uptight with homosexual panic, yelled taunts and wolf-whistled at them. All-American girls in their cashmere sweaters with round necklines and circle pins, wearing straight fifties-style skirts, came up and asked the band why they didn't carry purses and wear lipstick. There was hostility backstage too, and Mick Jagger got into a shoving match with the guitar player of country singer George Jones's band, which was also on the bill. Mick ended up in a headlock until Jones—disgusted by the Stones' look—told his ol' boy to let go.

After the San Antonio shows, the Stones were photographed at the Alamo, shrine of Texas independence. They complained bitterly to road manager Bonis that they weren't pulling any girls, what Keith termed "a distinct lack of crumpet." Alarmed by constant taunts and insults from strangers, scared by random violence reported on the TV news, Keith and Bill bought cheap automatic pistols in Texas. Keith never toured America again without a gun close by, especially when he learned that Muddy Waters carried a .25 wherever he went.

2120 South Michigan Avenue

Andrew Oldham wanted to record the next Stones album in America. They were all frustrated that the gutsy sound they'd been getting live in England never came close to being duplicated on record, which they blamed on sterile London studios and inadequate engineers. They were determined to get it right in a more sophisticated American studio. Phil Spector suggested they go to Chicago and work where their R&B heroes made their records. They flew to the Windy City on June 9. The band wanted to visit some famous blues clubs that night, but were told that racial tensions were running high and they'd better stay out of the South Side. Brian Jones spent the evening writing postcards to both of his pregnant girlfriends.

The next day, the Stones arrived at Chess Records at 2120 South Michigan Avenue. They walked into the studio and saw a big black man with a familiar-looking face, up on a ladder, painting the place. It was Muddy Waters.

Keith: "He was painting the goddamn ceiling, dressed all in white, with white paint like tears on his face, 'cause he wasn't selling any records at the time. That throws you a curve: here's the king of the blues painting a wall. When we started the Rolling Stones, our main aim was to turn other people on to Muddy. We named the group after him. And now I was getting to meet The Man. He's my fucking God, right?—and he's painting the ceiling!"

Bill: "We're unloading our van, helping Stu take the equipment in, when this big black guy comes up and says, 'Want some help here?' It's Muddy Waters, and he starts helping us carry in the guitars, the amps, the mike stands. It was unbelievable. Here's the great Muddy Waters carrying my guitar into the studio. I mean, it was unreal."

Muddy Waters had been following the Stones' progress for a while. He'd toured England in late 1963 (disappointing R&B fans by playing only acoustic blues because Chess was trying to reposition him as a folksinger) and had said complimentary things about the Stones.

Muddy was also one of the inspirations for a new American generation of young white musicians beginning to update R&B. In New York, John Hammond, Jr., was reviving Robert Johnson's songs. Ronnie Hawkins and his band the Hawks were recording Bo Diddley jams, and in Chicago, white kids—Paul Butterfield, Mike Bloomfield, Charlie Musselwhite, and Elvin Bishop—were adapting R&B styles for a new audience. The Stones had an advantage over the local white musicians: they had the British Invasion momentum and a sexy, hip-swiveling lead singer who had never been advised by Muddy—as had Mike Bloomfield—that he wasn't man enough to sing the blues yet.

The Chess studio was basically unchanged from the late 1950s. Although Andrew was nominally producing the sessions, they began working with resident engineer Ron Malo, who'd recorded classic sides by Muddy, Chuck Berry, Howlin' Wolf, and the Stones' other idols. It was the first time the Stones had recorded in a modern four-track studio, and Malo surrounded them with the trademark Chess echo that gave the blues a misterioso depth and dramatic edge. Over the next two days, the Stones taped their next single, a second British EP, and most of their next album in a burst of inspired creativity. On the first day, they cut "It's All Over Now" and the first version of Irma Thomas's "Time Is on My Side." Muddy smiled as he watched twenty-two-year-old Brian Jones play his skilled bottleneck guitar on "I Can't Be Satisfied" and some instrumental tracks featuring Stu on piano. Chess's resident composer Willie Dixon dropped by to sell the Stones some songs, but the band was more interested in covering some of their newly bought American soul records. Guitarist Buddy Guy and other blues stars came in and shook hands.

The next morning, Andrew staged a typically provocative press conference on a traffic island outside the *Chicago Tribune* building in the middle of the Loop. As reporters shouted questions, fans surged around them and traffic jammed up. An irate Chicago police captain showed up, threatened everyone with arrest, and the conference moved to the sidewalk before it broke up.

Back at Chess that afternoon, the band continued to record the soul tunes and R&B covers that would appear on the next album. In the middle of the session, Chuck Berry showed up, having been alerted that the English band was cutting a bunch of his songs. He had snubbed the boys earlier that year at one of the shows on his post-prison English tour, but now, with visions of royalties dancing in his head, Berry was much more friendly. He walked in while the Stones were playing "Down the Road Apiece," and afterward he smiled and said, "Wow, you guys are really getting it on. Swing on, gentlemen."

Bill Wyman: "Chuck Berry was the nicest I can ever remember him being, but don't forget we were making money for him. We all stood around talking about guitars, amplifiers, all that. We played 'Reelin' and Rockin' ' for him and he really liked it and said most of the cover versions of his songs didn't swing."

The Chess sessions produced a cornucopia of fresh material. Brian was brilliant on harmonica, Stu was prominent on boogie piano, and Mick slurred his vocals like an Arkansas sharecropper. Among the outtakes were Big Bill Broonzy's "Tell Me Baby," Willie Dixon's "Meet Me in the Bottom," "High Heel Sneakers," and Chuck Berry's "Don't Lie to Me" and "Reelin' and Rockin'." And in an incredible moment, as the Stones were recording the atmospheric Nanker Phelge instrumental "2120 South Michigan Avenue," Muddy Waters picked up a guitar and began to jam with the band. When the song was released later that year, Muddy's guitar had to be edited out—except for a single note—for contractual reasons.

In between takes, the Stones gave interviews to radio and TV crews, ate soul food from local rib joints, and chatted with Chicago blues idols who dropped in, curious about the strange English kids who had picked up on their thing. The Stones got a big dose of Chess ambience. Keith: "[There was] some incredible music going on in the back room while we were there. Sometimes we would open the door and peep in. Some *amazing* stuff going on."

The session lasted until two that morning, and then the Stones packed up and flew to Minneapolis, where they played that night. The tour was back on. Only four hundred kids showed up for the Minneapolis gig. Then to Omaha, where the Stones got a taste of old-style frontier justice.

Keith: "We really felt like a sore pimple in Omaha. The only people to meet us off the plane were twelve motorcycle cops, who insisted on doing this motorcade thing right through town. And nobody in Omaha had heard of us. We get to the auditorium and there's six hundred people in a fifteen-thousand-seat hall.

"There was this ridiculous cop scene. It was then that I realized what [satirist] Lenny Bruce was talking about. We were sitting back in the dressing room, drinking whiskey and Coke out of paper cups, waiting to go on. Cop walks in. 'You can't drink whiskey in a public place.' I was just drinking Coke, actually, and he says, 'Tip it down the bog [toilet].' I said, 'No, man, I've just got Coca-Cola in here.'

"The cop pulled his gun on me! I look up and I've got a .44 lookin' at me, right between the eyes. That's when I realized what it could get into."

The tour continued through Detroit, Pittsburgh, Cleveland, Harrisburg—only handfuls of kids in big arenas. The band continued its record-buying binge, picking up Motown and Stax records, stocking up on the soul music that was the cultural expression of the civil rights movement. The great soul artists—James Brown, the Supremes, the Temptations, the Miracles, Sam Cooke, Stevie Wonder, Otis Redding, Martha and the Vandellas, Wilson Pickett, the Four Tops, Mary Wells, Junior Walker, and others—were the dominant and most progressive force in American music, and the Stones had to deal with it. The soul records they bought on the road in America made them believers, and they knew they had to cover these songs to stay current.

The tour ended with New York concerts at Carnegie Hall. The first show was a mini-riot, with screaming girls jumping out of their seats and rushing the stage. When scissor-waving chicks besieged the stage door after the first show, the cops insisted that another band close the second show so the Stones could sneak out of the building alive.

Two days later, the Stones flew home, having begun their effort to restore a lost American folkway—the blues—to its homeland. But there were some unpleasant surprises waiting for them in England. Mick and Keith had moved into a new apartment in Hampstead just before leaving for America, and while they were on tour someone had robbed the place. Most of their clothes and gear were gone. And Keith's girlfriend, Linda Keith, had been in an accident and gone through the windshield of a car, leaving her scarred and disfigured. "Keith came to the hospital," she remembered, "and he leaned down and kissed me on the face and showed me I wasn't a monster and I wasn't revolting. And that *was* Keith."

———

The Stones came home with very mixed emotions about the American journey. The tour had been badly organized and premature, with no hit record to promote, and no one felt good about it except Brian, who was itching to get back to Los Angeles, where he'd been received as a living god.

Mick: "The grown-up world was a very ordered society in the early sixties, and I was rebelling against it. America was even more ordered than anywhere else . . . a very restrictive society in thought, behavior, and dress. And touring outside of New York and L.A. . . . we found it the most repressive society, very prejudiced in every way. There was still segregation, and attitudes were fantastically old-fashioned. Americans shocked me by their behavior and narrow-mindedness."

Things would be different when they returned to America a few months later. The Rolling Stones had indeed made an impression. "The Beatles want to hold your hand," Tom Wolfe wrote, "but the Stones want to burn your town."

The Three-Chord Wonders

Late June 1964. More TV shows in England during a lull after the U.S. tour. On June 26, the band's appearance on the BBC's *Juke Box Jury* (where a panel of pop stars rated records) caused a furor when the bored-looking, cigarette-dragging Stones slagged all the records. Outraged headline: THE UGLIEST GROUP IN BRITAIN.

Marianne Faithfull's "As Tears Go By" was climbing the charts (her photographs alone were a sensation). Howlin' Wolf, Sonny Boy Williamson, and Little Walter Jacobs were touring England, riding the blues boom opened by the Stones.

Eager to get their fresh Chicago music out to Stones fans, Decca released "It's All Over Now" with its harmonized chorus, proto-rock dynamics, and classic Stones dual-guitar attack—Brian's chiming drone and Keith's chunky rhythm riffing. The single quickly became the Rolling Stones' first no. 1 record. London issued it in the United States a month later.

In New York, the song's composer, Bobby Womack, was righteously pissed off. His group the Valentinos were signed to soul star Sam Cooke's label, and Cooke's manager, the savvy New York accountant Allen Klein, had given Andrew the song for the Stones to record. "I was very angry about it," Womack recalled. "I knew their record was going to go far, and our version was going to quit." But Womack felt better when the royalties began to click in. "Sam Cooke put me straight. He said, 'Bobby, one day this is gonna be history. Them boys are gonna be huge, and you'll be glad because you'll be the writer whose song broke 'em in this country.' When I saw the first check, I was shocked. It was *huge.*"

On July 23, Linda Lawrence gave birth to Brian's son at her parents' house. Brian was living in a new flat in Chester Square. In a typically perverse twist, Brian insisted the boy be named Julian Mark, which was the same name as his son by Pat Andrews. Brian hid out at a country cottage owned by Nicky Wright, the photographer who shot the band's first album cover. "Brian used to drive down in his Humber Hawk," Wright says, "often to escape these girls' fathers. We'd hide his car in the woods in case they came looking for him. He was like a tomcat, really, that summer in '64." Brian would drink too much and get paranoid, complaining that he was being ignored by Mick and Andrew. One day the paranoia really got to him. "Suddenly Brian stood up in my tiny kitchen. 'I'm fed up—this will show them!' He took a knife and slashed it across one wrist. My brother punched Brian on the chin and he went out like a light. His wrist was just scratched, with no serious damage."

Dick Taylor and other members of the Pretty Things, who had the flat upstairs at Chester Square, could hear Brian and Linda fighting, and were often shocked by Brian's brutality.

―――――――

July and August 1964 were shaping into the two most horrendous months of the Stones' stage career. Almost every show ended in mayhem, and some of them in extremely destructive and bloody riots.

Mick Jagger had returned from the States with a new thing, turning his back and shaking his ass directly at the audience, offering up his bum in a raw gesture of sexual incitement that provoked immediate bacchanalia and carnal violence. Facing Charlie, wiggling his hips, Mick became throbbing gristle, an anarchic invitation to let it rip. *Rip it up.* It was his way of combating the tedium of what they were about in those days, a teen pop band.

Mick: "We started out playing for a college crowd, so we were used to older people, y'know, blues enthusiasts. And to go from that to playing for thirteen-year-olds with the [flash] cameras, who are just screaming and not knowing any of the tunes, really, was kind of weird . . . We just got bored playing, because all they wanted to hear was the hits, and they didn't want to know about the blues, and we were feeling very blues purist right then."

The worst riot of the summer occurred on July 24 in the northern resort town of Blackpool during Scots Week, when thousands of vacationing Scots took over the town. Ten thousand drunk Tartans, some of the toughest people in the kingdom, even the girls carrying knives and stilettos, jammed into the cavernous Empress Ballroom. Beery football chants—"Scotland, Scotland"—filled the hall. Fights began the moment the Stones walked onstage, plugged in, and began "Walkin' the Dog." Mick and Keith looked scruffy, like they'd just been dragged from their beds. Mick turned his back and shook his bony arse in their faces. Brian— playing his pear-shaped white Vox guitar—began to tease the hysterical, screaming girls up front, who were quickly displaced by a rowdy gang of thugs who fought their way to the edge of the stage. Aroused by Brian's provocative, contemptuous glaring, they spat all over his legs.

One of these hoods then unloaded a big gob of saliva on Keith's Chelsea boot. Keith stomped his Cuban heel down on the guy's hand, then stepped back and kicked him in the head. Keith: "This guy in front was spitting. In those days, for me, I had a temper. 'You spit on me?' I kicked his face in."

The show imploded as the riot began. Stu rushed onstage to try to save the equipment and shouted at Keith, "For fuck's sake get out of here while you're still alive!" As the Stones ran for the exit, cops began fighting with the rioting Scots. The drum kit (borrowed from the band that had opened the show) was wrecked. A white Steinway grand piano was pushed off the stage as Stu watched in horror. Even the hall's immense chandelier was shattered. The band was smuggled into an armored van, but fighting continued in and out of the hall for hours.

At three in the morning, Stu arrived at the band's hotel, which, though twenty miles from the gig, had to be guarded by police all night to prevent the Stones from being lynched by a vengeful mob. Stu held a few splinters of wood hanging by wires. "There we are, kiddies. This is your amp," he told Keith, "and here's your guitar . . ."

"It was very nearly the date on my gravestone," Stu said afterward. A week later, the Stones' Belfast concert was stopped after twelve minutes. Half a dozen crazed girls were carried out of the hall, trussed up in straitjackets.

————

In August, the Stones returned to Richmond for the last time, headlining the National Jazz and Blues Festival. On the eighth, they flew to Holland to play a show at the Kurhaus, an elegant nineteenth-century opera house in The Hague. Surrounded by cops and filmed by a Dutch TV crew, the show ran through "Beautiful Delilah," "Dog," "Sneakers," "Susie Q," and "Mona," whose subversive Diddley throb set off a chain re-action as berserk fans—almost all boys—stormed the stage, ripped down the curtains, tore out the microphone leads. Seats were ripped from the floor. The majestic room was being sacked before the band's disbelieving eyes. They tried to continue with just drums, tambourine, and maracas, but then gave up and ran for cover. Stu was smashed on the head by a fly-ing bottle and rushed to the hospital. The Kurhaus was left in shambles.

In mid-August, Decca released the Stones' second EP in England, *Five by Five,* to showcase the new Chicago tracks. "Around and Around," the Chuck Berry song that had been on the tape the Blue Boys sent Alexis Korner two years previously, featured Stu's barrelhouse piano and an ex-plosive chordal guitar tag by Keith at the end. "Confessin' the Blues," an old Jay McShann swing-era tune covered by Chuck Berry, had Brian's in-timate harp in an echoing solo, as did "Empty Heart," written by the band, with Mick's lyric improvised from boilerplate blues vocalese. "2120 South Michigan Avenue," basically a duet between Stu on organ and Brian on harp, came minus Muddy Waters's impromptu guitar part. "If You Need Me" dated from Wicked Wilson Pickett's days as a member of the Falcons (also covered that year by Solomon Burke, an important Stones source); it had a hilarious "black" soul-style spoken verse by Mick.

Five by Five went to no. 1 almost instantly.

More riots on the island of Jersey and all over southern England amid teen subcult wars, the mods (fashionable, middle class) against the rockers (working class biker types). "Right, my little three-chord won-ders," Stu would bark to the band, "you're on!" In Wales, Charlie was hit in the head with an air-gun pellet and kept the beat going with a bloody face.

THE
'STONES

Come to the Klondike with the incredible **Rolling Stone** at **Eel Pie Island** on: **Friday** July 12 from 7.30-12

Twickenham Department of Graphic Design

Rare art college poster for "The 'Stones" at Eel Pie Island, July 1963.

The Rolling Stones backstage, late 1963.

DFE 8590

DECCA

Rocking out "I'm Moving On" with Mick on harmonica
at Wembley in 1965.

Brian Jones rehearsing on a London television stage, 1966.

Marianne Faithfull, radiant in black leather, on the set of her film
Girl on a Motorcycle, France, 1968.

Mick and Keith go acoustic in the *Aftermath* era, circa 1966.

The Stones recorded Howlin' Wolf's "Little Red Rooster" at Regent Sound in early September, plus three extraordinary numbers that throbbed with greasy funk: "Off the Hook," "Grown Up All Wrong," and "Susie Q." There were hard feelings in the band. Brian arrived at what he thought was the "Rooster" session with Phil May of the Pretty Things. No other musicians were there, just a note from Mick telling Brian where to overdub his slide guitar. The Stones had recorded the track the previous night without telling Brian. "I can't believe this," he moaned to Stu. "You guys had a session, and now I'm just to fill in?"

On September 5 the Stones went back on tour with the American soul duo (and mod faves) Inez and Charlie Foxx, who had a hit with "Mockingbird." At the end of it, Charlie Watts married his older art student girlfriend, Shirley Ann Shepherd, without telling the Stones or their manager, who was already nervous about Bill's family and Brian's legion of bastard children. Andrew himself married Sheila Klein that month.

———

October 1964. In America, London Records released haphazardly selected tracks from Chicago and Regent Sound as the Stones' second U.S. album, *12 X 5*. (Their second English album, *The Rolling Stones No. 2*, came out three months later with half the tracks different.) The album's jacket featured the unsmiling Stones in a dark, brooding photograph, faces half in shadow, by David Bailey. Kicking off with "Around and Around," the album included the Chicago tracks from *Five by Five* and a collection of covers: "Time Is on My Side" (rerecorded in London) featuring a good Brian Jones blues guitar solo, Merseybeat harmonics, and the famous triple-"Time" tag; "It's All Over Now"; the Drifters' "Under the Boardwalk" (recorded in London) with its articulate British soul feeling; and "Susie Q," Dale Hawkins's 1957 bayou romp with crazed double guitar frenzy over the handclap rhythm.

There were also three Jagger/Richards originals. "Good Times, Bad Times" (recorded in London) was an acoustic blues with a lazy Brian harmonica line. "Congratulations" was a downbeat, sarcastic love song beloved by young American (male) fans—it was not released in England—

with an acoustic guitar solo by Brian. And "Grown Up All Wrong" was a variant on the "Susie Q" rhythm, Brian sliding on bottleneck, a killer pastiche, stomping country blues straight outta Soho.

These songs marked the crucial beginnings of the Stones' core creative structure: Mick and Keith writing words and music, while Brian overlaid his own riffs and harp mojo onto their ideas. But it was only Jagger/Richards on the songwriting credits.

Keith: "Andrew's logic after the first album was that if we didn't start to find a source of new material . . . we'd only be able to scrounge around for another album or two before we ran out of top-notch rock and roll and R&B. You run out of classics eventually. In those days, the original versions were far superior to ours; we were just learning them. We got our music across because white kids had never heard it before, even though it was in their own backyard in [America]. But we were white and eighteen and looked sort of cute, whatever."

A New Delinquent Aristocracy

The Rolling Stones were already huge in France in late 1964. The French never much liked the Beatles, but they loved the louche and grungy Stones, probably because they had always understood black American music more than white Americans had. When the Stones arrived in Paris on October 19, they had three records in the French charts, and their concerts at venerable L'Olympia theater (home of the cancan) were complete sellouts (fans attacked the box office when tickets ran out). The Stones played an expanded set that added "Carol," "If You Need Me" (with acute vocal harmonies by Keith), "Tell Me," and "Confessin' the Blues" (with Brian terrific on harmonica). The cops planted stooges in the audience, and if some poor kid got rowdy, he was quickly frog-marched out of the hall, which annoyed the Parisian kids and got them ready to rumble.

The set ended with "Bye Bye Johnny," which set off anarchy and violence. As the Stones crowded into the armored riot police van with machine guns bolted to the walls that was waiting at the stage door, their audience went berserk, wrecking the ornate lobby and fighting in the street outside, breaking every plate-glass window around, attacking civilians and wasting cafés. The gendarmes made 150 arrests. Despite the Paris violence, the promoter told the press the Stones could come back to L'Olympia anytime.

After the show, the band hung out with semicrazed English rocker Vince Taylor, an old friend whose French R&B band had opened the show. Mick and Keith went drinking with Taylor's tambourine player, Stanislas Klossowski de Rola, known as Stash de Rola, the son of the painter Balthus, beginning a long and significant friendship. The group ended up at the disco New Jimmy's, *the* place to be seen in 1964 Paris. Bill scored a French girl and left early.

———

Long transatlantic flight to New York on a BOAC 707. Hundreds of fans at the airport. Band packed into Cadillac, swamped by fans at the Astor Hotel in Times Square. Outside the hotel, the girls chanted, "Time, time, time is on my side." Andrew ordered London Records' press rep, Connie deNave, to feed the straight press a hot flash: "The Rolling Stones, who haven't bathed in a week, arrived here yesterday." The image of the unwashed Stones was teletyped on the wire services and gained national notoriety instantly, guaranteeing the Rolling Stones would get noticed on this tour.

The Stones took Manhattan by storm the next day. When they appeared on the radio with "Murray the Kunt" (as Keith called him), the station was mobbed, resulting in another mad dash for the cars. They taped some songs for Clay Cole's dance show on Channel 11, then played two complete shows at the Academy of Music on 14th Street. The four thousand fans who saw the second show included Andy Warhol, Baby Jane Holzer, reporter Tom Wolfe, David Bailey, the Shrimp (but not her little sister, who was left behind in London to write her teen columns for *Tiger*

Beat), Diana Vreeland, editor of *Vogue,* who had championed the Stones the previous spring; the high-camp crowd of art directors and fashionistas; the in-crowd (Dobie Gray's song a big hit that month), as well as almost anybody cool in town that weekend. Because David Bailey had spread the word: the Beatles are over, too sweet, even your mum likes them. The Stones are *switched on,* man, totally *now.* They're rebels with a cause, an R&B rebellion against the bourgeoisie and suburban values, rock and roll guerrillas in tight pants.

Tom Wolfe: "In the center of the stage a short thin boy with a sweatshirt on, the neck of the sweatshirt almost falling off his shoulders, they are so narrow, all surmounted by this enormous head . . . with the hair puffing down over the forehead and ears, this boy has exceptional lips. He has two peculiarly gross and extraordinary red lips. They hang off his face like giblets. Slowly his eyes pour over the flaming bud horde, soft as Karo syrup, and close, and then the lips start spreading into the most languid, most confidential, the wettest, most labial, most concupiscent grin imaginable. Nirvana! The buds start shrieking, pawing toward the stage."

The air was thick with a rain of objects hurled at the stage: candy, lipstick, sneakers, paper plates with scrawls on them, stuffed animals, compacts, dozens of pens and pencils, wallets, coins, garbage, junk and trash, every one a love letter and a message of lust.

Later that night, the band went to a party thrown for them at photographer Jerry Schatzberg's huge studio loft on Park Avenue South. While hundreds danced to *12 X 5* and the Supremes asked "Baby baby baby, where did our love go?" the Stones, in jeans and sweatshirts, lounged in the private pad upstairs, too shy and exhausted and stoned to come down. Keith was hanging out with Ronnie Bennett. Mick had Jane Ormsby-Gore, daughter of Lord Harlech, British ambassador to Washington, in a dark corner. Only Brian went down to the party to meet and greet.

The next day, Sunday, was spent rehearsing for *The Ed Sullivan Show,* the only national live exposure then available to pop music. The cops guarding the theater refused to let the Stones leave the building for their own safety, since it was surrounded by girls. That night, the Rolling

Stones made their live American coast-to-coast TV debut amid screams and tumult in the studio audience. On a stage set with giant wheel-shaped "stones," they did "Around and Around" at the top of the show and "Time Is on My Side" near the end. Seventy million Americans watched.

The Stones performed in stark contrast to what Americans had seen coming out of England. America west of the Hudson finally got a load of sweatshirted Mick's leering sexuality, Brian's suggestive aggression, Keith's pimples and attitude, Charlie's Neanderthal look, and—perhaps worst and most shocking of all—the saturnine, older, knowing, lock-up-your-daughters gaze of His Otherness Bill Wyman.

It was America's introduction to what critic Nick Kent later called "a new, delinquent aristocracy." And it scared the shit out of normal people. The switchboard at CBS was overwhelmed with angry messages from parents objecting to the Stones. Thousands of them. A shaken Ed Sullivan gave a statement next morning to the press: "I promise you they will never be back on our show. If things can't be handled, we'll stop the whole business. We won't book any more rock and roll groups and we'll ban teenagers from the theater. Frankly, I didn't see the group until the day before the broadcast . . . It took me seventeen years to build this show, and I'm not going to have it destroyed in a matter of weeks."

The Stones were called slobs and riffraff in the papers that day, but they were already on a plane to a more receptive scene in L.A. Six months later, unstoppable, they were back on *Ed Sullivan* too.

No Peace in the Barnyard

Late October 1964. A Cold War presidential campaign had America—still paranoid and traumatized by the Kennedy assassination—locked in a political death grip. Atom bombs and mushroom clouds were on TV as anti-Republican propaganda. Roy Orbison was big on the radio with "Pretty Woman." The new Supremes single was "Baby Love." The

Beatles' *A Hard Day's Night* was the no. 1 album. The Beach Boys were moving out of the surf and into Brian Wilson's autoerotic love calls like "Don't Worry Baby."

The Rolling Stones made only a small splash in this cultural maelstrom, but at least in Los Angeles they hit like one of Lyndon Johnson's bombs on Vietnam a few months later. Their arrival coincided with the Teen Age Music International (TAMI) show, an old-style rock and roll show shot on videotape and kinescoped to be shown in movie theaters. The cast included Chuck Berry, Marvin Gaye, the Beach Boys, some second-division English bands, and the Barbarians with their one-armed drummer. As spearheads of the cash-generating British Invasion, the Stones were shocked to learn they were headlining: this meant they had to follow James Brown and the Famous Flames—the best, most exciting, most impossible-to-follow band in the world. Even worse, Soul Brother Number One was mad as hell that the Stones were closing the show, rasping, "Tell those crazy motherfuckers they gonna wish they never left London." Mick badgered Andrew to get the billing changed, but the producers refused. Musical director Jack Nitzsche couldn't help. It was finally agreed that it would be ten minutes after the wringing-wet James Brown was helped from the stage by his retainers that the Stones would go on.

Only the Supremes deigned to greet the Stones and say hello. None of the other American acts would speak to them.

While Brown did his wild act—the spins, the double splits, the slippery moves, the razor-sharp band, the choreographed manic episodes—the Stones trembled in the dressing room while the other acts, watching a video feed, cheered Brown on. Finally Chuck Berry and Marvin Gaye took pity on them and smiled. Marvin told them, "Just go out there and do your thing." The Stones calmed down and played a perfect set: "Around and Around," "Off the Hook," "Time Is on My Side," "It's All Over Now," and "I'm All Right."

Afterward, James Brown walked up to the Stones, shook their hands, and complimented them. After that, Mick decided to *become* James Brown.

———

The Stones in L.A. Hot sunshine and brown haze. California girls. Major wood at the Hollywood Roosevelt Hotel. New pal Jack Nitzsche laughing as he finds Mick and Keith, naked in the hotel corridor, after a girl locked them out of their suite. Brian cruising Sunset Strip, a Stones sensation in his tailored mod jacket, collar and tie, big shades and tight white Lee Riders jeans. Mick and Keith huddled in the hotel, working on new songs for sessions Andrew organized in Los Angeles. They banged out "Surprise, Surprise" and "What a Shame" and reworked "Heart of Stone," which they had composed back in July. They bought new soul records and learned Marvin Gaye's "Hitch Hike" and Otis Redding's "Pain in My Heart." They went to parties and did radio interviews. Charlie Watts told a disc jockey that American teenagers were like kids everywhere, except they had a lot more money. The Stones played shows in Sacramento and San Bernardino. Old-fart London Records promotion man George Sherlock tagged along and did no promo, which intrigued the band to no end. A show in Long Beach ended with a riot, with the Stones' getaway car engulfed and damaged by a mob of girls.

The next day, the Rolling Stones began working in RCA Studios with Jack Nitzsche on keyboards. Nitzsche, twenty-seven, was the key studio musician in L.A., a cool hipster with a Beatle haircut, wraparound shades, and a primo track record. He'd worked as Phil Spector's arranger since 1962, creating the thunderous orchestrations behind the Ronettes and the Crystals. He'd written "Needles and Pins," a big hit for the Searchers, one of the hottest bands in England. Now Jack Nitzsche basically joined the Rolling Stones as their indispensable arranger, playing on and helping produce almost all the records they would make in California over the next four years.

At RCA, the Stones cut Mick and Keith's new songs and redid "Heart of Stone" (recorded earlier in London with Jimmy Page on guitar) and Solomon Burke's "Everybody Needs Somebody to Love." They covered "Down Home Girl," written by tunesmith Jerry Lieber as an R&B

parody, by playing it straight like the honkies they were. They started at 11 A.M. and astounded the studio crew by working for seventeen hours. No one did that in L.A.

Jack Nitzsche wasn't used to working this way, and he was deeply impressed by the Stones' stamina and intensity. "They were the first rock and roll band I met that was actually intelligent," he said. "They could all talk! They were all really bright. We couldn't believe it. The Stones were also the first ones I ever saw say 'fuck you' to everybody. There was no guidance at all on those records and very little need for it . . . They changed my whole idea of recording. I'd just been doing sessions, three hours to get a tune down. This was the first time [I saw] a band got together and just played. That was the first really free feeling I had in the studio."

———

Back on tour. In Cleveland, fans exploded in sex frenzy during "I'm All Right" and a girl got pushed over the balcony. Tough Rhode Island girls with beehive hair wrecked Loew's Theater in Providence when cops stopped the show after five songs. Night train to New York. The next night, the boys—Keith, Mick, Andrew—were driven to Harlem to catch James Brown at the Apollo Theater on 125th Street. They were the only white faces in the audience. James was glad to see the hot English band and invited them onstage to take a bow during his show. Backstage afterward, James noted that even black women screamed at the Stones' long hair, and he offered them good champagne from an ice-filled tub in the corner of the room.

In New York and L.A., Brian Jones was the Stone the in-crowd wanted to know. Andy Warhol's hard-chic entourage in Manhattan took up Brian, who whispered to them, drew them in, his "china-cat smile of evil assurance" (Nick Kent) causing sexual havoc in the girls who encountered him. Brian told *New York Post* reporter Al Aronowitz that he'd fucked sixty-four girls in the past month, and showed him the dog chain Brian claimed he beat them with afterward.

The Stones downtown: hip Charlie in his Ivy League suit digging the Mingus band with the incomparable Danny Richmond on drums at the Village Vanguard, Dizzy Gillespie at the Village Gate with Max Roach on the skins. Bill Wyman was hanging out with John Hammond, Jr., and the buckskin-fringed, pot-puffing Village folk-blues crowd. Mick and Keith wrote songs in their hotel.

————

On November 8, the Stones flew to Chicago to work at Chess, mostly without Brian, who collapsed with alcohol poisoning and exhaustion, sparking an industry-wide rumor that he had overdosed on pills. They put him in the hospital and said he had bronchitis. The Stones and Stu cut "What a Shame" at Chess and early versions of "Mercy, Mercy," with Mick trying to reproduce the Afro-bayou falsetto of its original singer, Don Covay. Mick had a great respect for Covay's style. "You get a real contrast between the falsetto and the butch, harsh voice," he said. "It's nice for a singer to have another voice."

By then the Stones felt more at home in Chicago. Keith: "Long as you knew cats, you was cool. They'd nurture us. 'These guys are cool. They're weird but they're cool.' We'd become like their mascots. 'You want a bitch tonight? She'll love *you*. She never had nothin' like *you* before.' You'd get laid and fed late at night. The white side of town was dead, but it was rockin' across the tracks. An incredible education."

The Stones played most of their Midwest dates without Brian that November. Stu sat in on piano and they'd mike him way up to fill out the sound. In Dayton, Ohio, there was a titanic moan of disappointment at the announcement that Brian was ill and wouldn't appear, and several hundred girls got up and left. The Stones sucked without Brian—"You can't cover what you want from the Stones with one guitar," Keith told biographer Stanley Booth—but there was desultory talk about getting rid of him.

The last stop was in Chicago. Brian rejoined the band, and the show was a killer, a wild success. But after a week without him, with Keith struggling to play Brian's trademark riffs, they dumped on Brian for being erratic, a drunk, and an asshole. They all hated his guts for letting them down. Mr. Jones's paranoia index in turn jumped off the chart. It had been his band, but now he was shut out of the loop.

"The thing about Brian," Mick later said, "is that he was an extremely difficult person . . . and he did give everyone else an extremely miserable ride. Anyway, there was something very, very disturbed about him. He was so jealous of everybody else; that was his personality failing. . . . And you can't be jealous and be a leader. He was *obsessed* with the idea of being the leader of the band."

Keith: "Brian was great. It was only when you had to work with him that he got very hung up. The harder the work got, the more awkward he got, and the more fucked up he would get himself . . . Mick and I were being merciless on him, because you don't have the patience at the time."

Bill: "He could be the sweetest, softest, most considerate man in the world and the nastiest piece of work you ever met."

Charlie: "I think he wanted to be the lead singer. Well, of course he wasn't. His breathing would never allow him to be. And he wanted to be leader, and he wasn't a leader."

Stu hated Brian most of all. "Brian was very Welsh," he told an interviewer, "and Welsh people are very devious. They are basically dishonest . . . I think Brian's sin was being so goddamned stupid about himself. There was no need for him to get in that out-of-it state that he used to get into. He did it because he thought that was the way rock and roll stars should behave."

————

After a photo call in New York for *Billboard* (because *12 X 5* was selling so fast), the Stones flew back to London on November 17. They found "Little Red Rooster"/"Off the Hook" the no. 1 record in England, an incredible coup to have finally lifted a pure blues song atop the charts after two long years. Brian's once-cherished ambition had come to pass. It was his masterpiece, his inspired guitar howling like a hound, barking like a dog, crowing like a rooster.

But there was "no peace in the barnyard" for Brian. He learned that Andrew had told Eric Easton that he wanted Brian out of the group and that the idea had been vetoed by Mick, who didn't want to face the girls alone on the front line of the Stones. Mick still felt he needed Brian up there beside him. And Mick knew that Brian was bigger than *he* was in America, where the real action was.

Soul Brother Number Two

Mick Jagger came back from America in his new chameleonic guise, Soul Brother Number Two, the white James Brown. He consulted a choreographer to see if Brownian moves could be learned, was told that James moved too fast to deconstruct the moves properly. "I do a bit of James Brown now," he told a reporter, "but a very watered-down version."

On November 20, the Rolling Stones were back on *Ready Steady Go!*, miming "Little Red Rooster" for a segment that opened on a stark close shot of Mick's lips and mouth. They also mimed "Off the Hook," Mick slipping into tastefully understated dance steps, playing with an imaginary telephone. After "Around and Around," Keith collapsed in the dressing room because he'd been speeding for five days straight.

The rest of feverish 1964 was devoted to promoting their records, mostly on TV because of a serious feud between their management and the BBC that started when the Stones didn't show up for a radio gig. In turn, the no. 1 smash "Rooster" was ignored by *Top of the Pops*. They scrambled to patch things up with the Beeb, playing four Chicago-style covers on the *Saturday Club* radio program, including "Beautiful Delilah" and Willie Dixon's "Down at the Bottom."

Brian was busy denying that his recent illness would cause him to leave the Stones, a major rumor of the day. Charlie Watts denied the rumors about his two-month-old marriage, then admitted it when confronted by his annoyed band. Andrew thought two married members would kill his carefully nurtured image of the Stones as Bad Boys. They gave Watts a hard time about the secret marriage, but that was all. There was a certain integrity at stake here. The Stones, if they were really rebelling against anything, were protesting suburban values and outmoded bourgeois social rituals symbolized by marriage and family life. Mick and Keith constantly mocked Brian's pretentions and genteel manners, and Mick would soon begin attacking the underbelly of suburbia's hypocrisy in his songs. "My great thing against suburban life was that it was, first of all, petty," he later told an interviewer, "and secondly, boring, based on consumer values, at best unambitious, and full of tittle-tattle and jealousies and things like that. I was trying to look for a music that wasn't a reflection of that society."

———

The Rolling Stones had two million-selling singles that year in "It's All Over Now" and "The Last Time." In their flat in Hampstead, Keith and Mick were writing a new song, using a method that became standard procedure. They would play old blues riffs over and over until they mutated into something else, a new composition. That's how they came up with "The Last Time," based on an old gospel chant that had been updated by the Staples Singers and absorbed by Keith in the six months since he'd bought the Staples album in Chicago. They also had another tune going, a song about the skewed families of the rich girls the Stones were meeting—a threatening slow pop blues they called "Mess with Fire."

Now it was 1965, and "The Sixties" were about to really begin, with the Rolling Stones as their generation's point men and outriders, brave scouts in a terra incognita of changing consciousness that would soon shake the world.

three:

No Satisfaction

19th
BREA
THE
STON

"Could you walk on the water?" The American
sleeve of "19th Nervous Breakdown," 1965.

RVOUS
DOWN
LLING

LONDON®   45-9823

I do the bits you can't hear.

Brian Jones

Knee-to-Knee

Year zero for rock music was 1965, the pivot of the decade, when postwar baby boom culture took over the Western romantic tradition and turned the volume way up. In England, the Beatles and Stones tuned pop music into the new drug culture. In America, Bob Dylan invented rock by making strapping on an electric guitar a quasipolitical statement. In 1965 the novel was dead and the movies hopelessly behind the times. Music, fashion, and pop art carried the spirit of the day, and in the vanguard of this were the Rolling Stones.

They had been working nonstop now for fifteen months. They were regarded by other rockers as the best live band in the world. Their concerts were interactive lust fiestas with a backbeat, and no one who saw the Stones play live in those times ever forgot it.

During this period, Mick Jagger and Keith Richards sat knee-to-knee in hotel rooms and tour buses, writing songs. "It's the best place to write," Mick said, "because you're totally into it. You get back from a show, have something to eat, a few beers, and just go into your room and write. I used to write about twelve songs in two weeks on tour. It gives you lots of ideas."

The germ of the songs usually came from Keith. He played old blues licks, transformed them, sang along wordlessly in mostly vowel sounds. Mick would translate them into lyric ideas ("vowel movement"). Often Mick would speed the tempo, and the little riff would evolve into a nasty radio anthem like "Get Off My Cloud" or "19th Nervous Breakdown" or one of the brilliant pop art manifestos the Stones were inventing in those exhilarating days.

In January, *The Rolling Stones No. 2* was out in England and spent the winter at no. 1. *Clockwork*-obsessed Andrew's liner notes suggested mugging the blind for the money to buy the album until Decca changed the sleeve. The Stones refused to appear on England's Sunday night TV variety show *Live at the London Palladium* because it was a family program. Keith told a reporter the Rolling Stones were atheists, but then hedged: "When you really get to know us, we're pretty good guys at heart."

On January 16, the Stones flew to Los Angeles for two days in the studio before going on to tour Australia. Working with Jack Nitzsche and engineer Dave Hassinger at RCA Studio, they began building "The Last Time," combining Keith's rhythm with Brian's serpentine guitar hook. Hailed by some as one of the first rock songs, "The Last Time" used Brian's repeating, curling riff to hypnotic effect. " 'The Last Time' was the first song we actually managed to write with a beat," Keith said. "It was our first nonpuerile song." "The Last Time" took all night to get on tape, and Brian, Bill, and Charlie had passed out on the studio couches by the time they got to a demo called "Mess with Fire," an acoustic ballad about the dysfunctional families of the rich girls Mick knew. Retitled "Play with Fire" and recorded while the others slept, Keith played guitar, with Jack Nitzsche on piano and harpsichord and Phil Spector on bass. Mick displayed his keen sense of London's social geography in a somber lyric of blunt warning that was unprecedented in its negative passion. It was a star solo turn for him, the emergence of the sexual outrider who would haunt the airwaves for years to come.

Later that day, the Stones flew to Australia, where three thousand girls rioted at the Sydney airport, smashing a chain-link fence and breaking rails in the customs hall in a suicide charge to get their hands on the band.

There were twenty-four shows on this long tour. *Do you feeeel it?* Mick asked the squealing little girls, and they let him know that, yes, they felt it. "A blatantly sexual act which the chaste Beatles had not prepared our tender teens for," opined the *Sydney Morning Herald,* and press hostility continued for the whole tour.

Brian Jones and Bill Wyman took advantage of this by embarking on a carnival of intercourse, stealing each other's girls, sometimes several girls a day, according to Bill. A Melbourne barbecue in the Stones' honor turned into an orgy (Mick fucked both the hostess and her daughter).

On to Singapore, the first English band to play there, as guests of the British high commissioner and his family. The promoter laid on a dozen beautiful Chinese whores for the band that night. The girls were hot, professional sex stars, not the little teens the Stones were used to, and even Bill Wyman was intimidated. His girl took matters in hand when he failed to become aroused; she filled her mouth with toothpaste and gave him a foamy menthol blow job that did the trick.

While the band was Down Under, *The Rolling Stones Now* was released in America. It was another black album from the Stones, with black-and-white snapshots by David Bailey. *Now* was a rowdy grab bag of 1964 English singles ("Rooster," "Heart of Stone"), soul covers, and newer up-tempo jams like "Everybody Needs Somebody to Love" and the excellent "Down the Road Apiece" from Chess Studios. Even the primal, swampy "Mona," still throbbing in the can from the earliest Stones sessions, got on *Now*. So did "Pain in My Heart," Otis Redding's arrangement of New Orleans producer Allen Toussaint's song, cut by the Stones in L.A. So ramshackle was this U.S.-only release that an inferior take of "Everybody Needs Somebody to Love" was put on the album, supposedly because Chrissie Shrimpton delivered the wrong can of tape to the studio for mastering.

But to their audience, *The Rolling Stones Now* appeared as a cohesive manifesto from a barrier-smashing band equally comfortable with rock and roll, R&B, and the blues. "Surprise, Surprise" ended the record with Mick's snarling accusations over Charlie Watts's hard backbeat. Mick preached the lyric soul-style, and this last track's tough love carried over to the onslaught of "The Last Time" a few weeks later.

———

After Australia and New Zealand, the Stones returned to Los Angeles. At RCA Studio, they added vocals and guitars to "The Last Time," layering echo and reverb into the song's groundbreaking mix. Keith's famous single-note guitar break was a dramatic mirror of Mick's angry threats in the lyric, an insistent emphasis of the number's bloody-minded attitude.

While Mick, Keith, and Charlie worked in the studio, Bill and Brian hit the Sunset Strip dance clubs, where the Byrds were a hot young band playing folk music on electric guitars, turning Bob Dylan's "Mr. Tambourine Man" into a folk rock anthem. Brian moved around L.A. like an English prince, inviting young girls back to his room at the Hollywood Ambassador Hotel for threesomes and orgies. The girls staggered out of Brian's room after dawn, carrying rumors of sadism, perversion, and rough treatment from that freaky, insatiable maniac who played guitar for the Rolling Stones.

Mama's Cookin' Chicken Fried in Bacon Grease

February 1965. With "The Last Time"/"Play with Fire" rushed out in England and hot on the radio, Mick was hanging out in the Ad-Lib club high over Leicester Square with the Beatles, strategizing so their singles wouldn't get in each other's way. "A meticulous piece of work going down between the Beatles and the Stones," according to Keith, "not to clash with each other."

In early March, the Stones began a two-week British package tour with the Hollies and other bands. As they progressed through Liverpool and Manchester, engineer Glyn Johns crudely recorded shows by hanging a single mike from the balcony. In Manchester a girl sailed *off* the balcony, losing some teeth when she landed on some other girls. Girls jumped the stage, clamping onto Mick in death grips, burying Brian in a rugby scrum until cops dragged them off.

On March 18, last night of the Hollies' tour, after escaping rioting fans in Romford, the band was banging back to town in a Daimler when Bill Wyman announced he had to pee. Then they all wanted a piss. They stopped at a service station, but the attendant took one look and told them to get lost. Mick gave him some lip and was told to get off the forecourt. "Get off my fucking foreskin," yelled Brian, pulling a repulsive nanker. "We'll piss anywhere, man," Mick said, and the Rolling Stones lined up, peed on the wall, marking their territory, and roared off in a derisive blast of naughty language and rude gestures. Someone got the plate number, and the incident was splashed all over the press. Months later, they were dragged to court, charged with insulting behavior and obscene language, and fined five pounds each.

———

Spring 1965. "The Last Time" was no. 1 in England. There were furious bids for the Stones by other record companies because their Decca contract was expiring in May.

In April, Brian moved to a supposedly haunted mews house in Chelsea, which he outfitted in velvet drapes, precious guitars, turntable and record collection. He had become the outsider of the band and saw Mick, Keith, and Andrew only at the shows. Andrew kept talking about throwing Brian out of the band.

Mick and Keith moved to a new flat in Hampstead after fans besieged their old place. John Lennon came by and listened to Keith's superior collection of American records. They wore out the new Bob Dylan album, *Bringing It All Back Home,* a phantasmagoria of rock and roll recorded with young white bluesmen from Chicago. The songs were biting zeitgeist arrows, full of lyric trickery, surreal social protest, and soul force: "Subterranean Homesick Blues," "Maggie's Farm," "Gates of Eden," "Bob Dylan's 115th Dream."

The odd thing was that Dylan was said to be obsessed with charismatic Brian Jones and wanted to meet him on Dylan's upcoming English tour in May. Dylan even phoned Brian from New York, but the paranoid Mr. Jones didn't believe it was really Dylan until Dylan's manager, Albert Grossman, came on the line and convinced him. Dylan told Brian that the Stones were the best band in the world. Brian explained to Dylan that the Stones would be touring the United States in May; they could get together when Dylan came back to New York. (Brian spent so long on the phone with Dylan over the next year that the Stones' office staff dreaded getting the bills.) Inspired by the Stones, Dylan would make this his last solo tour. Soon he would put on a modernist checked suit, Chelsea boots, and an electric guitar—like a rolling stone—to howls of protest from his fans.

The Stones returned to L'Olympia theater in Paris for three sold-out shows.

Mick: "The Beatles had done very badly in Paris. They did a very unsuccessful series of shows with a terrible bill. Typically French, they knew that everyone else loved the Beatles, so they didn't. And we did this series of shows at the Olympia, which was great."

Mick did some soul-style preaching on "Everybody:" "Listen to mah song, it'll save the whole world!" Keith played a country-style guitar solo on "It's All Over Now." Mick sardonically introduced Charlie to the French fans: *"Charles ne parle pas la Francais,"* he drawled as Charlie Watts ambled up to introduce "Little Red Rooster." The crowd was out for blood, chanting between songs in Gallic delirium. The last song of the night was "Hey Crawdaddy": Mick sang one verse and then did the crawdad dance as the band vamped on the Diddley rhythm while the stomping, clapping, chanting audience got its rocks off. *YEAH!* Mick yelled at the end, running for the wings as the band unplugged and followed him off.

After the last show, English friends took the Stones to an intimate party at the apartment of Donald Cammell. A bit older than the Stones, the formidably hip Cammell was a talented English portrait painter who'd forsaken his studio in Flood Street, Chelsea, for a Left Bank atelier. Cammell was brilliant and attractive, with wide social connections and esoteric knowledge of the occult and the far out. Cammell and his beautiful girlfriend, fashion model Deborah Dixon, were avant-garde stars and very much a team. The party was chic and bohemian—low lights, hashish smoke, Miles Davis on the stereo—and the uncouth Stones were the least cool of Cammell's guests. But Cammell was interested in the Stones because he was getting into the movie business, and he befriended first Brian, then Mick, with fateful consequences down the road.

When the band returned to London, Brian stayed behind to hang out with his actress girlfriend Zou Zou and French pop star Françoise Hardy at Castel, the hot Paris club that year, basking in the atmosphere and adulation he enjoyed in Paris. He may have been the outcast of his band, but Paris treated Brian Jones like a god.

————

The Rolling Stones' third North American tour began in Montreal on April 23, with "The Last Time" radiating its bitter energy from America's fifty-thousand-watt clear-channel radio stations. It was scream-a-rama at the Academy of Music on 14th Street in New York City as Mick stepped over the footlights and jabbed a finger into the steamy bedlam during the Stones' first number, "Everybody Needs Somebody to Love." A piercing inhuman din was the audience's response to his torrid declaration—"I want you! You! You!" Ticket demand was so intense that promoters booked three more New York shows for the end of the tour.

The next day, the Stones were driven to Philadelphia for a concert featuring Little Anthony and the Imperials, Reperata and the Delrons, Bobby Vee, and the hot English headliners Herman's Hermits. The Hermits were a British Invasion bubblegum group with a current hit record, "Mrs. Brown You've Got a Lovely Daughter." Their singer was a younger, cuter, friendlier Jagger clone, and they were so popular that they would outsell both the Beatles and the Stones in America the following year. Mick hated the Milquetoast, teenybopper band so much that he still recalled, thirty years later: "Herman's Hermits were top of the bill and we were second, and there was some argument about the dressing rooms. Herman [Peter Noone] was complaining because his wasn't big enough.

There we were, and he was top of the bill because Herman's Hermits were *huge*. And then the most impossible thing was going out to have a hamburger, and some guy would go, 'Are you guys Herman's Hermits?' It would *kill* us! We'd say 'Fuck you! Herman's Hermits is *shit!*' "

If this touched a nerve in twenty-two-year-old Mick Jagger, it may have been because the similarities between the artistically valid Rolling Stones and the manufactured pop of Herman's Hermits (and other, younger English groups flooding into America) were much closer than anyone wanted to admit in 1965.

No Satisfaction

May 1965. The Rolling Stones were so big in America now that mighty Ed Sullivan had to eat his words. On May 2, they played "The Last Time," "Rooster," and "Everybody Needs Somebody to Love" on Sullivan's Sunday night show.

On the southern leg of the tour, at the Gulf Motel in Clearwater, Florida, Keith woke out of a fitful sleep with a riff in his head. Half-awake, he reached for his guitar and recorded the riff—like a reversal of the clarion horn vamp of "Dancing in the Street," Martha and the Vandellas' current hit record—on the cassette player next to his bed. Then he fell back into a deep sleep. When he woke in the morning, he rewound the tape and discovered the little riff. Later in the day, Keith played it for Mick and told him, "The words that go with this are 'I can't get no—satisfaction' " a line in Chuck Berry's "Thirty Days."

That night, Brian Jones picked up a beautiful young girl, a model, in the bar of the motel. The next morning, she emerged from Brian's room in tears, covered in bruises, both her eyes blackened. She told her girlfriend, who'd spent the night with Bill Wyman, that Brian had raped her and then beat her up. The girlfriend told Bill and said something about calling the cops. Panic! They were all so disgusted by Brian's brutality that, after a quick conference (Andrew: "Don't mess up his face!"), one of their English roadies, Mike Dorsey, stormed into Brian's room and thrashed him, breaking two of Brian's ribs. They took Brian to the hospital, where he was taped up and given painkillers. They made up a story that he had fallen while practicing karate by the motel pool. Brian spent the rest of the tour depressed, humiliated, schwacked on pills and drink.

By May 9, the Stones were in Chicago for a gig at the Arie Crown Theater. The next day, they went to Chess Studios for a round-the-clock session with engineer Ron Malo that produced cover versions of Don Covay's "Mercy Mercy" and Otis Redding's "That's How Strong My Love Is." They also cut the hilarious put-down "The Under Assistant West Coast Promotion Man" (supposedly about London Records' lazy promo guy George Sherlock: "sure do earn my pay, sittin' on the beach every day"); and the first acoustic reference track of "(I Can't Get No) Satisfaction," which sounded to Keith suspiciously like contemporary California folk rock, which he hated. They also cut six R&B covers, including Little Walter's "Key to the Highway" and "Fannie Mae," whose riff they took from "Promo Man." This was the Stones' last recording session in Chicago. Brian, sick and stoned on pills, didn't play on them.

A couple days later, they flew to L.A. and went back into RCA Studios with Jack Nitzsche and Dave Hassinger to finish "Satisfaction." In the studio, Keith hollered for more distortion on his guitar. "This riff's gotta hang hard and long," he kept saying. They turned the amps up, burning them to get a jagged sound, but it still wasn't rough enough. Ian Stewart went over to Wallach's Music City and came back with a new Gibson fuzz box, the first one the company made, and told Keith, "Try this." It *made* the record, goosed Keith's double-tracked guitar into the mechanized roar of a Panzer division cruising the Autobahn. The acoustic track from Chicago was buried under fuzz-tone guitar, a new bass line from Bill, and harder drum and percussion tracks. Mick's vocal track was deliberately buried in the mix by Dave Hassinger on orders from Andrew, who was worried about censorship if it was too obvious that lack of sexual satisfaction was what was really on Mick's mind.

Jack Nitzsche played tambourine on the new backing track. Brian

Jones was loaded on pills and didn't play much on these crucial sessions. Higher-echelon L.A. scenesters visited and brought cocaine to the Stones' sessions for the first time.

The final stereo mix of "Satisfaction" was finished by 5 A.M. on May 11, 1965.

These sessions also produced much of the Stones' next album: Solomon Burke's "Cry to Me," the Temptations' "My Girl," Sam Cooke's "Good Times" (only a few months after Cooke's murder in a local motel). They also cut two new Jagger/Richards songs: "One More Try" and "The Spider and the Fly."

————

In San Francisco, where the Byrds opened for the Stones, the Diggers—a proto-hippie anarchist street commune led by Emmett Grogan—published broadside flyers saying the Rolling Stones were "the embodiment of everything we represent, a psychic evolution . . . the breaking up of old values."

In Long Beach on May 16, the Stones did a complete show for nine thousand kids, who rioted outside afterward. The Stones' limo was engulfed in a terrifying crush of humanity as the kids threw themselves on the car. The band began to scream as the roof caved in and had to push it back up with their legs to keep from being crushed. Keith: "We could hear the roof cracking. We're all panicking! A hundred kids on the car, everywhere, outside, trying to force the door handles, trying to smash in the windows. We couldn't move or someone would get killed . . . the most frightening thing of my whole life." Police waded in with nightsticks and started to beat people. Blood spattered on the windows as the horrified musicians cringed. A cop was knocked off his motorcycle and badly injured; one girl lost part of her hand. Finally a helicopter landed next to the almost flattened limo; the Stones climbed aboard and were flown to safety back in L.A.

Ken Kesey and his Merry Pranksters had driven down from Frisco to party with the Stones, and they gave Brian a load of acid. The still-legal LSD-25 was billed as the door to a new consciousness by such apostles as Harvard's Dr. Timothy Leary, who under its influence advised the young to turn on, tune in, and drop out, reject the constipated values of the older generation, and build a new society based on expanded consciousness and communal, millenarian values.

Brian took to acid like someone who'd found God. Tripping his brains out, stepping over hallucinatory snakes, he took his harmonica to the clubs along Sunset Strip and spent his nights jamming with any band that would let the dissolute, wild-eyed young rock star onstage. After dropping a few cubes of Orange Sunshine, Brian even disappeared for a few hours, causing a frantic search so the Stones could make their May 17 gig in San Diego. They were so late for the show that the Byrds began to play Stones songs to placate an angry and restless crowd of kids.

Shindig was the big pop music network TV show in America in 1965, appearing Wednesday nights on ABC. Taping in Los Angeles on May 20, the Stones lip-synched "The Last Time," "Play with Fire," and "Little Red Rooster" on a set decorated with a new Rolls. During rehearsals, the Stones met Billy Preston, the keyboard player for the show's house band, the Shindogs, who later became a regular Stones collaborator. The Stones had pressured the show's English producer, Jack Goode, to feature a real blues musician on the program with them, and chose Howlin' Wolf when Goode told them to take their pick. Wolf arrived from Chicago with his great guitarist, Hubert Sumlin, and another man whom no one recognized.

Mick: "During rehearsal, Howlin' Wolf said to me, 'I want you to come meet somebody.' We went up into the audience—all these children—and this old black man wearing worn denim overalls—before it was fashionable—was sitting with all these kids. And Wolf said, 'This is Son House.' " Son House, sixty-three at the time, was *the* primeval Delta bluesman, one of the teachers of Robert Johnson, the source of his devil-at-the-crossroads story. "He said, 'This is Son House, and Son House did the *original* "Little Red Rooster." ' I didn't know what he was talking about, because he [Son House] was a little recherché at the time. But he told me not to worry because he wasn't the first person to do the song anyway."

Howlin' Wolf made his network TV debut with a raspy, spat-out "How Many More Years?" as the Stones symbolically sat at his feet. Brian cut short an interview and told *Shindig*'s host to be quiet so Wolf could begin the number. It was a great moment.

———————

Before the band left California, they struggled over "Satisfaction." The label said it was the best Stones song ever and wanted it out immediately. Keith didn't even like it. "It sounded like a dub [demo] to me," he recalled. "I couldn't get excited about it. I'd really dug it that night I wrote it in the motel, but I'd gone past it. I didn't want it out. It sounded all right, but I didn't really like that fuzz guitar. I wanted to make that thing different . . . you needed either horns or something else that could knock that riff out. The riff was going to make the song or break it on the length you could drag it out, and it wasn't meant for the guitar. Otis Redding got it right when he recorded it, because it's actually a horn riff."

Keith was adamant. He didn't want it as a single, but was outvoted. (Only Mick sided with Keith. The band was still a nominal democracy— even Stu had a vote.) So a monaural mix of "Satisfaction" was released in America later in the month and became the Stones' first no. 1 record in the U.S.

Brian Jones was disturbed by this. He still wanted the Stones to play R&B, the only thing that interested him. Later, while the band did "Satisfaction" at the end of their shows, Brian would play "Popeye the Sailor Man" as a countermelody because it's what he thought "Satisfaction" sounded like. It made the rest of the band crazy, and there was more talk (mostly from Andrew) of getting rid of Mr. Jones.

After the final California shows in San Jose, Fresno (cut short by police), and Sacramento, the Stones split up and traveled back to New York separately. Brian stayed in L.A. and dropped as much acid as he could, trying to develop new music under LSD's lysergic veil. Frustrated by these often-tuneless or modal experiments, Brian always erased his tapes the next day. Brian was a high-concept musician, great at coming up with a hook or a color, not good on details, and his total inability to write songs would help seal his fate in the Rolling Stones.

Like a Rolling Stone

The Stones regrouped in Manhattan the day before the first of three sold-out shows at the Academy of Music and found themselves the focus of intense interest by the downtown demimonde. London Records rushed out "Satisfaction" ("Promo Man" on the flip), and Keith's roaring fuzz-toned riff was buzzing out of radios everywhere. Bob Dylan was back in New York after his English tour. Wanting to meet Brian, whom Dylan regarded as *the* Rolling Stone, he arranged an introduction through reporter Al Aronowitz, who brought Dylan and entourage up to Brian's room at the Lincoln Square Motor Inn.

Dylan was in his 1965 speed-driven prime, about to stun the pop world by strapping on an electric guitar and playing his visionary, Stones-inspired rock and roll in public. Bushy-haired, hawk-beaked, nasal-voiced, black-shaded, sharp-dressed poetic champion bonded with articulate, pilled-up acidhead Welsh bluesman. Guitars came out and joints were lit by Dylan cohorts Bobby Neuwirth and Al Kooper. Brian's nervous paranoia about marijuana tickled Dylan. Jones had been told he was out of the group if he got busted for pot in America and couldn't work, so he was very uptight. Dylan couldn't believe it and teased him. "Brian, man, *fuck*, you're even puttin' *me* uptight."

Another night Dylan and Brian hung out at Andy Warhol's midtown studio during a big party. Warhol, ultimate voyeur and reporter, was filming the lost moths drawn to his flame as they destroyed themselves acting out sex and drug fantasies. It was the only scene in town. Rudolph Nureyev was there, dancing with pretty men to "I Get Around," "The

Name Game," "Come See About Me," and the Kinks blasting "You Really Got Me." The sexual tension in the Factory was intense. Edie Sedgwick was there, the "Girl of the Year," a lithe, half-mad, self-absorbed heiress type from an ancient Massachusetts family. Her starring roles in Warhol's underground movies had catapulted her into *Vogue* fashion spreads and general subterranean goddesshood. She had a low, sexy voice that always sounded like she'd just stopped crying. With her cropped hair dyed platinum, Edie was the promiscuous young queen of the Warhol superstars, an American icon at twenty-two. Every young man in New York wanted her.

Including Bob Dylan . . . who knew enough to keep his distance. But it still bothered Dylan when Edie went over and started to rub Brian's shoulders, muss his hair, whisper in his ear. Edie and Brian put their heads together and talked and laughed a long while on the famous Factory sofa while Dylan, glowering in the corner with his people, watched them carefully, stunned for once into complete silence.

Mick met Edie too, on another night at the Scene, the basement rock club on West 46th Street. The meeting was much anticipated by the Warholians, excited that their superstar was going to meet the sexy English singer. Their union seemed predestined, but nothing happened. Mick was in the vestibule when Edie arrived. She went right up to him.

"How do you do? I really like your records."

Shy smile from Mick, eyes down. "Um, oh . . . Thank you."

Eye contact . . . and an explosion of people burst into the tiny space. Flashbulbs blinded everyone. Manhattan frenzy, a swirl of hip-huggers, tight blue jeans, Pucci slacks, little-girl mod dresses. Edie fled. They never had a moment.

––––––––

June 1965. Back in London, Mick and Keith gave up their flat, unable to escape their fans. Keith bought a pad in St. John's Wood, while Mick stayed with David Bailey before moving into a new flat near Marble Arch. Mick bought Chrissie Shrimpton a white Austin Mini car, not knowing she'd been two-timing him with singer P. J. Proby while he was away. Keith bought a car for his mum. The Stones' new EP, *Got Live If*

You Want It (a play on Slim Harpo's "Got Love If You Want It") was released on June 11 with five tracks from the March U.K. tour and attendant chanting and screams. Despite blistering live versions of "Route 66" and "I'm Movin' On," the record only sold moderately, as the Stones now competed with records by newer mod bands like the Yardbirds and the Who, which appealed to younger kids with their speedy, jamming energy.

"Satisfaction" was held off in England so it wouldn't hurt the EP, but in America it was on its way to no. 1 and instant anthem status, despite being censored on some radio stations. In New York, powerhouse WABC programmed their own two-minute version with the "trying to make some girl" verse edited out. It was the Rolling Stones' decisive moment, a cautious but somehow powerful statement of the individual against mass culture and sexual norms. "I can't be satisfied," sang Muddy Waters in 1948, and by 1965 national alienation was so corrosive that even the postwar children, the baby boomers, members of the wealthiest, most secure, and best-educated generation in history, were saying no, we can't get any satisfaction either.

The deep roots of "Satisfaction" in Motown made it a great dance record. "It was the song that really *made* the Rolling Stones," Mick said much later. " 'Satisfaction' changed us from just another band into a huge, monster band. You always need one song. We weren't American, and America was the big thing, and we always wanted to make it there. It was very impressive the way that song and the popularity of the band became a worldwide thing."

———————

"Satisfaction" was huge as Bob Dylan cut a new song with an electric band featuring Al Kooper (Dylan: "Turn that organ up!") in New York on June 15. "Like A Rolling Stone" started out, according to Dylan, as ten pages long, "a rhythm thing on paper telling someone something they didn't know, telling them they were lucky." None of the musicians present had heard the song before, the performance was completely improvised, and it was immediately recognized as arguably Dylan's most important, if not greatest, song.

Later that year, Dylan told an audience in Carnegie Hall that "Like A Rolling Stone"—which always closed his electric shows—was about Brian Jones. ("Ballad of a Thin Man" is also said to relate to "Mr. Jones," and Dylan also recorded—but didn't release—a version of "I Wanna Be Your Man" titled "I Wanna Be Your Lover" late in 1965.)

"Like A Rolling Stone" was released as a seven-minute single in July 1965, got immediate airplay despite its length, and became an unlikely hit. It shattered the ironclad three-minute single format that dominated American radio, paving the way for longer songs and the looser FM format that took over pop radio later in the decade. For at least the next year, Dylan and the Stones operated in an unspoken, mutually influential alliance. Mick appropriated the flashing imagery of Dylan's lyric style, while Dylan adapted the Stones' electric clamor and immediacy, plus their sharp London look. The result for both Dylan and Stones was some of the best work of their careers.

————

In July, "Satisfaction" went to no. 1 and London released the new Stones album, *Out of Our Heads,* with a David Bailey band portrait that endearingly spotlit Keith's acne. *Heads* was a compilation album— singles and B sides, soul covers—but it was also one of the pivotal records in America in 1965. For the first time, a pop group represented themselves as artists whose black influences were as crucial as the new songs they were writing for their white audience. In America that year, torn by race riots and civil rights protests, this counted for something. It was the zenith of the Rolling Stones' greatest achievement, showing its huge white audience that black music had been ignored and despised and segregated for too long. Nothing the Rolling Stones ever did was as important as their giving respect to the music that had inspired them.

Out of Our Heads quickly became a no. 1 album and stayed in the American charts for the next nine months.

The Bounty Hunter

July 1965, and the Stones' loony young manager was trying not to lose his mind. Coping with mounting pressure and increasing manic-depressive episodes, his psychic resources stretched thin, Andrew Oldham took anything that kept his flash, anarchic flame on full burn. He was driven around London in an aquamarine Chevrolet Impala by his bodyguard, Reg "the Butcher" King, scattering pedestrians as they roared through the sooty streets. Andrew had a mean streak and enjoyed playing with it, insulting and pushing people around when he could get away with it. His twenty-one-year-old tycoon's brain was full of plans for the Stones, new bands like the Small Faces, and even his own record label, but he knew he wasn't equipped to cope with the complex financial dealings required to fulfill his ambitions. So in July 1965, Andrew hired a New York accountant to manage his, and the Stones', business affairs. Allen Klein's first task was to negotiate the Rolling Stones' new recording contract.

Keith: "Andrew got Klein to meet us, to get us out of the original English scene [contract]. The first time we met was in London. The only thing that impressed me about him was that he said he could do it—get us the money we were making. Nobody else had said that to us."

Mick: "Andrew sold him to us as a gangster figure, someone outside the establishment. We found that rather attractive."

Indeed, no one was more outside the establishment than Allen Klein, an accountant and talent manager who described himself as a bounty hunter. Klein had been raised in a New Jersey orphanage and struggled through college with an appreciation for the mysteries of cash flow. Breaking into show business, he'd made a successful career of signing on as a performer's business manager, then ransacking his record company's usually crooked books to ferret out unpaid, often substantial royalties. The tools of his trade were lawsuits, writs, and sometimes U.S. marshals if the company was recalcitrant about letting him into its accounts. Klein had started with singer Bobby Darin in 1962, got into big-time soul music with Sam Cooke, then made his move into the hot London scene. By mid-1965, Klein had a piece of the British Invasion as business manager for the Dave Clark Five, the Animals, Donovan, and Herman's Hermits. He wanted the Beatles too, the premier act of the whole movement, but had been rebuffed by Brian Epstein. So he settled for the Rolling Stones.

The band was eager. They'd sold roughly 10 million singles and 5 million albums by July '65, and reportedly earned about $5 million on the road. But they were each drawing fifty pounds a week in salary from Impact Sound and were chronically short of cash. Keith in particular was tired of being broke and ripped off. He'd recently punched promoter Robert Stigwood in a London nightclub after Stigwood failed to pay the Stones their percentage from the recent Australian tour.

Klein would negotiate the Stones' new record deal and take over as business manager. Eric Easton would be completely forced out. Andrew would be free to manage the Stones and start his own company, Immediate Records, the first independent label in Britain.

Most people who knew what was going on assumed that Allen Klein would sideline Andrew and take over the Stones within a year. Actually it took two.

––––––––

Mick, Keith, and Andrew met with Allen Klein in his suite at the London Hilton on July 24, just after the Stones had been fined and scolded by a judge for the pissing incident at the gas station the previous spring (which was front-page news in London for two weeks).

"Which one makes the records?" Klein pointedly asked Oldham when they were all sitting down with a drink.

"That one," Andrew said, pointing to Keith. At first, Mick and Keith were unsure about the thirty-two-year-old accountant. Klein was short and chubby with greasy hair, a thick New Jersey accent, and wore what Keith described as "diabolical" clothes, usually a turtleneck shirt under a mismatched cardigan. Klein smoked a briar pipe, was rough, brusque, and rude, and there wasn't much eye contact. But he also was a charmer, a character, and made them laugh with his streetwise act. He told them he'd double their royalties, clean up their taxes, make them millionaires within a year. He'd be their Big Daddy, look after them, take care of things. He'd promised Andrew a Rolls-Royce with tinted windows like John Lennon's. He promised the Stones the moon if they went with him.

Two days later, Monday, July 26, there was a band meeting in Andrew's office in Gloucester Place. Brian, Bill, and Charlie were informed that the others had hired Klein without bothering to check with them first. It was a done deal. Wyman suggested that they get a lawyer to negotiate with Klein. "Don't be so fucking mercenary," Keith shouted at him. "We've got to trust *some*one."

Keith: "I really pushed them. I said, 'Let's turn things around. Let's fucking *do* something. Let's go down to Decca with this guy and scare the shit out of them.' "

So the band accompanied Klein to the showdown at Decca House, the company headquarters on the Thames Embankment. Deploying his New Jersey gangster face, flanked by his New York lawyer, who looked like a hungry barracuda, Klein refused to negotiate with anyone but Decca's chairman, Sir Edward Lewis. In a paneled boardroom overlooking the river, Klein spewed a torrent of profanity, insults, and threatening demands at Lewis and Decca's senior executives.

Keith: "He told us each to get a pair of shades and just stand behind him in a row while he talked. 'Whatever you do, don't say a *word*. Don't open your mouth.' So we stood there, and they just crumbled in front of our eyes, these hard-boiled English lawyers. And we came out of there with the best record contract anyone had. That impresses a guy. He did a good job."

The Stones' new deal with Decca was for $1.25 million for world rights to their recordings, exclusive of North America, to be paid in New York by London Records to Nanker Phelge Music Ltd., the Stones' publishing entity. Klein also negotiated a 9.25 percent royalty, higher than the Beatles were getting. Their new contract guaranteed annual payments of $35,000 ($7,000 per Stone) for the next ten years.

On July 29, the band and Andrew signed the Stones' five-year deal at Decca House. Klein returned to New York, where he got another million from London Records for their American rights. Klein, true to his word, had done what he'd promised.

When these advances were paid sometime during the autumn of 1965, Klein had the checks made out to "Nanker Phelge Music USA," a different company, owned and controlled by Allen Klein.

This turned out badly for the Stones and later became a disaster. For the next five years, Klein kept their money in his pocket. He made them beg for it. According to Bill Wyman, if one of them wanted to buy a car or a house, Klein loaned them their own money and charged them interest. They were completely dependent on him and his New York office, and often desperate for cash. At the end of the deal, the Stones never got their money, and had to pay Klein to go away. They lost control of their publishing rights and their back catalog as well. For the Stones, negative repercussions from their 1965 deal with Allen Klein still echo, many years down the road.

But . . . at first they were all happy. They thought they were in Fat City. This crude Yank was Taking Care of Business and making them rich. Charlie Watts bought a Tudor mansion in Sussex. Bill Wyman moved into a house in Kent. They got new cars and spent real money on clothes. The Rolling Stones had turned a giant corner, and over the next few years Klein ratcheted them up many levels, turning the Stones' "brand" into a global money machine and worldwide legend. The Stones, and later the Beatles, would pay dearly for his services.

Fraser the Razor

August 1965. Two shows at the London Palladium. Brian, splendiferous in white, his amps turned so loud they drowned out Mick. With their new management in place, the Stones took a break. Keith and Linda vacationed in the south of France, while Brian and Linda Lawrence flew to Tangier to escape a paternity suit over Brian's other son Julian. They were joined by Mick and Chrissie, who went to Tangier at the urging of their friends Robert Fraser and Christopher Gibbs.

Fraser and Gibbs were the two most interesting young men in London: art dealers, Old Etonians, and friends since the age of thirteen. Both were gay, clever, and ultrahip. They set styles and trends in mid-sixties London; the writer/painter Brion Gysin would later claim that Fraser invented Swinging London by himself. Strawberry Bob Fraser (as Keith called him for his preference for pink suits) introduced pop art to London in his Duke Street art gallery, where he represented Andy Warhol and Jim Dine and brought British pop artists like Richard Hamilton into view. Chrissie Gibbs dealt in antique furniture and the exotic orientalism of Moroccan decor, which he popularized when he started bringing things back from his homes in Tangier and Marrakech. Fraser was dark, kinetic, stoned, adept at bringing the right people together. Gibbs was blond, reserved, in control, and his flat in Chelsea was *the* salon of the so-called Chelsea Set, the demimonde of artists, photographers, musicians, and their women that made London cool and sophisticated. As Gibbs recalled: "My apartment at 100 Cheyne Walk was in a seventeenth-century house with these huge paneled rooms. It was at the bend in the river where the houseboats are, the light bouncing off the water. It was Moorish in mood, quite spare, with straw mats mixed up with Renaissance things. We kept an open house there, nice people coming around, smoking and dropping acid. Brian Jones was about, lots of to-ing and fro-ing. Cecil Beaton photographed the place, and then Antonioni shot the party sequence of *Blow Up* there. A lot went on. The landlord was not a bit pleased and I almost got thrown out. They shot another film there when I was away one weekend, with three hundred people dropping acid on a Sunday, loud music, gypsy girls breast-feeding their babies . . . All that's ages ago, but that was the scene."

Fraser was drawn to the young, glamorous, reckless pop world, and together, he and Gibbs met the Stones, tried to sell things to John Lennon and Mick Jagger. Fraser and Paul McCartney were good friends. Brian was close to him too, and Fraser and Gibbs were always telling him about Morocco, how he had to go there and see for himself.

Tangier was to be a perfect creative incubator for the Stones over the next few years, as was the red-walled desert city Marrakech, to the south. Going to Morocco was like time travel to the medieval world, with great music, plentiful dope, superb food, and the kind of privacy the Stones rarely got anywhere else.

Tangier was a sunny white city that slept during the dry, hot summer days. When the wind was northerly, the call of the muezzins from Tangier's mosques on the shoulder of Africa could drift five miles across the Strait of Gibraltar and be heard in Andalusia. Since Roman times, Tangier had been the place where Europe and Arab North Africa uneasily intersected. It was an international city for many years, ruled by its European consulates, a haven for shady characters, European exiles, and artists like Delacroix and Matisse. It was a world capital of Anything Goes, with few cops and a relaxed attitude toward anyone with a (false) passport and a few dollars in any currency. The leading literary light in the city was the American writer Paul Bowles, author of *The Sheltering Sky* and collector of Moroccan tribal music. His salon attracted Beat Generation stars like William Burroughs, who wrote *Naked Lunch* in Tangier, and his friends Jack Kerouac, Allen Ginsberg, Brion Gysin, and Timothy Leary. There was also a colony of well-off cosmopolitans like Paul Getty Jr., at whose house Mick Jagger and his girlfriends frequently stayed.

Plus, the climate was soft, the beaches were empty, the Moroccans were friendly, and there was plenty of *kif,* a powerful blend of cannabis and black tobacco that gives the smoker a friendly blast of clarity. Or there was *majoun,* a candy made of honey and hashish paste. Morphine, speed, and the entire pharmacopoeia were available over the counter. Tangier was as far out as one could get and still be on the fringe of Western civ, a perfect place for angel-headed hipsters like Mick, Brian, and Keith to hide from the cold, commercial world to the north.

———

Mick Jagger was pulled out of this idyll halfway through August to fly to New York to meet with Allen Klein about the Stones' American record deal. While in town, he and Keith went to the Beatles' immense concert at Shea Stadium. At the time, it was the biggest pop concert in history. The Beatles were almost totally drowned out by screaming girls.

Back in England, there was a big round of summer parties. The Ormsby-Gore girls came out, and Mick was best man at David Bailey's wedding to the ravishing French actress Catherine Deneuve (the Shrimp was history). "Satisfaction" was released in England and went to no. 1 like a shot. Brian Jones started seeing Nico, a serenely luscious blond German singer signed to Andrew's new Immediate Records label.

Late in August came the initial press reports about the Stones' new management team and record deals. Eric Easton was fired as the Stones' booking agent, replaced by the more tuned-in London veteran Tito Burns. Andrew also announced the Stones had a deal to make five movies. The first would be *Only Lovers Left Alive,* based on a 1964 cult novel by Dave Wallis that posited a Stones-like gang taking over a postapocalyptic world. Over the next year, Andrew generated massive press about this project, which never got made.

Anita

Under time pressure, the band flew to Los Angeles on September 5 for two days of recording at RCA to finish tracks they'd worked on in July. The city was still tense from the race riots that had torched the Watts section a couple weeks earlier. *Out of Our Heads* was still at the top of the charts.

Working with their usual studio team, the Stones finished "Get Off My Cloud," the first of an astounding five-single sequence of anarchic pop art masterpieces that over the next year attempted to "exorcise the demonic ghosts of the Oedipal family romance and all forms of social hypocrisy" (critic Jonathan Cott). These songs—"Cloud," "19th Nervous Breakdown," "Paint It, Black," "Mother's Little Helper," and "Have You Seen Your Mother, Baby, Standing in the Shadow?"—were a concentrated barrage of the Stones' trademark cynicism, deeply influenced by Bob Dylan's flashing-chain imagery that liberated song lyrics into new realms of poetic beatitudes.

As the follow-up to radio-friendly "Satisfaction," the Stones could hardly have come up with anything more weird than "Get Off My Cloud." Keith wrote the melody and Mick wrote the words with their ninety-ninth-floor Manhattan/Metropolis imagery and pop-artsy unfurling of the Union Jack as, in Mick's words, "a stop-bugging-me, post-teenage-alienation song." The rushed, offbeat vocals (set to the "Twist and Shout" rhythm) were so buried that the lyrics were muddy and unintelligible. Brian's sitarlike slide guitar supplied a strange Carnatic ambience as "Cloud" hurtled along to a thunderous drum track.

Keith hated this new single too.

"It's true. I never dug it as a record. The chorus was a nice idea, but we rushed it as the follow-up to 'Satisfaction.' We were in L.A and it was time for another single. But how do you follow 'Satisfaction'? I wanted to do it slow, like a Lee Dorsey thing. We rocked it up, and I thought it was one of Andrew's worst productions."

After finishing the tracks that would fill out their next album, the Stones rushed back to England, where on September 8 they played their last-ever ballroom show on the Isle of Man. To avoid a violent mob, the group had to squeeze into the hall through the bathroom window, and they swore it would never happen again. It would be many years before the Rolling Stones again played together on a small stage in a sweltering room.

———————

On September 11, the Stones began a short but fateful tour of Germany and Austria. After the show in Munich, there was a bitter argument with Brian, who had again played "Popeye" during "Satisfaction." They told him to his face he was out of the band if he did it again, and Brian got really upset. Andrew also slagged Brian for abandoning Pat Andrews and their child, an impending bad publicity disaster, as Pat was threatening to go to court.

Backstage in Munich that night was twenty-three-year-old Anita Pallenberg, already famous as the most beautiful model in Europe. She was blond, beautiful, stacked, trendy in miniskirt, tight sweater, and knee-high white boots. With their usual studied cool, the Stones made a show of ignoring Anita. Only Brian spoke to her, in German, and introduced himself as the leader of the Stones.

Anita: "I first met Brian at the Oktoberfest Circus. I told a photographer I wanted to meet the Stones and got backstage with him. There were the Troggs, the Spencer Davis Group with Stevie Winwood—they were the opening acts. Backstage, it was where the horses walk, a beer-hall atmosphere. I had a piece of hash and some amyl nitrite poppers.

"I went straight to Brian: he was the one I fancied. I tapped him on the shoulder and had a big smile ready when he turned around. I could hardly believe it, but he was upset, on the verge of tears, and I thought somehow it was my fault. I asked him if he wanted to smoke a joint, and

Brian says, 'Yeah, yeah, let's smoke a joint. Come back to the hotel. I don't want to be alone tonight.'

"Brian was tearful that night because Mick and Keith had teamed up on him, and I really felt sorry for him. He was devastated. He cried in my arms all night. It wasn't a sex thing. He just wanted someone to be with him. We had a little fling together. That was how I met him."

The other Stones, Keith in particular, were foaming with envy when they saw drop-dead-lustrous Anita go off with Brian that night. It was the epochal entry of Anita Pallenberg into the Rolling Stones, and over the next five years she would be the only woman who ever became one of them.

The Stones moved on to West Berlin the next day, and all Brian could think about was Anita, who turned up at the concert again. He asked her to come to London with him, but she said she had a modeling job in Paris. They all visited the Berlin Wall before sneaking into the big outdoor gig in the Waldbuhne (where Hitler Youth rallies used to be held) through bunker tunnels left over from Nazi days. They played before 23,000 kids and sparked one of the worst riots of their career. Any Nazi-era gesture was strictly illegal in Germany, so provocative Andrew suggested to Mick that it would be trippy if Mick did the Nazi goose step during the instrumental break of "Satisfaction"; Mick took it further and started doing the *Sieg Heil* routine, throwing stiff-armed salutes. The German kids went ape and stormed the stage. Blitzkrieg! Police waded in with truncheons, and one policeman reportedly lost an eye in the ensuing battles. All the seats were destroyed as well as several trains taking the kids home afterward.

After the final show in Vienna, the Stones returned to London without Brian, who went to Paris to rendezvous with his ravishing new girlfriend.

———

Anita Pallenberg was born in Rome in January 1943. "My family," Anita says, "followed the Goethe dream of moving south," settling in Italy to live as artists. Her father, Arnaldo Pallenberg, painted and played piano. Her mother, Paula Wiederhold, was a secretary at the German Embassy in Rome. Their first daughter accidentally put an electric plug in her mouth and was disfigured, so the Pallenbergs had another child, hoping for a son. "I was supposed to be a boy named Martin," Anita says, "but here I am. I grew up rather poor in a fabulous Roman villa with illusions of being rich, because my grandfather gave most of his estate to the Nazis. We had concerts of chamber music on Fridays, but no money at all really."

The Pallenbergs were pan-European, with family and friends everywhere. Anita grew up speaking four languages in an artistic and literary milieu. She was sent to a Swiss school in Rome, which she mostly skipped to wander about the ruins of the classical city. She was then sent to her father's "decadent" (as she described it) boarding school in Bavaria, 180 boys and 20 girls, mostly the children of ex-Nazis. She excelled at Latin and pottery, went sailing in the summer and skiing in winter. But Anita hated her school and was finally expelled for hitchhiking to Munich for fun. While visiting an aunt in Berlin, she watched the Berlin Wall go up in 1961. (She happened to be there to watch it come down in 1989 as well.)

"I left school to make some money," she says. "I studied graphic design and art conservation in Munich for six months, lived in the Schwabing cafés, meeting people." In 1963, she went to New York with an Italian painter and stayed with a cousin in Greenwich Village. The mischievous blond with the sculptural body and sensational, diamond-hard smile became part of the art scene that included Jasper Johns, Robert Rauschenberg, and Willem de Kooning. She met poets Frank O'Hara and Allen Ginsberg, satirist Terry Southern, and playwright LeRoi Jones, who was fluent in German. The avant-garde Living Theater was around, heirs of Antonin Artaud's theater of cruelty, and Anita hooked up with them too, "as a hanger-on," she says. "I've always been a hanger-on. Whenever I liked something, I really got into it. How better to get into it than to *be* with them, you know?"

Anita's Italian boyfriend got jealous, started beating her up, so she left him and began working as an assistant to an Italian fashion photographer. She met Andy Warhol and his crowd, then a New York model agency spotted her and sent her off to Paris and Sicily on modeling assignments. "I liked to travel, so I got a lot of swinging jobs all over Europe. I was always on the run and my poor father thought I was a prostitute. He would stay up all night waiting for me to come home, but my mother was envious of what I was doing, my kind of life." She was the quintessential sixties girl, happy to get on a jet plane with nothing more than a rucksack on her back and a credit card in her pocket.

Anita was also connected in London: she knew the whole scene, the club-hopping aristocrats Tara Browne and Mark Palmer, whose mother was a lady-in-waiting to the queen, and the Chelsea Set artists, handsome young photog Michael Cooper, Robert Fraser and Chrissie Gibbs. In Paris, she knew Donald Cammell through Deborah Dixon. Anita was white-hot all over, an incandescent light in any room. Her magazine image appeared all over Europe in the futurist clothes of the day, and she was already working in experimental films with the German director Volker Schlöndorff.

Anita: "When I first bumped into the Stones, they were like schoolboys. Brian was so far ahead of them you wouldn't believe it. Here are Mick and Keith up onstage trying to learn how to be sex objects, and Brian already had a bunch of illegitimate children! Brian was *very* well spoken, soft-spoken, spoke German as well. He captivated me with the way he moved, his hair, his soft manner. He wanted to capture your attention when he was speaking. He was sensitive, highly strung, totally ahead of his time. And also part of *another* time, the dandy with his clothes and all of that.

"As I got to know Brian, I really fell for him. He was so talented and found everything so easy. He had time to be interested in other things, wasn't narrow-minded like the others. I dare say that, but . . . yeah! Brian was a pain in the ass and very vulnerable to a lot of shit, but he was *way* ahead of his time."

How's Yer Paranoia
Meter Runnin' Now?

Late in September '65, the Rolling Stones started a British tour to promote the U.K. version of *Out of Our Heads,* mostly soul music covers. Brian wore all white, sporting the fleecy lining from a coat he'd gotten in Sweden, setting a big trend for shaggy caveman vests—the Neanderthal look—throughout the rock and roll world. Bill Wyman noted the thunderous applause at every show when Brian Jones unstrapped his Gibson Thunderbird guitar and moved to the organ for "Time Is on My Side." Mick was swinging his mike stand, thrusting it like a weapon, and doing new dance moves he'd picked up from black soul stars.

As the band careered through England, they started to get hurt by the hail of debris that rained onstage. Keith got knocked out by a flying seat in Manchester. In Stockton-on-Tees, a shilling hit Mick in the face, cutting him over his eye. The crowds were almost all children and got really wild as Brian's slide guitar and wailing harp on "I'm Movin' On" whipped them into foam. Keith got knocked cold by an armrest in Northampton: Brian waved the curtains shut while Bill cut the power, and they stopped the show for fifteen minutes until Keith recovered.

In October, "Cloud" was released and performed on *Ready Steady Goes Live.* It reached no. 1 and reigned for three weeks. Brian bought a white Rolls-Royce Silver Cloud (from George Harrison) which came with the plate DD 666. Right away the girls who hung around Brian's door (who were occasionally allowed in to tidy up and do the dishes) decided the DD stood for Devil's Disciple.

On October 26, Mick and Keith recorded their version of "As Tears Go By," with Mick singing the ballad alone with an orchestra arranged by

Mike Leander. (They also cut a version in awful Italian, "Con Le Mie Lacrime.") But for Keith's nimble acoustic guitar, it was Mick Jagger's first solo recording, produced by Andrew as a copy of Paul McCartney's "Yesterday," leading John Lennon to publically remark that the Stones did everything the Beatles did, six months later.

In fact, the fall of 1965 saw a critical repositioning of the Rolling Stones by its songwriters, Mick and Keith. They had begun as an R&B group and changed into a rock and soul band. Now, the Stones turned into the first avant-garde rock band, blending R&B with "underground" culture and folk rock trends from Southern California, where they made their records. It was an instinctive move that consciously veered away from the Beatles' act and established the Stones on the dark side of the bulging baby boom youth movement, hairy prophets of sexual freedom, chaos, and drugs.

———

To New York to begin their fourth U.S. tour in late October 1965. Looming over Times Square like a vengeful Olympus was an enormous billboard with a David Bailey image of the Stones in uncommonly sullen and dark mien, promoting their upcoming American album, *December's Children (and Everybody's)*. Andrew was really beating the drums now: even the Beatles never had this. Their agency announced the Stones would make $1.5 million on this tour.

Turned down by the Warwick Hotel, they took over two floors of the City Squire Motor Lodge; the lobby was besieged by eager young women and girls for the duration. Edgy press conference with reporters unnerved by the glaring, chain-smoking Stones, especially Charlie Watts's Cro-Magnon look and murderous level stare when asked a stupid question. Then there was the slept-in hair, the unsmiling mugs, Keith's icy gaze. *Hey! You!* Jagger called out of the radio, sinister as a switchblade, *get offa my cloud!,* as this new rant made him into the most potent rock vocalist on earth. And it hardly ever got any better than this, this new kind of song where the lyrics didn't matter. The music was all about attitude anyway.

Opening acts on the Stones' shows were variously Patti Labelle and the Bluebells, the Vibrations, and the Rockin' Ramrods from Boston. Watching over things on tour dates in Canada and New York State was the formidable Pete Bennett, Allen Klein's song plugger, who rammed "Cloud" onto radio playlists and into the charts within days of its release. Bennett (Benedetti) had deep connections in both the Democratic Party and the Five Families. The Stones dubbed him their Mafia promo man. They also got a new road manager, Mike Gruber, and a traveling accountant, Ronnie Schneider, Klein's nephew.

Performing in sports jackets, tight jeans, and checkered trousers, with Mick and Brian sporting white Capezio ballet shoes, the Stones continued on through Rochester, Providence, New Haven, and Boston Garden, playing their American set, starting with "Everybody Needs Somebody," Mick standing over the footlights, *I want you! You! You!* They played fewer soul covers in America, only "Mercy Mercy" and "That's How Strong My Love Is" (with Brian on organ) and more jams like "Around and Around" and "The Last Time." A fast and furious "Cloud" came before "I'm All Right" and "Satisfaction."

November 6. Brian was blasted on pills, downs and ups, recovering from two shows in Newark, real screamfests. He was having a hard time on the tour. In addition to his stage wounds, a girl had hit him on the head with a beer bottle when he got rough with her in his hotel room. A couple nights earlier, someone had hassled him at a club called the Phone Booth, and Brian had broken a glass and slashed the guy's face. They'd hustled Brian out and he'd gotten away with it so far, but he was paranoid about being arrested for the attack.

He was headed across town from a party in his chauffeured blue Cadillac when the lights went out.

Brian looked out the window. The lights were out everywhere. New York was dark, and the only illumination came from the bright full moon and the headlights of cars in the chaos of the streets. Brian started to freak and reached for his asthma inhaler and his pills. The entire northeastern United States had lost power, the famous blackout of '65.

They gave Brian a candle in the lobby of the Lincoln Square Motor Inn (where the Stones had moved after the City Squire, annoyed by fans crowding the lobby, asked them to check out), and he climbed the five floors to his room. Total blackout. Paranoia. A few hours later, there was a knock on the door. Brian froze! He cracked open the door with the chain on. In the gloom of the hall he made out Dylan's craggy face.

"Hey, Brian," Dylan sneered. "How's yer paranoia meter runnin' *now*!" Brian opened his door. In came Dylan, Robbie Robertson, Bobby Neuwirth, other people. "It's an invasion from Mars," Dylan announced. "Let's turn on, man. What better time—the little green men have landed!" They all jammed for the rest of the evening, the famous "Lost Jam" because there was no electricity to record it. Brian blew harp till his lips were bloody.

Eventually Dylan had enough of Brian's hyperparanoia. Late one night at Max's Kansas City on Park Avenue South, goaded by Neuwirth, Dylan started to attack. He told Brian the Stones were a joke, told Brian he had a lousy voice, no wonder they didn't let him sing; told Brian he was the *weak link* in the fuckin' chain, man. Brian, Dylan insisted, had the wrong image, and the Stones oughta get rid of him sooner rather than later. It was a game Dylan and Neuwirth had, pushing a person to the precipice—Dylan had savaged Warhol at the Ondine disco a few nights earlier—but it was all too horribly true and Brian cracked like an egg. He broke into drunken tears, which made Dylan and Neuwirth goof on him even more for his emotional state.

"Aw, come on, Brian," Dylan finally drawled. "You can always join *my* band."

December's Children

November 1965. The tour headed south, to Greensboro, North Carolina, where Brian scored a mountain dulcimer, chiming lyre of Appalachian folklore, which he had long desired after hearing one played by Richard Farina. Within a few hours, Brian was playing it like a hillbilly, but two days later in Baltimore, someone stole the dulcimer from the Stones' unguarded dressing room during the day's second show.

On through the South, Mick and Keith—missing their girlfriends—wrote feverish, conflicted, lovesick songs in their shared hotel suites, in the back of the plane, in dressing rooms in Oklahoma and Wisconsin. Anita flew in from London and spent a week traveling with the Stones, which fueled rumors, published in London and Paris, that she would marry Brian—with Dylan as best man. The other Stones were jealous, deeply impressed, intimidated by Anita's obvious intelligence, radiant vibe, her predatory international cool. She was sharper than any of them and could put down even Mick with a look or a cutting remark. She was the ultimate rock star's girlfriend, emitting as much white light as her lover. The two of them, Brian and Anita, even looked alike after she dyed their already blond hair an even lighter color. They were a pair of incestuous, impossibly glamorous twins. Brian became more difficult when she was around to renew his confidence. Now he played "Popeye the Sailor Man" all the time, in the middle of everything. "It didn't matter anymore," Keith recalled. "Nobody could hear shit anyway, with a load of thirteen-year-old girls wetting themselves."

———

At Memorial Auditorium, Sacramento, Keith Richards was almost killed. The first show went great. Twenty minutes into the second,

Keith touched an ungrounded microphone with the neck of his guitar as he tried to swing it into place so he could sing the chorus of "The Last Time." There was a horrible electric buzz, and a blue bolt of light surrounded Keith. He collapsed like a rag doll, flat on his back. There was a bad smell in the air, and the shocked girls in the first ten rows thought Keith was dead.

The band stopped playing. Bill rushed over and unplugged Keith's guitar. Keith didn't move, and the whole scene was frozen disbelief. The curtain crashed down. After a few minutes, a policeman came out and told the hushed crowd to stay calm, that Keith was alive and on his way to the hospital, where the doctors told Keith that the rubber soles of his new Hush Puppies had saved his life. Later Stu showed Keith the guitar: three strings had burned open, like blown fuses.

———

December's Children (and Everybody's) was released in December in the United States, another dark album cover with a black-and-white photo of the Stones framed by dumpsters. It was a powerful but ramshackle sampler of old and new material, starting with the raw, atomic R&B of "She Said Yeah," cut at RCA the previous May in the speedy mod-beat style of the Yardbirds and the Who. Then into the "shuffle and eighths" of "Talkin' 'Bout You" and some older blues and R&B material from 1963. "Cloud" started side two, and both sides ended in the Dionysian live tracks from the spring '65 British tour, "Route 66" and "I'm Moving On."

The Stones didn't like the album, which they regarded as disparate tracks randomly assembled for the U.S. tour. Keith later described the album as something they couldn't have gotten away with releasing in England. Brian Jones called it "an album of rejects."

December's Children carried Andrew's bleak, Burgess-like liner notes about the unquiet times—the Vietnam War, the murdered Kennedy, the Watts riots—and references to Dylan and Elvis. The ragtag sampler still came off as a blue, shadowy work that seemed to explore emotional undertones and maturing ambivalence. The core of the album was four recent and related songs, all in a rolling, acoustic style. "The Singer Not the Song," "I'm Free," "Gotta Get Away," and "Blue Turns to Grey" were all folk rock jams, Keith's melodies and vocal harmonies, with ringing guitars and marimba vibes in an easy, loping groove. Adding the orchestral "As Tears Go By" made it the softest of the band's albums to date. "I'm Free" was the only one of these songs played by the Stones onstage. Beloved by its teenage audience for its aggressive arrogance, "I'm Free" stayed in the Stones' live show for years, and still occasionally rears its cocksure head as an anthem of compressed adolescent yearning. "I'm free . . . to do what I want . . . any ol' time."

The California shows were the last of that long tour. The West Coast was the epicenter of the political earthquakes that would soon rock America, with turbulent student protests spreading through various universities. The Vietnam War was still heating up. The civil rights movement, led by Martin Luther King, conducted sit-ins and demonstrations. The Free Speech Movement at the University of California at Berkeley had galvanized college students into thinking about issues of social control. *I can't get no satisfaction* was a rallying cry, despite Mick's deliberate refusal to write overtly political songs. In many ways, the Rolling Stones' indirect social protest in their songs was more subversive than clumsy, folk rock anxiety anthems like the current hit record "Eve of Destruction."

Their girlfriends all flew in for the L.A. shows. Mick told Chrissie Shrimpton to stay away from Anita Pallenberg, telling her that Anita was poison. Keith and Linda and Brian and Anita attended the Second Acid Test run by the Merry Pranksters, with Electric Kool-Aid, costumed freaks tripping their brains out, and a swirling psychedelic light show that supplied the "mixed media" environment in vogue with the new bands in the San Francisco area.

Brian was flying on acid all the time now. Anita: "The first time he took it, he saw creatures coming out of the ground, the walls, the floors. He was looking at cupboards for all the people: 'Where are they?' That's when he said to me, 'Dress me up like Françoise Hardy.' I powdered him, dressed him up like a chick, you know." Then Anita seduced him, and it changed Brian's life. "It's like he came out of it a haunted man," Anita recalled.

————

The Stones were totally exhausted after six weeks on tour. Mania and hostility were aimed at them everywhere they went. Despite having more muscle around them, they were still insulted and spat on. Middle America hated them on sight. They were beat. "Dunno about you blokes," Mick had said at the end of the grueling tour, "but I'm about ready for my nineteenth nervous breakdown."

On December 7, the Stones began four days of work at RCA Studios, where they produced their next two singles and most of two albums. They worked with Jack Nitzsche in the windowless studio, where time seemed to stand still as they built their songs in twenty-hour sessions. Andrew kept them locked in the studio, afraid they'd collapse if they even went out to eat. Brian was often comatose, on his back with his guitar strapped on. Sometimes he didn't show up. When he did, he was often brilliant, dubbing in apposite piano or harpsichord tracks.

All the tracks were written by Mick and Keith during the five-week tour and reflected the dislocation of life (and love) on the road. Their new single, "19th Nervous Breakdown," was cut to the "Diddley Daddy" rhythm with a clarion guitar flash. The lyrics were a Dylanesque take on an insane party girl, the kind of person you meet at certain dismal, dull affairs (Chrissie reportedly thought it was about her). At the end of the wild, rackety tune, Bill Wyman copied the dive-bomber bass lick from Bo Diddley as well.

With Jack Nitzsche, Ian Stewart, and Brian on piano, organ, and harpsichord, the new songs had a bitter, lovelorn tone and a lot of echo. The new singles, "Breakdown" and "Mother's Little Helper," were folk rock jump tunes. The others, a sequence of great songs of romantic remorse like "Sittin' on a Fence," "Think," and "Ride On Baby," would appear over the next two years as album tracks on the two versions of *Aftermath*, the compilation LP *Flowers*, and on the flip sides of singles.

(One song, "Looking Tired," was never released.) The long blues jam "Goin' Home" was recorded at an all-night studio party hosted by Andrew that drew Brian Wilson, dancers from *Shindig*, and many local friends. There was a black girl wearing a long fur coat and nothing else. Some remembered a white duck walking around the studio. With this audience on hand, Mick, wearing a striped shirt, his collar buttoned up, spent hours on his knees, singing soul riffs into a handheld mike. Keith, in shades and a leather jacket, comped along impassively on guitar, swigging Pepsi from a bottle.

Each member of the Stones made about $50,000 on the tour. Their money was held by Allen Klein in New York. Bill and Charlie flew home to London. Keith and some tour people went to Arizona, bought cowboy gear and Colt .45s, and spent a few days riding and camping in the desert, sleeping under the stars. Target practice, Apache shepherds in the hills, coyotes howling at the moon: it was Keith's boyhood Roy Rogers fantasy come to life.

Brian and Anita flew to the Virgin Islands. Mick headed to Jamaica, then back to New York, where he finally met a comatose, newly married Dylan in Bob's crowded flat at the Chelsea Hotel. (Dylan's entourage sniggered at Mick's foppish black-and-white-checked suit while they tried to revive Bob long enough to say hello.) Brian and Anita came to New York too, hanging (uneasily) with Dylan, who was about to record his masterpiece *Blonde on Blonde*: the title may have come from his impression of the two dazzling European kids who liked to beat each other up and then parade around the clubs with their black eyes and bruises, a love supreme all black-and-blue.

four:
Catch Your Dreams
Before They Slip Away

The Stones in their prime at a photo call

in Green Park, London, January 1967.

We're making our own statement. Others are

making more intellectual ones.

Brian Jones

King of Clubs

In 1966, inspired by the formidable women around them, driven by the twin engines of ambition and drugs, the Rolling Stones continued a run of visionary hit singles and began to release albums that stood as crucial works of the era. The influence of a powerful new female energy on the Stones was undeniable. Anita Pallenberg restored the faltering Brian Jones to his place in the band and in the Rolling Stones mythos. Keith Richards fell in love with her too, and their romantic triad realigned the precarious political axis within the Stones, an unresolved fulcrum until Mick Jagger hooked up with Marianne Faithfull late in the year. Marianne's wild spirit and noble erudition would soon contribute another strong female persona to the band's creative identity. Now the Stones and their women moved in a glamorous flash of pop celebrity and artistic validity, the vanguard of the new generation's cultural heroes. Nobody in those times was more beautiful than they, or more doomed.

At the same time, it was the era of "Stupid Girl" and "Under My Thumb," misogynist songs of dominance set to the Stones' darkest, most ardent music. While these were in production, a battle raged between the Stones and Decca over Andrew's proposed title of their next album, *Could You Walk on the Water?* This was supposed to be a deluxe gatefold album with six pages of color pix shot on the last American tour and a cover featuring the Stones walking atop a California reservoir like pop messiahs on the Sea of Galilee. But the record company coughed: in the bitterness (over lack of control of their work) that followed, the album was called *Aftermath* for want of another concept.

In January 1966, the Beatles' *Rubber Soul* was hot with acid imagery and exotic influences, particularly the new sound of George Harrison's sitar on "Norwegian Wood." One night George put the massive sitar in Brian's hands, and within an hour Brian was working out little melodies on the complex twenty-six-stringed instrument.

In America, the Stones' version of "As Tears Go By" was a hit single. The U.S. audience hadn't yet heard Marianne Faithfull's earlier record, and Jagger's "Tears" got to no. 6 in January. That month, Keith went on a spree. He bought a dark blue Bentley S Touring Continental that he couldn't as yet drive. He mounted a Confederate flag on the front bumper, had a record player installed, and named the car Blue Lena, after singer Lena Horne. Then he bought Redlands, a half-timbered, four-bedroom Tudor farmhouse in the country near West Wittering, Sussex, on the south coast of England. The thatched old farm, still surrounded by a medieval moat, needed complete refurbishing. Redlands would become Keith's refuge and the scene of much drama to come. Keith and his dog, Ratbag, moved into it the following spring.

"19th Nervous Breakdown" came out in February, with the powerfully dolorous "Sad Day" on the U.S. B side, and got to no. 2 in both the U.S. and the U.K. ("Sad Day" was an atmospheric experiment never issued on any Stones album.)

Meanwhile, there was a revolution under way within the Stones. Mick Jagger's affair with Chrissie Shrimpton was winding down in ever more rancorous public bickering, jealousy, and recrimination. Keith's girlfriend Linda Keith was dabbling with heroin, and their thing cooled. As these romantic energies subsided, Brian and Anita were launched on one of the great sadomasochistic love affairs of the century. Brian's new pad in Elm Park Lane, Chelsea, was a silken carnival of sex and LSD, with Brian's houseguests spreading lurid tales of the two "enchanted siblings" (Terry Southern) beating each other with whips in cross-dressing furies of love. In the clubs they frequented—Dolly's, Blaises, the Scotch of St. James—Brian would punch Anita in the face at the slightest provocation. The beautiful blond woman took it with a smile and displayed her bruises with seeming pride.

Some of her friends were appalled, but Anita told them she had never known such love for a man. Their bond seemed unshakable. It's well known in the literature of sadomasochism that some women believe that to stay in an abusive relationship is to be strong; she takes pride in finding her own voice, even if it means she'll be hit. Couples like this live through intense cycles of violence and redemption, and their bond is sometimes intractable. The love they share, although some may find its expression perverse, is often profound and very real.

There's little doubt that Anita Pallenberg knew that in her, Brian Jones, breaker of women, had finally met his match. By falling in love with Anita, he had finally found a woman so strong he couldn't destroy her. With this young goddess on his arm, Brian recovered some of his dissipated aura. Dressed as a dandy in sharp pinstripes, outlandish broad-brimmed hats, and flamboyant women's costume jewelry bought at Saks Fifth Avenue in New York, Brian was the King of Clubs. Even the East End hoodlums stepped back when Brian walked into a club. At Annabels, movie stars and decadent aristos gawked at Brian and Anita like bumpkins. At home, fueled by LSD, he began experimenting with tape recorders, making atmospheric "free-form" tapes of inchoate melodic ideas that he would erase before they had a chance of turning into a song. He told friends that the other Stones would only laugh at him if he tried to bring his ideas into the studio. "I would like to write," he told an interviewer, "but I lack confidence and need encouragement."

Keith Richards was mesmerized by Anita because she scared him silly. "She knew everything and could say it in five languages," he told Stanley Booth. Plus, Brian had turned Keith on to LSD, and they became close again under its influence. After Anita moved in with Brian in May 1966, she presided over the household with a seductive haze of astrology, magic spells, and hash smoke. Film director Kenneth Anger referred to Brian and Anita as the "occult unit" within the Stones. Keith moved in with them (and frequent guest Tara Browne) later in the year and became a regular member of their blond acid cult, which left Mick Jagger and his unfashionable girlfriend—"you're *obsolete,* my baby"—out in the cold. Mick was afraid of acid, hadn't taken it yet, and so for a time became the butt of jokes and object of derision as the bourgeois, suburban "straight" man of the group.

In early 1966, Brian Jones was sitting at the bar in Blaises, flying on acid with a pocketful of speed, when he was approached by a pair of incognito reporters for *News of the World,* the muckraking Sunday paper with the largest circulation in Britain. One of them politely asked Brian if he was a member of the Stones.

"That's right," Brian said softly, looking at the man from behind a fringe of blond hair almost covering his eyes.

"Which one are you, then?"

"Mick Jagger," Brian lied, and turned away with a sigh, tired of being hassled in clubs. But the reporters settled in and told Brian they'd be honored to buy him a drink. At some point, the conversation turned to LSD, and Brian told them that he'd been tripping a lot lately, but added, "I don't go out much on it now that all the other cats have taken it up. Do you know what I mean? If too many people get turned on to it, it will just get a dirty name very quickly, do you see?"

"When did you first try the stuff?"

"On tour," Brian answered. "With Bo Diddley and Little Richard." This was absurd, but Brian loved to put people on. He still told people he was the leader of the Rolling Stones. Meanwhile, he was popping pills, and after some more desultory drug talk he was joined by some friends. Brian took a foil-wrapped chunk of Moroccan hash out of the pocket of his velvet-trimmed jacket and showed it to his pals, inviting them to his house for a smoke. As they left, the two reporters called out, "Bye, Mick!" Brian and his gang had a good laugh at this.

February 1966. To New York, with the band staying at different hotels for the first time. The next day, there was a photo session for the new album at Jerry Schatzberg's studio, followed by a party for the Manhattan hipoisie in the Stones' honor. Andy Warhol arrived with a huge entourage. Smoke and music: Stevie Wonder's "Uptight"; Nancy Sinatra's "These Boots Are Made for Walking."

On February 13, they arrived at Ed Sullivan's theater (Studio 50) on Broadway for the morning rehearsal to find a crush of girls waiting for them. They ran for the stage door, but the doorman wouldn't open up and the Stones were roughly mobbed, their hair pulled, clothes torn by the devouring young Bacchae. When the badly rattled Stones finally got in, Keith threw a trash can at the doorman. There was another row when Sullivan's producer wanted to bleep out the "trying to make some girl" line from "Satisfaction" (this had been done on *Shindig*), but Andrew threatened to walk out and the line went out uncensored. That night, they managed to build some energy for "Satisfaction" amid squeals and screams from the girls in the audience, followed by Mick and Keith duetting on "As Tears Go By." The show's finale was a hectic, riffing take on "19th Nervous Breakdown" that put the Stones' rude 1966 insolence over to Sullivan's huge national audience.

After two days in Los Angeles, the Stones flew to Australia to tour. They played to 25,000 people in Sydney and suffered through a riot in New Zealand on Brian's twenty-fourth birthday. Keith's face got cut and Brian hurt his leg when a phalanx of hysterical girls stormed the stage. Bill Wyman scored a career-high total of thirteen girls on this tour, one of whom told him that she'd had his baby the year before. Around this time, Wyman and the band tallied their chick scores thus far. Bill came out with about 250, Brian 130, Mick about 30, Keith 6, and Charlie Watts none.

On the way back to California afterward, the group stopped in the South Pacific paradise of Fiji for a brief holiday. Brian took advantage of Fiji's large Indian population and culture, buying a beautiful new sitar in a music shop in downtown Suva. The fragile instrument developed a big crack almost immediately; Brian taped it up and kept playing it anyway.

During a day at the beach in Fiji, Brian amazed them all—Keith, Mick, Stu, Charlie, and Shirley—with his swimming prowess, venturing far out into the rough, breaking waves like a porpoise, without a care in the world.

What a Draaag It Is, Gettin' Old

Back in L.A., the Stones recorded the rest of their dark masterpiece, *Aftermath,* in four days (March 6–9, 1966). The eleven songs included "Paint It, Black," with Brian deploying his new sitar's mystical tones. Two versions of "Out of Time" were cut, along with "Stupid Girl" and "Under My Thumb." These angry, hard-core, proto-rock songs were softened by the madrigal-like "Lady Jane" and "I Am Waiting." Jack Nitzsche played harpsichord on both. Rejuvenated Brian used a whole palette of instruments—dulcimer, piano, vibraphone—to add subtle shades and sophisticated, flickering lights to the new music.

Keith: "Brian had pretty much given up on the guitar by then. If there was [another] instrument around, he had to be able to get something out of it, just because it was there. At that point it was a great thing; it gave the Stones on record a lot of different textures and sounds we wouldn't have done otherwise . . . little touches that make you think at the time, 'Oh no—he's gonna play the bloody *marimbas,*' but afterwards you think, 'Yeah, right, that did it.' "

Even Andrew Oldham paid tribute to Brian's work: "His contribution can be heard on every track, and what he didn't know how to play, he went out and learned . . . It was more than a decorative effect. Sometimes Brian pulled the whole record together."

Later in March, the compilation album *Big Hits (High Tide and Green Grass)* was released in the United States, using the *Could You Walk on the Water?* package and photos. Here the Stones glared on the shore of the reservoir, instead of walking on it. The concert and studio photos included a very unflattering shot of Brian in half-nanker pose as if to say, "Look at what a snotty asshole we have to deal with every day." With its mix of old songs and "19th Nervous Breakdown," it got to no. 3 and sold well for the rest of the year.

Late March. Ten-day Euro tour started with another riot in The Hague. Anita joined up in Paris. The shows began with "The Last Time" and moved through older soul covers and hits like "Time Is on My Side" and "Play with Fire." Then it built through "Breakdown" and "Cloud" before the "I'm All Right"/"Satisfaction" meltdown. Smoke bombs were thrown at L'Olympia in Paris during the second show: sixty fans were arrested by the gendarmes. The aftershow party at the hotel featured Françoise Hardy and Brigitte Bardot, reigning European movie sex bomb since her 1956 role in *And God Created Woman*. Bardot asked Mick and Keith to write a song for her next film. Marianne Faithfull was at the party too, at the height of her beauty and pop stardom, twenty years old, without her husband, famously promiscuous. (She had a role in Jean-Luc Godard's new film *Made In U.S.A.*) Brian moved around Paris like a national hero, mobbed for autographs wherever he went.

———

Decca released the (superior) British version of *Aftermath* in April. It had a rose-tinted cover shot of the band by Guy Webster, with four shots from Jerry Schatzberg's intimate New York photo session on the back. Dave Hassinger's liner notes talked about the Stones' cool professionalism at RCA, taking note of the long hours it took to build a song, from the moment Mick and Keith ran it through for the band to the final track.

After-Math (spelled this way on the jacket) had fourteen tracks and ran longer than contemporary pop albums usually did. For the first time, all the songs were Jagger/Richards compositions, making this, for serious fans, the first real Rolling Stones album. By turns tender and offensive, *Aftermath* disturbed and delighted everyone who listened to the Stones' blatant attack on motherhood and the common decencies of traditional courtship and other sexual mores. "Mother's Little Helper"—set to the same frantic rockabilly rhythm that Keith used for "Breakdown"—used sci-fi guitars and the sitar, plus the weird "doctor, please" C&W bridge, to

talk about tranquilized suburban housewives. "What a draaag it is, get-
tin' old" seemed like an attack on middle-aged values and echoed Pete
Townshend's "Hope I die before I get old" line from the Who's "My
Generation."

"Stupid Girl" was a 4/4 stomp about Mick Jagger's love life. "I
wasn't in a good relationship," he said later. "Or I was in too many bad
relationships." Describing someone as "the sickest thing in the world" can
be seen as a stake in the heart of his long affair with Chrissie Shrimpton,
but shouldn't be taken so literally. "It's a caricature," Mick said, "and it's
in reply to a girl who was a very pushy woman. I had so many girlfriends
at that point, I was obviously in with the wrong group."

The mood lifted a bit for "Lady Jane," Mick's "unconscious" pastiche of a Tudor love song. Brian Jones played an amplified dulcimer over
Jack Nitzsche's harpsichord, as Mick sang lines supposedly inspired by
Henry VIII's love letters to Lady Jane Seymour. (Some related the song
to Mick's friend Jane Ormsby-Gore.) Others heard "Lady Jane" as marijuana, "Lady Ann" as amphetamine.

Then back to the dirty business of male chauvinism with "Under My
Thumb," Brian's marimba playing lead to a gentle rocking beat that accelerated into a groove toward the end. "Thumb" had serious, fuzz-tone
guitar, a lyric that mixed love and hate—"under my thumb's a squirming
dog who's just had her day"—and Otis-type soul riffing at the end. Mick
later called this searing song "a jokey number," but it stirred a sense of
outrage in many of the women who heard it as a triumphalist expression
of domination. They followed this with "Doncha Bother Me," a Chicago-
style R&B tune with slide guitar and harmonica. Mick's sneering vocal—
"Not knowing why / Trying to get high"—was flush with bad attitude.

"Goin' Home" finished the side with a landmark blues jam, mostly
Mick riffing over understated layers of harmonica and guitar, building
momentum over eleven tense minutes. The song had been recorded at an
all-night studio party during the first *Aftermath* sessions the previous
December, and carried the crack-of-dawn feeling of the best white blues.
"Goin' Home" was an homage to Wilson Pickett and the other soul
shouters the Stones loved, a way for the Stones to crack open the short

form demanded by the standard song formats of the time. The drums even drop out at one point, when someone threw something at Charlie Watts and the band kept playing.

Side two: "Flight 505," a rocker about in-flight paranoia. "High and Dry," the other side of "Thumb," a corny C&W song about getting dumped by a rich girl. "Out of Time," a pointed attack on Chrissie Shrimpton—"my poor old-fashioned baby"—with rich marimba and guitar countermelodies and some of Mick Jagger's best singing on record. "It's Not Easy" was organ R&B and chugging boogie. "I Am Waiting" was a "Lady Jane" clone with enigmatic lyrics and eccentric phrasing. "Take It or Leave It" had scat lyrics and a sad, lovelorn feel that appealed to young men. "Think" featured fuzz-guitar slabs, great drumming, and loads of romantic recriminations: "Tell me whose fault was that, babe!" "What to Do" ended *Aftermath* on a note of confusion familiar to all young lovers.

Aftermath's audacious and seemingly cruel attitudes antagonized some listeners as an attack on women. Others saw it much differently. In a critique published in *New Left Review,* Richard Morton described "Stupid Girl" and "Under My Thumb" as ironic anthems designed to expose sexual exploitation: "The enormous merit and audacity of the Stones is to have . . . defied a central taboo of the social system: mention of sexual inequality. They have done so in the most radical and unacceptable way possible: by celebrating it. The light this black beam throws on the society is too bright for it. The triumph of these records is their rejection of the spurious world of monadic personal relationships."

In the end, *Aftermath* was a somber, troubled letter from the band to its audience, who made the record no. 1 within days of its release. Even Mick Jagger, rarely given to praising the Stones' work, was proud of it: "[*Aftermath*] was a big landmark record for me. It's the first time we wrote the whole record . . . It had a lot of different styles, and it was very well recorded. So it was, to my mind, a real marker."

Aftermath was an important part of its times, contemporaneous with Dylan's *Blonde on Blonde,* Antonioni's *Blow Up,* Catherine Deneuve in the film *Repulsion,* Truman Capote's nonfiction novel *In Cold Blood.* The

Stones were entering their mighty midperiod, and there was nothing now—almost nothing—that could stop them.

Not that they wouldn't try . . .

The Sun Blotted Out
from the Sky

April 24, 1966. Tara Browne's famous twenty-first-birthday party at Luggala, a Guinness family estate near Bray, Ireland. Outlandish period costumes and huge blocks of black hashish. Brian and Anita as Cupid and Psyche in feathers and silk. Mick and Chrissie having a row. She was embarrassed because people generally identified her with the scathing put-downs in *Aftermath*.

These were the days of "Paint It, Black," released in early May 1966. (The comma in the title, inserted by someone at Decca, aroused much curiosity and even charges of racism.) There was nothing else like it on the radio. This lurid tone poem seemed to describe a funeral procession amid haunting, existential self-doubt. Brian's sitar stated the melody with an otherworldly dolor, and pounding drums launched the song into a high-noir ambience of anxiety and hopelessness, desirous to see the sun blotted out from the sky. Leonard Bernstein, conductor of the New York Philharmonic, called it one of the greatest songs of the century. It seemed to have social echoes as well, reflecting recent waves of immigration to England from India and Pakistan.

Keith: "We cut it in L.A., as a comedy track. Bill was playing the organ, doing a piss-take on our old manager [Eric Easton], who started as an organist in a cinema pit. We'd been doing it with funky rhythms and it hadn't worked out and he started playing it like this [a sort of unintentional klezmer parody] and everybody got behind it. It's a two-beat; very strange. Brian playing the sitar makes the whole thing."

"Paint It, Black" was an instant hit record, no. 1 in both England and America. It also marked the Rolling Stones' commercial apogee as a singles band in the sixties. "Black" was their last no. 1 for more than two years.

———

May 1966. Keith moved his record collection and guns down to Redlands; the rooms were still empty of furniture except for Keith's bed. He bought the cottage across the moat for a music room. His girlfriend Linda Keith moved to New York, leaving Keith high and dry. An old gardener named Jack watched over Redlands while Keith hung with Brian and Anita, who moved in permanently with Brian that month.

At the end of the month, Bob Dylan and his band, the Hawks, returned to London for climactic performances at Royal Albert Hall. Playing electric rock in the second half of his shows, with a giant American flag as a backdrop, Dylan had been reviled as a sellout and a Judas for almost four months. People threw things at the stage in disgust. His old fans were pleading with him to get rid of the band, but Dylan ignored them. Dylan's shows invariably ended with searing electric versions of "Ballad of a Thin Man" and "Like A Rolling Stone" during massive audience walkouts.

Dylan had been on the road, around the world, since February, and was said to be running on speed and heroin. In London, he ran into Keith and Brian at Dolly's, a private club in Mayfair. Dylan had to be carried into the place by Stones chauffeur Tom Keylock, who was minding Dylan while he was in town. Dylan and the two drunken Stones started to get into it. No way, Dylan told Keith, were the Stones the best rock and roll band anymore. Opaque behind his black shades, Dylan told Keith that the Hawks were the best band nowadays.

Keith, taken aback, asked, "What about us?"

"You guys may be the best *philosophers,*" Dylan slurred. "But the Hawks—they're the best band, man."

Keith didn't need to hear this and began to brood. Dylan began to twist the blade in Keith's guts. "Y'know, man, I coulda written 'Satisfaction'—easy," he told Keith. "But there's *no fuckin' way* you guys coulda written 'Mr. Tambourine Man.' You know that? *Think* about it."

Keith thought about it, and a few drinks later decided that "Like A Rolling Stone" was really kind of taking the piss out of his band. Keith made a lunge for Dylan, expertly parried by Keylock. There was a little scuffle. Dylan got uptight and Keylock hustled him out of the club, into the car, and back to the Mayfair Hotel. As Keylock turned into Park Lane, he noticed Keith and Brian behind them in Brian's Rolls, and then Brian tried to get past to cut them off. Brian was drunk, swerving in and out of traffic, and they seemed to want another go at Dylan. Keylock pulled into the hotel driveway and got Dylan into the lobby just as Brian's Rolls jumped the curb and tried in vain to ram through the revolving doors. None of this was mentioned the next night (May 26), when the Stones visited Dylan backstage after his show ended in massive booing, catcalls, and walkouts. The Stones had taped *Top of the Pops* in the afternoon and shared a box at Royal Albert Hall that night. Afterward, they all went to the Scotch of St. James and got loaded. A few weeks later, Dylan would fall off his motorcycle near his home in Woodstock, New York, and effectively retire his electric mod persona for good. The Hawks became The Band.

By June 1966, the Stones were burned out.

"We were actually trying to [accomplish] something by taking a few chemicals and making this wrench," Keith told Stanley Booth. "The ideal behind it was very pure. Everybody at that point was prepared to use himself as a laboratory, to find some way out of this mess. It was very idealistic and very destructive at the same time for a lot of people. But the downside of it now is that people think that drugs are entertainment . . . We weren't taking drugs just for fun, recreation. *Creation,* maybe."

Brian and Anita went to Spain for a week and stayed in the resort town of Marbella. But their fun was strenuous, and he returned more ex-

hausted than before he left. Mick suffered some kind of physical breakdown and went into seclusion at his flat in Harley House. A couple of TV
shows were canceled because Mick's doctor told him he was suffering
from nervous stress and had to rest for a week before going back to
America. It was going to be a hard tour. The American version of
Aftermath had failed to make no. 1. "Mother's Little Helper," with its derisively cruel images of women tranquilized by little yellow pills, was released as a single that month and only made no. 8. A lot of American fans
thought "Little Helper" was a real downer. There was a feeling in the
band that the Stones had to prove themselves all over again.

Oh Baudelaire!

The Stones landed in New York on June 23, 1966, to begin
their fifth American tour and discovered no hotel would book them.
Andrew threatened to sue amid much publicity, and the band made do at
the down-market Holiday Inn. That night, Bill played bass on a John
Hammond Jr. blues session. Brian and Dylan showed up to hang out, their
relationship patched up, and later Dylan played Brian the acetates of
Blonde on Blonde. Like everyone else, Brian was floored by the power and
humor of the music, particularly the shouted chorus of "Rainy Day
Women #12 & 35":

Everybody must get stoned!

————

The American version of *Aftermath* (with "Paint It, Black" as
lead track) was climbing the charts but didn't look to make no. 1. On June
24, the band held a tense, sullen press conference aboard Allen Klein's
motor yacht anchored in the Hudson.

Reporter: "What's the difference between you and the Beatles?"

Mick: "There's five of us and four of them."

Reporter: "I want to do a piece about the reality of being a Rolling Stone."

Mick: "The reality of being me? It's fucking nasty today."

Boston was the first stop of the tour. The most Anglophile of American cities, Boston craved English bands and was a main beachhead of the British Invasion. The Stones played the Manning Bowl in Lynn, about twenty miles north of town, in the rain before fifteen thousand zealots. Cops dosed the stampeding crowd with tear gas during "Satisfaction," and there was panic, trampled kids, plenty of arrests. Drunken fans surrounded the limos and tried to smash the windows. Others chased the band all the way to the airport.

Back in New York, the Stones' gear was stolen out of the equipment truck, including custom-built Vox guitars and Brian's electric dulcimer. Playing their noir rockabilly anthems in a new soul band style, they sold out shows in Washington, Baltimore, Buffalo, Hartford. The McCoys and the Standells were opening shows. Allen Klein added dates to the tour daily, often two shows a day.

At Marine Ballroom, Atlantic City, a nineteen-year-old poetess from Pitman, New Jersey, named Patti Smith was crammed up against the stage:

"Mick ripped off his flowered shirt and did a fandango. Satisfaction. Tambourine on head, he strutted like some stud . . . this was no TV, this was real. I could enter the action. I got set to out-stone-face Bill Wyman, the cornerstone of the Stones, relentless as Stonehenge, as a pyramid. Any hard-edged kid took to him. He was onstage right to catch some spit from Mick. Then hell broke. Handkerchiefs folded like flowers, a million girls busting my spleen. Oh Baudelaire! I grabbed Brian's ankle and held on like a drowning child. It seemed like hours. I was getting bored. I looked up and yawned. Bill Wyman cracked up. Brian grinned. I got scared and squeezed out and ran."

On July 2, the Stones played the Forest Hills tennis stadium in Queens. Cops waded into the crowd with nightsticks and deployed tear gas. The band flew back to Manhattan by helicopter, then motorcaded to the Cafe Wha? on MacDougal Street to see a new guitarist that Linda

Keith had hooked up with. He was this black hippie from Seattle, an ex-paratrooper, who turned up like a psychedelic Martian in Greenwich Village playing left-handed Fender Stratocaster, upside down, in a group called Jimmy James and the Blue Flames. The Rolling Stones' collective jaw plunged as they first beheld Jimi Hendrix, a few months before his arrival in London, already controlling an improvised arsenal of blues licks and feedback developed in the road bands of Little Richard and the Isley Brothers. To the Stones' horror and delight, Hendrix deconstructed some Dylan songs and "Wild Thing" and blasted out an incendiary new music that threatened to make them all obsolete within months.

Linda, somewhat to Keith's consternation, was crazy about Hendrix. She even took one of Keith's new Stratocasters and loaned it to him. But Hendrix was involved with someone else and the vibes were weird. Keith was concerned about Linda, and didn't like her scene with this flaming black warlock.

War Memorial Arena, Syracuse, July 6. The Stones flew in on their private turboprop. Radio people came on board for snapshots and interviews with Brian and Mick. Brian was wearing his flamboyant lemon/pink/blue-striped blazer. As the band entered the hall, Brian saw a big American flag stretched out to dry and grabbed it for a souvenir, inadvertently dragging it on the ground. This sent the stagehands into apoplexy. Their brothers were dying for this flag over in Vietnam! There was a scuffle, some angry curses, and the cops threatened to bust the Stones for insulting the Stars and Stripes. Klein and Andrew forced Brian to apologize. The Stones played a shortened set and left town quick.

Back in New York City, Keith and Brian met an LSD dealer named David Schneiderman, aka the Acid King. Dude had a briefcase full of Blue Cheer, Windowpane, Purple Haze. Keith invited him to drop by when he was in London.

Brian and Andrew stayed out all night with three black courtesans who cruised Manhattan in a Rolls-Royce. At 3 A.M. Brian took Andrew to see Max Jacobson, legendary Dr. Feelgood. The doctor treated Andrew's raging case of herpes, then shot them both up with the powerful amphetamines for which he was notorious.

On through the American Midwest and out to California. High times as everyone was stoned on good Mexican pot, and a hazy, unfamiliar air of unity took over. Everyone was getting along, and even Brian was doing relatively okay. They were playing like demons every night. "Under My Thumb" raged with an explosive Memphis drive. "Cloud" was taken fast, with Brian's metallic sitar licks. "Not Fade Away" was a jungle rave, Brian on harp. "19th Nervous Breakdown" was a dual-guitar orgy, with Keith doing great vocal harmony. Deafening screams from the girls during "Time Is on My Side" and "Lady Jane." The Stones gave "Satisfaction" a fuel-injected trajectory, usually with Stu on piano, and a cool, stop-time ending amid the mayhem.

The Rolling Stones were now giving the hottest, most exciting shows of their careers. Mick was bumping and grinding, wiggling his can at the fans, stirring them into estrus. Many shows were attended by violence: cops were beat up, dozens of arrests, multiple injuries.

Los Angeles in the summer heat. The Stones only went out at night. Brian and Anita moved through the clubs and parties like movie stars, only they were the real thing. Brian told friends he was dazzled by the Cadillacs prowling the Strip, and loved the big Hollywood Hills houses, with their pools shimmering in David Hockney blue. He'd like to live there, he said, except for being constantly mobbed on Sunset Boulevard, hassled by both locals and tourists.

The Hollywood Bowl show on July 25 (opened by Buffalo Springfield) packed 17,500 fans and got rave reviews, no problems, and a great vibe as the band played a perfect set in front of huge photographs of themselves from the *Aftermath* album. The 1966 American tour ended in Hawaii on July 27, where the (dateless) rest of the band got annoyed with Bill for scoring a pair of pretty sisters. Wyman and Keith both finished their American adventure with a sexually transmitted disease caught from a beautiful flower child in Los Angeles, and both ended up on penicillin. Wyman's long-suffering wife, Diane, had to have the shots too.

Brian Jones would never play music for an American audience again. It was his last American tour.

———

Keith Richards: "In those days, Mick and I were into a solid word/music bag, unless I thought of something outstanding that could be used in the title. I would spend the first two weeks of the tour [on writing songs], because it was done on the road, all of it was worked out . . . an American tour meant you started writing another album. After three, four weeks, you had enough and then you went to L.A. and recorded it. We worked very fast that way, and when you came off a tour, you were shit-hot playing, as hot as the band is gonna be."

Three versions of "Have You Seen Your Mother, Baby, Standing in the Shadow?" were recorded between August 3 and August 7 at RCA, involving different instrumental tracks. The Stones' next single was pure murder: using electronic feedback, distortion, and battle-hardened fuzz guitar (only weeks after their obviously influential encounter with Jimi Hendrix), "Mother, Baby" was both a demolition of constipated pop song formats and a Rimbaudesque declension of the shadow world of illicit sexuality. The wildly experimental song suggested not only maternal prostitution and incest but fraternal lust as Jagger asks if you've seen your brother standing in the shadow too.

He might well have asked if you'd seen yourself. "You took your choice at this time," he sings: "The brave old world, or the slide to the depths of decline." The song ends in an echo of Jimi Hendrix's slashing "Wild Thing" chords.

The Stones left L.A. "with pockets full of acid" (Keith) and took the rest of the summer off. Mick and Keith went to Acapulco to write the rest of the new album. When Mick returned to London, he smashed up his new Aston Martin in a car wreck. Both he and Chrissie Shrimpton were uninjured. Keith called Linda's parents and told them she was in a bad scene in New York. Her father brought her back to London, and friends thought it probably saved her life. Keith went to see her, but came away knowing it was all over between him and the beautiful, adventurous Ruby Tuesday.

————

Late in August, Brian and Anita arrived in Tangier and checked into the luxurious Hotel El Minzeh, where they met their friend Christopher Gibbs.

"Brian was a very difficult person to spend a lot of time with," Gibbs recalls. "He was a willful, spoiled, demanding, heroically selfish and self-centered being with a lot of sweetness and charm. And part of that charm was this glorious musical gift, of being able to pick up any instrument from any culture in the world and fiddle about with it until he could make it do what it was meant to do.

"And of course he was *very* rough with the ladies. Once Brian and Anita and I went to Tangier, staying at the Minzeh. On the second day, Brian had a fight with Anita and went to strike her. She managed to duck and he hit his fist on the iron frame of the window. I had to take him to the Clinic California, where they put his arm in a cast."

Brian sent a telegram to Andrew Oldham in London on August 31, saying he'd broken two bones in his hand while climbing in the mountains, and would be unable to play guitar for two months. Before he left Tangier, he spent some time with Brion Gysin, an expatriate artist and writer who was a key member of the Tangier Beat-expat scene. Gysin started to tell Brian about a mysterious village of master musicians up in the Moroccan mountains, in a place called Jajouka. Wild music, dancing boys, plenty of *kif,* stay up and rave all night. Brian Jones, bored to death with the Rolling Stones, was intrigued and made Gysin promise to take him to Jajouka someday.

The Ultimate Freak-Out

September 1966. Tom Driberg, righteous, somewhat bo-hemian Labour M.P., spoke on the Stones' behalf in Parliament after a Scottish judge gratuitously insulted the band while sentencing some poor kid to the workhouse. It was the first inkling that the judiciary class had it in for the Rolling Stones. The judges, the cops, the law: they couldn't wait to get their hands on the band.

Mick and Keith were at IBC Studios working on a horn track for "Have You Seen Your Mother, Baby?" Brian and Anita returned from Morocco on September 4 so Brian could begin work on the sound track to Volker Schlöndorff's new film, *Mord und Totschlag,* about to begin pro-duction and starring Anita in her first feature film.

Anita: "It was called *A Degree of Murder* in English. They needed a German-speaking face. I auditioned in Paris and got the part. Then the di-rector asked Brian to do the music, and it became a big thing for us. The Stones movie wasn't getting made, so Brian got into it on his own." Brian's injured hand prevented him from playing. His band included Jimmy Page, Small Faces drummer Kenny Jones, and ace London studio musician Nicky Hopkins on piano. The music was dark and gloomy, to go with a script about a waitress who accidentally kills her ex-boyfriend and goes through changes while disposing of his body.

After finishing their new single in Los Angeles, the Stones gathered in New York on September 9. Dressed in high-retro World War II women's clothes and wigs, with heavy makeup supervised by a stun-ning transvestite Brian, they posed for a series of drag photos on an East Side street on a quiet Saturday afternoon. Brian pushed a distastefully

retarded-looking Bill Wyman in a wheelchair for an extra dash of contempt. After the photo shoot, they repaired to a bar, still in drag. Keith:
"Hey, let's go and have a beer. But what voice do you do? We sat there
and had a beer and watched TV and no one said anything, it was just so
outrageous." Later, while shooting Peter Whitehead's drag promo film for
"Mother, Baby," Brian yawned, smirked wickedly, lifted his skirt, and
started masturbating. The camera kept rolling. Mick Jagger rescued this
bit from the cutting room floor and played the footage for his dinner
guests for years.

The Stones appeared on Ed Sullivan's show the next day,
September 10, doing "Paint It, Black," "Lady Jane," and "Mother, Baby."
Mick, in a floral shirt, sang with a live mike to prerecorded backing tracks
because of Brian's injured hand. Brian, in vestal white, sat down and
smiled while pretending to play the sitar. Keith stood at the piano during
"Mother," wearing a provocative Wehrmacht field jacket. The Stones had
bought loads of Nazi uniforms and memorabilia in L.A. at the end of the
U.S. tour. Around this time, Anita dressed Brian in a black SS uniform
with a swastika armband and had photos taken of him stomping on a
baby doll. In November, another shot from this series, with Anita kneeling submissively in front of Nazi Jones, ran in London papers to univer-
sal distaste, since no one "got" this supposed antifascist protest.

A couple days later, "Have You Seen Your Mother, Baby, Standing
in the Shadow?" was released in the U.S. and the U.K. as a horn-driven,
wall-of-noise attack on motherhood and apple pie. Keith Richards was
unhappy with the record, claiming it was rushed out before it had been
finished, and that the wrong mix was released, one that buried the rhythm
section. The flip side was a nasty psycho-blues, "Who's Driving Your
Plane?," recorded over the summer in L.A. with Brian blowing harp over
a slow, metal guitar riff.

"Have You Seen Your Mother, Baby?" was the last of the Stones'
great pop art singles, ending a five-song mockery of family values marked
by ethereal gloom and strident antagonism. Despite great reviews, the
record was way over the heads of their mass audience and stalled in the
middle of the Top Ten in England and America. The Stones' old fans

found "Mother" off-putting and sleazy. Even Charlie Watts's parents complained that the Stones had gone too far this time.

But those speed-spiked negativity records shook people up and made them think. "Jagger's got this marvelous sense of the day in which a family breaks up," wrote Norman Mailer years later. "The son throws acid in the mother's face, the mother stomps the son's nuts in, and then the fat cousin comes in and says: What is everyone fighting for? Let's have dinner. And they sit down, the son has no nuts left, the mother's face is scarred, but they go on, and British family life continues. Jagger's got that like no one else's ever had it."

Mick: " 'Have You Seen Your Mother, Baby?' was like the ultimate freak-out. We came to a full stop after that. I just couldn't make it with that anymore—what more could we say?"

On September 23, the Stones began another English tour. Opening were the white-hot Yardbirds, with Jeff Beck and Jimmy Page in the band, and the Ike and Tina Turner Revue. The Stones hadn't toured England in more than a year, but any doubts about their fans were erased the minute they walked onto the stage at Royal Albert Hall in their velvet jackets and trendy white loafers. The cream of the London pop world was there, as was Brigitte Bardot. As soon as they hit "Paint It, Black," all five musicians were taken down by a wave of girls, who had to be pulled away so the band could flee. Order was restored, the concert resumed, but the kids rushed the stage again, only to be thrown back into the crowd by the security goons. Six songs into it, some fans got on the stage again. Keith was knocked down, and Mick was strangled. But the Stones played a full set that ended in "Satisfaction" while screaming, hysterical girls were punched and kicked by sadistic security men.

As the tour progressed through England, the Stones enjoyed watching Tina and the Ikettes, these four wild women—the personification of the sexual yin energy in rock and roll—doing their shag-shag-step-and-a-kick. Mick: "A lot of women performers are quite static, or certainly were in the sixties. They did their best, but they weren't like Tina. She was like a female version of Little Richard and would respond to the audience—really go out and grab them." It was a trick Mick Jagger wanted very much to learn.

Brian and Bill pestered Ike to show them the piano licks he'd played on the old Howlin' Wolf records, while twenty-six-year-old bombshell Tina was teaching Mick the sideways pony in backstage dressing rooms. She would laugh at Mick's spasms and show him how to move. Glowering Ike Turner was not too pleased and thrashed his wife in a London hotel room. Mick had a fling with new Ikette Pat Arnold, who later cut a record for Immediate. Bill was driving a couple of the girls from Glasgow to Newcastle in his Mercedes when he smashed it up. They all went on the tour bus after that.

———

That autumn, Anita bought an apartment where she and Brian could crash. It was at 1 Courtfield Road in South Kensington, and they moved in that October. Keith virtually lived there as well, all previous hatchets having been buried amid a mellow haze of reefer plumes during the summer's American tour. The flat was on two levels, with an oak-paneled minstrel gallery, and it quickly became the main hangout of the Stones. Dropping acid and rolling joints of Nepalese "Temple Ball" hashish were the main activities in the candlelit, incense-fogged household draped with geometric Moroccan textiles. Nina Simone and California bands were on the record player. Brian was reading Truman Capote's *In Cold Blood* and a textbook called *The Psychology of Insanity*. He was playing a lot of saxophone, deep into John Coltrane's new, blowing energy music. Robert Fraser was a regular, along with his protégé Michael Cooper, an intuitively invisible photographer who quickly replaced Gered Mankowitz as the main eye on the Stones. Tara Browne had broken up with his wife and was in residence and miserable. Brian was having daily paranoiac fits on LSD, which flooded into London that fall in solar flares of orange sunshine.

Keith would taunt him. "Is it the fucking *snakes* again, Brian?" Mr. Jones spent a lot of time in a fetal position in the corner while the party went on around him.

Marianne Faithfull bonded with Anita and soon joined the Brian/Keith/Anita unit as an intimate member. Married to art gallery owner John Dunbar, the marriage failing, the mother of a year-old son, she plunged into the Stones' seductive family. Slender, voluptuous, even more beautiful than Anita, she radiated a blue-eyed innocence that belied her fierce intelligence and passionate appetites. She'd had a string of minor hit records after "As Tears Go By," her singing style a mixture of exceptional maturity and soulful vibrato. She was a pop star in her own right. Allen Klein was besotted with her. Bob Dylan was said to be in love with her, like so many men drawn to her charismatic orbit, but his amorous advances had been rebuffed.

She had awkward sex with Brian—"leaning over me, like an asthmatic god"—at Courtfield Road during an acid trip, and ended up spending the night with Keith (which, in her memoirs, she called "the best night I've ever had in my life"). In the morning, Keith told her that it was Mick Jagger who fancied her the most: "Go on, love, give him a jingle. He'll fall off his chair. He's not that bad when you get to know him."

Marianne thought this a bit of a stretch. Mick was considered to be unhip and uptight by the Courtfield Road denizens, not part of the in-crowd, an uptight bourgeois cat with a nowhere girlfriend. (Mick occasionally appeared at the flat to smoke a joint, but the unwashed dishes, piles of dirty laundry, and general crash-pad grunge appalled his fastidious sensibilities, and he rarely hung out.) Marianne thought Mick was narcissistic, manipulative, and as tight as two coats of paint.

As the Stones stormed through England, they were playing some of the best, toughest music of their lives. The audience was younger and crazier than on recent tours, and Brian told interviewers he thought they helped bring some of the Stones' lost magic back. "It was like it was three years ago when it was all new," he told the *Rolling Stones Monthly*. Songs like "Under My Thumb" and "19th Nervous Breakdown" were played with the gritty funk of a Memphis soul band. The funkafied lessons of Otis Redding's version of "Satisfaction" was now fully integrated into the Stones' live sound. "Lady Jane" was delicately thrummed by Brian on his dulcimer. "Mother, Baby" and "Satisfaction" went off like grenades. The rhythm section—Wyman and Watts—supplied a powerful, churning bottom over which Jagger, Keith's guitar, and Brian's harps and sitar floated like stinging bees. Some fans think these were the best shows of the original Rolling Stones' career.

The audiences may have been more excited, but they were also smaller. The Stones couldn't help notice a lot of empty, unsold seats on the tour.

After a show in Bristol one night in October, everyone gathered in Mick's room. Michael Cooper had brought a print of *Repulsion*, Roman Polanski's new movie starring Catherine Deneuve. By dawn, Marianne Faithfull, who'd been invited to the gig by Brian and Keith, found herself alone with Mick Jagger and Pat Arnold. Pat finally left. Mick and Marianne went for a walk together just before dawn. A devotee of Holy Grail lore, she quizzed Mick on his knowledge of Arthurian material, a test he passed with gentle humor. The two young stars returned to the hotel and made love for the first time that fateful morning in Bristol.

My Mouth Is Soaking Wet

In the fall of 1966, the Rolling Stones were not exactly the hottest group in London. Though the Beatles had retired from performing, they were still the kings (John Lennon's statement that the Beatles were more popular than Jesus set off a press furor on both sides of the Atlantic). The Stones had become passé among the younger mods, who preferred the Small Faces and the Who. Eric Clapton, erstwhile Crawdaddy Club acolyte who'd quit the Yardbirds after their first album, was *the* guitar star of the time, with the graffito CLAPTON IS GOD scrawled on walls where youth hung out. Clapton's new band, Cream, a speed-rocking power trio, was the sharpest in the land.

Then Jimi Hendrix arrived in London. When Hendrix came to a club one night and asked to jam with Cream, he lit into Howlin' Wolf's "Killin' Floor" and ended up playing with his teeth. Clapton had to leave the stage. A new genius had fallen into their midst like a cast-out angel. Jimi shocked all the British pop stars, who suddenly realized that Hendrix, not one of them, would be the true avatar of rock music—as long as he lived.

———

The Stones' English tour ended in Southampton on October 7. They wouldn't tour again in England for five years.

Mick continued to see Marianne Faithfull in secret. He started spending more time at Courtfield Road, since that's where she hung out. Her feelings for the ardent Jagger began to change. He was sweet to her, generous, really seemed to want her. Mick and Mrs. Dunbar finally appeared together in public on October 15 at the launch of *International Times,* London's new underground newspaper, which generally championed the Stones in its pages.

Meanwhile, Brian was dropping more and more acid, flying all the time, working on doomy soundscape tapes for his film project. He followed Anita to Munich, where the movie was in production. He and Anita fought tooth and nail, and as his hand healed, he started hitting her again in violent spasms of jealously every time another man even looked at her.

That November, *High Tide and Green Grass* was released in the U.K. with an updated track list. In America, London Records' semifraudulent *Got Live If You Want It* concert album featured recent live tracks from London, Manchester, and Bristol recorded by Glyn Johns. It was filled out with ancient studio recordings ("Fortune Teller," "I've Been Loving You Too Long") augmented with screams from the tour. Since the shows were often disrupted, there were major instrumental drop-outs on the tracks, and much overdubbing of the guitars was necessary. Over the years, the U.S. *Got Live* developed a bad reputation as exploitative and subpar, but it stands as the only surviving example of the Stones' ferocious attack in its last year as an R&B band.

————

Mick and Keith, inspired by the women in their lives and strong drugs, were writing some incredible new music. Keith was playing with hard rhythms and grungy acid guitar. He banged out a new riff on piano that eventually became "Let's Spend the Night Together." Mick was feverishly moved by his hot liaison with Marianne. His new lyrics— the tongue getting tired, the soaking-wet mouth—were full of images of devouring cunnilingus. "She Smiled Sweetly" was the first real love lyric Mick wrote. If *Aftermath* had foretold the downfall of Mick's rhetorical punching bag Christine Shrimpton as *maîtresse-en-titre*, the new music for *Between the Buttons* hailed the rise of Marianne Faithfull as Jagger's new muse.

It was recorded in the new Olympic Studio, which had moved from Soho to Barnes, in southwestern London. Built as a film stage, owned by a London advertising mogul, Olympic started out as a jingle factory. The Stones brought in their engineer, Glyn Johns, who in turn brought in other rock and pop clients. Olympic had great engineers, like Eddie Kramer from South Africa, and a young tape operator named George Chkiantz, who would develop key sonic tools such as automatic double tracking and "phasing," a tricky soundwave distortion technique that would be used to psychedelic effect on recordings by Hendrix, the Small Faces, and many others.

The Stones loved Olympic. It was the only London studio with technical capabilities that approached their lab at RCA in Los Angeles. Jack Nitzsche flew over for the sessions. Also on keyboards on some tracks was Nicky Hopkins, the young blues piano player who'd started with Cyril Davies in the All-Stars. Hopkins had left the Royal Academy of Music at sixteen to play in R&B groups, but a serious digestive illness sent him to the hospital for over a year. Since 1965, he'd been confined to doing sessions, where he'd worked with the Who and the Kinks. Hopkins fit in well with the Stones (except for Stu, who found Nicky's playing too slick) and played with them in the studio and on the road for years.

The *Buttons* sessions ran for three weeks through November and early December 1966, producing some of the Stones' greatest songs. The Stones needed a new hit single; they came up with "Let's Spend the Night Together" and what evolved into "Ruby Tuesday," which was worked out by Brian and Keith as a sketch of Linda Keith. Sensing that power within the band lay in monopolizing Keith, Brian succeeded for a while in freezing Mick out. Brian played the song's madrigal line on his recorder, while Keith and Bill Wyman managed to coax a countermelody out of a cello: Bill held the instrument and fretted the fingerboard while Keith bowed. The track was long known as "Title 8" until it finally got its lyrics near the end of the sessions.

Keith's pounding piano drove the lusty "Let's Spend the Night Together." Charlie Watts, still hot from the English tour, was playing with new jazz-inflected polyrhythms, affecting up-tempo jams like "Miss Amanda Jones" and "Connection," which Charlie cut alone with Keith in the studio. Brian's luminous marimba and Charlie's jungle tom-toms powered the brilliant "Yesterday's Papers," the first song Mick wrote by himself for a Stones record. A demo titled "Sometimes Happy, Sometimes Blue" evolved over three weeks into the halcyon outtake "Dandelion."

The new studio scene also gave the Stones new problems. Working with four-track tapes, they took full advantage of new opportunities for overdubbing, sometimes stepping on their tracks so much that the tapes took on a muffled, compressed quality that spoiled the sound of *Between the Buttons* for them in the end.

There was a big social scene going on in the studio during the sessions, reflected in jokey collage-style tracks like "Something Happened to Me Yesterday." Mick and Marianne would often disappear to a storeroom upstairs to smoke a joint and make love. There were lots of visitors, parties, serious smoke and speed. The scene at Olympic included characters like Jimi Hendrix; Spanish Tony Sanchez, a Soho hustler who scored dope for Keith; "Prince" Stash de Rola; Michael Cooper snapping away, bonding with Keith and Brian; UFO/paranormal researcher John Michell; Tara Browne in and out, floating in his sweet lysergic coma;

Robert Fraser, who had just been outrageously busted by the cops and fined for obscenity because his art gallery had exhibited a sculpture of a pink phallus by American pop artist Jim Dine.

As the sessions wound down, the tracks recorded in Los Angeles the previous summer got new vocals relating to Mick's passion for Marianne. Mick toned down the brutal lyrics to "Yesterday's Papers," whose early versions were bitter and harsh. On a misty December dawn, at the end of an all-night session, Gered Mankowitz took the Stones to Primrose Hill in North London for the new album's jacket photo. With his lens smeared with Vaseline, he shot the Stones bundled against the morning chill, an enervated dead-eyed Brian sunk deep in his muffler, his red eyes averted, a village idiot's grin on his gray face. It seemed to Mankowitz that Brian was deliberately screwing up the shoot.

———

When Jack Nitzsche returned to Los Angeles, Brian, Anita, and Keith went with him. Mick had planned to take Chrissie for a holiday in Jamaica. The Stones had done good work at Olympic, with a dozen strong tracks in the can and many interesting outtakes like "I Can See It," a tough rocker with piano and slide guitar; "Looking Tired," a C&W blues they'd written in Nashville; the great "Ride On Baby" (written in Ireland, the only one to be released); "If You Let Me"; and "Gold Painted Nails."

But things began to fall part. Tripping Tara Browne was killed in a car crash on December 17, shocking both Beatles and Stones deeply. Browne had been racing his Lotus down busy Redcliffe Gardens in Chelsea when he ran a red light and smashed into a van. His girlfriend, model Suki Potier, was unhurt, but Tara died instantly. "I heard the news today—oh boy," wrote John Lennon. Brian Jones was devastated at the loss of one of his closest friends. "It affected Brian *very* deeply," Anita said. "It made it seem like the whole thing was a lie."

After Tara was killed, Brian didn't want to return to London, and he and Anita and Keith spent Christmas 1966 in a Paris hotel suite. They were all tripping one night when Keith said to Brian, *"You'll* never make thirty, man."

Brian looked away and said, "I know."

———

Mick canceled the Jamaica holiday and went Christmas shopping at Harrods instead with Marianne. They had lunch together in Knightsbridge and talked things over.

Marianne: "If Mick hadn't been hanging around and courting me, I suppose I would have stayed with my husband. But Mick's life was too tempting, this very powerful man with lots of money, promising me the moon with my name on it. I fell for it." On December 19, Mick and Chrissie both issued statements to the press that they had broken their long unofficial engagement.

Bill Wyman also left his wife around this time and moved into a flat in London.

An era was ending, one that had begun for the Stones four years earlier in Richmond. The long-running *Rolling Stones Monthly* fan magazine folded. Their reign as a teen act was over, as was their role as high priests of R&B. The midnight hour had passed, and the new dawn would bring a much different world for the Rolling Stones, one that would spin way out of their control.

Just before Christmas, depressed by the horrible public humiliation of the forthcoming "Yesterday's Papers" (which asked, "Who needs yesterday's girl?"), Chrissie Shrimpton tried to kill herself with sleeping pills. Her recuperation bills were sent to Mick, who refused to pay them. Instead, he had her things moved out of Harley House. A few weeks later, Marianne Faithfull moved in with Mick. When he confided his anxieties to her, she smiled sweetly and said, "Don't worry."

Catch Your Dreams
Before They Slip Away

The sensational new Rolling Stones album, *Between the Buttons,* was released in January 1967, a Charlie Watts tour de force, a hard-hitting pastiche of rock styles and erotic fervor. "Let's Spend the Night Together" was a piano-driven oral-sex chant with crashing drums, Keith on bass, Nitzsche's droning organ, and a *Pet Sounds* harmonic bridge. "Yesterday's Papers" glowed in marimba hues and had Hendrix-influenced fuzz guitar; it was the last of the Stones' stupid-girl songs. "Ruby Tuesday" had Brian's owl-hooting flute and Jacobean cello vibe. The raucous "Connection" was Keith Richards's first lead vocal on a Stones record (its images of injections, customs searches, and paranoid longing prefigured the rest of his career). Keith played organ on "She Smiled Sweetly" in a muffled drum duet with Charlie, as Mick unreeled his first unabashed love song, echoing Dylan's "Just Like a Woman." Nicky Hopkins's piano and some hillbilly dulcimer competed for attention with a kazoo on "Cool Calm Collected," an arch music hall throwback that speeds up until it screws itself into the studio floor amid laughter as the needle skidded off the album's first side.

"All Sold Out" opened side two with a strange, nasty diatribe against "a girl so strangled" amid two weaving guitars and heavy drums. "My Obsession" was a dark foray into sexual appetites and pussy-eating, full of ominous drums and faraway piano. Bob Dylan's folk rock harmonica songs were evoked on "Who's Been Sleeping Here," an anguished, explicit complaint to Marianne ("just like Goldilocks") about her famous love life. The tempo picked up and the theme continued with "Complicated," another Marianne song: "she's very educated, and she doesn't give a damn." Round and round she goes, as "Miss Amanda Jones," the darling of the discotheque crowd, was unleashed in a capacitor burst of pop energy. The jokey acid trip of "Something Happened to Me Yesterday" (Brian on saxophone) was delivered as a comic mocking of squares, the cops, and even the trad jazz musicians in the song's fade. The British *Buttons* also contained the sentimental "Backstreet Girl," backed by a Parisian accordion line—Mick's favorite song on an album he didn't much like—and the Bo Diddley rave "Please Go Home."

The last Stones album to be released in two versions ("Ruby" and "Papers" were left off the U.K. disc), *Buttons* was the key transitional work between their early black R&B albums and the apocalyptic masterpieces that came later in the decade. The album title was an accident. Charlie Watts, who drew cartoons for the back of the jacket, asked Andrew what the record was called and was told the title was between the buttons, meaning it hadn't been decided. Charlie's droll six-panel cartoon was titled "Between the Buttons," and it became the album title as well. The cover shot disturbed Brian's fans, who could see their idol's glazed, shadowy eyes. It made him look, wrote critic David Dalton, "like a doomed albino raccoon."

The first single was controversial from the minute the song pluggers brought it to the radio stations. "Let's Spend the Night Together" was viewed as sexually explicit and thus taboo. In America, the disc jockeys flipped it over and played safer "Ruby Tuesday" instead, and the record eventually went to no. 1.

The band didn't really like *Between the Buttons*. "We recorded it in London on four-track machine," Mick later told an interviewer. "We bounced it back to do overdubs so many times we lost the sound of it. [The songs] sounded so great, but later on I was really disappointed with it."

The Stones bought some new clothes that month: colorful jackets, floral scarves, broad-brimmed hats, costume jewelry, reflecting the peacock revolution in men's fashion in 1967. They did a photo call in London's Green Park, Keith in his woolly white caveman vest, Brian in a flamboyant white hat that became his trademark that year. They all went to see the flaming Jimi Hendrix Experience in various London clubs.

On January 15, they played *The Ed Sullivan Show* in New York. Again the doorman didn't recognize them and wouldn't let them in the theater. There was a melee and Mick's hand was cut by scissors wielded by a girl trying to cut a lock of his hair. Keith punched the doorman hard when they got in. They played "Ruby Tuesday" and, after a big fight and self-loathing when they caved in, a censored version of their new single. Sullivan was adamant: "Either the Stones go, or I go." Rolling his eyes with sarcasm, Mick had to sing "Let's spend *some time* together" for Sullivan's immense national audience. The band clashed with Andrew Oldham over this, accusing him of giving in too easily to Sullivan's demands. Mick felt intense shame at being censored. "We should have walked off," he said later.

Back in London a few days later, Brian, Keith, and Anita went shopping in Chelsea, buying clothes at the boutique Granny Takes a Trip for the band's atypical gig on ITV's *Sunday Night at the London Palladium,* the big variety show. Mick had to deny press stories that the Stones were changing their rough image to pander to the show's family audience. There was another blazing row when the Stones refused to appear with the rest of the cast, waving the traditional good-bye, on a revolving stage at the end of the show while Jack Parnell and His Orchestra played "Startime." This was everything the Stones had been fighting for four years. The producer told the Stones they would be insulting not just him and the show but the British public as well. Mick told him to fuck off. Andrew sided with the TV producers, and the resulting shouting match and bad feelings—Andrew stormed out of the studio—diminished Andrew's involvement with the Stones. The Stones performed with Keith and Brian tripping on strong acid. The band snuck out a side door after miming to four songs, having managed to avoid the constipated censorship imposed in America, but they caught some negative publicity when they were conspicuously absent from the revolving stage. After this rupture with Andrew Oldham, Mick assumed the role as spokesman for the Stones and hired the veteran London press agent Leslie Perrin to handle the Stones' fractious relationship with the press.

———

Brian and Anita fought like tigers. She knocked him down with a punch in a crowded Chelsea nightclub. He'd steal her movie scripts and rip them up because he was jealous. Once, after Brian had beaten her up, Spanish Tony asked Anita what had happened and was told it was none of his fucking business. Sanchez arrived at Courtfield Road one day to find Brian freaking because he thought Anita was dead from an overdose of sleeping pills. They got her to the hospital, where her stomach was pumped. When she came to, Anita and Brian clutched each other and wept like babies.

Mick and Marianne were also drowning in each other. "They were like a couple of rabbits," Ian Stewart said. "I'd go over there and she'd be sitting up in bed, radiant and smiling, and he'd be completely wasted and wiped out. They would just fuck all the time."

In late January, Mick flew to Italy, where Marianne was appearing at the San Remo Song Festival. Marianne had rented a villa in the old fishing village of Positano, and the two lovers spent a week swanning around the Italian and French Riviera. At a nightclub, Marianne bought a bottle of French pep pills from the deejay and fatefully stashed it in the pocket of Mick's handsome green velvet jacket.

On Sunday, February 5, Mick and Marianne were in bed at Harley House, reading the Sunday papers. Suddenly he jumped up, waving the mud-slinging weekly the *News of the World*.

Mick Jagger has taken LSD at the Moody Blues' house in Roehampton.

It was the latest report in the paper's ongoing exposé "Pop Stars and Drugs."

Jagger told us: "I don't go out on it (LSD) now the cats (fans) have taken it up. It'll just get a dirty name. I remember the first time I took it. It was on tour with Bo Diddley and Little Richard."

During the time we were at the Blaises club in Kensington, Jagger took about six Benzedrine tablets. "I would just not keep awake in places like this if I didn't have them."

. . . Later at Blaises, Jagger showed a companion and two girls a small piece of hashish (marijuana) and invited them to his flat for "a smoke."

Marianne laughed. "It's *Brian,*" she said. "They've confused you with Brian. He still goes around telling one and all that he's the leader of the Rolling Stones."

Mick was livid. The *News of the World* was trying to kill the Stones the way the paper destroyed the lives of the wayward vicars and philandering politicians it usually pursued. But this was absurd. Cautious Mick told friends he'd never taken LSD and was unusually circumspect about doing drugs at all, unlike Brian and Keith, who were flying on acid a lot of the time. Mick prided himself on being discreet and in control of his private life.

Late that afternoon, he called his solicitor. That night, he appeared as scheduled on an ITV talk show hosted by Eamonn Andrews, who cautiously asked him about the drug story. Mick announced that the *News of the World* story was a complete lie and that he would take action to clear his name. Two days later, Mick's solicitor obtained a writ for libel against the paper.

It was a declaration of war, ill advised as it turned out. Robert Fraser called it "the Oscar Wilde mistake."

Jewels and Binoculars

Late January 1967. A weird and sinister campaign of harassment and surveillance targeted the Rolling Stones. If the *News of the World* could prove that Mick had used drugs before his day in court, the paper would avoid an embarrassing and expensive libel verdict. Mick noticed an unmarked van parked in the service road behind his flat at odd hours, and his phone sounded tapped. Someone was watching.

It was also more than just the drug thing. The Stones had been picking at the scab of postwar England for years now and were regarded with unease by the establishment they were mocking. The Stones were the dangerous, shadow side of the Beatles, who had the sense to hide their appetites in vague pop imagery. The Rolling Stones were agents of change, heralds of foreboding and dangerous times, and they were out of their heads. Scores of cops had been injured in riots at Stones shows, and some police officials felt they had a score to settle with these rich, arrogant punks. To them, the Stones were the sound of sedition. The sixties were heating up toward a frenzy of civil unrest, generational revolt, and a brutal war in Vietnam. "Street Fighting Man" was only a year away, and anyone with eyes could see him coming. The cops tried like hell to kill him before he arrived.

Marianne Faithfull went on a chat show on the BBC that month and stuck the dagger in deeper. Some, Mick included, wanted to blame her for what happened afterward.

"Marijuana's perfectly safe, you know," she said in her sweet, tuneful voice. "It's an old scene, man. And drugs really are the doors of perception. Something like LSD—it's as important as Christianity. *More* important . . . I'd like to see the whole structure of society collapse.

Wouldn't it be lovely? We're taking orders from a bunch of dead men. It's insane. I mean, how much longer can it go on?"

The press had a field day with Marianne preaching anarchy on the BBC. The satirical magazine *Private Eye* began to refer to her as Marijuana Faithfull.

Robert Fraser called Mick's libel suit "the Oscar Wilde mistake" because, a hundred years earlier, Wilde had sued after being called a sodomite in public. At the trial, it was established that Wilde *was* homosexual and he was sent to jail for it. Now Mick was suing because he had been called an acidhead in public and he spent the rest of that week organizing an acid trip for himself and his friends at Keith's house in the country. The Acid King was arriving from New York, and this was going to be Mick's first proper trip, and his first with Marianne. His phone was clicking like a telegraph. Marianne answered one day and a young West Indian voice warned her the line was tapped (this turned out to be a phone engineer who was a Stones fan). The warning was ignored.

Brian and Anita were in Munich, and Keith had tagged along. Work started without them on the Stones' new single at Olympic, just Mick and Charlie playing on a demo called "She Comes in Colors," with Nicky Hopkins on piano. Keith returned the next day and joined Mick and Marianne at Abbey Road Studios, where the Beatles' session for "A Day in the Life," the climactic song (about Tara Browne's death) on their new album, was being filmed in a party atmosphere of champagne and hash joints. Mick knew the Beatles were preparing a psychedelic masterpiece, and he was concerned how the Stones would look if they followed the Beatles with an acid-drenched record of their own a few months later.

At the session, Mick invited George and Patti Harrison to the weekend house party at Redlands.

The *News of the World* claimed to have received a telephone tip, supposedly from an employee of Keith's, that the Rolling Stones were taking illegal drugs at a weekend house party in West Wittering, Sussex. The managing editor called Scotland Yard and informed the police of the allegations against these common little shits in the band who had snubbed all England.

There had been a lot of tripping at Redlands over the past few months, with Keith and Brian larking and looning around the village and countryside, high as the clouds, laughing and ostentatiously freaking out. A few weeks earlier, Mick left Keith's house after one of these acid festivals, muttering his feelings of foreboding to Donald Cammell. "This is getting out of hand," Mick told him. "I dunno where it's gonna end."

By midnight, all the guests had arrived. There were Mick and Marianne, Keith, the Harrisons, Robert Fraser and his Moroccan servant Mohammed, who did the cooking, Christopher Gibbs, Michael Cooper, a Kings Road hippie named Nicky Kramer (a fringe member of Keith's entourage), and the American acid dealer David Schneiderman. A fire was going in the great Tudor hearth, the guitars came out, joints were passed. In connection with his own recent obscenity bust, Fraser talked about his friend Stephen Ward, the society osteopath who had killed himself after being framed for pimping in the Profumo Scandal. "I saw what they did to Stephen," he said darkly. "They can do anyone they want." Then they all went to bed and slept until noon, when the Acid King started making his rounds.

David Schneiderman, as he called himself, had an act: LSD was a sacrament, and he was the priest. Marianne: "He was very West Coast, opinionated, pompous. Getting high came with a little moral. He was, 'This is the Tao of lysergic diethylamide, man. Let it *speak* to you.' It was all a bit too reverent for our taste, but Robert told us he was the Acid King, and he did have the goods."

Late Sunday morning, the Acid King appeared in each of the five bedrooms, bearing a pot of tea and doses of Orange Sunshine. It was a beautiful winter day, and after breakfast most of the guests piled into the cars and embarked on a mystery tour of the countryside while the acid wormed its way into their brains. Michael Cooper's photographs show the flared trousers, white loafers, bug-eye mirrored shades, floppy hats, and bushy Afghan jackets so in vogue that year. After visiting the cold pebbled beach along the Sussex coast, they tried to find the famous purple country house of the aesthete and surrealist patron Edward James, whose furnishings included several red sofas, designed by Salvador Dalí, shaped like the lips of sex queen Mae West. But the house, in West Dean north of Chichester, remained elusive, and the party returned to Redlands late in the afternoon.

Keith and Mick both wanted to rest, and Mick enjoyed his quiet acid trip. "He was great to be around," Marianne wrote. "Very calm and cool, without his usual nervous energy." As night came on, they all gathered around the fireplace in the long lounge with its fur carpets and Moroccan cushions. Mohammed served a delicious couscous, and after eating, George and Patti Harrison left for their own house in Surrey.

Marianne went upstairs to have a hot bath.

Outside, in their hidden positions around Redlands, the waiting force of cops watched George drive off. To this day, Keith thinks nothing would have happened with a Beatle in the house. "They were out there all day, waiting for George to leave. From then on, we were fair game."

The most famous drug bust of the sixties began shortly after Marianne returned from her bath, wrapped in a furry bedspread because she hadn't brought a change of clothes down to the country. The eight men were relaxing, passing a joint to take the edge of the day's tripping. Christopher Gibbs was resplendent in a silk costume; the scent of Moroccan cooking wafted in from the kitchen, and *Blonde on Blonde* was on the stereo.

Someone mentioned there was a face peering in through one of the leaded windows. Probably some fucking fan. Then a furious pounding on the heavy oak door. Reluctantly Keith got up to answer it, and into the room stepped Chief Inspector Gordon Dinely at the head of nineteen cops from the West Sussex constabulary.

"Mr. Keith Richard, pursuant to the Dangerous Drugs Act of 1964, we have a warrant to search these premises." Just then, Dylan let go at top volume:

"The ghost of electricity hooooowls in the bones of her face . . ."

Squads of cops poured into the room from every entrance as "Visions of Johanna" blared on. The TV flickered with the sound off. The police ogled their pale, costumed victims, sitting amid candlelight and incense like a painting by Burne-Jones. Then they began to search. They were polite to everyone except Mohammed, and they began to hassle Gibbs as another distastefully dressed foreigner until he informed them, in his plummy Old Etonian voice, that he was wearing the national dress of Pakistan.

Keith was on the phone to his solicitor in London. Marianne looked at Mick. *Poor bugger,* she thought. *His first trip, a lovely day, and now this.* When a fumbling cop proposed to search her, she purposefully let slip the fur throw, exposing her ample breasts for a moment, two of the most glorious big tits in Albion, giving the scene the immortality it deserved. As the chief inspector was formally asking if Keith was the owner of the premises, Dylan let go again:

"Jewels and binoculars haaang from the head of the mule, but these visions . . . of Johanna . . . make it all seem so cruuuuuel!"

Keith turned on his strobe light. Mick and Robert started to laugh at the lurid absurdity of the scene. A cop turned the record player down. Keith turned it back up again, louder, and asked the cops to keep their muddy boots off the Moroccan cushions that covered the floor. The cops were going through the kitchen, confiscating mustard packets Keith had brought back from American drive-ins. Some female cops asked Marianne to come upstairs to be searched in private. "Darling," she called to Mick, "this old dyke wants to search me!" They took her upstairs while the men lined up to be searched. They found twenty-four pills in Robert Fraser's pocket. He told them they were insulin tablets, but they were government-issue heroin tablets Spanish Tony had scored for him, good for six months in jail. Mick was searched and nothing was found. Same with Keith and the others. Schneiderman had a small tin of hash and a plastic bag of grass, which were duly impounded. One of the cops reached for the Acid King's LSD-filled briefcase. "Please don't open that case," Schneiderman begged, explaining it contained valuable exposed film that would be ruined. The chief inspector nodded his assent, and the case was never opened.

One of the policewomen came downstairs with the green velvet jacket Mick had been wearing for about a month. The jacket pocket still contained a glass vial with the speed pills Marianne had bought a few weeks earlier. Mick told the cops what they were and, gallantly, said they were his. He lied and said he'd got them from his doctor. Good for a year in prison, pep pills having been outlawed after the 1965 mod/rocker riots.

After an hour, Chief Inspector Dinely announced the search was over. He warned Keith that he would be liable for prosecution if they had been using drugs. "Yes, I see," Keith said, dripping with sarcasm. "They pin it all on me." Schneiderman asked if they were being arrested. Not necessarily, he was told. That'll come later. As the police filed out the door with their booty, Keith went over and dropped the needle onto "Rainy Day Women #12 & 35":

"But I would not feel so all alone, everybody must get stoned!"

————

As the police convoy drove back down Redlands' lane to the Chichester Road, they carried away some old pipes, an ashtray, all the incense, the pills they'd seized, and any chance that Mick could win a libel judgment against the *News of the World.* Christopher Gibbs recalls that the atmosphere was relaxed and philosophical after the police left. A bit of grass and some uppers; what could happen? (Fraser didn't mention the heroin.) No one could believe their good luck that the massive acid stash hadn't been discovered.

The phone rang a few minutes later. Brian was calling from London to say he and Anita would be down to Redlands in a couple of hours.

"Don't bother, man," Keith told him. "We've all just been busted. Yeah, you heard it right. Busted!"

Blue Lena

News of the raid on Redlands was a major bummer and scared a lot of people. It was the end of Swinging London, as the smart set retreated into their houses to have their fun in private. The cops put out a scurrilous lie that they'd found Mick lapping a Mars bar protruding from Marianne's bum. The *News of the World* got an exclusive story on the raid, published the following Sunday. Chaos and paranoia in the Stones camp. All work on their next album stopped.

As press scrutiny tightened, bribing the police—standard procedure in these affairs—became more difficult. Mick, Keith, and Fraser raised seven thousand pounds and gave it to Tony Sanchez, who claimed he gave it to a police contact to make the evidence disappear, but nothing ever happened. "David Schneiderman" disappeared immediately after the raid. It could only be determined that someone resembling the American left the country within days. Keith's minders fingered Nicky Kramer as the traitor and had him beaten up, but Kramer denied everything. Many (including Keith) thought the East End villain who did the beating, David Litvinoff, who sometimes drove for Keith, was a more likely suspect.

When the lab reports came back, Mick was charged with possession of speed, Fraser with heroin, Keith with allowing his house to be used for drug taking. Court dates were set for June. Their well-connected lawyer, Michael Haver, a future attorney general, told them that it looked to him like someone was out to get them. Convictions on these charges could mean prison time, the cancellation of their record contract, and the end of the Rolling Stones.

Advised to stop making provocative gestures and disappear for a while, the band had a few weeks off before a Euro tour in late March. They decided to go to Morocco, a place where even pop stars could vanish. Mick flew to Tangier. Keith, Brian, and Anita would drive down. In Tangier, Robert Fraser arranged to meet up with Brion Gysin, who could take them up to his village of musicians in the mountains. From there to Marrakech at the edge of the Sahara. They wouldn't be bothered there.

––––––––

The voyage of the Blue Lena began in Paris. Tom Keylock had ferried the car over, meeting Keith, Brian, and Anita at the George V. Along for the ride was the beautiful Deborah Dixon, who lived with

Donald Cammell. It was a cozy foursome that headed southwest to Aquitaine, Spain and Morocco beyond. Little did Deborah Dixon know that she'd stepped into a complex web of conflicting loyalties, sexual tension, and intrigue that would lead to the dissolution of the original Stones.

The Blue Lena was furnished with fur rugs, pop art cushions, and outrageous Swedish sex magazines. The car's cassette player blasted soul music, a live Hendrix tape, the new Beatles single "Penny Lane." Brian's birthday was coming up and he was in a good mood, relieved it wasn't him that got busted. He was drinking brandy, smoking heavily, crumbling chunks of hash into joints and sucking them down, outwardly oblivious to the smoldering looks between his best mate and his girlfriend.

After they'd been on the road for a day, Brian turned blue, unable to breathe. At the hospital in Toulouse, he was told he had blood in his lungs and would have to stay a few days. Gallant Brian told the others to carry on to Tangier, and he would meet them there. When they checked into a hotel for the night, Keith told Keylock to book only three rooms. He and Anita spent the night together. The next day, Deborah Dixon flew back to Paris. On Brian's twenty-fifth birthday, they left him in Toulouse and drove to Spain. Tom Keylock could barely keep his eyes on the road because Anita and Keith were making love in the back.

Keith: "A lot can go on in the backseat of a Bentley. What can anyone say? Shit happens, man."

They spent a couple days relaxing in Marbella, on the Costa del Sol. They got hauled down to the *comisaría* by the tough Spanish cops when Keith's credit card was rejected at an expensive restaurant. Finally Brian's frantic telegrams found them. Anita was ordered to return to Toulouse to help him get back to London. Glumly they drove to the airport and put Anita on a plane. Back on the road to Tangier, Keylock asked Keith what the hell was going on. "She'll be back" was all Keith would say.

The dusty Blue Lena pulled up to the luxurious Hotel El Minzah in Tangier on March 5, 1967. Mick, Michael Cooper, Robert Fraser, and Brion Gysin were sunning at the oasis-like swimming pool, and Keith went to join them. Keylock went across the street and scored a big block of fresh hash from their friend Achmed the rug dealer.

A few days later, Brian, Anita, and Marianne flew down from London via Madrid and Gibraltar, where they visited the colony of rare apes that inhabit the Rock. Tripping Brian played the monkeys one of his tapes, and the apes went completely berserk, shrieking in displeasure, running away. Brian began to cry, devastated that the Gibraltar apes hated his music.

Marianne: "Anita was watching Brian with an aghast expression on her face, and I knew right then and there that this was going to be a fatal week, because all that day Anita had been asking about Keith, how I felt about him, comparing him to Brian."

Square of the Dead

Brion Gysin, then in his early fifties, was the hippest man in the world and an old Morocco hand. He was an artist whose work was so avant-garde he'd been expelled from the surrealist movement in Paris by André Breton thirty years earlier. As a writer he had devised the experimental "cutup" method, which his friend William Burroughs adapted for his artfully scrambled narrative technique. Through a Moroccan friend, in 1952 Gysin had discovered the Master Musicians of Jajouka, an old tribe of the hills south of Tangier. The Jajouka musicians played therapeutic trance music and preserved Arcadian rituals that Gysin thought dated to deepest antiquity. Gysin occasionally took selected friends like Bill Burroughs and Paul Bowles up into the hills to hear this music. The previous year, he'd taken Timothy Leary. Now Robert Fraser wanted Gysin to take the Rolling Stones.

Brion Gysin: "Fraser the Razor, the man who invented Swinging London, brought them to my pad overlooking Tangier Bay. It was Mick and saturnine Keith with his eye on miniskirted Anita Pallenberg, and Brian Jones with a fringe of pink hair over his beady red rabbit eyes. Plus Fraser and Tom, their egregious chauffeur. Is this the whole group? I ask, and they all snicker. 'No, there's Charlie Wattsisname and the other one and their wives,' Fraser says. On cue the rest mockingly echo: 'The wives! The wives!' Michael Cooper is taking pictures of the Stones curled on my bed like writhing iguanas. Paul Bowles stops by to meet the Stones, takes one look at these costumed freaks, and immediately splits in a state of shock. At the end of the evening, I took Fraser aside and told him *no way* was I taking this circus up the mountain to hear my music, because once the youth of the tribe got a load of these cats and their women, it would be all over up there. They'd already thrown Tim Leary out of the village for giving acid to some of the boys.

"So we went to Marrakech a few days later, where there was a lot more music on hand and the desert climate was more to their liking."

They checked into the Hotel Marrakech in a palm oasis under the city's red walls. On a clear day, they could see the snowcapped peaks of the Atlas Mountains.

––––––

The loud voice echoing down the hallway belonged to Brian Jones. He was screaming at Anita because he knew something had happened between her and Keith, and so she told him all about it, rubbed his nose in it. So he beat her up with a new ferocity that really frightened her.

Outside, around the pool, Cecil Beaton, doyen of British celebrity photographers, had hooked up with the Stones and was taking snapshots of a shirtless Keith lounging in his new "antique" coral necklaces and Tuareg wedding baubles. Anita emerged from the hotel with fresh bruises on her face. She sat in a rocking chair and watched her new lover being photographed.

Cecil Beaton (from his diary): "They were a strange group, the three Stones: Brian Jones and his girlfriend Anita Pallenberg—dirty white face, dirty blackened eyes, dirty canary drops of yellow hair, barbaric jewelry— Keith R. in 18th century suit, long black velvet coat and tightest pants, and of course, Mick Jagger . . . He asked, 'Have you ever taken LSD? Oh, you *should.* It would mean so much to you: you'd never forget the colors.

For a painter it's a great experience' . . . He is sexy, but completely sexless. He could nearly be a eunuch. As a model, he is a natural . . . Their wardrobe is extensive. Mick showed me rows of brocade coats. Everything is shoddy, poorly made, the seams bursting. Keith himself had sewn his trousers, lavender and dull rose, with a band of badly stitched leather dividing the two colors . . . None of them is willing to talk, except in spasms. No one could make up their minds what to do, or when."

Brion Gysin: "We take over the top floor of this hotel for a playpen hanging over the swimming pool. That night, Brian and I dropped some acid. Anita took some sleepers and went off to bed. Keith plugs in his guitar and sends throbbing sounds after her into the moonlight. Robert puts on an old Elmore James record and gets Mick doing little magic dances for him. For the first time, I understand that Mick really is Magic! Tom the chauffeur comes in and whispers in Brian's ear. They want me to find some Berber girls for Brian, but I tell them I can't make that scene. Room service arrives with huge trays of food; the food goes over the balcony and the trays are used to toboggan around the floor."

Tom Keylock ran into Brian late that night in the lobby of the hotel. "He was completely off his crust, staggering through the lobby, sandwiched between these two dodgy-looking Berber whores, the ones that have peculiar blue tattoos all over them. They were holding Brian up and heading toward Anita's room. I followed them up the stairs, trying to point out the error of his plan, but he wasn't having any of it. All hell broke loose when they reached the room. Brian had the idea that he was going to get Anita to perform with these two birds. Anita naturally declined the offer and Brian smashed the room to bits. Anita grabbed her clothes and legged it to Keith's room, leaving Brian with these women amongst the wreckage. It was very symbolic. Looking at Brian, I thought, 'That's yer lot, mate. You've really blown it this time.' That moment was the beginning of the end for him and you know what? I think he knew it too."

Anita: "When Keith saw what Brian had done to me, he tried to console me. 'I can't watch Brian do this shit to you any more. I'm going to take you back to London.'

" 'What about Brian?' I asked. 'He won't let me leave—he'll kill me first.' "

Keith told her not to worry, he would sort it out and they'd make their escape. Tom Keylock made up a story about a planeload of British reporters landing in Marrakech to bother them, which got Brian properly paranoid. Then Keylock got Gysin to disappear Brian for a few hours, to get him out of the way. No sooner had they gone than Keith and Anita were throwing her bags in the car, lots of luggage filled with feather boas. Keylock asked what would happen when Brian returned. "Fuck 'im," said Keith. "We're leaving the bastard here, and you're driving."

Brion Gysin: "Around the hotel swimming pool, I saw something I can only call mythological. Mick is screaming about his hotel bill, getting ready for takeoff. The cynics among us are snickering because it looks like love at first sight. At the deep end, Anita is swinging in a canvas seat. Keith is in the pool, dunking up and down in the water, looming up at her. When I go to pass between them, I see that I can't. I can't make it. There's something there, a barrier. I can see it. What I see looks like a glass rod, a twisted glass rod, revolving rapidly. Between Keith's eyes and Anita's eyes, it shoots back and forth at the speed of light. Tristan and Isolde stuff, as red as a laser beam. I don't like the looks of this one bit, so I check out of the hotel immediately and move in with a friend who has a house in the medina, the old Arab quarter.

"Somehow the sinister chauffeur finds me the next day, tells me the press is looking for them and they need to hide Brian so he won't say anything stupid. He says, 'Brian thinks the world of you, y'know. You both have the same tape recorder, your Uhers. Why don't you take him to that place you were talking about so he can tape some music? Bring him back at five or six, there's a good chap.'

"So I took Brian Jones over to the Jma al-Fna, the Square of the Dead, the central plaza of Marrakech. Under the winter sun at three in the afternoon, the Jma al-Fna was full of snake charmers, acrobats, medicine men, storytellers, and musicians. We stopped at a flying carpet full of Mejdoubi—holy fools banging away on drums and smoking *kif* from an outrageous pipe strung with evil amulets, rotten teeth, old trinkets, carcasses of small animals. The Mejdoubi dig Brian for what he is and pass him this pipe, his eyes glistening with pure greed. One hit, and he almost coughs out a lung! Brian wants this pipe badly, but it's bad medicine and I refuse to translate for him.

"I drag him to my friend's house. Brian was sulking, furious. He wants that fucking pipe, told me he'd be willing to pay a fortune for it. On the way back, the Mejdoubi sell it to him for some astronomical price. (Returning through customs at Heathrow, he loses it, since it reeks of dope.)

"That ain't all he loses, as he discovered when he got back to the hotel. Half an hour later, he's on the phone to me, sobbing: 'Come quickly, can you please? They've all gone and left me—cleared out! I don't know where the fucking hell they've gone; there's no message and the hotel won't tell me anything. I'm here all alone, man. Can't you come at once?'

"I go over there. Get him into bed. Call a doctor to give him a shot and stick around long enough to see it take hold on him. I don't want him jumping down those ten stories into the swimming pool . . . And now, looking back into that time pool, I see how I got set up to help the Stones lose Brian. And I see another ghostly swimming pool somewhere in the future.

"Those whom the gods love, die young."

Jumpin' Ja

five:

Che Guevara with a Band

"Jumpin' Jack Flash" single sleeve, 1968.

sh The Rolling Stones   882 156-7   LONDON

Five strings, three notes, two fingers, and an asshole,

and you've got it! You can play the darned thing. That's all

it takes. What you do with it is another thing.

Keith Richards

The Psychic Debris Field

March 1967. The Blue Lena made its return voyage north, flee-
ing the wreckage left behind in Marrakech. Across the Strait of Gibraltar,
up through Andalusia, Catalonia, Languedoc, across France and the
English Channel, suffering through a massive British customs search, escaping arrest only because Tom Keylock hid the hashish under the gas
cap. Anita Pallenberg's brutal ordeal with Brian Jones was almost over.
And yet she was filled with regret, didn't really want to leave him,
wouldn't have left if she wasn't afraid for her safety. As Marianne Faithfull
later wrote, Keith would never have gotten Anita if Brian hadn't been
such an asshole.

Thirty years later, recalling feelings from those somber days, there's
still sorrow in her voice as Anita says simply of Brian Jones, "He was, I
think, the *passion* of my life. There's a difference between love and passion. Brian had that passion, and I think I was passionately in love with
him."

"Brian really was an easy victim," Keith told Stanley Booth. "He
needed to be in a fucking hospital. But we were all working too hard to
expect it [intervention] from the guys you're working with. Then I get
myself right out of the picture. I make friends again with Brian and then
steal his old lady. So I really screwed up."

When they got to London, Keith cleaned out the Courtfield Road
apartment, taking half the records and half the dope. Anita never went
back there again. The fugitive couple settled in Redlands.

Brian flew from Marrakech to Casablanca, and then on to Paris,
where he threw himself on the mercy of Donald Cammell, who was

shocked to find the disoriented Stone on his doorstep, with no luggage, looking like a tramp and smelling of brandy. "They left me," Brian told Cammell. "They fucked off and left me." Brian was a wreck, a psychic debris field. Cammell helped him get back to London, where Brian found Anita's clothes gone from their flat.

Keith: "Later in London, Brian caught up with us. Anita says, 'No, you're just too much of an asshole to live with. Keith and I got something going' . . . That was the final nail in the coffin for me and Brian. He never forgave me for that. I don't blame him."

———

The Rolling Stones had a European tour coming up, one they couldn't cancel because the whole band was desperate for cash, especially Mick and Keith, facing astronomical legal fees. On the day that Mick, Marianne, and Christopher Gibbs arrived in London, the *Daily Mirror* published details of their drug bust, naming names and revealing that the two Stones could expect drug charges to be filed against them. It would cost a fortune to get out of this one—if they even could.

There was a question whether Brian would do the tour. He told friends he might have to quit, had forgotten how to play guitar, that he was fed up. There was also serious talk of firing him, since no one wanted to see him, much less go on the road and play music. But Mick vetoed this, according to Bill Wyman, because he thought it would do too much damage to the Stones' image, since Brian was still a crucial visual part of the band. In the end, Brian said, Anita persuaded him to do the "Polish tour" by telling him they'd get back together if things went okay. Brian took some guitar lessons to prepare for the tour.

On March 24, 1967, the Rolling Stones flew to Malmö, Sweden (body searches at customs), to begin a twenty-eight-show European tour that ran through early April. It was the usual: smoke bombs, baton charges, police dogs, riots inside the halls and out. The youth of Western Europe was getting ready for 1968, with the Stones beating the jungle drums of unrest and revolt. Ironically the Stones were playing well, even though the rest of the band wasn't speaking to Brian and he wasn't speaking to them. They didn't even look at each other.

During the German leg of the tour, Keith had a torrid affair with a pretty model, but Anita finished filming *Mord und Totschlag* and joined the tour in Paris on April 3. They moved on to Italy, where Jane Fonda, about to star in her husband Roger Vadim's seriocomic sci-fi film *Barbarella*, came to the Stones' Rome show, invited by Anita, who wanted a part in the movie. Their friend Stash de Rola's father, the painter Balthus, was director of the French Academy in Rome. With Stash, the Stones spent time smoking hash at the palatial Villa Medici, the academy's High Renaissance headquarters.

Every time they crossed a border the Stones were subjected to hostile, provocative drug searches and humiliating immigration delays as nervous officials harassed them. As the Stones were leaving Paris on April 12, there was a stupid hassle about their passports at Le Bourget airport. Keith dissed the inspector, and the enraged *fonctionnaire* punched him, then Mick. He kept at it until Tom Keylock stepped in.

———————

The first Rolling Stones show behind the rock-starved Iron Curtain took place in Warsaw, Poland, on April 13 in a 2,500-seat hall in the Palace of Culture. The best seats had been scalped to the children of the *nomenklatura*.

Keith: "All very uptight. There's army at the airport. Get to the hotel, which is very jaillike. We get there to do our gig. *'Honski de boyski boisk! Zee Rollingstonzki!!!'*

"And who's got the best seats down front? The sons and daughters of the hierarchy of the Communist Party. They're sitting down there in their diamonds and pearls, with their fingers in their ears."

Three songs into the set, as the dulcet strains of a bored version of "Lady Jane" die away, Keith turned around to face the drums. "Stop fucking playing, Charlie!" He walked to the front of the stage and started to yell at the first five rows. "You fucking lot, you can fucking get out and let the bastards in the back down front!" Keith just stood there until the first four rows emptied out, and then the show went on. The audience kept chanting "I-can't-get-no!" Outside, the army turned water cannon, dogs, and tear gas on ten thousand kids who couldn't get in. It was clear to Keith Richards at that moment that the days of the Iron Curtain were numbered.

The tour ended in Athens on April 17. This was the Rolling Stones' last series of shows for more than two years. Mick told *Melody Maker* the Rolling Stones were down on touring and would probably never tour in America again. This was also Brian Jones's last tour with the band he had started five years earlier. Bill Wyman and his stunning new girlfriend, Astrid Lindstrom, stayed in Greece for a vacation. The rest flew back to England without Keith, who went to Rome for Anita's audition for *Barbarella*. Screenwriter Terry Southern insisted she would be perfect as the lesbian Black Queen. Anita got the part.

Flower Power

May 1967. On the cusp of the Summer of Love, the Rolling Stones were looking at jail time.

Not Brian, though, to his amazement. He kept telling people he'd been warned he was next. The cops were out to get him. He told Linda Keith, who'd hooked up with Brian after Anita left him. He told Tina and Nicky, the lesbian girlfriends who lived with him for a while. He told Anita, whom he saw in Cannes when *Mord und Totschlag* made its debut (with his music) at the film festival. He and Anita got on okay until he beat her up in his hotel room after the screening, and she fled back to Keith.

On May 10, Mick, Keith, and Robert Fraser had breakfast with their lawyers, Allen Klein, and Les Perrin at Redlands, then drove to Chichester courthouse. Several hundred people waited outside, not all of them fans. Charged with drug offenses, they opted for a trial by jury and were bailed at 100 pounds apiece. The trial date was June 22, 1967.

While this was going on, the notorious Scotland Yard detective Norman Pilcher ("Semolina pilchards" in John Lennon's bitter "I Am the Walrus") and his drug squad busted Brian and Stash de Rola for a piece of hash and a little cocaine at Courtfield Road. The cops also took a lot of Brian's stuff, beginning a series of corrupt shakedowns when the drug squad realized they had an easy mark. The newspapers headlined Brian's arrest the next day. Shaken and upset, he sent his parents a telegram that night: "Don't jump to hasty conclusions and don't judge me too harshly. All my love, Brian."

Brian's lawyers told him to stay away from the other Stones while his drug case was pending, and his social separation from Mick and Keith became somewhat official.

The Stones were making a new record that month, a droning Moroccan anthem of defiance called "We Love You." The first session at Olympic didn't start well. Mick, Keith, and Brian arrived at two-thirty, but Charlie Watts didn't show. They hadn't seen him since their court dates and knew he wasn't happy about Brian getting busted. They waited and waited. Charlie finally came down the stairs and glared at his bandmates. Slowly a big grin spread across his face and he said, "So how are our jailbirds, then?"

"We Love You" was a message from the band to its fans, expressing appreciation for support in the wake of the drug busts. It was a psychedelic collage of jail sounds, Nicky Hopkins's piano riff, tape-delayed vocal effects (featuring John Lennon and Paul McCartney on high harmonies), angry drums, and Brian Jones's extraordinary coda on his favorite new instrument, the Mellotron. This icon of "progressive rock" was a tape-driven English keyboard that looked like a small Hammond organ and was actually an early sampling device. Thirty-five keys activated tape-recorded notes; the Mellotron was supplied with sets of tapes for brass, strings, flutes, a choir, and a cheesy-sounding orchestra. The Beatles had famously used it for the beginning of "Strawberry Fields Forever" a few months earlier. It was cutting-edge electronics at the time, and a very hard ax to play.

"*You* try playing a Mellotron," says engineer George Chkiantz, who worked on "We Love You" at Olympic. "Just *try*. There's a horrible time lag, depending on how many notes you push down, and most people, even great musicians, screwed it up. A terrible instrument—dreadful, very hard to play, impossible to maintain tempo—unless you were Brian Jones. *Nobody* else could have gotten anything like that."

Allen Ginsberg was in London for a pro-marijuana rally in Hyde Park. He met Mick at Paul McCartney's house, and Mick invited the Beat poet to that night's session with Paul and John Lennon to record backing vocals for "We Love You." Ginsberg, waving his Shiva beads and a Tibetan oracle ring, conducted the singers from the other side of the studio glass to the tempo of the stuttering Mellotron track. "They looked like little angels," he wrote later of the Stones and the Beatles, "like Botticelli Graces singing together for the first time."

There *was* something epic about Brian's panoramic Mellotron fanfare at the end of "We Love You." In forty-two seconds of powerful energy music, it took in the whole sweep of the turbulent year, the travel across continents and oceans, the sheltering sky over the desert in southern Morocco. As brilliant as anything else in the Stones' career, the solo was perhaps Brian's last great contribution to his band, recorded in the last days in which he was physically and mentally able to make a contribution.

After that, Brian Jones was mostly a debauched vision on chemicals, drink, and pills. Ostracized by his band, he attracted a new sleazy entourage of pop-world leeches. An American turned him on to Quaaludes, a hypnotic downer sold as Mandrax in Europe. He took up with Suki Potier, who'd been with Tara Browne when he was killed. Brian and Suki—an Anita look-alike—shared their grief over Tara for the next eighteen months. On June 2, Brian and Stash, immaculately coiffed and dandified in tailored suits, answered drug charges at West London Magistrates Court. Shown a vial of cocaine, Brian blurted, "No, man—I'm not a junkie.

That's not mine at all." Brian and Stash were bailed at 250 pounds apiece, and trial was set for later that summer.

———

During all these busts and trials, Andrew Oldham made himself scarce. There was a harsh climate of contempt in Soho and London showbiz circles for the Stones' legal troubles, which some thought the band had provoked by their behavior. In America, Phil Spector openly ridiculed the Stones for getting themselves busted, and advised Andrew to lay low. There was a rumor that Andrew had had some kind of nervous breakdown anyway.

"That was the death knell for me," Oldham has said. "The band thought I should have been standing next to them in court and I wasn't. Basically, I lost my bottle. As far as the police were concerned, I was a notorious figure and they wanted to bust me the same way they busted the Stones and [later] the Beatles. [Unlike Mick Jagger] I would have been classified as a drug-dealing businessman and been stitched up like a kipper. So I kept a low profile for a lot of that period, staying in California when I knew my number was up."

———

June 1967. The Beatles' revolutionary *Sgt. Pepper's Lonely Hearts Club Band* was the main pop artifact in Western youth culture. It was a "concept album," a new thing in rock and roll, a show in itself: the Beatles playing a band giving a concert. The album was the climax of a four-way transatlantic pop olympiad between the Beatles and Stones on one side and Bob Dylan and Brian Wilson on the other. *Blonde on Blonde* and the Beach Boys' *Pet Sounds* had set a new standard in 1966. In 1967, the Beatles answered them with *Sgt. Pepper,* a kaleidoscopic whirligig of music hall pastiche, emotional ballads, and an apocalyptic evocation of the death of Tara Browne. *Pepper*'s phantasmagoric album cover was designed by Peter Blake and shot by Michael Cooper. It was a tough act to follow.

But the Stones themselves, crippled by drug busts, were faltering.

Their new album, inevitably seen as their response to *Sgt. Pepper,* was made, as Mick said, "under the influence of bail." The staff at Olympic now watched in horror as the Stones settled into a more relaxed method of recording. Since the *Aftermath* sessions, the Stones had been notoriously slow in building tracks into songs. Now hours and whole days would be wasted in waiting for someone to show up. It looked like the Stones would respond to the Beatles' bright, cohesive variety show with a sullen, contrived record by an almost broken-up group.

In America, London Records needed product for the beach that summer. They released an album titled *Flowers* in June 1967, another grab bag of tracks the Stones had lying around. The Flower Power–era album jacket was unpromising, a crude rendition of the Stones as the heads on weedy-looking stems. Side one featured the album debuts of "Have You Seen Your Mother?" and "Out of Time," plus tracks from Decca's *Buttons* and a great version of Smokey Robinson's "My Girl," cut at RCA back in 1965. Side two was assembled as an emotional, regret-filled series of songs left over from recent U.K. albums. "Backstreet Girl" and "Please Go Home" had been left off the American version of *Buttons.* The great "Take It or Leave It" had been left off the U.S. *Aftermath.* Marimbas, harpsichord, drums, and the Mellotron flavored "Ride On Baby," and "Sitting on a Fence" had some fine guitar picking and harsh lyrics dating from Mick's breakup with his old girlfriend. Individually they were all good songs. Packaged together, they were sort of a downer.

Keith: *"Flowers* was put together in America by Andrew Oldham because they were begging for product. All that stuff had been cut a year before and rejected by us for not making it. I was really surprised when people dug it, surprised when it even came out!"

Flowers played against the grain of the Summer of Love that year. Its dark themes, impassioned singing, and lovelorn music implied that the halcyon excitement of that summer was but a veneer, and underneath lurked the same old doubts and fears. Many fans loved it anyway. "The *Flowers* album was for loners and lovers only," Patti Smith wrote. "It provided a tight backdrop to a lot of decadent fantasy."

Iridescent Ghost

Spring 1967. Marianne Faithfull had been playing the role of Irina, the youngest of Anton Chekhov's three sisters, opposite Glenda Jackson at the Royal Court Theater in Sloane Square since April. She'd gotten good reviews, though she once collapsed onstage while tripping. Mick came every night, at least for the last act. Then he'd go on to the studio, where the Stones continued to work on their album. "She Comes in Colors" was moving along, and Brian Jones kept experimenting with the Mellotron's eerie artificial sounds. He was often so pilled-up and befuddled they had to prop him up with pillows while he played. Mick bought an early Moog synthesizer, but didn't know how to play it. Bill Wyman had a track called "Acid in the Grass," which Mick refused to sing on. "It's your fucking track," he haughtily told Bill. *"You* fucking sing on it." This became Bill's trippy "In Another Land" as the sessions went on. Keith's "Sometimes Happy, Sometimes Blue" demo mutated into "Dandelion."

―――――

On June 13, Brian Jones and Jimi Hendrix flew to San Francisco, then by smaller plane to Monterey, where the Monterey International Pop Festival was held the following weekend. Brian didn't play a note at Monterey, but he was a smash anyway. Dressed variously in exquisite Chinese silk robes and a lustrous golden coat, dripping with Berber jewels and a crystal swastika, blasted out of his mind on STP (a newly formulated psychedelic speedball that lasted about three days), Brian floated around the festival's backstage area with luminescent blond Nico on his arm, the two looking exactly alike. With the aura of an imperious acid czar, Brian was, David Dalton wrote, "like an iridescent ghost on the threshold of the drugs that sustained him." (The joke among the backstage crew was: Have you seen that chick that looks just like Brian Jones? Hey, man, that *was* Brian Jones.)

Monterey (organized by John Phillips of the Mamas and the Papas and record executive Lou Adler) was the first major rock festival to feature all of the sixties' musical currents, and boasted some spectacular events: the Grateful Dead's all-night set; the Jefferson Airplane's hallucinogenic nighttime LSD opera in front of the Joshua Light Show; Otis Redding's soul show for what he affectionately called "the Love Crowd." On June 18, Ravi Shankar sent the festival off on an extended, blissful Indian reverie as Brian Jones and Nico watched from the front row. The Who came on next, louder than bombs, as Pete Townshend and Keith Moon destroyed their instruments amid smoke bombs and sonic chaos.

Brian's job was to introduce the American debut of the Jimi Hendrix Experience. To prepare himself, he dropped some acid with actor Dennis Hopper. Brian came onstage, took the mike, and whispered, to almost dead silence, "I want to introduce you to a very good friend of mine and a countryman of yours—Jimi Hendrix, the most exciting performer I have ever seen." Hendrix made the audience forget the Who. Playing on two hits of the house acid, Monterey Purple, he played his guitar behind his back and with his tongue. He worked a one-handed version of "Strangers in the Night" into the power chords of "Wild Thing." Kneeling as if in prayer, he torched his broken instrument in a holocaust of lighter fluid and sacrifice. When the flames died down, he swung it around his head and smashed it to bits. The Monterey Festival was where the guitar players—Hendrix, windmilling Pete Townshend, Mike Bloomfield—became the Voice of God in rock music.

Brian returned to England loaded with the new California chemicals: DMT (a variant of hog tranquilizer) for a heavy downer, STP for psychedelic speed. "That was the worst," Anita recalled. "Too chemical. No one could handle that stuff."

———

London, June 25. On a Sunday afternoon, Brian, Mick, and Marianne joined the Beatles to sing along with "All You Need Is Love" in a pioneering multinational satellite TV broadcast called *Our World*. Brian had played sax on the Beatles' obscure "You Know My Name" at Abbey Road studios a few days before.

On Tuesday, June 27, Mick and Robert Fraser were back in court. Presiding was Judge Leslie Block, a vindictive pillar of the Sussex squirarchy. Fraser admitted possession of the heroin pills. His lawyer cited his Eton background and military service in Africa. The prosecutor dredged up his recent obscenity conviction for Jim Dine's pink penis sculpture, and he was found guilty. Mick's jury, instructed by Judge Block not to buy the idea that he had a prescription for the speed they found in his pocket, then found Mick guilty. The judge sent Mick and Robert off to Lewes Prison for the night, to be sentenced after Keith's trial the next day. Mick was prepared for this: he had a bag of clothes, books about Tibet, and a jigsaw puzzle to pass the time.

On Wednesday, it was Keith's turn to plead not guilty to allowing his house to be used for drugs. The prosecution kept harping on the nude girl the cops had seen at the party. Mick's lawyer tried to keep Marianne's name out of it—"she is described as a drug-taking nymphomaniac with no chance to say anything in her defense"—but outside court, smirking cops were feeding the press their obscene Mars bar story. Marianne visited Mick in his cell during the lunch break and found him crying and distraught, facing prison and the end of his career. (The Stones got no support from Decca, ostensibly because they weren't signed directly to the label. When the Beatles had drug problems later on, EMI helped considerably.) Keith also visited Mick and Robert, who were then taken back to jail to wait for the conclusion of Keith's trial. Michael Cooper snapped a photo of Mick in his cell, but lost his film to the jailers on his way out.

It was glum at Redlands that night. Keith packed his bag, ready to be jailed. They learned that police had broken into Courtfield Road after a false telephone report that Brian had overdosed. Marianne and Michael Cooper consoled each other in bed. The headline in the *Evening Standard* blared: NAKED GIRL AT STONES PARTY.

On Thursday, Keith Richards defiantly took the stand. He told the jury that the Stones had been framed by the *News of the World* in retaliation for Mick's libel suit. Dressed in a sharp black suit, he contemptuously told the court, "We're not old men, and we don't worry about petty morals." The jury found Keith guilty after deliberating for five minutes.

Judge Block gave Keith a year in prison. Keith looked at the ceiling, went pale, stayed silent. Robert Fraser got six months and sarcastically clicked his heels. Mick got three months. He reeled back in the dock, stifling a burst of tears, as the judge pronounced sentence and the girls in the gallery yelled out protests. Outside, six hundred fans cried out at the harsh verdicts. Shame! Unfair! Let them go!

Marianne got in to see Mick in his cell afterward, and he was so upset he could hardly speak. Anita was in Rome, working on her film. Allen Klein was called in New York, and he left for London immediately, determined to get the Stones out. Mick was driven to Brixton Prison in South London, while Keith and Robert were delivered to the dungeon-like Wormwood Scrubs to begin their sentences.

There was a small street protest in London that night. Kids demonstrated on the Kings Road and in Piccadilly Circus. Deejay Jeff Dexter led kids out of the underground club UFO and into the streets and was beaten up by the cops for his trouble. Labour M.P. Tom Driberg, who knew Mick socially, said in Parliament that the Stones had been made scapegoats for the drug problem. The Who took out ads in the papers, protesting the "grave sentences imposed upon the Stones at Chichester" and announcing they were releasing a single, "The Last Time"/"Under My Thumb" (quickly recorded the previous day), with proceeds going to the Stones' legal costs. Drummer Keith Moon joined two hundred demonstrators outside the Fleet Street offices of the *News of the World.* His girlfriend carried a sign that read FREE KEITH.

In Wormwood Scrubs, they took Keith's clothes, gave him a blunt spoon to eat with, told him they were going to cut off all his hair, told him he was going to spend a year sewing mailbags. He wrote to his mother and told her not to worry. As he settled in, the other inmates started shoving bits of tobacco and rolling papers under his cell door. Keith dragged his chair to the cell window and spent his first hours staring at his little square of sky.

"Most of the prisoners were great," he recalled. "It was, 'What are you doin' in here? Bastards! They been waiting for you in here for ages.' " During the daily walk in the courtyards, Keith was offered hash and even acid. "Wot? Take acid? In here?" That afternoon, "Ruby Tuesday" came on the radio and the whole jail erupted in cheers. "They were banging on the bars. They knew I was in and wanted to let me know."

At Brixton Prison, Mick Jagger, depressed and lonely, was writing the verses of "2000 Light Years from Home."

———

Keith: "That afternoon [Friday, June 30], I'm lying in my cell, wondering what the fuck is going on, and suddenly someone yelled, 'You're out, man, you're out. It's just been on the news.' So I started kicking the shit out of the door. I yelled, 'You let me out, you bastards! I got bail!' "

It was true. Their lawyers had gone to the High Court of Criminal Appeal in London and gotten Keith and Mick bailed at 5,000 pounds apiece, pending their appeals. Robert Fraser, out of funds, stayed in Wormwood Scrubs, eventually serving four months of his sentence. Tom Keylock picked them up from prison, took them to a meeting with Michael Havers, and then to a pub in Fleet Street, where Les Perrin arranged an informal press conference. "It's great to be out," a relieved Mick Jagger told the reporters. Keith told them he was so stunned at his sentence he just went limp.

That night, they met with Allen Klein in his suite at the London Hilton. Klein confiscated a chunk of hash from Marianne as she was rolling a joint, and flushed it down the toilet. Mick and Marianne went off to her father's cottage in the country for a few days, away from London and prying eyes.

Meanwhile, Les Perrin went to work. The veteran press agent got in touch with William Rees-Mogg, the editor of the august *Times* of London. On Saturday, July 1, the *Times* published an editorial that has been credited with saving the Stones from further jail time.

The Real Butterfly

WHO BREAKS A BUTTERFLY ON A WHEEL, thundered the *Times* on the morning of July 1, 1967. The Alexander Pope headline, a reference to the trial of Oscar Wilde, was an indication of the moderate moral dudgeon to come. Noting that "Mr. Jagger" got three months for some pep pills, the paper warned the same thing could happen to the archbishop of Canterbury on his way back from visiting the pope in Rome. "One has to ask, therefore, if this technical offence, divorced as it must be from other people's offences, was thought to deserve the penalty of imprisonment." (The editorial never mentioned Keith or Fraser.) Maintaining that it would be wrong to speculate on Judge Block's reasons, the *Times* cut to the chase:

> There are many people who take a primitive view on the
> matter, what one might call a pre-legal view of the matter. They
> consider that Mr. Jagger has "got what was coming to him." They
> resent the anarchic quality of the Stones' performances, dislike
> their songs, dislike their influence on teenagers, and broadly
> suspect them of decadence . . .
> One has to ask: has Mr. Jagger received the same treatment as
> he would have received if he had not been a famous figure, with
> all the criticism and resentment his celebrity has aroused? . . .
> There must remain a suspicion in this case that Mr. Jagger
> received a more severe sentence than would have been thought
> proper for any purely anonymous young man.

With this, the *Times* killed the case against Mick, and by extension, Keith.

No one took the case seriously after that, except the lawyers who went through the motions in court for another six weeks. The *Times,* it was observed, had acted with some courage, it being technically illegal to write about a criminal case in progress. Old Fleet Street hands realized that Les Perrin had saved the Rolling Stones' arses.

Keith stoically accepted the *Times*'s deep condescension. "The *Times* people, they're the ones who can say, 'You're just a butterfly. Let's just keep you a butterfly and leave it at that.' "

————

Brian Jones spent the month of July in and out of clinics and nursing homes, under psychiatric care. He was deeply upset because his mother had been insulted in the streets of Cheltenham after his arrest; once again he'd brought disgrace to his family. The Stones were in the studio after July 7, working on new songs with Nicky Hopkins on piano, under the influence of bail. "2000 Light Years from Home" was in pro-duction, along with "Citadel" and further work on "We Love You." Brian would come in from the clinic for the sessions, dabbling on saxophones, tablas, even a harp. Ian Stewart would watch this in distaste. "It was tragic to see, because Brian really was a good player, but all he wanted to do was fiddle with reed instruments and Indian drums. He was too far out of it to play anything. Being a 'star' just got to him—totally."

At the end of the month, Mick, Keith, and Marianne made a promo film with Peter Whitehead for "We Love You," based on the Oscar Wilde trial, with Mick as Oscar, Marianne as his boyfriend, and Keith as a hang-ing judge in a ridiculous wig.

On July 31, Mick and Keith won their appeal in a courtroom filled with kids wearing Stones T-shirts. At the judge's polite request, Mick turned around and asked the fans not to make any noise. Mick's convic-tion was upheld, but he received a probationary discharge. Keith's con-viction was thrown out amid screams of pleasure from fans that disturbed the decorum of the law courts. Keith, suffering from chicken pox, had to wait for the verdict in another room. "When I got up," Keith recalled, "I was covered in spots. It was the last straw—they couldn't take it. They couldn't even get me into court because I was diseased." He went right back to Rome to be with Anita.

Mick and Marianne were promptly whisked by helicopter to a country house in Essex, where a TV discussion was filmed with him, William Rees-Mogg, politician Lord Stow-Hill, and the bishop of Woolwich, concerning the problems of youth. Tranquil on Valium, according to Marianne, Mick didn't have much to say, but the broadcast managed to enhance his shaky stature as a spokesman for his generation.

"I hated the bust," Mick later said, "because it stopped the band and slowed us down . . . It wore me out. It wore my bank balance out. Cost a fortune! And those horrible, gray people that get you off . . . I mean, they put us through a lot of hassle and took a lot of bread off of us. It's just a lot of games they play between different lawyers. We were just there, you know. Nothing *real* happened." Robert Fraser, his appeal denied, stayed in prison and subsequently lost his art gallery.

———

Keith Richards was transformed by Anita Pallenberg in Rome that summer. They lived in a suite in the Ritz Hotel atop the Spanish Steps. After working at Cinecitta all day, the Black Queen—totally into her occult role—presided over a salon that included Terry Southern, director Pier Paolo Pasolini, Warholite Gerard Malanga, and Julian Beck and Judith Malina of the Living Theater. Mick and Marianne visited as well, and one night they all dropped acid in the haunted, splendiferous Villa Medici with Stash de Rola. The next day, Mick wrote the melody that became "Sister Morphine" on his guitar.

Keith started wearing Anita's jewels, then her clothes and her makeup, and got his unruly hair together in the unkempt shag that became his trademark. Keith had always been somewhat shy, but under Anita's thumb he became flamboyant and cocksure, the very picture of the English rock star, the pretender to the throne being abdicated by Brian Jones in free fall.

————

The Stones spent much of August 1967 working at Olympic on what would become *Their Satanic Majesties Request.* At the same time, Steve Winwood's new psychedelic soul group, Traffic, was making its first album in Olympic's Studio A. Traffic was being produced by an affable, Brooklyn-born drummer named Jimmy Miller, who had moved to England to work for Chris Blackwell's label, Island Records. Mick Jagger was a Traffic fan, hung out with them, noted Jimmy Miller's laid-back production style, and realized the Rolling Stones would need a new producer when they showed Andrew Oldham the door.

Mick was taking a lot of acid, reflected in songs like "2000 Man" and free-form psychedlic jams like "Gomper." His spacey lyrics were heavily influenced by his current reading: the Taoist classic *The Secret of the Golden Flower,* the occult anthology *The Morning of the Magicians,* and *A View over Atlantis* by the Stones' friend John Michell. No one was happy with the seemingly directionless music, but Allen Klein and Decca insisted the Stones have a new album ready for Christmas. After a deliberately sloppy blues jam at Olympic one night, Andrew Oldham walked out of the studio and never came back. His era was over.

To celebrate the court verdicts, the Stones released the sensational "We Love You" on August 15, with "Dandelion" on the B side. Mick had finished the lyrics during his night in jail. Prison footsteps and a slamming cell door started "We Love You," which ended in Brian's martial Mellotron coda. (Both sides of the record concluded with brief snatches of the songs on the flip.) "We Love You" failed to make much impact, with its defiant "we don't care" lyrics buried deep in a drone of white noise, and only reached no. 7 in England. In America, the soaring, nursery-rhymish "Dandelion" was released as the single's A side. It was the Stones' contribution to Flower Power and the Summer of Love, but, Keith pointed out, "We didn't have a chance to go through too much Flower Power because of the bust. We were 'outlaws,' man."

Mick was helping Marianne with her new album, producing a couple of tracks. Paul McCartney came to the studio to hear her record "When I'm 64." In late August, Mick and Marianne went to Wales with the Beatles to meet George Harrison's new guru, Maharishi Mehesh Yogi. In London, Brian Epstein, despondent that his contract with the Beatles was about to lapse, took his own life with sleeping pills. It killed the weekend in Wales, and later killed the Beatles as well when Allen Klein tried to take them over.

The Stones finished most of the work on the new album in early September, amid published rumors that Brian Jones was leaving the band and would be replaced by Jimmy Page. Ace session player John Paul Jones, who would join Page in Led Zeppelin the following year, arranged the strings that glistened behind "She's a Rainbow."

Brian Jones hated the Stones' psychedelic new album and predicted to one and all that it would bomb. Stu hated it too. On September 13, they all flew to New York with Michael Cooper to build a set and shoot their album cover in lurid and expensive 3-D. For three days, the Stones built the outlandishly exotic set in a Manhattan photo studio, assembling colorful shrubbery out of scraps of paper, painting the red Saturn that hung over the Himalayan backdrop. "The whole thing, we were on acid," Mick said later. "We were on acid doing the cover picture. It was like being at school, sticking on the bits of colored paper and things. It was really silly, but we enjoyed it. Also, we did it to piss Andrew off, because he was such a pain in the neck. The more we wanted to unload him, we decided to go on this path to alienate him." Dressed in blatantly Pepperish outfits rented from a costume supplier in Manhattan, the Stones posed for Cooper's shimmering 3-D picture, shot on September 17, and then flew back to London.

On September 27, the Rolling Stones confirmed three months of rumors by announcing they had fired Andrew Oldham as their manager and in the future would produce their records themselves. Andrew, Keith later said, "was no longer into what we were doing, and we weren't sure what we wanted to do, because of the busts. He didn't want to get involved, so it seemed the right time. It just fell apart."

At this point, Mick Jagger actually took over day-to-day management of the Stones. He hired Marianne's assistant, Jo Bergman (an American who had worked with Brian Epstein on the Beatles' fan club), to run the Stones' new office on Maddox Street in Mayfair. To Bill Wyman's disgust, she took orders only from Mick and seemed interested only in catering to his every whim.

————

Mick's flat in Marylebone Road had been robbed of clothes and jewelry earlier in the month, so it was time to leave. He rented a posh house in Chester Square for himself and Marianne, had Christopher Gibbs decorate it with period furniture and Moroccan orientalia, and moved into it that October. He liked to stay up all night, reading and smoking, listening to records, seeing visitors in his study on the second floor, where he worked on lyrics in a notebook with the words "Songs for a Cold Winter" hand-lettered on the cover. He also bought a sixteenth-century country house called Stargroves, near Newbury in Berkshire. It was a gloomy old pile with Cromwellian associations on fifty acres, bought with half an idea of turning it into a cool place to make records.

For three months that autumn, Marianne was in France starring in her first feature film, the soft-porn *Girl on a Motorcycle* with Alain Delon. When Mick found out she was having an affair with the production's still photographer, he flew over to keep an eye on her. For her role as a doomed, free-loving bikerette in the erotically charged film, Marianne wore nothing under a skintight black leather suit as she tore through the film on a motorbike, her long blond hair flowing behind her.

The papers were full of stories that October that the Stones and the Beatles would team up on various business ventures: a new studio, perhaps even their own record label. Keith was in Rome with Anita, Brian in Spain with Suki Potier, worried (according to his letters to the band's office) about paying his bills. Mick was talking with Donald Cammell about starring in a film based on a screenplay Cammell was writing titled *The Performers,* about a rock star and a gangster.

On October 30, Brian Jones dressed formally in a gray pinstripe suit and foulard tie. He was still recovering from a night out with Jimi Hendrix at a Moody Blues show. He and Stash de Rola were driven in Brian's silver Rolls-Royce to Inner London Sessions, where they had their day in court.

Stash's case was dismissed. Brian pleaded guilty to allowing drugs to be used at Courtfield Road and to possessing hashish. His lawyers produced several psychiatrists who had treated Brian; they testified that a prison sentence would send Brian into a psychotic depression and that he might kill himself. Then Brian stood in the dock and swore that he'd never smoke dope again. Unmoved, the judge gave Brian a year in prison, and Brian was hauled off to Wormwood Scrubs in a state of shock.

More street protests that night on the Kings Road. The next day, Brian was bailed out of prison, but his spiraling vortex of decline was in whirlpool mode. Now, while no one was looking, the cops decided to break the *real* butterfly on their dirty wheel.

Where's That Joint?

Their Satanic Majesties Request was a parody of the wording on the British passport: "Her Britannic Majesty requests and requires," etc. The album was released in mid-November 1967 in a lavish package whose gatefold sleeve included a maze puzzle: its original goal was a nude picture of Mick Jagger, but this had been vetoed by the record company. The maze was surrounded by an incoherent Hieronymous Bosch collage mixing floral designs, Indian imagery, Renaissance painting fragments, and science-fiction motifs superimposed on a map of the world. Cheeky puffs of hash smoke decorated the album cover and inner sleeve.

Demand for the album was immense and it "shipped gold," a commercial success even before its release. (It reached no. 2 in America, no. 3 in the U.K. The American single "She's a Rainbow"/"2000 Light Years from Home" got to no. 10.) As the Stones had expected, the album foundered under *Sgt. Pepper*'s overwhelming backwash, but *Majesties* is still a fascinating exemplar of post-*Pepper* psychedelia, and many of its songs retain a certain transportive power for the generation that first heard them under the influence of the bong and the acid-soaked sugar cube.

It began with a blast of discordant horns that introduced the strained bonhomie of "Sing This All Together," with the Stones inviting their audience to close their eyes, open their heads, and let the pictures come. This melted into the Manhattan dreamscape of "Citadel," which used fuzzbox guitar and the Mellotron to move through "the woods of steel and glass," Warholian New York, with a nod to Candy (Darling) and Taffy, two of the drag queens that floated through that world. The song's industrial clanking parodied the Velvet Underground, while Mick's spat-out vocal recalled the angry and vengeful Dylan.

A bizarre harpsichord and the winds of Thor introduced Bill Wyman's "In Another Land," with Bill's lambent singing (augmented by Steve Marriott from the Small Faces) alternating with Mick's snarled, swaggering chorus: "And I awoke—is this some kind of joke?" This cut to a half minute of Bill Wyman snoring in the studio before continuing with "2000 Man," an acoustic guitar breakdown backed by drums echoing across the universe, which mutates into a Beatles-like rock jam before returning to acoustic mode. Suddenly we're at a pot party. Marianne coughs, a Mellotron plays, laughing voices. Marianne: "Flower power, eh?" Laughter. Mick: "Where's that joint?" And so into a reprise of "Sing This All Together," subtitled "See What Happens." This was a long filler track with noodling guitar, percussive jams, freak-out groans, bad-trip screams, an embarrassing mix of borrowed ideas and uninspired chants. The side ended with a doomy electronic wash of "We Wish You a Merry Christmas" and a jarring, whispery noise that sounded, to those listening under headphones, as if the Rolling Stones were saying, *we hate you, we hate you, we hate you.*

Side two. Sound of cockney voices: we're being sold fish in Billingsgate, vegetables in Soho. A celeste and a violin, and into the great "She's a Rainbow" to Ringo Starr's Beatles beat, with fey backing vocals and Marianne coming in colors, a blithe poem of psychedelic fantasy sex.

"Have you," the song gallantly asks, "seen a lady fairer?" A tolling bell and sepulchral organ in "The Lantern" introduced three verses of phased meditations on communication with transmigrating souls. This was the Stones in a new hermetic mood, in the spirit of Aleister Crowley, the Great Beast 666, late weirdo British magus and newspaper whipping boy. "The Lantern" was about theosophy, narcosis, and the lure of the occult, and it seemed to go on forever.

"Gomper" was sitars, a tambura, tablas, the Stones sitting cross-legged on the floor, the music playing inside the 3-D bubble on the album cover. Birds of love hovered over moaning lovers in a Persian miniature, with Brian playing many of the instruments, jamming along a trippy fly-way.

The album's one masterpiece came next. Written in prison, "2000 Light Years from Home" had Kubrickian undertones a year before *2001: A Space Odyssey* appeared. A whooshing Mellotron slipstream soared over fast drumming and percussion, and Mick's singing echoed the exalted isolation of freezing red deserts and the cold light of distant stars. An oscillating theremin sent faint signals from Aldabaran, clearing Mick's ship for a landing. It was high-degree psychedelia to the max, one of the few great artifacts the movement produced. "2000 Light Years" ends in a morbid tag of tolling chords and the eerie subterranean light of Brian's Mellotron.

Suddenly—back in Soho. A smooth-talking tout was murmuring on the wet sidewalk at midnight. "Great live show, they're naked and they dance. It's twelve and six to come in, sir, there's a one o'clock show tonight, sir, nonstop, continuous show, stay as long as you like, there's a bar downstairs . . ."

The finale, "On with the Show," was an affectionate satire on the *Sgt. Pepper* nostalgia act that sent up the Beatles' "concept" and all of show business as well, ending with a frantic piano straining to be heard at a loud, boring party.

Their Satanic Majesties received the worst reviews of the Stones' career, but still shifted half a million units by Christmas. Even the band slagged it, Mick describing it on a London TV show as a bunch of "dirgy

The Stones in late 1967.

Anita and Mick on the set of their film *Performance*, September 1968.

Keith and Mick with career-saving American producer Jimmy Miller, Los Angeles, 1969.

The Rolling Stones' new lineup, with Mick Taylor in Brian Jones's old spot, onstage in Boston, November 1969.

Mick throws rose petals into the crowd while the Stones
vamp on "Street Fighting Man," Boston, 1969.

Muddy Waters, whose song "Rollin' Stone" gave the band its name, in 1976.

Below: Beat Fathers and mentors to the Stones: William Burroughs and Brion Gysin in London, 1972.

toe-tappers." In the press, *Majesties* was routinely attacked as pretentious and a terrible mistake, slavishly imitative of the Beatles.

———

Brian was back in court on Tuesday, December 12, to appeal his drug conviction. Three psychiatrists testified that he was "an extremely frightened young man" and "a very emotional and unstable person." A sympathetic judge commuted his jail time to three years' probation and a 1,000-pound fine, provided he continue to seek treatment. Mick and Keith came to court in support of Brian, who left after the judgment to have some rotten teeth pulled. Two days later, stoned on downers, he collapsed in his new flat in Chelsea and wound up in the hospital.

At a press conference around this time, Mick let fly at Brian. "There's a tour coming up, and there's obvious difficulties with Brian, who can't leave the country." He talked about how the Stones wanted to tour Japan, "except Brian, again, he can't get into Tokyo because he's a druggie."

Some people around the Stones were appalled by Mick's callousness toward Brian. They wondered why Mick saw him as such a threat. Spanish Tony Sanchez, working now for Keith as a drug courier, thought it was because Brian lived the life that Mick only pretended to live. "Brian was genuinely out of his skull on drugs most of the time, while Mick used only minuscule quantities of dope because he worried that his appearance would be affected. Brian was into orgies, lesbians, and sadomasochism, while Jagger lived his prim, prissy, bourgeois life and worried in case someone spilled coffee on his Persian carpets."

———

The Stones scattered for the Christmas holidays. Keith and Anita joined Robert Fraser, just out of prison, and Christopher Gibbs in a rented house in Marrakech. Brian and Linda Keith journeyed with Stash de Rola to Ceylon, where Brian spent time with the astronomer and novelist Arthur C. Clarke. Mick and Marianne and her son, Nicholas, went to

the sleepy island of Barbados and then on to Brazil. They were listening
to the new Dylan bootleg *Great White Wonder* (later released as *The
Basement Tapes*), and Marianne was reading William Burroughs's *Naked
Lunch*, which, she told Mick, made her want to be a junkie. One night, in
the city of Bahia, they stumbled into a *candomblé* ceremony, with drumming and dancing in the streets outside the city's rococo old cathedral.
Mick was heavily bearded, with long flowing hair, Marianne was carrying
Nicholas, and they were the only white people on the scene. Some of the
locals made a negative connection with the two English freaks and
chased them out of the plaza with curses and stones. This incident was
the germ of the voodoo dread that came out later in "Sympathy for the
Devil."

The Fifth Dimension

The Rolling Stones went back to work in 1968, a frenzied
year of great music, intense film work, radical politics, business battles,
sensual adventures, and personal tragedies. Keith: "1968—it's got a hole
in there somewhere."

It started in the Fifth Dimension, the name given to Keith's studio
in the old cottage on the grounds of Redlands. Redlands was Keith's play-
ground. Activities included shooting the water rats that lived on the banks
of the moat, riding motorcycles, archery, throwing knives, rolling joints,
playing with the changing cast of dogs that kept disappearing as neigh-
boring farmers poisoned or shot them for bothering their sheep. The entire Living Theater would arrive for a weekend. Legendary Euro hippies
like Joe Monk came and went (Monk was shot by a farmer for poaching
pheasants). The house was burglarized every few weeks until Keith had a
nine-foot wall built around the house and its two-acre garden. Redlands
was full of friends and music all the time. For the Fifth Dimension, the
cottage's walls were knocked down to create a big central room, which

George Chkiantz wired for sound with huge speakers. "Great echo in the long room," he says. "Great for listening to Wagner records." Keith was listening to old Blind Blake records for inspiration, fascinated by the "open" guitar tunings this great blues virtuoso of the 1920s deployed on the discs he cut for Paramount. In the Fifth Dimension, primitive Philips and Norelco cassette recorders were used to capture jams and demos.

Keith: "They just had a little microphone, and I'd overload the crap out of it. Just slam the mic right down the acoustic guitar and then play it back on a little extension speaker, put a microphone on that and then put it on tape. That's how 'Street Fighting Man' and 'Jumpin' Jack Flash' were done. Push it through and then double it again. A piano in the background, Nicky Hopkins or Ian Stewart. Maybe a sitar. And it would all become one track creating this sort of eerie space. Fairy dust!"

Early demos like "Stuck Out All Alone" became "You Can't Always Get What You Want." Ideas born during an endless jam on "Two Trains Running" would turn into "Midnight Rambler." The driving chords of "Primo Grande" developed into "Everybody Pays Their Dues," which in turn became "Street Fighting Man." A new bootleg recording (then available only by mail order from underground blues sources) of unreleased Robert Johnson songs (like "Love in Vain") inspired new blues forays such as "Meet Me at the Station," which became "No Expectations" on *Beggar's Banquet,* the first of the four classic midperiod Rolling Stones albums released between 1968 and 1972.

———

In January 1968, the Beatles' *Magical Mystery Tour* was atop the album charts. Brian was seeing a lot of Hendrix, was in the studio when Jimi recorded Dylan's new "All Along the Watchtower" on January 21 at Olympic, played his sitar with Jimi on recorded jams titled "Little One" a couple days later. Trying to mend fences, Brian was hanging out at Redlands, showing up at Stones rehearsals sometimes. The Stones' new office was up and running, and Stu was scouring South London for a rehearsal studio for the band. Everyone was short of money, and continuous telexes were sent to Allen Klein in New York, imploring him to release money to the band for houses, offices, instruments, dope. Mick finally got 25,000 pounds to pay for semidelapidated Stargroves.

In March, the Stones hired Jimmy Miller as their new producer. He had worked with the band Family and on the Spencer Davis Group's records. The Stones met Miller while he was producing Traffic at Olympic. Keith especially appreciated Miller's approach, what he later called "the chemistry behind the board." Miller was a drummer himself, heavy into rhythm, skilled in capturing a band's live sound, and his quiet enthusiasm coaxed the Stones through a fresh round of inspired creativity.

Early on, Brian approached Miller and told him he didn't think he had much to contribute. Miller checked with Mick, who told him, "Look, you can't force him, but he'll be okay." A two-week band rehearsal in a Surrey studio resulted in a clutch of new songs: "Stray Cat Blues," "No Expectations," Howlin' Wolf's "Rock Me Baby," and the earliest versions of "Jumpin' Jack Flash." The song's great riff began with a bass line Bill Wyman created while warming up in the studio. Later Keith and Mick were jamming at Redlands, trying to work in new guitar tunings like open E and open D, contrified tunings that consciously moved away from the blues tunings they'd always written in.

Keith: "It was about six in the morning and we'd been up all night. The sky was beginning to go gray and it was pissing down rain. 'Jumpin' Jack Flash' comes from this guy, Jack Dyer, who was my gardener, an old English yokel who'd lived in the country all his life . . . So Mick and I were sitting there, and suddenly Mick starts up. He hears these great footsteps, these big rubber boots—*slosh, slosh, slosh*—going by the windows. He said, 'What's that?' And I said, 'Oh, that's Jack. That's Jumpin' Jack.' And we had the open [E] tuning on my guitar. I started to fool around, singing 'Jumpin' Jack,' and Mick says, *'Flash!'* And suddenly we had this wonderful alliterative phrase. So we woke up and knocked it together. It's really 'Satisfaction' in reverse, except it's played on chords instead of a fuzztone."

The Stones recorded a supercharged early version of "Jumpin' Jack Flash" in sessions with Jimmy Miller and Glyn Johns at Olympic in mid-March that also produced "No Expectations," "Parachute Woman," and "Child of the Moon." "Everybody Pays Their Dues" was a track that started out as a Redlands demo on Keith's cassette player. The band tried it in the studio but couldn't get anything going. Then Charlie Watts produced an antique toy drum and cymbal he'd just bought, and set it up on a carpet on the studio floor. Keith sat cross-legged next to him and they began to play. This sounded great, so Keith recorded it on his cassette. They transferred this crude demo to four-track, and two nights later transferred this to eight-track tape, with myriad overdubs. Now it had dramatic ringing guitars and a buzzing Indian drone and looked like a possible new single.

March 16. After an all-night session, Brian Jones returned home to his Belgravia flat to find that the police had broken down the door to rescue Linda Keith, who'd taken an overdose of Mandrax. She was rushed to the hospital and recovered, but Brian's landlord evicted him that afternoon, throwing his clothes and his gear into Chesham Street. Brian moved into a hotel. The headline next day was the predictable NAKED GIRL IN STONES FLAT.

That day, Sunday, March 17, there was a big peace demonstration in London, part of worldwide protests against the war in Vietnam. Like most artists, Mick Jagger was appalled by the war and had been speaking out in interviews since 1965. Persuaded by London's leading radical editor, Tariq Ali of the Vietnam Solidarity Committee, to join their march on the American Embassy in Grosvenor Square, Jagger put on his street-fighting clothes and sallied forth.

The march began in Trafalgar Square, with about ten thousand people listening to actress Vanessa Redgrave denounce Harold Wilson's Labour government for its complicity with the war. Red and blue Vietcong flags fluttered in the cold breeze. The unruly crowd then marched down Oxford Street and swarmed through Mayfair on the way to the "imperialist fortress," as the embassy was called in march literature. Mick and his companions joined up in South Audley Street, linking arms with demonstrators for photographers, before the crowd massed in Grosvenor Square, where riot cops were waiting. Mounted police charged the crowd, and a hippie who offered flowers to the cops was truncheoned to the ground. Protesters threw marbles under the horses and burned them with cigarettes, and Mick joined in the rock-throwing and running for a few minutes before disappearing into the afternoon. The demonstration petered out after that, with the militant German SDS contingent angry at the English kids for the general lack of action. Later Mick told Tariq Ali that he, too, was disappointed at the peace movement's lack of battle readiness.

"What can a poor boy do?" he asked in the new lyrics he wrote to go with the backing track of "Everybody Pays Their Dues." What good would it do anyone to battle with the cops? How would that stop a war half a planet away? "It was a very rough, very violent era," Mick said later. "The Vietnam War, violence in the streets, pillaging and burning. And Vietnam was not war as we knew it in the conventional sense . . . It was a real nasty war, and people didn't like it. People objected and didn't want to fight it. The people that were there weren't doing well. It *had* to influence what we were doing at the time."

Che Guevara with a Band

April 1968. Anita was in Rome, where she had a part in *Candy,* based on Terry Southern's satiric soft-porn novel. When Keith heard she might be having a scene with costar Marlon Brando, he flew out to be with her. Bongo-playing Brando kept putting down the Stones, but they all got along well enough that Keith and Anita soon named their son after him.

Mick and Marianne were visiting friends in Ireland, where, in the almost medieval quiet of an Irish Georgian country house, they conceived a child. Mick bought a house for his new family at 48 Cheyne Walk in Chelsea. The house was modest and charming, with a wisteria vine running up the iron balcony along the river-facing front of the house. Legendary Cheyne Walk was the prime artistic neighborhood of London and had been home to Oscar Wilde, George Eliot, Rossetti and a whole flock of Pre-Raphaelites, John Singer Sargent, Ian Fleming. It was entirely apposite that one of England's brightest young romantic poets should settle there.

Charlie and Shirley Watts were at home in rural Sussex with a growing herd of Arab horses and their month-old daughter, Seraphina.

Brian Jones took Suki and engineer Glyn Johns to Morocco, where Brian wanted to record the rhythms of the Gnawa brotherhood. Brian, fired by boredom and fear of the Stones' obsolescence, was desperate for a new context to replace R&B as the basis of the Stones' music. He'd been embarrassed by the insipid psychedelia of *Satanic Majesties* and wanted the next Stones album to shift toward the earthiest North African rhythms he could find. The Gnawa were the descendants of West African slaves brought north in the same diaspora of the Bambara people that fueled the slave trade to the Americas. Like their musical cousins in the New World, the Gnawa were bluesmen, known for their affinity with the jinn and other dark forces, and for their penetrating trance rhythms. On previous Moroccan voyages, Brian had heard the trademark Gnawa rhythms played on big iron castanets, a sound that sent him into altered states as effective as any drug he'd ever taken.

Glyn Johns disliked Brian intensely. The engineer was almost one of the Stones and shared the rest of the band's general contempt for Brian. But Johns respected him as a musician and was persuaded to do the Morocco recordings. He agreed with Brian's idea of taking the tapes on to New York and dubbing black musicians over the tracks.

They flew first to Tangier and put up at the Hotel El Minzeh. Christopher Gibbs was also there. "Brian was his usual self, the same old brawl, this time with Suki. She jolly nearly died when I was with them that time at the Minzeh. She had smashed her wrists on a mirror and was bleeding badly. And Brian, instead of calling a doctor or the concierge, rang *me*. 'Can you come and sort this out for me? Can you ring the doctor? Can you talk to the management? Can you clean up the blood? Do you know how a tourniquet works?'"

On to Marrakech, where the Gnawa were. The session was

arranged by Brion Gysin, but there were serious technical problems with Brian's Uher recorder, and the sessions were abandoned when Glyn Johns impatiently split for London.

———

London. The Stones' office was abuzz with multiple projects. The new single was "Jumping Jack Flash"/"Child of the Moon," and word was out that the Rolling Stones were back, better than ever. The Stones began working with movie agent Sandy Lieberson, and film deals were afoot, real ones this time. Jean-Luc Godard wanted them in his new movie. Donald Cammell's brilliant script *The Performers* was green-lit by the new Warner Bros.–Seven Arts film company, with Cammell directing, conditional on Mick Jagger taking the part of the rock star Turner. Mick was talking about producing something he was calling a "rock and roll circus." At the end of April, the Stones made promo films for their new record with Michael Lindsay-Hogg. "Jumpin' Jack Flash" was shot in two color versions in a studio, with the band wearing elaborate war paint and bug-eye shades. It was broadcast on TV all over the world the following month, one of the first proto-videos credited with making its song a hit record.

"Jumpin' Jack Flash" bore down on the world in May 1968 like an emergency bulletin while Paris burned and America writhed in agony. Acoustic guitars, a zooming bass, and the trademark Jimmy Miller tonal drop in the main riff began the song. Then Mick introduced his new persona, Jack Flash, in the lingo of Delta mysticism and hoodoo. Jack was demonic, born in a cross-fire hurricane, jinnlike, supernatural. He was related to Happy Jack somehow, and to Union Jack, that once-proud banner of a lost empire, now a pop art icon on jackets and tea trays. Halfway through, as the song hurtled even faster, maracas kicked in, Jimmy Miller providing a hint of Gnawa-Diddley sizzle. (The maracas also kicked *out* for a few bars, the result of a catastrophic split in the tape just prior to mastering.) Jack Flash didn't really have much to say—"It's a gas!"—but it was all in the way he said it, driven by the best band in the world. Again there was a stone groove of a coda, thirty-five seconds of riffing guitar, droning organ, buzzing Eastern sounds (Brian playing a tambura), and Charlie Watts making great time.

"Child of the Moon" was something else, a California pastorale with a dramatic chordal riff (related to "Stray Cat Blues"), trumpets that sounded like the Byrds, and sweet lyrics that sketched Marianne Faithfull's "misty-day, pearly grey, silver silky-faced, wide-awake, crescent shaped smile."

The record jump-started the Rolling Stones' career. "Jumpin' Jack Flash" was their first no. 1 in England in more than two years. It wiped the slate clean for the Stones, surpassed all their previous work. Mick: "It's about having a hard time and getting out, just a metaphor for getting out of all the acid things." In America, it got to no. 3 and served as the transistor anthem at the riots during the summer's political conventions in Chicago and Miami. It was played constantly on the radio in Paris, where in May 1968 a coalition of rebellious students and striking factory workers almost toppled the government of Charles de Gaulle in a monthlong series of violent demonstrations and real street fighting. France was as close as any of the '68 protests came to an actual revolution, and Jumpin' Jack Flash seemed to preside over this youthquake like Che Guevara with a band.

———

The Stones owed Les Perrin a lot for getting the *Times* to pry the law off their backs, so as a favor to Les (who had an interest in the *New Musical Express*) they played a surprise gig at the NME Poll Winners show at Wembley arena. Voted by readers Best R&B Group for five years running, the Stones did a surprise encore to the show, playing "Jumpin' Jack Flash" and "Satisfaction" on a stage in the middle of the hall. Pandemonium in the house as Mick threw his tambourine, then his Capezio dancing shoes, into the pulsing crowd. The band had to walk through the crowd at the end, and it got a little rough on the way to the dressing room. "Just like the old days," Bill Wyman said, with satisfaction.

It was Brian Jones's last performance.

Next day, it was back into Olympic for a week. The control room was full of girls, friends, and musicians as the Stones cut several albums' worth of songs and demos with Jimmy Miller. "Street Fighting Man" got its new words. Old blues licks, worked out sitting cross-legged on the floor, produced "No Expectations," "Stray Cat Blues," "Love in Vain," "Prodigal Son." "Memo from Turner," based on *The Performers* screenplay ("You schmucks all work for *me*") was demoed with Steve Winwood and Jim Capaldi from Traffic. Jimmy Miller brought in Rik Grech, the bass player from Family, to play a beautiful country fiddle on "Factory Girl." A demo called "Blood Red Wine" produced enough ideas to later generate three different songs. The earliest guitar versions of "You Got the Silver" dates from this week. Outtakes included "I'm a Country Boy," "Silver Blanket," "Hamburger to Go," "Lady," "Family," and Bill Wyman's sexy "Downtown Susie."

The Stones' sessions that May were, for George Chkiantz, like working in a nightclub, one that opened just as the London clubs closed. Friends and hangers-on would turn up at four in the morning. It was an exclusive after-hours club with the best music on offer, albeit in a workshop state.

———

Brian Jones was renting a peer's flat in Royal Avenue House, just off the Kings Road. It took two hours to walk down the street now because it was so crowded with freaks in costume—uniforms, Indian silks, fringed buckskin, tiny sunglasses, snakeskin boots, floppy hats. The whole street looked like Sgt. Pepper's band.

Brian picked up the phone and called the Stones' office as cops broke into his apartment through the garbage chute on Tuesday, May 21. Brian tried to stay cool. The previous night, the Stones and their ladies, many of them on acid, had seen a screening of Stanley Kubrick's monumental *2001: A Space Odyssey,* and Brian was still flying. When the dope-sniffing cops found a ball of wool with a chunk of hashish in it, Brian lost it. "Oh no, man. No. C'mon—this *can't* happen again—just when we're getting back on our feet."

The narcs frog-marched Brian over to Chelsea Station and booked him as Lewis Brian Jones, twenty-six, musician. He told them the stuff wasn't his, that he never smoked hash because it made him dizzy. They hauled Brian over to court and displayed him, dazed and disheveled, to press photographers. The office sent the Stones' accountant over with 2,000 pounds, and the real butterfly was bailed into the life of a permanent target for the police.

The Devil Is My Name

Country music was in the air in 1968, and the Rolling Stones had to breathe it like everyone else. Bob Dylan's *John Wesley Harding*, recorded in Nashville, sounding like new acoustic psalms, looked back on frontier America from Dylan's rural hideway in Woodstock, New York. In California, the Byrds had produced a soulful countrypolitan jam called *Sweetheart of the Rodeo*, outfitted with neo-Nashville twang and great rediscovered songs. Dylan's touring band, the Hawks, transformed themselves into The Band, avatars of "country rock." Their new album, *Music from Big Pink*, was so influential that Eric Clapton disbanded Cream when he heard The Band's acetate that spring, and headed to Woodstock to try to join the group.

The Byrds toured England at the end of May with their newest member, Gram Parsons. Gram was twenty-two, a star-quality Georgia-born musician, tall and handsome, a southern gent and Harvard dropout. He was obsessed with the tender mysteries of modern country music and its acknowledged masters: Hank Williams, Buck Owens, Jimmie Rodgers, the Louvin Brothers. Gram had an encyclopedic knowledge of old songs, a substantial trust fund, and the cavalier charm of a southern troubadour. He'd started the first country rock group, the International Submarine Band, then took over the Byrds with his bell-clear country singing. Gram had sung most of the original *Rodeo* tracks, but a lawsuit over an old record contract had caused Roger McGuinn to overdub new vocals.

Otherwise *Rodeo* was Gram Parson's record, widely hailed as a master-piece and the birth of so-called "country rock."

The Stones stole him almost immediately when they went to the Byrds' gig at Middle Earth in Covent Garden. Gram was spirited to Mick's house in Chester Square to help out with songs. At dawn, they all piled into a Rolls and drove down to Stonehenge, then still accessible to anyone. Michael Cooper shot several rolls of Keith and Anita and Mick and Marianne cavorting around the ancient sarsen stones with Gram Parsons and a bottle of Jack Daniel's. They took Gram to Redlands, stoned, wined, and dined him, and he started teaching Keith—on piano—the old country songs he knew.

Keith: "Gram probably did more than anyone to put a new face on country music. He brought it into the mainstream of music again. He said, 'Don't forget about this shit' . . . I think I learned more from Gram than anybody else." Gram was soon immersed in the Stones' soft machine of druggy glamour and aristocratic fantasy. The Stones in turn were charmed by the naive young star. They were all naturally wary of new hangers-on, but Gram had the means to keep up with their appetites. G.P. could pay his own way.

When the Byrds moved on to South Africa after playing Albert Hall late in the tour, Gram Parsons quit the band to hang with Keith.

"He was a warm, down-to-earth guy," Keith said later. "He didn't know much about the [apartheid] situation in South Africa, so Anita and I explained it to him in Robert Fraser's apartment. It was quite an intense way to meet a guy. So . . . he stayed in London, and he started to show me the difference between Nashville and Bakersfield. We just used to sit around the piano and sing and get high." The effects of this new friend-ship would be heard on the next four Stones albums.

———

Earlier in the year, Marianne Faithfull had given Mick a copy of *The Master and Margarita,* a newly translated novel by the Russian author Mikhail Bulgakov. Mick read it in his study in Chester Square, absorbed in the horrific story of the devil's visit to Moscow in the 1930s in the company of a naked female vampire and a cigar-smoking black cat who's a dead shot with a .45 Browning. Omnipotent, well-spoken Lucifer kills people, drives them mad, spirits others to distant places. Women are vulnerable; he gives them magic ointment to rub on their bodies to make them fly through the air, naked, on broomsticks. Only the Master, a writer working on a book about Christ and Pilate, has the moral authority to stop the devil in his tracks.

Out of this came "The Devil Is My Name," a lyric Mick took into Olympic Studio the week of June 4, when the Rolling Stones were filmed in rehearsal by Jean-Luc Godard for his hotly anticipated new radical propaganda film, *One Plus One*.

Mick respected Godard and was flattered he wanted the Stones' energy for his movie. Godard was the shooting star of French cinema, a former critic who'd filmed heroic works of existentialist adventure like *Breathless* and *Contempt*. His recent *Weekend* was an avant-garde reading of Maoism, with cannibal hippie drummers thrown in. It marked the end of the old, romantic Godard. His latest, *Le Gai Savoir*, was an open call to social revolt. He was one of the few New Wave directors to see beneath the conventions of the genre and scrape at the rot in the system. Writing in February 1968, the American critic Susan Sontag called Godard "one of the great culture heroes of our time," and compared him to Picasso.

The project began as a film about abortion financed by a Greek woman, Eleni Collard, which Godard would direct. Then England's abortion laws loosened up. Godard told the producer he would still make a film in England if they could get him the Beatles or the Stones. Working through actor Ian Quarrier, who knew Mick through Marianne's theater connections, Mme. Collard got Godard the Rolling Stones, hot actor Terence Stamp, and a budget of 180,000 pounds.

Jean-Luc Godard arrived in London on May 30, haggard from *Les Evénements du Mai*, the Paris street riots that he'd shot on the run with 16mm cameras. Godard was distracted and felt he should be in Paris, where the national riot cops in their long black raincoats were still tear-gassing students and kids; but he was already behind schedule and he needed to shoot right away.

Mick: "There were lots of meetings in London hotel rooms, trying to get out of Jean-Luc Godard what the film was all about. Never did find out." Godard tried to explain it in a jumble of disconnected images: an abortion film, Black Panthers lusting after white women, a character named Eve Democracy reading Hitler's *Mein Kampf* aloud in a porno bookstore, music and suicide, quasidocumentary comic strips, a political cartoon. Godard told them he wanted to create a new cinema, converting political dialectic into film scripts. The Stones listened politely, nodded wisely, hadn't a clue. No one did. "I want to make this film as simply as possible," Godard told a reporter. "What I want, above all, is to destroy the idea of Culture. Culture is an alibi of imperialism. There is a Ministry of War. There is a Ministry of Culture. Therefore, culture is war."

No one was at their best. Godard seemed under a strain. Mick told friends he was stuffy. Brian Jones's arrest had left him a zombie. Terence Stamp got busted too and had to drop out of the film. Producer Quarrier ended up reading Hitler's book himself.

There was some method to Godard's madness. He intended to show the Stones building a song as a metaphor of growth, intercut with images of the radical deconstruction of outmoded bourgeois society. As he began to film in the brightly lit Olympic Studio, he caught Mick teaching Brian the guitar chords to "The Devil Is My Name." As the long session unfolded, the Stones took off their pink jackets, Keith removed his shoes, Charlie loosened his tie. They ran through the song at different tempos with Nicky Hopkins on electric piano as Mick sang guide vocals, lyrics that later evolved into "Sympathy for the Devil." Keith moved to bass guitar, while Bill played maracas after Keith suggested a rhythmic shift to samba mode. Hours passed as the Stones started, stopped, chatted, and chain-smoked Marlboros. Godard filmed Brian's utter isolation as he sat by himself in a booth, ignored by everyone, strumming an acoustic guitar that no one had bothered to hook up to the control room. Godard shot long sequences of the back of Brian's head, allowing the camera to linger on his hair.

During the day, Godard shot outdoors in Battersea, completing long, excruciating scenes of black radicals reading from LeRoi Jones and Eldridge Cleaver in an auto junkyard before executing beautiful white girls with machine guns.

When Godard resumed filming at Olympic, "The Devil Is My Name" had mutated into a *samba nova,* with African drummer Rocky Dzidzornu (Keith called him "Rocky Dijon") pounding out a Niger River counterrhythm. The lyrics asking who killed Kennedy were changed to "the Kennedys" after Robert Kennedy was assassinated in Los Angeles on June 5. Godard's camera, roving around the studio, caught an interesting visitor to that night's session. Sitting in a dark corner was "Chas," glowering in a well-cut dark suit. This was actually the actor James Fox, a friend of Mick's who'd been cast in the role of the slick gangster in *Performance.* When the camera got too close, Fox got up and walked out of the frame.

Godard's footage of the Stones in the studio is the only coherent portrait of the band working in its prime. The bright movie lights cast an unreal glow because the studio was usually almost dark, but otherwise it was pure documentary. "Godard happened to catch us on two very good nights," Mick said later that year. "He might have come every night for two weeks and just seen us looking at each other." The most dramatic footage was shot as Mick overdubbed his vocal, while Keith, Anita, Brian, and Suki sang the famous hoodoo whoops in the background. This was the era when Anita Pallenberg joined the Rolling Stones, became as crucial as anyone in the band, something that Godard managed to capture with a few moments of film.

On the last night of filming, Godard's hot lights set the studio ceiling on fire. It burst into flames as the Stones were jamming at four in the morning. The Stones and everyone else ran out of the building as the ceiling began to collapse. (Godard couldn't believe this, and muttered that he was being sabotaged by the English because it had always rained on his outdoor locations.) Fire crews arrived and drenched their equipment, but the precious tapes were salvaged by Bill Wyman and Jimmy Miller.

Godard went back to Paris, then returned to London to reshoot the

Stones, without Brian, jamming with Nicky Hopkins. Linda Keith listened intently on the other side of the wall. Tom Keylock lit everyone's cigs as the finished version of "Sympathy for the Devil" finished the sound track.

There was a huge row later on because Godard intended to leave the song unfinished, while Quarrier and the film's financial backers insisted it end with the Rolling Stones performing the complete song. Godard asked for a reason, and was told, "ten million teenyboppers in America alone."

"*One Plus One* does not mean 'one plus one equals two,'" Godard complained when they changed the end of the movie. "It means what it says, so we are obliged to take it as it stands: a series of fragmentary fragments." After its initial release as *One Plus One* (Godard punched Ian Quarrier at the premiere), the film was retitled *Sympathy for the Devil.* The following year, Godard said he was disappointed in the Rolling Stones for not supporting him. "The Stones are more political than other bands, but they should be more and more political every day. The new music could be the beginning of a revolution, but it isn't. It seems more like a palliative to life. The Stones are still working for scientific experiment, but not for class struggle or the struggle for production."

Music from Big Brown

Brian Jones's future in the Rolling Stones became even more doubtful on June 11, 1968, when a judge ordered him to trial on the new drug charges. Already on probation, Brian might go to jail for a second conviction. This killed plans for a Stones tour of America later in the year. Rumors flew around London that Brian was out of the band. The Stones were looking for a new creative force to help Keith Richards. "Jumpin' Jack Flash" was still no. 1 in England, and they couldn't afford to lose any more momentum.

The new Stones album, due out that summer, was almost finished. Mick decided to reposition the Stones as the heirs and legatees of the courtly troubadours, time-tripping, Grail-seeking jongleurs on a mission to preserve the romantic mysteries for a self-destructive nuclear world. So the band was photographed for their album's inner sleeve dressed as medieval minstrels attending a dissolute feast in a crumbling manor. Christopher Gibbs, who styled the photo session, came up with the album title: *Beggar's Banquet.* Another photo shoot, at an old ruin near Derby, depicted the Stones playing cricket in troubadour costume.

The Stones scattered around Europe for a week in June: Brian in Spain, Mick in Paris, Keith back to Rome, where he and Anita were living. On June 26, they regrouped at Redlands to rehearse with a twenty-one-year-old slide guitar expert from California who turned the Stones on their ears.

Jack Nitzsche brought Ry Cooder to London to jam with the Stones. Born in Los Angeles, Ry developed into a slide guitarist after hearing folk legend John Fahey's bottleneck style. At fifteen, he was playing at the Ash Grove folk club, where in 1965 he was discovered (backing Jackie DeShannon) by Henry Fredericks, a six-foot-four National-steel-guitar-playing blues singer (with an M.A. in agronomy from the University of Massachusetts), who performed as Taj Mahal. They formed an electric blues band called the Rising Sons. The Sons played gigs in L.A. during 1965–66, got a good reputation as an integrated band, but had a run of bad luck. Their album for Columbia (Dylan attended some sessions) was never released. They were blown off Johnny Carson's *Tonight* show at the last minute. Cooder's next gig was with Captain Beefheart's Magic Band, and he was also working in L.A. as a studio musician.

Marianne Faithfull was recording a new Jagger—Richards song, "Sister Morphine," whose lyrics she had written. Nitzsche thought Cooder should play on the track. Nitzsche also had been asked to compose the sound track music for *The Performers* and had enlisted Cooder to bond with the Stones so that back in L.A. he could reproduce the groove the Stones were mining at the time.

Instead, Cooder turned the Stones on to *his* groove. It was an open
G tuning, for five strings only. Until 1920 or so, the five-string banjo had
been the string instrument favored in bands. In the Roaring Twenties,
Sears, Roebuck began selling cheap guitars, and black musicians would remove the bottom string and tune them like banjos. The style had faded a
decade later, preserved only in recordings by "country" blues musicians
like Fred McDowell and Arthur Phelps—Blind Blake.

Ry Cooder arrived at Redlands on June 25. Anita: "He came down
to visit for the weekend. He was just passed out, I remember, on the
couch. Then he'd get up and play—really good. He was a very quiet person, but then I was probably as passed out as he was."

The next day, sitting on the floor of the Fifth Dimension, Cooder
began to play slide guitar as Charlie Watts tuned his drums and Jimmy
Miller rolled tape. Even Brian Jones was impressed as Cooder's lurid, serpentine playing boomed through the room's speakers. It was a new way
of approaching rock music, and Keith Richards, unable to depend on
Brian for any input, paid close attention to Cooder's style. They jammed
on and recorded Muddy Waters's "Still a Fool" and a lick of Keith's titled
"Highway Child."

Keith: "Ry Cooder came to play on 'Sister Morphine.' I'd been playing with the open G and he was using it too. I picked up a lot of tips on
how to handle it. I eliminated the sixth string so it wouldn't rumble and get
in the way . . . I started to get into that, and the high-stringing 'Nashville
tuning' the country boys use [shown to Keith by Gram Parsons: the bottom four strings are restrung and tuned an octave higher than usual]."

Keith had grown up playing in Chuck Berry's blues tunings; the new
open G style he learned from Cooder would affect his style from then on.
Out of it came "Honky Tonk Women," "Gimme Shelter," and the other
guitar hooks that would soon earn Keith the soubriquet "the Human Riff."

Keith: "Five strings, three notes, two fingers, an asshole, and you've
got it!"

The ruthless police harassment of Brian Jones continued relentlessly. Crooked cops would knock on his door, ask if he had any drugs, and try to shake him down for money. He came down to Redlands late in June to talk to Mick about the situation, worried that the Stones would dump him if he went to jail. This developed into an argument as Mick tried to placate him. "We've *all* been busted," Mick shouted at Brian, "and none of us has gone to prison yet. Why should you be any different? Don't be so fucking stupid."

Brian started to scream that he was going to kill himself. He dashed out of the house, ran across the lawn, and threw himself into the moat. Keith told people the moat was very deep, and Brian appeared to be struggling, so Mick reluctantly waded in to save him after Spanish Tony and Keith refused to do the honors. But the moat was only a few feet deep, and Brian was only pretending to be in distress. When Mick got to him, he was furious. He grabbed Brian's hair and pushed his head under. "You want to drown, you bastard? Well, I'm going to bloody well drown you, then. Look at these velvet trousers—cost me fifty quid!—you've ruined them. You stupid bastard, I hope you *do* go to jail!"

Brian drove back to London that night and seemed to be feeling a little better.

———

By early July, they had the basic tracks for *Beggar's Banquet* and a new sonic highway to follow. "Sympathy for the Devil" would open the record as a devilish showpiece with intimate voodoo rattles, sinister piano chords, and Keith's spiky guitar playing. It ended in a rave for piano and guitar, with Mick screeching over the music like an Amazon shaman, donning the dangerous mantle of a new plutonian persona—"Call me Lucifer"—to succeed impish Jack Flash.

"Street Fighting Man" had been built with acoustic guitars only, flavored by single drum strokes and maracas that supplied a hypnotic fervor to Mick's lyrics about compromising with bourgeois complacency, about why he was *not* a street fighter and never would be, despite the need for

violent revolution to stop a brutal war and retool society. The song ended
in a quiescent drone of tambura and an Indian double-reed *shenai,* played
by Traffic's Dave Mason, which seemed to point to meditation and inner
strength as an antidote to the futility of political struggle. The ringing effect of the guitars came from open tuning. Keith: "What's fascinating
about open stringing is that you get these other notes ringing sympathet-
ically, almost like a sitar. Unexpected notes ring out, and you say, 'Ah,
there's a constant. That one can go all the way through this thing.' "

These were the two rock centerpieces at the banquet. The rest of
the album evolved from cleverly recycled blues licks and country tunes
that Jimmy Miller managed to pull from the chaos around the Stones
amid film shoots, drug busts, and tension. "It was on the point of dis-
persal," Keith said. Miller's calming approach allowed the Stones to relax
and play the roots music they enjoyed, as if they were a bunch of players
on the front porch of a house on an old country road, the same one The
Band was living on in Woodstock. (The words "Music from Big Brown"
were scrawled—by Keith—on the cruddy toilet stall depicted on the
album's soon-to-be-rejected cover.)

"No Expectations" evolved out of the pre-owned country blues
"Meet Me at the Station" and starred Brian Jones in his last moment of
greatness with the Stones, playing shimmering Hawaiian guitar lines over
the sober lyrics of blues desolation. Mick: "That's Brian playing. We were
sitting around in a circle on the floor, singing and playing, recording with
open mikes. That was the last time I remember Brian really being involved in something really worth doing. He was there with everyone else,
but he had just lost interest in everything."

"Dear Doctor" was a parody country song, a send-up of hillbilly traditions complete with a corny harmonica, Band-like mandolin, and a narrative about a shotgun wedding that didn't work out. Country music was
still a joke to the Stones. "We're just playing games," Mick said at the time.
"We aren't really into country music enough to know."

"Parachute Woman" came out of the new Robert Johnson bootleg,
reinterpreted by Jagger/Richards (on cassette at Redlands) as a gutbucket
country-blues riff. The basic cassette track was used on the record.

George Chkiantz: "They fell in love with the sound of this mono cassette recorder. If they got the distortion just about right, it had this curious warble, a remarkably gutsy sound." "Jigsaw Puzzle" echoed with pedal steel guitar and Keith's bottleneck as Mick spun out Dylanesque chains of imagery—the gangsters, tramps, and a bishop's daughter—that ends in Burroughsian images of the queen killing twenty thousand grandmas, who thank Her Majesty for her trouble. The song built to an orchestral climax of stride piano and winding electric guitars.

"Street Fighting Man" opened side two, followed by a country blues, "Prodigal Son," stolen from Memphis bluesman Rev. Robert Wilkins's recording "The Prodigal Son." The Stones cut the song as an intense acoustic jam, Charlie brushing his drums and cymbal, Mick retelling the old Bible story with understated fervor, like a jackleg preacher by a campfire. When the album was released, "Son" was credited to Jagger/Richards. But Rev. Wilkins was still alive, still appearing at blues festivals in America, and the Stones got into trouble for thieving.

"Stray Cat Blues": shuffle and eighths, down and dirty sex talk, a carnal sketch of what Terry Southern referred to as "groupie-poon," the (very) young girls who wanted to dally with the Stones. Patterned roughly on the Velvet Underground's buzzing "Heroin" drone, "Stray Cat" was about spreading and biting: bongos, drums, and piano joined the chiming guitars of "Street Fighting Man," then the whole band with Mellotron in a long jam after Mick's modest proposal of a threesome with the stray cats. It was a brilliant, explicit Hogarth print from the Stones' candlelit underworld, and one of their greatest songs.

The endearing "Factory Girl" was an Indian country jam, with guitar, mandolin, and tabla played expertly by Charlie. The sweet fiddle part was overdubbed by Rik Grech.

Mick's "Salt of the Earth" ended the album with his deep cynicism and anarchic irony. It started quietly with piano and slide guitar, built to anthemic strength, then laid back as Mick contemplated the masses through a lysergic lens. "Salt of the Earth" then went gospel, with piano and a gospel choir added in Los Angeles when Mick and Jimmy Miller flew to California on July 5 to supervise the mixing and overdubbing of

Beggar's Banquet. The night they landed in L.A., they went out to dinner with the Doors, who were widely viewed as America's version of the Rolling Stones. Mick Jagger sat in the front row of the Hollywood Bowl with Marianne and Jimmy Miller as Jim Morrison moaned and writhed in the deepest oedipal throes of "rock theater." On the way back to their hotel, Mick told Jimmy Miller that he thought the Doors were really boring.

Jajouka Rolling Stone

July 1968. While Mick and Keith were finishing *Beggar's Banquet* in Los Angeles, Brian was back in Morocco, continuing his quest to expand the Stones' music. His aim this time was to capture the elusive magic of the Master Musicians of Jajouka.

Brian had been trying to get to Jajouka for a couple of years. The village had been discovered by Brion Gysin after he and Paul Bowles had attended a religious festival near the Caves of Hercules, on the coast near Tangier. There Gysin heard the keening wooden oboes of the Jajouka musicians for the first time. He told Bowles, "That's the music I want to hear every day for the rest of my life." Within a year, he managed to visit Jajouka, a hidden mountain village in the Djebala hills, about seventy miles south of Tangier. One of the first Europeans to witness Jajouka's tribal rites, Gysin recognized carefully preserved rituals that stretched back to the religious ceremonies of Rome and Carthage and even further back to Arcadian Greece. Gysin also found that the village's traditions were in great danger, as its young hereditary musicians left the mountains for city life. Gysin dedicated himself to preserving Jajouka, opening a restaurant, famous in the annals of expatriate Tangier, where groups from Jajouka could play every night for a stable clientele.

After the restaurant closed following Moroccan independence in 1956, Gysin began taking friends to Jajouka to experience the astounding spectacle of Bou Jeloud dancing. A village boy was sewn into fresh goatskins and a straw bonnet for seven days. Fueled by *kif* and infused with the spirit of Pan, the goat-god, the boy danced for hours, even for days, in front of a wailing line of drummers and men playing the *rhaita,* a double-reed wooden trumpet. Thirty of these together sounded like Allah's bagpipes, and the drums provided a trance-inducing North African backbeat. Bou Jeloud ("Skin Father") danced until he dropped during the Aid el-Kebir, the "Great Feast" of the Muslim calendar. Sometimes the boy dancing the role of Bou Jeloud died afterward, the ultimate performance.

———

July 1, 1968, was a lovely summer morning in London. George Chkiantz had been up all night at Olympic Studio when the studio manager asked him if he had a passport, and could he leave for Morocco that day? Brian Jones would pay him a hundred quid a day to help him make some tapes of tribal music. George went to Brian's flat in Chelsea and picked up his Uher tape recorder and some microphones. The batteries were dead and would take fourteen hours to recharge, but George had to catch a plane to Gibraltar. From there an old Dakota ("full of gays") deposited him at Tangier's half-built airport, with goats grazing on the runways. To George's amazement, Brian was there to meet him at nine in the morning. No one had ever seen Brian at nine in the morning before. George told him about the battery problems with the Uher but said they could run off the car batteries if he could find some cable. Brian showed him some Indian-owned electronic shops on the Boulevard Pasteur, and soon Chkiantz had what he needed to record tapes in a village with no electricity.

Brion Gysin: "They came to Tangier that summer. It was Brian, his girlfriend Suki, and a very good soundman. They wanted to record Bou Jeloud's music during the Aid el-Kebir, but it wasn't that time of year, so they settled for whatever they could get. I tried to get them to leave the girl in Tangier, told them Jajouka was primitive—no place for a woman—but she absolutely insisted on coming. So I had her cut her hair, and she dressed in jeans and a simple white shirt to try to look more like a man. (Actually she looked a lot like Brian.) Off we went, into the hot Moroccan summer. We met my friend Hamri, whose mother was from the village, in the town of Larache, then hired a taxi and got to the foot of the mountain. We had to walk the rest of the way."

The village was on a plateau halfway up the mountain. Flocks of goats wandered among the adobe houses, most of them thatched, others with newer tin roofs. No foreigners found their way up there, and the newcomers were followed by an entourage of curious children. They were greeted with glasses of steaming mint tea and long pipes of locally grown *kif* and quickly got to work.

Brion Gysin: "We arrived late in the day and set up the tape machine, and they played until four or five in the morning. It was incredible, with drums and flutes and dancing boys in pink dresses. The musicians wore their turbans and brown mountain djellabas, and you'd think you were in a medieval world. Which, in a sense, you were. The chief drummer, Berdouz, served as emcee, pouring tea, passing pipes of *kif*, keeping the party going. At midnight, all the dogs in the village started barking, and Jones got upset that this would spoil his tapes. So Hamri had them round up the dogs and move them off somewhere.

"It was the first time serious recording had been done up there, apart from my own little Uher, and there was some uncertainty among the older musicians. But the younger kids in the tribe were very keen. They loved putting on the headphones to listen to the playback. It was the first time they had ever 'heard' themselves. They thought Brian Jones was very funny and not really of this world, with his long blond hair and furry hippie clothes. This was 1968, and they'd *never* seen anybody like this before.

"Brian, meanwhile, was in ecstasy, half passed out under the headphones as he listened to the music. The countertones and 'partials' produced by the dueling flutes could put you into trance by themselves. We finally crashed around dawn. We slept a few hours in the morning until the musicians became impatient. At eleven o'clock, the whole group gathered in front of our house with their *rhaitas* and blew one tremendous blast—our wake-up call. Then they ran away, falling over each other laughing. We spent the rest of the day on further recording." George Chkiantz: "We recorded them outdoors underneath a great hedge of blue cactus, the earth very dry and hot. I found it difficult to stand still and wished I'd brought a mike stand. Since their festival wasn't happening, we tried to arrange for them to play various 'scenes' from the Bou Jeloud music, so we could get a kind of synopsis of the long ceremony. Gysin had tried to record them before, but he told us he was frustrated by the gender segregation imposed by the village. He was unable to hear the women's music to get a complete picture of the village, which prevented him from proving his theories about their supposed pagan survivals.

"The *rhaitas* were incredibly loud—twenty of them lined up in an L-shape with the drummers. The Uher was set to 'minimum' and it was already overloading. I had to point the two mikes at the ground and take the sound reflected off the earth. We went through the batteries, then rigged up the car hookup. I finally got the sound I wanted by having them move around me as they played in a reverse figure eight, with me in the middle holding the two mikes. When the reel started to run out, I'd wave and they'd just stop and smile. In the end, we had about five hours of tape.

"We recorded the flute music at night, and even got some women's music the next day, with the girl singing lead playing a *bendir,* like a snare drum with a wire over it. Brian told me he was looking for a contribution to the next Stones album, that he wanted compressed segments of a seven-day festival. I think we came close to getting what he wanted in the short time we were there."

Brion Gysin: "Something strange happened that day. I was sitting on the ground with Brian and some of the younger musicians, who were digging on this Rolling Stone cat in his furry Afghan coat. We were under the thatched eaves of a farmhouse where they were going to cook lunch for us. Two musicians came in the courtyard leading a white goat. Brian looked at the goat, watched it disappear into the shadows with the two men. One of them held a knife. Catching the glint from the blade, Brian realized the goat was going to be slaughtered. He staggered to his feet, made a choking sound. He gasped, 'That's me!'

"We all picked up on it, and said, 'Yeah, man, okay. Right! It looks *exactly* like you.' Because it was perfectly true. The goat had a blond fringe hanging over his eyes. 'Yes,' I stammered, 'it *is* you.' Brian turned white, as if he had a premonition of something. Twenty minutes later, we were eating grilled chunks of the goat's liver, and it was never mentioned again.

"We spent the rest of that day recording the music of the *rhaitas* and drums. They put on a little Bou Jeloud performance for Brian so he could get a taste of it on tape. They made him promise to come back for the next Aid el-Kebir, and they would sew him into the goatskins and he could dance as Bou Jeloud. Can you imagine?

"Brian was happy on the way down the mountain. We'd only been there a night and a day, but he had all he needed, I guess. We went back to Tangier, checked into the Minzeh, and Brian began to listen to the tapes."

George Chkiantz: "Brian in Jajouka was at his most considerate and charming, the perfect guest. Back in Tangier was another story. He beat up Suki right off. He was crazed when we returned from Jajouka. When he couldn't make the Uher work, he freaked out, woke me out of an exhausted sleep, demanded I stagger naked down the hotel corridor to push the right buttons. A few hours later, Suki called me to come quick. Brian was wrecked, standing on the balcony and insulting Arabs on the street below. I went over to calm him down, and he just blacked out, keeled over, and smashed his head on the iron railing. He looked dead to me, and I began to panic. What do we do now? 'Nothing,' said Suki. 'It happens all the time.' She covered him with a bedspread and left him on the balcony.

"I needed to get back to London, but before I left the next day, Brian and Suki took me to the famous beach at Cap Spartel [on Morocco's Atlantic coast]. The guard told us not to swim because the current was too strong. He said, 'If you go in today, next week we find your body ten miles down the beach at Asilah.'

"We put our towels down and I took a nap. I woke up twenty minutes later to see Brian swimming a quarter mile offshore, just his head in the waves. He waved to me! Expertly fighting the current, he eventually regained the beach, his footprints coming out at the exact place they went in. It was the strongest swimming I've ever seen. It made me think, later on."

————

A few weeks later, Brian was back in London, playing the Jajouka tapes at Olympic with George Chkiantz, happy with what he'd gotten. He felt the rhythms he'd captured were the antidote to the boredom people felt with R&B. Anticipating the world music movement ten years before it happened, he realized it would be amazing to dub guitar solos over the Jajouka polyrhythms. Brian and Chkiantz experimented with this a bit, but George hated the result.

"It wasn't a good idea," Chkiantz said later. "After a couple of weeks, I sold him on the idea of making an impression of the trip to Morocco, like seeing a play in a theater through a scrim. I talked him into leaving the flutes alone, except for a bit of echo at the end. For the *rhaitas*, the goat-god dance, we introduced 'phased' procession music that takes you on a little trip through our experience, in and out of consciousness. The whole thing was done in a few days, down to mastering, with Brian present every minute. I sent the tapes to the Stones' office late in the summer."

No one had seen Brian this involved in anything since Anita left him. There was a brief flicker of hope that Brian Jones was being recalled to life. Brion Gysin: "It was a big deal in Jajouka for months afterward, this idea of Brian Jones returning to dance as Bou Jeloud. They pestered me about it for months. They even wrote a song for him, a Moroccan jump tune with funny English lyrics in the chorus":

Ah Brahim Jones
Jajouka rolling stone
Ah Brahim Jones
Jajouka really stoned!

What Can a Poor Boy Do?

July 1968. Six thousand miles away, Keith and Mick were mixing *Beggar's Banquet* at RCA and Sweetland studios in Los Angeles. Charlie flew in, then Anita. Gram Parsons had a connection for pharmaceutical cocaine from a dentist in Watts, and some grudgingly felt Gram was buying his way into the Rolling Stones. Gram, Keith told friends, got better coke than the Mafia. He and Keith bonded like brothers as Gram took Keith through country music, teaching him songs. One night they drove out into the California desert to watch the sunrise at Joshua Tree National Monument, an out-of-this-world moonscape of cactus and canyons and prehistoric trees. Wrapped in blankets, guitars at hand, Anita as beautiful and gray-eyed as Minerva, they climbed atop the Cap Rock promontory and felt like gods watching Apollo begin his blazing ride across the desert.

The Stones went to hear Taj Mahal and his band, and really dug the big Harlem-born blues singer, who had the same reverence for country blues they did. Taj's version of "Corinna" was a big favorite. (He had replaced Ry Cooder with a young Indian guitarist from Oklahoma, Jesse Ed Davis.) Taj played a National steel guitar like Muddy Waters or Robert Johnson, and Keith recognized they shared the same approach to the blues: once removed, from another generation. Mick told Taj about his plans for a circuslike concert he wanted to stage later in the year, and invited Taj to come to London and be part of the show. Marianne decided that if her baby was a girl, she would name her Corinna.

Marianne's out-of-wedlock pregnancy was big news in England. It was mentioned from the pulpit of Westminster Abbey, discussed in the papers, and later was the undeclared subject of debate between velvet-booted Mick and Mary Whitehouse, an advocate of sensible shoes and conservative family values, on David Frost's TV show in London. Mick, while acting as a spokesman for permissiveness, ardently wanted to marry Marianne, but she was still married. Also unknown, except to a few close friends, was that Anita Pallenberg was in the early stages of pregnancy herself.

———

The Stones worked hard in the studio. Jack Nitzsche was surprised to see Anita tell Mick that his mix of "Stray Cat Blues" was crap because the vocals were too forward. He was even more surprised when Mick remixed according to Anita's suggestion. They put the gospel choir on the end of "Salt of the Earth" after Marianne found them.

She was complaining she had nothing to do, so while they were still mixing *Banquet* Mick produced two tracks for Marianne at RCA. "Sister Morphine" and "Something Better" both featured Ry Cooder, Charlie on drums, and Jack Nitzsche on keyboards. "Sister Morphine" was five and a half minutes of a dying accident victim's desperate craving for narcotic relief (the lyrics were addressed to his nurse). Nitzsche scolded Marianne for snorting cocaine in the studio. "Everyone in the band can get wrecked except the drummer and the singer," he told her. Delivered in a quavering voice (recorded later at Olympic) over languid slide guitar, the song was a desolate cry of pain from a pregnant girl feeling herself coming apart at the seams.

———

July 26 was Mick's twenty-fifth birthday. That day, he flew back to London from Los Angeles with the first acetate pressings of *Beggar's Banquet*. There was a party that night at Spanish Tony's new club, Vesuvio, in the Tottenham Court Road, in which both Mick and Keith had a financial interest. Decorated with cushions, water pipes, and Moroccan tapestries, the club was designed to cater to rock stars tired of being ripped off by the expensive clubs they frequented. The opening party featured mescaline punch and hash cake, and was full of Beatles, Stones, and their friends. Mick arrived late from the airport and played the *Beggar's Banquet* acetate at top volume. Everyone realized that after the debacle of *Satanic Majesties,* the new Stones album was make-or-break; there was relief in the room when everyone seemed to enjoy it immensely. Congratulations all around, and many mescalined toasts were offered to its success. Mick played some other records fresh from California: Dr. John the Night Tripper's Creole murk, and Al Kooper's new group, Blood, Sweat and Tears. Then Paul McCartney modestly asked Spanish Tony if he'd mind playing the new Beatles single on the house P.A. It was "Hey Jude." The other side had John Lennon wailing on "Revolution." It was the first time London's elite had heard these climactic Beatles songs, and there was huge applause afterward. Mick Jagger, Sanchez recalled, was annoyed at being upstaged at his own birthday party. (The Vesuvio Club was torched a few months later in a fire the authorities termed suspicious.)

————

Decca executives could only shake their heads that month when shown the cover the Stones wanted for *Beggar's Banquet.* Photographed by Barry Feinstein (husband of Mary Travers of Peter, Paul and Mary) in a toilet at a Mexican car repair shop in Los Angeles, the cover included graffiti insults (by Keith and Mick) aimed at Allen Klein, Lyndon Johnson, the U.S. Marines, Herb Alpert (whose album had prevented *Aftermath* from reaching no. 1 in the United States), and Bob Dylan (the words "Bob Dylan's Dream" pointed to the toilet's flush handle). The album credits were on the other side, along with thanks given to Strawberry Bob (Fraser), St. Christopher (Gibbs), Spanish Tony, John and Michelle Phillips, Lenny Bruce, John and Yoko, Taj Mahal. Other graffiti: "Ronald Reagan is a sissy"; "Lyndon Loves Mao"; "Zappa's in the cistern"; "Leicester Square [notorious gay cruising spot] at 11 A.M."; "God rolls his own"; "Music from Big Brown."

Both Decca and London Records refused to release the album until another cover design was submitted. The Stones dug in their heels and a stalemate developed. The original July 26 release date came and went with both sides refusing to cave. Keith Richards was especially adamant about the cover. "What the Beatles and ourselves wanted—the most important thing—was to break the record companies' control. If you're writing songs and you're playing 'em, nobody should have the right to tell you how it should be done. You make the record, and you give it to the company."

The Stones told their label it was merely a distributor of their product with no censorship rights. The company had other ideas and said no. This delayed *Beggar's Banquet* for four months and poisoned relations with the Stones, who resolved that their next album for Decca would be their last. Around this time, the band also learned that the corporate parent of Decca was using the record company's vast profits to underwrite research for its military radar and arms business. Incredibly the Stones realized they'd been contributing to the Vietnam War effort.

———

In America, the summer of 1968 was known as the Long Hot Summer. Race riots torched inner cities, and there was civic instability that hadn't been felt by Americans since the Depression of the 1930s. A cultural chasm divided the generations, and tear gas was in the air of the cities. London Records released "Street Fighting Man"/"No Expectations" as a single in August, just after the Democratic Party's presidential convention in Chicago, where riot cops brutalized demonstrators and anyone in the streets they could get their hands on. The single's red sleeve had a photo of L.A. cops clubbing a young demonstrator. When Chicago stations boycotted the record, other radio outlets followed suit, and London hastily withdrew "Street Fighting Man" and recalled all copies in the stores. It was the first banned record of the Stones' career. Naturally the single didn't even make the charts. The Stones' brilliant, timely follow-up to "Jumpin' Jack Flash" completely bombed.

Keith: "They told me that 'Street Fighting Man' was subversive. 'Of *course* it's subversive,' we said. It's stupid to think you can start a violent revolution with a record. I wish you could."

six:

Let It Bleed

Star-quality blues guitarist Mick Taylor

replaced Brian Jones in 1969.

Either you're dead, or you move along.

Mick Jagger

A Different Persona
Every Time

The Rolling Stones were at loose ends in the early fall of 1968. Their new album was delayed, and they were unable to tour because of Brian Jones's drug problems. The Jeff Beck Group was London's hottest band. Ex-Yardbirds guitarist Beck, brilliant but moody, had Rod Stewart on vocals and young Ron Wood on bass. They were about to invade America to great acclaim, paving the way for Led Zeppelin later in the year.

Donald Cammell had been shooting the first half of his film, now called *Performance,* in London since mid-July. Mick Jagger was about to disappear into his movie role as the retired rock star Turner for the month of September. Anita had landed the role of his consort, the script called for sex scenes, Cammell was a student of the polymorphous perverse, and Keith was feeling weird about it.

———

The Stones' organization in this critical period was headed by Jo Bergman, who had been brought to the U.K. by Brian Epstein and then switched to working for Marianne Faithfull. Mick Jagger was unhappy with Allen Klein's control and decided to set up an independent management operation in late 1967. Marianne gave Jo to the Stones.

According to Peter Swales, a young promo man who worked with the band at the time, "Jo Bergman ran the office with a lot of strength. She had serious entrée and ability to fix things, like a friend in the consular section of the American Embassy who could facilitate Keith's visa problems. Jo was abrasive, manipulative, devious, and there was always some question among the staff about her loyalty because she was close to Allen Klein. But Jo was the boss because she controlled the lines of communication, especially with Mick, who made himself available by phone twice a day. Ian Stewart ran the Stones' rehearsal studio and storage space in a basement in Bermondsea, South London. I loved seeing Stu because he was so honest about things. You hear that he wasn't embittered about the Stones, but I beg to differ. He *always* spoke about them sarcastically, didn't take their music seriously, regarded Mick as a bit of a ponce. Stu loathed Brian, yet always claimed he was the greatest guitarist in England—at least in his prime.

"Before I was formally hired, they sent me to Cheyne Walk to talk to Mick. I was shown upstairs to the lounge, and there was Mick, dancing in front of a full-length mirror with music blasting. I was amazed, and unnerved too. The room was done in Moroccan textiles, with a Buddhist altar overlooking the river. We sat cross-legged on the floor in front of the fire and Mick handed me a joint, which I reluctantly smoked with him despite these lurking feelings of intimidation. Mick was full of unrealistic marketing schemes in the wake of their troubles with Decca. He wanted to know if I thought *Beggar's Banquet* could be distributed from the backs of lorries, and I had to say no, I didn't think that was feasible.

"By the time I came along, Brian Jones was just a wreck. I mean, I was shocked. He was on the borderline of obesity, in his body and his face, although his hair hid that a bit. He perspired all the time and smelled of brandy. He seemed like both a sweet, gentle man who spoke beautiful, pristine English and an utterly pathetic creature who was seeing a psychiatrist for severe paranoia. My experience, contrary to what else one hears, was that Mick Jagger bent over backwards to try to accommodate Brian. They didn't really want to dump him—that wasn't on their agenda at all. It was just that he'd become completely unreliable. He was a passenger in the band, but he couldn't even remember to get on the bus.

"We never saw much of Keith, who hardly ever came to the office.

Mick was always in and out, a different persona every time. He'd show up in a proper brown pinstriped suit for business meetings with Sandy Lieberson, who was producing *Performance*. Sometimes he came in jeans, looking disheveled, stealing my Rothmans and smoking them like a woman, *very* camp. He was so totally secure in his masculinity that he could really camp it up with the best of them."

The Only Performance That Makes It

Mick and Anita began working on *Performance* early in September 1968. Filming continued for seven weeks, following the improvised mind fuck of the second half of Donald Cammell's script—an occult stew of hallucinogenic sexual confusion. The collateral damage from the filming had fatal consequences for the Stones, their women, and almost everyone connected to the movie. *Performance* would be delayed for years, was then heavily censored, would get bad reviews when finally released.

But thirty years later, *Performance* would be called the best film ever made in England. Some believe that when advanced technology renders Rolling Stones CDs as obsolete as Edison cylinders, say in a hundred years, *Performance* will stand as *the* glittering Stones-related document of London in the late 1960s.

Cammell wrote *Performance* to test the affinities between the sadistic violence of London's criminal gangs (the Krays, the Richardsons) and the sadomasochism Cammell saw in Brian Jones and others in the London pop world. The Chelsea Set, of which Cammell was a member, mingled art dealers, actors, musicians, aristocrats, and villains, providing the back-story of the film.

Performance tells the story of Chas, a psychopathic enforcer for Harry Flowers, a homosexual mobster loosely patterned on Ron Kray, half of the notorious Kray twins who had ruled London gangland. The first half of the film, lurid with homoerotic innuendo and tortuous imagery from Francis Bacon's paintings of naked male torsos, places Chas in his milieu of extortion, beatings, and revenge. (Production of *Performance* happened only because both Krays were in prison for murder.)

When Chas kills a former friend, he's marked for death by his own gang and forced underground. Through a ruse, he becomes a lodger in the Notting Hill house of Turner, a retired rock star, and his weird girlfriends. Reclusive Turner, out of boredom, decides to mess with Chas: turn him on, break up his macho pose, and see what's underneath. He manipulates Chas with his seductive world of smoke and mirrors, sex and drugs, music and the occult.

Performance is an extended tribute to the avant-garde masters of the sixties. Jorge Luis Borges, William Burroughs, Georges Bataille, and James Brown are constantly referenced. The script—an explicit homage to Borges—calls for hundreds of jump cuts and flashbacks derived from the cutup method derived by Burroughs and Brion Gysin. Burroughs's obsession with the legendary dope-crazed Assassins of Hassan Sabbah is a leitmotif of the film. Satan is openly evoked as Jagger/Turner sings Robert Johnson's "Come On in My Kitchen."

Performance is about the madness that occurs when personal boundaries dissolve and people merge into each other. As they trip on magic mushrooms, the *chi* of the two men transmigrates. Cammell shows a mystical confluence as rock star/*hashishin* and gangster/assassin interfuse. As Chas's gang closes in on him, he shoots Turner as the ultimate madness. The camera follows the trajectory of the bullet as it burrows through Turner's brain, evoking a flash image of Borges, whose stories celebrated outlaws, their knives and killings. Chas is led to his fate in a white Rolls-Royce, but it's Turner's face that looks out the car window as it drives off.

Performance had been written the year before in St. Tropez by Cammell, with the help of Deborah Dixon. Anita remembers working on her dialogue while they were at the beach, loose pages blowing away and landing in the water. As the son of Aleister Crowley's biographer, Cammell was interested in magic, not politics, but his screenplay makes many subtle points about the class system. In London, Cammell recruited David Litvinoff to help with the cockney gang-speak that gives the script its immediacy. Litvinoff was the link between the Chelsea Set and the (gay) underworld, and he used his own beatings at the hands of the Kray gang as material for the script.

Cammell had worked on a couple of mid-sixties movies but was frustrated at the utter failure of the film world to capture the visceral excitement of the times or anything even remotely hip. He'd been talking to Mick about doing a film for two years, and in the end it didn't take much convincing. Cammell's magnetic personality encompassed interests in literature, cinema, art, metaphysics, philosophy. "If he said, 'Come with me to hell,' " one friend said of Cammell, "you'd say, 'Okay—how bad can it be?' " When Mick signed on to play Turner (for $100,000 and 7½ percent of the net), Cammell and Sandy Lieberson, acting as producer, persuaded the new management of Warner Bros.–Seven Arts to finance the project. They were given a large budget and an extraordinary amount of freedom to create what the studio hoped would be a mystery film about a pop star played by Mick Jagger. It was an extraordinary leap of faith by Warners. Donald Cammell had never directed a film, Sandy Lieberson had never produced a movie, and Mick Jagger had never starred in one, yet the studio agreed to an unsupervised shoot. *Performance* was made by a group of amateurs with no one looking over their shoulders, probably the main reason for its authenticity and greatness.

The first half of the film had been shot around London that summer after Cammell brought in cinematographer Nicholas Roeg to codirect. While Cammell rehearsed the actors and dictated the action, Roeg blocked the cameras and actually shot the film. James Fox, who played Chas, was given an education in thuggery at the Thomas a Becket pub in South London, headquarters of the British boxing world. The old Harrow boy, who normally played posh types, emerged as one of the chaps, with a body taut as cable. His character was modeled on an East End tough named Jimmy Evans. Real Chelsea villains like John Bindon—famous for biting a man's ear off in a fight—were recruited to play members of Harry Flowers's gang.

Cammell and Roeg shot in sequence, and the first half was finished by mid-August 1968. The exterior shots of Turner's house were filmed in Powis Square, Notting Hill Gate. The interiors, decorated by Christopher Gibbs with his Delacroix mélange of antiques and orientalia, were shot in an elegant house in Lowndes Square, Knightsbridge, that had previously housed a crooked gambling club. The doors and windows were sealed shut for the production, and Cammell conjured a hermetic, occult environment for his actors to play their fateful parts.

Mick and Cammell had talked endlessly about the characters in the film, especially Turner. "Turner was an amalgam," Mick said, "with more than a bit of Brian Jones." Turner (played by Mick with his hair dyed almost black) whispered in Brian's semiprecious lisp and moved through the darkened rooms of his house with Brian's devious detachment. His "secretary," Pherber, was completely patterned on Anita Pallenberg, who won the role of herself after the American stars Warner's wanted became unavailable. Mia Farrow, their first choice, broke her ankle as she was about to come to London. Tuesday Weld actually arrived in London, but her shoulder was accidentally broken by Deborah Dixon during some New Age "therapy" for Weld's chronic backache.

Anita got the part. Pregnant when she signed the contract for *Performance*, she had an abortion a few days later and went on with the film.

The role of Lucy, the young girl in Turner's ménage à trois, was played by Michelle Breton, a boyish, twenty-year-old waif who Cammell and Dixon had met in St. Tropez and taken into their ménage, Cammell being big on threesomes. Breton was the free-spirited paradigm of the hippie kid that Cammell needed to balance his two jaded rock stars.

Where the first half of *Performance* closely follows Cammell's script, the second half was mostly improvised on the set, depending on how the players interacted. It was pure Theater of Cruelty, Antonin Artaud made flesh in the film's most famous line, spoken by Turner to mind-blown, disoriented Chas:

"The only performance that makes it, that *really makes it*, that makes it *all the way*, is the one that achieves madness."

Now Cammell threw out the script the studio had financed and approved. Dialogue was made up on the spot. Anita wrote most of her own lines. From the beginning, Mick and Anita relentlessly teased James Fox, trying to break him with psychic jujitsu, the same way Turner tries to break Chas.

Anita thought Fox a total square and was openly contemptuous of him. She'd laugh in his face and mock him without mercy. Mick and Marianne had a social friendship with Fox and his girlfriend, Andee Cohen, that involved lots of flirting and sexual tension. Fox had been warned by his father, a prominent talent agent, that the film's advocacy of drugs and bisexuality would hurt his career; his girlfriend was so worried she broke up with him. "Mick's a ruthless tease," Cammell said later, "and he worked on Jimmy Fox for three days until he had a crack-up." Spanish Tony found Mick and Fox smoking dusty DMT in the greenroom, to give some extra flash to the drug scenes they were about to do. Halfway through the shoot, Anita slipped some acid into Fox's coffee without telling him, which sent Fox off the deep end. "I was a real brat," she said.

Things got really complicated when Cammell started to shoot the sex scenes. The bathtub scene alone took two days to film on a closed set. Anita had already seduced Mick three days into filming, according to Tony Sanchez, after secretly wanting him for years. At Cammell's urging, Mick and Anita made love in the set's big bed while he called the action and Roeg shot them with a 16mm Bolex. After the camera stopped rolling, they kept going, kept at it in the greenroom while the crew waited in disbelief. Word got around. Keith heard it from Robert Fraser and was freaked out. He and Anita were living in Fraser's Mount Street flat, rented to Anita for an enormous sum paid by the production. But Fraser had neglected to move out, and he and smoldering Keith were both there when Anita got home from the day's work. Keith, working on the songs for *Let It Bleed,* hated the film that had thrown his woman into bed with his best friend. He ignored Cammell's request to write some music for the film, refused to visit the set, realizing that a confrontation with Mick would harm the Stones. Instead, Keith waited for Anita in his Bentley, parked in front of the house, and worked on the melody to "You Got the Silver." Anita Pallenberg was a woman with rules of her own, but this was an almost public sexual humiliation. Keith sunk into a depression that he began to treat with heroin and cocaine speedballs, which quickly became his favorite drug for writing songs. He wrote "Gimme Shelter" on Mount Street under this influence.

When the horrified studio executives saw the rushes of Cammell's explicit sex scenes, especially the soft porn threesome sequences of Turner, Pherber, and Lucy, they shut down the film. Sandy Lieberson had to beg them to resume production. Then the lab processing the 16mm footage complained that it contravened England's obscenity laws and insisted they were required by law to destroy the film. Cammell and Lieberson managed to get the negative back, but had to watch the lab's director censor the print with a hammer and chisel.

Later, unknown to his stars, Donald Cammell edited his footage of Mick and Anita into a thirty-minute blue movie and submitted it to a porno festival in Amsterdam, where it won the Golden Schwantz.

The pressure only built as the production continued through October. "Memo from Turner," the Jagger/Richards song that limned the obsessions of *Performance,* providing the artistic high mark of the film (in what could be considered the first modern music video), was unfinished. Keith wouldn't work on it, and Mick's demo lyrics about licking policemen's balls had to be rewritten. Donald Cammell was the only man in England who could pressure Mick Jagger, getting up his nose to finish the lyrics and record a new arrangement so they could finish the film.

Anita: "Donald could reduce Mick to tears over not coming up with the right piece of music, or the feeling that he wanted for a scene—and then to tears of joy when he finally hit it. Mick and I would be terrified by his tirades and rages, but when we got it all right, it was great. And even through all that, Donald and Keith still remained friends."

When the film ended, everyone went into deep shock. Keith and Anita went back to Italy and it was rocky. Marianne knew everything and was doing so much cocaine Mick feared for the baby, now almost to term.

Marianne Faithfull: "It was soon after *Performance* finished shooting in the fall of 1968 that drug use among our inner circle took a quantum leap. It's when things become completely unacceptable to the human spirit that you turn to alcohol, to drugs, to help you get through. It was right after *Performance* that Anita went off her rocker for years. Into an abyss."

She wasn't the only one. The events around *Performance* set off a chain reaction of disasters that kept exploding. James Fox freaked out, underwent a religious awakening, disappeared for years. Michelle Breton became a heroin dealer, disappeared, was soon presumed dead. David Litvinoff killed himself in Christopher Gibbs's house. John Bindon, later convicted of murder, became a junkie and died young.

Only Mick was okay, perhaps even stronger than before. He emerged from the film with a new persona he never let drop, the untouchable rock shaman, the magus of the airwaves, the midnight rambler in love with his own beauty and power.

As for Donald Cammell, he knew he had a masterpiece. Everything in his film had been real but the blood and the bullets. He and Nick Roeg vanished into their editing room, but it would be a year before they showed a working print to Warner's. Their cut was so violent, and violently edited, that an executive's wife vomited at the screening and the whole audience fled in revulsion.

Performance was shelved until 1970.

The Baby's Dead

At the end of September 1968, Brian Jones was back in a London court, looking fat and wiped out, pleading not guilty to having a chunk of hash in a ball of wool. Mick and Keith arrived to support Brian, who was duly found guilty. The girls in the gallery cried out at the verdict, and Mr. Jones had to be helped back to his seat. Suki was sobbing, and Keith seemed freaked out. If the judge sent Brian to jail, the Stones would finally have to replace him. But Brian groveled, his psychiatrists testified, and miraculously he was let off with a fifty-pound fine and a scolding.

Outside the court, Brian danced a jig with Mick and Suki. It looked like a brand-new day. Holding Suki's hand afterward, he told the press, "I was sure I was going to jail for at least a year. I never expected that I would be going home. It's such a wonderful relief." Asked for a quote, Mick said, "We're very pleased Brian didn't have to go to jail. Money doesn't matter."

Brian was staying at Redlands. Tom Keylock drove him there with Cynthia Stewart, Stu's wife, to look after him. She put her arm around Brian, and he cried most of the way.

While Mick and Keith were preoccupied with the *Performance* shoot, Brian worked on his Jajouka project. He wrote notes for the album sleeve that touched on his pride in capturing the wild music of the tribe Ahl Sherif in the field. He carefully noted that the recordings were impressionist rather than ethnographic. "I don't know if I possess the stamina to endure the incredible, constant strain of the [Bou Jeloud] festival," he wrote, "such psychic weaklings has Western civilization made of so many of us."

In October, the Rolling Stones caved in to Decca's demand that the toilet sleeve be dropped from *Beggar's Banquet.* A plain white sleeve, styled as a banquet invitation, would be substituted for the late November album release. This would draw unfavorable comparisons with the Beatles' *White Album,* also released that autumn.

Around this time, the Labour Party dispatched M.P. Tom Driberg to convince Mick Jagger to become a politician. Harold Wilson's government had gained forty seats in the 1966 election and was on a roll. Driberg was a longtime ally of the Stones, and he and Mick met to talk politics over lunch at the Gay Hussar in Greek Street. (They had first met when Allen Ginsberg had taken the homosexual Driberg to Mick's flat in Marylebone Road, where Jim Dine's pink phallus sculpture dominated the room. They were drinking tea when Driberg looked longingly at Mick's crotch and gushed, "Oh my, Mick, what a *big* basket you have." Jagger turned red and smiled, Ginsberg reported.)

Driberg now told Jagger that there would be 6 million new voters in the next British general election and that Mick would surely win if he stood for Parliament. Mick listened carefully and gave it much thought, since politics had been one of his early career choices. When Marianne returned to London, she could see he was vacillating. Driberg would come to Cheyne Walk for the evening, find Mick and Marianne playing records and cooking dinner, and keep trying to recruit Mick for the Labour Party.

It almost worked. Marianne recalls that Mick would be convinced at the end of the evening, but would change his mind in the morning when Donald Cammell called screaming for Mick to finish the lyrics to "Memo from Turner." But in the end, instead of winning Jagger for Labour, Driberg was almost talked out of the party by Mick, who was disgusted by the government's support for America in Vietnam, its recent, humiliating devaluation of the pound, and for supporting the Nigerian regime during the civil war in Biafra province.

One night in November, Driberg showed up at 48 Cheyne Walk to have supper with Mick and Marianne. As he arrived, Mick called from Olympic to say he'd be at the studio all night. Marianne burst into tears. Sobbing, she asked the startled politician to please go to the pub next door and buy a few bottles of wine, because she had no money.

————

With the filming complete, the Stones were back in the studio with a vengeance, trying to heal themselves, working on the songs for the album that would become their unrivaled masterpiece, *Let It Bleed*.

The first number they cut was "You Can't Always Get What You Want," on the weekend of November 16 at Olympic. Mick's lyric was an explicit plea to Marianne about her drug use, and an essay on how heroin had infiltrated the lives of the Stones and the people around them. Like "Gimme Shelter" and "Monkey Man," the song described heroin use as a text containing all the bittersweet sadness of the times, in which people felt powerless and turned inward for solace and security. "If God made anything better," Charles Mingus said of heroin, "he kept it for himself." Musicians loved the drug because it made them feel secure and focused.

Al Kooper arrived at Olympic early on the sixteenth, a Saturday night. Then Charlie and Bill, whom Kooper had met in New York, came in. Jimmy Miller was producing, and conga player Rocky Dijon was rolling the massive hash joints required for the sessions. Soon Keith and Mick crashed through the door, Mick in a huge fur coat, Keith in a Tyrolean mountaineer's hat with a pheasant feather stuck in the band.

Soon everyone was on the floor in a circle, just guitars and percussion, as Mick and Keith taught them the chord changes and rhythms of "You Can't Always Get What You Want." Kooper started playing a groove from an Etta James record, and Keith picked it up on guitar. As the session wore on, Jimmy Miller tried to show Charlie a certain drum accent that Charlie failed to master. When Charlie took a break, Miller sat down at the drums and kept playing when they recorded the take (Charlie was unhappy about this but said nothing). Mick and Keith both played acoustic guitars, with Bill on bass. Brian Jones was slumped in a corner, reading *Country Life* magazine during the entire session.

Keith overdubbed his part on electric guitar, and Kooper put his signature organ on the track. At two in the morning, folding tables appeared in the studio laden with an enormous banquet of roast lamb, curries, salads, deserts, and an impressive wine selection. The session broke up at dawn. Kooper told Jagger to call him if he wanted to put horns on the track, because Al thought he heard a good horn part for the song.

———

Two days later, Marianne lost the baby she'd been carrying for seven months. Both she and Mick were distraught. It was a devastating blow that doomed their long affair. Marianne had been anemic, blamed herself, felt blamed by her doctor and Mick for taking drugs. Now she retreated into barbiturates and drink. "He really wanted that baby," she said of Mick, "and so the miscarriage did both of us in."

Mick commemorated their tragedy, inserting the lines "The baby's dead / my lady said" into the new version of "Memo from Turner," and the song was finally complete.

In late November, while *Beggar's Banquet* was released in America and its Luciferian imagery began to seep into youth culture, Brian Jones bought a house in the country. The place was in Hartfield, Sussex, fifty miles southeast of London and not far from Charlie's house. Cotchford Farm, as it was called, was better known around the world as the House at Pooh Corner, because it had been the home of A. A. Milne, who had written his tales of Winnie the Pooh in the house. There was a statue of Christopher Robin in the garden, which the Milne Society had the right to visit annually. It was an almost ridiculously perfect home for a reclusive, semiretired rock star. Christopher Gibbs set about fixing the place up, and everyone close to him talked about how much Brian, who loved to swim, would enjoy the outdoor pool when summer came around again.

The Rock & Roll Circus

December 1968. Planning for *The Rolling Stones Rock & Roll Circus* had been in production for several weeks. Mick Jagger's strategy was to match the Beatles' *Magical Mystery Tour* TV film and get the Stones in front of an international audience. Mick had a fondness for old-fashioned English traveling circuses. His idea was to combine the Stones and their favorite bands with the clowns, jugglers, and animal acts of one of the small circus companies still touring bucolic English fairgrounds, with Brigitte Bardot as the ringmaster. The Stones put up their own money so they could retain control over the film.

Peter Swales: "The Stones weren't a functioning band at that point. Mick, Keith, Charlie, and Bill desperately wanted to get the show back on the road. Mick had told the press the Stones would tour in 1969, and the *Rock & Roll Circus* was supposed to be the first step. Mick was the 'spiritus rector,' the guiding spirit behind the *Circus,* which was done without the input of—indeed was done almost in spite of—Allen Klein."

Mick originally wanted the Stones to appear with the Who, Marianne Faithfull, Dr. John, Gram Parsons's new band, the Flying Burrito Brothers, and a "supergroup" led by Steve Winwood, whose band Traffic was just breaking up. (As the great sixties bands began to disintegrate, their principal stars began linking up with stars from other bands: "supergroup" was a major buzzword of the era.) Keith wanted Johnny Cash, who declined. The Isley Brothers were too busy.

Peter Swales: "Allen Klein tried to sabotage the *Circus* by withholding money and completely failing to book Dr. John and the Burritos. Tom Keylock and I went to Steve Winwood's flat to beg him to do the *Circus* ('No shame in trying to blackmail him,' said Tom), but Winwood said he was physically ill and wouldn't budge. Then Glyn Johns played me an acetate of Jimmy Page's new band, still called the New Yardbirds [soon to be Led Zeppelin], and pleaded with me to get them on the *Circus.* Jagger said no without hearing the record, and I thought there may have been some bad blood there.

"By now it was getting close to taping, but we had no acts except the Stones and the Who. So Mick played his trump card and called up his idol—John Lennon. Mick didn't really want to do it because he didn't want to be beholden to John, but he did it. Lennon said he would do the supergroup and brought in Eric Clapton. Mitch Mitchell [from the Jimi Hendrix Experience] would play drums, and Keith elbowed Bill Wyman aside and insisted on playing bass.

"The final show came together only days before the taping. Taj Mahal and his band were recruited too late to get them work visas, so they flew in as tourists and had to work secretly. I found a new band called Jethro Tull after hearing 'Blues for Jeffrey' at Pie Studios. Then Brian Jones, who'd been given no role in the *Circus* other than a few lines, insisted that Ivry Gitlis be flown in from Paris to perform. [Gitlis, a Paris acquaintance of Brian's, was one of the last living inheritors of the great European violin virtuosos. At forty-seven, he was the embodiment of the romantic tradition and a champion of modern composers like Bartók and Stravinsky.] Brian was obviously under a huge emotional strain. He was sozzled on vodka at the meetings, often crying in the office. Brian insisted that Gitlis was a genius, and we accommodated him." Puzzled by the invitation, Gitlis accepted out of respect for Brian.

———

On December 5, the Stones hosted a drunken press party for *Beggar's Banquet* at a London hotel that ended in a pie fight. Brian Jones was the favorite target; even Les Perrin mashed a pie in Brian's face. Lord Harlech, former British ambassador to Washington, took a direct hit. So did Prince Rupert Lowenstein, Mick Jagger's new financial adviser and éminence grise, a London merchant banker descended from Viennese Jewish aristocracy with a millennium-old Bavarian title. There was a delegation in town from the San Francisco scene—writer Ken Kesey and Rock Scully, who managed the Grateful Dead—hanging out at the Stones' office. They got pied too.

As it turned out, the press didn't need much prodding. *Beggar's Banquet* got rave reviews as critics realized the Stones had rediscovered their blues and country roots and were building something admirable out of them. Mick Jagger described the album to *International Times* as "just a hazy mirror of what we were thinking last summer when we wrote the songs." The hazy mirror was a Top Ten album in England and America, a sharp reflection of the convulsive psychic currents coursing through the Western world. Nothing else captured the youthful spirit of Europe in 1968 like *Beggar's Banquet.*

———

On December 6, the Stones and the Who rehearsed at the Marquee to test the new French TV cameras that would be used for the *Circus,* shooting film and videotape at the same time.

Peter Swales: "The rehearsals for the *Rock & Roll Circus* were held at the Londonderry Hotel. Nobody had seen the Stones play in England since 1966 and there was a lot of suspense. Could they still do this? Eventually the gear got set up [with Nicky Hopkins on piano and Rocky Dijon on congas] and the Stones started to play 'Sympathy' in a re-arranged format, and I watched Jagger just *whip* the Stones back into form. It was incredible!

"But, no Brian. He was tinkering, fiddling, couldn't get his guitar in tune. But I had the sense that, even then they were still willing to give Brian the benefit of the doubt."

———

The *Rock & Roll Circus* was filmed over three days, December 10 to 12, at InterTel studios in Wembley. Beseeching telegrams to Allen Klein to send money for the production went unanswered, so Mick Jagger had to put up 10,000 pounds to secure the studio. On the first day, the cast rehearsed on the set, half a circus tent with a sawdust ring in the center. Ringmaster Jagger presided over an archway, flags, colored lights, and a four-track mobile studio parked outside, in which Glyn Johns recorded the tracks. Sir Robert Fossett's traveling circus provided trapeze artists, clowns, and even a tiger. John Lennon, Eric Clapton, and Mick jammed on "Peggy Sue." Lennon insisted his supergroup be called the Dirty Mac, a play on guitarist Peter Green's hot new blues band, Fleetwood Mac, then taking London by storm with its faithful Elmore James revival.

The main *Circus* taping began at noon on Wednesday, December 11, and would last for eighteen hours. The audience, picked from fans who'd sent in coupons from *New Musical Express*, were given bright ponchos and floppy hats, and sat around the circus ring. Technical problems with the cameras and the lights kept interrupting the flow of the event, with many delays and retakes for each artist. The Kesey/Dead entourage, accustomed to the spontaneity of California happenings, complained about the canned, media-event nature of the show and left early.

Most who stayed enjoyed themselves. Jethro Tull did their number between clown acts. Taj Mahal and band played the old Homer Banks song "Ain't That a Lot of Love." Keith, outfitted in top hat and black eye patch, introduced a fire-eater, assisted by top model Donyale Luna (who got asked out by Brian backstage). Charlie introduced Marianne's number, "Something Better," which she mimed motionlessly seated in a flowing purple dress, looking tragic and sedated.

Peter Swales: "Marianne was nervous, really very tense. At one point, she was sitting near the entrance when six London cops trotted in. The dressing room area was fragrant with hash smoke; Marianne thought it was a bust and flipped! She went bananas, totally hysteric, until it became clear they only wanted to have their tea in the studio canteen."

To introduce the Dirty Mac, Mick dressed up as Allen Klein, in a pastel blue sweater and turtleneck shirt. Mimicking Klein's accent and delivery, he interviewed Lennon as "Winston Legthigh" backstage, while John ate a plate of rice with chopsticks. The Dirty Mac took the stage just after ten and ran through "Yer Blues," a track from *The White Album* that featured the line "I feel so suicidal, just like Dylan's Mr. Jones." Yoko Ono reclined in a black bag at John Lennon's feet and held his hand between takes. Eric Clapton played a couple of fiery guitar solos, earning his place in what became the Plastic Ono Band after the Beatles broke up a year later. After "Yer Blues," Ivry Gitlis joined the band for an R&B jam, with Yoko adding her piercing banshee cries to the mix (this was later titled "Her Blues").

Next came the Who, just off an American tour and impossibly hot. They did several takes of Pete Townshend's mini-opera "A Quick One (While He's Away)," each better than the last, ending in a molten climax of windmilling power chords and Keith Moon's explosive fusillade of drumrolls. The Who were so powerfully *on* they proved impossible to follow.

Three hours now went by as the musicians broke for a meal and the Stones' T-shaped stage was set up by Stu. Some of the audience left to catch the last trains of the night. Finally, at two in the morning, the Rolling Stones with Nicky Hopkins and Rocky Dijon began to warm up. The band looked great: Mick's hair was longer than ever, still dark brown from his role as Turner. Keith had his trademark shag cut, and even

Charlie's hair was below his shoulders. Brian looked okay, but he strummed his guitar listlessly off to one side (he had tried to introduce one of the circus acts but could hardly manage his lines). Bill Wyman wore pink velvet boots and played great, as usual.

The lights and cameras were turned on, and the band started running through songs—"Jumpin' Jack Flash," "Parachute Woman," "No Expectations"—again and again. Long pauses between songs were taken up with discussions with the director and Glyn Johns about whether another take was required. "You Can't Always Get What You Want" was given its debut performance around 4 A.M., with Mick singing directly to Marianne, who was sitting off to one side. Another take, played to the camera, was lurid and alive as Mick relaxed and began to dance. Brian couldn't get through the chords, so Keith had to get the song over without the rhythm guitar.

Exhausted and drained, the Stones did a couple takes of "Sympathy" at 5 A.M., with Rocky Dijon beating his congas and Nicky Hopkins pounding the piano keys as Mick stripped off his shirt, revealing a painted devil covering his chest. Keith tore off a blazing guitar solo as Mick writhed on the stage floor. It was a serious, passionate performance that revealed the darkness lurking in the heart of the song.

The night ended at six in the morning, with Keith and Mick singing along with the backing track of "Salt of the Earth" while seated in the audience, with the Who and their roadies clowning around them. With everyone dancing and making merry, the remaining audience filed out to waiting buses. Mick and Keith shook their hands and thanked them for staying. Bill Wyman thought the whole thing was "a load of laughs and a great spirit."

It was Brian's last appearance with the Stones.

————

Mick Jagger was disgusted when he viewed the taped footage of the *Rock & Roll Circus* a couple days later. The Rolling Stones had sucked. They were obviously off their form and had been badly upstaged by the rip-roaring Who. With some early interest in the film from

London Weekend Television, Michael Lindsay-Hogg edited the footage down to an hour.

Peter Swales: "We all went to see the first version of the *Circus* in a little preview theater in Soho. Allen Klein sat next to Jagger and—right there—killed the movie.

"He said, 'I don't like it. Why? Because the Who blew you off your own stage!' It was all he had to say."

In near-panic mode, the Stones planned to reshoot their own sequence of songs, but it would have cost another 10,000 pounds and never happened. The *Circus* was obsolete when Brian Jones died the following year, and when the Stones split with Klein in 1970, he took the film with him. It would be another twenty-five years before Klein finally released the film as a videocassette, one that almost everyone agreed was a quite wonderful period piece.

———

At the end of 1968, Mick and Marianne and Keith and Anita took ship for Brazil, telling the press they were making a pilgrimage to visit a famous magician. The two couples were trying to patch things up after a difficult year. Anita was pregnant with Keith's baby, but she liked to tease Mick about it being his. On the crossing, Anita hemorrhaged, inspiring "the clean white sheets stained red" in Marianne's final version of "Sister Morphine." New Year's Eve was spent at a macumba voodoo ceremony on the beach in Rio.

And on a hot and dusty cattle ranch where they tarried before they continued their adventure in Peru, Keith wrote a honky-tonk cowboy tune on acoustic guitar, a song about the black ranch hands and their ponies that would change and grow over the next few months until it became something else entirely.

Blow with Ry

January 1969. Brian was in Ceylon over New Year's. He had problems checking into good hotels that didn't want a disheveled hippie as a guest. He visited visionary *2001* author Arthur C. Clarke and saw an astrologer who reportedly told him to be careful around water in the coming year. While he was in Ceylon, a London court turned down his appeal of his second drug conviction. Not even Jo Bergman's friend in Grosvenor Square could get Brian an American work visa now.

It was almost all over for the Beatles as well. On January 30, they played their final concert on the roof of their office building, filmed by Michael Lindsay-Hogg for the *Get Back* film. The cameras also caught the Beatles' discontent and burnout in the studio, as they recorded with Billy Preston on keyboard. Allen Klein took over management of the Beatles after John Lennon was persuaded by Mick that this would be a good idea. Paul McCartney, opposed to Klein but outvoted by his band, was bitterly upset, and the seeds for the end of the Beatles were sown. Conventional wisdom has Mick helping get the Beatles for Klein as a way of getting him off the Stones' back, but Jagger has denied this.

————

The Rolling Stones were back in Olympic Studio in February, working on "You Can't Always Get What You Want." Jimmy Miller—"Mr. Jimmy" in the lyric—was producing, with Jack Nitzsche helping out. On March 15, Nitzsche arranged and recorded the song's soaring chorale, using singers Doris ("Just One Look") Troy and Madelaine Bell and actress Nanette Newman, as well as thirty-five members of the London Bach Choir in an inspired display of tasteful incongruity. Brian Jones, hopeless psychic cripple, was befuddled. "What can I play?" he asked Jagger one night. "I don't know," Mick aridly replied. "What *can* you play?" After that, Brian missed a lot of these sessions, and people wondered if he was still in the band.

Peter Swales: "Brian showed up for only a few recording sessions. He put some Moroccan drums on 'Midnight Rambler.' It was about the limit of his capability. And Jagger would lay it down this way, and not in any *mean* way: 'We *can't* deal with this any more. If he doesn't fucking show up tonight, he's out of the band.' He said this six times.

"I had to communicate these ultimatums to Brian, not too pleasant a task. He'd become so paranoid about the band that he couldn't tune his guitar if Keith was around.

"Some people have since depicted Jagger and Richards as mind-fucking Brian, but I've got to say that I never saw anything of the sort. They tried to accommodate him. They extended themselves, indulged him. But . . . *this guy!* Nobody could save him."

Keith was snorting heroin, offered some to Jack Nitzsche in the studio, told people he wasn't a junkie, had it under control. But anyone who knew Keith and Anita could see how they had changed.

Meanwhile, the music was running hot. Keith and Mick had written the episodic "Midnight Rambler" and "Monkey Man" during a holiday in the hill town of Positano (near Naples) in 1968. Most of the episodes in "Rambler" were worked out in cafés, with Keith on acoustic guitar and Mick on harmonica. Keith had found "Love in Vain" on the new Robert Johnson bootleg and was determined to record it. "You Got the Silver" was taking shape during late nights at Olympic.

During one of these, while Mick Jagger was working, Stash de Rola climbed the wisteria up the balcony of 48 Cheyne Walk, entered the bedroom, and stayed with Marianne until dawn. It was dangerous, but Stash knew Mick would be at Olympic until six in the morning. Then Marianne began having sex with Spanish Tony in return for drugs, because she had no money of her own to buy cocaine and smack.

Decca released Marianne's "Sister Morphine" as a single that February. This wild cri de coeur was an extraordinary artistic statement by a twenty-two-year-old pop singer, but two days later Decca pulled the

record off the shelves because it advocated narcotics use. Mick had produced the song, and he visited the company to try to sort it out. But Sir
Edward Lewis was adamant, and "Sister Morphine" was suppressed.
Marianne was crushed, and Mick disappeared back into the studio. "I
began to lose heart," she later wrote. " 'Sister Morphine' was my inner vision and no one would ever know about it. That was the most depressed
I ever felt." Later that spring, she took on the part of the tortured Ophelia
in a new London production of *Hamlet* starring Nicol Williamson. Some
nights she played Ophelia on LSD, and some nights she made love with
Williamson in the dressing room before they went onstage.

————

Mick Jagger wrote to artist M. C. Escher to invite him to design the cover for the new Stones album, *Let It Bleed,* but Escher bluntly
declined. Peter Swales was dispatched to Paris to approach surrealist photographer Man Ray, who also couldn't be bothered.

Mick invested in the British edition of *Rolling Stone* magazine, which
had been named for the band, but pulled out the following summer (too
busy, no editorial control), and publication stopped.

More successful was the Rolling Stones' Mobile, a truck-mounted
studio control room that was delivered to the band that winter. Rolling
on the back of a British Leyland BMC lorry painted in military camou-
flage, the Stones' Mobile would record much of the next two Stones albums and many other landmark sessions and concerts, and would
continue operating for the next three decades.

————

Ry Cooder arrived at the *Let It Bleed* sessions in May 1969,
brought in by Jack Nitzsche to fill out the Stones' sound. Cooder was put
up in a little apartment near Earls Court. Some felt he might be asked to
join the Stones as a perfect foil for Keith and were disappointed when he
wasn't. Playing his fluid slide guitar themes and original interstellar riffs,
bursting with new ideas and approaches to the music, Cooder was involved in long taped jams with Mick, Charlie, Bill, and Nicky Hopkins

that contained the germs of many *Bleed*-era arrangements. (Excerpts would be released three years later as *Jamming with Edward* on the Stones' own label.) On May 16, Cooder played on a band version of "Sister Morphine" (with different lyrics), as well as adding mandolin to "Love in Vain." The Stones also worked on "Midnight Rambler" and "Monkey Man," and Ian Stewart played piano on the fatalistic new "Let It Bleed," which seemed to sum up the general gloom at the end of the sixties. It was the antithesis to the Beatles' quiescent song "Let It Be."

Cooder didn't like what was going on. "The Rolling Stones brought me to England under totally false pretenses," he told *Rolling Stone* a year later. "They weren't playing well and were just messing around the studio. There were a lot of very weird people hanging around the place, but the music wasn't going anywhere. When there'd be a lull in the so-called rehearsals, I'd start to play my guitar. Keith Richard would leave the room immediately and never return. I thought he didn't like me! But, as I found out later, the tapes would keep rolling. I'd ask when we were going to do some tracks. Mick would say, 'It's all right, Ry, we're not ready yet.'

"In the four or five weeks I was there, I must have played everything I know. They got it all down on these tapes. *Everything*...

"Brian was still alive then, definitely a phased-out person, a sad character. Sometimes when we'd begin playing, Brian would grab a harp and start blowing into a mike. But most of the time he just sat in a corner, sleeping or crying. Jagger was always very contemptuous of Brian and told him he was washed up. They're *bloodsuckers,* man."

––––––––

Brian came to a session to play autoharp on "You Got the Silver." George Chkiantz was the tape op that night. "You know where we ought to be?" Brian whispered to Chkiantz. "Right now, we should be in Jajouka. The festival's going on. I should be dancing in a goatskin. I wish I were there. I *really* wish it."

In the middle of May, Brian's parents visited him at Cotchford Farm. He'd broken up with Suki Potier and had a new girlfriend, a Swedish girl named Anna Wohlin. There was a crew of boisterous builders working on the place, living on the property, charging their drinks in the village pub to Brian's account. Brian showed his parents the Christopher Robin garden, the purple velvet walls, the Moroccan hangings. They found him in good spirits, until he came across a picture of himself and Anita Pallenberg in happier times. He stared at the photograph for a long time, absently whispering her name over and over again.

––––––––

May 1969. "Harlem Shuffle" was a big hit in England, a cool late-soul dance number by Bob and Earl. Keith and Anita were staying at the Ritz while trying to buy the big brick house at 3 Cheyne Walk, down the street from Mick, but getting money out of Klein's office in New York was difficult. Anita was seven months pregnant. One night she and Keith were driving down to Redlands at top speed in a huge Mercedes Keith had bought. Supposedly a Nazi staff car earlier in its life, it had already been smashed and repaired once during Keith's brief ownership, since he liked to drive after a snort of heroin and then would nod off at the wheel. He did it again that night. The speeding car missed the turn at a roundabout, hit the curb, skidded off the road and down an embankment. Covered in blood and glass, Keith hid the dope, dealt with the police, and later got Anita to the hospital, where they found her collarbone broken. Soon Keith was back at the wheel of the Blue Lena.

––––––––

Mick got word to Brian Jones that if he didn't turn up for the photo session for the cover of *Through the Past Darkly,* the Stones' new oldies album, he was out of the band for sure. Brian duly arrived at Ethan Russell's studio, and the band was then photographed lying in a star shape on the deck below St. Catherine's Dock, near Tower Bridge. The actual cover was shot behind some smashed glass near South Kensington Station. Afterward, the Stones stepped into a workingmen's pub for a drink. Dead silence for a while, then someone murmured, "Fucking

Rolling Stones. 'Oo bloody cares?" His back to the crowd, Keith slammed his glass down on the table, hard. Dead silence after that.

It was the last time all five Stones were together.

On Wednesday evening, May 28, the Chelsea cops raided 48 Cheyne Walk. "Marianne, don't open the door!" Mick yelled. "They're after the weed!" But the cops got in, busted them, suggested a bribe to a disgusted Mick. "Why don't you leave us alone?" Mick asked. Mr. Jagger and Mrs. Dunbar, as she was identified, were bailed at fifty pounds apiece.

Around this time, Ry Cooder walked in, unexpectedly, to Olympic Studio and found Keith working on a new song that had developed from tapes Cooder had played on a few days earlier. Cooder freaked out, complained to Nitzsche that the Stones were doing "a sponge job" on him. "They took a number of my best licks," he told *Rolling Stone*, "but more important, they took the basic groove I was playing. He [Keith] had been listening to those tapes. I told Jack Nitzsche we were getting out of there immediately.

"When Mick heard about it, he called me and said, 'What's the matter, Ry? Is it money? C'mon, man, don't leave us now. Let's have *fun*.'

"I told Mick they had all they needed already and that I was leaving. A lot of what I did over there showed up on *Let It Bleed,* but they only gave me credit for playing mandolin on one cut. 'Honky Tonk Women' is also taken from one of my licks. They even admitted this to John Phillips. What bothers me most is the theft of songs . . . The Rolling Stones are a reptilian bunch of people."

Keith: "I heard those things he said. I was amazed. I learned a lot of things off a lot of people. I learned a lot watching Bukka White play. He [Cooder] taught me the tuning [open G] and I got behind it.

"Yes, he came by, and we played together a lot. I mean, he's a gas to play with. He played beautifully, man. But I wasn't there for a lot of it. Charlie and Bill dug to play with him. I mean, *he's so good.*"

The Honky-Tonk Blues

May 1969. The cowbell, then the snare and the bass. The tone-drop riff that opened like a switchblade. Chords in spine-tingling open G, a sonic slash of electric blue: guitar runs, a pedal steel. Memphis, New York City, the divorcée that got laid. Some piano, horns, more guitar. Big band break, big final chorus—she's a hooooonky tonk *woman!*—and that final orgasmic shout, *Whooo!*

"Honky Tonk Women" was the joyous, ballsy med-tempo rocker that made its audience believe it was listening to the greatest rock and roll band in the world. It was recorded in five hours, from eleven on Friday night, May 30, to about four the next morning. Jimmy Miller showed Charlie the drum kick, then played the cowbell that rocked out Keith's cool Brazilian cowboy song. The horn section (much more prominent in the early mixes) was three guys from a recent Fleetwood Mac tour. Nicky Hopkins was on piano. The next morning, Mick Jagger called the office and said, "We done a number one last night."

It was also the advent of Mick Taylor, new guitar player for the Stones.

Eric Clapton had been approached to join the band to replace Brian several times, always informally, but it never happened. They thought of asking him again when they decided to sack Brian at the end of May so they could tour America in the fall, but Clapton was already committed to Blind Faith, his supergroup with Steve Winwood, Ginger Baker, and Rick Grech. Other names were mooted, including Ronnie Wood, a genial twenty-one-year-old smoker and drinker with a great laugh, pinprick eyes, and the right hair, black and scruffy like crow feathers. Recently fired as Jeff Beck's bass player, Woody had just hooked up with the rest of the Small Faces after Steve Marriott left the band. Ian Stewart loved the Faces and let them use the Stones' rehearsal room in Bermondsey, which is where Mick phoned to ask if Ronnie Wood might be interested in joining the Stones. Bassist Ronnie Lane took the call, said no thanks, and only told Woody about it five years later.

———

Mick Taylor was a twenty-one-year-old blues guitarist with the liquid style of an Andalusian singer. His playing was incredibly fluid, with an ear to harmonics and arabesque decoration. As a musician he was a romantic melodist. Physically he was a slight, pasty, innocent-looking youth with long wavy hair, and obviously younger than the Stones.

Born in Hertfordshire on January 17, 1948, Mick Taylor taught himself blues guitar by listening to B. B. King records. He'd first seen the Stones in Soho clubs in 1963, the year he left school. His bands were the Juniors in 1964, then the Gods in 1966–67 before joining John Mayall's Bluesbreakers, replacing Peter Green in 1967. He left the Bluesbreakers in 1969 to go solo.

Mick Taylor was puzzled to get a call from Mick Jagger. He hadn't been a real Stones fan until he'd heard *Banquet* the year before, especially "Street Fighting Man." He arrived at Olympic the night the Stones recorded "Honky Tonk Women," on which his guitar was later overdubbed. Mick Jagger was in a room doing an interview with the London underground paper *International Times*. Jimmy Miller just sat there waiting for Keith, who showed up three hours later. Taylor played on some tracks they were developing—"Gimme Shelter," "Live with Me," an early "Loving Cup"—and thought that was it. "Well, I enjoyed it very much," young Mick told old Mick, thanking him. A few days later, Jagger rang up and asked Mick if he wanted to join the Stones, and Taylor asked for a week to think about it. "It was a very good period for the group," he said later. "They'd made a decision to really get back into touring again. There was a very special atmosphere surrounding the whole thing."

Taylor called Jagger back. "I said, 'I'd *love* to be a Stone!' And that was that." His initial salary was 150 pounds per week, until he became a made member of the Rolling Stones by proving himself on tour. "We got the right guy now," Mick told Peter Swales. "He's really young and cute-looking."

Mick Taylor gave the Stones something it never had, a blues guitar virtuoso. For the next five and a half years, Taylor's charged, cliché-free playing would be the foil for Keith Richards's spiky style as the Stones kept on rolling.

June 1969. The Stones were working on the heroin confidential anthem, "Monkey Man." Brian Jones missed the sessions. He stayed in Sussex, talking to other musicians, especially Alexis Korner, about forming a new band. John Mayall and Mitch Mitchell both visited. Brian consulted Jimi Hendrix who told Brian he needed to write some up-tempo jams. "If you don't see little kids skippin' to your music," Hendrix said, "You got nothin'." Ian Stewart declined the opportunity, saying, "I started one fucking group with you, and that's enough."

On Saturday, June 8, Mick barked to Peter Swales, "Get me a fucking taxi," and went off to see Blind Faith play a free concert for 150,000 kids in Hyde Park. Pink Floyd's free acid rave in the park was even bigger the year before. Promoted by Blackhill Enterprises (who managed Pink Floyd), with the huge crowd expertly controlled by a hip, buckskin-clad emcee named Sam Cutler, the event came off without a hitch. Backstage, Cutler suggested to Mick that the Stones play for free in the park too. A free concert, Jagger realized, would be a trippy way for the Stones to introduce their new guitar player and "Honky Tonk Women" to the world. The date was set for July 5.

They sacked Brian Jones from the Rolling Stones the evening of June 9, one of those early summer English nights when it doesn't get dark until late. Mick, Keith, and Charlie Watts drove down to Sussex to talk to Brian at Cotchford Farm.

Keith Richards: "Mick and I had to go down and virtually tell Brian, 'Hey, old cock, you're fired.' Because there was no serious way we could go on the road with Brian. The fact that he was expecting it made it easier. He wasn't surprised. I don't think he even took it all in. He was already up in the stratosphere. He was like: 'Yeah, man, okay.' "

Mick softened the blow as best he could. He told Brian they would put out any statement he liked. He could say he was leaving the band or just not touring this time, whatever he wanted. They offered him 100,000 pounds in ready cash and 20,000 pounds a year as long as the Stones lasted. Yeah, man, okay.

Keith: "We said, what do you want to say? Do you want to say that you've left? And he said, 'Yeah, let's do it. Let's say I've left and if I want to, I can come back.' [We said,] 'Because we've got to know, and we've got Mick Taylor lined up.' He said, 'I don't think I can. I don't think I can go to America and do those one-nighters anymore.' "

When the meeting was over, the Stones drove back to London to finish mixing "Honky Tonk Women." Brian sat by himself for a while, watching the Christopher Robin garden paint itself black, crying softly to himself.

———

The next day, Les Perrin issued a statement from Brian: "I no longer see eye to eye with the others over the discs we are cutting. The Stones' music is not to my taste any more . . . I have a desire to play my own brand of music rather than that of others. We had a friendly meeting . . . I love those fellows."

The other Rolling Stones would express a certain amount of regret and guilt over the years about what happened to Brian. Mick Jagger: "We carried Brian for quite a long time. We put up with his tirades and his not turning up for over a year. So it wasn't like suddenly we just said fuck you. We'd been quite patient with him, and he'd just gotten worse and worse. He didn't want to come out of this rather sad state. We had to baby him, and it was rather sad.

"What we didn't like was that we wanted to play again onstage, and

Brian wasn't in any condition to play. He was far too fucked up in his mind to play."

Charlie Watts: "I felt sorry for him, for what we did to him then. We took his one thing away, which was being in a band. I'm sure it nearly killed him when we sacked him. That's my opinion."

Awakened from the Dream of Life

Late June 1969. The Rolling Stones were working on "Midnight Rambler" at Olympic, the lyrics inspired in part by the published confessions of the Boston Strangler, Albert DeSalvo, who killed six women in the sixties. They all met at a strip club in Frith Street, Soho (Keith and Mick arrived in Mick's spiffy yellow Morgan), where Ethan Russell photographed the sleeve of "Honky Tonk Women." They rehearsed for the July 5 Hyde Park concert in the Beatles' basement studio at Apple in Savile Row; Charlie and Keith played for hours, jamming on Jimmy Reed numbers, trying to get something going. The next day, they held a press conference in Hyde Park to introduce Mick Taylor as their new guitar player. "He doesn't play like Brian," Mick was quoted. "He's a *blues* player. He gets on well with Keith and wants to play rock and roll, and that's OK with us." They taped their first TV appearance with Taylor, doing "Honky Tonk Women" and "You Can't Always Get What You Want" for David Frost's American program.

Mick and Marianne were learning their lines for their roles in Tony Richardson's new film, *Ned Kelly,* based on the Australian outlaw and folk hero. Mick had been cast as Ned (with Marianne as his loyal sister), provoking a brief outcry from Australian newspapers, which thought Mick too epicene for the role of badass, cop-killing Ned.

While Marianne was drowning herself every night in *Hamlet,* Mick had been seeing a lot of a black American actress, Marsha Hunt, who'd been in the London production of the rock musical *Hair*. He was trying to get money out of Allen Klein for repairs at Stargroves, his country place, which was serving as a commune for some of his friends. And he was helping his new banker, Rupert Lowenstein, plan a big party, a White Ball, at the banker's Holland Park home. Peter Swales hired a new band called Yes to play, and it was a big deal because Princess Margaret, movie stars, and politicians were expected.

Keith needed money to close the deal on 3 Cheyne Walk, but Klein's office in New York didn't respond to his frantic calls and telexes. So Keith sent Tom Keylock to New York. Tom vaulted the receptionist's desk, stormed into Klein's office, sat down, and told Klein he wasn't leaving until he had Keith's money. Rupert Lowenstein was waiting in the wings to assume control of the Stones' finances. Their Decca contract would expire in 1970, and the Stones anticipated a bidding war for their services.

Things had been quiet at Cotchford Farm in June, and Brian seemed better than he had in years. Charlie and Shirley Watts visited him a few times that month, since they lived nearby, and found him upbeat and better. Alexis Korner came and jammed in Brian's fully equipped music room. Brian was heavy into Creedence Clearwater Revival's swampy hit "Proud Mary" and liked to blast "The Ballad of John and Yoko" with his favorite line, "They're gonna crucify me." Stu asked if he was coming up for the free concert, and Brian laughed and said no, because he'd be the only person who'd have to pay.

He was living with Anna Wohlin, a pretty, raven-haired Swedish dancer. She was twenty-two, in love with him, and was trying to help him get back on his feet. They were enjoying the long days of the English summer, taking walks with Brian's dogs, Emily and Luther, picking flowers. Also living on the property, in a flat above the garage, was a builder named Frank Thorogood and his girlfriend, Janet Lawson, a nurse.

Brian had problems with Thorogood and his building crew. Thorogood, forty-four, had been hired by Tom Keylock, having done some work at Redlands. His crew was a raucous bunch of lads and riffraff, openly contemptuous of the stoned rock stars for whom they worked. Thorogood had been working at Cotchford Farm, but Brian felt over-charged and taken advantage of, and had given Thorogood the sack. He allowed him to continue living on the property, possibly because Brian owed him money.

———

Over the years, there have been many attempts to make sense of what happened on July 2, 1969, the night Brian Jones died. In the official version, the people in the house that night claimed that an unsteady Brian was swimming by himself after an evening of drinking, possibly suffered an asthma attack while in the water, and was found drowned at the bottom of his pool. No one believed this except the East Sussex coroner.

Another version, related by an unnamed source years later to an investigating journalist, claimed that Brian was accidentally drowned during a drunken party while "playing" with some of the straw dogs who were working for him. Everyone scattered after a dead Brian was pulled out of the pool, and, threatened and intimidated by Frank Thorogood, no one ever said anything to the police.

Anna Wohlin published her own account thirty years later. According to her, only four people were there that night: Brian, Anna, Thorogood, and Janet Lawson. Brian had fired Thorogood a few days earlier, but hated falling out with people, and invited Frank and Janet to spend the evening with them by the floodlit heated pool.

It was a hot summer night. According to Wohlin, Brian tried to talk to Thorogood, to make up with him. But Thorogood was truculent and kept bringing up the money he said Brian owed him. Brian was conciliatory, teasing, needling Thorogood, drinking his favorite wine, Blue Nun. He suggested they all have a swim. Janet Lawson wasn't in the mood and went into the house to get a drink. Brian, Frank, and Anna jumped into the pool.

The teasing continued in the pool, Wohlin says, and Thorogood got upset. He grabbed Brian and dunked his head underwater. Brian came up sputtering, coughing up water, supposedly still laughing at Thorogood and taunting him. From the house came Janet's voice, telling Anna there was a phone call for her, and Wohlin left Brian and Frank alone in the pool for about fifteen minutes.

"I was chatting on the phone," she related, "when I heard Janet cry from below the bedroom window. 'Anna! Anna! Something's happened to Brian!' I found Frank in the kitchen. His hands were shaking so badly he had difficulty lighting his cigarette . . . When I got outside there was no sign of Brian. Then I saw him, lying on the bottom of the pool." Thorogood and Janet got Brian out of the pool and onto his back in the grass. "He looked so alive when we got him out," Wohlin said. "Unconscious, but not dead." She thought she felt Brian grip her hand. Bill Wyman said she told him that she felt Brian's pulse. Janet tried artificial respiration, but it didn't work, and she told Anna that Brian was dead and ran to call for help.

"I refused to believe Janet when she told me he was gone. I kept giving him resuscitation until the ambulance people pulled me away. I was devastated—Brian had been murdered, by Frank Thorogood."

According to Wohlin, Thorogood threatened her life if she told the police what she had seen. She was taken to London, hidden from the press by Les Perrin, kept away from the funeral. Within a week, she was put on a plane for Sweden and told not to come back to England if she knew what was good for her. She stayed silent until her account was published in England in 1999.

Frank Thorogood called Tom Keylock's home to tell him what had happened, and Keylock arrived—possibly before the police were called. After Brian was pronounced dead shortly after midnight on July 3, the police took conflicting statements from Thorogood, Janet Lawson, and Anna Wohlin. Les Perrin found Brian's asthma inhaler by the side of the pool at three in the morning and gave it to the police. After they left, Brian's house was looted of some valuables—money, tapes, guitars, clothes, and a William Morris tapestry.

Ian Stewart picked up the phone at Olympic Studio at two in the morning of Thursday, July 3. It was Tom Keylock's wife, saying Brian was dead. The Stones had been recording a Stevie Wonder song, "I Don't Know Why." They all looked at each other and went into what passed for shock among the Rolling Stones. They lit a couple of joints and sat on the floor. Charlie Watts wept for a while, then called Bill Wyman at his hotel to tell him Brian was gone.

BRIAN JONES OF THE 'STONES' FOUND DEAD was the headline on that morning's *Daily Mirror*. The London press reported the events as given them by the police, based on the three people they'd interviewed.

At 10 A.M., the Stones appeared as scheduled at the BBC studios to tape "Honky Tonk Women," since the single would be out the following week while Mick was in Australia. That night, he and Marianne went to Prince Rupert's White Ball. Mick wore the skirted white suit that he would later dance in at Hyde Park. Marianne, deeply affected by Brian's death, wore black, much to the annoyance of the Lowensteins. The rock bands Peter Swales hired for the party did their thing, and Rupert Lowenstein was pleased as punch when the next day's papers reported that his party had kept the neighbors awake until three.

The Stones met at their Maddox Street office later that day amid doubts whether to do the concert, but decided to carry on in memory of Brian. "He would have wanted it to go on," Mick told a reporter, straight-faced.

———

"Brian's death will always be suspicious," Keith Richards said years later, reflecting the disquiet about the case that lingered for decades. Everyone knew that Brian was the strongest swimmer they'd ever seen, and it was absurd that he could drown in a backyard pool unless he'd had a lot of help.

After he died, rumors that Brian had been accidentally killed circulated immediately. Police reopened their investigation six weeks after the coroner issued his preliminary report of "death by misadventure" due to a combination of drugs and alcohol. Some who worked on the case reportedly wanted to charge Frank Thorogood with manslaughter, but it never happened.

Keith Richards: "We were completely shocked. I got straight into it and wanted to know who was there, and couldn't find out. The only cat I could ask [Tom Keylock] was the one I think got rid of everybody and did the whole disappearing trick so when the cops arrived, it was an accident. Maybe it was. Maybe the cat just wanted to get everyone out of the way so it wasn't all names involved. Maybe he did the right thing. I don't even know who was there that night, and trying to find out is impossible. It's the same feeling [as] who killed Kennedy. You can't get to the bottom of it.

"Maybe [Brian] was trying to pull one of his deep-diving stunts and was too loaded and hit his chest and that was it. But I've seen Brian swim in terrible conditions. He was a goddamn good swimmer and it's hard to believe he died in a swimming pool."

As the years went by, the Stones came to agree that Brian died accidentally. Keith said that he, Keith, had more reason to kill Brian than anyone. Mick dismissed all the conspiracies, as did Charlie Watts: "I think he took an overdose. He took a load of downers, which is what he used to like, and drank, and I think he went for a swim in a very hot bath . . . Quite honestly, I don't think he was worth murdering, because he was worth more alive than dead."

Mick: "Brian drowned in his pool. The other stuff is people trying to make money."

Yet Brian Jones's death remains a mystery to many people unconvinced that any of the legends of his fall are accurate. He gave the Stones what Nick Kent has called "the full force of authentically damned youth," and so it seems apposite that the details of his death are unclear.

Nevertheless, some believe that Frank Thorogood, dying of cancer in 1993, confessed to killing Brian Jones. "I done Brian," he allegedly gasped to a friend, and expired shortly thereafter.

Shelley in Hyde Park

Saturday, July 5, 1969. The bands opening for the Rolling Stones in Hyde Park started playing for the huge crowd of about 300,000 at one o'clock on a hot, sunny afternoon. King Crimson, Family, and Alexis Korner's New Church played short sets. The stage, the largest ever built for an outdoor show in England, was ringed by cameras and protected by about fifty local "Hell's Angels," actually a bunch of yobs in studded leather costumes. Sam Cutler had heard from Rock Scully how the Oakland chapter of the Hell's Angels motorcycle gang had provided hip security for the Grateful Dead's famous free shows in San Francisco's Golden Gate Park, and so these ersatz London bikers were hired to do the same in Hyde Park.

Mick Jagger had laryngitis but was itching to get onstage. Keith was stoned. Mick Taylor was scared shitless. Ronnie Wood bumped into Keith and Charlie on his way to the show and wished them luck. The Stones gathered in the nearby Londonderry House Hotel on Park Lane, where Bill Wyman saw Jagger in tears, deeply affected by Brian's death. The Stones were driven to the backstage enclosure in an old army ambulance. They rehearsed for fifteen minutes, trying to tune the guitars to a harmonica. Then they gave one of their worst performances ever.

Before the Stones went on, Mick asked Sam Cutler to quiet the crowd. Costumed in his white party dress and a studded dog collar, standing in front of a backdrop showing a drunken Brian from the *Beggar's Banquet* photo sessions, Mick then addressed the crowd: "Now listen, cool it for a minute. I really would like to say something about Brian, about how we feel about him just going, when we didn't expect it." He took out an edition of Percy Shelley and read two stanzas from the heroic threnody "Adonais":

Peace, peace! he is not dead, he doth not sleep—
He hath awaken'd from the dream of life—
'Tis we, who lost in stormy visions, keep
With phantoms an unprofitable strife . . .

Keith hit the opening chords of Johnny Winter's "I'm Yours, She's
Mine" as the Stones began their first show in England in two years and
Tom Keylock released two thousand white moths in memory of Brian.
But most of the creatures had suffocated in their boxes, one of which had
been crushed by a drunken "Angel" who'd fallen on it, and the gesture fell
flat as dead moths littered the stage.

The Stones did their best under the circumstances: "Jack Flash";
"I'm Free"; "Mercy Mercy"; "No Expectations," with Mick Taylor playing
Brian's slide part expertly. "Here's one about a groupie" before "Stray Cat
Blues." The air was so humid the guitars kept going out of tune, and the
Stones struggled to keep up with their perspiring drummer. "Tempo!"
Mick shouted at the band. "Get your tempo together." In the crowded
VIP area in front of the stage were Marianne and her son, Paul
McCartney and Linda Eastman, Eric Clapton, Donovan, Allen Klein,
Robert Fraser, Michael Cooper shooting away, Marsha Hunt in tight
white buckskin. The Stones managed the public debuts of "Loving Cup,"
"Love in Vain," and "Honky Tonk Women" in a protracted format that
differed from the recorded version and sounded ragged. "We got lots
more to do," Mick told the crowd after the Stones had badly mangled
"Loving Cup," "and we're gonna get better as we go along!"

They didn't. They bungled "Midnight Rambler" too, then stumbled
through "Satisfaction," "Street Fighting Man," and ten minutes of
"Sympathy for the Devil" with a troupe of South African dancers until
Mick got bored and signaled that the Zulus be thrown off the stage.

After an hour, having disgraced themselves, the Stones were done.
A confetti drop covered Charlie and his tom-toms in colored paper. But
the event was judged a great success in the press because the giant, docile
crowd had even picked up their litter as they left. The positive, peaceful
buzz from the show helped reestablish the Stones as the leading band in

England. Afterward a car took a dope-sick Marianne and Nicholas back to Cheyne Walk, while Mick squired his girlfriend Marsha Hunt to see Chuck Berry and the Who at Royal Albert Hall.

The next day, Mick and Marianne flew to Australia to begin work on *Ned Kelly*. During the long flight to Sydney, Marianne had a chance to think things over. When they arrived at their hotel, she took 150 Tuinal pills and said good night. Mick couldn't wake her the next day and thought she was dead. They pumped her out, but she was in a coma for six days, during which, she told Mick, a ghostly Brian urged her to join him on the other side.

Tony Richardson gave her part in the film to a local actress, and production went forward during July.

———

Brian was buried in Cheltenham on July 10, the day after a coroner's inquest concluded he'd drowned accidentally. Charlie and Bill attended with Shirley and Astrid. Suki Potier came, as did Ian Stewart. Linda Lawrence came from America with her five-year-old son, Julian. Mick and Marianne sent a wreath. Due to his local notoriety, Brian's parents had to beg for the service to be held in the Anglican church in whose choir he'd sung. As a possible suicide (to say nothing of his reported six bastard children), permission was denied for Brian to rest in the churchyard.

Bill Wyman was astonished to see the crowds lining the streets to witness the funeral cortege. There were hundreds of women, many in tears, throwing roses at the hearse. Canon Hugh Hopkins, who'd known Brian as a boy, gave a diffident eulogy that many found offensive in its faint praise for Cheltenham's pop outlaw. The scriptural reading was the Prodigal Son.

On the way out of the church, Brian's bronze coffin (flown in from New York) was saluted by the police. This gave Charlie Watts his only laugh of the day.

During the funeral, the workmen who'd been grafting off Brian held a party at Cotchford Farm, even using Brian's bed for their fun. A truck was backed up to the house and filled with furniture, artwork, and instru-

ments, including an organ and Brian's Mellotron. These were never seen
again. Local people who'd befriended Brian were troubled to see his
clothes, papers, and other effects burned in a series of bonfires over the
next few days. Suki Potier arrived the following week to find the house
looted and almost empty. Luckless, she herself died in a car wreck within
a few years.

––––––––––

Most people were fatalistic in the wake of Brian's death, especially those who knew him. Anita was angry that no one had been around
to take care of him. The office staff took it hard. So did Keith. Others were
almost relieved.

George Chkiantz: "I had my doubts whether he could ever get anything together. I'm sorry to say that it might have been fortunate that
Brian died before he found out how few friends he really had. I felt sorry
for him, felt that when the Stones' money ran out, it wasn't going to be
so good for him."

"No one wanted to imagine Brian growing old," Peter Swales adds.
"He was one of those types of characters you never wanted to see shuf-
fling down the Kings Road later in life."

When asked for a comment on Brian's death, Peter Townshend
said, "Oh, it was a normal day for Brian. Like he died every day, you
know?" George Harrison was quoted: "I don't think he had enough love
or understanding."

It was the first major death of anyone in the rock movement, fore-
shadowing many tragedies. In Los Angeles, Jim Morrison wrote a long
poem, "Ode to L.A. While Thinking of Brian Jones, Deceased":

You've left your Nothing
To compete with Silence
I hope you went out Smiling
Like a child
Into the cool remnant
Of a dream.

————

There was an accident on the *Ned Kelly* set as Tony Richardson shot his movie in the pale light of the Australian winter. An old revolver exploded in Mick's hand as he was rehearsing for a gunfight scene, and while recuperating the doctors told him to exercise his injured wrist. One day he was alone in the outback with his valet, Alan Dunn, playing electric guitar through a small amp, when the chords to "Brown Sugar" materialized in the air. The lyric came next, "brown sugar" being a play on potent Asian heroin and the charms of black girls like Marsha Hunt. The song was the only positive thing to emerge from Mick's Australian ordeal. His girlfriend had tried to kill herself, and he wouldn't make another movie for twenty years. He described the disastrous *Ned Kelly* as "that load of shit" when it came out the following year.

————

That summer, around the time of Hyde Park, Keith got his ear pierced by some Living Theater people one night. He hung from his lobe a heavy bone earring he'd gotten in Peru. It became his trademark over the next few years, along with his no-limits gaze and the endearing gap where his front teeth had rotted out of his head.

The Bleeding Man

The Rolling Stones' hot new single "Honky Tonk Women" ruled the airwaves in the summer of 1969, a raunchy jam with a stripper beat that made hearts beat harder and sold its way to no. 1 everywhere. A truncated mix of "You Can't Always Get What You Want" appeared on the single's flip side. Al Kooper had volunteered to arrange horns for the track and received the master tape for this song in the mail one day from Mick. Kooper arranged and recorded a full horn section for the song, but only his French horn introduction was finally used. Kooper was credited on the single's label with organ and piano as well, an unprecedented gesture by the Stones attesting to Kooper's exalted stature as a studio wizard.

Anita and Keith's son was born on August 10, 1969, and named Marlon Richards, after Marlon Brando. Bill Wyman divorced his wife, and the press delighted in publishing his real age, thirty-two, considered ancient for a pop star. In mid-August, the Woodstock music festival was held in upstate New York. (Mick Jagger had turned down an invitation for the Stones to perform.) Billed as "Three Days of Peace and Love," Woodstock mingled a half million muddy, tripping rock fans with the star performers of the day (the Band, the Who, Hendrix, et al.) without much trouble. This spawned the communitarian notion of "Woodstock Nation," an idealized global village of rock music–loving youth supposedly self-sufficient enough to feed, police, and care for itself without the help of the "straight" world. It was a hippie myth that lasted until the Stones toured America four months later.

In London, Mick was trying to disengage with Allen Klein. Mick told Peter Swales not to give Klein the Stones' Hyde Park tapes, so Peter hid them in the toilet. When Klein showed up at Maddox Street to collect the tapes, Swales tried, "Sorry, I can't give them to you." Klein grabbed Swales by the throat and threw him across the room. He got the tapes. Swales then carried a note from Mick to Paul McCartney that read, "Do what you want about Allen Klein, but I don't trust this guy."

In September, Decca/London released *Through the Past, Darkly— Big Hits Vol. 2*, dedicated to Brian's memory. The album collected "Honky Tonk Women" and other, more recent singles and album tracks. Issued in a six-sided die-cut sleeve, the album carried an epitaph, as if it were Brian's tombstone: "With this you see, remember me and bear me in your mind. Let all the world say what they may, speak of me as you find."

The music business is like shark life—keep moving or die. The Stones needed money, had to tour America now to support their new album, so the autumn of 1969 was taken up with planning: eighteen shows in fourteen cities during three weeks in November. It would be a new kind of tour, arenas only, ratcheting up the entire game, with the same stage, lights, and sound system every night, all designed by technical director Chip Monck from San Francisco promoter Bill Graham's organization. Opening acts would include the Ike and Tina Turner Revue, B. B. King, occasionally Chuck Berry, and the young London rock singer Terry Reid, who had turned down Jimmy Page's offer to join Led Zeppelin.

The Rolling Stones were basically without management. Allen Klein was preoccupied with the Beatles after his new client John Lennon told the other Beatles in September that he was quitting the band. Working through Klein's disaffected accountant nephew, Ronnie Schneider, who had carried their bags on the '65 tour, Mick set up a tour that got the band a 60/40 cut with American promoters. Mick had originally wanted to book the tour himself, bypassing the agencies and earning the band an 80 percent share, but this was too difficult. (Nobody got this kind of deal until Led Zeppelin's manager, Peter Grant, forced it on the concert business in 1972.)

Peter Swales: "This is where we all saw Jagger prove himself as a natural leader, where he just took the thing over. He really knew how to consult; he'd listen and consider any opinion, especially Charlie's. Charlie could kill one of Mick's pie-in-the-sky plans with a few words. He was a very savvy, very dry and lovely bloke. Mick handled Keith differently. Keith didn't have much to say—these weren't his best years—but what he *did* say had major weight. They'd hammer things out together and could be very ruthless with others. I'd see them break people down, and it was scary. But you *never* saw them go at each other."

The Stones were uneasy. They hadn't toured America in three years, and now they were returning to a nation that had become a cauldron of weirdness and mayhem. The Vietnam War had poisoned America's spirit, and race relations were volatile after Martin Luther King's assassination the year before. In Los Angeles, the Stones' first stop, Charlie Manson's hippie "family" had just butchered a houseful of celebrities.

It was a witchy time. There was black magic in the air, amateur necromancy that made Stones pal Kenneth Anger's occult dabbling in London look tame. Astrology was immense. Hippie girls cast the tarot and threw coins to consult the I Ching. Gurus were afoot, and hip youths were "getting back to the land," with communes sprouting everywhere. The rock music scene was totally wild. Los Angeles groupies began to spread rumors about Led Zeppelin signing a pact with the devil in exchange for their incredible new success. It was a replay of Robert Johnson at the crossroads, a new blues legend for the Atomic Age.

It had never been easy for the Rolling Stones in America, but now it seemed even more dangerous. Mick Jagger must have had an inkling that any performer playing Lucifer in America was in for trouble. On this tour, there was a new emphasis on muscle, bodyguards, and various layers of security (in part because of union problems with the Stones' nonunion crew, in part because of "some paranoia among the organizational people about Uncle Allen," as Keith put it). Hyde Park honcho Sam Cutler, longhaired cockney in fringed buckskins and a cowboy hat, exuding laid-back rock know-how, was hired as road manager.

Touchdown at LAX. The band scattered. Mick and Keith shared a house owned by Stephen Stills in Laurel Canyon. Bill and Astrid and Mick Taylor and girlfriend Rose Miller checked into the Beverly Wilshire Hotel, while Charlie and Shirley and their daughter stayed in a rented house above Sunset Boulevard that became Stones headquarters. The band set up at Elektra Studio in Hollywood for further recording and mixing for *Let It Bleed.*

Almost as soon as they arrived, a torrid scene gathered around the Stones. Mick took up with Miss Pamela, teenage shirtmaker to L.A.'s ascendant country rockers and leader of the GTOs, the groupie clique attached to Frank Zappa's band. She was in the middle of an affair with Jimmy Page, but Page was back in London. Keith hooked up with the black groupie Emeretta Marks, having left Anita and Marlon in London. Gram Parsons was in and out on his big motorcycle with his fabulously plentiful cocaine and his charm, very tight with Keith (to Mick's annoyance), playing soulful country songs on the piano, shoving coke up every nose in sight. At night, they went to clubs to catch Taj Mahal opening for blues legend Big Boy Crudup, or Gram's Flying Burrito Brothers at the Corral in Topanga Canyon, or Ike and Tina at PJ's. Back in Laurel Canyon at dawn, they'd play "Love in Vain" on guitars. They'd replay the stuff they'd done in the studio that day. Miss Mercy of the GTOs would be laying out her tarot deck while Mick tried to persuade Miss Pamela to get into bed with him.

The autumn evenings in Los Angeles were soft and balmy, there was tons of good dope and pretty girls everywhere—Sam Cutler found he couldn't keep them away—and soon everyone calmed down. They threw a thirty-third-birthday party for Bill Wyman at the end of October, but the guest of honor suffered an anxiety attack after eating a hash brownie and left early.

Let It Bleed was finished during the last two weeks in October after almost a year in production. Jimmy Miller and Glyn Johns rolled tape at Elektra Studio in Hollywood. "Live with Me" was filled out by local musicians Leon Russell on piano and Bobby Keys on tenor sax. Mick Taylor, warming to his new job, played red-hot lead guitar on "Live with Me" and "Love in Vain." Merry Clayton, an Afro-headed soul singer who worked in the studios, was chosen for the crucial female vocal part in "Gimme Shelter." Mick and Keith were also writing, cutting early versions of "Shine a Light" (with Leon Russell) and "All Down the Line."

By early November, the album that is arguably the Rolling Stones' great masterpiece was in the proverbial can. "Gimme Shelter" opened *Let It Bleed* with its haunting heroin music, the aural equivalent of cooking junk in a tingling fever of anticipation, conflating sex, violence, drugs, and music in a boiling stew of rambling blues harp, guitars, scrapers, and maracas. Merry Clayton's raving cries of rape gave the song its crazy edge; she was the first woman ever to play a major part on a Rolling Stones record.

"Love in Vain" came next, augmented with extra chords and given a primitive reading by Mick. Ry Cooder played the crying mandolin, and

Mick Taylor added atmospheric, trainlike slide guitar. In a publishing scam when *Let It Bleed* was released, "Love in Vain" was credited to the fictitious "Woody Payne," prompting more accusations of thievery.

"Country Honk" was a Gram Parsons remix of "Honky Tonk Women," closer to Keith's Brazilian original. Gram brought in young country fiddler Byron Berline, who overdubbed his part outdoors, in the parking lot of the studio, as Jimmy Miller honked a car horn.

The up-tempo rocker "Live with Me" marked the debut of reedman Bobby Keys into the Stones' orbit. Keys was a seasoned road musician of twenty-six who'd met the Stones on their first tour, when he was in Bobby Vee's band. He had a raw, honking tenor sax style and worked regularly in recording sessions when he was in L.A. Leon Russell, who arranged the number, brought Keys to the studio to add some old-school rock and roll ambience to the track. "Live with Me" became a preview of the Stones' horn-augmented seventies sound. Keys's tenor solo, fiery with roadhouse grease and Dexedrine energy, would be good for nearly thirty years as an adjunct Rolling Stone.

"Let It Bleed" ended side one with its ironic look at friendship and Stu's barrelhouse piano underscoring Mick's generous offer to come all over him. The Beatles had left themselves open to ridicule with their idealized wish to "Let it be." In the Stones' less delusional worldview, it was more realistic to "Let it bleed." (Keith's preferred title for this album had been *Hard Knox and Durty Sox,* which was duly printed above the track list on the record's inner sleeve.)

Bleed's second side was a nearly perfect sequence of rock songs. The dramatized episodes and violent lingo of "Midnight Rambler" so warped against the prevailing cultural grain that the song commanded instant recognition as something special. "Rambler" built climaxes with an almost sexual dynamic before hurtling to a final, orgasmic rush. (The song's connection to the au courant rock theater concept was Doors engineer Bruce Botnick, who had mixed "Rambler" in Los Angeles.) It also established Mick Jagger as a serious blues harmonica stylist, the possessor of a unique and recognizable sound.

A startling and surreal love song, Keith Richards's perilous journey through the diamond mines of romance, "You Got the Silver" was his first solo track, with Nicky Hopkins on organ between the verses. The full band came in halfway, with Keith shouting over his spidery guitars.

"Monkey Man" and its satanic, apocalyptic imagery nailed the album cold. "All my friends are *junkies,*" Mick Jagger howled, not far from the truth. The song was a Burroughsian peek into hell, with swooping cones of guitar and an almost savage glee as shrieking apes clawed the back of the song's riff as it faded into . . .

The plummy English choir that kicked off "You Can't Always Get What You Want," Mick Jagger's sad chronicle of his circle's descent into drugdom. With a sob in his voice, he told his story of despair at a fashionable party, of seeing the doomed junkie Mr. Jimmy at the Chelsea Drugstore, of seeing his girlfriend's beauty and persona begin to slide into narcotic decline. The poignant last verse, with its image "in her glass was a bleeding man," was a psychic coronary before the organ and choir climbed celestial octaves as Jimmy Miller's drums beat a tattoo into overdose, death, and transfiguration.

"It's a kind of end-of-the-world thing," Mick later said of *Let It Bleed.* "It's Apocalypse; the whole record's like that."

The London Bach Choir, heard on the album's last song, was offended at *Let It Bleed*'s relentless drug ambience. Its director denounced *Bleed* when it was released late in November. No rock record, before or since, has ever so completely captured the sense of palpable dread that hung over its era.

The Greatest Rock and Roll Band in the World

On October 27, 1969, the Rolling Stones held a press conference at the Beverly Wilshire to announce their tour schedule and to counter attacks in the press. When it was reported the Stones would take home a million dollars from the tour, the influential San Francisco columnist Ralph J. Gleason scolded the band for high ticket prices ($7.50) and general arrogance. Recalling the good vibes in Hyde Park, Mick Jagger parried by offering to play a free outdoor concert in the Bay Area after the tour. American fans didn't exactly buy into media criticism of the Stones, and the whole tour sold out within hours. Extra dates in L.A. and New York sold out within minutes.

Rock Scully and Emmett Grogan, leader of the Diggers, came to L.A. to discuss the free concert with Jagger and his brain trust of tour executives: Ronnie Schneider, security consultant John Jaymes, and Sam Cutler. The Grateful Dead's organization would try to secure Golden Gate Park and get the other San Francisco bands to play. It would be Woodstock West, but better. The Hell's Angels would handle security, no problem.

When rehearsals began, there was initial fear in the entourage as they heard how badly the Stones played, stopping and starting, ragging each other. Rehearsals scheduled for 7 P.M. only got going when Keith arrived at one in the morning, a pattern that continued throughout the tour. The Stones adopted an arrogant "make 'em wait" attitude that infuriated promoters and arena personnel all over the country as the band often went on three hours late.

After a week, to general relief, the band started playing like the Rolling Stones. It was just the five Stones, plus Ian Stewart on piano for the Chuck Berry rockers that Keith and Mick Taylor could play together. Mick Taylor was shocked by how loud the Stones' new Ampeg amplifiers were set. "If you don't play as loud as Keith," Stu told him, "you might as well go home."

The concert business in America had been professionalized since the Stones had last toured, with vast changes in the format of the commercial rock show.

As Keith recalled, "It had changed while we'd been off the road for three years. Suddenly we had to work with P.A. systems. Now there's an audience who's listening to you instead of screaming chicks. Before, we'd go out and play and there'd be one speaker hanging off the wall for the voice and that was it. The band just played, the girls screamed, and we ran away. Instead of playing full blast to try and penetrate the audience, now we gotta learn to play onstage again. So for us it was like a school, that '69 tour."

Mick Jagger: "The whole thing became more organized. Had your lights, had your own crew. Up to then rock and roll tours were much more ramshackle. You played every kind of place, very disorienting for the performer. It's much easier to play the same kind of place every night, the same stage, the same configuration. It becomes like a second home."

———

On Friday, November 7, 1969, the Stones flew to Fort Collins, Colorado, to begin the tour at Colorado State University. The band's security unit, under the massive black bodyguard Tony Funches, was made up of moonlighting New York City narcotics detectives, armed to the teeth. Their job was as much to protect the Stones from local police as it was to hold their rabid fans at bay. And from the beginning, the fans, especially the girls, tried to throw themselves at the band in reckless waves of adulation and lust. America seemed really crazy for the Stones.

Sam Cutler introduced the band in Colorado with what became his famous boast: "Ladies and gentlemen, the greatest rock and roll band in the world—the fabulous Rolling Stones!" Mick professed to be shocked at Cutler's ballsy slogan, instant buzzwords that caught like a prairie fire around the land, provoking much comment and wonder. Was it really true? Mick: "It was a stupid epithet, like we were a circus act. I used to say, '*Please* don't use that, it's too embarrassing.'" Sam Cutler ignored him.

Mick was performing in his black "Omega" jumpsuit, the legs of his and Keith's trousers fashionably studded with silver Mexican conchas. Trailing a long pink silk scarf and with blue-beaded moccasins on his feet, Mick danced and whirled on a purple carpet with a white starburst, bumped and grinded, minced and pranced, carrying the visual part of the show by himself in Brian's absence, as the other Stones played almost impassively around him.

Next day, two shows at the Los Angeles Forum. Mick started eyeing Claudia Linnear, the statuesque Ikette whose pelvic astonishments were a highlight of the Ike and Tina Turner Revue. Just before "Honky Tonk Women," Mick asked for the house lights to be turned on "so we can see you," and the rest of the show was played in bright electric light.

On November 9, the Stones had their first fiasco, at the Oakland Coliseum, where it went bad even before the music started. Promoter Bill Graham was abusing fans, slapping teenage girls, which made Charlie livid. Graham then got into a fistfight with Sam Cutler. After they were pulled apart, Graham began shouting at Pete Bennett, Allen Klein's tough New York promo man, who smashed Graham in the crotch with his briefcase. Graham went ape, and two competing teams of security goons squared off in the backstage corridors. Graham threatened to cancel the second show and demanded to speak to Mick, whom he worshiped as the living apotheosis of Rock Spirit. Jagger received Graham in his dressing room, hardly looked at him, continued to apply his mascara and rouge, and haughtily told Bill to please stop shouting and quit being silly. "The show," Mick told him, in not much above a whisper, "must go on."

It did, but the amps burned out right after "Jack Flash."

Mick: "Shit! Hang on a minute. Can you hear that?" The guitars were dead, so they moved the acoustic bit up to the front. Power restored, they tried to regain their footing. "Carol" built into a propulsive swing with the two guitars weaving together. There was hardly any applause. Same after "Sympathy." The crowd was completely sedated. Mick: "Oh, it'd really be a groove if you'd shake your arses!" Nothing, a few cheers. "O-kaayy, here we go, slowly rocking on." This led into "I'm Free," which killed the show like a shot in the head.

"I think we've got a problem," Mick said into the mike, a wild understatement. He plunged into the harp intro to "Midnight Rambler" with its sadomasochistic floor show. He took off the heavy studded belt that Marianne had bought in the Kings Road and whipped the stage floor in diabolical time to Keith's deafening guitar chords during the song's rape scene. When the belt struck the stage, Chip Monck flashed a gory strobe of red light, like an explosion of blood in the pitch-black hall. The effect was dramatic, violent, enthralling.

This woke the soporific audience, provoking the first real applause of the show, ten songs into the set. But it wasn't really the crowd's fault. The hall was too big, the sound was bad, and the Stones didn't really come alive until "Little Queenie" got rocking good. "Come *on*, San Francisco!" Mick shouted. "Let's see how you can shake your arses! Come on! Gonna have a good time! Wooooo! Come on! We want to hear the chicks hit the high notes of this next one." This was "Honky Tonk Women," which started slow and stately, played awhile as a sing-along, and got really good when Mick Taylor remembered why he was there and started to play his wild Arabian blues fills. The show ended, on fire at last, with "Street Fighting Man," Keith setting off his dynamite riff with energy, feedback, and flame-throwing liquid spears of sound. Mick threw a big basket of rose petals into the crowd, as he did at every show. The second Oakland show only happened because some Grateful Dead crew people in the audience raced over to the band's Marin County headquarters, got the Dead's amps, and loaned them to the Stones.

The Stones made a quick getaway to their chartered plane after the show. Instead of flying back to L.A., a demoralized Mick ordered the pilot to take them to Las Vegas, where they spent the rest of the dark morning gambling. At one point, with no limos, the band started stumbling across desert roads from one casino to another, looking to lose even more money.

Both of the Oakland shows had been recorded by Bill Graham's staff and broadcast over the San Francisco FM station KSAN. Within weeks of the tour, the edited tapes were bootlegged on an album with the stamped title *LIVEr Than You'll Ever Be*. The first unauthorized Stones record—the disc label said Lurch Records—it appeared in early 1970, sold hundreds of thousands of copies, and received rave reviews in the underground press.

———

The Stones' tour continued through November, coursing through the western United States amid immense publicity and increasing fan abandon. The cops at Southern Methodist University's field house reminded the band's security squad that Texas judges awarded up to ten years in prison for possessing a single joint, so the Stones—guarded by their own narcotics police—discreetly snorted their coke while Chuck Berry opened the show, then played a perfunctory set and got the hell out of town.

The next show was at Auburn University in Alabama in front of a segregated crowd of ugly-lookin', cannon-fodder crackers too stoned to dance. Mick hated this so much he insisted on flying out that night instead of staying in the local motel. They waited hours for a chartered plane to show up, then took off uneasily in an ancient DC-3 during a rainstorm that blew them into Chicago airsick and thoroughly disgusted.

Sunday night, November 16, in the Chicago International Amphitheater, Chuck Berry refused to play until he got his $3,000 fee in cash. Abbie Hoffman got backstage to ask for money for the trial of the Chicago Eight, the radical antiwar leaders indicted for disrupting the Democratic convention the previous July. He left empty-handed. As Tina Turner and the Ikettes gyrated in hip-high silver minidresses, Mick watched from the wings, licking his lips, eyes glued to Claudia Linnear. This annoyed Ike Turner, who packed a gun onstage and had proprietary feelings toward Claudia himself. After the show, Tina Turner took Mick aside and warned him to lay off sister Claudia or there was going to be a problem with Ike. Mick cooled it for a while, then got into the lubricious dancer when Ike wasn't around. When he found out, Ike Turner was mad as hell.

Wild Horses in Alabama

Late November 1969. The Stones were crisscrossing America now, playing better every night. "Midnight Rambler" took over the show, a six-scene play-within-a-play, a blues allegory on rape and murder. By the time the lights came on for "Honky Tonk Women," whole buildings were rocking. In some of the halls, the Stones could see the balconies actually sway. It was Keith's favorite part of the show. "The whole place looks the same, when the house lights are up, when the stage looks just as tatty as the rest of the hall and everybody's standing up. That's the real turn-on, not the 'theater' [of "Rambler"]. It's when the audience decides to *join,* that's when it really knocks you out."

Traveling separately from the band was a mysterious friend of Keith's named Fred Sessler. He was forty-six, looked sixty-six, an international businessman born in Poland. He'd seen the Stones in their Crawdaddy days and later befriended Anita and Brian. Sessler had what he called a legal license to import pharmaceutical cocaine from a Swiss drug company. On the tour, he traveled by himself and stayed in his own suite at the band's hotel. When the musicians ran out of coke, a gofer would deliver an empty 35mm film can. He'd fill the can from a large plastic sack, run a jack of diamonds over the edge, and screw the cap back on—always with a smile. Anytime, day or night. Over the years, Sessler became a legendary companion and benefactor of many rock stars and can still be found backstage at Stones concerts.

Around this time, Mick Jagger learned that Marsha Hunt was pregnant with his child and that Marianne Faithfull—having learned of this—had run off to Italy with an ex-boyfriend of Anita's, Mario Schifano. Anita had arranged for Mario to stay with Marianne while Mick was away; she took him to bed, then left Mick for him. It got into the press immediately, leaving Mick publicly cuckolded during his triumphal American tour.

On November 26, the Stones held a press conference in the Rainbow Room, atop the RCA Building in Rockefeller Center. Mick announced that the Stones would play a free concert in San Francisco at the end of the tour to say thank you to their American fans. The concert, he predicted, would "create a microcosmic society which sets an example to the rest of America as to how one can behave in large gatherings."

A reporter asked him if, after recording "Satisfaction," the Stones were more "satisfied" now.

"Sexually, do you mean?" Mick asked amid press laughter. "Or philosophically?" Told both, Mick answered, "Sexually, more satisfied.

Financially, dissatisfied [Allen Klein was standing behind him]. Philosophically, still trying."

———————

The Stones' contract with Decca was expiring in a few months, and much intrigue now began. The Stones were in contact with Marshall Chess, the son of Leonard Chess, whose death the previous year ended the family's involvement in Chess Records, which had been sold. Marshall went to Jagger, looking for work, and was eventually made president of their new vanity label, Rolling Stones Records. Mick began to talk with Ahmet Ertegun, the debonair chief of Atlantic Records, the R&B-loving son of a Turkish diplomat. Atlantic Records was the founding label of the R&B movement, the company where every blues-loving English rock band wanted to be. Ertegun had signed Led Zeppelin earlier in the year and was presently selling tonnage of *Led Zeppelin II,* affectionately known as the Brown Bomber. He wanted the Rolling Stones, and Mick Jagger wanted Atlantic to distribute Rolling Stones Records.

Decca wanted a live album of the tour, so Glyn Johns recorded shows in Baltimore, New York, and Boston. A film crew had also joined the tour, led by documentarians Albert and David Maysles, who would film the Madison Square Garden shows and stay with the Stones through the free concert in California.

The three Madison Square Garden shows were sellouts and the best music of the tour; everything had to come together for the live album and the film. By this time, the Rolling Stones probably *were* the greatest rock and roll band in the world. People thought Mick Jagger believed it, anyway. Terry Reid opened all the concerts. Janis Joplin watched the first show from the side of the stage, after duetting with Tina Turner during the Revue's set. Janis was taking an occasional nip from her omnipresent bottle of Southern Comfort. When Mick sang "Live with Me," drunken Janis yelled back, "You don't have the balls!" Jimi Hendrix came backstage on the last night, looking blasted but jamming deftly, playing Mick Taylor's guitar upside down. Mick Jagger worked on his makeup and ignored Hendrix, still annoyed because Jimi had put a move on Marianne years before. After the Stones played their best show of the tour, Mick stole Hendrix's beloved girlfriend, the celestial black groupie Devon Wilson, and brought her back to his hotel for three days of piece and love (Jimi commemorated their tryst in his great song "Dolly Dagger"). Keith and Charlie went late to Slug's, the stygian jazz bar on the Lower East Side, to hear drummer Tony Williams's fiery jazz-rock band Lifetime, with John McLaughlin playing guitar.

Let It Bleed was released at the end of November. The cover was a surrealist collage depicting the band as plastic figures on a wedding cake assemblage whose layers contained a pizza, a tire, a can of tape, all atop an old turntable (the assemblage is shown destroyed on the verso). The album was immediately recognized as a climactic masterpiece in reviews. "The Stones have never done anything better," wrote Greil Marcus in *Rolling Stone*. "This era and the collapse of its bright and flimsy liberation are what the Stones leave behind with the last song of *Let It Bleed*. The dreams of having it all are gone, and the album ends with a song about compromises with what you want—learning to take what you can get, because the rules have changed with the death of the Sixties."

Let It Bleed got to no. 3 in America against withering competition (*Abbey Road* and *Led Zeppelin II*) and was no. 1 in England for months.

Two shows at Boston Garden, where "Live with Me" shook the house. Before "Street Fighting Man," with the house lights up, Mick said (with a wicked smile parting famous lips, revealing overbite): "We'd like to say a special hello tonight to all the minority groups here with us, all the *fags*, all the *junkies*—good evening, *junkies*! [sneaks a look at Keith, who's using]—and all the *straight people*, the *cops*, all you *minorities* out there." The Stones returned briefly to New York, waited in a broken plane for nine hours, flew to Florida on November 30 to play the Miami Pop Festival, held in a swampy drag strip inland from Palm Beach. This was the last show of the '69 tour, and the Stones were brain-fried but still able to take nourishment. They were topping a bill that included the Jefferson Airplane, Big Brother, and Johnny Winter, and they thought it would be a good prep for the big outdoor show in San Francisco the following weekend.

The Stones had been starting their shows two hours late, building up fan anticipation by keeping 'em waiting. Now they were eight hours late: 55,000 kids had been waiting outdoors in a grove-killing Florida rainstorm in battlefield conditions. There was political trouble as well, with right-wing groups agitating against the festival and the corrupting power of the Stones specifically. The Stones were flown in by chopper. Freezing, wrapped in a blanket, Keith hit the chords of "Jumpin' Jack Flash" at three in the morning, and thousands of cold kids started dancing. They played until dawn broke over the Everglades, and the "festival" was counted a ragged victory for the band, performing in the open air with frozen fingers. Exhausted, the Stones jammed a little for their film crew in their Palm Beach hotel, then disappeared off the map for a supposed rest. Instead, they flew to northern Alabama and checked into the Holiday Inn near Sheffield for a few days of recording, arranged by Ahmet Ertegun and kept secret from Allen Klein. Klein controlled the Stones' song copyrights, tape masters, and royalty payments. He had the Rolling Stones by their throats, and they couldn't afford to rile the volatile accountant.

At Muscle Shoals Sound Studio, a squat bunker in a factory zone where Aretha Franklin and other Atlantic soul stars did some of their most down-home recording, the Stones worked with Memphis musician Jim Dickinson and engineer Jimmy Johnson. A big old porcelain toilet bowl in the middle of the funky studio held a microphone for special plumbing resonance, "a shitty sound," according to the locals.

At Muscle Shoals, the Stones began working on their next album and the rest of their career. The first night, they recorded "You Gotta Move," a retitled version of Mississippi bluesman Fred McDowell's "Got to Move." Keith took the high part sung by McDowell's wife, Annie Mae, as he had when they did the song as part of the tour's acoustic set. The second night, playing guitar, Mick taught Keith his Australian outback song, originally titled "Black Pussy" but renamed "Brown Sugar," partly in honor of sepia beauty Claudia Linnear. "Brown sugar" was also the street name of unrefined heroin from Southeast Asia. ("Drugs and girls," Mick later said of the lyric. "All the nasty subjects in one go.") Charlie got into a classic rock groove ("Do it like 'Tallahassee Lassie,' Mick told him"), and Ian Stewart played good boogie piano. Mick wrote the three verses on the spot, and the band got it right after half a dozen takes. In "Brown Sugar," the Stones had what they came for: a furious and alive record of a coked-up band rocking out in the Deep South.

The next night, after drinking half a fifth of Jack Daniel's and playing country songs on the piano, Keith high-strung a guitar in a Nashville tuning. Prompted by Mick for a song ("C'mon, you must have *hundreds*"), Keith disappeared into an office and worked out the melody line to "Wild Horses" and the words of its chorus, thinking of Anita and baby Marlon back in London. Plugging into Keith's riff, with the "dull aching pain" of his own love life in mind, Mick wrote out the song's verses of regret and his unwillingness to let his graceless lady slide through his hands. Stu hated any song with minor chords, so Jim Dickinson played piano, and by dawn the Stones had their newest love song, a conflated portrait of their feelings for the wild, untamed blondes in their lives.

At the dawn end of these sessions, mindful of bootlegging, Mick Jagger carefully erased all the extra tapes of their work before he left the studio. On December 4, the Rolling Stones flew to San Francisco and their shared destiny in the cold, empty hills south of the city.

The Battle of Altamont Speedway

December 1969. While the Rolling Stones were in Alabama, their halcyon free concert in the Bay Area was on its way to hell. San Francisco's main rock promoter, Bill Graham, still angry with the Stones, queered them playing Golden Gate Park by bad-mouthing the show to the cops and mayor's office. Another site was found at Sears Point Raceway. The Stones, the Airplane, the Dead, CS&N, the Burritos, and Santana were all set to play. The national press ran with the story, and thousands of Stones fans were heading west for the final mammoth rock festival of the sixties, a groovy tribal gathering that would make Woodstock look sick. Then, three days before the show, with the stage already built, the raceway site fell through when its film studio owners demanded movie rights to the concert. At the last minute, another site was offered by the owner of a demolition derby track in the barren hills of Alameda County, thirty miles south of Oakland, in a place called Altamont. The name seemed to indicate a pinnacle of some sort, perhaps an auspicious new height.

Working overnight, the crew organized by the Grateful Dead's office dismantled the stage, trucked it down to Dick Carter's Altamont Speedway, and rebuilt it at the bottom of a wash in treeless hills covered in sand-colored winter scrub. This high desert landscape was immense, empty, and unforgiving, looking like the arid *bled* in northern Morocco, traversed by gigantic power lines and drainage ditches. A perimeter was set up backstage amid heaps of wrecked cars that recalled Godard's junkyard sets in *One Plus One*. The Oakland, San Jose, and Frisco chapters of the Hell's Angels were invited by the Grateful Dead's organization to protect the stage, much as they had done, peacefully, at previous San Francisco festivals. This was no big deal. Payment was said to have been a busload of beer, but this was later indignantly denied by the seething Angels after they'd been blamed for what happened at the Battle of Altamont Speedway.

————

The wan, crescent-shaped moon—and much was later made of this—was in Scorpio.

The Rolling Stones flew into San Francisco on Friday, December 5, and checked into the Huntington Hotel. That evening, Mick and Keith drove out to Altamont with the film crew to check out the scene. They found an immense hippie encampment surrounding floodlit scaffolding and the stage being built. Chip Monck was on the job, as were hundreds of volunteers who labored through the night. Volunteer medical teams were setting up field clinics. It seemed like San Francisco was working overtime to show the world what could be done for free. Beyond the perimeters, friendly campfires burned in the darkness as hundreds huddled together for warmth. Jugs of California wine were proffered, joints, good vibes: so good that Keith decided to stay the night and crash in one of the trailers behind the stage.

By noon the next day, December 6, an estimated 300,000 carpeted the hill in front of the stage. Roads were blocked ten miles around Altamont, so the only way in and out was by foot, motorcycle, or the helicopters landing on the nearby racetrack. There was weak sunshine, and all the bands were supposed to play in daylight. Santana went on first, jammed a set of their conga-driven Chicano rock, played "beautifully," according to Charlie. Young Carlos Santana watched in alarm as knife fights and stabbings broke out at the side of the stage while he was playing. A naked fat man was badly beaten when he tried to approach the stage, which was only four feet high. Then the Flying Burrito Brothers started their pure country rocker, "Six Days on the Road," with Gram Parsons up front as the hero of the rodeo.

Excited by the young Burritos, the girls in the crowd surged to the edge of the low stage—some guys too—and the Hell's Angels in their black leather jackets and greasy denims lost control. Fights broke out in front of the band and the music stopped. Gram tried to soothe it—"Let's not hurt each other"—but some people were bleeding badly.

The Stones arrived early in the afternoon by helicopter—without Bill Wyman, who missed the flight. Mick got off the ship, accepted some flowers, and was punched in the face by an acid-crazed kid. He found Keith in his trailer, getting briefed by Gram Parsons on the vicious fighting the Burritos had seen during their show. Wary of the whole thing, Charlie Watts chatted up a couple of the Angels minding the trailers and found them quite pleasant. Waiting for Wyman, insulated from the growing chaos outside, the Stones and Gram Parsons spent the afternoon smoking weed and yodeling country tunes.

Out front it was a bummer. The acid, the mescaline, the DMT, the alcohol had a death grip on the afternoon. A thin greasy line of stoned bikers under the watchful eye of the formidable Oakland Angels chieftain Sonny Barger faced an increasingly hostile mob of freaks and suburban high school kids. Crazed Stones fans fought to get up close. Tripping kids who'd gotten rid of their annoying clothes and were only trying to hurl their shivering naked bodies onstage were beaten with pool cues the Angels had thoughtfully packed for crowd control.

In his most soothing tones, Sam Cutler, the Voice of Hyde Park, announced that a baby had just been born and appealed for blankets. Nothing. More fights in front of the stage as the Jefferson Airplane started up. Grace Slick vainly appealed for calm. Singer Marty Balin saw a Hell's Angel savagely punch a black man and leaped off the low stage into the crowd to stop the fight. The Angel stepped back and knocked Balin out with one punch. They got him back on the stage, where he sat dazed while his band played "Volunteers." When Balin came to, he cursed at the Angel who'd hit him, and the enraged biker smashed Balin in the head and knocked him out again.

When the Grateful Dead's helicopter landed, Jerry Garcia and the others ran into Michael Shrieve, Santana's drummer, who told them what was going down. The Dead got right back on their chopper and didn't play that day.

Crosby, Stills and Nash went on late in the afternoon with their fey songs about Judy Blue Eyes and the Marrakesh Express. They watched, horrified, as the bikers continued to defend the stage, and the line of Harleys now parked in front of it, with their pool cues. When some poor victim went down, brained by a cue, the Angels stomped him bloody, and crew people watching from the stage assumed that people were being beaten to death. There was no official police presence anywhere at Altamont.

After CS&N, there was a long wait as the sun sank behind the hills, the evening turned cold, and the crescent moon shone with a baleful light. Sam Cutler kept announcing the Stones wouldn't appear until the stage was clear of everyone, including the Angels who occupied it like a drunken crew of pirates. One of these, a saucer-eyed devil wearing a wolf's-head hat, even whipped out a flute and played into the microphone for a few moments of horrifically apposite *Boujeloudiya*.

Bill Wyman finally turned up after dark; he had been shopping with his girlfriend. The Stones tuned up in a tent behind the stage. It was late and very cold when the Rolling Stones finally came out and played one of the musically better shows of the 1969 American tour.

——————

Seven P.M. Suddenly the hot lights flashed on, a harsh splash of current in the cold black night. Sam Cutler: "I'd like to introduce to you, everybody—from Britain—the Rolling Stones!" Dull roar. Bright white floodlight outlined the packed stage against the gloom. Mick appeared in an orange and black satin suit, a little drunk, with silver satin pants tucked into knee-high velvet boots with three-inch heels. The "Omega" on his chest was the last letter of the Greek alphabet, signifying The End. Keith was in a tight red leather jacket and ruffled lace shirt, Jack Daniel's at hand on the drum riser. Mick whooped it up, Charlie hit the drums and into "Jack Flash." Then "Carol" and "Sympathy," where the Stones' invocation to Lucifer broke down as a motorcycle exploded in front of the stage and a mini-riot flared up. Mick stopped the band. "Hey, people, sisters and brothers . . . Come on now, will you *cool out*, everybody." After a while, Charlie and Keith started up again and Mick said into the mike, "Okay, we can groove—something very funny always happens when we start that number." The Stones kept playing "Sympathy" while the Angels pushed a guy off the stage, then cut him down with their cues, then gang-stomped him. It looked like they'd killed him and Keith stopped playing, really upset. Mick: "I mean, like *people*, who's fighting and what for? Why are we fighting? *Why are we fighting?* Every other scene has been cool . . . We've gotta stop them right now, you know, we can't, there's no point..."

Tumult. Leather in swirling motion. Sound of heads cracking. Sam Cutler took the mike, trying to talk to the Angels as the pool cues were raised and smashed down horribly.

Keith, livid, pointing: "Either those cats *cool it*, or we don't play. I mean, there's not that many of them." Sonny Barger looked at Keith. The Stones' security men, impassive New York cops in windbreakers, moved in closer to the band. Another fight in front of Keith: "That guy *there*! If he doesn't stop it—"

An Angel grabbed the mike, an ugly brute, and addressed the night: "Hey! You don't cool it, you ain't gonna hear no more music! You wanna all go home, or what?!" After a woman on the stage, a member of the local band Ace of Cups, was cut by a thrown beer bottle, the Stones' cops suggested to Jo Bergman and the women in the Stones' entourage that they leave. The Hell's Angels had assumed control, and the cops could smell what was coming.

Stu took the mike: "We need doctors down here now, please. Can we have a doctor down now to the front?" Mick gazed at the Hieronymous Bosch tableau in front of him and said, "Keith, man . . . *these scenes*!" Nearby sat Timothy Leary, apostle of LSD, looking scared and pale, aghast.

Keith called for some "cool-out music" and the Stones launched into "The Sun Is Shining," a Jimmy Reed blues, trying to calm things down. Then Keith called "Stray Cat" as small pockets of mayhem continued to erupt in front of them. Then "Love in Vain," with Mick Taylor's inspired guitar solo soaring into the blackness. Bill Wyman hit the bass line of "Under My Thumb," and things actually began to cool out a little.

A flurry on the left side of the stage. All night a tall black kid in a lime-green suit and a black pimp's hat had been grooving away, irritating the Angels near him. His name was Meredith Hunter, known as Murdock on Telegraph Avenue in Berkeley. He was eighteen. Halfway through "Thumb," he pulled a gun out of his pants and pointed it at an Angel who was grabbing at his throat. There was a scuffle, and the kid pointed the gun briefly at the stage. An Angel stabbed him in the head, pushed him out of sight of the stage, and stabbed him twice more in the back. When he was down, a dozen more Angels stomped him to death. Then they stood on his head. Witnesses reported his last words: "I wasn't going to shoot you."

The band quit and Keith started yelling again, but stopped when the

Angels told him they'd taken a gun off a guy who was shooting at the stage. They finished "Under My Thumb," and Mick Taylor, who'd come to play, suggested the brand-new "Brown Sugar." No one knew they'd just seen someone killed.

" 'Brown Sugar'?" Keith asked, incredulous.

"Wot?" Charlie said.

Jagger: "He wants to do 'Brown Sugar.' "

Keith switched guitars, and the Stones' new rocker was given its premiere performance under the hot movie lights as the Maysles brothers' cameras rolled. The Stones played the rest of their usual show, with a truncated "Rambler" and the band bearing down as it blasted its way through. At the end of "Street Fighting Man," two Hell's Angels threw baskets of roses into the writhing crowd, and the Stones left fast.

The Stones' whole entourage piled into one waiting helicopter, desperate not to be left behind. The pilot was afraid to take off, but Cutler was screaming at him to fly as an unruly crowd surged under the whirling rotor blades. The pilot got his overloaded ship off the ground, and the Rolling Stones lurched into the night, leaving the damned and blasted heath of Altamont behind them, along with any lingering illusions of Woodstockian groovyness and a significant piece of their reputation.

Pearl Harbor
for Woodstock Nation

The Stones gathered in Keith's hotel suite in the early morning of December 7—Pearl Harbor Day. A tape of moaning old blues songs was playing. Keith was furious at the Hell's Angels for wrecking the day. Emeretta was doing her best to console him, and Mick was trying to get Miss Pamela and Michelle Phillips down to his room for a threesome. Gram Parsons was nodding against the wall in black leather and eye makeup, while Keith was wearing flash cowboy duds; Miss Pamela had the impression Keith and Gram were turning into each other. Gram was bummed because he thought Michelle, radiant ex-Mama, was with him. Keith cheered him up by giving him a demo tape of "Wild Horses," only days old.

There was powder going up noses, serious gloom and doom. Mick thought he'd been shot at, and talked about quitting while he was alive. He told them he blamed himself, that it shouldn't have happened. "I'd rather have had the cops," he sulked. Miss Pam noticed Mick was a nervous wreck. "I thought the scene here was supposed to be so groovy," he said. "If Jesus Christ had been there, he would've been fucking *crucified.*" No one could believe what had gone down. For years, the Rolling Stones had seen weird scenes in front of them while they played, but this was the first time one of their concerts had featured human sacrifice. They tried to follow the radio reports of multiple deaths, beatings, overdoses, and other casualties. Bitter callers were blaming the Stones and the Angels equally, and it was clear that an almost infinite bummer and hassle was coming. Time to get out of town. Sam Cutler was delegated to stay behind and try to patch things up with the locals. He met with the Hell's Angels after his personal safety was guaranteed. The Angels demanded the incriminating films made at Altamont, meaning the Maysles's footage, and weren't thrilled when Cutler explained the film was back in New York already, and the Stones were gone too. Real gone, as Sam Cutler soon found out. From then on, his phone calls to the Stones or their office in London were never returned.

———

Later on December 7, Mick and Jo Bergman flew to Switzerland to deposit the Stones' tour money, almost a million dollars, in a Geneva bank recommended by Rupert Lowenstein. When they arrived, they were escorted by Swiss police to the rubber glove room, where their body cavities were searched. From Switzerland, they went to the south of France to look for a house for Mick to rent. Marsha Hunt was waiting for them. Facing ruinous taxes, drug charges, and total lack of privacy, Mick had decided to leave England and live, at least for a while, the life of an exile.

When Keith arrived at Heathrow airport, he was greeted by Anita and baby Marlon. "Keith!" she cried when she saw him. "They're throwing me out of the country!" Her Majesty's government had indeed seized Anita's passport and threatened to deport her unless Keith married her immediately. So Keith made plans to get out too.

When Mick arrived in London a few days later, Marianne and Nicholas met him at the airport. "Hullo, girl," Mick said to her when he got off the plane. "Wop in yer bed, eh?"

————

Four people died at Altamont. One executed, two run over by a Plymouth, one drowned in a drainage ditch. About a hundred victims were treated for stabbings and beatings by the Angels. Seven hundred bad trips. An awful day for everyone, including the Hell's Angels.

The national media ignored Altamont. *Time* and *Life*, still rhapsodizing about Woodstock, didn't mention it. The *New York Times* ran a small story in a late Sunday edition. *Newsweek* ran a piece three weeks later. San Francisco, however, was trauma city. PEARL HARBOR TO THE WOODSTOCK NATION, read a headline. The *Berkeley Tribe*: STONES CONCERT ENDS: AMERIKA UP FOR GRABS. The Airplane and CS&N said they wouldn't play any more outdoor festivals. The Grateful Dead went into hiding. When the Stones appeared to criticize the Hell's Angels for the disaster at Altamont, the Angels went public, with Sonny Barger furiously claiming that his bikers just did what they were asked to do, and that the dead guy was pointing a gun at the stage. "We *told* 'em," Barger rasped, "we told 'em we weren't gonna play cops for the Rolling Stones." Barger later claimed he stuck a gun in Mick's ribs to make him finish the show at Altamont. According to court testimony years later, unknown members of the Hell's Angels put a murder contract out on Mick Jagger as a result of the confused events *after* Altamont.

In its exhaustive, embittered coverage of Altamont, *Rolling Stone*, never shy about its total adulation of its main inspirers, called it "perhaps rock and roll's all-time worst day."

Let It Bleed took on new resonance. Right after Altamont, it broke into the Top Ten.

Much was made of the absurd notion that the Altamont disaster was the end of Innocence, Community, the Movement, the Sixties, the Stones. It was an easy tag for the media, and the Stones suffered for years. Mick Jagger had little time for it. "Of course some people wanted to say Altamont was the end of an era," he said later. "People like that are like fashion writers. Perhaps it was the end of *their* era, the end of their . . . naiveté."

Debate continued for years. Keith tried to be philosophical about it when interviewed two years later. He said Rock Scully and the Dead should have known what would happen, but that it all had fallen apart too fast. All the planning occurred while they were making a record in Alabama. They didn't know. The Dead told them that Ken Kesey had cooled the Angels out.

Keith thought the gang-stompings were cowardly. "If someone tries to do [me], it's between him and me. I don't call in Bill Wyman to come in and do him *for* me, with one of his ankle-twisters or vicious Chinese burns."

Still, "Who do you want to lay it on? Do you want to blame somebody, or do you want to learn from it? I don't really think anyone is to blame.

"Altamont, it could only happen to the Stones, man. Let's face it. It wouldn't happen to the Bee Gees."

On Sunday night, December 21, in London, the Stones played at the Lyceum Theater, the last Rolling Stones concert of the sixties. Two shows, at five and eight, tickets sold out for weeks, thousands of fans in the streets and enough cops to stop a riot. It had been seven years since they started. Brian Jones was dead, and the new guy would never become one of them. Some think their best work was already behind the Rolling Stones, and that they would spend the next three decades and the rest of their career defending, often successfully, their self-bestowed heavyweight title as the greatest rock and roll band in the world.

seven:
The Devil's
Right-Hand Man

Keith Richards during the Los Angeles studio

sessions that completed Exile on Main Street,

spring 1972.

Music's meaning to people is one of the great mysteries.

Keith Richards

Blame It on the Stones

In early 1970, the Rolling Stones were still in England, but their Blue Period was over and their lives would now evolve and change. The Beatles disbanded that year, and Bob Dylan retreated into near seclusion. This left the Stones standing alone in the arena, soon to be outdone in heavyosity by the younger, louder, more intense Led Zeppelin.

The Stones adapted to the 1970s by mutating into a gypsy band, always on the move, adding and dropping musicians for a tour here, an album there. Moving beyond its roots in blues, R&B, soul, rock and roll, and rock, the Stones added horns to become a Memphis-style roadhouse band, used Mick Taylor to explore jazz-style textures, delved into the seventies pop discoveries—funk, reggae, disco, power pop—in order to stay alive. The Greatest R&R Etc. would become a ballad band, at least on the radio ("Wild Horses," "Angie," "Fool to Cry"), until forced to deploy a stripped-down response to the punk bands later in the decade.

The Stones remained stoic about Altamont. To Keith, "It was just another gig where I had to leave fast." The Stones' more pretentious critics postulated that the contemptuous politics of *Beggar's Banquet* and *Let It Bleed* had come to life in the bleak California hills. Incredible blather was written about the death of the sixties and the loss of innocence by the Stones and their generation, but in the end no one really cared except the lawyers who worked the lawsuits that began to fly around California like bats at sunset. A young Hell's Angel, already doing time in Soledad prison on a parole violation, was charged with murdering Meredith Hunter at Altamont after six crews documented the knifing on film. He was acquitted by a jury in 1971.

"After Altamont," wrote Stanley Booth, who'd been on the '69 tour with the band, "the Stones would for reasons of self-preservation turn toward comedy." Songwriter Kris Kristofferson composed a funny ditty called "Blame It on the Stones."

————

In January 1970, the Stones remixed and overdubbed their New York concert tapes at Olympic and Trident studios in London. Mick tried to sell Decca a double live album, with B. B. King and Ike and Tina on the second disc. "Decca wasn't interested," Mick said later. " 'Who is B. B. King? Who are these people?' So in the end I gave it all up. I've still got that part of the album and it's good."

David and Albert Maysles came to London and filmed the Stones watching their grisly Altamont snuff footage. Mick walked out without saying a word, followed by the rest of the band. The Maysles couldn't find a distributor for the film and wondered if it could even be released.

Blasted by postpartum depression and loneliness, Anita Pallenberg had become a heroin addict while Keith was on tour. When Keith returned, he joined her in the arms of Morpheus, an addiction that would last for seven years and cede near-total control of the Rolling Stones to Mick Jagger. Keith and Anita holed up in their house in Cheyne Walk, employing Spanish Tony Sanchez, who talked like Peter Lorre on pills, to buy their drugs. Keith avoided marrying Anita after Les Perrin's press campaign got the government off their backs.

————

The Stones began recording new tracks that winter, about the time Bill Wyman—who didn't use drugs—stopped talking to Keith, a silence that lasted until 1981. They set up in an empty parlor off a main hall at Stargroves, the mouldering country manor that Mick had bought years before. The room's old oak floor and plaster walls gave the music an intimate, woody flavor. The Stones' thirty-four-foot mobile studio (with a nervous Andy Johns, younger brother of Glyn, at the controls) was outfitted with sixteen-track tape machines, mixing board, microphones, and effects units. "Sway" was the first song cut, with Mick Taylor's amp placed in the big fireplace and the microphones in the chimney. Charlie's drums were in a big bay window. Nicky Hopkins was on piano, and Mick Taylor began to deliver the solo virtuosity that marked the first important directional change for the Stones since 1968. Mick Jagger's "Bitch" evolved from a jam between him, Charlie Watts, and Bobby Keys, a rhythm with a horn kick. Keith's demo melody called "Japanese Thing" later became "Moonlight Mile." Other Stargroves tracks included the second version of "Cocksucker Blues," Mick's low, moaning soliloquy about a teenage hustler; "Mean Woman Blues"; "Alladin Story"; "Good Time Woman," an early version of "Tumblin' Dice" with Stu on piano and Mick Taylor on slide guitar; a track called "Green Bent Needles" that became "Sweet Black Angel"; and Robert Johnson's boasting blues "Stop Breakin' Down." Keith also overdubbed his National steel guitar onto the Stones' 1969 version of "Sister Morphine." Already in the can from the Muscle Shoals sessions: "Wild Horses," "Brown Sugar," and "You Gotta Move." All the Stargroves tracks would be worked on over the next year, especially when Bobby Keys and Jim Price joined the band that fall.

———

It was a turbulent time for Mick Jagger. Contemptuous of drug addiction, he got addicted to love instead. After their pot bust was resolved, he won Marianne back and they were living together again by March 1970. But she was miserable, using smack, and spoke openly of her desire to *really* get into it, to experience the doomed floating freedom of the junk world, while he worried that they could get busted for heroin at any moment. She despised her acting career and let it go. She called Mick at the studio, crying and complaining of loneliness, while he was trying to work, which led to big fights and more tears. Marianne's public behavior began to slip. Mick would take her for a country weekend at a duke's castle and she'd nod off into the soup. They'd have to carry her upstairs, and Mick would be embarrassed. He was spending more time with Marsha Hunt at her place in St. John's Wood.

One day that summer at Cheyne Walk, after Marianne overheard

Ahmet Ertegun tell Mick she was a business liability, a possible obstacle
to the Stones' signing with Atlantic Records, she packed up her little boy,
slung a favorite Persian carpet under her arm, and walked out of Mick's
house, never to return. Mick tried to get her back. He played "Wild
Horses" and said he'd written it for her, but Marianne was already out the
door. She let herself go and put on weight so Mick wouldn't want her
anymore. Her husband divorced her and got custody of their son. True to
the legend she'd decided to write for herself, Marianne Faithfull traded life
with Mick Jagger for the existence of a registered heroin addict on the
streets of Soho.

Mick rarely spoke about any of this. For a time, he took up with
Patti D'Arbanville, a good-lookin' American girl of nineteen who was a
friend of Miss Pamela's. Years later Mick remembered, "Marianne,
y'know—she almost *killed* me. Forget it! I wasn't going to get out of there
alive! Marianne and Anita, I mean—*help!*"

Rupert Lowenstein, the Stones' new financial adviser, gave
them the bad news that summer. They all had to get out of England.
They were all broke and in debt. Their business manager hadn't paid their
British taxes in years, and each of them had a six-figure tax bill. Allen
Klein's contract with the band was about to expire, but he still controlled
their publishing and catalog and would probably not let go without a
fight. Lowenstein told them there was no chance of settling their debts
and rebuilding their fortunes unless they made an immediate break with
Klein and left England to avoid its ruinous taxation and possible bankruptcy proceedings. Keith didn't want to be forced out of England, but he
was eventually convinced to join the Stones' exile by April 5, 1971, the
start of the next British tax year.

On July 30, 1970, the Rolling Stones announced that Allen Klein
was no longer authorized to act on their behalf. Their Decca recording
contract expired the same day. Owing one more new single to their despised label, they sent Decca a tape of "Cocksucker Blues," the explicitly
obscene demo whose lyrics asked, "Where do I get my ass fucked? Where

do I get my cock sucked?" Decca declined to release the single. "I'd rather the Mafia than Decca," Keith said later.

Performance was released in America in August 1970, only weeks after the awful *Ned Kelly* had bombed. Heavily reedited and censored after Warner's executives objected to nude sequences of Mick and the explicit sadism of the violence, *Performance* still had a shocking impact that bore witness to its turbulent creation. Donald Cammell had fought the studio for two years while they shelved the project, then revived it after a management shake-up. Cammell reedited the film using cutup techniques that caused his codirector, Nicholas Roeg, to try to take his name off the film. Dialogue was redubbed when studio executives complained they couldn't understand the cockney accents of the gangsters. Repeatedly delayed and almost sabotaged by the studio, *Performance* delighted and mystified Stones fans but bored the mainstream critics, who didn't understand it. Stones fans flocked to see Mick, and the film did respectable business during its first run. Released in England the next year, it was recognized as a serious work of art, but ran for only two weeks before being pulled out of the theaters. Decca released the scorching song "Memo from Turner" as a Mick Jagger single in England, and it became for many the most thrilling rock moment of the year, quivering with devilish malice and bad attitude, a cynical, perverse rock masterpiece featuring Ry Cooder's menacing slide guitar. "Memo from Turner" kept the Stones' street cred alive until their next album came out months later.

Let It Rock

Summer 1970. The Rolling Stones announced the formation of Rolling Stones Records right after their Decca contract expired. Marshall Chess became the new label's president. He was short, dark, bearded, funny, intense, full of entrepreneurial energy and ideas of how to sell the Stones. He made the effort to get to know the whole band, not just Mick and Keith, and succeeded in winning their trust. It didn't hurt that he'd filled Mick Jagger's mail orders for blues records in his role as stockroom boy at Chess ten years before. "He was a hustler, street," Keith said of Marshall. "He was Chicago, the South Side, and the world of black records that none of us *really* knew." Marshall Chess also became the band's de facto manager in the first part of the seventies. He lived on the top floor of Keith's house in Cheyne Walk for a year, and soon got in dope trouble too.

————

In August, the Stones began rehearsing for a European tour scheduled for that fall. Bobby Keys and Jim Price were hired as the new horn section when their gig with Eric Clapton's band Derek and the Dominos fell through. One night Keys ran into Mick at a club in London. Mick: "We're out here in the country. Why don't you drop by and bring your horn?" Keys played sax on "Can't You Hear Me Knocking?" He also played a blistering solo on "Brown Sugar," and he and Price overdubbed their horns on "Bitch."

Bobby Keys: "After we played on *Sticky Fingers,* Jim Price and I weasled our way into a gig. We'd woven our way into the fabric, and we thought, 'Thank God.' These guys had some real rockin' *fans.* People were going to burn the place *down.*"

Keith was thrilled to have Keys in the band. The twenty-six-year-old Keys, a big and beefy Texan with a helmet of brown hair and serious reedman jowls, had been on the road since he was thirteen, had played on Buddy Holly's first record date at KLLL radio in Texas, had played with Holly and the Crickets at Alan Freed's first rock and roll show at the Brooklyn Paramount in 1958. "It's a gas not to be so insulated and play with some more people like Bobby Keys," Keith told Robert Greenfield in *Rolling Stone.* "Bobby's like one of those things that go all the way through. He was *there,* man."

It was the first Stones tour of Europe in three years, with a sixty-five-man crew, American-style production, and high ticket prices that bought criticism from angry fans. The Stones played an augmented 1969 set, with Stu on piano for the Chuck Berry songs and no encores. According to Jo Bergman, who planned much of it, the entire tour schedule revolved around year-old Marlon Richards, who came along with his mum.

The tour opened on September 2 in Helsinki. Opening was guitarist Buddy Guy's white-hot Chicago blues band with elite soloist Junior Wells on harmonica—often booed by loutish young fans on the tour. The first few Stones shows were like public rehearsals, but they soon tightened up. The new song "Dead Flowers" was played fast and fierce. A turbocharged version of Chuck Berry's late boogie chef d'oeuvre "Let It Rock" was added to the set a few shows in. Mick Jagger, inspired by Junior Wells's star-quality nightly improvs, blew his harp the entire length of "Midnight Rambler," joining the band as an instrumentalist, breaking into jazzy jams prior to the "Don't Do That" segment of the Stones' rock theatrical.

Bobby Keys and Keith bonded well because they liked the same things, and he joined the self-contained Richards family entourage. Their heroin was carried across borders in custom-built devices such as hollow fountain pens and fake shaving cream bottles. When they ran out of dope, they forced the local promoters to find some. "No smack, no show, baby." Audiences were kept waiting for hours until the necessary drugs were supplied.

While they were touring, Decca and London released *"Get Yer Ya-Yas Out": The Rolling Stones in Concert,* overdubbed live tracks from the '69 tour. This was the last authorized Rolling Stones album on their old label. David Bailey's cover photo depicted many layers of inside jokes. Charlie Watts jumps in the air, clutching guitars and wearing Mick's Uncle Sam stage hat. Behind him a donkey, bearing his drum kit and another guitar, has necklaces and binoculars hanging from its neck, a reference to the jewels and binoculars hanging from the neck of a mule in Dylan's "Visions of Johanna." The "Ya-Yas" in the title was a phonetic mishearing of an old New Orleans term for bosoms. The album's real charm lay in its nonmusical moments: the cutup tape collage of Sam Cutler's introductions; the girl who yells, "Paint it black, you devil"; Mick's stage patter about the busted button and "Charlie's good tonight, inne?" The album got to no. 1 in England and no. 5 in America.

———

September 22, 1970. By the time the tour got to Paris, the Stones were back on form. The fans were too, with many arrests in Berlin and minor trouble in Hamburg. The Paris show at L'Olympia was a big event, with many friends of the band backstage and at a big party at the Hotel George V afterward, where Mick met a stunning twenty-one-year-old Nicaraguan girl, Bianca Perez Moreno de Macias. She was introduced to Mick by the French record executive Eddy Barclay as his fiancée.

Bianca Perez was tiny, birdlike, dark-complected, and utterly beautiful, with a cheekbone resemblance to Mick that everyone noticed. She was intelligent, had won a scholarship to study in Paris at seventeen, before entering the party circuit on the arm of actor Michael Caine. Mick Jagger fell for this sultry gamine immediately, and she ditched Barclay for him. She wouldn't sleep with Mick, which intrigued him no end. He left for Vienna with Bianca much on his mind.

When the tour got to Rome, Anita contacted her family. She hadn't seen them since taking up with Brian Jones, but had made contact again after her son was born. "We sent a limo for my father," she recalled, "so he could come to the show. Outside the hall, the car was attacked by anarchists who threw rocks, thinking the Stones were inside. This was my father's introduction to the world I was living in. But he was fair-minded about it, enjoyed the show, and I think he was pleased that I was with a musician, because that's what he was."

Bianca Perez arrived in Rome to be with Mick and then stayed with the tour. Bianca and Mick merged into a top-secret and passionately inseparable, look-alike, glamour-radiating couple. The tour ended in Munich on October 11. Mick and Bianca flew back to London together. She moved into Mick's London home within weeks and became pregnant that winter.

On November 10, Marsha Hunt gave birth to Mick's first child, a daughter she named Karis. This was at first kept secret from everyone, in-

Mick Jagger married Bianca Perez in St. Tropez in 1971.

Issue No. 89
August 19, 1971
60¢
UK 15 p

The Rolling Stone Interview:
Keith Richard

The Rolling Stone Overview:
Grand Funk

Keith's landmark interview with writer Robert Greenfield made the cover
of *Rolling Stone* in 1971.

LIFE

The Stones Are Rolling Again

The New Role for Fathers Begins at Birth

The Boom in Dome Homes

What Is Barbara Walters Trying to Prove?

Mick Jagger, Stones' leader

JULY 14 · 1972 · 50¢

Smokin' Ron Wood replaced Mick Taylor as the Rolling Stones' lead guitar in 1975.

Riding the flying phallus.

Mick lets it rip in Europe, 1976.

The Rolling Stones as *Some Girls* is released, 1978.

Glimmer Twins and Rolling Stones Records artist Peter Tosh, 1979.

Mick sported athletic gear during the Stones' 1981/1982 tours.

cluding Mick's family. He didn't want his mother to know. With the advent of Bianca, Mick's relationship with Marsha Hunt was officially over.

––––––––

Further recording took place at Olympic Studio that autumn to finish *Sticky Fingers*. Billy Preston played gospel organ on "I Got the Blues." "Can't You Hear Me Knocking" got its guitar overdubs, with Mick Taylor playing in Carlos Santana's jazzy, repetitive style. String sections for magisterial "Sway" and evocative "Moonlight Mile" were scored by Paul Buckmaster, Elton John's arranger, in November. "Moonlight Mile" was Mick, Jim Price on piano, and Mick Taylor playing what Jagger called a "real dreamy, kind of semi–Middle Eastern piece." Keith was too stoned to make it to the studio, so "Mile" became the first Rolling Stones track whose credits didn't include him.

Around this time, the Stones gathered in a Soho screening room to watch the Maysles brothers' film, now titled *Gimme Shelter* and ready for release. Afterward, they had an argument about whom the late Meredith Hunter had wanted to shoot. As they were leaving, Mick said to Keith, "Flower Power was a load of crap, wasn't it?"

––––––––

Work on the new album continued into December at Olympic. "Good Time Woman" was in development, and "Sweet Virginia" came to life as another Stones hillbilly joke. On December 18, a studio party was held for Keith's twenty-sixth birthday. Eric Clapton, George Harrison, Bobby Keys, and Al Kooper all came, and all but Harrison played on a convulsive live version of "Brown Sugar," recorded after the party had been cleared away. With Clapton burning blue on slide guitar, this new version of "Brown Sugar" was so good it almost made it onto *Sticky Fingers*.

A Sunny Place
for Shady People

The seventies got under way in January 1971 with the Rolling Stones' affairs in flux. The Beatles had officially disbanded the month before when Paul McCartney sued the others, who had signed with Allen Klein. The Stones were bitter about their losses and leaving England, furious about their tax situation, and concerned about their new record deal. Atlantic Records, designated distributor of Rolling Stones Records, had been sold to a corporation that managed parking lots, and despite Ahmet Ertegun's assurances to Mick that he retained control, no one quite knew what would happen.

Keith didn't want to move to France, but the United States was off limits because Mick's recent drug conviction prevented him from even visiting for a year. Keith was also upset because Mick was besotted with Bianca Perez, and Keith was jealous. He hated Bianca almost at once. He thought her pretentious, self-absorbed, square, too young, and not at all rock and roll, and he worried that she would come between Mick and the Stones.

Keith was addicted to heroin and lived permanently in its twilight world with Anita and their fellow junkie Michael Cooper. Keith skin-popped his doses, injecting them into his muscles instead of his veins, which provided an illusion of self-control. Concerned about his health and probable supply problems, he decided to clean up before the move to France. He spoke to Mick about it, and Mick consulted William Burroughs, with whom Mick was meeting at Burroughs's Duke Street flat about a possible movie based on *Naked Lunch*.

Burroughs had been famously cured of a twenty-year narcotics habit by a British doctor, John Dent, who used the metabolic regulator apomorphine to achieve controlled and relatively painless withdrawals for his patients. Burroughs explained that although Dent had died, his veteran nurse, known as Smitty, continued to get satisfactory results from the apomorphine protocol.

Smitty duly arrived at Redlands in early February and put Keith through four howling, shivering days of heroin withdrawal, which left Keith a pale, emaciated ghost, though free of his usual craving for dope. The cure lasted about seventy-two hours, when Michael Cooper arrived at Redlands with a taste of good smack. Then Gram Parsons arrived in mid-February to hang out, which snuffed the whole cure idea. Keith now switched from pure heroin to skin-popping speedballs, a heroin-cocaine cocktail he found particularly conducive to songwriting. The drugs occasionally percolated in the muscle tissue of his arms, causing abscesses that left ghastly-looking scars.

Anita saw that the apomorphine cure didn't take, so a month later she tried a seven-day sleep cure at Bowden House clinic. While she was away, Keith nodded off in the London suburbs while driving down to the country, wrecking the now Pink Lena. Grabbing his stash, with police sirens wailing in the distance, he vaulted a nearby wall and found himself in the back garden of Nicky Hopkins's house. Nicky, home from a stint playing with Quicksilver Messenger Service in San Francisco, offered Keith a cup of tea. The Pink Lena was replaced with a red E-type Jaguar.

———

With *Sticky Fingers* almost completed, the Stones booked sessions at Olympic in February to begin the next album. They played badly, usually without Keith, and the tapes were later scrapped. Howlin' Wolf, the grand master of the blues, was in town to record with English rock stars in sessions arranged by Marshall Chess. Charlie, Bill, and Ian Stewart served as Wolf's rhythm section while he taught Eric Clapton the right way to play "Little Red Rooster." Ringo Starr and Steve Winwood sat in as well. The sometimes-thrilling tracks would be released later in the year as *The London Howlin' Wolf Sessions* on the Stones' label in England and by Chess Records in America.

————

In March 1971, the Rolling Stones undertook a farewell tour of England. Their first English tour in five years, and they stunk. Everyone said so.

They went out as an eight-piece show band, with the horns and Nicky Hopkins on piano, playing mostly in the north. The rhythms were sluggish because Keith was so stoned. Traditionally Keith set the tempos. He would start playing, quickly followed by Charlie, but if Keith was off— and he was really off that year—it could take time, often the whole set, for Charlie to catch up. Mick couldn't hear the piano through the stage monitors, so his vocals were often off too.

Keith was traveling with his gang (Anita, Marlon and the nanny, Gram Parsons) and his dog, a puppy named Boogie. After the Glasgow show, he tried to smuggle the dog onto a commercial flight, but the pilot wouldn't take off. The cops were called. Keith was holding enough heroin to land him back in Wormwood Scrubs for a few years, but he gave the cops a hard time anyway. After a big hassle, Boogie rode in the cargo hold and the band got back to London that night.

Although almost all the shows on the farewell tour sucked, the set did have its moments. Mick, in a pink satin suit with a floppy, multicolored cap, still got the girls screaming every time he turned his back and wiggled his bum. "Midnight Rambler" got a major rethink, with the harp, drums, and piano providing a Bo Diddley overture to a cool, fast version of the three-year-old charger. During the rape scene, Mick gurgled, "Go down on me, bay-beh, ooooh yeah," and assorted blow-job-recipient moans. "Satisfaction" had a vamping, soul-show intro, bump-and-grind with the horns, and then a long jam with Mick Taylor improvising floral arrangements. The unfamiliar new songs—"Wild Horses," "Dead Flowers," "Bitch" ("a song for all you whores in the audience")—were received quietly by the fans. The chugging finale "Let It Rock" woke everyone up when Keith started to play his ass off, sometimes taking three hot guitar choruses when his tired blood got boiling. No encores on this tour either. Keith kept missing trains and planes, and shows would start hours late. The Stones were so-so in Bristol, sloppy in Leeds, late in Liverpool. Bill Wyman got upset that they were playing so badly. "I just want everyone to say it *was* shit," he complained in the Liverpool dressing room, after a show that started five hours late. Bored Mick Jagger told Bill and everyone else that he just didn't care. Mick had the label deal to worry about, and still had to cut verses out of "Moonlight Mile," sequence *Fingers*, supervise the cover, design the new logo, and leave the country. Plus, Bianca was along, distracting him, her cruel features a mask of elegant, hot-blooded *froideur*. She was a couple of months pregnant and lovelier than ever as her tiny figure began to blossom. Completely upstaged in the crucial glamour department, Anita started to hate Bianca too, tried to mind-fuck her and put her down, but Bianca had a steely determination and the adoring support of Mick. She treated Anita with blithe detachment, like a vulgar relative, which made Anita really livid. Mick told Bianca she had to put up with Anita. Anita was one of the Stones.

The tour ended with shows at the Roundhouse in London. The band's families came, everyone's parents. "It was weird wigglin' me bum at me mum," Mick said, "like an incestuous thing." On March 26, the Stones played before an invited audience at the Marquee, taping TV shows for Europe and Brazil. Backstage, Keith cursed at his old enemy, the club's owner, Harold Pendleton. Keith swung at him, missed. It took Mick an hour to persuade Keith to get onstage. Keith was schwacked, played poorly, and the audience got bored with the band stopping numbers and starting again. So Mick had them all thrown out, and the band taped a set in an empty club. The result was so inert that the tapes weren't broadcast.

In England, the Labour government was again raising taxes. Denis Healey, chancellor of the exchequer, talked about squeezing the rich "until the pips squeak." On March 30, a few days before they left for tax exile in France, the Stones threw a farewell party at an old inn in Maidenhead. John and Yoko, William Burroughs, Eric Clapton, and many friends came to say good-bye. They were jamming at 2 A.M. when the sound went dead. The hotel had cut the power because the neighbors were complaining. Drunk and enraged by *jam-us interruptus,* Mick picked up a table and threw it through a huge plate-glass window that gave onto the placid Thames. Then he ran out into the night and was across the English Channel within hours, having bid a Byronic farewell to Albion.

————

The Rolling Stones were all in France by April 6, 1971. Mick and Bianca were in a hotel in Paris. The rest of the band settled into exile in the south of France in the tradition of English artistic exiles like Graham Greene and Somerset Maugham, who called the Riviera "a sunny place for shady people." They all rented houses amid the most beautiful springtime landscape in the world, a subtropical garden of jasmine and lavender. Bill and Mick Taylor's family were in Grasse, perfume capital of Provence. Charlie and family were in the Cévennes, the arid hills to the west. Mick leased a chateau near St. Tropez.

The Richards family rented a palatial villa called Nellcote for 10,000 pounds a month. Overlooking the deep harbor of Villefranche, near Cap Ferrat on the Riviera, the villa had wide balconies, hanging gardens, and endless blue vistas of the Mediterranean. Nellcote had a suitably shady past. The nineteenth-century British admiral who built it had later thrown himself off the roof. Germans had occupied it during World War II, and the vaulted cellar was supposedly the scene of Gestapo interrogations. It turned out to be a good place to record the next Rolling Stones album.

————

On April 6, the Rolling Stones sailed into Cannes on a yacht and appeared at the Carlton Hotel to sign their new record deal with Kinney National, an American parking lot corporation that now owned the Atlantic, Elektra, and Warner Bros. labels. Kinney boss Steve Ross and Atlantic chief Ahmet Ertegun presided. The deal required the Stones to produce six albums in the next four years, including *Sticky Fingers.* "The band is *not* retiring," Mick said. "We'll remain a functioning group, a touring group, a *happy* group." The Stones were horrified by the tacky public breakup of the Beatles in December 1970, and would avoid this fate at all costs.

"Rolling Stones Records was a licensing deal," he later admitted, "not a real record label for other artists. It gave us at least the *image* that we were independent." The Stones were still tied to Allen Klein, whom they were about to sue for millions, but—under new management and with their precarious finances controlled by someone they trusted—the band was on its way out of near bankruptcy.

"Control was what Ahmet and Prince Lowenstein had to offer the Stones," wrote George Trow in a contemporary *New Yorker* profile of Ertegun. "Both offered access to productive adult modes—financial and social—that could prolong a career built on non-adult principles." The suave socialite Ertegun became Mick's entrée to the international jet set and the upper Manhattan bohemia, a world that had eluded him so far.

There was a party that night in Cannes. The press had been flown in, and the photographers mobbed Bianca, who wore nothing under a black voile blouse. Keith Richards, outlaw junkie trouvère, who cared nothing for any of this, left early. "I have to find my dog," he told a journalist. "He's my only friend at the party, man."

The Tongue of Kali

"Brown Sugar," the first Stones single on their new (yellow) label, was released a few days later, April 16, 1971, with "Bitch" on the flip side. The English single had a bonus track, "Let It Rock," recorded at the Leeds show on March 15. The rocking taste of sex and race in "Brown Sugar" propelled it to no. 1 in America, no. 2 in England.

Sticky Fingers followed in early May. The album's jacket, a pop art assemblage of jeans (with a real zipper) that opened to reveal well-hung white underwear, was designed by Andy Warhol. This evolved from artwork Warhol had submitted in 1969 for *Let It Bleed,* which had the vinyl record in girls' panties inside cutoff Levi's (and which had been misplaced by the Stones' office staff). In case anyone missed the design's phallic statement, the Stones cataloged their first album on their new label as COC 59100. The album also marked the debut of the Stones' new logo, a cartoon of lips, teeth, and lolling tongue in red, white, and black. Often attributed to Warhol, it was actually devised by Mick Jagger and graphic designer John Pashe in homage to the iconographic tongue of Kali, the Hindu goddess of creation, life, and destruction.

Sticky Fingers kicked off with "Brown Sugar." A tenor sax break instead of a guitar solo signaled that this was the New Look Stones. "Sway" and its heroin-inflected tale of "this demon life" ended with a stirring string section. The darkness continued with "Wild Horses" and its dull, aching pain of separation and loss. The mood was lifted in "Can't You Hear Me Knocking?" as the Stones built a Chicano acid rock groove with Mick Taylor's riffing, Bobby Keys's fluttering sax, and Rocky Dijon's congas. "You Gotta Move" closed side one.

"Bitch" opened side two with its all-time riff and Moroccan-sounding horns. Mick Taylor's hard-edged guitar seemed to assert its rights to rule the Stones' new style. "I Got the Blues" cast Mick as a begging soul man, reinforced by Billy Preston's gospel attack on the organ. "Sister Morphine" was the Stones' version from the spring of 1969, credited to Jagger/Richards with no mention of Marianne Faithfull. It starts with just acoustic guitar, joined by Ry Cooder's slide guitar on the second verse. By the third verse, the band joins, and there's a very doomy tag with Cooder and Jack Nitzsche on "treated" piano that carried the morbid song into a blue, mystifying underworld.

This was followed by the black parody of country rock "Dead Flowers," with its drug paraphernalia, the needle and a spoon, and its farewell to Little Suzy, Queen of the Underground. Keith loved country music (Mick treated it as a joke), and country-style songs of varying degrees of irony would appear on almost every Stones album to come. The album ended with the Pacific Coast sonic highway of "Moonlight Mile," a swooning California vibe best appreciated with "a headfull of snow." This beautiful song of dreamy fatigue featured guitars by the two Micks,

Jim Price on piano, and an orchestral wash of strings that ended *Sticky Fingers* on a majestic note of long distances traveled before coming to rest at home. Keith's acoustic guitar, uncredited on the album, appears at the end of the song, left over from the original demo when it was titled "Japanese Thing."

Sticky Fingers was a sensation, no. 1 in America and Europe—proof that the Rolling Stones would survive into the uncertain seventies. There wasn't a lot of great pop music around in 1971. American rock fans were preoccupied with bombastic Grand Funk Railroad and the macabre theatrics of Alice Cooper. In England, fans had Deep Purple, Humble Pie, Rod Stewart, and the Faces. London's glam movement was moving out of its underground beginnings of Warholesque, cross-dressing rockers (T. Rex, David Bowie) mocking sexual norms in high heels and glittery makeup. With powerful and daring "Brown Sugar" and "Bitch," with their Memphis-style horns, orchestral colors, and Mick Taylor's cool blue guitar, the Stones now positioned themselves as keepers of a hard rock flame they'd ignited almost a decade earlier.

May 1971. Mick Jagger called the Stones' London office to say he was going to marry Bianca, now four months pregnant, in St. Tropez. He gave Shirley Arnold his guest list. The press got wind of it, and his intimate wedding in an old stone chapel turned into another Stones media riot.

Mick and Bianca flew from Nice to Paris on May 2. He gave a dinner party for her, gave her a diamond bracelet, visited a jeweler to have a pair of matching wedding rings made. Roger Vadim and his wife, actress Natalie Delon, agreed to serve as witnesses. On May 7, a chartered flight brought the wedding guests: Mick's family, Paul and Linda, Ringo and Maureen, Eric Clapton, Keith Moon, sundry aristocrats, Ronnie Wood from the Faces, Robert Fraser—seventy-five people in all.

On the morning of May 12, Bianca was presented with a harsh prenuptial agreement that severely limited the amount she could collect from Mick in the event of a divorce. They had a terrible fight, and

Mick threatened to call off the wedding if she didn't sign. She later said this marriage contract had never even been discussed, that she hadn't a clue what it meant, that she only signed it reluctantly, and that it ruined her day.

They were staying at the Hotel Byblos in St. Tropez. That morning, a rabid pack of photographers occupied the town hall where the civil ceremony would take place. Mick didn't want to marry in public, and the wedding was delayed until finally the mayor threatened to walk out. So, amid a perspiring scrum of paparazzi, the wedding couple arrived in their beautiful clothes, the bride's rouged nipples peeking out of her jacket. Fights broke out among the press during the brief ceremony. Keith smashed a camera, a wild gleam in his eye. A few hours later, they were married again, this time in private, in the old Chapel of St. Anne, by a priest who had (supposedly) been giving Mick some pointers in Catholicism. As requested by the bride, a selection of music from *Love Story* was played in the chapel.

The party that night at the Café des Arts was a blowout. Caviar, champagne, lobster. The bride wore a turban and a see-through lace top. Bobby Keys ran the jam session, joined by Steve Stills, Nicky Hopkins, and Michael Shrieve, Santana's drummer. Mick got up with Doris Troy and Pat Arnold for a medley of soul hits. Bianca left early. So did Joe and Eva Jagger, still holding their wedding present. They'd been unable to secure a private moment in which to give it to their son and his bride.

Mick had wanted the Stones to play at his wedding. Keith, who'd pleaded with him not to marry Bianca, had nodded off in a corner, snoring, and some guests wondered if he was turning into Brian Jones. His friends knew that Keith was despondent. Bianca was his enemy: a snooty petite bourgeoise who disdained him and Anita (Bianca referred to Anita as "that cow"). To Keith, Bianca was a pampered party girl who hung out with the elderly squares that Keith liked to mock, and she was stealing his friend and posing a serious threat to the band.

Mick left the party with the last guests at four in the morning. Later that day, Mick and Bianca boarded a yacht in Cannes for a honeymoon at an Italian cliffside palazzo, accessible only by boat. One can only imagine what Bianca thought was in store for her as she experienced the whirlwind events of her wedding, but she later was famously quoted: "My marriage ended on my wedding day."

––––––––––

That June, Nellcote, Keith's villa in Villefranche, was a hectic rock and roll commune as the Stones and their allies gathered to record the Stones' crucial next record. Nellcote was set in a park planted with palm and cypress trees brought from around the world by its nautical builder. A long flight of steps led to a private beach. There was a water bed on the balcony, a bright parrot in a cage in the front garden, a rabbit in a hutch in the back. Keith's dogs had the run of the place. In the rooms downstairs, the ceilings were thirty feet high and the mistral howled down the chimneys. A giant *Sticky Fingers* promo poster of Mick was propped on the mantel of the main fireplace. Country music—Merle Haggard, George Jones—blared from the record player, alternating with Chuck Berry and Buddy Holly albums. Hired chefs fed large stoned groups of musicians and friends at long tables at odd hours; at the height of the sessions, Keith was spending $7,000 a week on food, rent, and dope. The hot ambience of Nellcote reminded journalist Robert Greenfield, who was on the scene to interview Keith for *Rolling Stone,* of F. Scott Fitzgerald's Riviera novel *Tender Is the Night* crossed with *The Shirelles' Greatest Hits.*

The Stones were supposed to record in a separate house, but Stu couldn't find one near Keith, who insisted he had to work close to his family and his stash. So Stu drove the Stones' mobile studio to France, and they built a recording room in Nellcote's cellar. The old villa's frail wiring couldn't handle the new demands for current, so the crew illegally tapped into the French railway system's nearby power lines and ran heavy cables through the kitchen window and down to the dark, humid basement. So *Exile on Main Street* became Keith's trip, done on his time at his house. The rest of the band also moved into Nellcote when they realized that Keith would only be working downstairs as Marlon's erratic sleep schedule permitted. The Stones' sidemen, engineers, and technicians rented other houses nearby, and Anita often had twenty-five guests for meals. She asked Keith, "Why is it no one ever says goodbye?"

The proximity of Marseilles, heroin capital of Europe, assured that no annoying dope shortages occurred. Mafia-level dealers arrived at Nellcote carrying top-grade Thai heroin (called cotton candy for its bright pink sheen) in smart attaché cases. Cocaine was often smuggled in by the van making weekly runs between London and Nellcote. After partying with Keith, John Lennon threw up all over the villa's grand marble stairs.

Villefranche was a deep-water port of call for battleships of various navies. Reasoning that the sailors might have opium or hash to sell, Keith bought a sleek Riva powerboat so he could buzz out to the huge gray ships moored offshore. Anita, pregnant with their second child (because Marlon was lonely), would watch Keith put to sea from her balcony, unsure whether he would make it home, as the sky turned sunset pink over Cap Ferrat. He ran the boat over rocks, crashed into other boats, and ran out of fuel a few times. Since he had no radio, he drifted until someone rescued him. He named the boat Mandrax.

One evening in late May, Keith and Spanish Tony went to see Errol Flynn's old yacht, moored in nearby Beaulieu. As they were leaving, an Italian tourist accidentally dented Keith's red Jaguar. Keith got mad and displayed his switchblade. The Beaulieu harbormaster intervened, knocked Keith down, and got punched out by Spanish Tony. Keith then produced Marlon's toy pistol from the glove box, so the harbormaster drew his own quite real revolver and called the gendarmes. This fracas was resolved over dinner at Nellcote with the local police chief, who was bought off with some autographed albums and promises to behave.

The police, however, started watching Keith and the British invasion of freaks that had followed him to town.

Tropical Disease

July 1971. The Stones had been jamming almost every night for several weeks and began recording in Keith's basement around July 10. They had songs left over from both the last album and Stargroves, and were also writing new material as the "Tropical Disease Sessions," as Keith called them, got under way.

It was rough. Everyone was stoned out of their minds, disconnected from familiar surroundings, in exile. There were serious cash flow problems, and the Stones were suing Allen Klein, Andrew Oldham, and Eric Easton. Since Keith was a junkie, the recording schedule ran on heroin time. Charlie and Bill would arrive around 8 P.M., and Keith would show up at midnight. After working for a while, he would go upstairs, saying he had to put Marlon to bed, and be gone for three hours. This drove Mick crazy; tempers often flared, and then Mick would leave to be with Bianca, who refused to come to the Riviera and was living in a Paris hotel. Keith would come back downstairs, find Mick gone, often for days, and flip out.

"Everybody was stoned on something," Mick later said. "So it wasn't particularly pleasant. I didn't have a very good time. It was this communal thing when you didn't know whether you're recording or living or having dinner. You don't know when you're going to play, when you're going to sing. Very difficult. Too many hangers-on. I went with the flow, and the album got made [but] it got impossible. Everyone was so out of it. And the engineers, the producers—all the people that were supposed to be organized—were more disorganized than anybody."

These guys (Jimmy Miller, Andy Johns) were themselves shocked at how badly the Stones were playing—unfocused and out of tune. Andy Johns thought they sounded like the worst band on the planet and wondered if the tracks would even get released. Mick Taylor was upset because this was his first complete Stones album and things seemed so fucked-up. He was also freaked that Mick Jagger was coming on to his wife, Rosie.

But over the summer, some of the songs began to gel, and the Tropical Disease music started to sound like a new, lurid, really drugged-out version of the Stones. "Rocks Off" was an early success, a lurid tale of lust and impotence that Keith nailed in two takes at nine in the morning after the engineers, who had left at dawn, had been summoned back from their beds. Mick and Keith wrote upstairs, Mick mumbling vowel movements while Keith riffed on the guitar, and by the time they came down to the basement they had something, like "Rip This Joint," that they could show Bobby Keys and Jim Price. "Casino Boogie" and the new lyrics for "Tumbling Dice" were influenced by the lavish gambling casinos just down the road in Monte Carlo. Mick was either rushing his lines or slurring them, so the lyrics were unintelligible, a technique copped from bluesman Slim Harpo, whose style so influenced the boogie "Hip Shake" that his name got into the song. "Torn and Frayed" was one of a series of cracked country tunes inspired in part by the brief presence of Gram Parsons at Nellcote. Keith summoned him from L.A. early in July, and Gram arrived with his wife, Gretchen, whom Anita loathed. Gram stayed up nights with Keith, played some guitar and piano, and later claimed to have sung on a couple of the finished songs. With Mick not around much, it was good for Keith to have Gram to bounce ideas off, but Parsons was strung out on heroin and going downhill. After weeks of Gram snorting up all the drugs while his old lady complained, Keith threw them out. Crushed and suicidal, Gram headed to London, never again to find himself completely welcome in the Stones' fickle milieu.

While the Stones were working downstairs, the parade of characters continued in the spacious salons upstairs. William Burroughs and Terry Southern arrived to hustle a Stones sound track for a *Naked Lunch* movie. Corsicans arrived with half kilos of heroin, 6,000 pounds per, and were paid in cash. The Bauls, a tribal band from Bengal, came to Nellcote to tape some drums that eventually weren't used. A gang of petty criminal "cowboys" from the St. Tropez underbelly was installed by Anita in the villa's gatehouse, where they dealt drugs and stole everything they could. Half-naked Anita smoked opium with Marshall Chess. A chef was hired to prepare the gourmet luncheons served daily to one and all. Keith drove him crazy by ignoring the sumptuous buffet and demanding a cheeseburger. After lunch, Keith would sit on his verandah, shirtless and barefoot, strumming his guitar, thinking up the words to a new, autobiographical song called "Happy." Anita hired the chef's daughter as a nanny for Marlon and shot her up with heroin. The girl got sick and Anita made her swear not to tell her father. Everyone knew that eventually there would be hell to pay.

Bill Wyman found Nellcote's narcotic vibes distasteful, so he stayed away and took up smoking grass. He only played bass on eight of *Exile*'s eighteen tracks. Down in the cellar, Mick Taylor earned his only songwriting credit on a Stones album by coming up with the guitar lick of "Ventilator Blues" during a humid Mediterranean summer night when the only air in the room came from a little fan hung above Charlie's drums. Some nights the temperature reached a hundred degrees, and the band played with their pants off. It was so humid Mick and Keith couldn't sing. They medicated their vocal cords with Jack Daniel's and kept working.

The sessions carried on into the autumn, with Mick shuttling between the Riviera and Paris, since Bianca refused to go anywhere near Nellcote. Tempers and the band were starting to shred. The basic track for "Happy" was cut one night with Keith on guitar and vocals, Bobby Keys on sax, and Jimmy Miller playing drums. These three, along with Mick Taylor on bass, formed the core group that did the basic tracks of *Exile on Main Street.*

In August, *Rolling Stone* published Robert Greenfield's long interview with Keith, a landmark of Stonesology that introduced Keith's often-hilarious facility as a wordsmith and quote-factory to the world. Keith was surprisingly candid about the lure and the danger of heroin. "If you're going to get into junk, it takes the place of everything. You don't need a chick, you don't need music, you don't need nothing. But it doesn't get you anywhere. It ain't called 'junk' for nothing. Why did [William] Burroughs kick it, after 25 years? He's thankful he kicked it, believe me.

There's a lot of Chinese shit around. That's all I can say. That's another one of those rumors."

——————

Rolling Stones Records, the band's new label, released its first album in September 1971. *Brian Jones Presents the Pipes of Pan at Joujouka* was a spacey-sounding version of Brian's 1968 Moroccan tapes, electronically enhanced and edited into a post-psychedelic orientalist fantasia that still captured the time-tripping essence of the village's music. The Stones' vast audience remained indifferent to the late Brian's epic quest for the square root of the blues, and few who bought the album understood the dark North African spirits it conjured. But the perceptive critic Bob Palmer aptly described the record's magical ambience in *Rolling Stone:* "a backward drum track here, a phased melody there, an electronic undercurrent that suggests the menace of the darkness outside the circle of firelight." The record was Brian Jones's final bow, two years after his death, and was later seen as the alpha project of the world music movement, which integrated non-Western music into the mainstream of popular culture. And up on Jajouka's mountain, the tribal musicians put a photo of Brian on the wall of their clubhouse and continued to sing their Brahim Jones song. The old glossy photo of Brian seemed to jiggle in its frame every time they sang it.

——————

By October 1971, the bright Mediterranean days were getting shorter, and darkness of the soul began to settle around Nellcote. Bianca delivered her daughter Jade in Paris, and Mick informed Keith he wasn't coming back. On October 11, thieves broke into Nellcote and stole eleven guitars while everyone slept upstairs. Keith's eyes filled with tears when he was told. Friends like Bobby Keys and Michael Cooper had never seen him cry before. A second burglary relieved Keith and Anita of cash and clothes. Bobby Keys's behavior was getting him thrown out of casinos, and a local boy complained to the cops that he'd been molested at Nellcote by someone from the Living Theater. When Jacques the chef learned that Anita had given his daughter heroin, he tried to blackmail Keith and was fired. The police arrived the next day, took statements, asked about drugs, and demanded to know why Corsican dope dealers had been seen visiting Nellcote.

The other Stones got nervous about doing any more work at Keith's. Someone organized a bust drill at Nellcote, and the occupants made plans to skip town. The Stones had twenty new songs, enough for a double album, so they decided to finish recording in Los Angeles. The police learned of the move and tried to prevent Keith and Anita from leaving France while their investigations of heroin trafficking were going on. Keith's lawyers persuaded the cops that Keith would continue to rent the expensive villa as assurance of his intent to return. So in late November, the Rolling Stones all slipped out of the country. Mick and Keith and their families flew to L.A., with Keith and his new guitar technician, an affable southern lad named Ted Newman Jones III, detouring through Memphis so they could begin to replace the vintage Gibson, Fender, and Martin guitars that had been stolen from Nellcote.

Jackson Pollock in Stereo

January 1972. The Stones were working at Sunset Sound in Los Angeles, polishing the muggy, hellish Nellcote tracks, recording new songs and overdubs with the cream of L.A.'s musicians. Billy Preston was a huge presence with his gospel keyboard on "Shine a Light." He took Mick to Rev. James Cleveland's church one Sunday to listen to the soaring choir as it lifted its voice to the heavens. Keith brought in Dr. John— Mac Rebennack—who showed up with his crew of Creole percussionists to work on "Let It Loose" and other numbers. Rebennack also brought in the female voices—Tami Lynn, Clydie King, Shirley Goodman, and Vanetta Lee—that effectively painted *Exile* black. "They weren't necessarily totally stand-up people," Dr. John later said of the Stones, "but I dug working with them." With Bill Wyman still sulking in France, bassist Bill Plummer, a jazz player who'd worked with George Shearing and Paul Horn, played upright acoustic "doghouse" bass on "Rocks Off," "Turd on the Run," and "All Down the Line."

Mick Jagger was living in a rented mansion with Bianca and Jade, deep into planning the Stones' year. The new album would come out in the spring, followed by a big American tour. The tour would spawn another live album, perhaps a double with Stevie Wonder, who would open the shows, and at least two films: one an underground newsreel, the other a full-blown concert film. Mick went to see the Who play in L.A. and hired away their road manager, Peter Rudge, to run the Stone's 1972 tour. He also hired star L.A. publicist Gary Stromberg, who suggested helping the best writers in the country to get magazine assignments and then taking them on tour with the band for a few days each, giving them a taste of life on the road.

The Stones were out on the town a lot. Charlie was in the jazz clubs, digging Dexter Gordon. Mick went to see Merry Clayton, who had made a career out of her star turn on "Gimme Shelter." One night Mick, Keith, and Ian Stewart showed up at a club where Chuck Berry was playing. Berry's road manager invited them onstage, so Keith plugged in and started to play along with "Sweet Little Sixteen." Berry glowered at Keith, told him to turn down, screwed up the rhythms, and threw them all off the stage after two songs because the audience was going crazy. Chuck later explained that Keith was playing too loud.

Anita was due to have her baby in April and was taking three shots of heroin a day. When she couldn't stop and her time grew short, Keith moved his family to Switzerland, where the situation could be managed discreetly. Anita entered a private clinic, while Keith and Marlon checked into the Hotel Metropole in friendly Montreux on Lake Geneva, where local music promoter Claude Nobs looked after English bands. On March 17, Anita gave birth to a daughter, Dandelion, born with a cleft palate. Naming the girl after a weed ("Go away dandelion" ran a famous Stones chorus) was perhaps an indication of how things ran in the Richards family in those days.

With the rumor of a vague Hell's Angels death threat in the air, Mick and Bianca left L.A. with *Exile* almost finished and headed for Bali, soulful South Pacific isle of cultured peace and spiritual tranquillity. Mick was back in New York by early May 1972 to settle the Allen Klein lawsuit. So anxious were the Stones to get out from under Klein's thumb that they gave him the farm. Their original suit for multiple millions in back royalties was dropped. ABCKO Industries, Klein's holding company, wound up with the publishing rights to all Jagger/Richards and Nanker Phelge songs through 1969; the master tapes to the Stones back catalog through *Get Your Ya-Yas Out* and subsequent anthology albums; and a reported $14 million. Basically the Rolling Stones had to give Klein the entire recorded output of the past ten years, and Mick Jagger convinced the rest of the band it was worth it. The deal was announced on May 10, 1972. "The settlement," Mick told the press, "is that Allen Klein never has anything else to do with us."

Keith was doing so much dope he was unable to complete some of the final overdubs on *Exile on Main Street*. Studio guitarist Al Perkins played slide guitar on "Torn and Frayed" while Keith returned to Switzerland for a three-day heroin detox. (For years, Richards maintained that the Stones' best album was created during his heaviest period of addiction, a tribute to both his drug of choice and his physical stamina.) The rest of the Stones arrived in Montreux on May 17 for several weeks of secret tour rehearsals in a movie theater with Nicky Hopkins, Bobby Keys, and Jim Price.

They were all around thirty now, with separate lives and interests. Mick and Keith were no longer as close as they had been, and the rehearsals were a way to bring the Stones together as friends as well as musicians. The show, Mick Jagger insisted, must go on.

———————

Exile on Main Street came out in May 1972, while the first single, "Tumbling Dice," was climbing into the Top Ten. This epochal eighteen-song double album still stands as the best Rolling Stones album for many fans. A damp, drunken-sounding collection of riffs, incomprehensible lyrics, and jam-type songs, *Exile* also marked the end of the Rolling Stones' protean midperiod, the last of four albums in the band's glory days, the foundation on which their career still rests.

The album cover was a montage of black-and-white photos by Robert Frank, the Swiss-born filmmaker whose classic photo book, *The Americans,* had a foreword by Jack Kerouac. Frank's 1959 beatnik film *Pull My Daisy,* with Kerouac, Allen Ginsberg, and Gregory Corso, was considered the first underground movie, and Frank had been hired to film the upcoming tour in cutup underground style.

The album was sequenced as four discrete sets, one on each side of the two records. Mick said the record shouldn't be played all at once, that it was designed as twenty-minute bursts. The first side of *Exile* was a missile launch of energy with "Rocks Off." "Rip This Joint" was a lightning tour of southern cities, the fastest song the Stones ever recorded until "Flip the Switch" outran it twenty-five years later. "Hip Shake" was a fast boogie homage to Slim Harpo, with Mick on harp and Ian Stewart on piano. "Casino Boogie" was a Nellcote basement jam with Bobby Keys that led into "Tumbling Dice," a homage to good-time women that had only come to life when it got its chorus of black singers in Los Angeles.

"Acoustic" side two delved into country matters. "Sweet Virginia" was a mock country tune about hiding pills and speed in somebody's shoe. "Torn and Frayed" introduced Joe the Guitar Player, a take on wild Keith Richards and his accelerated lifestyle. "Sweet Black Angel" was a lilting calypso about Angela Davis, the fire-breathing Black Panther activist who had just faced down murder charges in California. The marimba on this track and others, credited to "Amyl Nitrate," was actually played by Didimus (aka Richard Washington), one of Dr. John's Cajun conjurers. The set ended with "Loving Cup," an acoustic song that built over four minutes into a funky grandeur that typified the louche ambience of the album.

Side three. "Happy" with Keith on vocal, his trenchant, anthemic, open G autobiography and hard rock manifesto for two guitars and horns. "Turd on the Run" was a country shuffle in overdrive that described the pain of giving diamonds and getting disease in return.

"Ventilator Blues" transported the Stones fan into Keith's humid Gestapo basement. The darkly shimmering "Just Wanna See His Face," with Keith on electric piano, had been given a Delta gospel treatment in L.A. and emerged as a hoodoo, churchy reverie of atmosphere and fervor, the most overtly spiritual of all Stones songs, ever. This song bled into "Let It Loose," with Dr. John and the moaning girls, which ended the side.

Exile on Main Street concluded with four upbeat soul numbers. "All Down the Line" was an old *Bleed*-era Stones jam goosed by Jimmy Miller's percussion and the L.A. studio singer Kathi McDonald. "Stop Breaking Down" was Robert Johnson on the Riviera, mostly Stu and Mick on harmonica (the track was miscredited as "Trad." on the album). "Shine a Light" was a West Coast gospel treatment of a 1968 Stones demo: terror in Room Ten Oh Nine on a Sunday morning, and it introduced Billy Preston as a sometimes-sanctified Stones sideman who would continue in concert and on record for five more years. ("Shine a Light" has been called Mick's love song to Keith.) The album's finale, "Soul Survivor," really just a verse and a lick, anticipated the stripped-down, semidesperate Stones of *Black and Blue*.

Exile had a mismatched, random, brain-fevered quality, like a Jackson Pollock splatter. It was all over the place, random, hard to handle. "It ran the gamut of the Rolling Stones' interests at that point," Mick said later. "It was recorded in a very amateurish fashion." *Exile* was an instant no. 1 album, a huge success for the Stones, and, promoted by a publicity-rich tour that summer, stayed high in the charts for the rest of the year.

STP

June 1972. Mick wanted a state-of-the-art professional tour this time. They had their own plane, a Lockheed Electra turboprop with the Stones' red lapping tongue logo painted on the fuselage and tail. They had a real tour manager, Peter Rudge, a large, efficient English public school type with long hair and acceptable manners. They had a film crew, headed by Robert Frank, on hand to film a documentary. They had a forty-man crew and a phalanx of security, especially after the segregationist presidential candidate George Wallace was gunned down in May. Both Mick and Keith carried loaded .38s, and they hid behind LeRoy and Stan, their famous linebacker-size black bodyguards. The Stones were scared. The Hell's Angels supposedly had a murder contract out on Mick, left over from Altamont, and were trying to extort money from the Stones. After the tour, Mick told Robert Greenfield, "Don't say I wasn't scared, man. I was scared *shitless.*"

Technical director Chip Monck rigged a huge mirror over the stage and bounced the lights off it from the sides and behind, instead of lighting the stage from in front and above. This bathed the musicians in reflected beams of pale light, frontlit and backlit, that gave the frenetic Stones experience a weird, dreamlike aura. (Monck's innovation was supposed to be the wave of the future, but the system was so awkward it was barely used again.)

Robert Frank's film crew joined the band in L.A. during rehearsals on a soundstage at Warner Bros. and pre-tour interviews in a house above Sunset Boulevard rented from aviation heir Michael Butler. Guaranteed "access all areas" and adept at getting through closed doors, Frank was shooting in Super 8, and he gave one of his Eclair cameras to Mick for some rock star vérité. Marshall Chess was the producer of Frank's doomed-from-the-start documentary, and Keith's pal Stash de Rola was put to work holding the microphones.

Ticket prices were held to $6.50. The laminated backstage passes had the letters STP printed on them for "Stones Touring Party," alternately "Stop Tripping Please." Fred Sessler was on the case as pharmacist to the band. "He was incredibly important to the Stones," Gary Stromberg says. "Everyone deferred to him. Fred was the only one on that tour, other than the band, who could write his own ticket." No one really knew where Fred got his amazing stash; word was he had a license to import cocaine manufactured by Merck Pharmaceutical in Switzerland. Everyone marveled. What a guy!

———

First show, Vancouver, June 3. On the plane, drinks were served, and the tequila sunrise, a vitamin-rich cocktail of O.J., grenadine, and cactus liquor, became the official drink of STP. Motown hero Stevie Wonder and his tight soul band Wonderlove opened the show with rippling, intensely musical versions of his great soul hits. The blind master musician blasted out "Uptight" and shook every arena on the tour. The Stones then opened their shows with a roaring "Brown Sugar." Mick had two main costumes: a jumpsuit in ivory-colored silk with a red sash by Michael Fish, and Ossie Clark's blue silk and velvet number with plastic and metal studs, both set off by thick golden chains around his neck and Balinese bracelets around his wrists and arms. He wore white dance shoes with little bells and never stopped bopping, exhibiting all his trademark struts, feints, and jabs.

The Stones' ninety-minute show mixed recent hits with new *Exile* tracks like "Tumbling Dice," "All Down the Line," and "Happy." Mick's pre-break line—"Keith's gonna sing 'Happy' for ya now"—often drew the biggest cheers of the show as Keith, cruising on smack and wrapped in a yellow scarf covered in red Tibetan mantras, took over the mike and bawled out his life story as the horns, stage left, blared joyously behind him. Nicky Hopkins played keyboards on the melodic stuff. Stu took over when it was Chuck Berry time.

Keith told friends he hated the big arenas the Stones were playing, hated Peter Rudge, hated the tour. He carried his drugs in a small black doctor's bag. The Stones also had their own staff physician in tow, Dr. Larry, who was equipped to treat any malady from depression to gunshots. Dr. Larry also had a taste for the youngest of the young girls who flocked to the hotels to meet the Stones. "People on the tour started trading him girls for drugs," Gary Stromberg recalled, "and we later learned he almost lost his license for writing too many prescriptions."

In San Francisco, the Stones played the Winterland Ballroom for promoter Bill Graham. Mick diffused lingering tensions with Graham by being charming, and the poison left over from 1969 was forgotten. No longer were they the greatest R&R band in the world: understated Chip Monck now simply said, "Ladies and gentlemen, the Rolling Stones." Everyone except Stu was wrecked, and the Stones played so out of tune that Nicky Hopkins was disgusted by the people who came backstage to tell them how great they were. At the airport, a young woman tried to serve Altamont-connected subpoenas to Mick. Keith smacked her and threw the papers on the runway before they flew south.

Two shows at the Forum in L.A. inspired a media frenzy and an ungodly guest list. Bianca earned the loathing of the Stones' office ladies by commandeering precious tickets for her friends. Less than friendly when on tour, Bianca was much reviled by the STP crew for putting them uptight. They liked it better when Mick took up with photog Annie Leibovitz later on the tour when his wife wasn't around.

In Denver, Keith threw overweight, glamour-deprived Gram Parsons out of his hotel suite, which as usual was Party Central. A story went around that Gram had threatened Keith with a knife after having been denied all the cocaine in the room, and that he was told to stay away from the tour.

"Some nights," wrote Robert Greenfield, "it was as though they brought Keith to the hall in a cage and his hour and a half onstage was the only freedom he was going to get. There was no way of telling when he'd crash into an amp or fall the last three steps off the back of the stage. He was dangerous and unpredictable, which made him exciting to watch." Typical 1972 set, circa midtour: "Brown Sugar" with solos by Keys and Mick Taylor; "Bitch" with Charlie on the attack (some think this was, musically, Mr. Watts's greatest tour); "Rocks Off" with its lazy mid-song bridge and busy horns; "Gimme Shelter"; "Happy" croaked and quacked by Keith, goosed by the brass; "Tumbling Dice" delivered in Mick's new "preaching" style, spoken more than sung; "Love in Vain," mostly a showcase for Mick Taylor's spellbinding blues solo; "Sweet Virginia," Keys taking the sax solo; "You Can't Always Get What You

Want" with Jim Price playing the intro on trombone; "All Down the Line" as fast as Charlie could make it; "Midnight Rambler" full throttle too, the centerpiece of the show and another side of the Stones' incredible young virtuoso, Mick Taylor. Introducing him, Mick liked to say, "The lady with the lipstick—Mick Taylor on guitar!"

After the rock rape scene of "Rambler," the shows geared up to the finale of "Bye Bye Johnny" with Keith playing blocks of Chuck chords as the solo; an even crazier "Rip This Joint"; "Jumpin' Jack Flash" with Keith's new stuttering guitar at the end; and a set-ending, erupting "Street Fighting Man"—blazing chords and supercharged drumming that built to a breathtaking peak. Then it was rose petals and good night.

————————

June 19 and 20. Three shows in Chicago International Amphitheater. The Stones were happily entertained with Bunnies and blow at Hugh Hefner's Playboy Mansion, where they stayed for three nights enjoying the underwater bar and the game room with rows of pinball machines. The Bunnies were highly buffed midwestern prom queens on Quaaludes, up for just about anything English in tight pants. Sad-eyed Charlie Watts played pinball. With the boys on coke and the girls on 'ludes, the Stones' visit turned into a seventy-two-hour orgy. Hugh Hefner wisely refused to let Robert Frank and his cameras into his house, and Frank was furious.

In Kansas City, Gary Stromberg began bringing in his star writers to hang out. Truman Capote had a *Rolling Stone* assignment and brought along celebrity photog Peter Beard and his girlfriend Princess Lee Radziwill, sister of Jackie Onassis. Capote appeared to be on tranquilizers and was bluntly ignored by Mick, despite Capote's extreme visibility quotient. Rumpled, bearded Terry Southern was covering the tour for *Saturday Review* and was as high as anyone in the band.

"Terry Southern was so stoned you had to look out for him," recalls Gary Stromberg. "This was uncool, but Terry was close to Keith, so you couldn't say anything. One night in Mobile, Alabama, he was standing by Keith's amp during the show, with the uniformed Mobile police chief standing next to him. Terry was fumbling in his pockets and dropped all his drugs—pills, powders, Baggies, amyl nitrite poppers, hash pipe—on the floor in front of them. He fell on his knees to gather them up while Keith was laughing and kicking the pills and phials that had rolled onto the stage over to him, while still playing. The cop never said a thing."

"Princess Radish," as Keith called her (Capote was "that old queen"), ratcheted the tour up a notch in the publicity department. She and Capote gave the Stones an uneasy sheen of celebrity beyond the world of rock music, which annoyed other bands like Led Zeppelin, who were touring at the same time and found themselves ignored even though they were outselling the Stones in every city. It was the beginning of the nexus of the Rolling Stones and Big Gossip, items that got them mainstream daily publicity instead of mere ink in the rock press.

With this new celebrity entourage milling in the dressing room, the Stones played badly in Kansas City. It was the worst show of the tour, which the princess then left in a huff when told she couldn't fly with the Stones on their plane.

Only Stones Left Standing

Bianca rejoined the tour as the Stones blasted through the southern states. Chic as ever, she wore a light pastel summer suit, with matching straw derby and a gold-topped ebony walking stick (Keith was incredulous). To get away from their onerous forty-man crew, the Stones drove across the South in a small convoy of station wagons, listening to the radio, passing joints, and stopping in drive-ins to eat. "The South is the only place in America where you can get decent food," said Mick. "And it's fucking great to get away from all those people." They were thrown out of a whites-only roadhouse in Louisiana because of their black bodyguards.

Truman Capote gave a small dinner for the band in New Orleans before quitting the tour. Ahmet Ertegun threw a large party for the Stones, with blues heroes Roosevelt Sykes and Professor Longhair for entertainment.

By early July, the Stones were burned out, with another three weeks still to go. On July 4, they played a sold-out RFK Stadium in Washington, D.C., while a riot raged outside. Marshall Chess crashed and burned. Stash de Rola was caught shaking down dope dealers for drugs and money. The security posse decided to get rid of Stash, so in Indianapolis one of the bodyguards put a gun to his head, then beat him to a pulp and suggested he disappear. But their plans to lose de Rola were foiled by Keith; in an extremely tense meeting, he insisted that Stash had to stay.

In Montreal, Anglophobe Quebec separatists issued threats against the Stones and firebombed the Stones' equipment truck on July 17. Replacement gear had to be flown in from California. The next day, the Stones flew to Boston for two shows at Boston Garden. Fog forced a landing in Rhode Island, where a local photographer caught them at the airport and started snapping. Keith punched him, beginning an absurd fracas. The cops arrested Keith, and also Marshall Chess and Robert Frank for getting in their way. In Boston, Stevie Wonder played for two hours to an impatient crowd while the Stones were hauled off to jail. Meanwhile, a Latino race riot was raging in Boston, and part of the city was on fire. The mayor of Boston came to the hall and begged the Stones' crowd for patience and discipline so the large police concert detail could be diverted to the riot. He got a standing ovation, then called the governor of Rhode Island and managed to spring the Stones from jail. Gary Stromberg: "So we drive up to Boston, really worried because the Stones are five hours late, and as we get near the city we can see this fearsome red glow from the fires, and we figure that the Stones fans are sacking Boston! We got to the hall, the band tuned up in just a few minutes and played one of the greatest shows of the tour."

The STP tour wound down now and Robert Frank complained he wasn't shooting enough sleaze, so a mock orgy was staged for the film crew on the flight to Pittsburgh. The roadies stripped naked a couple of braless, bosomy young groupies and pretended to eat and screw them while Mick, Keith, and Mick Taylor gathered round, rattling shakers and tambourines. Bill Wyman stayed in the front of the plane with his son. Charlie thought the whole film was a mistake. Famous groupie Cynthia Plastercaster was filmed in a postcoital spread, and Frank shot as many blow jobs as he could. Another groupie, Cynthia Sagittarius (who said she'd been raped twice while hitching rides to follow the Stones), was filmed shooting up Keith and then herself. Mick was caught snorting white powder off the tip of a switchblade. Keith: "Since it was being filmed, a lot of it was performance, like the chicks on the plane. It was only done because the camera was turned on." Keith was filmed nodding off into a heroin stupor in the locker room before the Pittsburgh show, while Mick talked business with smiling Ahmet.

The last shows were in New York City. The Hell's Angels asked for a sit-down with Peter Rudge and demanded the Stones play a concert to help them recoup legal expenses from Altamont. Rudge told the Angels he would discuss it with the band, then changed hotels and hired extra security instead. The final Madison Square Garden show ended in a massive pie fight. Ahmet Ertegun threw a huge party for the band after the last show on July 26, Mick's twenty-ninth birthday. Muddy Waters, gracious blues Buddha still recovering from a near-fatal car wreck, played "Rollin' Stone Blues" for his erstwhile protégés. Count Basie's orchestra also entertained, with Charlie Watts impressed by Basie's ancient drummer, Papa Jo Jones. A stripper emerged from the cake. Bob Dylan came; so did Woody Allen, Zsa Zsa Gabor, Andy Warhol, and Truman Capote. Capote, consummate publicity hound, had disliked traveling with the Stones, where the only limelight was reflected. He slagged the Stones to his friends and didn't bother to write his article for *Rolling Stone*.

Capote on the Stones: "They're complete idiots." On Mick Jagger: "He's about as sexy as a pissing toad." On Mick Taylor: "Pretty, dumb, uninteresting." On Nicky Hopkins, chronically ill with a digestive disorder and painfully thin: "Has the mark of death on him." On Bobby Keys: "Totally undisciplined and headed for disaster." The novelist, himself addled on pills and drink, could have been talking about himself, because he never wrote anything of value again.

————

The Stones returned to California after the tour. There was another birthday party in L.A. for Mick, at which Little Richard entertained. The band had survived two months on tour in America during the summer of 1972, unlike most of their entourage, who were never the same again. The casualty list was high. Marshall Chess was addicted to heroin. Jimmy Miller was a pale ghost of himself. Gram Parsons had lost it. Jo Bergman and Chris O'Dell left. Gary Stromberg was so wasted that friends kidnapped him after the New York shows and left him on a boat off Fire Island with no dingy so he could dry out. Robert Frank's film, a ropy, *cinéma-vérité* newsreel titled *Cocksucker Blues,* was never released because the Stones feared they wouldn't be allowed back into America. A concert album of the tour was killed when Decca refused permission to use live versions of songs recorded on their label. The concert film, *Ladies and Gentlemen, the Rolling Stones,* was mediocre and never went into general release.

Only the battle-hardened Stones were left standing. They'd made about $1.5 million on the tour: each took home perhaps $250,000. Mick was upset when he learned that Led Zeppelin, touring at the same time to larger crowds than the Stones, had demanded and got a 90/10 split with the local promoters.

Mick took his family and went back to England to watch cricket matches. Keith returned to his family in Switzerland. He rented a house near Montreux and resumed a relatively quiet life. His cars were brought over, dope deliveries arranged, and when it snowed, he took up skiiing. He immersed himself in the revolutionary new reggae music coming out of Jamaica, turned on by the Wailers' first album, *Catch a Fire,* and the brilliant songs on the sound track album from the film *The Harder They Come.* Still passionate about music, Keith knew reggae was the wave of the future, much as R&B had been ten years earlier. Keith would ride this cultural wave as adroitly as any white musician who ever tried to master reggae's steel pulse.

The rest of the band returned to France, where they were arrested, harassed, and investigated by the police for the rest of 1972, based on widening allegations of heroin trafficking and other crimes at Nellcote the year before.

The Third World Nashville

By late 1972, the Stones had been rolling for a decade. The old band of ambitious kids and the bonds that had unified them were history. They were all turning thirty now, lived in different countries, were often out of touch. From then on, their music came much harder, and at a greater cost. *Exile on Main Street,* still selling well by year's end, was the last of their four midperiod, era-defining masterpieces. With Keith debilitated, barely capable of even living up to his cartoonlike "outlaw" persona as the Human Riff, Mick Jagger was forced to assume complete control.

Quite cleverly, he turned the Rolling Stones into a ballad group, which succeeded in keeping them on the radio through the seventies, when soft rock and disco made it hard to get a real rock and roll song played on the air in America. During the next four years, the Stones' mid-seventies albums were less like Bulletins from the Edge and more like formulaic "product": a hit single, some ballads, two cool rock and funk numbers, and plenty of filler. Coasting on their mystique, the Rolling Stones rode out the seventies until they found their new muses later in the decade.

———

In November 1972, Mick went to Montreux to work on new songs with Keith. But there was contempt between them, and their old collaborative flame was just a glimmer. Keith mostly ignored Mick, or kept him waiting, or thrust half a riff at him. "This one goes, 'Angieeeee,' " he'd say, and expect Mick to make a song out of it.

"Up to then Mick and I were inseparable," Keith said later. "We made every decision for the group. We loved to get together and kick things around. But after we split up, I started going my way—downhill to Dopesville—and Mick ascended to Jet Land . . . Mick and I have different attitudes, and during the seventies I was living in a different world from him. I don't blame him; he's earned the right to do what he wanted. And even if I could've related to it, I was too busy being busted, which is equally dumb. But it got up my nose, his jet set shit, and the flaunting of it. But then he's a lonely guy too. He's got his own problems."

The Stones had to go somewhere to record the new album, but where? France was out because the cops were after them. Their American work visas had run out. They were in tax exile from an England preoccupied with David Bowie and glam rock, which Keith despised. There was no creative vibe in Switzerland. Almost stateless, Keith came up with the idea of recording in Jamaica while listening to the Slickers sing "Sweet and Dandy" on a throbbing reggae album in the Richards chalet in the cold mountains above Montreux, as the Swiss winter began to close in.

Kingston, Jamaica, was the new third world Nashville. The funky port city's recording studios were churning out an incredible stew of innovative music that would propel reggae's new stars—Bob Marley and the Wailers, Burning Spear, the deejay Big Youth, Toots and the Maytals—into planetary sainthood within just a few years. Jamaica also had tropical beaches and an experimental socialist government, and the whole island was a garden of the best marijuana in the world. Kingston's studios were known to be primitive, but singer Paul Simon had recently recorded at bandleader Byron Lee's Dynamic Sound Studio (where Jamaican star Jimmy Cliff had cut his hit single "Wonderful World, Beautiful People"), so the Stones decided to try Jamaica themselves.

On November 23, 1972, they moved into small rooms at the Terra Nova Hotel in uptown Kingston, once the family home of Chris Blackwell, the owner of Island Records and the man behind Bob Marley's rise. Kingston was a violent town, locked down at night by factional fighting in the ghettos, and there were huge bullet holes in the heavily guarded studio's control room walls. Bill Wyman's girlfriend Astrid was reportedly raped in their hotel room while Bill was forced to wait under the bed until her attacker had left.

The Stones plunged into new music with Nicky Hopkins and let fly. Byron Lee had upgraded the studio for them, adding previously unknown amenities like headphones, vocal mikes, a grand piano, and a Hammond B3 organ. The Stones worked from sundown to dawn, seven days a week.

Keith: "The backing tracks [for *Goat's Head Soup*] were all done in Jamaica. We started off with 'Winter,' which was just Mick strumming guitar in the studio. 'Angie' and 'Dancing with Mr. D' came in the middle of the sessions. 'Starfucker' was about last." Mick resurrected "A Hundred Years Ago," an elegiac song about his days with Marianne, written three years earlier. Keith wrote and sang the stark sexual infidelity confession "Coming Down Again," while "Starfucker" was all Mick's. The voodoo stew of "Dancing with Mr. D" was Keith's riff and Mick's lyric. Outtakes included "You Should've Seen Her Ass," "Four and In," and early versions of "Waiting on a Friend" and "Tops." The sessions were productive because the Stones had nothing else to do. There wasn't much of a scene because reggae was then mostly recorded music, not a live one, so there weren't any bands to go see. They would leave the studio and return to the hotel, where they had trouble finding things to eat once their taste for curried goat and boiled akee began to wane.

———

In late November, the Stones flew to Los Angeles to plan a Stones tour of the Far East that would take them back to Australia, and then to Japan for the first time. While in L.A., they jammed at Elektra Studio, producing high-grade experimental tracks starring Mick Taylor and Nicky Hopkins. These included rambling jams like "Travellin' Man," "Leather Jacket," "Potted Shrimp," and a later version of "Blood Red Wine" that was close in spirit to "Winter." Never officially released, these Elektra jams would take on lives of their own in the bootlegged netherworld of fascinating but unfinished songs.

The Japanese shows sold out as soon as they were announced, and the Stones looked forward to going there despite portents that the government wouldn't let them into the country because of their drug arrests. To help clear the air, the Stones (without Keith) returned to France in early December. French arrest warrants had been issued for Keith and Anita; the charges involved distribution of heroin to minors. Press stories implied the whole band was involved, which Mick, Bill, Charlie, and Mick Taylor all heatedly denied. The Stones released a statement that they had not been arrested in France and were free to come and go.

While his band was dealing with the cops in Nice, Keith and his family went to Ocho Rios, on Jamaica's tropically lush north coast. Installed in a rented house called Casa Joya overlooking Mammee Bay, Keith and Anita fell in love with the lush scenery, the relaxed "soon-come" atmosphere, and the local Rastas who emerged from jungle villages to hang out and turn Keith on with the giant ganja cigars called spliffs. These included local stars like singer Justin Hines, who showed up one evening with a band of Rastas bearing hand drums, coconut shell "chalices" for smoking ganja, and the hypnotic Rasta *burru* rhythm that induced a trancelike state of meditation and peace. Keith Richards had found a new spiritual home. He and Anita bought a villa (from British rocker Tommy Steele) called Point of View for its 360-degree panorama of the mountains of St. Anne parish and the aquamarine waters of the Caribbean. For Keith, Point of View would become as important a refuge as Redlands had been.

Billy Preston joined the last two weeks of the interrupted Kingston sessions, which were over by Christmas. Mick's cool hard rock demo of the groupie tribute "Starfucker" was one of the last tapes in the can. Japanese reporters trooped down to interview the Stones about their impending series of concerts at Tokyo's Budokan martial arts arena. A reporter from *Melody Maker* found Keith frail and gaunt, and noted Jagger's obvious concern and support for him. "This album will be less freaky, more melodic than the last one," Mick told the reporter. "We've recorded a lot of fast numbers, maybe too many." The tracks would be mixed in L.A. in the new year.

Lead Guitars and Movie Stars

January 1973. The Rolling Stones were poised to tour the Far East, but with French arrest warrants out for Keith and Anita, the Australian government banned them, followed by the Japanese. Australia soon relented, but Tokyo stood firm, refusing to allow convicted drug users Mick and Keith to enter. This left a ten-day hole in the tour, but the band decided to go ahead. On January 18, they warmed up with a benefit show in L.A. for Nicaraguan earthquake relief before flying to Hawaii for two shows. Instead of touring in Japan, the Stones returned to Los Angeles to work on their Jamaican tracks at the Village Recorder.

In February, the Stones played Hong Kong, Australia (body searches at customs), and New Zealand with Nicky Hopkins, Bobby Keys, and Jim Price. Keith returned to Jamaica after the tour to try to put his house in order. Bored and lonely while he was away, Anita had taken up with the local Rastas, dreadlocked and red-eyed, who now flocked to Point of View. But Keith's house was in an elite enclave of Jamaican politicians' and millionaires' gardens, where Rastafarians were regarded as dangerous. Anita's public affection for her Rasta friends began to draw fire, and Keith was bluntly warned that the law would come down on her if she didn't cut it out. Humiliated, he left the island and went to London, where he binged with Spanish Tony for a few weeks, picking (and losing) fights with Italian gangsters in sleazy clubs like Tramps in Jermyn Street.

Anita Pallenberg was too wild to let colonial social pressure stop her from playing with her Rasta entourage. While Keith was away in London, Jamaican cops raided Point of View and arrested Anita for ganja possession. They threw her into a cell with male prisoners, who beat and repeatedly raped her. Some of the guards had their way with her as well. It took a $10,000 cash bribe to get her out of jail, and when Keith met her at Heathrow, Anita was badly bruised. Sobbing, she ran into Keith's arms. The doctor who examined her at Cheyne Walk confirmed evidence of multiple rape. Chastened, the couple tried to resume their lives in Cheyne Walk and at Redlands, but Keith was mad as hell.

Sessions for *Goat's Head Soup* continued in London during the spring of 1973. "Hide Your Love" was recorded at Olympic with Mick Jagger playing piano, as was "Heartbreaker." "Silver Train" (originally written for guitarist Johnny Winter) was recorded by the Stones at Island Records' studio in Basing Street. Several unreleased songs date from this era, including "Criss Cross Man" and "Through the Lonely Nights," with Jimmy Page adding a bit of guitar. New horn players (Jim Horn, Chuck Finley) were brought in to shore up the faltering Stones brass section as Keys and Price became drug casualties. Andy Johns was also strung out; unable to finish the sessions, he was replaced by Keith Harwood, who worked with Led Zeppelin. Jimmy Miller was reduced to playing on percussion tracks with African master drummer Reebop Kwaku Baah. One of the last songs recorded was "Starfucker," a backhanded rock and roll tribute to the band's groupie friends. The song's title and graphic lyric about "giving head to Steve McQueen" caused the album to be delayed when Atlantic's lawyers balked. "But it's *our label*," Mick complained to Ahmet Ertegun, who wouldn't budge. They changed the name of the song to "Star Star" and got a release from Steve McQueen, who didn't mind the publicity.

————

When he was in Jamaica, Keith was in his element, guarded by his Rasta pals, playing with his collection of ratchet knives. One night the drummers who came to Keith's house to play and chant in the evenings took Keith to meet the master drum maker in the hills above nearby Steertown. Keith bought a set of his *akete* drums and was told that the drums needed to age for twenty years. To Keith, that was no problem. He could wait.

On June 26, there was, as usual, a party at Keith's house at Cheyne

Walk. Reggae records were blasting away. Marshall Chess and Stash de
Rola were there, very high. Keith was playing his psychedic piano in his
purple music room. Others were in the tripping parlor with its huge
gothic candlesticks and a shrine to Jimi Hendrix. Suddenly, police broke
into the house. Keith, Anita, and the luckless Stash were arrested for possession of heroin, cannabis, Mandrax, and firearms—three of Keith's
guns—and released late that night on bail.

————

Keith and Anita were down at Redlands on July 31 when the
house caught fire. They carried antiques out of the burning farmhouse,
but the thatched roof lit up and soon collapsed. A few things were saved,
but Keith lost some guitars. Redlands needed to be completely rebuilt and
would be lost to him for years.

Goat's Head Soup was released that August. The first single, "Angie"/
"Silver Train," was their first American no. 1 single in five years, since
"Honky Tonk Women." As a touching ballad of uncharacteristic vulnera-
bility, "Angie" was wildly popular in Latin countries and signaled a major
switch for the Stones into the saccharin power ballad. A simple performance video for "Angie" was taped in London by Michael Lindsay-
Hogg.

The Stones were photographed by David Bailey for the album's
gatefold sleeve in makeup and glam-style gauze. The title, *Goat's Head
Soup,* meant to evoke the atmosphere of Jamaican obeah voodoo in which
they pretended the album had been recorded, was unsubtly illustrated by
an insert photo of a goat's head boiling in a stewpot.

"Dancing with Mr. D" started the album with Keith's devilish, repeating guitar riff as Mick droned a chanting lyric about possession and
fear. Like many of the tracks on *Soup,* "Mr. D" was held together by Mick
Taylor, whose tastefully eloquent guitar unified this disparate collection of
songs. "100 Years Ago" continued with its changing tempos, moving from
poignant pastoral reverie to urgent jamming, with Billy Preston on organ.
It was one of Mick Jagger's best, most emotional vocals ever. "Coming
Down Again" was Keith's song, illuminated by Nicky Hopkins on piano.

A pretty drug ballad with a turgid sax solo by Bobby Keys, it had an unnerving air of edgy quiescence, the wistful downside of a good high. It was also a stark message to Anita, as Keith sang about sticking his tongue in someone else's pie, and how good it tasted.

Billy Preston's urgent clavinet stutter empowered "Doo Doo Doo Doo Doo (Heartbreaker)," a hard-rocking number about a ten-year-old girl addicted to smack in New York. Mick sang his tough lyric in a fury as the horns backed him up with martial flourishes. The first side of *Soup* finished with "Angie," a lovesick bohemian rhapsody that turned out to be highly radio-friendly. "Let me whisper in your ear—*Angie*," sang Mick with an intimacy that hadn't been heard from the Stones before. A swelling string section helped move "Angie" along with a bit of sonic grandeur.

The shimmering bottleneck riff of "Silver Train" started side two. Mick's harp was a loaded freight train rolling down the Cotton Belt over Stu's pounded piano. "Hide Your Love" came off as a loose and relaxed jam over Mick's basic piano track. "Winter" (on which Keith didn't play) was another big production ballad that drew upon the cold malaise of *Let It Bleed* for its atmosphere of melancholy and longing. Mick's lyric evoked a curious combination of Californian languor and intellectual cravings (Mick as Van Morrison), with strings again supplying an orchestral cushion.

This was followed by the curious pastiche of "Can You Hear the Music." Tibetan bells, shepherds' flutes (played by Jim Horn), burbling clavinet, and inchoate chanting aimed for cave-light ritual as the Stones tried to capture a tribal feel. More to the point was *Goat's Head Soup*'s final track, the censored "Star Star." This was more like the old Stones, a faux Chuck Berry anthem about a bicoastal groupie into "lead guitars and movie stars." The Steve McQueen line had stayed in the song, but on the American pressings Atlantic Records bleeped through Mick's line "I bet you keep your pussy clean." "Star Star" had a great, vamping rock tag at the end, a thrilling burst of raw energy that would accompany giant inflatable penises sprouting from their stage in years to come.

Goat's Head Soup received middling and puzzled reviews, *Exile* being a tough act to follow. Ian Stewart, the conscience of the Rolling

Stones, called the album "bloody insipid" when it came out. It was the no. 1 album in America and England that autumn.

The Devil's
Right-Hand Man

While staying in London in the spring of 1973, Keith was at Tramps one night when he met Chrissie Wood, sultry blond wife of matey lovable Ron Wood, who played guitar in the Faces, everyone's favorite drunken rock band. Keith fancied her, offered her a ride home in his yellow Ferrari. When they got to Ron's house, a Georgian mansion in Richmond called the Wick, she invited him in for coffee. Keith couldn't believe his luck.

Chrissie showed Keith around the beautiful house, which had been owned by the actor John Mills. She showed him the bedroom of Hayley Mills, the child actress who had grown up in the Wick. Keith was about to make his move when Chrissie asked him if he'd like to come downstairs and meet Ronnie, who was working in his basement studio. Somewhat crestfallen, Keith descended the stairs to find Mick Jagger, working on "It's Only Rock 'n' Roll" with Ron Wood.

It was an awkward scene for a few moments. Keith, like everyone else, had heard the rumors that Ron Wood might be asked to join the Stones if Keith's drug problems got any worse. But Ronnie's bluff good humor, liquid hospitality, and brittle laughter diffused the tension, and things got sorted out eventually. They were upstairs in the Wick's oval living room, sipping cognac, when a beautiful blond German model named Uschi Obermeier walked in. Mick immediately hit on the Woods' sexy houseguest, but she seemed to prefer Keith. Knowing a cool scene when he fell into one, Keith immediately moved into a small cottage in the garden of the Wick. He cemented his brotherly new friendship with Ronnie Wood while seeing Uschi constantly, and for the next year the Wick became Keith's London squat. It was the beginning of Ron Wood's eventual absorption into the Rolling Stones.

————

The Stones toured Europe, with Billy Preston on keyboards, during September and October 1973—a depraved drug tour, everyone out of their minds. Even once-innocent Mick Taylor was using heroin now. The tour started with a ten-day rehearsal in a Rotterdam warehouse at the end of August and opened in Vienna on September 4. They played some dates in Germany and did several shows at Wembley after a big publicity party at Blenheim Palace, Winston Churchill's birthplace, on September 6. *Tout* London was there, the press and Mick's posh friends. Anita refused to attend the party and waited in the car instead. When Keith spent too long inside fixing smack with Bobby Keys, she marched into the party—disheveled, hair akimbo, Teutonic fury—and started to scream at Keith for keeping her waiting. Mick whispered to Keith to get her out at once or it was fucking front-page news tomorrow. Keith took Anita to the car, got in, and she tried to scratch his eyes in full view of partygoers as the car sped off into the night. Their son, Marlon, looked quietly out the window, pretending to ignore what was going on as his parents punched each other in the backseat.

Keith was at one of his lowest points, and there were even rumors in London that the Human Riff was dying. Drugs had wrecked his crucial musicianship. He only played rhythm guitar on that tour, kept dropping his pick, forgot the words to "Happy" most nights. Mick was making sarcastic onstage comments when Keith disgraced himself, saying, "Thanks, Keith, that was . . . amazing," and rolling his eyes. Stu called him "a walking bloody tragedy." Bill Wyman let it be known that this tour might be his last. The music business projected its collective death fantasies on him as the Next OD (like Nils Lofgrin's pleading song "Keith Don't Go.") Writers competed for lurid metaphors to describe Keith's skeletal aura. Now he became "the devil's right-hand man" and "a bone-faced hoodlum raunch connoisseur toting a powerful drug-oriented misterioso." Keith took it all in stride. "The drugs thing was just an extra side of the image that was forced on us by political circumstances," he said. "You've got a particular image, and people expect you to live up to it, so I continued to get very wasted. I was the odds-on favorite as rock's next celebrity death. It didn't happen, despite everything. I'm a survivor."

The Stones were playing in Manchester in September when Bobby Keys told Keith that Gram Parsons had overdosed and died alone in a seedy Los Angeles motel. Gram's road manager had then stolen his body from an airport loading dock and tried to burn it on a makeshift pyre in the desert at Joshua Tree. Keith and Keys retired to the hotel bar to meditate on this, staring into their drinks, saying little. Keith's friends were dying all around him. Michael Cooper, wasted on heroin and confined to a wheelchair, had killed himself with an overdose. Keith's beloved grandfather Gus Dupree also passed away. In Manchester that night, Keith assumed control of the Stones and seemed to be playing for his own life, running off poignant guitar solos and singing his throat raw.

Keith tried to get off dope again after the Stones played in Innsbruck, Austria, on September 23. He and Marshall Chess rented a Swiss villa and underwent a three-day hemodialysis treatment that slowly filtered heroin from their bloodstreams, which led to the urban legend that Keith was having his blood regularly transfused in Switzerland to support his narcotics habit. This was widely interpreted as an extreme new low mark in rock star decadence.

In October, Bobby Keys collapsed in Germany, too sick with heroin addiction to play any more. The Stones were furious at Keys for letting them down on the road, an unforgivable fuckup. Peter Rudge had a roadie dump Keys in a taxi and put him on the first plane back to America. Bobby Keys was forgotten. It would be decades before he was allowed onstage with the Rolling Stones again.

On October 19, the Stones played the Deutschlandhalle in Berlin, and played really well, meshing gears on a killer five-song finale: "Silver Train," "Honky Tonk Women," "All Down the Line," "Jumpin' Jack Flash," and "Street Fighting Man." It was a great show before a hyped-up crowd. No one knew then it would be the last concert ever played by Mick Taylor as a member of the Rolling Stones.

There was a party for the Stones in an elegant Berlin hotel afterward, with naked girls in high heels dancing with record company executives. At three in the morning, as Mick and Keith watched from two thronelike chairs, two girls stripped to some Turkish music and then proceeded to make love on a fur rug. One of Billy Preston's band threw a candle at them, the rug caught fire, and the girls got singed. Naked and humiliated, one of the girls got up and spat some guttural German curses in Jagger's impassive face.

––––––––––

While the Stones were touring, Keith and Anita were fined and given suspended sentences by a French court for their drug use at Nellcote two years earlier (both were banned from France for two years), and on October 24 a London court fined them for the dope and gun charges from the Cheyne Walk bust. Celebrating at the Londonderry Hotel a few days later, Keith nodded off and set his bed on fire.

Keith and Mick were both spending time with Ronnie Wood, enjoying the continuous good vibes and woozy hospitality at the Wick. "It's Only Rock 'n' Roll," the Stones' next anthemic single, came from these basement jams, with the basic track laid down by the band Wood was rehearsing for his upcoming first solo record. As they prepared early material for their new album, Mick and Keith decided to jettison dope-addled Jimmy Miller and produce the new record themselves. "Jimmy went in a lion and came out a lamb," said Keith later. "We wore him out completely. Jimmy was great, but the more successful he became, the more he became like Brian. [He] ended up carving swastikas into the wooden console at Island studios. It took him three months to carve a swastika. Meanwhile Mick and I finished up *Goat's Head Soup*."

Keith was also philosophical about the death of Gram Parsons (whose remains were retrieved and buried in a New Orleans cemetery under a small stone inscribed "God's Own Singer"). "Anything that Gram was involved in had a touch of magic about it. Unfortunately many of my closest friends have died suddenly . . . While they were with me, I could always hold 'em down. I could take care of Gram. But once he'd moved

back to L.A., I started to hear stories. Oh, shit!" The Eagles took over
Gram's country rock music and spun it into multiplatinum success.

The Stones needed a change, a new act. This is when Mick and
Keith began to recast themselves as a newly productive post-glitter unit
within the Rolling Stones—the Glimmer Twins.

eight:
The Glimmer Twins

The Glimmer Twins' motto was "Give Us a Glimmer."

Just to put yourself up on that stage, you've got to have an

enormous ego. It's what you do with it in your spare time. People

expect me to be a wild man: "Keith Richards—crazy fuck."

Keith Richards

Give Us a Glimmer

The Glimmer Twins—jet-riding rock nomads, heavy-duty tax exiles, funk-faking jive turkeys—got started in Munich in November 1973 when the Rolling Stones began their German Period in the easygoing, artsy Bavarian city where Adolf Hitler had risen to fame fifty years earlier. Hitler was endlessly fascinating to Keith Richards, who could speak knowledgeably and admiringly of Hitler's mesmeric stage presence and uncanny control over immense crowds—attributes only a contemporary rock star could really experience.

All the big English bands wanted to record at disco producer Giorgio Moroder's hot new Musicland Studio in the basement of the Arabella Hotel, but Mick Jagger was able to get a priority booking on short notice. All the Stones came to Munich in the middle of November except Mick Taylor, who was officially ill but actually disgruntled with being the underpaid, uncredited, and disrespected guitar player in a group that failed to appreciate him. They woke like vampires at sunset, had some breakfast and an alcohol fix, walked a little if it wasn't raining, and then went down to the studio. They worked long hours past midnight with Billy Preston, so hot a property in 1973–74 that Miles Davis named a track on his new album after him. The Stones began rebuilding "It's Only Rock 'n' Roll" (originally recorded at the Wick by Mick and Ron Wood with Faces drummer Kenny Jones, American bassist Willie Weeks, and David Bowie adding some sub-rosa vocal hysteria on the song's laddish chorus). Keith erased Wood's guitar track and dubbed in his own Berryish riffing, and Wood later had to be content with an album-sleeve

noncredit for *inspiring* "It's Only Rock 'n' Roll" instead of a (very lucrative) credit for cowriting it.

———

When in doubt, the Rolling Stones had always turned to black
music for direction. In 1973, lining up with prevailing contemporary taste
and Billy Preston, they began to reposition themselves as a funk band.
Funk was the bass-driven pop music of black America, a hybrid of James
Brown's precision-tooled groove, the black hippie chants of Sly Stone,
and the flamboyant styles of the Black Panther Party and professional
procurers. The stars of early-seventies funk (Earth, Wind and Fire;
Funkadelic; Ohio Players; Curtis Mayfield; the Meters) were the ghetto
superstars of the era. Mick Jagger especially liked their stage clothes, colorful costumes that cast the musicians as space travelers, African princes,
and wildly successful pimps.

So in Munich, the Stones began to fake the funk in earnest, relying
on Billy Preston's expert chops. They covered the Temptations' 1966
Motown hit "Ain't Too Proud to Beg" in a crypto-funk arrangement. They
tried a new song, "Luxury," in the same groove, but it later developed into
a lame reggae experiment. (Reggae's pulse proved difficult for Charlie
Watts to master. A contemporary Jamaican conceit held that only illiter-
ate, spliff-nourished Rastafarian drummers could play reggae's backward,
inside-out "riddims.") More successfully the Stones cut the first versions of
"Fingerprint File," Mick Jagger's funk-saturated take on modern paranoia,
powered by his own crudely evocative lashes of blaxploitation guitar.

Breaking for Christmas, the band dispersed. Bill Wyman booked a
studio in Los Angeles to record his first solo album, *Monkey Grip,* a tuneless and charmless LP released by Rolling Stones Records in the spring of
1974. *Monkey Grip* had an all-star cast that included Mick Jagger on some
backing vocals and Mick Taylor on guitar, but Keith hated it and was
openly resentful that any Rolling Stone would go outside the band to
make music on his own.

Mick Taylor finally joined the Stones when they regrouped in
Munich in January 1974. Engineer Andy Johns, deemed unfit for duty due

to heroin use, wasn't invited back. His brother, Glyn Johns, completed his mixes on "Fingerprint File." The young English engineer Keith Harwood, a favorite of Led Zeppelin's, was brought in to replace Andy Johns and finish the album.

These second Munich sessions were hard on Mick Taylor, and people around the studio thought that Keith was trying to humiliate him. Taylor would get to Musicland early to work on a bass part or try something on guitar, and Keith would erase the tapes later that night. Mick Taylor wrote the melody and played beautifully on "Time Waits for No One," but despite vague promises got no songwriting credit. At one session, Taylor was playing well when Keith began to curse him. "Oi! Taylor—you're playing too fuckin' loud." Keith stopped playing and let fly. "I mean, you're really good *live,* man, but you're fucking useless in the studio. Lay out, play later, whatever." Some thought this was Keith's way of letting Taylor know he wanted Ron Wood in the Stones.

While they were working, Mick summoned the Dutch graphic artist Guy Peellaert to Munich to design the album jacket for *It's Only Rock 'n' Roll.* Peellaert's sensational 1972 book *Rock Dreams,* a vivid fantasia of airbrushed photomontages, had depicted the Stones as sadomasochistic child-molesting Nazis. For their album cover, Peelaert painted them as triumphant gods descending from a classical temple, feted by hundreds of diaphanous, petal-strewing handmaidens.

The new tracks were mixed down at Island Studio in London that spring. "Time Waits for No One," originally from the 1970 Stargroves sessions, was resurrected for the album and got a sinuous slide guitar treatment from Mick Taylor. Percussionist Ray Cooper, from Elton John's band, overdubbed almost every track.

Keith was living with Uschi Obermeier in the garden cottage at the Wick, spending days in bed with her, working on Wood's solo album in his basement by night, along with both Micks. By living at the Wick, Keith was avoiding both Anita and the constant police surveillance of his house in Cheyne Walk. "It was pure accident that I started helping Woody on his first solo album," Keith said later. "I went over to his place one day and stayed three months, working and playing snooker, worked nonstop putting Ronnie's album together. That was my first extended period of working with somebody else outside the Stones, because up till then it was the Stones or nothing. I wasn't inclined to work with anybody else, but Ronnie caught my fancy."

Mick and Keith wrote "Sure the One You Need" and "Act Together" for Wood's album. Keith sang on several tracks with Wood, while Mick's voice was prominent on the reggae-style "I Can Feel the Fire." Wood's American producer had brought in a load of MDA, brain-damaging psychedelic speed, so some of these sessions got a little nuts. When released later in 1974, Wood's *I've Got My Own Album to Do* sounded more like an adjunct Stones album than a solo project by one of the Faces. The title was a poke at Rod Stewart, who always used to whine that he couldn't work with the Faces because he had to work on his own solo album.

———

Summer 1974. Keith wanted the Stones to tour, but Mick vetoed the idea. With Mick running the Stones, Keith was in no shape to organize anything himself and had to defer.

Keith: "I was devoting most of my time to scoring dope. I was completely out of it, and Mick had to cover for me. He took over completely. I managed to make the gigs and write some songs, but Mick took care of everything through most of the seventies. He covered my ass."

Keith wanted to go out because, he told Barbara Charone, "every minute spent off the road I either turn into an alcoholic or a junky, 'cause I've got nothin' else to do." Instead, Keith played—looking cadaverous— at a couple of Ron Wood's London solo gigs in July, cuffing rhythm guitar and singing with the band. With their black shag hairdos, Keith and Ron looked like identical crows when they sang together at the mike— "degenerate Everly Brothers," according to Nick Kent.

After finishing the new Stones album, Mick and Bianca spent the rest of the summer at Andy Warhol's six-acre compound of houses at Montauk, on the eastern tip of Long Island. Warhol adored Bianca's aloof, hard-edged chic. He called her "the greatest movie star who never made a movie," and remained close friends with her for the rest of his life.

Warhol and Mick Jagger—two master manipulators—were never close, but they did use each other, each to his own advantage.

In August 1974, the Stones made some videos with Michael Lindsay-Hogg. "It's Only Rock 'n' Roll" was mimed to a new backing track, with the band in heavy makeup, camping in U.S. Navy uniforms as soap bubbles gradually filled the tent in which they were supposed to be playing. With the Stones off the road that year, the videos were a newly crucial promotional tool broadcast on *Top of the Pops* in England and on the late-night syndicated American rock TV shows *Midnight Special* and *Don Kirshner's Rock Concert.*

It's Only Rock 'n' Roll was released in October 1974 with a blare of radio play for the Stones' anthemic title single, a dumb song (with a great hook) about the perils and satisfactions of being a rock star, suggesting suicide right onstage. Recognized as a muddled holding action by critics, indifferently received by European fans, the album went to no. 1 in America and definitely had its moments. "If You Can't Rock Me" led off in a laddish, Faces-style rock-funk groove. "Ain't Too Proud to Beg" continued the funk thing in a soul context. "It's Only Rock 'n' Roll" was a philosophical statement—"Well, I *like it*"—set to a relaxed chug. The lyrics seemed to echo the opening track's threat of romantic abandonment in the face of marital strain. "Till the Next Goodbye" was an insincere love song set in Manhattan, where Mick was spending much of his time. The first side ended with "Time Waits for No One," Mick Taylor's luminous swan song with the Stones, a pretty ballad of fateful regret that seemed to definitively close out the band's fruitful midperiod.

The dreadful, faux-reggae "Luxury" started side two. Actually more ska than reggae, Mick essayed a lame parody of Jamaican patois, giving the song the same jokey treatment Jagger applied to the Stones' "country" songs. "Dance Little Sister" was a hard, stuttering funk jam with Stu on piano. "If You Really Want to Be My Friend" was an attempt at soul music neoclassicism, with the vocal group Blue Magic (an Atlantic Records act) on background vocals. "Short and Curlies" was another riffing jam with Stu, a taunting song from Keith full of mockery and resentment: "She got you by the balls!" The album ended with Mick's "Fingerprint File." His great guitar lick—discordant, disturbing shards of nervous racket—led to a black Hollywood movie about suspicion and surveillance, complete with coke-sniffing effects and an expertly timed one-sided phone contact. "All secrecy, no privacy," Mick whispered. "Lay low, bye bye."

It's Only Rock 'n' Roll was the first Rolling Stones album whose production was credited to the Glimmer Twins, Mick and Keith. Asked about this by an interviewer, Mick said, "Our motto has *always* been 'Give us a glimmer.' " This was a long-standing joke dating from their 1968 ocean voyage to South America, when a fellow passenger tried to discover the identities of Mick and Marianne, Keith and Anita, who were traveling incognito. This woman kept saying, "Give us a glimmer," to the mysterious hippies, who thought this very funny.

Keith's take on the Glimmer Twins: "A touch of glimmer can be more addicting than smack."

The Great Guitar Hunt

By the fall of 1974, Mick Taylor had his fill of life in the Rolling Stones. The band hadn't toured in more than a year, and he was bored. His marriage was coming apart. He was alienated by not being credited with cowriting songs on *It's Only Rock 'n' Roll*. Recording with the Stones was so painful that he didn't like listening to the records. He was getting more deeply into heroin as well. It was all over for Mick Taylor. He'd never really been one of the Stones anyway.

The band met in November in Montreux to plan a tour for 1975 and discuss recording plans. Mick Taylor—under pressure from his wife to leave the Stones, already talking to bassist Jack Bruce about forming a new band, and unable to confront Mick Jagger (with whom he was friendly) and Keith (with whom he was not) about his many grievances—said nothing.

Mick Jagger was all over the place: Paris nightclubs with Rudolf

Nureyev, New York parties with Bianca, London rock concerts. While he and Bianca were in Nicaragua in late November, Mick Taylor phoned the Stones' office to say he was leaving the band. Bill Wyman thought he was bluffing, trying to cut a better deal for himself.

But after an Eric Clapton show on December 4, at a party at promoter Robert Stigwood's house, Taylor tried to hand Jagger his resignation. "Mick told me he wanted to do something else," Jagger said. "He'd played with us for five years and he felt he wanted to play some different kind of music. So I said, 'Okay, that's fine,' and that was that." Later that evening, Jagger was sitting in a car with Ron Wood and Marshall Chess. Jagger told Wood, "Look, I don't want to split up the Faces. I really dig the band, but if you ever want to move on, would you come with us?"

Wood was incredibly flattered, but still felt committed to the Faces and told Mick it would be better to find someone else. "If you get *real* desperate, though," Wood said, "ring me up."

The Rolling Stones were furious with Mick Taylor. Their guitar player was quitting the band three days shy of going back into the studio. On December 7, the Stones returned to Munich to begin the *Black and Blue* sessions as a quartet with Nicky Hopkins. On December 12, in a series of polite but clipped press releases, the Stones announced Mick Taylor's departure from the band. Everyone tried to put a good face on it. Keith sent Taylor an insincere telegram: "Really enjoyed playing with you the last five years. Thanks for all the turn-ons. Best wishes and love." (Taylor's wife said he cried when he read this.) Jagger, in mischievous mode, told the press, "No doubt we'll be able to find another six-foot-three guitarist who can do his own makeup."

Within a week, the London papers were full of rumors that Taylor had quit the Stones because of money, which he repeatedly denied. "There was no personal animosity in the split," he told *Sounds*. "There was no row, no quibbling. I'm very disturbed at the stories going around that it was all to do with credits and royalties. I'm very upset because I like all the guys in the Stones."

Keith was raging. "No one leaves this band except in a fucking pine box," he fumed to friends. Later he said, "The man's timing was incredi-

bly bad. Why wait until a few days before we were going to start [record-
ing]?" The others—having seen how Keith had treated him—were more
puzzled than angry.

"He wanted to leave to make his own records," Charlie Watts said
later. "I thought he'd be incredible, like a Pat Metheny or something. And
it didn't happen. Nothing happened when he left us." Keith was less sympathetic. "Mick figured he'd learned enough. He was bored and thought
he was now a songwriter of great stature. He had a million plans. Mick is
a beautiful guitar player, amazing. But I'm still waiting."

"I still don't really know why he left," Mick Jagger said. "He never
explained, at least to me. He wanted to have a solo career. I'm guessing
he found it difficult to get on with Keith."

Mick Taylor would spend many years recovering from being a
Rolling Stone. "The whole experience made me more cynical," he said
long afterward. "One of the reasons I don't bother to make records on my
own is because I don't get paid for some of the biggest-selling records of
all time. Frankly, I was ripped off. You get cynical about the music business, and it stops you playing."

———

Munich, December 1974. The Stones worked, sullenly, with
Nicky Hopkins on a series of long, funk-based jams. Glyn Johns was back
as engineer/producer, totally bored as Keith slogged the band through
nine-hour versions of the new ballad "Fool to Cry," Eric Donaldson's
early reggae smash "Cherry Oh Baby," and a track labeled "Black and
Blue Jam" (with visiting Jeff Beck), which years later developed into
"Slave." The Stones' turn to funk was another intraband compromise, in
the same way R&B had been the medium between Brian's blues and
Keith's rock and roll. Now funk—the dominant black American popular
music of the time—became the meeting ground of Mick's fascination
with disco/dance music and Keith's scholarly obsession with reggae.
"Hot Stuff" was the result.

With Mick Taylor gone, over the next five months the Stones

turned their recording sessions into auditions testing the world's best electric rock guitarists. When word got out there was a vacancy to be filled, a parade of famous ax heroes dutifully made the trek to studios in Rotterdam and Munich, with varying degrees of success. Fiery Irish guitar star Rory Gallagher dropped by to play, prompted by Glyn Johns, who thought he'd be perfect for the Stones, but Mick and Keith barely said hello to him. Peter Frampton was reportedly considered, highly recommended by Bill Wyman and Stu, then dismissed. Rumor had it that Eric Clapton again declined the job.

Keith moved back to the Wick, where Ron Wood was working on another solo album. They were joined by Wayne Perkins, a longhaired Texas session star and slide guitar wizard who'd rocked up the Wailers' first album, *Catch a Fire,* and a host of big-name sessions. Keith and Perkins meshed nicely in London, and when Keith invited him to Munich for the March recording sessions, Perkins thought he had joined the Rolling Stones. In Munich, he played (superbly) on "Fool to Cry" and "Hand of Fate," and the job seemed to be in Perkins's grasp. But Keith was starting to feel that he played too much like Mick Taylor.

Mick invited the brilliant but erratic Jeff Beck to Munich. Beck was a big star and hot off his best-selling jazz-rock *Blow by Blow* album. Beck cut several (unused) tracks with the Stones, then left Germany after saying insulting things about the rhythm section. Mick vetoed Wayne Perkins as a Rolling Stone and brought in another American blues virtuoso, Harvey Mandel, who played on "Memory Motel" and "Hot Stuff," the Stones' new tribute to James Brown's "The One" funk riff.

Ron Wood arrived in Munich late in March 1975. His wife, Chrissie, had run off with Jimmy Page, so Woody was at loose ends. He worked on "Crazy Mama" and "Hey Negrita" and was pressured by Keith and Mick to join the Stones, not as a permanent member, but as a temporary hired guitarist on the tour scheduled to begin in only a couple of months.

"Either you're joining," Mick told Wood, "or we aren't doing the tour."

Keith: "Ronnie Wood walked in and any other consideration collapsed. We had to own up that we were an *English* rock and roll band, and not just English, but *London*. That's why Ronnie and I burst into gales of laughter at a certain word. Those little things become a big advantage on the road."

Many Rolling Stones fans were disappointed by Ron Wood's elevation. He wasn't a soloist like Mick Taylor or a sonic avatar like Brian Jones. He was an entertaining, journeyman-quality rock guitarist with contagious energy and a prodigious life force. Glyn Johns thought Wood the worst choice the Stones could have made, a major disaster both for the talented Wood's development and for the Stones. Ron was often stoned silly, usually half-drunk, appeared stupid at times. He was Keith's butt-boy and became the Rolling Stones' clown and jester, sometimes appearing to degrade himself by flattering his new bosses—the least threatening bloke they could have found. People closer to the Stones realized Wood was hired as a surrogate younger brother, foil and mediator between Mick and Keith. "He brought musical vitality and a powerful, likeable personality into our ranks," Bill Wyman wrote. "He has always been a positive force in soothing tensions in the band. He's able to hang with all of us in turn. Acting as a foil for both Keith and Mick, on and off stage, couldn't have been easy."

Ron Wood's temporary appointment to the Rolling Stones was announced on April 14, 1975, and he was put on salary for the duration of the tour. This arrangement continued when Rod Stewart left the Faces at the end of the year and Woody joined the Stones for good. It would be eighteen more years before Ron Wood was officially made a member of the Rolling Stones and invested with a commensurate financial share.

A Certain Magic in Repetition

A fascist-looking jet-propelled eagle was the logo of the Rolling Stones' 1975 Tour of the Americas—TOTA for short—a money-spinning forty-seven shows in twenty-seven venues throughout Gerald Ford's disco-besotted United States that summer, to be followed by a tour of South American capitals that fall. Charlie Watts helped supervise the design of the tour, with its two lotus-shaped stages, one with "petals" extending into the audience, the other with hydraulic petals that unfolded around the band at the start of the shows. It was to be a showbiz tour, with Mick relying on stage props for the first time. Outlandish inflatables, trapeze swings, and Billy Preston's minstrel-like disco act would, he hoped, compensate Stones fans for what was missing from that tour—any new creative edge and a sense of mission. The spark of the band was low, so they depended on old-fashioned flash to get them through. Much of the year, flash worked well for the Rolling Stones, who managed to play some of the best rock shows ever performed.

The Stones assembled in April to begin rehearsals at a Montauk Point house rented from Andy Warhol's film director, Paul Morrissey. Keith's U.S. visa problems had been fixed by Mick, who intervened with a social contact, American ambassador Walter Annenberg. After another Swiss hemodialysis cure, Keith passed a blood test in London and got his visa. Ron Wood finished mixing his album *Now Look* at Electric Lady Studio in New York and went directly to Montauk to join the Stones. Security around the house was tight due to renewed threats from the Hell's Angels, still bent on Altamont revenge and rumored to be planning an amphibious landing on the beachfront property.

Billy Preston was the tour's musical director, helping to plan the set and rearranging some of the Stones' warhorse numbers. Drummer Ollie

Brown was hired away from Stevie Wonder's band to play percussion, and his timbales, cowbells, and congas freed Charlie Watts from rock timekeeping, allowing him to play in a lighter, more swinging style. Preston's manager had demanded his client perform a mini-set of his two radio hits, "Outta Space" and "Nothin' from Nothin'," during the shows, so the Stones got even deeper into funk during rehearsals. Preston's songs would come near the end of the concerts so Mick could rest for the five-song finales. Missing entirely was Bobby Keys; Keith wanted him back, but Mick refused. Keys was broke and living in Los Angeles, where he played bar gigs as "Mr. Brown Sugar." The Stones toured without horns that year.

A press conference was scheduled to launch the tour in Manhattan on May 1. They needed a gimmick, something catchy. Charlie remembered that the old Harlem jazz bands used to advertise their shows by playing in the streets on flatbed trucks. So as a big crowd of the New York press gathered at lunchtime at the Fifth Avenue Hotel in Greenwich Village, the Rolling Stones pulled up front in a light drizzle, blasting "Brown Sugar" with amps set at ten on the back of an eighteen-wheel tractor trailer. Surprised journalists poured into the street, and Ian Stewart threw them leaflets listing the tour dates. The truck pulled away, the band in full cry. Two blocks away, the Stones jumped into waiting limos and disappeared.

Mick and Bianca were living in Manhattan, but soon Mick was back in Montauk as rehearsals continued, and Bianca began to be seen around New York on the arms of other men. Andy Warhol made the series of Jagger photos that were turned into silkscreen portraits, and took pictures of the Stones biting each other. On May 18, Mick accidentally slashed his wrist on a glass door in a restaurant, requiring twenty stitches. A few days later, the band gathered in an airplane hangar at Stewart Airport in Newburgh, New York, to rehearse on their lotus stages for the first time. The new production included lights designed by Broadway technical director Jules Fisher and huge speakers suspended above the stage, since the lotus wings had no room for amps. Mick used a wireless microphone for the first time, freeing him from the tyranny of wires forever. Mick also test-drove the giant inflatable white penis that burst out of the stage during the guitar vamps on "Starfucker" in a coup de théâtre of ironic ribaldry and blatant self-parody. Another balloon, a confetti-spewing green dragon, would be manipulated by Mick and Ollie Brown during the last song of the set.

Mick did a round of interviews to promote their tour, answering innumerable queries about the new Rolling Stone. "I wanted someone that was easy to get on with and that was a good player and used to playing onstage . . . Woody's personality seemed to fit the bill. Onstage he's got a lot of style, and it's got to be fun on the road. That's what it's all about." *Rolling Stone* reporter Dave Marsh asked him why he was touring. "It's my *job*," Mick said. "My vocation. No musician is beyond that, until he gets too old. There's a certain magic in repetition."

With no new album to promote, Rolling Stones Records released the compilation *Made in the Shade,* a ten-track post-1971 anthology that delivered hit singles and concert faves in a poolside-by-the-pyramids sleeve. Allen Klein trumped this with *Metamorphosis,* a mislabeled, scattershot collection of old Stones demos and outtakes recorded in the sixties. Though not without interest for the band's hard-core followers, *Metamorphosis* had replaced a Bill Wyman–proposed project known as *The Black Box.* This was an insider's collection, assembled by Wyman from the Stones' archive, with carefully selected rarities and historically minded production notes. The *Black Box* project was ultimately vetoed by ABKCO for not including enough publishing-rich Jagger/Richards songs. The Stones were annoyed by *Metamorphosis* but powerless to make it go away.

Old friends also noticed the Stones were a cranky lot. "The money's got them in trouble," Stu told press rep Lisa Robinson. "They can't even live in their own country. They have to go from one hotel to another." Mick complained bitterly that the tax laws had forced a whole creative community into exile and had killed British music.

May 1975. The Stones gathered in New Orleans for the final rehearsals. Their new press agent, Paul Wasserman, an older, bearded guy from L.A., introduced himself to Keith and said he'd be handling the press. Keith hugged him, whispered, "Better you than me," and walked away. The band sounded good. Ron Wood trembled in fear, but his blazing slide guitar gave the Stones a new screeching jolt. Playing with a younger black drummer woke up laconic, thirty-four-year-old Charlie Watts, empowered him to play with a funky kick in his drums. It was like the whole band had gotten its blood changed, and they came out swinging. The '75 shows were the longest of the Stones' career, as if they thought they had to compete with the three-hour marathons of the other big English bands like Led Zeppelin and Jethro Tull.

The shows began, tongue of Kali firmly in cheek, with the recorded trumpets of Aaron Copland's *Fanfare for the Common Man*. The Stones emerged onstage to cherry bomb wargasms as the roadies set off explosions and Keith fired off the chords to "Honky Tonk Women." "If You Can't Rock Me" segued through Ollie Brown's congas into a jokey, disco-tinged "Get Off My Cloud," now a stage-business duet with Billy Preston. The show progressed through a sequence of hits and high spirits: "Happy" got a scorching slide guitar lift-off from Ronnie while Keith shouted his slurred, smacked-out lyrics, his voice now lost to tobacco abuse but still full of gruff character. Ron Wood's choppy chord solos replaced Mick Taylor's fluid groove on "Tumbling Dice." "Starfucker" had a thrilling vamp section at the end while Mick rode the white penis that blew up into an arena-size erection. The live performances of "Fingerprint File" had an extra-cool guitar lick over dub-style fills and an interlude for some paranoid stage business: "Who dat man in de corner? Not *dat* corner, de one over there!"

"You Gotta Move" was transformed into a vocal quartet, as Mick, Keith, Wood, and Preston gathered around the mike and sang soul-style harmonies over Charlie's Salvation Army drumbeat. This often got a gospel-style reprise from Billy Preston. With no horns, Billy played the intro to "You Can't Always Get What You Want" on the synthesizer instead. Ron Wood played Brian Jones's slide guitar licks expertly on "Little Red Rooster." They ignored "Satisfaction" entirely.

Billy Preston's set usually ended with Mick coming out in his Giorgio di Sant'Angelo striped crepe "clown suit," tied at the waist and

fashionably cross-gartered, and dancing the bump and suggestive homoerotic grinds with Preston, who performed in stacked heels and a massive
Afro wig. The finale was a burning "It's Only Rock 'n' Roll," "Brown
Sugar," "Street Fighting Man," "Jumpin' Jack Flash" (with Mick flying
around the halls at the end of a trapeze rope), and the winding guitars and
samba drums of "Sympathy for the Devil."

TOTA had no single opening act. Instead, various bands—the
Meters, Little Feat, the Eagles, the Outlaws—opened in different parts of
the country.

For the TOTA shows, limos were out. The band was driven in low-
profile station wagons and vans. Peter Rudge had hired a new, heavyweight layer of security. Despite the anti-FBI jibes in "Fingerprint File,"
moonlighting FBI officers and Secret Service agents protected the Stones
from local police departments. Spanish Tony claimed that Keith told him
he was supplied unusually pure heroin by these operatives. Fred Sessler
was also along with his licensed Peruvian marching powder. Carefully de-
lineated lines of cocaine and heroin on the amplifiers were available during the shows, and any roadie who put his flashlight on them was fired.
The heroin lines were for Keith and Woody exclusively, while the coke
was for the rest of the band. Keith and Woody also smoked "dirty fags"—
heroin-laced cigarettes—during the shows.

The Stones opened far out of town on June 1, 1975, at
Louisiana State University. The Meters, Creole-funk heroes from New
Orleans's 13th Ward, opened with their strutting "second-line" syncopa-
tions and the mellow harmonies of the Neville brothers. Then to the airport and the waiting Starship, a customized Boeing 720 jetliner with a bar,
an organ, sofas, maroon shag carpeting, a fireplace, various lounges, and
a bedroom in the back. The Starship was the ultimate new amenity in the
booming world of seventies rock, affordable only by the Stones, Led
Zepp, and Elton John. Peter Rudge and security chief Bill Carter, a lawyer
and former Secret Service agent, ran such a tight ship that Bianca Jagger
referred to the atmosphere around that tour as "a fascist state." But tough

measures were often required. At the second stop, San Antonio, the local vice squad threatened the band with arrest if they deployed their flying penis. Cops flooded backstage during the show, ready to pounce, but were faced down by Bill Carter, who knew how to talk to local police chiefs.

Ron Wood put his mark on the tour early, made himself indispensable, worked hard to fit in, got people drinks. Manic laughter in the tuning room before the show did wonders for the Stones. He was everyone's little bro. Keith: "Good to be with in a tune-up room and inspiring to all in attendance, Ronnie is. He gives everyone courage for the show." Wood was the first antic stage presence Mick had to deal with since 1967, with his flash guitar posturing and his attempts to bait the stone-faced Wyman, who barely moved or smiled during the shows. Mick bounced off Woody during the shows, jumped on him, kicked him, mugged in his face, did physical shtick, licked his cheeks onstage.

Kansas City, June 5, with the Eagles opening. The Stones played outdoors for the first time under a white stage tent for eighty thousand kids, a sea of waving arms, topless girls hoisted onto brawny shoulders, and a constant, chanting roar. Backstage the musicians and crew wore T-shirts that asked "Who the fuck is Mick Jagger?" Keith, who'd been awake for a week, jamming through the night and listening to reggae with Ronnie, debuted a pair of skintight white leather pants in which he would live for the rest of the tour.

Municipal Stadium, Cleveland, 83,000 customers on June 13. Next day, before the Buffalo show, the crew took a boat ride under Niagara Falls. "Don't show this to Jagger," Rudge said as they beheld the mammoth cascade. "He'll want it onstage."

In Toronto, word got backstage that a young girl, blind since birth, was following the tour, hitching from show to show. Keith started noticing her up front every night, squeezed in the crunch of fans, and became concerned for her. He arranged for the roadies to look after her, let her ride in the trucks, see that she got in all right every night. It was a simple gesture, a karmic gift that would pay off down the road.

Six shows at Madison Square Garden in New York at the end of

June, with the blossoming lotus stage deployed for the first time. A round of parties and jams with Eric Clapton at Jimi Hendrix's old studio. Bob Dylan backstage one night, with Carlos Santana onstage with the Stones on the last night of the week. At this show, the Stones were joined by a hundred steel drummers, masters of pan music recruited from Brooklyn's West Indian community to add a Carnival vibe to the New York finale. When Keith crashed into "Happy," the Garden brimmed with communal joy as the fans sang along with the bombed-out guitarist. After this show, the Stones threw a big party for the Steel Band Association drummers and their girlfriends in Brooklyn, with reggae songs turned up to full watts all night. The next day's papers reported that the six shows had grossed over a million dollars.

———

Fred Sessler drove the Stones crazy by disappearing for a few days. A New York record executive, Stu Werbin, got some cocaine for Ronnie and was invited to have a snort with the band. He observed that Mick was playing games with Bianca, pretending not to notice that she wanted a toot. This went on for a while until Keith, in spiteful defiance of Mick, served Bianca several crystalline lines. Sessler reappeared before the Stones left town, his supplies replenished. Money never changed hands with him because he never sold drugs and wasn't a dealer. His only compensation was hanging with the Stones and being seen with them.

After a few days off, the Stones plunged right back in with a Washington, D.C., show on July 1. To Mick's annoyance, Bianca was photographed in the embrace of President Ford's son Jack while visiting the White House with Andy Warhol. She was spotted dancing with Disco Jack at decadent Studio 54 in New York a few days later, which got Mick *really* steamed.

Memphis a few days later. The Starship arrived late at night without Mick, who was driving. They were greeted on the runway by eighty-three-year-old Beale Street blues legend Furry Lewis, who sat on a couple of cases of whiskey, singing "Let Me Call You Sweetheart." Enchanted, Keith sat down on the tarmac to listen awhile. Later that afternoon, at the

Stones' July 4 show at Memorial Stadium, they refused to play until Furry
Lewis did a couple of songs for 51,000 half-nekked kids who'd already
been waiting five hours in the hot summer sun. Furry told them a joke
about eating pussy, got a big roaring laugh, and played the crowd "Let
Me Call You Sweetheart."

The Stones blasted off at nine, Mick in a lavender silk cape, Keith in
a Bob Marley T-shirt, tearing off the chunky chords to "Honky Tonk
Women" as the whole stadium began to quake. Police in riot gear threatened to arrest the Stones if they performed "Starfucker" and exposed their
big balloon dick in Memorial Stadium. Bill Carter took the police chief
aside and advised: "If you bust the Stones tonight, these kids will burn
down this stadium and your city along with it. Plus, this band will litigate
you forever. These ain't some broke hippies, Chief. I guarantee you, *they
will sue!*" The Stones played "Starfucker" that night like it had a nitrous
oxide hookup, and the flying phallus wasn't exposed in big outdoor shows
anyway. After the show, in honor of American Independence Day, Mick
had Jimi Hendrix's bitterly sardonic "Star-Spangled Banner" played over
the P.A. Afro-headed Ollie Brown earnestly read a selection of revolutionary texts (Lenin, Che, Thomas Jefferson) chosen by Mick, ending
with Chairman Mao's rhetorical query "Is one revolution enough?"
Thousands of Stones fans remained in the stadium to listen to Jagger's
Godard-like guerrilla theater piece.

The next morning, Keith and Woody left Memphis by limo, along
with Fred Sessler and their big English security man, Jim Callaghan, to
drive through the South to the next gig at the Cotton Bowl in Dallas.
They stopped for some pork barbecue in tiny Fordyce, Arkansas, where
the car and the two exotic musicians attracted not a little attention. Keith
was wheeling the limo out of town when he swerved across the road
while trying to tune in KFFA in Helena. A cop pulled them over and
busted Keith for carrying a ratchet knife. They went back to Fordyce,
where the cops pried open the trunk and arrested Sessler for cocaine possession. As a crowd of longhairs gathered around the courthouse, some
calls were made, and Arkansas native Bill Carter soon arrived. Keith's bail,

set at $162, was paid and he was released. Sessler, described in subsequent press reports as a hitchhiker, paid $5,000. A chartered plane hastily ferried the miscreants off to Dallas.

Most Glamorous Gladiators

That summer of 1975, the Stones stayed on the road in America, playing some nights much better than others, standing on their laurels, a strategy that almost begged for contempt. Their presentation was criticized as "a generally unrevealing set of reinterpretations of their old songs." Critic James Miller, covering the tour for *Newsweek*, wrote that "the Stones became the Seventies' most glamorous gladiators, but the shows grew slick and the music slack. Here was rock royalty gone cynical . . . fabulously moneyed superstars with enough nasty habits and jet-set sidekicks to keep the gossip juicy."

When TOTA reached Los Angeles, the Stones were joined by their wives at the Beverly Wilshire. Anita, recently deported from Jamaica after her drug conviction, was absent, so Keith stayed at a canyon hideaway owned by Fred Sessler. Movie stars—Raquel Welch, Liza Minnelli, Bianca's rumored boyfriend Ryan O'Neal—clamored for tickets and backstage passes. Bianca commandeered the best seats for her friends. "You should write something bitchy about her," Mick told Lisa Robinson. "She's very rude to people." Ron Wood and Bill Wyman skipped Ahmet Ertegun's party for the Stones at Diana Ross's house and went to see Bob Marley and the Wailers play at the Roxy nightclub instead.

In San Francisco, the Stones were in the middle of the second of two desultory concerts when Mick's assistant, Alan Dunn, passed him a note onstage that read, "She's on the plane." Bianca had left the tour and gone home, to Mick's relief. Later that night, he and Keith went to see reggae stars Toots and the Maytals. Stray cats were soon observed padding out of Mick's hotel room in the morning. The daily tour memo warned "Loose lips cost wives." Fred Sessler flew in Uschi Obermeier to elevate Keith's flagging spirits.

Elton John called Mick at his hotel and asked if he could sit in with the Stones in Denver that night. Though Mick had agreed to let him join for only one number, Elton refused to leave, stayed for six songs, fucked up the arrangements, and annoyed everyone.

In Chicago, Mick and Billy's disco grind got a little Out There, with Mick stripping and Billy miming fellatio, drawing accusations of poor taste in the papers. Keith crashed in Chicago after a five-day binge. He woke up to find a "Dear Keith" letter from Uschi, who had fled. Keith crumbled for the rest of the tour despite Ron Wood's strenuous efforts to keep him going. "You want a psychiatrist," Keith mused, "go see Ronnie. He's a one-man suicide line. I could make a fortune selling tickets. Suicide court! They'd come out laughing their heads off, with a new vision of life."

By early August, the Tour of the Americas should have continued in South America, but these shows were canceled due to political chaos, security concerns, and Stones burnout. Keith didn't want to stop. Peter Rudge added a few more big American shows—Louisville, Hampton Roads, and a final outdoor show in Buffalo. The Louisville show on August 4 was harassed by police acting on a tip that mass quantities of narcotics were being used in the dressing rooms. The cops were held off by a defensive force of lawyers, bodyguards, and extra security men. Bill Carter called the local district attorney and demanded he appear in person to call the cops off. The official duly arrived, posed for some pictures with Mick, and told the police to leave the band alone.

For the last show in Buffalo, Mick, Keith, and Ronnie all dropped LSD, annoying Charlie and Bill Wyman. The big crowd had been drinking beer outdoors all day, with more than a hundred arrests during the Outlaws' opening set. Then a long delay because Mick didn't want the Stones to play until dark. The crowd got tense, with medical teams treating six hundred for injuries and ODs, provoking nervous jokes about another Altamont finale on this tour. The Stones finally took the stage and played a long, loopy show. Mick performed "Street Fighting Man" while the band was playing "Brown Sugar."

———

At tour's end, the Stones scattered to the winds. Mick went to New York, Charlie to England. Bill Wyman started his second solo album, *Stone Alone,* in L.A. Unable to return to Jamaica without Anita, Keith reunited with her in Los Angeles, where she became pregnant in a holding action to preserve her family.

Keith was back in Montreux by October, when the rest of the Stones and Ron Wood arrived to work on their new album at Mountain Studio. These *Black and Blue* sessions continued in December at Musicland in Munich, where Jimmy Page was just completing the guitar overdubs on the new Led Zeppelin album, *Presence.*

Ron Wood had gone directly from the Stones' tour to Miami, where the Faces were rehearsing for their tour, but the writing was on the wall. Wood dutifully played with the Faces that fall, but at the end of 1975, he was staying in a rented house in Munich where the Stones stashed their auditioning guitar players, when he learned that Rod Stewart had quit the Faces, leaving him free to join the Stones. "I've got a plan," Keith told him. "Let's not tell the press you're in the band or make any announcement." "I just *appeared,*" Wood later said. In the studio, when Wood tried to get the Stones to listen to a new song he'd written, Charlie Watts stopped and cracked, "Fucking hell, will you look at him? He's bossing us around *already*!" But it was said in a kindly way. "I kind of got a clue that I was in," Wood later said. "It was like coming into a gang that I knew I would be at home with."

The London police happily welcomed Wood and his family into the Stones. While he was in Munich, they raided his home in Richmond, probably looking for Keith, since they broke into the garden cottage before forcing their way into the Wick. The cops found Chrissie Wood in bed with a girlfriend, arrested them both for cocaine possession, and leaked the sleeping arrangements to the press. It would take many months and 12,000 pounds in legal fees to get Chrissie Wood off.

January 1976. The Stones in New York. Mick was buying a house on West 72nd Street, preparing to move from the hotel where he and Bianca were living. Business talks with Ron Wood, haplessly negotiating his permanent entry into the gang. The Stones decided to keep him on salary, which over the years would lead to occasional (relative) poverty and dependence on his sideline as an artist for cash flow. In London, Mick Taylor sold his gold record of *It's Only Rock 'n' Roll* at auction for seventy-five pounds.

The new Stones album, *Black and Blue*, was being mixed in New York at Atlantic Studios, heavy on drums and funk, faux-black vocals, and pseudo-reggae chops. The Stones flew to Florida in February to be photographed for the album sleeve at sunset on a Sanibel Island beach by Japanese fashion photographer Hiro. Ron Wood's membership in the band was announced in New York on February 28, 1976, when the Stones confirmed that they would tour Europe that summer. Wood relocated his family to a beachfront house in Malibu and started hanging out with Eric Clapton at The Band's cozy Shangri-La Studio, near Bob Dylan's cliffside home.

Keith and Anita were living in Switzerland that winter while she waited for her third child. On March 26, she had a premature baby boy in a Geneva clinic. They named him Tara, after Tara Browne.

Not the *Chandelier!*

There was seismic activity in pop music in 1976, and the tremors forced some changes on the Rolling Stones. In America, hard rock's big era was over. Led Zeppelin, plagued by car crashes and addiction, was off the road, its empire in shambles, leaving American rock acts Aerosmith, Ted Nugent, and Lynyrd Skynyrd to carry the flame. Disco music was in its Babylonian ascendance, fought to the death by reggae musicians. English soft rock avatars like Peter Frampton and a reconstituted Fleetwood Mac began selling megamillions of albums in America on the strength of two or more hit singles per album. Overnight, many stations that used to play the Stones switched to soft rock or disco formats. In England, the scuzzy young underground musicians in their spiky hair and torn clothes, a coalescing shock wave of punk bands—the Sex Pistols, the Clash, the Jam, the Damned, the Slits, Generation X—despised the Stones, Zeppelin, Elton with a passion. The punk bands blurted out inarticulate antirock manifestos and condemned rich, dope-addled, out-of-touch rock stars as—and this hurt—"boring old farts." Their revolt was partly against the bombastic grandiosity of rock as a rite of worship, and partly simple hatred of decadent older musicians. Punk music was crude, simple, jam-packed with speed and crazed energy, and it put the older musicians to shame. (Among the Stones, it was Mick the punks reviled; Keith's open defiance and lack of pretense seemed to earn him an unspoken pass from the pantheon of punk.) In the vanguard of the punk bands, the Clash issued a widely publicized antirock challenge, demanding the death penalty: "No Stones or Who in '77."

It was into this roiling pop cultural stew that the Stones released "Fool to Cry"/"Crazy Mama" as a single at the end of April 1976: it reached the Top Ten in both England and America in May. The album *Black and Blue* was initially promoted by a blatantly sadomasochistic ad campaign that displayed a tied-up, beaten, and bruised blond model, her clothes torn, her legs spread wide, tongue out, her face a mask of demented desire. Angry women defaced the *Black and Blue* billboard when it went up over Sunset Boulevard in L.A., and the ads were withdrawn.

Black and Blue was a funk-informed collage of guitarists, ballads, and halfhearted stabs at reggae. It led off with "Hot Stuff," the Stones posing as the Ohio Players, hanging on a riff and a prayer, with Billy Preston on piano, Harvey Mandel on guitar, and Mick rapping in dreadful urban blackface, the Al Jolson of rock. "Hand of Fate" was an old-time rocker with Wayne Perkins on guitar, playing like a Mick Taylor clone. "Cherry

Oh Baby" was Keith and Ron's half-earnest, semiparodic cover of a classic Jamaican hit, with lead-footed Charlie Watts failing to play properly and Keith shouting the Rastafarian hail—"Irie!"—in the middle of the track. The side ended with "Memory Motel," the story of Hannah, a honey of a girl from Boston, an unusually romantic and affecting ballad of admiration. Keith sang the bridge—"She's got a mind of her own"—with more soul than he'd put into a song since "You Got the Silver." Mick and Keith both played keyboards on this song of road fever, wounded loneliness, and bittersweet recollection.

Ron Wood played chopped-up lead guitar over Billy Preston's chaotic piano on "Hey Negrita" on side two, a slice of Wood-inspired funk/reggae. (Negrita was a nickname Mick had for his dark-complected wife.) "Melody" (which Bill Wyman said was actually written by Billy Preston) was a lounge-gospel throwaway. "Fool to Cry" was another Mick Jagger ballad, haunted and newly vulnerable, about his love for a woman in a poor part of town. With Mick on keyboard and Nicky Hopkins on string synthesizer, it had a long, hypnotic carousel of an instrumental tag as Mick begged and pleaded with a sincerity that seemed real. The winding guitars and old-school crunch of "Crazy Mama" ended the album in a molten lava of fanfare guitar and big rock chorale.

Black and Blue was a hit album that spring. It reached no. 1 in America and no. 2 in England, surprising everyone, including the Stones. But the record sickened the rock critics who'd grown up worshiping the Stones. The acerbic Lester Bangs, the conscience of the rock press, let fly in *Creem* magazine: "There are two things to be said about the Stones' album before closing time. One is that they are perfectly in tune with the times (ahead some times, trendies), and the other is that the heat's off, because it's all over, they really don't matter anymore or stand for anything, which is certainly lucky for both them and us. I mean, it was a heavy weight to carry for all concerned. This is the first meaningless Stones album, and thank god!" Bangs's ironic relief was nothing compared to the poisonous critical venom spewed on the Stones by English writers imbued with fashionable punk no-future ideology.

The Rolling Stones' eight-week European tour began in Frankfurt on April 28, 1976. A hundred-strong crew of roadies, techs, accountants, and assistants hurtled the Stones along with fifteen big trucks, tons of lights and speakers, Keith's twenty-two guitars, a big custom stage, a pagoda-shaped white tent for the outdoor shows, and the flying penis and green dragon. The superb Meters, powered by the impeccably sharp drummer Joseph "Zigaboo" Modeliste and probably the best band in America, opened the shows. There was major drug traffic around the tour, with Keith personally signing laminates for his favorite dope dealers. Skeletal and supposedly "elegantly wasted," according to his press agents, Keith looked awful and played worse. He fell down on opening night during the finale, couldn't get up, kept playing anyway.

There was so much heroin around the tour that even the crew was scoring in the special dealers' lounge, found backstage at every show. There was serious harassment as they crisscrossed European borders, with constant luggage and body searches. Keith's seven-year-old son, Marlon, was along with him, playing wildly with his expensive toys backstage, or calmly sitting on a barstool watching his dad drink doubles of Scotch whisky, keeping him company, providing a bit of focus in the blur.

The after-show action was usually in Woody's room, with blues tapes (Furry Lewis, Big Maceo, Robert Johnson) alternating with throbbing reggae: Peter Tosh's "Legalize It," Culture, Max Romeo, Gregory Isaacs, the Itals. One night some British writers were allowed upstairs to interview the Stones. They found Keith chopping cocaine and candidly dumping on outcast Bill Wyman for the mediocrity of his solo album *Stone Alone*. When Mick discovered they were the same journos who had slagged *Black and Blue*, he became agitated. "Throw these cunts out," he hissed to their press agent. Keith, ever the gent, apologized to the hacks as they were herded out. Mick usually kept his distance from the rest of the tour. "Nobody hangs out in *my* fuckin' room," he told one writer, "except the band. What are *you* doing here, anyways?"

As if to prove to the punks that they were right and the Stones were truly obsolete, they played terribly almost every night: long shows with draggy tempos, sloppy guitar work, phoned-in funk, pathetic sing-alongs, ending with Mick flying around like a doomed Wallenda at the end of his trapeze. Keith found playing "Fool to Cry" so boring that he occasionally nodded off during the song. On May 19, Keith was driving Marlon and some friends home at dawn from a viscerally bad Stones show in Stafford when he nodded off at his customary 100 mph, bounced off the center barrier of the M1 motorway, and ditched his Bentley in a field. He got rid of most of the drugs before police arrived, but forgot about the silver coke stash and spoon he wore around his neck. The cops arrested him for the cocaine and also found some LSD in the car.

That night, the Stones began a sold-out six-night stand at cavernous Earls Court, an acoustically challenged exhibition hall with the ambience of an airplane hangar. "This is the worst toilet I've played in," Mick was quoted, "and I've seen toilets." Even the usually sharp Meters sounded terrible. Sleepless for five days, ill from heroin, out on bail again, Keith was unable to conjure up his requisite Evil and played like a zombie. Mick yelled at the band—"No mistakes this time!"—as he moved to his keyboard for "Fool to Cry." The Stones got the worst reviews of their career. Their act was called a sham, and "a charade inflated into a carnival." (Martin Amis on Mick Jagger: "This well-put-together, vitamin-packed unit of a human being does not really dance any more: it's simply that his head, his shoulders, his pelvis, both his arms, both his legs, both his huge feet and both his buttocks are wiggling, at great speed, independently, all the time . . . Mick is, without doubt, one of our least sedentary millionaires.") Mick's friend Princess Margaret, sister of the queen, popped backstage one night, further wrecking the band's street cred.

While playing in London, Mick called up Bryan Ferry, effete lead singer of the group Roxy Music, and invited him to one of the Earls Court shows. Ferry came with his fiancée, Jerry Hall, the ravishingly beautiful blond Texas girl who was one of the highest-paid fashion models in the world. They went to dinner with Mick after the show, Mick in his "mockney" persona, then went back to Ferry's house, where Mick flirted outrageously with his host's girlfriend until the disgusted Ferry stomped upstairs to bed. When Mick finally left, Jerry wouldn't kiss him good night, but Bryan Ferry's days as Jerry's man were numbered from that moment on.

The Stones knew the tour sucked. "I don't think our capabilities are stretched enough. We're slightly locked into being the Rolling Stones," Mick said. After the London debacle, the Stones went back to Germany, then to Spain and Yugoslavia for the first time. In early June, they arrived in Paris for three concerts at Les Abattoirs that would be recorded for a live album. Backstage on the first night in Paris, the jealous boyfriend of a girl Mick was seeing pointed a pistol at Mick before he was tackled by the bodyguards and hustled away.

Anita was in Switzerland with the children. On June 6, the final night of the Paris shows, Keith was called to the phone. He was told that his eleven-week-old son, Tara, had suffocated in his crib. The news was kept from the rest of the tour, so no one except a few insiders knew why Keith Richards came to life that night in Paris, playing long and luscious blues guitar solos on "Hot Stuff" and a painful, crying aria on "You Can't Always Get What You Want." Most of the tracks used on the concert album *Love You Live* were taken from this show.

Anita flew to Paris to be with Keith. Dumb with grief, they clung to each other like two wraiths with a hellhound on their trail. "No longer the Scott and Zelda of the rock and roll age," wrote Nick Kent, "they looked like some tragic, shell-shocked couple leading each other out of a concentration camp . . . I thought they were going to die." There was talk of canceling the remaining dates, but Keith refused, and would have carried on even longer. The last show was in the Stadthalle in Vienna on June 23. Afterward, the Stones wrecked their hotel in a furious orgy of vandalism. "No, no!" Mick could be heard shouting. "Not the *chandelier*!" The bill for cleaning this up was 5,000 pounds. Mick later blamed it on Ahmet Ertegun.

Tara JoJo Gunne Richards's earthly remains were cremated in Geneva. After the tour, Keith and Anita flew to London and checked into a hotel. They never returned to Switzerland again.

Two Sevens Clash

Summer 1976. John Phillips, ex-Papa, forty years old, former pop king and alpha wolf of Los Angeles, was living in London, working on the sound track for Nicholas Roeg's movie *The Man Who Fell to Earth* (starring David Bowie). He and his wife, actress Genevieve Waite, lived near Cheyne Walk, around the corner from Mick. While Mick was on tour that summer, Phillips enjoyed a dalliance with Bianca Jagger. His suspicious wife burst in on them one night, and there was a small scandal in Chelsea. Keith and Anita, deep in drugdom and crippled by guilt and despair, were then invited to vacate their suite at Claridges by the management. They brought Marlon over to play with Phillips's son one day and then didn't leave. Within a few weeks, John and Gen were junkies too.

Mick responded to Phillips's seduction of Bianca by inviting him to cricket matches, staying up all night, and playing guitar with him. Phillips, composer of "California Dreaming" and "Monday Monday," had a batch of new songs, which Mick suggested they record, using the Stones as the studio band.

On August 21, the Stones headlined a huge outdoor rock festival at Knebworth Park. It was their last show of the year and was widely rumored to be the last Stones show ever, since Keith Richards was expected to die at any moment. The Stones went on at eleven-thirty after Lynyrd Skynyrd, 10cc, Hot Tuna, and Todd Rundgren had played. The Stones' thirty-song set included oldies like "Route 66" and "Dead Flowers" and was judged a huge success. Keith and Ronnie finally relaxed and played as a team, bouncing licks and runs off each other. Mick worked the ten-yard catwalk that extended into the crowd, a harbinger of the future, and a massive fireworks barrage was set off right after "Street Fighting Man."

Right after that, the Stones began working with John Phillips at

Olympic Studio. Mick was enthusiastic, and Phillips got Keith and Mick Taylor into the studio for the first time since Taylor had left the Stones two years earlier. Phillips had a handshake deal with Mick to have the Stones play on his album and release it on their own label, an incredible opportunity to which he responded by self-destructing. The sessions went well until Phillips's heroin addiction alienated Mick. Then, in late September, session engineer Keith Harwood was killed in a car wreck when, floating on heroin, he nodded off at the wheel. When Mick lost interest, Keith Richards took over helping Phillips, but then Keith's own drug problems got in the way.

John Phillips's career-reviving project with the Stones was shelved. Some saw Mick's avenging hand in this, but Ahmet Ertegun was also reportedly reluctant to have the Stones competing with their own next album. Mick wasn't quite through with Phillips, though. A few months later, he invited Papa John and his daughter Mackenzie to his place for lunch. She was then an eighteen-year-old TV star with a sitcom and a thousand-dollar-a-day cocaine habit. While he was making sandwiches, Mick sent Phillips out to buy mayonnaise and then locked him out of the house. Mick told Mackenzie, "I've been waiting for this since you were ten years old," and jumped her in a flash. When Phillips returned and realized what was going down, he pounded on the door in a rage, then eventually left. Mackenzie Phillips later revealed that her tryst with Mick Jagger was "unbelievable. One night. Wham-bam. Bye-bye."

October 1976. The Stones were in Los Angeles, where Ron Wood had relocated with pregnant Chrissie. He and Mick spent nights listening to 150 hours of concert tapes, picking tracks for the new live album. Mick talked to record execs—MCA, EMI, Polydor—about the Stones' new record deal. The British papers were publishing rumors that Mick's marriage was over. "I got married for something to do," he told a reporter. "I've never been madly, deeply in love. I'm not an emotional person."

Mick resumed an earlier affair with Bebe Buell in New York that autumn. The gorgeous former *Playboy* pinup loved Mick without being in love with him, and as an expert on affairs was keenly observant of Mick as a lover. "The first time I was with him I was a bit shocked," she says, "shocked by how small he was, how frail he seemed with his tiny bones. I was two inches taller than Mick, but he seemed to love it. He was aggressive in the sack, very self-assured but considerate too. When I would be with him, I knew that flowers, perfume, or something in silk would arrive next day.

"You didn't just go out with Mick. He wanted his women to look the part. He'd check me out before we left my house, and if he didn't approve, I was sent back for another outfit. He was also a total genius with skin. He'd come into my bedroom and say, 'Let me look at your face, Bebe.' He'd take out a little jar of specially formulated cream and start putting it on for me. He taught me how to steam my face, what herbs to use. He knew more about facials and cosmetics than any woman.

"No one was monogamous back then. Everybody in that world cheated, but I think that Mick loved Bianca much more than he ever admitted to anyone. He called her B, and I thought she was a good woman. She referred to me as Mick's little friend."

Mick had other girlfriends as well: Sabrina Guinness in London, socialite Barbara Allen in New York, and model Apollonia von Ravenstein, among others. Bebe says that she was once invited by Mick and David Bowie to an orgy with four black men on Long Island. "There's no stopping Mick Jagger," she says. "Sexually, he's completely without prejudice, and he pushes himself to the limit."

When Bebe Buell became pregnant that fall (by Aerosmith's Steven Tyler), Mick proudly told his New York friends that the child was his.

Ron Wood joined the Malibu gang of Bob Dylan confederates, started a new solo album at The Band's Shangri-La Studio, became a father when his wife had a baby boy they named Jesse James. Woody appeared briefly with The Band in their Thanksgiving Day concert in San Francisco in late November, a farewell show famous as The Last Waltz. Ron and Chrissie Wood separated shortly after that.

In December, Keith was listening to concert tracks when he decided to use the studio time to cut a Christmas single. He played guitar and bass on Chuck Berry's "Run Rudolph Run," with Stu on piano and Mike Driscoll (from Mick Taylor's blues band) on drums. The song was released in time for Christmas—two years later.

In Jamaica, where Keith was living toward the end of 1976, the big reggae song was "Two Sevens Clash" by Joseph Hill's group, Culture. The song prophesied that the year 1977, when two sevens clashed, would be an apocalyptic one. Sure enough, in 1977 martial law was declared in Jamaica to prevent civil war. In England, reggae musicians linked up with the punks (the Clash named themselves after Culture's song), an alliance commemorated by Bob Marley's militant jam "Punky Reggae Party." For the Rolling Stones, 1977 would bring enormous changes, portents of dissolution, threats of prison, international scandal, and, ultimately, some of the finest music they would ever create.

February 1977. The Stones were on a roll just before the whip came down in Toronto. They had a good live album in the can, the last record they owed Atlantic under their old contract. There was stiff competition for their services among other record labels, a deal potentially worth tens of millions to the musicians. The Stones were rehearsing, playing well, the new guy working out nicely. Mick and Keith had some early songs for the next album—Keith's "Beast of Burden," Mick's "Faraway Eyes"—which they felt was going to be very strong, the first complete Stones album with their new lineup.

It was Mick's idea that the Stones convene in Toronto, Canada's cultural capital, in February. Keith had been found guilty of cocaine possession in January and fined, which again made his entry into the United States a problem. The Stones wanted to record some classic R&B songs in a nightclub atmosphere to include on their live album, partly as a "golden handshake" for departing executive Marshall Chess, whose family's publishing company still controlled the rights to the old Muddy Waters, Bo Diddley, and Chuck Berry numbers the Stones would cut. By recording in Toronto, Mick could commute to the ongoing label negotiations and his family in New York, where the live album was also being mixed.

On February 16, the Stones announced their new record deal with the British company EMI to distribute Rolling Stones Records everywhere except America. One of the deal's perks involved EMI providing cheap studio time to the Stones at the company's famous Pathé-Marconi Studios in Paris, where they would record their next five albums. It was Marshall Chess's last deal for the Stones. Later that year, the Stones resigned their North American distribution deal with Atlantic Records after Ahmet Ertegun coughed up a reported $20 million.

The Stones and their huge entourage, still captained by Peter Rudge, arrived in Toronto in mid-February to rehearse for a three-night stand at the suitably sleazy El Mocambo nightclub early in March. They checked into the Harbour Castle Hotel and waited for Keith, who didn't show up.

He and Anita were wintering at Redlands, where their only visitors seemed to be dope dealers making smack and coke runs from London. Still trying to recover from the death of their baby, struggling to cut down their drug intake by themselves, the couple seemed to sense that they were approaching some kind of tragic catharsis. With writer Barbara Charone present, Anita tore into Keith one night as he stared vacantly at the flickering TV. "It's impossible to get *laid* around here," she yelled. "I'm going to walk the streets of the town. I'll probably have better luck." When Keith pointedly ignored her, Anita let him have it.

"You think you're Superman, don't you? Well, you're only Superman when you play the guitar! You think you can handle drugs, but you can't! I know what I am, and I've been that way for seven years. You pretend! You're *afraid*. You pretend that you don't have a drug habit. You just go upstairs to the bathroom! You think people don't *know*? You're no different than anybody else. You can't handle drugs either!"

It had been a long time since Keith's last detox, and he was in a state of physical decline and a week late getting to Canada. He'd insisted the Stones rehearse before the club dates, but was unable to pack his things and get his family to Canada. Mick and the band sent him frantic "Where are you?" telegrams every day. Without Keith, the Stones were going into panic mode.

On February 23, Keith and Anita finally packed their clothes, guitars, and toys into twenty-eight cases, and locked Redlands up tight. They took Keith's dog Tabasco over to Doris Richards's house in Dartford and said good-bye to Angela, as daughter Dandelion was now called. Dressed in flamboyant, matching black and white silk suits, with Marlon in his usual shorts and Wellington boots, Keith and Anita boarded the British Airways flight that would take them to the final act of their ten-year romance.

Watch Yer Bottoms, Keith

Toronto, February 24, 1977. At the airport, Keith looked like Lazarus before Jesus sorted him out. He'd cooked his last shot of smack on the plane, then gallantly tossed the burned spoon into Anita's bag. Anita seemed agitated going through customs and made a scene, so they brought in the dogs, found a lump of hash, the spoon, and the usual traces of residue in her luggage. The police busted her for suspected narcotics violations, but let her go on to the Stones' hotel.

Three days later, acting on a tip that Keith had a large stash on hand, the Royal Canadian Mounted Police came looking for him. Keith was sleeping in one of the many "floater" suites the Stones kept in the hotel, so it took the Mounties a couple of hours to even find him. When they did, his door was mysteriously unguarded by the security detail that usually protected him. Keith was deeply asleep, almost comatose. The cops were unable to wake him during a prolonged search, which uncovered enough dope to charge him with being a heroin trafficker under Canadian law.

One of the cops started slapping him. He came around enough to hear the cops say, "You're under arrest for conspiracy to traffic in narcotics."

Next day: major headlines. The Stones borrowed $100,000 in cash from Canadian promoter Michael Cohl, but Keith was bailed at only $1,000. He begged the cops for a couple of grams of heroin to tide him over, but they weren't amused. Meetings with lawyers, who confirmed that Keith could go to jail for life for this sixth drug arrest in ten years (no one in Canada had beaten a drug-dealing rap lately). The Stones were upset, Mick despondent. Their new record deals were seriously threatened, and there were fears the new live album could be the Stones' last.

There was nothing to do but press on. Keith tried cold-turkey withdrawal in his bathroom. Ronnie and Bill Wyman dropped in while he was having a seizure. Worried that Keith was dying, they found some heroin for him. Keith then pulled himself together enough to work. The Stones, with Billy Preston and Ollie Brown, rehearsed at El Mocambo early in March. Under pressure, they morphed into a bar band again and just let it rock. Keith: "Everyone's talking doom and disaster, but we're up onstage and never felt better. We sounded great! People were asking, 'Is this the end of the Rolling Stones?' In actual fact, it was a period of real productivity for us."

The first gig took place on March 4 in front of three hundred radio contest winners. Opening was local band April Wine, which got the slot as a favor to the guy who had helped out the Stones when their truck was bombed in Montreal in '72. Keith recalled how purely amazed the packed Canadian kids looked as they jammed in within touching range of the band. The Stones played a long set in the wild, smoky atmosphere, enjoying the lost intimacy of a club date. Sitting near the front of the crowd was a large saucer-eyed woman, grooving and having a good time. She was twenty-eight-year-old Margaret Trudeau, the wife of the Canadian prime minister, and she was about to enter the Rolling Stones legend forever.

Madcap Maggie (as the Canadian press called her) had married Pierre Trudeau, almost thirty years older, six years earlier. He was the preeminent Canadian politician of his era, holding power between 1968 and 1984, a dashing liberal intellectual who symbolized an invigorated Canada. The Trudeaus had been the nation's golden couple, with three children and a seemingly happy marriage. But free-spirited, ex-hippie Maggie had chafed under the tight security forced on her family by the same Quebec separatists who'd firebombed the Stones in Montreal in 1972. She had been hospitalized for mental strain several times and was considered unstable, with a taste for pot and recklessness. In early 1977, she and her husband had separated, secretly and informally, and she was visiting a friend in Toronto when the Stones came to town that winter.

Mrs. Trudeau moved into a suite at the Harbour Castle and joined the party. "Someone said she wanted to go to the gig, so we took her," Mick said. "I had never met her before, but I guess she likes to go out to clubs and go rocking and rolling just like everyone else—a young girl, you know." Margaret threw a champagne party for the Stones in her suite after the show. Mick took her aside and pointed to his portly press agent. "Don't talk to Wasserman," he whispered. "He's trying to get publicity for us, but he's an arsehole." Later that night, Maggie answered a knock on her door, in her white pajamas, to find the press agent offering her a bottle of champagne. She accepted it and closed the door. In the morning, Paul Wasserman leaked a story that Mrs. Trudeau had been seen in the corridors of the Stones' hotel in her pajamas. The next day's headlines— PM'S WIFE AND ROLLING STONES—signaled the end of her marriage as the rumor spread that she was having an affair with Mick Jagger. But it was actually Woody she was friendly with. They were both going through marital separations, and they bonded with each other over mutual pain. Bill Wyman described their relationship as a "liaison." On Saturday, the second night at El Mocambo, Ronnie invited her along with her camera to take pictures of the band. Sitting up front as the Stones blasted forth, she shot Mick with his jumpsuit unzipped to his pubis as young ladies fondly massaged his crotch, trying to get him hard between songs. "It was great up to a point," Mick said the next day, "but then it got difficult to sing." The Stones were paid half the night's bar money, $371.

The Stones stayed in town for a few days after the shows, mixing the Toronto tapes in a local studio. Mrs. Trudeau had dinner with Woody and Charlie Watts, and ended up shooting dice and smoking hash with Wood and friends until nine the next morning, which fueled further headlines: SEX ORGY IN CANADIAN PM'S WIFE'S SUITE. Late that afternoon, a frightened Marlon Richards knocked on her door. "Where's everybody gone?" the little boy asked. "Daddy's lying on the floor crying, and I don't know what to do."

Margaret went with Marlon to Keith's filthy, cluttered suite. Anita had gone shopping. Keith was lying in a fetal position and moaning. She knew he was due in court to face narcotics charges the next day. She got Keith into bed, covered him up, and played with Marlon until Anita returned.

The press fury grew into a crisis and the prime minister was under fire. The Canadian dollar dropped in value. Pierre Trudeau had to deny that his wife had run off with the Rolling Stones. Opposition newspapers attacked the credibility of the government, and Margaret Trudeau's official duties were suspended. Charlie Watts sniffed, "I wouldn't want *my* wife associating with us."

On March 7, Keith appeared in court to hear that he was being charged with possessing cocaine in addition to heroin. On the way out of court, he was pushed and spat on by unknown bystanders. That afternoon, there was a heavy-duty band meeting. Keith was still using heroin and Mick was jittery, worried they were under surveillance and certain another bust was coming down. The hotel was full of undercover cops, and the Stones fretted there was an informer on their staff. Mick decided the Stones would leave Keith in Canada until his case was resolved. The album had to be mixed while Keith tried another detox. Bill Carter was deputized to somehow persuade the U.S. government to let Keith enter the country on an emergency visa, to try to save his life.

On March 8, Keith was bailed again for $25,000 and given his passport back. Disgusted, Mick left Canada, but was stopped at the airport and searched before he was allowed to get on a plane. The rest of the band followed him the next day. Ron Wood's departure hurt Keith badly. "They all *vanished*," Anita said bitterly. Margaret Trudeau flew to New

York as well, further igniting press speculation that she and Jagger were an item, despite firm denials by both of them. Whatever had or hadn't happened in Toronto, she never saw any of the Rolling Stones again. Her marriage ruptured, and she spent two years in New York, becoming part of the Studio 54 disco scene. Bianca, undisputed sultana of Studio 54, believed the stories about her and Mick and refused to speak to her.

Stranded with his family in Toronto, facing an uncertain future as he shuffled between court dates, Keith sought some solace in music. Ian Stewart booked him into Sounds Interchange studio on March 12–13, where he cut a sequence of brokenhearted country songs in a Bakersfield mood, with Stu on piano, to have product in the can if his bail was revoked and he went to prison. The songs, never released but often bootlegged, plumbed the depths of his feelings in the poignant voice of the debauched ex-chorister that Keith had become.

Keith's situation in Canada gave new meaning to the concept of persona non grata, but in New York and Washington, Keith's people pleaded with the new administration of President Jimmy Carter to let Keith enter the country to detox. Early in April, he and Anita were permitted by special dispensation to fly to New York for treatment. No one was more shocked by this than Keith. "I was down-and-out in Toronto, stuck there, right? And America let me in to clean up—gave me a medical visa to clean up. And that *amazed* me, y'know? You don't ever expect from government the helping hand, y'know?"

Keith entered a private rehab clinic near Philadelphia and was on ice for the next six weeks. Mick sent him cassettes of his favorite New York reggae radio shows to help keep his spirits up. He and Anita went through a "black box" cure that used electric shocks to stimulate the brain to overproduce narcotic-like bio-endorphins, allowing a narcotics addict to detox slowly.

The cure worked—for a few weeks. But although Keith got into heroin again, he now really wanted to let it go. The thing that most pleased him was the looks on the faces of the drug dealers when he began to turn them down. He later admitted that the Toronto bust had been a huge blessing and had saved his life. "I wanted to come back," he said, "and prove that what I had gone through had made a difference, to justify this kind of suffering."

The Human Riff in Paris

May 1977. Bianca Jagger's birthday party at Studio 54 featured Mrs. Jagger riding around the club on her husband's present, a white Arab pony led by almost naked, glitter-sprinkled black model Sterling St. Jacques—a tabloid image flashed around the world. The waiters all wore diapers and nothing else. The other Stones could only shake their heads. The Jaggers' marriage was over, a casualty of his serial infidelity and her longtime affair with actor Ryan O'Neal. Mick now made a big play for Jerry Hall, the brassy, sensual Texas model with a sense of humor and a straight-up sexuality. Everyone always had fun around Jerry Hall. When Jerry danced, the whole world seemed to undulate around her, and she was known for dispensing cheerful, up-to-the-minute tips on oral sex. She liked to say the best method of keeping a man was to drop everything for two seconds and give him a blow job. When her father died while Bryan Ferry was touring in Australia, Mick was there with massive bouquets and sympathy. He won her heart by the end of the year.

In June, Mick and Keith began the final mixes of *Love You Live*. Billy Preston brought his own mixing engineer to Atlantic Studios one night, an act of hubris that got him fired from the band by Keith. (Preston had never signed his 1975–76 touring contracts with the Stones, and was able to hold up the live album for a considerable percentage of the action.) As part of their new record deal, Atlantic gave the Stones an office suite in the Warner Communications building in Rockefeller Center. Atlantic executive Earl McGrath replaced Marshall Chess as president of Rolling Stone Records. Chess was grateful to the Stones, who'd backed him up as a heroin addict in charge of their careers. "They stuck up for me," he later said. Within a year of leaving, Chess recovered from his addiction.

They were also writing songs. Keith was living at the Mayflower Hotel in a suite stuffed with reggae singles acquired in nightly forays to Jamaican shops in the Bronx. If a primal reggae group like the Heptones was playing out on Long Island, Keith was there. He and Wood were jamming from 3 A.M. to noon, often at Mick's West Side house, working on his last plea to Anita, "Beast of Burden."

Bebe Buell's baby girl, Liv, was born in New York on July 1. Her first visitors were Mick and Ron Wood. Mick tried to convince Woody the tiny thing with huge lips was his child, and there *was* some slight resemblance, since her real father, Steven Tyler, had big lips too. ("Aerosmith was *really* wild," Bebe Buell said later. "They made the Rolling Stones look like a kindergarten!")

That summer, Keith and Anita moved to a secluded estate in South Salem, New York, about an hour north of Manhattan. Commuting to the city to work with John Phillips, Keith stumbled back into heroin use. He went through yet another rehab at the Stevens Clinic in New York and was told by his lawyers that he had to live separately from Anita if he intended to stay dope-free and out of prison. Blamed by Mick for the Toronto bust and for Keith's decline, Anita began to be treated as a scapegoat and an outcast. It was the end of her era as a member of the Rolling Stones.

Mick flew to Paris to look at the studios they would start to use later in the year. Then he and Bianca took off on a cruise around the Aegean Sea on a last attempt to patch things up. By the time they returned to New York, they had broken up.

———

With a lurid cover by Andy Warhol, part of a sequence of distasteful photos of the Stones biting each other, *Love You Live* was released in September 1977. It bore a dedication to Keith Harwood: "Those whom the gods love, grow young." The Stones held a party for the album at Trax, the West Side music hangout. Three sides of the double album were from the previous year's Paris shows, with one side reserved for a selection of Chicago blues cut at El Mocambo. *Love You Live* was a Top Ten album on both sides of the Atlantic that fall.

In October, the Stones gathered in Paris to begin recording. Keith and Woody flew in on the Concorde supersonic jet. Keith got in a cab, forgot the address of the apartment he'd owned for years in Paris, and had to be rescued. Mick was staying in L'Hôtel, small and discreet, where he was joined by Jerry Hall, who moved in with Mick permanently soon after.

It was now do-or-die for the Stones, who had to make a great album in the wake of the punk/new wave challenges of pathetic Old Fartism. And there was serious strain within the band. Ron Wood was firmly allied with Keith, who openly ridiculed Mick's artificial, chameleon personality and social pretentions. Mick patronized Keith, telling Nick Kent they would never tour "with a geezer pushin' a heroin charge." Charlie was put off by the bitchiness, and extremely annoyed that his daughter, Seraphina, was taunted at school with "Your dad's a junkie too." Hardly anyone spoke to Bill. Stu was alienated and had to be begged to come to Paris at all.

When they first looked at Pathé-Marconi, the Stones were unimpressed by the sterile facilities in the quiet suburb of Boulogne. Disliking the actual studios, Keith instead picked out a large rehearsal and storage room as the Stones' new Paris atelier. Keith: "The *room* is as important as the band and the song and the producer and the engineer. The room is *at least* as important as all that to the total sound. You can't separate rock and roll music, instrument by instrument. It can only be recorded by jamming the sound all together." At Pathé-Marconi, he reconfigured a space to his specifications, and all or part of the next five Rolling Stones albums were recorded at 62 rue des Sèvres.

———

The *Some Girls* sessions began on October 10, 1977, and went through late November. Mick hired London engineer Chris Kimsey to work on the album because he admired the crisp bass and drum sounds

Kimsey had given Peter Frampton and Bad Company. The rhythm section was ecstatic for once. "He [Kimsey] did get beautiful sounds for me and Charlie," Bill Wyman said, "and that inspires you and turns everyone on to your playing." Ian Stewart wouldn't play on any of the Stones' driven, demonic new songs, so Mick started playing rhythm guitar, giving the band a raw, three-pronged attack on the early demos. These were Ron Wood's first official sessions as a member of the band, since he'd mostly played bass or sung backup on *Black and Blue*. They worked on a track titled "Rotten Roll," an early version of "Before They Make Me Run." "Lazy Bitch" was the working title for what became "Hang Fire." "Start Me Up" was birthed as a reggae song. They were prolific and very *on*, producing demos of "So Young," "Everything's Turning to Gold" (with Mel Collins, who'd played with Alexis Korner and King Crimson, on saxophone), "Fiji Jim," and "I Can't Help It," among many others. Expectations for the new album started to build. Everyone knew the *Some Girls* music was the best the Stones had come up with in five years.

The sessions broke in November, when Keith had to return to Toronto for a court date. He told the judge of his efforts to get off drugs, and frankly explained that, as an addict, he was compelled to take them again when the band resumed touring. Case continued to 1978. Keith may have seemed contrite in court, but both privately and publicly he remained defiant. "I've *never* had problems with drugs," Keith told an interviewer. "Only with policemen."

Back in Paris in December, the sessions continued to run hot, especially after they found Sugar Blue, a twenty-two-year-old blues harmonica virtuoso named James Whiting. Born and raised in Harlem, he'd moved to Paris and was just scraping by, playing his harp in the Métro, when he let loose one night at a party at a friend's place. As the party broke up, a man who Blue thought was in the film business gave him Mick Jagger's phone number and told him to call. Sugar Blue thought it was a joke, but he was broke and called the number. He ended up playing harmonica on the next three Rolling Stones albums.

Sugar Blue was one of the few outsiders to play on what was mostly an insular Stones album. Also joining the December sessions was ace keyboard player Ian "Mac" McLagan, late of the Faces, who turned up in Paris after Ron Wood strongly recommended him to replace Billy Preston.

Mac had been one of the kids pressed up close to the Stones at the Crawdaddy Club in Richmond in 1963. He'd been a mod pop star since 1965, when he joined the Small Faces, then spent five years in the Faces with Ronnie. He played Hammond organ and keyboards with a sharp London pop twist. Best of all for him, he was liked and respected by Stu, who'd cared for neither Nicky Hopkins nor Billy Preston.

He arrived at Pathé-Marconi to find the Stones listening to a playback of pumped-up, hard-rocking "Shattered." Woody put a couple of white lines on the piano for Mac and yelled, "Hey, Keith, look who I've got here!" Keith glanced at Mac snorting away. "Oh it's 'im. I see Woody's taken care of you, then." Within an hour, Keith and Charlie started to play, then Wood and Bill fell in. Mac sat down at the Hammond, Stu at the piano. Pinching himself, Mac realized he was playing with his favorite band. Mick picked up his harmonica and started blowing, and the next incarnation of the Rolling Stones was in place.

After dinner at an African restaurant, it was back to Keith's place, where they played Mac some of the new songs. "Claudine" was a down and dirty, libelous riff about Claudine Longet, the ex-wife of crooner Andy Williams, who had just gotten off lightly after killing her skiing star boyfriend. "When the Whip Comes Down" had a heavy punk influence in its rent boy lyrics and blazing tempo. They played a funkafied version of the Temptations' "Just My Imagination" and told Mac it needed an organ part.

Later in the evening, just to embarrass Charlie, Keith jabbed a needle full of smack through his jeans and into his bottom. He left the syringe hanging there, walking around the room and laughing. "He's fucking 'orrible," Charlie murmured.

Mac spent two days in the studio with the Stones, playing on both "Imagination" and "Miss You," Mick's love song for Jerry Hall; played them over and over and over again, settling into the Stones' method of beating a song to death before recording the definitive version. Needing to get back to London for another session, Mac asked Woody about compensation for his work. Woody had a word with Mick, who looked pained. He came over to the Wurlitzer electric piano Mac was playing and said, "I've only got a few francs, is that all right?"

"Sure, Mick—whatever you can afford." Mick Jagger emptied his pockets and paid McLagan 120 francs—about twenty dollars.

Because We Can't Remember Their Fucking Names!

Early in 1978, after breaking for the holidays, the Rolling Stones returned to Paris to finish *Some Girls* amid sometimes-bitter hassles. Mick wanted a streetwise, minimalist disco-punk sound, while Keith was into dub reggae and rootsier styles. "[It was] the kind of edgy, punk ethos," Mick said of the sessions. "The whole thing was to play it all fast, fast, fast. I had a lot of problems with Keith about it, but that was the deal at the time." Mick's new songs tended to be speedy guitar riffs in F. Strung out and disillusioned, Keith missed many sessions, so Ron Wood added pedal steel colors to "Faraway Eyes" and "Shattered." Wood also come up with the flashy blues "Black Limousine," closely related to Elmore James's "Dream Girl."

By March 1978, the Stones had more than forty new songs on tape, enough for their next three albums. These rich sessions even produced great outtakes: "Indian Girl," the country rocker "Misty Roads," a long reggae jam titled "Jah Is Not Dead," and multiple versions of "Claudine." Keith's "We Had It All" was a fully realized country love song, *very* sad and sentimental, with a weeping pedal steel wash. "Start Me Up" almost got on the album as a reggae song, but was left off because Keith worried that he'd unconsciously copied the main riff from something he'd heard on the radio.

Mick Jagger exercised almost total control over the new album, but

Keith had the last word, recutting his epic "Before They Make Me Run," with engineer Dave Jordan using the Stones' mobile studio. They gave the track a sonically different feel from the rest of the album, with Keith singing in a serpentine nasal drone that sounded like an Arabian vocal from Mars.

Ron Wood had met a pretty ex-model named Jo Howard at a party in Kensington the year before. She'd been a pinup girl for the London tabloid *The Sun,* was dating Egyptian playboy Dodi Al-Fayid, hated rock music, thought Woody a "flash sod." She told him she worked at Woolworth's in Oxford Street, so he actually staked out the employee entrance until he realized she'd been pulling his leg. He finally tracked her down, won her with his sincerity, gallantry, his manic laugh and charm, and got her pregnant in Paris while working on tracks for his third solo album, for which he'd just signed with CBS. When she heard about it, Crissie Wood filed for divorce.

They finished recording early in March. Mick took Jerry Hall to see Stargroves, which he was selling. Poking around the musty old house with its sixties orientalist trappings, she found Marianne Faithfull's love letters to Mick in an old chest. She was a bit jealous when she realized how much Mick must have loved this wild woman, who was then rumored to be recording a stunning new album and planning a comeback.

Then Mick and Keith returned to New York, where *Some Girls* was mixed at Atlantic Studios. A tape of "Miss You" was sent, sight unseen, to remix engineer Bob Clearmountain, who produced an eight-and-a-half-minute disco-mix version of the song for dance clubs—the Stones' first extended twelve-inch "disco 45." Mick and Jerry were living in posh East Side hotels, while Keith was with his family north of the city.

In April 1978, they signed their first major act to Rolling Stones Records, an attempted linkup between the rock and reggae movements.

Both Keith and Mick had been interested in Peter Tosh for years. With Bob Marley, Tosh was the founder of the Wailers and a key figure in the reggae world. More radical than Marley, the tall and fierce Tosh (short for Winston Hubert MacIntosh, born in 1944) had left the Wailers and made a strong series of records that included furious reggae jams like "Steppin' Razor," "Legalize It," and "Equal Rights."

"I don't want no *peace*," Tosh sang, "I want equal rights and justice." He was an uncompromising Rastafarian street revolutionary who lived on a massive ganja intake and fearlessly sang, "Legalize it, and I will advertise it." It also appealed to the Stones that Tosh fronted one of the best bands in the world, Word, Sound and Power, whose rhythm section—drummer Sly Dunbar and bassist Robbie Shakespeare—had invented a harder rocking form of reggae called rockers, which goosed the steady reggae beat with faster offbeats and flying cymbals. By signing Peter Tosh, the Stones would also get one of the hottest drummers in the business and would promote this new, coked-up Jamaican style.

On April 22, Mick and Keith flew to Kingston to see their new act perform at the National Stadium in the legendary One Love Peace Concert, a historic show in which Bob Marley tried to unite the island's two warring political gangs. Protected by armed troops, the entire Jamaican political and judicial hierarchy attended the concert. As a preamble to his part of the show, Peter Tosh stood onstage with a blazing ganja spliff and lectured the prime minister, the judges, and the cops, in an often obscene and hilarious rant, about how they were Babylonian oppressors who were down-pressing the children of Jah. Mick and Keith watched from the wings as Tosh and the band then played a stinging set of hard-core protest reggae that moshed down the place and justified their faith in him. A few weeks later, in retaliation for his public insolence, the Kingston police arrested Tosh for smoking ganja at Aquarius Studio in uptown Halfway Tree, where he was making his album. They took him to the station and beat him almost to death.

———

Some Girls was released in May 1978 and saved the Rolling Stones' career. Edgy, tender, and tough, with a steaming asphalt ambience, it was a reflection of the Stones pandering to dance music, punk rock, and new wave rock and roll. The die-cut album jacket, a pop montage of celebrity faces in an ad for cheap wigs, had to be recalled when the annoyed celebs (Lucille Ball, Raquel Welch) demanded their images be removed. "Miss You" was the album's signature song and first single, a 4/4 dance jingle with a falsetto chorus and Mick's put-on pimp's voice selling Puerto Rican girls. Mel Collins played the sax solo, and Sugar Blue's harp sounded like a night train in the Delta. "Miss You" was the Stones' first American no. 1 single in seven years.

"When the Whip Comes Down" followed, a raunchy rocker that toured the pre-AIDS Manhattan leather-bar underground with a crashing, punkish tag at the end. Bill Wyman's superb bass line propelled the Whitfield/Strong soul classic "Just My Imagination," with Charlie playing in-the-pocket drums and featuring cool, sustained ringing guitars. The Stones had boiled down the original riff, used "all the girls in New York" as a new text, and included the Temptations' original (and difficult to sing) interior-monologue vocal bridge. Keith played a long guitar solo round the fade.

"Some Girls" was the album's parodic title track. Starting in a blast of blues harmonica, Mick sang of his sexual obsessions in an arch, jokey voice, running down the (de)merits of French, Italian, American, English, Chinese, and black girls in a lewd and politically incorrect diatribe that caused Atlantic to slap a warning label on the copies of *Some Girls* distributed to radio stations. The reference to "a house in Zuma Beach" was an insolent jab at Bob Dylan, who had lost his famous copper-domed palace north of Malibu in his recent divorce settlement. Asked by an interviewer why the album was called *Some Girls*, Keith laughed and said, "Because we couldn't remember their fucking names!" The first side ended with "Lies," a splendid punk homage to the manic speedball energy of the Sex Pistols and Sham '69, with Ron Wood and Mick exchanging rapid-fire bursts of guitar noise.

"Faraway Eyes" started side two with a typical Stones country parody. "Respectable" was Mick's less-than-fond three-chord farewell to his wife: the rag trade girl, the queen of porn, the easiest lay on the White House lawn. "Get out of my life! Don't fuck my wife! Don't come back!" The song also referenced Keith's legal troubles in the "Talking heroin with the president / If there's a problem, son, I'll bet it can be bent" lines, chanted to hard-core Chuck Berry changes.

Keith Richards's extraordinary "Before They Make Me Run" was a different type of farewell, a tacit commitment to retirement from a life of calamitous addiction and permanent death watch. Keith also wrote the love song "Beast of Burden," another Stones salute to Motown cut in the same groove as "Imagination." "Beast" was an explicit plea from Keith to Anita to not drag him down into degradation and despair. It was the most passionate song on a snake-eyed, dispassionate, market-calculated album.

Some Girls ended with the subway rumble of "Shattered," a journey through the Seventh Avenue anxieties of New York life in the seventies, when the great city seemed to be deteriorating into a bankrupt, decadent Calcutta. "Looka me!" shouted Mick, summoning all the sleazy, coked-up neurosis of an urban hustler desperately on the make.

Some Girls recaptured the Rolling Stones' distracted and aging audience. The record's fearless attack and astute, nonpreachy social commentary was an artful mirror of the times. In England, the album reached no. 2, but in America, it was an almost instant no. 1 and stayed high in the charts for the rest of 1978. After selling 8 million copies, *Some Girls* proved to be the biggest Stones album ever.

Summer Romance

May 1978. The Rolling Stones convened in Woodstock, the old bohemian village a hundred miles north of New York City, to rehearse for their summer tour. Mick and Jerry moved into a rented house and prepared to start work at the nearby Bearsville studio complex owned by Albert Grossman, ex-manager of Bob Dylan and The Band. Keith arrived in Woodstock with Anita. He was so wasted from heroin toxicity that he had to be carried from the car to his house. With millions of dollars in the balance, Keith had to get off heroin so the tour could be insured. He moved in with Mick and self-administered another black box cure, this time using pot, pills, and alcohol to ease the excruciating pain of withdrawal instead of going cold turkey. All the Stones tried to support Keith in what seemed his most dire hour. When the electrodes fell off his head, Jerry Hall (whom Keith disliked) would plug them back in again. Writhing in a semiconscious state on the living room couch, Keith managed to wean himself from heroin. Now he turned into a serious alcoholic instead, but one who could at least function well enough to rehearse and undertake a lucrative national tour.

Peter Tosh's first album for Rolling Stones Records also came together in Woodstock that spring. Recorded mostly in Kingston studios with synthesizers playing the melody lines, two of Tosh's tracks got guitar overdubs by Keith and Wood: "Stand Firm" and the title song, "Bush Doctor." Mick worked on Tosh's first single, a reggae-soul version of Smokey Robinson's Motown classic "Walk and Don't Look Back." It had a popping Sly and Robbie "riddim" format and a funny spoken dialogue between Mick and Tosh, who wasn't exactly known for comedy routines. This was an attempt to tone down Tosh's stern outlaw image (although Tosh had previously recorded the song in Jamaica in 1966) and replace it with a more dance-friendly vibe. This was incongruous because Tosh was foremost among reggae's rabidly antidisco preachers, denouncing disco's "get down" philosophy, urging his black audience to "get up" instead. But the Stones were totally committed to him, and he would open for them in stadiums all over America that summer. When they finally toured Africa, Tosh told Mick, the Stones would open for *him*.

––––––––

The Stones' 1978 American tour started in Florida in June. Backstage at Lakeland, the first stop—where they appeared incognito as the Stoned City Wrestling Champs—Keith bought a stolen .38 Special revolver from a local security man. Ian McLagan had to learn twenty songs on two days notice, since Ronnie had brought him in at the last minute. A few days into the tour, having summoned Mac to his reggae-drenched hotel suite, Keith taught him how to skank, reggae style, with left and right hands bouncing off the keyboard. Mac had some problems with the tour contracts the Stones' management ordered him to sign. When he balked, Mick sarcastically demanded to know if Mac was going to hold them for ransom, as Billy had done.

By the second date in Atlanta (where they played as the Cockroaches), the Stones were already dispirited. They were trying to re-tool their arena shows for football stadiums, playing on a bare stage surrounded by a huge red lips and tongue logo painted on a scrim. A pair of giant tonsils floated over Charlie's drums, the old 1960s Gretsch kit which he'd gotten out of storage for the tour. Mick was dressed in his concept of cheap disco fashion, dubbed the "F train look" after the New York subway that ran through immigrant Queens: red Puerto Rican trousers, white After Six dinner jackets, rakishly tilted Kangol cap. He looked too dopey for words, and the Stones were getting condescending reviews.

Hard times for the Stones, despite creative revival and a hit album. Mick and Wood were both being divorced. Their trusted press agent, Les Perrin, died. Black radio boycotted the album because of the line "black girls just wanna get fucked all night," which prompted Rev. Jesse Jackson, the civil rights activist, to denounce the Stones. Threatened with jail in Canada, Keith and Anita had split. When Anita left Woodstock, Keith moved in with Ronnie and his new girlfriend, Jo Howard, who was pregnant. Keith started seeing a friend of Jo's, a beautiful blond Danish model named Lily Wenglass. Lil, as she was called, was intelligent and sexy. She brought Keith back into the world of desire after his cure had taken hold, and made a lot of enemies early on by keeping his old friends away from him while he was trying to stay (relatively) straight.

As the tour progressed, the shows often split in two, with the Stones playing listlessly on the old battle hymns, and with a brittle power pop surge on the new songs—"Respectable," "Beast of Burden," "Miss You," and especially "Shattered," which turned into an explosive trance riff that blew minds all over the United States that summer. It was Keith's band on the old stuff, but Mick drove the new songs, playing fast rhythm guitar. Early in the tour, they taped a New Jersey theater show that captured a screaming, maniacal "When the Whip Comes Down" and Keith croaking out "Happy" with a saw-toothed fury that showed that even on this, perhaps the low point of their concert career, the Stones were still capable of transcendence on any given night. Few missed Billy Preston's fuzzy gospel stylings, and on their best nights the Stones still managed to play stripped-down, grease-gun rock and roll. When shows went well, Keith credited the new guy. "With Ron Wood, the band's playing more like the way it did when Brian and I used to play at the beginning." Asked about writing songs, Keith said he was "more interested in creating sounds, something that has a different atmosphere and feel to it." Asked what inspired him, he answered, "The latest stuff coming out of Jamaica."

The tour divided into camps—vivacious Mick and Jerry versus truculent Keith, with Wood as the tenuous link. Keith avoided Jerry and didn't like that she was now making appearances with the Stones. Emerging from his long drug stupor, he tried asserting himself in business matters, annoying Mick, who had run the Stones alone for most of the decade. "I thought I was doing Mick a favor," Keith said later, "but he saw it as a power grab."

Off heroin, Keith was becoming more human. He even let Woody bring Bill Wyman to his room one night for a hatchet-burying session that allowed the two Stones—who'd never gotten on—to begin speaking again. "Woody's come along and pulled both sides together," Wyman told an interviewer. "He's the reason for the band getting closer, being able to talk to each other, even saying unheard-of things like 'You were great tonight.' Woody started to get that happening. He's *fabulous!* He made this band come to life again."

After playing Soldier Field in Chicago in July, the Stones (without an ailing Bill) jammed with their mentor Muddy Waters and Willie Dixon at Muddy's regular club gig at the Quiet Knight. Muddy was on a high, riding a successful album (*Hard Again*) recorded with Johnny Winter. The Stones gathered round the venerable Delta legend, who performed sitting on a stool, and did hammy versions of "Mannish Boy" and "Rollin' Stone Blues."

The Stones were flying this tour on a smaller plane, a Convair 580 turboprop. In Texas, Mick explained the Stones' lackluster performance to their restive audience: "If the band seems slightly lacking in energy, it's because we spent all last night fucking. Ha ha! We do our best." In Tucson, hometown girl Linda Ronstadt (in silk hot pants) joined Mick onstage to sing "Tumbling Dice." Keith freaked out when he saw the sign outside the hall billboarding "Mick Jagger and the Rolling Stones."

The tour began to wind down in California. Bobby Keys and Nicky Hopkins joined the Stones for the finales of the huge Anaheim Stadium shows—listless disasters that the band tried to phone in. Keith was doing heroin again ("Hollywood—it always kills you in the end"), the crowd choked on the red dust of the baseball infield, and everyone said the shows sucked. Marsha Hunt's lawyers tried to seize Mick's money from these shows for unpaid child support.

The final Stones shows were in San Francisco. Keith wanted to keep the tour energy going, so the Stones and Ian McLagan stayed in L.A. and cut some tracks at an old haunt, RCA Studios in Hollywood. The sessions were closed, with only drummer Jim Keltner allowed in to hang with his pal Charlie Watts. Working from midnight on, the Stones cut a dozen songs, including the basic tracks of "Summer Romance" and "Where the Boys All Go." On his own, Keith cut a version of Jimmy Cliff's reggae anthem "The Harder They Come," with Ronnie on guitar, which would be the B side of "Run Rudolph Run" later in the year.

For a while, Keith, Woody, and Jo lived in a house rented from the Getty family. Keith and Ron bought pure Iranian heroin from a Los Angeles dealer named Cathy Smith and spent their time "chasing the dragon"—smoking fumes from smack cooking in foil. Keith dropped an ice pick on his bare foot while cutting chunks from an opium ball, but didn't seem to mind. Then Woody and Jo moved into a new house they'd bought in Mandeville Canyon, while Keith and Lil hid out in a house nearby. It caught fire while they were in bed one morning, and they had to climb out a window, naked. With fire engines wailing in the distance and Keith's ammunition exploding in the burning house, Keith and Lil were trying to cover themselves when a car pulled up, driven by a cousin of Anita's who lived nearby. They jumped into the car and disappeared just as the police arrived.

The Blind Angel

Autumn 1978. Keith Moon, the Who's volcanic drummer, the raucous Bacchus of London pop excess, overdosed on antidepressants after detoxing from drugs and alcohol. Bill Wyman and Charlie Watts went to the funeral representing the Stones, who all felt that they'd lost a friend.

By October, *Some Girls* had sold almost 4 million units. "Respectable" was released as a single, quickly followed by "Shattered" (with the quasi-reggae "Everything Is Turning to Gold" on the B side). To promote these, the Stones agreed to appear on American TV's premier venue—the opening show of that season's *Saturday Night Live,* in New York's NBC studios.

The show was in its fourth year and at the zenith of its hipness. Hot comedians John Belushi and Dan Aykroyd had spun their Blues Brothers skits into a hit album and a crack R&B homage band (with Steve Jordan on drums). It would be the Stones' first live television broadcast in ten years.

The Stones rehearsed with the *SNL* cast the first week in October, staying at the Plaza Hotel. But Olympian intoxication sabotaged this meeting of the gods. The Stones, especially Keith, proved incapable of delivering comedy lines, and the druggy skits involving the band were dropped. Regarding Keith, who could barely stand, let alone remember the single line he was given, cast member Laraine Newman observed dryly, "It's interesting to be standing there working with someone who's dead." The Stones guzzled Scotch and vodka and openly snorted lines of cocaine in the studio. The network's censor told producer Lorne Michaels that Mick would have to wear underwear for the broadcast because of the bulge problem. After hours, there was jamming and high-octane dope intake in Belushi's "vault," a soundproof music room in his apartment. On the day of the broadcast, the Stones showed up at NBC mostly drunk. Mick had rehearsed till he was hoarse, and they had to play "Beast" an octave lower so he could sing it. They played brilliantly at the dress rehearsal but choked at airtime, giving mediocre and nervous performances of "Miss You," "Beast of Burden," and "Shattered." Mick grossed out the nation by licking Ronnie's lips during a close-up at the microphone. The consensus at the show was that the Stones had blown it. *SNL* broadcast the Stones' better dress rehearsal tape when the show was rerun later that year.

––––––––

Ronnie Wood's daughter Leah was born later that month, just before her dark Uncle Keith had his big day in court. It was eighteen months after the Toronto busts, a period of strategic delays and legal maneuvering that had its denouement when Keith appeared in court on October 23, 1978. Supporting him were his girlfriend Lil and Canadian citizens Dan Aykroyd and Lorne Michaels. Press interest in the case had intensified after the Sex Pistols' recent disintegration on their first American tour, and the subsequent indictment of bassist Sid Vicious for murdering his American girlfriend in New York. The press gallery was jammed with reporters eager to report Keith Richards's sad downfall as well. But the detective who had arrested Keith had been killed in a car accident earlier in the year, and there were rumors that the Canadian government was embarrassed and that Keith might walk.

As the hearing began, the judge threw out some of the prosecution's evidence and declared Keith's arm-long rap sheet inadmissible. When the heroin trafficking and cocaine possession charges were also dropped, seasoned observers had the impression that a colossal and costly fix was in. After Keith made some properly contrite noises and pleaded guilty only to heroin possession, he received a year in jail, suspended to probation. Other wrist-slap conditions included continued drug treatment and a benefit concert for the Canadian Institute for the Blind within six months.

Keith raised his fist in the air when the judge was finished, immensely relieved he wasn't going to prison. Fists in the air and cheers outside the courtroom. The deal and the legal fees had cost him a reported $3 million, but he didn't care. The best part was who *really* got him off—if the legend is true.

Keith: "There was this little blind girl, Rita, following us around on the previous [1975] tour, and I asked the roadies to look after her . . . It turns out that this little girl knows or is related to the judge who's trying the case. So totally unbeknownst to me, she goes to see this judge at his home, tells him a simple story—how I've looked after her and all that, and the upshot is that he passes a ruling that as the major payment for this offense we have to play a free concert at this blind school. My blind angel came through, bless her heart." In addition, the sentence settled Keith's legal situation enough that he was ultimately able to get a green card, the permanent entry visa to live in the United States.

There was some outrage in Canada's conservative press and judiciary circles over the leniency of the sentence, and the government was forced to announce it would appeal. Things dragged on for another year, until the heat died down. Keith Richards has never been arrested since.

November 1978. Keith recuperated in Jamaica, then flew back to New York. Peter Tosh's *Bush Doctor* album was out and selling well along with its single, Peter and Mick duetting on "Don't Look Back." This gave the Stones massive new credibility in the music world because it seemed so right for the band that had helped rescue the blues to now use its resources to catalyze a new black music that inspired them. Tosh and his band were selling out their shows, playing the militant "rockers" style with astonishing drama and power, riding the true cutting edge of popular music. Mick caught their act at the Bottom Line in New York. When Tosh called on him to sing, Mick was bodily lifted up and passed over the heads of the audience from the back of the room to the stage. On December 12, Mick and Keith arrived at NBC, where Mick would sing "Don't Look Back" with Tosh on *Saturday Night Live*. There was a tumult of Rastas, comedians, and rock stars in the dressing room as Mick and Keith smoked a spliff with Tosh and posed for photographers. More spliffs, and Mick bounced around the nerveless Tosh as Sly and Robbie popped their rhythms. Then Mick disgraced Tosh (in the eyes of all watching Jamaicans) by licking Tosh's lips in a lunatic replay of his lingual assault on Wood a few weeks earlier.

On December 18, Keith went to a thirty-fifth-birthday party for himself in New York, then flew home for Christmas with Marlon and Anita. Airport photographers didn't recognize her. Bloated from alcohol, with stringy hair and gaps in her teeth, the hag who was once the toast of Europe staggered past them incognito.

The New Barbarians

January 1979. Jamaica was so politically unstable that reggae's international wing had to relocate. Chris Blackwell built a new recording studio at his Compass Point property in the Bahamas, where the Rolling Stones gathered that month to work on their next album, the hotly anticipated follow-up to *Some Girls*. The new album had cynical working titles like *Certain Women* and *More Fast Ones*. There was a lot left over from Paris the previous year: "Start Me Up" and "Claudine," with its funny chant "Clau-dine's back in jail again" to a rub-a-dub reggae beat, a little like what a new wave band called the Police was doing: a few bars of reggae whipped up in the chorus by a burst of rock rimfire. "Jah Is Not Dead" was another experiment with rockers-style reggae and R&B, Mick vocalizing in fake West Indian patois. Visiting San Francisco musician Boz Scaggs also played at that session. The tape features Mick angrily telling some coke-snorting hangers-on to leave the studio.

The Stones long disco-rock piece called "Dance" began as a Latin jam at Compass Point with Michael Shrieve playing percussion and Max Romeo on vocals. "I am what I am," Mick sang on the early versions, "and I know I've got my faults." He was fighting Bianca in court at the time; she wanted half of his estimated 10-million-pound fortune (she wouldn't get close). He was also battling Keith, who began to assert himself regarding production details he'd ignored during years of drug coma. The control-driven Mick Jagger couldn't believe Keith was back and wanted in, and often responded with eye-rolling contempt at his suggestions.

––––––––

Keith had to play his Canadian benefit concert by the end of April to fulfill his sentence. This coincided with Ron Wood having to promote *Gimme Some Neck,* his third solo album and his first for Columbia. The label, in a major coup for Wood, had loaned him the services of Bob Dylan and a new Dylan tune called "Seven Days," which Wood had recorded in Malibu, with Mick Fleetwood on drums. *Neck* was Wood's best record. Its songs about anxiety, reggae jams, Faces-style raunch, and acoustic interludes amounted to a proto-Stones album, since most of them played on it.

So Keith and Ronnie put together a road band, the New Barbarians (name courtesy of Neil Young; the "New" had to be tacked on when they learned there was already a Barbarians). The band included the two guitarists, Bobby Keys on sax, Ian McLagan on keys, Meters drummer Zigaboo Modeliste, and jazz-rock star Stanley Clarke on bass.

The New Barbarians rehearsed in Los Angeles in February 1979, playing all night at Wood's house in Mandeville Canyon as John Belushi laid out generous lines of the devil's dandruff. They were buying Persian Brown heroin from Belushi's friend Cathy Smith and chasing the dragon to relax. The comedian was also the master of ceremonies when the New Barbarians made their world debut in front of five thousand fans in Oshawa, Ontario, on April 29, opening for the Rolling Stones.

Belushi: "I'm just a sleazy actor on a late-night TV show, but here's some real musicians! Come on up here! Keith Richards! Ron Wood! The

New Barbarians—*go nuts!!*" Powered by one of the best drummers of the era, the New Barbs gave the basic Richards/Wood guitar attack a funky second-line hop. They did Wood's songs in a loose, jamming style, then powered up for Keith's numbers: "Happy" and "Before They Make Me Run." Both of these benefit shows concluded with the unrehearsed Stones, whose entire touring apparatus had been driven up from storage in Dallas for the only concerts the Stones would play anywhere that year.

The New Barbarians spent April and May on the road, selling out all their shows. Keith was traveling with his girlfriend Lil and played well almost every night, usually drinking a quart of vodka during the shows. He sang "Love in Vain" with Woody and did solo turns on Sam Cooke's "Let's Go Steady" and "Apartment #9" in the heartache style of his Toronto recordings. Living on alcohol and cocaine, Keith assumed a particularly spectral appearance as his hair began to gray and his face caved in, and rumors of his impending demise again spread through the music industry. Reporters who got backstage noted that the post-performance Keith looked like he'd just been crucified. Bobby Keys was redeeming himself after years of scuffling in bars. His playing on the big finale, "I Can Feel the Fire," was often the high point of the set. The tour ended at the Forum in Los Angeles on May 21. Expenses had been so lavish that Woody and Keith made no money, and *Gimme Some Neck* stiffed as well. Keith and Woody's brotherly bond began to strain under financial pressures and Wood's rapid ascent into drugdom's First Division.

————

On June 21, Anita was at home with her son and some houseguests, Fred Sessler's son Jeffrey and seventeen-year-old Scott Cantrell, a local kid Anita had taken in. Cantrell was lying in Anita's bed, watching television and toying with the .38 pistol that Keith had bought in Florida on the previous Stones tour. While supposedly playing Russian roulette, Cantrell shot himself in the head and died in what the headlines called Keith Richards's bed.

The police arrested Anita. They later cleared her of involvement with Cantrell's death but charged her with possession of stolen firearms.

Suddenly "Claudine" didn't seem so funny when Anita was looking at four years in prison. If the suicide weapon could be tied to Keith, no one knew what would happen. The New York papers smeared Anita with accusations of black magic, animal sacrifice, orgies with the local youth, witchcraft, and poor housekeeping. Keith called her from Paris, furious that she had lost his gun.

This was the final nail in the coffin of the Keith and Anita saga. Keith's life with Anita in all its bloody and sordid glory was the subject of Spanish Tony's recently published memoir, *Up and Down with the Rolling Stones,* which portrayed them as callous libertines and pathetic junkies. Keith's Canadian case had been reopened, to appeal the perceived leniency of his sentence, and that decision was hanging in the balance. His American visa was jeopardized, and now the lawyers warned him to stay clear. "That boy who shot himself in my house really ended it for us," Anita said later. "It was the end of our personal relationship." Separated from his family, Keith was virtually homeless. He spent most of the summer of 1979 hiding at Fred Sessler's house in Florida, and his long affair with Lil began to cool.

————

In the wake of *Some Girls'* massive success, there was a spurt of Stones-related music released that year. Another anthology, *Time Waits for No One,* featuring tracks from 1971 to 1977, was released in Europe as the last album due under the old WEA contract. The one true masterpiece of this era was Marianne Faithfull's *Broken English,* a harrowing song cycle about betrayal and decay, declaimed in a ravaged gravel-alto amid a ferociously new wave band setting. It was a stunning comeback for Marianne after years of living her Burroughsian dream of abject addiction and helplessness, an existential conceit that fundamentally worked out, considering the magisterial power of the *Broken English* music and persona. (Critic Camille Paglia claimed Marianne's album was one of the greatest works of art ever produced by a woman.) The title song was about the anarchist Baader-Meinhof gang in West Germany and burned with a low flame that caught the edgy, terror-obsessed mood of 1979, the year of the Red

Brigades. The searing "Why'd Ya Do It?" was perhaps the most directly penetrating song about infidelity ever written, and took enormous courage and skill to pull off. *Broken English* was an avant-garde sensation, one of the great Rolling Stones albums, even though none of them played on it.

Less successful were the other Stones-related records. *Gimme Some Neck* was followed by Mick Taylor's first solo album, *Leather Jacket*, a Big Statement album without any real songs. The title track was a bitter portrait of Keith and Anita, while the rest of the album sounded like familiar, recycled guitar moves. The third album in this continuum was Ian McLagan's *Troublemaker*, recorded in Los Angeles later that year.

In November, while Ron Wood was working on Mac's record in L.A., Bobby Keys brought something special to the studio one night. It was a new kind of cocaine, little rocks one cooked and smoked instead of snorted. One big toke provided a bolt of crystal-clear energy. It wore off a few minutes later: time for another hit. "Freebasing" cocaine was even more addictive than heroin, even more of a job, involving a chemistry set of retorts and burners that often exploded in the user's face. It was the immediate precursor of the crack epidemic that seriously threatened black culture later on.

Woody got totally addicted right away. John Belushi started freebasing at his house. Mac got totally hooked. The dope bills skyrocketed as *Troublemaker* was recorded in a haze of reggae smoke and the jivey backbeat of Faces rock and roll. Mac's album soon joined *Gimme Some Neck* and *Leather Jacket* in the bargain bins after its release the following year.

———

The Stones tensely finished the major recording for *Emotional Rescue* in Paris that fall.

They took their tapes to New York in November, mixing at Electric Lady. Epic struggles in the studio over mixes, levels, sequencing, everything. "Dance" was supposed to have been a Stones instrumental jam, but Mick insisted on putting words to it, writing what Keith derided as an opera. Keith: "It was supposed to just have this *minimal* lyric. Instead, Mick comes up with *Don Giovanni*." Huge fight over whether "All About You" or "Let's Go Steady" would be the token Keith song on the album. Stories of serious bad blood circulated around New York amid published (and denied) reports that Bill Wyman was leaving the Stones and that Ron Wood was killing himself with freebase. Mick took Keith's pithy criticisms in the studio as personal attacks and saw his primacy over the Stones threatened. Word got back to Keith that Mick wished out loud that Keith would go back to being a full-time junkie.

The seventies were all over now, and the Rolling Stones were tattered but erect. Bianca got her divorce and custody of Jade. Mick and Jerry bumped into her at Woody Allen's 1980 New Year's party in New York, and everyone got on well. Charlie and Stu were touring in a boogie-woogie revival band called Rocket 88. Bill Wyman was photographing his neighbor, artist Marc Chagall, in Provence. Ron Wood was making his next album with a glass pipe. Anita Pallenberg pleaded guilty to a reduced weapons charge and was fined. Marianne Faithfull stayed true to her vocation, refusing to give up her beloved drugs. Keith Richards remained the standard-bearer of the old rock star style. "I've *studied* this shit," he said of dope. "I'm a walking laboratory. I'm Baudelaire rolled in with a few other cats." But his tone, and his attitude, soon changed after he found a new girlfriend in New York, one who helped him grow into another way of living.

nine:
World War III

Mick Jagger and reggae star Peter Tosh share a smoke

backstage at Saturday Night Live, New York, 1979.

We were just tired of being the Rolling Stones, and since we couldn't find a way out, we started fighting and smashing it all to pieces. If we made it through the eighties, we can go on forever.

Keith Richards

From the Neck Down

Keith Richards was thirty-six years old on December 18, 1979. His old London friend David Courts made him a silver skull ring as a present, a grinning death's head that became a trademark, emblematic of its owner's precarious address on the edge of mortality. Keith was wearing the ring at the birthday party held for him the night he met his wife.

She was a twenty-two-year-old model named Patti Hanson. She was a wholesome, bright-looking blonde with lovely eyes and a perfect smile. She had been modeling since she was sixteen, had been in a couple of movies, was one of that year's top models in New York. She was the youngest daughter of a religious family from Staten Island, very intelligent and sweet, and mutual friends had been trying to fix her up with Keith for weeks. Playing Cupid, Jerry Hall had invited her to Keith's party at the Roxy Roller Disco, but Anita had also showed up in case Keith wanted to come back to his family in the wake of breaking up with Lil.

Keith called Patti a few days later and she joined his midnight entourage—Fred Sessler, poet Jim Carroll, Max Romeo, and assorted Rastas—in lightning raids by limo on Trax, restaurants, crash pads, and obscure reggae shops in Brooklyn and the Bronx. Patti Hanson started to really like this guy. He was kind to her, didn't bother her for sex, seemed to want a friend more than anything else. She saw he needed someone to keep away the dope dealers who pestered him day and night. It wasn't exactly love at first sight, but on the last day of 1979, she went home to Staten Island to be with her family. When she returned after midnight, she found Keith sitting on the steps of her apartment building, waiting for her in the cold. After that, with this American girl at his side, Keith's worst days were behind him. She even gave him a set of keys to her apartment.

Supposedly off heroin, Keith had been scoring dope in secret armed forays to Eighth Avenue by himself, buying just enough to keep going. Patti helped him clean up after he moved in with her in March 1980. "After ten years of trying to kill myself," Keith reported, "I decided I'd better get on with my life." Keith again switched his addiction to a more socially acceptable alcoholism. Patti kept the dealers away, and even old comrades like Fred Sessler were taboo for a while. Keith was dead drunk the first time he met Patti's parents, who weren't thrilled their girl had brought home the prince of darkness. But as their affair stabilized into domestic routine, Keith actually managed to stay off smack.

But people could only shake their heads about Ron Wood, raving freebase fiend. In January 1980, he and Jo were busted on the Caribbean island of St. Martin with 260 grams of cocaine. After three days, they were released and deported without being charged, after they complained that the police had planted the coke in their rented house. Five years after joining the Stones, Wood was impoverished from keeping up with Keith's and Mick's lavish styles while earning less than half of what the other Stones made. His drug use so enfeebled him that he spent the next five years expecting to be fired at any moment.

Bill Wyman told the press he was quitting the band in 1982. At a dinner party in New York, Mick Jagger told Warhol and Burroughs that the Stones probably wouldn't be around for the band's twentieth anniversary. Charlie Watts, now famous in certain English country circles as a sheepdog breeder, told an interviewer that rock and roll was just a load of bollocks anyway, and he hated playing it.

———

The early-1980 skirmishes of the War of the Stones began in various Manhattan studios as Mick and Keith traded volleys while they mixed their next album, *Emotional Rescue,* that spring. Keith chafed at

Mick's autocratic control over the band and its hundred employees. Mick hated dealing with Keith in his often-incoherent, ratchet-knife-flicking state. Keith wanted to go on the road, while Mick wanted to go on vacation. The band wanted "Claudine" on the album, but the lawyers said it was libelous and the song was killed. Keith almost took "All About You" off the album as well, fearing he'd stolen the melody from something he'd heard on the radio. The only thing they agreed on was the first single, "Emotional Rescue," which was released in June 1980 with "Down in the Hole" on the B side. Despite its fey, quasi-reggae structure, the song defied some pessimistic predictions and was a Top Ten record in America and Europe in the summer of 1980.

The *Emotional Rescue* album was also released that month. Eclectic and sometimes daring, it turned out to be a genre-crossing experiment that honorably ignored its obvious opportunities as the sequel to *Some Girls*. Keith and Ron Wood's "Dance" began the album as an attempt to fuse rock's dynamics and spaciousness to the disco format. Mick locates the album on the corner of 8th Street and Sixth Avenue in the opening lines, continuing the Londoner-in-Gotham ambience of their previous album. "Dance" introduced a newly martial Stones persona, backed by Bobby Keys's growling, multitracked saxes. It had the epic feeling of a sound track to a war movie and seemed to launch the Rolling Stones into the 1980s with an almost militant seriousness.

Rescue continued as a sometimes-bizarre mélange of styles. "Summer Romance" was fast and punky. "I'm a serious man with serious lusts," Mick bawled, "and have to do away with this crucifix stuff." An original Stones reggae song followed, "Send It to Me," Charlie having finally figured out reggae rhythm, with Ron Wood playing bass. "Let Me Go" was a country rocker with Woody playing pedal steel guitar and Keith applying some Jamaican "dub-style" mixing techniques. Side one ended with the bizarre lament "Indian Girl." Set in the Nicaragua of the Sandinista era as guitars strum, a marimba bubbles, and Jack Nitzsche's mariachi horns blare horribly, "Indian Girl" was Mick's sympathetic depiction of a revolution struggling against Yankee aggression, delivered in a series of absurd accents and skewed viewpoints. Critics and fans agreed that "Indian Girl" was one of the strangest things the Stones had ever done.

Side two: "Where the Boys Go" was more yobbo punk, music for soccer hooligans. Stu played piano, and there were some synthetic "girls" singing on the tag in what sounded like a chorus from the musical *Grease*. Keith played the blues on "Down in the Hole" as Sugar Blue wailed on harp and Mick went "down in the gut-tah" with his tale of trading sex for cigarettes and nylons in the American zone.

"Emotional Rescue" was set behind the surreal scrim of Mick's African "covered voice" falsetto, sung to a rub-a-dub reggae-disco format previously unknown to mankind. Stu played electric piano, Wood played bass, and Bobby Keys's sax entered during the vocal shift when Mick started his barefaced hokum (ad-libbed in the studio) about coming to Jerry Hall's emotional rescue on a fine Arab charger. This was followed by "She's So Cold," a tepid but sweet rocker that had evolved from an enervated studio jam in the Bahamas.

Keith Richards's "All About You" closed *Emotional Rescue* in what was widely interpreted as a devastating kiss-off to Anita Pallenberg. "So sick and tired of dogs like you—the first to get laid—always the last bitch to get paid." As the quiet ballad reached its climax, Keith audibly choked himself up and moaned, "So how come I'm still in love with you?"

———

The Stones spent the early summer of 1980 doing press interviews at their office at 75 Rockefeller Plaza in New York. Mick, dressed in pastel summer cottons, offered clipped bromides about *Rescue,* which he described as a piss-taking pastiche and the chaotic result of two years of recording. He said rock and roll was "a false vision" as a powerful social force and answered queries about whether Keith actually helped produce *Rescue* with, "You've *got* to be joking." Keith received the press with an open bottle of Jack Daniel's, generous helpings of snowy Peruvian crystals, and flamboyant flourishes of his ratchet knife. Stone drunk for many of his interviews, Keith often put a framed photo of Charlie Watts in front of his interrogators, explaining that Charlie *was* the Rolling Stones. After manfully fending off rumors about infighting among the band and Bill Wyman's supposed retirement, Keith inevitably had to answer questions on "All About You." He parried these by saying the song was about his constantly farting dalmatian, hence all the dog references in the song. Bobby Keys and others close to Keith thought the song was as much about Mick Jagger as about Anita.

Emotional Rescue was really hated by the British press. *New Musical Express* slagged the record as "devoid of passion, bloated with clumsy posing and artifice."

Even a revitalized John Lennon put down the Stones in an interview published in *Playboy:* "They're still congratulating the Stones for being together 112 years. Whoopee! At least Charlie's still got his family. In the Eighties they'll be asking, 'Why are these guys still together? Can't they hack it on their own? Why do they have to be surrounded with a gang? Is the little leader frightened someone's gonna knife him in the back?' . . . They'll be showing pictures of the guy with lipstick wriggling his ass and the four guys with the evil black make-up trying to look raunchy. That's gonna be the joke in the future. Being in a gang is great when you're a certain age. But when you're in your forties and you're still in one, it just means you're still 18 in the head."

———

Late in July, Mick took Jerry to Morocco for his birthday and telexed Keith in New York that the Stones wouldn't tour that year. Keith was livid but powerless to do anything about it.

———

October 1980. The Rolling Stones convening in Paris, decided to tour America in 1981 and Europe the next year. Peter Rudge was out as tour director, replaced by Bill Graham. With the tour on and a new album needed, engineer Chris Kimsey, who always taped everything if a Stone was working in the studio, told the feuding Stones that he could pull together an album's worth of songs from existing outtakes and lyric-less instrumental tracks already in the can. Later that month, they started work at Pathé-Marconi on "Start Me Up," transforming it from a reggae tune to a ballsy, anthemic rocker.

They worked in Paris for much of November, fieldstripping old songs and recycling less-than-magic riffs from the Stones archive. One day a technician asked Charlie Watts about some old bits of confetti stuck under the rims of the drummer's snares and tom-toms. "Hyde Park, 1969," Charlie deadpanned without missing a beat, as the startled roadie realized that Watts had never bothered to change his drumheads.

John Lennon was assassinated by a fan outside his Central Park West home on December 8, 1980, an event that deeply traumatized the Stones along with everyone else. Bill Wyman called a New York radio station from his house in France to vent his feelings over the air. When Mick returned to New York, he started carrying a gun.

Like Punk Never Happened

January 1981. Appalled at his deafening, block-rocking, arena-grade sound system, Keith Richards's neighbors tried to get him evicted from the downtown Manhattan flat he shared with Patti Hanson. Mick Jagger was in Peru filming Werner Herzog's gonzo conquistador epic *Fitzcarraldo* (Mick's first movie role in twelve years), but production was delayed when Amazon headhunters attacked the jungle location. Mick quit the film when Herzog's reshoot conflicted with the Stones' tour later that year.

In March, Rolling Stones Records released *Sucking in the Seventies,* a subpar anthology of late-decade tracks with a remix of "Dance Pt. 2" and a live "When the Whip Comes Down" from a 1978 theater gig. A long instrumental version of "Dance" was also issued on a twelve-inch single, closer in spirit to the stirring, thematic Richards/Wood rock-disco experiments of 1979.

That same month, Mick and Keith and their women met up in Barbados to plan the upcoming tours and work on song lyrics. Mick and Jerry went on to Mustique, a tiny private island in the eastern Caribbean, an exclusive tropical getaway for British aristocracy and millionaires. Mick would soon build a winter vacation home there. Keith worked on reggae crooner Max Romeo's album *Holding Out My Love to You* with Sly and Robbie at Channel One studio in Kingston, and kept an eye on Peter Tosh, who was about to release his third album for the Stones' label. Tosh's lung-busting ganja habit was making him increasingly deranged, and Bob Marley's death from cancer that May sent him off the deep end. He started waving a scimitar in his shows and had a guitar made in the shape of a machine gun. Tosh correctly predicted that he would be the next major reggae star to die.

Tattoo (the original title; "You" was added at the last moment by Mick) was in rush-job production. Chris Kimsey had been digging in the vaults, rounding up old riffs and ideas from as far back as Jamaica ten years earlier. Finding songs like "Waiting On a Friend" from the *Goat's Head Soup* and *Black and Blue* sessions, he added outtakes from the 1977–79 Paris sessions. When he had enough for an album, Kimsey gave the tapes to Mick, who quickly threw them together: "I recorded some of it in a broom closet, literally, when we did the vocals. The rest of the band were hardly involved."

Mick also supervised the saxophone overdubs in New York by Sonny Rollins, the hard-bop saxophone improviser who played in various styles on several tracks. Rollins got the inspiration for his melodic solo on "Waiting On a Friend" by asking Jagger to dance for him while he played, translating Mick's body language into jazz. The finished tracks were mixed uniformly by engineer Bob Clearmountain so the new Stones album didn't sound like the touring-fodder grab bag that it was.

———

In June, most of the Stones were in New York. They saw Jimmy Cliff's show at the Ritz nightclub, where a few days later Keith and Patti went backstage to greet Chuck Berry after one of his shows.

Drunk-looking Keith came up behind Chuck and pawed him—"Chuck, man, how ya doin'?"—whereupon the irascible legend whirled around and punched Keith in the face before storming out. Keith, eyes blackened, was philosophical: "He didn't recognize me." Berry later apologized to Ron Wood, thinking he was Keith.

With the tour starting in September and the band rusty after three years off the road, the Stones needed a place to regroup and rehearse. Late in July, Stu and Alan Dunn checked out Longview Farm, a studio complex in the quiet central Massachusetts countryside. A week later, Keith flew up to inspect the place, and liked the homey, farmlike vibe so much he crashed for three days.

Bringing their families, the Rolling Stones arrived at Longview Farm in Brookfield, Massachusetts, toward the middle of August and began six weeks of rehearsals, costume fittings, and business meetings with the burgeoning Stones tour staff and financial empire. The stadium-size tour would be seen by 2 million fans and gross $50 million. Newly designed merchandise—T-shirts, belt buckles, tongue decals—would bring in another $10 million. An obscure perfume company, Jovan, coughed up $4 million in production costs. This was one of the first rock tour sponsorship deals, which allowed Jovan to plaster the logo of their cheap fragrances over everything. Bill Graham Presents ran the tour with its massive apparatus—three stages, fleets of trucks, and huge crew—in a military-style operation designed to get the artists onstage in a contented frame of mind. Despite past battles, Graham still seemed to worship the Rolling Stones. "Wherever they went," he later said, "was the rock and roll capital of the world on that day."

Mick, his daughter Jade, and Jerry settled in at the farm, with Mick taking morning jogs along the country lanes. Bill and Astrid flew in from France, while the Watts family came in from England. Ron Wood and his family arrived a little later, with Woody in frail condition, barely able to play. Keith told him bluntly that his job in the band was in jeopardy if he didn't get himself together. Mick gave Ron an ultimatum that no hard drugs be present at the farm. Ian McLagan, playing keyboards on the tour, noted that Woody, hopelessly addicted to freebasing, was puffing base-laced cigs in the studio when he thought no one was around. A rumor circulated that boogie guitar expert George Thorogood, whose band the Destroyers would open many of the Stones' shows, would take Ron Wood's place on the tour if Woody proved too schwacked to play.

The Stones rehearsed on a specially built stage at the end of Longview's open-beamed barn, playing on small combo amplifiers without the usual Marshall stacks of amps. Ted Jones's tenure as Keith's guitar valet was over, and now all the instruments—the black Telecasters tuned to open G, the venerable Gibson Les Pauls from the sixties, the priceless customized Sunburst and rosewood Teles, the Stratocasters and Broadcasters, the Epiphones, Bill Wyman's basses—were handled by tech Alan Rogan. This would be the first completely wireless tour for the Stones, the guitars now free of electric cable forever.

On August 26, Mick announced the upcoming tour at a press conference in Philadelphia, where it would begin. A few days later, *Tattoo You* was released, and it was like punk never happened. The grandiose three-note riff of "Start Me Up" erupted from car radios all over America as a clarion blast from the past. It was the Stones calling in the faithful for a revival of classic rock values, and their audience responded by making the single no. 1 for nine weeks in the United States.

"Start Me Up" had begun as reggae. The Stones had cut twenty takes of it on the same night in the spring of 1978 that they recorded "Miss You." Only one take was done rock style, but it was the one Chris Kimsey salvaged. Growling, rubbery guitars were overdubbed, and Mick bawled out new lyrics about a girl who could make a grown man cry and make a dead man come. The next track, "Hang Fire," was also from 1978, an acid portrait of a lazy and backward England with a falsetto chorus and Stu on piano. "Slave" was a remixed *Black and Blue* track from 1974, with another hoodoo falsetto vocal and Sonny Rollins's tenor sax. Keith Richards's "Little T&A" was a cheerfully callous love song to Patti Hanson—"tits and ass with soul"—with minimalist guitars and a dub-style Keith mix at the end. "Black Limousine" was another old Paris track, with three guitars and Ian McLagan on keys. In 1981, it got a new guitar solo by Ron (who received a songwriting credit) and a strange harp part by Mick Jagger. *Tattoo You*'s first side ended with the New York saga of "Neighbors," the only new song on the record, inspired by Keith's community relations problems in his downtown 'hood, illustrated by Sonny Rollins's perfectly cubist, cutup sax solo.

"Worried About You" began side two with a remixed song that first surfaced in Munich in 1974 and was then revived in Paris five years later. Mick's original "Fool to Cry" falsetto got a new descant vocal from Keith, who was himself learning to sing again. "Tops" was a remix of a great Jamaica-era outtake, a brilliant conflation of cynicism and poignancy about the old show business come-on: "I'll take you to the top." (Mick Taylor heard himself playing guitar on "Tops" and later had to sue the Stones to receive his royalties.) "Heaven" came next, with its Latin mood and seductive falsetto mutterings, followed by "No Use in Crying" from the Compass Point sessions. Ron Wood got his unprecedented second songwriting credit for coming up with its bluesy melody.

Tattoo You ended with "Waiting On a Friend," from Jamaica in 1972. A perverse cha-cha with Billy Preston on piano and Sonny Rollins blowing tenor on the fade, "Friend" was not only an instant classic but also a clever attempt to repair the sleazy and feuding image of the Stones as they were about to make some real money again on the road.

It worked. *Tattoo You,* with its comic-art cover of a tribally tatted Mick Jagger, sold almost a million copies in America during the first week of September 1981 and became the Rolling Stones' first simultaneous no. 1 album in the U.S. and U.K. in years.

Who Are the Rolling Stones?

September 1981. Deep in tour rehearsals at Longview Farm in autumnal, maple-red Massachusetts, the Rolling Stones tried to get it together one more time. Mick Jagger, cementing his hard-won rep as rock music's ultimate showman, carried a calculator and appointment book around the farm, taking meetings, telling Woody's old lady, Jo, to keep her "brats" (Jesse and Leah) out of his face. Keith turned a basement room into his pool hall and barroom, where he and Woody drank, jammed, and complained about "Brenda," one of their many names for the prissy, diffident Jagger. Mick had insisted the musicians sign a "no dope at the gigs" clause in their tour contracts, and Keith, who hated freebase, had personally guaranteed that Ron Wood wouldn't use base on the tour. Another clause provided that Mick stay completely off the stage while Keith did his single number of the set, "Little T&A." Mick had made a lot of unilateral decisions about the tour that annoyed Keith. He didn't like the cheap-looking Japanese pop art stage sets. He didn't care about the film and cable TV rights Jagger was selling, and didn't think the Stones were in any shape to do a concert film. He was irked that Mick refused to hire Bobby Keys for the tour and instead had signed up Ernie Watts, a black reed player with a big, muscular tone (from Quincy Jones's Los Angeles studio team). Keith despised Mick's industrial "cherry picker," a crane-mounted bucket that would project Mick way over the heads of the kids in the stadium shows like a ludicrous pop preacher. This was such a sore point that Mick tried to leverage Keith with it, offering to lose the cherry picker if Keith promised there would be no hard drugs on the tour. The cherry picker stayed in the show.

The band's huge entourage and visitors to the farm were all told not to give any drugs to Wood, who was in disgrace. Even Ian McLagan thought Wood a risky gamble on this tour. His per diem allowance was too small to buy drugs. Mick wouldn't even talk to him. When Woody staggered into an interview Keith was giving, he was ordered to disappear. "That's one boy," Keith muttered in disgust, "who hasn't got much longer the way he's going." Keith himself was guzzling rivers of vodka. His cocaine was flown in on a private plane once a week. He fell off a porch in the middle of a six-day binge, and it was feared for a horrid few hours that he'd broken his ankle, aborting the tour. But it was just a sprain, and painkillers were not in short supply.

Despite, or because of, the internal hatreds, the Stones started to roar like a Ferrari once again, and gradually the tour set cohered on a hundred-foot rehearsal stage. "Under My Thumb" started the show, a relaxed reading that got the band into a Memphis-sounding soul groove before Mick came out and began to sing. "When the Whip Comes Down" came next in murderous style, an incredible blast of energy in shattered mode. Ernie Watts on horn powered "Just My Imagination." Ian Stewart pounded the grand piano for Eddie Cochran's "Twenty Flight Rock" before Charlie went into the tom-tom Motown beat of the Miracles' "Going to A Go Go." A rocket-fueled "Satisfaction" was the lone encore, with scraping, riffing guitars that vulcanized football stadiums all over the country. Tickets for the tour were priced at $15, and astute rock tycoon Mick Jagger wanted his customers to get their dollar's worth.

———

On September 14, "Blue Monday and the Cockroaches" played a "surprise" gig at 350-seat Sir Morgan's Cove in nearby Worcester, Massachusetts. Five thousand fans showed up in jeans and black leather, and a riot was averted only when the club opened its doors so an abridged Stones set could be heard in the streets. The mayor of Boston banned two more small warm-up gigs at the Orpheum Theater. After another week of run-throughs, the Stones flew to Philadelphia, where they began a three-month, fifty-one-city American tour with a mistake-filled open rehearsal in front of eighty thousand fans that got clunker reviews in the press and demoralized everyone.

But as the Stones careered around the East Coast on their rented Boeing 707 jet, they found their sonic thing again. They were playing in front of giant stylized cartoons of guitars, race cars, and records (designed by Kazuhide Yamazari, the Warhol of Tokyo). A giant arc of colored balloons arched over the stage, which fell among the musicians during "Satisfaction." Mick played in sports gear—baseball jackets, football pants, big numbered shirts, kneepads. In the sweaty finale, he danced in a spectacular flag cape, fashioned out of a Union Jack and the Stars and Stripes by designer Giorgio di Sant'Angelo, which to some cynics seemed like a tacit endorsement of the go-for-broke right-wing politics of the new

Reagan-Thatcher era. Keith was resplendent in silver skull ring and steel handcuff bracelet, his unspeakable blue jeans tucked into his favorite Sherwood Forest brown suede boots, which Keith refused to go onstage without. A bandana kept Keith's salty hair off his face as, performing without heroin for the first tour in years, he began to play with his old passion again.

By the time the Stones reached the Fox Theater in Atlanta in mid-October, *Tattoo You* was no. 1 and the show was really clicking. The two guitars fought a saber duel in the hellacious "Shattered" as Bill Wyman's bass line churned a backwash of irresistibly funky bottom. "Twenty Flight Rock" and "Go Go" were the flash curios of the set as the Rolling Stones seemed intent on proving they were still the tits. If Charlie held the beat back, Keith would jump up on his drum riser and flail his playing arm until Charlie had to smile, give up, and kick the band up another notch.

As the tour moved around the land, attracting plenty of media attention (but without the frenzy of previous eras), the question now arose: Who are the Rolling Stones? Critic Robert Palmer tried to answer this with the sympathy of an old-school Stones fan: "They're a grown-up rock and roll band, with fans ranging in age from under ten to sixty and more, and with a history as rich and various as the histories of the early bluesmen and first generation rockers they've always admired. They have something else in common with those blues singers and early rockers, too: they have their dignity."

————

Various bands opened for the Stones: Van Halen, Heart, the Neville Brothers, Etta James, J. Geils, the Stray Cats, the Fabulous Thunderbirds, George Thorogood and the Destroyers. Thorogood was said to be rehearsing the Stones' set in secret in case Ronnie got fired or crapped out, an issue that came to a head in a California hotel when Keith heard a rumor (probably from Jo) that Ronnie was freebasing again and diddling girls in a floater suite. "I'd *guaranteed* he wouldn't do this shit," Keith said later, "and then I found out he was up there doing it." In a rage, Keith headed for the elevator, with Patti, Jo, Stones executive Jane Rose, and a few security guys trying to talk him out of murdering Woody. "My old lady was going, 'Keith, don't make a scene.' And by the time I'd gotten [to Wood's room], she'd ripped the back of my shirt off." Keith barged in with his shirt in shreds and a vigilante squad behind him. He took hold of Wood—"You stupid fucker!"—and punched him hard in the nose.

Keith: "The next day, Ronnie and I had a bit of a *hah-hah,* and it was all over." The little fight at least cleared the air, with both guitarists playing better together for the rest of the tour.

A new act called Prince opened shows for the Stones on some of the Southern California dates. Prince sang falsetto and spun like a dervish. Jagger thought he was totally hot. At the Los Angeles Coliseum on October 9, Prince came out wearing only a black knit bikini bottom, a tiny elfin boy in what looked like a pair of panties. The Stones, incredulous, watched the video feed in their dressing room (Charlie: "Cor! 'E's in his bloody *underwear!*") as a barrage of cans and homophobic curses started flying toward the stage. Prince stayed on for five minutes while flying objects and food landed around him. Then he was booed off the stage. The next night, he lost the black bikini and wore some clothes, but was still hit by fruit and a roasted chicken a few minutes into his act. He left the stage and the tour, abandoning five more gigs opening for the Stones, whose audience clearly hated him.

November 5, 1981. Tina Turner, shed of Ike and basking in solo stardom, opened for the Stones at their stadium shows in New Jersey's Giants Stadium. She came out at the end of the Stones' set to sing "Honky Tonk Women" with the man she taught to dance back in 1965.

After a month touring the Midwest, the Stones fetched up in Chicago. Before a run of three nights at the Rosemont Horizon, they showed up at the Checkerboard Lounge on the South Side to jam with Muddy Waters. On a crowded stage with Buddy Guy and Junior Wells, they backed Muddy as he ran through "Mannish Boy," "Long Distance Call," "Hoochie Coochie Man," and "Baby Please Don't Go." Keith: "For that gig, Ronnie and I dressed up in white shirts and black vests, like really going to work. When we play[ed] with Muddy Waters, we dressed for business." Sitting on a stool surrounded by his acolytes, Muddy was a magisterial presence in what was his last recorded performance, forty years after Alan Lomax turned up at his cabin in the Delta. Lung cancer had struck Muddy Waters, and he died at home in Chicago in 1983. The Stones sent a huge floral arrangement to his funeral with a note that read, "In memory of a wonderful man dear to us all. We shall never forget you Muddy."

———

December 1981. Immense crowds at the Silverdome in Pontiac, Michigan, and the Superdome in New Orleans, where the Stones threw a party on a Mississippi riverboat. Film director Hal Ashby, famous for *Harold and Maude, The Last Detail, Coming Home,* and extreme Hollywood drug use, joined the tour with a movie crew to shoot the Stones' Phoenix-area show in 35mm for a concert film. After a near-perfect show at Sun Devil Stadium (during which Keith tried to brain a stage-crasher with his guitar), Ashby overdosed on drugs at the party in Mick's suite and was carried out of the hotel on a stretcher with an IV needle in his arm.

The next night, Mick Taylor joined his old band in Kansas City for a chilly onstage reunion. The tour was almost over now, and the Stones were beat, but there was just enough petrol in the tank for the last two shows in Hampton Roads, Virginia. The first, on Keith's thirty-eighth birthday (December 18), was broadcast nationally on the HBO cable TV network. Directed by a recovered Hal Ashby, the show started with a Dionysian "Under My Thumb," after which Mick, nervously pacing the immense stadium stage, urged his national television audience to get drunk and smoke joints. It was a long way from Ed Sullivan on Sunday night.

The Stones cracked on with "When the Whip Comes Down," which hit like a heat wave, then played a long version of their show, augmented by Bobby Keys on "Brown Sugar" as Mick flew like a hydraulic angel over the seething crowd. Introducing the band, he called out Charlie Watts, who always got a huge cheer. Then the inevitable: "Ernie Watts on saxophone—no relation." After Mick had the big crowd sing "Happy Birthday" to Keith, they ended with "Satisfaction," the whole band riffing hard as Mick testified: "Luv ya, luv ya, luv ya, got ta leave ya. Wo-yay! Wo-yay! Wo-yay! Wo-yay! Good night everybody—thank you!"

And, with a wave, they were gone. Real gone, since the fractious 1980s would see "ism and schism," dissolution and spite within the Rolling Stones, and it would be eight years before they toured America again. There was a party backstage after the broadcast for Keith and Bobby Keys. Keith cut the cake. The next night, the last show of the tour, Keith gave Bill Graham a package wrapped in newsprint with a single rose attached. The gift was the brown boots he'd worn every night, good-luck seven-league boots patched with tape and holed through the sole, as tattered and beat-looking as their former owner.

Hijacking
the Cherry Picker

MTV changed the music business in America in 1982, and although the aging Rolling Stones never made a huge impact on youth market video, MTV had a huge impact on the Stones. Traditionally musicians had always traveled to their audiences to sell their music. Now, with a video in heavy rotation to a select audience, a band could appear before several million fans several times per day. For rich bands like the Stones, video obviated the ancient need to keep moving or die. MTV also became a major launching pad for solo stars: Madonna, Bruce Springsteen, Prince, and—in epic fashion—Michael Jackson, whose *Thriller* album became the biggest seller in recording history on the strength of short- and long-form videos. Among the video audience, bands became almost passé. The video revolution's cameras loved a face more than a band, a fact not lost on ever-ambitious Mick Jagger as the Stones' record contract was about to come on the market again. The fallout from all this would cripple the Stones in the 1980s and lead to damaging public rancor.

———

The year began with bad feelings between Mick and Keith over their executive assistant, Jane Rose, who had worked for the band since 1974. Mick had fired her at the end of 1981, and Keith had immediately hired her to look after his affairs as his manager. This made Mick crazy, and the more authority Keith gave Jane, the angrier Mick became. "If I'd given up on Jane," Keith said later, "I could have maybe kept the Stones together. It actually got down to things like that."

In London on April 28, Mick announced the Euro leg of the Stones' tour at a press conference. Ian McLagan was replaced on keyboards by Chuck Leavell from Macon, Georgia, late of the Allman Brothers Band. Leavell had been recommended to Mick by Bill Graham, and he'd first played with the Stones at their Fox Theater shows in Atlanta the year before. A facile musician and amiable team player, Leavell would become Mick Jagger's long-term arranger and accompanist. Ernie Watts was replaced by Bobby Keys, finally brought in from the cold at Keith's insistence, along with trumpeter Gene Barge.

———

The tour began at the end of May in Scotland with the same show as the American tour. George Thorogood and the J. Geils Band opened many of the shows, with Thorogood again prepared to go on if Woody broke down. Mick openly wanted Wood out, and banished him from the Stones' hotels in case his drug use drew police attention. Keith kept him in the band out of loyalty and bloody-mindedness in the face of Jagger's disdain. On May 31, they played the tiny 100 Club in Oxford Street, nearly twenty years after their Soho debut as the Rollin' Stones in 1962. Then on through stadiums and soccer fields in the Low Countries, Germany, France (a rocking "Chantilly Lace" added to the Paris dates), and Scandinavia (body searches at the Swedish border) in June before they landed back in London for two crucial shows at Wembley Stadium.

Keith and Mick did a round of interviews for the Wembley concerts.

With J. Geils and the reggae bands Third World and Black Uhuru opening, both shows sold out, much to the relief of the Stones. Mick complained (with a wink) that Princess Diana's new baby, William, was
stealing the Stones' limelight. Keith was asked how he was approaching
the Stones' big Wembley homecoming and quipped, "From Heathrow."
He continued to stubbornly defend his heroin addiction. "I don't like to
regret heroin," he told the *Evening Standard,* "because I learned a lot from
it. I'd regret it if I'd OD'd." Keith did regret Ron Wood's drug habit. At the
second Wembley show, when Keith forgot the changes to "She's So Cold"
and Wood failed to cover for him because he was spaced out, Keith
charged over and punched Ron hard in the face, nearly knocking the
drowsy guitarist off the stage, drawing a rousing cheer from fans in front.
The Stones got good reviews in England for the first time in years, and
the concerts were chalked up as victories for the band.

Keith hadn't seen his father in twenty years. While in London,
prompted by Patti Hanson, he was finally moved to renew contact. Bert
Richards, now in his seventies, an old tippler in a cloth cap who drank
even more than his son, had mellowed as well, and he immediately became a cosseted fixture in Keith's entourage. Keith astounded the crew
when he even offered his dad a slice of his sacrosanct shepherd's pie, the
classic English dish of mashed potatoes, ground beef, and gravy that was
the daily staple of Keith's touring diet. (Keith once pointed a loaded gun
at a roadie who had unknowingly tasted Keith's private pie.) Bert soon
started moving around with Keith and Marlon as they commuted between England, Jamaica, and New York.

The 1982 tour lasted through July. Mick and Keith weren't speaking
at all. When Jagger ranked on J. Geils's singer, Peter Wolf, for always
hanging out in Keith's room, Keith bitterly told Wolf, "That's a fair example of the kind of cunt I've had to deal with for twenty-five years." In
Norway, Keith hijacked Mick's cherry picker and played a long aerial guitar break while Jagger fumed below, ordering poor Ron Wood to somehow get Keith down. In Sweden, Keith collapsed, drunk, during "Beast"
and played the solo on his back, smoking a cigarette.

These final 1982 shows proved to be the last of the old-style Rolling

Bill Wyman married Mandy Smith in 1989. From left: Jo Howard, Patti Hanson, Shirley Watts, Jerry Hall, Keith, Ron, Mick, and Charlie.

Mick Jagger recording the Master Musicians
of Jajouka at Palais Ben Abou. Tangier, Morocco,
May 1989.

Dogging it during the *Voodoo Lounge* era at Ron Wood's
Irish farm, 1994.

Mick Taylor, still playing the blues. Martha's Vineyard, 2000.

Mick Jagger in Chicago, 1997.

Mr. Keith Richards, of late.

Old Gods prepare to traverse their bridges to Babylon,
Toronto, 1997.

Stones concerts, featuring the core band, keyboards, and a horn or two. When they started playing again late in the decade, the shows were transformed into immense spectacles with operatic stages, a chorale of backup singers, brass quartets, and a glitzy Las Vegas aura. Something precious was gone forever.

———

Autumn 1982. A London publisher signed up Mick Jagger's ghostwritten autobiography for a million pounds. The advance would later be returned when Mick supposedly couldn't remember anything of interest. Jerry Hall wanted to get married, but Mick couldn't be bothered. Soon she was seen in public with a portly, horse-owning plutocrat who, Jerry intimated, could buy and sell Mick with a phone call. Mick fled to New York, where he went out with a local debutante and, reportedly, actress Valerie Perrine.

In November, the Stones returned to Pathé-Marconi in Paris to begin work on their last album for Atlantic. Ahmet Ertegun wasn't interested in re-signing for the demanded tens of millions, and Mick was being courted by the flamboyant, shpritzing CBS Records chief Walter Yetnikoff, who wanted the Stones, plus Mick's much-rumored solo career. Back in their favorite room, the Stones and Stu ran through their stash of old material. Not much was left after *Tattoo You* had scraped the barrel, so Mick and Keith began writing in a rented basement room. They put "Wanna Hold You" together, with Mick playing drums and Keith singing. Mick was reading William Burroughs's visionary new sci-fi novel *Cities of the Red Night,* which would inspire the psychic template for the dance club politics of "Undercover of the Night," which Mick was working out on guitar by himself. Ron Wood had a promising track that the band worked on. Its creator's low status in the Stones was evident in the working title someone scrawled on the tape can: "Dog Shit."

On November 12, Jerry Hall flew in from New York, fresh from two months of horsey escapades and headlines. Mick started in on her in front of reporters the minute she stepped off the plane. But Mick told Jerry he would marry her, and they patched things up. She gave an interview to a

London paper about how weird and sexually dirty Mick was. When she had to get sexy at a photo shoot, she blabbed, she just thought of some of the nasty things he did to her. When the Stones broke off recording for Christmas, Mick took her to Mustique, where his new house was going up. Keith and Patti were also about to marry, but her father died and the wedding was postponed. Keith helped carry his coffin at the funeral early in January 1983.

Dream Things
I Can't Keep Inside

The tensions and psychic kung fu among the Rolling Stones sharpened the band's creative edge as work on *Undercover* progressed in Paris in January 1983. Keith's mature style in the studio was now becoming fixed. "The way I write songs," he said at the time, "is to sit down and play twenty-five great songs by other people, and hope one of mine drops off the end." Keith would arrive at the sessions in a long cape, brandishing a lethal sword-stick that alarmed the guests of the other band members. Mick had written rubbery raps that were evolving into the episodic scenarios of "Undercover of the Night" and "Too Much Blood." While tempers were sometimes short at Pathé-Marconi, with arguments over tempos and keys, the sessions (with Chris Kimsey as associate producer) hatched what some Stones fans consider to be the Stones' last authentic album, the culmination of the Paris cycle that had begun with *Some Girls*.

The concert film *Let's Spend the Night Together* was finished early in 1983 and released that spring to no great acclaim. Critics seemed to think that anything less than murder and mayhem in a Stones film seemed anticlimactic after the carnage of *Gimme Shelter.*

Charlie Watts bought an old estate deep in the Devonshire landscape, with stables for the family's Arabian horses and kennels for the eighteen Best in Show sheepdogs. Bill Wyman and his girlfriend of fourteen years, Astrid Lindstrom, returned to England after many years in France, then split up. Astrid told a gossip columnist that she was tired of sharing Bill with thousands of other women.

In May, Mick and Ron began mixing *Undercover* at the Hit Factory in Manhattan. Keith joined them late in the month, but left for Jamaica in June before the album was complete, a gesture that ignited further gossip. Mick finished the record by overdubbing riffing horns and some African percussionists from the Sugar Hill hip-hop tribe onto his violent songs about murder, repression, and sexual domination. Chuck Leavell overdubbed an organ part on "Undercover." Keith's guitar tech Jim Barber played guitar on "Too Much Blood."

In July, Keith flew to Los Angeles to appear with Jerry Lee Lewis on a TV broadcast. At the airport, he ran into Chuck Berry, who seemed to recognize Keith this time. So glad was Chuck to see him that, in the crush of Keith's embrace, he dropped a lit cigarette down the front of Keith's shirt.

Jerry Hall got pregnant that summer. Woody and Jo had a baby boy, Tyrone.

In August 1983, the Stones signed their new American distribution deal with CBS Records. The contract called for four new Stones albums at $6 million apiece. Guaranteed promo budgets brought the deal to the $28-million mark, which at the time was the richest ever signed by a pop group. More significantly the CBS contract included the rights to Rolling Stones Records' back catalog dating from 1971, which soon earned the company its money back after it reissued the old records on compact disc. Most important to Walter Yetnikoff, whose winning bid reportedly doubled his closest competitor's, was Mick Jagger's explicit commitment to make solo albums for Columbia.

In New York, desperate to get their new videos played on MTV, Mick hired the hot young British director Julian Temple, who'd made the Sex Pistols' film *The Great Rock and Roll Swindle,* to direct videos for "Undercover of the Night," "Too Much Blood," and "She Was Hot." On their first meeting, Keith swung open his ratchet, put the blade to Temple's throat, and told him he'd better not fuck up. Temple shot footage at the club Bains-Douches in Paris and in Mexico that October. Following the murky "Undercover" storyline of political murder in contemporary Central America, Temple depicted *bandito* Keith Richards kidnapping and then executing bourgeois oppressor Mick Jagger in a lurid romance of surreal wish fulfillment.

Undercover was released in November 1983, in a sleazy blue sleeve showing a vintage peep-show pinup whose earthly delights were strategically plastered with stickers. The title track, "Undercover of the Night," was a bubbling, gripping fantasia on the dirty war in El Salvador, the Contra revolt in Nicaragua, the "disappeared" young leftists in Argentina. Set in a humid, sadistic milieu of revolt and intrigue, "Undercover" was Mick's attempt at relevance in a vapid era of heavy metal bands and jive MTV fodder. Its long-form format was influenced by Michael Jackson's "Thriller," but had more serious ideas about the sex police, the race militia, and other agencies of social control.

"She Was Hot" moved into familiar territory as Mick shouted out a song about passion with a black girl he picked up on an unpromising Sunday night. It featured Chuck Leavell and Stu on piano in a lusty romp, with a passionately raunchy guitar solo from Ron Wood. "Tie You Up (The Pain of Love)" was an *Exile*-type jam (Ron Wood on bass) on the old Stones theme of sadomasochism. Keith's "I Wanna Hold You" was methodical generic rock. His reggae track, "Feel On Baby," was a sweaty bowl of goat's-head soup with Sly Dunbar on synthesized Simmons drums.

"Too Much Blood" began side two with Charlie playing Afro-beat drums and some "Moroccan" horn vamps. Based on the true-crime story of a Japanese student at the Sorbonne who killed and ate his girlfriend, "Blood" was rapped out by Mick in a mix of voices and personae to a beat-box dance floor rhythm that owed a lot to Michael Jackson's "Thriller." The sax solo was played by New York session man David Sanborn, who also played on the following track, Ron Wood's "Dog Shit" demo, retitled (by Mick) "Pretty Beat Up." "Too Tough" was an embittered and sardonic song of regret, followed by "All the Way Down," the contemptuous, morning-after side of "She Was Hot," sung in Mick's hilariously snotty "Shattered" persona. The album ended with "It Must Be Hell," a downer in honky-tonk open G, with Ron Wood on slide guitar and quasipolitical lyrics echoing the vibe of oblique engagement with the issues of the day in "Undercover."

MTV started playing the Stones' violent new "Undercover of the Night" video and it looked like the record might take off. The album made it to no. 1 in England, but in the United States *Undercover* only got to no. 4, and the "Undercover of the Night" single only reached no. 9. (A twelve-inch remix of "Undercover" was also released with the dub-style "Feel On Baby" track on the B side.) Reviews were predictably tepid for the Stones' last album for Atlantic, and there was contempt from feminists for the album's multiple songs about sexual domination, bondage, and pain. When British TV banned the "Undercover" video, Mick tried to protest on Channel 4's *The Tube:* "It just follows the song, and it's a song about repression and violence. We're not trying to glamorize violence. We're trying to say something that has a point." The video had to be reedited (without Mick's execution) so it could be shown on the BBC's *Top of the Pops.*

Despite the album's relative failure, *Undercover* had a certain integrity that became more evident with the passage of time. Subsequent Rolling Stones albums were blander and fragmented in comparison, as solo careers and old animosities sapped the band's strength. Some fans felt that after *Undercover,* the Stones flamed out, with only rare glimpses of that old black magic down the road.

———

December 1983. Keith and Patti decided to marry in Mexico. She had given up her career for Keith, and he was persuaded he could make a life with her and start a second family. "I know I couldn't have beaten heroin without Patti," he said. "I ain't letting that bitch go!" Mick flew in to serve as best man at the wedding, Keith's first, on his fortieth birthday, December 18. His parents, Doris and Bert, saw each other for the first time in twenty years. The jam session at the bachelor party featured old rock and roll songs, mostly Jerry Lee Lewis hits. (Anita

Pallenberg, who was living in London, had broken her leg falling out of bed and had gotten busted again, so was unable to attend.) The Lutheran ceremony was conducted in Spanish, and Keith broke a glass with his foot in the ancient Jewish tradition. At the reception afterward, he sang Hoagy Carmichael's "The Nearness of You" to Patti, and his smoke-coarsened voice cracked open with feeling.

Shortly after the wedding, the authorities in Baja quietly advised Keith that a good way of avoiding a Mexican prison stay for drug trafficking would be to make himself and his entourage scarce. Keith left town immediately and didn't come back.

On December 21, Mick and Jerry gave a Christmas party for the famous at their new house on West 81st Street in New York. Christmas meant a lot to Mick, and invitations to his annual party became prized tokens of social acceptance in the worlds through which he moved. Even then a new world was unfolding, since Mick Jagger was already writing songs for the solo album that would soon stop the Rolling Stones dead in their tracks.

World War III

Keith Richards would later refer to the Rolling Stones' mid-1980s crisis and collapse as World War III. Looking for an escape hatch from the not-happening Stones, Mick Jagger stretched his luck with a solo career that first sent Keith into a rage, then prodded him to seek his own artistic life beyond the Stones, which resulted in his best music in years. But acting out the mixed emotions of love and hate the two Stones felt for each other so damaged their once-conspiratorial bond that it would never be the same again. Years of negativity and bad karma eventually came home to roost, and all the other Rolling Stones went haywire as well.

January 1984. Alexis Korner died of cancer at fifty-five on New Year's Day. Pathé-Marconi Studios were bulldozed for a parking garage. The Stones would have to find a new room somewhere for their next record.

They returned to Mexico later in January for the video shoot of "She Was Hot." Julian Temple's piece featured Charlie as a talent agent and the voluptuous Broadway dancer Anita Morris doing Jayne Mansfield's bosomy sex goddess part in *The Girl Can't Help It.* As flaming Ms. Morris undulated to the song, the buttons of the band's bulging trousers popped off, an image that proved too risqué for MTV, which banned the video when "She Was Hot" was released that winter.

In February, Bill Wyman started dating Mandy Smith, aged thirteen, whom he had spotted dancing with her sister at the British Rock Awards at the Lyceum Theater in London. Mandy looked ten years older, and Bill—forty-eight years old and single for the first time in years—fell hard. "I was totally besotted by Mandy the minute I saw her." He sent Julian Temple over to arrange an introduction, then showed up at her family's home to ask permission of her mother to see her. Mandy Smith's real age stayed a well-kept secret for two years as Bill took her around with him. When the British press found out, the Bill and Mandy saga became a staple of the tabloids, tinged with ridicule for the supposedly menopausal Stones.

———

Walter Yetnikoff managed to convince Mick Jagger that his first solo album should be the first record released by Columbia under the Stones' new contract. Keith was apoplectic. "If he tours with another band," he hissed in an interview, "I'll slit his fucking throat." Undaunted, Jagger pressed on. After the birth of his third daughter, Elizabeth Scarlett Jagger, on March 2, 1984, he took his family to the Bahamas, where he would later record, then on to Mustique, where he wrote the bulk of *She's the Boss.*

In April, Keith took Patti to Point of View, his house above Ocho Rios on Jamaica's north coast. The idea was for the young marrieds to work on a baby, but the house had been occupied by a disgruntled Peter Tosh. Tosh had made two more albums (*Mystic Man* and *Wanted Dread or Alive*) for the Stones' label, but sales had fallen and the reggae star had stopped touring. Blasted on potent strains of Jamaica herb like Goatshit and Lamb's Breath, Tosh was irrationally claiming the Stones owed him millions. He was squatting at Point of View with an entourage of Rasta ganja traders and a flock of goats when Keith called him from the airport in Montego Bay and told him to get out. Tosh told Keith he'd be waiting with his AK-47.

Keith: "Then you better learn how to put the fucking magazine in, Peter, because I'll be there in an hour."

When Keith arrived, he found his house completely trashed, with goat shit everywhere. He never spoke to Tosh again. A little while later, Tosh told a Philadelphia radio interviewer that he would cut Mick Jagger's throat the next time he saw him. Time passed, and one day Tosh dropped by one of Mick's solo sessions in New York. Mick saw Tosh through the glass and stopped working. He ran into the control room, bared his throat, and taunted Tosh. "Here, man. You wanna fucking kill me? Go ahead and do it *now*. Let's get it over with."

Soon Peter Tosh was asking for his release from Rolling Stones Records. In 1987, he was murdered during a robbery at his home in Kingston.

In May 1984, Mick and Michael Jackson cut a riff-banging rock song called "State of Shock" for the Jackson brothers' album *Victory*. Michael insisted on singing two hours of scales with Mick before recording because he felt Jagger was singing flat. The simple chant was done in two takes. Released as a single, it went to no. 3, which Mick thought auspicious. Mick then returned to Compass Point in the Bahamas to make his solo record with producers Nile Rogers (Chic, Bowie, Madonna) and Bill Laswell. Jeff Beck played a lot of guitar, and Jagger also recruited Herbie Hancock, Peter Townshend, Jan Hammer, and "Fly and Rob-Me," as Peter Tosh called his old bandmates Sly and Robbie. The sessions continued through the year as Jagger, now a huge fan of Prince's megaselling "Purple Rain," sought to apply a similar sheen to his big solo debut.

The four original Rolling Stones convened in Paris in June 1984 without bothering to invite Ron Wood. Mick had insisted Wood enter an English clinic for drug detox when Wood's cocaine habit reached $5,000 a day and he seemed near death. (Wood left the treatment after three weeks, and Mick was annoyed that the clinic called him to complain.) During a contentious business meeting, in which Keith accused Mick of deserting the band, they agreed to start making the next Stones album in Paris that fall, and tour in 1985.

When Ron Wood got out of rehab, Keith took him on again as bosom buddy. They began jamming on song ideas in Wood's new basement studio in New York with soul singer Bobbie Womack, who'd written "It's All Over Now" and was making an (unreleased) album with Wood. Keith called the ever-hospitable and only partly rehabilitated Wood "the holy host," as he began to take Mick's place as Keith's songwriting foil.

In September, Keith Richards's oft-cleansed blood began to boil when Mick postponed the Stones' record because he was still working on his own album. Keith was mad Mick was writing all the songs by himself, the first formal breach of a twenty-year writing partnership. Worried that a Jagger bomb would damage the Stones, he bluntly warned Mick: "Don't make a shit album."

In early October 1984, the Stones gathered in Amsterdam to talk about the new album. Mick reassumed the role of dictator. He was condescending and preoccupied with his solo career, to which—he made clear—the Rolling Stones took a backseat in his datebook. One night Keith got Mick drunk. Mick picked up the phone in Keith's hotel room and called Charlie Watts upstairs. It was five in the morning. Charlie was asleep but picked up the phone.

"Izzat my drummer, then?" Mick bawled. "Where's my fucking drummer? Get yer arse down here right away!"

(Keith: "Mick, drunk, is a sight to behold.")

Charlie got up, shaved, put on a fresh white shirt and a tailored Savile Row double-breasted suit, tied his tie, slipped on bench-crafted shoes from Lobb in St. James.

"Charlie came down," Keith said, "grabbed Mick, went *boom*! Dished him a left hook that knocked him into a plate of smoked salmon and then he almost floated out the window and into a canal in Amsterdam. My favorite jacket, which Mick was wearing, got ruined."

"Don't *ever* call me 'your drummer' again," Charlie growled between clenched teeth. "You're *my* fucking singer."

Keith: "It was Charlie's way of saying, 'I've *had* it. It's *over*, man.' If there was one other friend Mick had, it was Charlie."

The Biff Hitler Trio

January 1985. It was rough in Paris when Mick showed up at the *Dirty Work* sessions with no material, having shot his wad on his solo album. Keith, of course, had known this would happen, and he was not pleased: "In 1985, we started getting into solo shit, and I *told* him I didn't want to be put in that position after all these years, because I *knew* it was a conflict of interests. I fought him like a dog—not to do that. I knew right then that I'm gonna write songs and think, 'That's mine. Stones can't have that. Oh, the Stones can have this.' What do I do? Give 'em the best I got? The second best?"

What dialogue there was on this issue was mostly carried on later in the press. Mick was defensive: "When we signed the contract with CBS, I had a provision to make a solo record. Keith knew all about it, so it wasn't a bolt from the blue. [All the sniping] was Keith's way of getting back at me. He just liked to mouth off about it. I thought he overreacted, because making a solo record seemed a natural thing for me to want to do."

When Mick left the Stones in Paris after a few weeks to promote his solo album, Keith took over the sessions and assumed control of the Rolling Stones. Ron Wood, who by then had been in the band longer than Brian Jones or Mick Taylor, stepped in as Keith's creative foil and wound up with four song credits on *Dirty Work*. Keith was Ron's best man when he married Jo in a country church in Buckinghamshire that month. Mick didn't show up.

Mick's all-star album was released in March. *She's the Boss* was a mostly opaque and colorless "product" that got mediocre reviews, though the album was a Top Ten record in America and England and sold a respectable 2 million copies. Mick was disappointed. To Keith's immense relief, Mick's solo career looked like it wouldn't happen. Keith kept threatening to kill Mick if he toured with another band and was contemptuous of Jagger's relative failure.

———

The Stones' sessions in Paris resumed in April 1985, after Keith had taken time off to attend the birth of his daughter Theodora Dupree Richards at New York Hospital. They draped a gown over him and led him into the delivery room, and he was close to tears as he watched a child of his born for the first time. Marlon was off in boarding school, while daughter Angela was living in Dartford with his mum. Anita Pallenberg, living through cycles of addiction and recovery in London, staying on peaceful terms with Keith and Patti, knitted a sweater for the baby.

Battle stations at the new Pathé-Marconi studio. Mick was annoyed that Keith was running the show and began using a different studio in the building, usually arriving at midnight from the flat he and Jerry were renting in suburban Neuilly. When Mick was finished, he often left without seeing the others. The vibe was terrible. Charlie Watts was having a bad time—his daughter had been expelled from her school for smoking pot—and he was medicating himself with drink and beginning to quietly use heroin, to everyone's shock. Bill Wyman was morose and bored. Ian Stewart thought the Stones were over and wouldn't play on any of the tracks. "We just got fed up with each other," Mick said. "You've got a relationship with musicians that depends on what you produce together. But when you don't produce, you get bad reactions. Bands break up."

Keith was determined to complete the new album, whose working title was briefly *19 Stitches* after a stoned tape op fell into a glass table with great loss of blood. They worked on the reggae oldie "Too Rude" (copped from a Frankie Paul record) and began to develop Bob and Earl's late soul classic "Harlem Shuffle," which Keith had been trying to get Mick to do for years. One day Mick came in, tore straight through the song in two takes, and left the studio. Bobby Womack later filled out the vocal in New York.

A lot of the anger Keith and Ron felt at Mick's defection went into harsh new songs of conflict and aggression: "Fight," "Had It with You," "One Hit (to the Body)." Wood later recalled, "There were a few times when Keith and I felt like killing people, but we picked up our guitars and wrote songs instead." They kept telling themselves that the Stones' open sores would heal when the record came out and they got back on the road.

In May, the Rolling Stones were approached to do the Live Aid concerts to be held in July in London and New York and broadcast around the planet to benefit Ethiopian famine relief. The Stones begged off as a group, but then Mick offered his services to organizer Bob Geldof as a solo act.

By early June, the Stones had about twenty-five new tracks finished, including "Cook Cook Blues," Mick and Bobby Womack singing "Strictly Memphis," and Keith's "You're Too Much." Abandoning Pathé-Marconi for good, they left Paris and moved the sessions to New York.

In London, Mick Jagger and David Bowie made a record and video of "Dancing in the Street" for the Live Aid broadcast. Later in the month, Mick began rehearsing with Hall and Oates's blue-eyed soul band. As an extra blast of energy for his first-ever solo show, Mick asked Tina Turner, now an international icon of survival, vitality, and glamour, to appear with him at Live Aid.

Two days before the July 13 concert in New York, Bob Dylan stopped by Ron Wood's house on New York's Upper West Side. Dylan said that Bill Graham, who was running the New York show, had arranged for Dylan to close the concert after Mick Jagger had performed. "It's a big charity thing," Dylan murmured to Wood. "Bill Graham's got a band for me, and I have to go along with it. Do you think maybe you and me could play together?"

Wood said he'd do it, and would get Keith too. He called Keith up. "Get over here," Ron rasped. "Bob wants us to do Live Aid with him."

There was a pause while Keith considered this reversal of fortune that could trump Mick's big moment. He said, "You better not be lying, Woody," and hung up. Keith came right over, and after some uncomfortable posturing by Dylan and some diplomacy by Wood, Dylan asked Keith to do the show. They began jamming in Wood's basement, working on Bob's songs and some acoustic Stones numbers.

———

Saturday, July 13, 1985, was a big day for the rock world, a vast communitarian revival show broadcast to 1.6 billion people around the world. In Wembley Stadium in London and JFK Stadium in Philadelphia, the top musicians of the day played for the starving in Ethiopia, inspired by horrendous scenes of famine and death televised daily in the West.

Mick Jagger's 9 P.M. performance in Philadelphia on Saturday was the triumph of the Live Aid broadcast. Wearing a bright yellow suit and working overtime, he did his new stuff and some crowd-pleasing Stones songs. Tina Turner was a sensation with her leonine wig and long legs as she sang "State of Shock" and "Honky Tonk Women" with Mick.

Bob Dylan's finale, backed by the two Rolling Stones guitarists, should have been a killer. But Ron Wood knew it was going to be a disaster when they arrived at the stadium that afternoon and Dylan muttered vaguely, "I wonder what Bill Graham wants me to do?" They jammed a little in the tuning room, but even when they went up the ramp to the stage, Keith and Ron still had no idea what Bob was going to play. As they were being introduced by actor Jack Nicholson, Dylan looked at them from behind his shades and said, "Maybe I should do 'All I Really Want to Do.' " Keith and Ron looked at each other. They didn't know the song.

They came out onstage with acoustic guitars and sat just behind Bob as he started "The Ballad of Hollis Brown" instead. Keith and Ron tried to fake it. Behind the stage curtain, Lionel Richie was rehearsing his hideous anthem "We Are the World" with the whole cast, so Dylan and the two Stones couldn't hear themselves. The set was ramshackle and inaudible, with Keith and Ron cringing in smiling embarrassment as they tried to keep up with an improvising Dylan. "We came off looking like real idiots," Wood said, "but I'd do it again for Bob." Keith said it was a privilege to work with Bob. "I'll play with that asshole anytime."

————

During the summer, the Stones worked at RPM Studio in New York amid deathly vibes. Bill Wyman played bass on only half the album. Ian Stewart was ashamed of the band, didn't play on the record, told friends he wanted to retire. After an August photo shoot for the album sleeve in which he looked vacant and refused to make eye contact with the camera, Charlie Watts went back to England in disgust. "In twenty-five years with the Stones," he complained to a reporter, "I've spent five years working and twenty years hanging about. I'd have been dead years ago if I'd thought about it." After he left, Ron Wood played drums on some of the tracks. New York drummer Steve Jordon, who worked in David Letterman's TV studio band, played on several as well. Keith called the nucleus of himself, Wood, and Jordon the Biff Hitler Trio.

Mick Jagger worked separately with Chuck Leavell and singer Bernard Fowler, mainstays of *She's the Boss*—when Mick was even around. The birth of his first son, James LeRoy Jagger, on August 28, further distracted Mick from the Stones' fractured sessions. Bobby Womack, who had known the Rolling Stones for twenty-one years, thought he was watching them break up that summer. At home in the English countryside, Charlie Watts fell down a flight of stairs in his basement and broke his leg. The Stones' album was delayed until Christmas, but still wouldn't be finished in time. Sitting alone in the studio at 5 A.M. with writer Robert Palmer, Keith kept muttering, "We've *got* to tour behind this fucker. It's our only hope." Keith at this point was thinking a lot about the future of the Stones. He'd seen worse times than these, and insisted there was still hope and a good reason to carry on. "We can make this damn thing *grow up*," he told a reporter during a break from a long jam with Wood on an Everly Brothers medley. "We're the only ones around who've kept it together this long. Is there a point in being a rock and roll band after twenty years? Can you make it grow up gracefully? Can you get it to mature, and make sense? I still love doing it, and we're at a point now where we'd like to make it grow up with us."

So Keith stayed in the studio, mixing what he considered a crucial first Stones album for CBS and cracking the whip. "I'll work 'em till they drop," he joked in an interview for *Spin* magazine, "but I'll drop with 'em." He and Ron initiated U2's singer Bono into the cult of the blues in October, and Keith cut a track with him for the anti-apartheid *Sun City* album at Right Track Studio, which Keith liked so much he moved the Stones' sessions into the facility the following month. The album was finished by the end of 1985. CBS made them remove the word "cunt" from the hand-drawn lyric sheet by the New York cartoonist Mark Marek.

Back in London, their absent drummer and Ian Stewart organized the Charlie Watts Big Band, featuring the cream of London's jazz players. They played a week at Ronnie Scott's club and later made an album, *Live at Fulham Town Hall*. It was Charlie's jazz ambition realized, a welcome respite from the dissolution of the Stones.

———

In December, Ian Stewart was in London, preparing to fly to New York to help put the Stones' album to rights, when he began having breathing problems. The forty-seven-year-old Stu, the acknowledged co-founder and conscience of the Stones, had been depressed over the band's chronic problems. On December 12, he died of a heart attack while waiting to see his doctor in a West London clinic. Stu's funeral, the capper to a horrendous year for the Rolling Stones, was attended by the whole band and the upper echelon of the English rockocracy. No one had ever seen Mick Jagger tearful in public before, as Stu's favorite song, "Boogie Woogie Dreams," was played at the end of the service. Keith nudged Ron Wood and whispered dolefully, *"Now* who's gonna tell us off when we fuck up?"

Stu's death sent the Stones into catalepsy. In New York, Keith told friends that it was the final nail in the coffin. Stu's bluff authenticity and common touch had been a long-term constant that had helped hold the Rolling Stones together. When asked to comment on Stu's death by the fanzine *Beggar's Banquet,* Keith blurted out, "Why'd you have to leave us like that, you sod?"

Straight to Jagger's Head

January 23, 1986. Keith Richards, fidgeting with nerves, half-drunk to avoid soiling himself, was in the kitchen of the Waldorf-Astoria in New York, waiting to induct the unpredictable Chuck Berry as the first member of the Rock and Roll Hall of Fame. Around tables in the ballroom sat the upper echelon of the music business and many of Keith's idols: Berry, Little Richard, Jerry Lee Lewis. Keith pulled it off by being candid: "I lifted every lick he ever played, man." Then a little magic happened for Keith in the all-star jam after the ceremony, as he and Chuck Berry, for once in a good mood, actually managed to play together for the first time. The thing meshed. It rang. It was *music.* Keith closed his eyes and seemed transported. It was a moment Keith would try to recapture later in a tumultuous year that saw the Rolling Stones stop working after twenty-four years on the job.

In the weeks after Ian Stewart's death, the Stones were grieving and traumatized. Those who understood the Stones knew that the loss would have a severely negative effect on the band's immediate future. "It was Stu's band, really," Keith shrugged to friends. On February 28, billed as Rocket 86, the Stones played a private tribute show for Stu at the 100 Club in Oxford Street, in part to squash rumors of the death of the Stones as well. It was the first time the Stones had played a gig together in four years. Charlie was late, subbed for by Simon Kirke of Bad Company until he arrived. When Watts sat down, the Stones played like a muddy R&B band again, with Keith ripping off ferocious leads and urging the others on. Eric Clapton sat in, along with Jeff Beck and other friends of Stu's, for a sweaty rock and roll wake for the Stones' irreplaceable straight man. At the end of the night, Keith and Mick left the club with arms around each other's shoulders, visibly moved by all the emotion of the night.

Dirty Work was ready for release that winter. In February, the Stones gathered in Manhattan to appear in a partly animated video for "Harlem Shuffle" directed by Ralph Bakshi. A cartoon also figured on the inner sleeve of the album, which had a funny strip about a sadistic gym trainer named Olga brutalizing her clients. In fact, the whole album was like a cartoon, including the nightmarish cover shot of the undead-looking Stones lounging in Day-Glo jackets, the first album photo of the band since *Between the Buttons* in 1967. In the photo, Keith appears to be kneeing Mick Jagger in the crotch.

Dirty Work was produced by Steve Lillywhite and the Glimmer Twins and dedicated to Ian Stewart. Often viewed as a flop and the least interesting Rolling Stones album, it can be seen instead as the model for Keith's solo albums and the beginning of a presentation style that would sustain the band when it regrouped several years later. The backing voices on the first track, "One Hit (to the Body)," prefigured the chorus of singers the Stones would later deploy in their shows. "One Hit" launched the album on its anxious, contentious course, a narrative program of the Stones breaking up over the course of a year. Jimmy Page rumbled two turbulent guitar solos over cowriters Wood and Richards, whose mean streak continued with the power chords of "Fight," another passive/aggressive challenge to Mick. "Harlem Shuffle" changed the mood of Sturm und Drang halfway through the first side (and this was the last Stones album to actually have sides, as the compact disc would be the dominant delivery system for music the next time they released an album). It was the old Stones "shuffle and eighths" adapted to the hitchhike rhythm, with Chuck Leavell's electric piano lick and Don Covay and Bobby Womack singing along with Mick. It clicked on the radio as a novelty Top Ten single that spring.

Back to hell on the next track, the tuneless chant "Hold Back," set to a Keith riff with Ivan Neville on funky bass. "Too Rude" was a dub-wise take on Sly and Robbie's reggae song, with Jimmy Cliff singing beautifully along with Keith and Ron.

Side two began with Mick and the girls (Janice Pendarvis and Dollette MacDonald) singing "Winning Ugly," a rollicking song about competition that could have been on *She's the Boss*. Same with a funk workout written with Chuck Leavell, "Back to Zero," another inter-Stones memo about dissolution. "Back to zero," Mick shouts (there being little "singing" on this mostly chanted and rapped-out record), "that's where we're heading." There was more of this on "Dirty Work," which actually sounded like a Stones song with an impassioned, no-nonsense vocal ("I'm beginning to *hate* you") from Mick before the track faded into humid, free-floating rage—the angriest song the Stones ever did. *Dirty Work* skidded toward the finish line with the great "Had It with You," a hot Anglo-rockabilly workout with Mick playing good harp and rapping a Slim Harpo vocal. Keith's "Sleep Tonight" was an ominous warning and threat delivered straight to Mick Jagger's head, a dark ballad (in homage to Hoagy Carmichael's vintage style) about the loss of dignity that built to a climax and ended in a strange and portentous chorus.

The last track on *Dirty Work* was thirty seconds of Ian Stewart playing some expert barrelhouse piano. The album's liner notes ended with "Thanks, Stu, for 25 years of boogie-woogie."

Dirty Work was Keith's album, and everyone knew it. He wrote the songs because Mick had gone off on his own. With so many guests, with the Stones' rhythm section mostly absent, there was grumbling at Black Rock, CBS's imposing headquarters on 52nd Street, that *Dirty Work* wasn't really a Rolling Stones album at all. But, in a pop era dominated by Bon Jovi, power ballads, and the big-hair metal bands that prevailed on MTV, *Dirty Work* did quite well, reaching no. 3 in England and no. 4 in America.

It would have sold a lot better if Mick Jagger hadn't decided it would be impossible for him to tour that year. He didn't like the album, couldn't see himself performing any of the songs, didn't think the Stones could physically make it on the road. Before leaving for Mustique to write his next solo album in early April, he sent the band a "Dear Stones" letter.

Keith was disturbed when he read it, incredulous that Mick didn't tell them in person, humiliated that he was the last to know. "He said, 'I don't need you bunch of old farts. You're just a millstone around my neck. You're too much of a hassle.' There's times I could've killed him." The Stones hadn't toured in four years, and Keith had been counting on playing with his band again. CBS was pissed off. The rest of the band was miserable at missing an estimated $40-million payday, but Mick wouldn't come around.

"Touring *Dirty Work* would have been a nightmare," Mick later told Jann Wenner. "Everyone was hating each other. Everybody was so out of their brains, and Charlie was in seriously bad shape. It would have been the worst Rolling Stones tour. Probably would have been the end of the band." He told a French writer, "The band was in no condition to tour. The album wasn't very good. Health was diabolical. I wasn't in good shape, and the rest of the band couldn't walk across the Champs-Élysées, much less do a tour."

So the Rolling Stones flamed out for three years, and Keith Richards had to get on with his life.

———

In London that spring, Charlie Watts was stopped by a reporter on the street near the Stones' office. Looking dapper but dazed, Charlie claimed he didn't even know *Dirty Work* was out because he'd been playing with his jazz band. "Does it sound good, then?" he asked. He also said he couldn't even imagine touring with the Stones.

It was a rough patch for the drummer. His wife, Shirley, had gone into a clinic for alcoholism treatment, and Charlie was using heroin. Later he recalled: "Mid-eighties, maybe toward the end of '86, I hit an all-time low in my personal life and in my relationship with Mick. I was drinking a lot. I nearly lost my wife and family and everything. I took more speed than heroin, though. I slept one day in four for two years. I liked speed, because I'm naturally lethargic . . . In the end, you need someone who loves you to tell you that you aren't there anymore, because when you look in the mirror, you see someone else."

By the end of 1986, after he'd brought his jazz band to America, Charlie Watts quietly cleaned up in London and got off drugs. Few knew of his problems until he had solved them.

———

In London in May, the Stones shot a video for "One Hit (to the Body)" that dramatized the hard feelings among them, with Mick and Keith glaring menacingly and taking stylized pokes at each other. Patti was pregnant and couldn't travel by air, so she and Keith were aboard the *Queen Elizabeth II* when it pulled out of Southampton, bound for New York, three days away. During the voyage, Keith had time to think about his predicament.

Keith to Lisa Robinson: "I couldn't just sit around waiting for Mick to snap his fingers and put the Stones together—if ever. I'd go berserk, right? I've *got* to work. It was frustrating because we were in a unique position, having been together for so long, seeing if we could make this thing grow up. But suddenly I'm asking myself: who the fuck am I going to play with after all these years?"

Jane Rose knew that Keith had to keep on moving, so she got him into business with a vengeance. When the ship docked in New York on June 6, Keith kept right on going on a course that led to a creative renewal that no one could have foreseen. That night, he joined Chuck Berry on-stage at a blues festival in Chicago's Grant Park, and a plan was hatched for Keith to take part in a concert on Berry's sixtieth birthday later that year. He flew on to Los Angeles where he joined blues singer Etta James at a bar gig. Then back to New York to promote the new Stones album on NBC's *Friday Night Videos*.

Mick Jagger and David Bowie appeared at the Prince's Trust charity show in London before the prince and princess of Wales. Bill had to leave England when he split up with Mandy Smith, now sixteen, and the story broke in the press. By the time the headlines appeared, Bill had escaped, driving down to his house near St. Paul de Vence in France to avoid arrest until he was assured that Mandy's family and the police wouldn't press pedophilia charges.

Robert Fraser had never quite recovered from the prison term he served after the famous Stones bust of 1967. He lived in India for a while before returning to England and a series of failed businesses and art galleries. Always ahead of the curve, Robert was one of the first people in England to contract AIDS, and when his finances collapsed, he was supported by Paul Getty. Mick Jagger stayed in touch. "Mick was constant in his friendship for Robert," Christopher Gibbs says. "He was very encouraging, tried to help Robert, stayed a good friend." Robert Fraser died in 1986. Brion Gysin, the Stones' protean connection with Moroccan mysteries, died of cancer that summer.

In early July, Keith and his entourage flew to Detroit to help Aretha Franklin record "Jumpin' Jack Flash" for a film sound track. The drummer on the session was Steve Jordon, Keith's main sticksman while Charlie Watts was indisposed. Jordon was a versatile, tuneful, and dependable pro, a black musician in dreadlocks who became Keith's new creative partner. After Aretha, Keith flew to St. Louis in July to negotiate with Chuck Berry about Keith's role as music director for a birthday tribute concert and movie deal that depended on Keith's participation. He convinced an initially reluctant Berry to include Johnnie Johnson, the St. Louis piano star who had helped write the melodies of some of Berry's classic songs. Berry himself suggested they use Steve Jordan, who had drummed on the Hall of Fame jam. When the deal was done, Keith went back to New York to teach himself how to put a rock and roll band of his own together.

Cheap Champagne, Brief Affairs, Backstage Love

The Rolling Stones' ten-year New York period came to an end in mid-1986. Mick Jagger began his second solo album, *Primitive Cool,* with producer Dave Stewart in Los Angeles and Holland. Ron Wood sold his house, returned to London, and set himself up in suburban Wimbledon. Bill Wyman was hiding in France from London headlines like JAIL THIS WORM WYMAN FOR LOVING MANDY. Charlie Watts was working on a brief American tour with his jazz band.

After the birth of his daughter Alexandra in July, Keith Richards moved his large female household to rural Connecticut, an hour north of Manhattan. Heroin-free, he sustained himself with daily doses of vodka, ganja, and the odd line of cocaine in the evening. He spent September assembling the band for the Chuck Berry gig: Bobby Keys on sax, Chuck Leavell on keyboards, Steve Jordan on drums, Joey Stampinato (from the New York band NRBQ) on bass. Eric Clapton, Robert Cray, Linda Ronstadt, and Etta James were recruited to appear in the concert and film, directed by Taylor Hackford (*An Officer and a Gentleman*). In October, Keith arrived in St. Louis to begin working with Chuck Berry, an ordeal that almost made heroin addiction attractive again.

Chuck Berry, self-described schizophrenic, was waiting for Keith at Berry Park, his public amusement complex in Wentzville, Missouri. Porno tapes played constantly in his music room, and Chuck would later be arrested when it was discovered that the ladies' toilet in his restaurant was equipped with a video camera—inside the bowl. Everyone was nervous about the concert. Berry was used to doing things his way, and Keith was after the kind of precision that would work on film, "a very intimate, combo thing," as he put it. Berry had never rehearsed in his life, and when the rock stars started to come in, there were diffident rows over interpretation. Berry was less than effusive and would sometimes go into a hypnotic trance in the middle of rehearsal. When he interrupted Keith's playing and reprimanded him for getting the opening of "Carol" wrong, Keith stifled his instinct to retaliate or walk out, and just took it. He let Berry patronize him, often when the movie cameras were rolling, since the rehearsals were being filmed. (Berry kept calling Keith "Jack.") Keith later said he worked on the concert "not so much as musical director as an S&M director—social director of the S&M band. When you're working with Chuck, you've got to be prepared for anything. I had to remind myself that, to be second guitar to Chuck Berry—'Shit, man, when you started, you'd have thought you'd died and gone to heaven.' "

Keith was on a crusade. He'd gotten Berry together with Johnnie Johnson ("two big guys with hands the size of plates"), who'd been driving a bus for twenty-five years and still gigged six nights a week. Keith felt this was a last opportunity to get some good live music out of them. Berry fought Keith right up to the two concerts on October 16 at the Fox Theater in St. Louis. Chuck refused to sing at the sound check until Keith kissed him on the cheek and begged, "Chuck, *please,* just once." When they finally took the stage after ten days of rehearsals, all their work was forgotten as Chuck launched "Maybelline," "Around and Around," "Sweet Little Sixteen," and his other hits in completely different arrangements, some in different keys. "The band's looking at me onstage," Keith later recalled, "and I could only look back at 'em, you know? *Wing it, boys.*' "

The concerts went well enough to be the basis for a successful film in 1987 titled *Hail Hail Rock 'n' Roll.* Anita and Marlon were in the audience as Eric Clapton played the blues on "Wee Wee Hours" and Robert

Cray did "Brown Eyed Handsome Man" with regal confidence. When it was over, an exhausted Keith Richards went back to a beautiful Connecticut autumn and slept for a month.

Keith came out of the Chuck Berry project still respecting his mercurial idol, and armed with a new, highly marketable skill. He told biographer Victor Bockris, "The whole process of putting those bands together for Aretha and Chuck made me realize I had this ability . . . to put certain guys together in the right situation and create a band. If you gave me the right guys, in ten days I could give you a band that sounded like they'd been together for ten years."

Meanwhile, Mick Jagger worked on his new solo album in Holland with Dave Stewart from the band Eurythmics until late in the year. He had a better fix on his solo style, some strong new songs, and Jeff Beck on guitar. In early 1987, Mick and Jerry Hall moved on to work at a studio in Barbados, where Jerry was arrested with twenty pounds of ganja at the airport on January 21. After a month of hearings in which she claimed she had been framed, she was let off and Mick's sessions moved to Right Track Studio in New York.

Across town, in a studio on Broadway near 19th Street, Keith Richards was writing songs with Steve Jordon, with Charlie Drayton playing bass. Ivan Neville was on keys. When Keith got wind that Mick was planning to tour his new album, he started to take his own solo career more seriously and opened negotiations with Virgin Records tycoon Richard Branson. When their studio caught fire on April 8, they dragged their amps into the street and kept jamming until the fire trucks arrived.

While Keith spent the summer of 1987 in Jamaica, Mick finished *Primitive Cool* with high hopes. He had bared his soul, made a Big Statement, sung some candidly personal lyrics. Released in September 1987, *Primitive Cool* sold poorly despite its hard rock attack from Jeff Beck and his drummer Simon Phillips on "Throwaway," with its jaded palette of "cheap champagne, brief affairs, backstage love." Mick wrote his most insightful and soul-baring lyrics in years for nostalgic songs like "War Baby" and "Primitive Cool." The album was a paradigm of slick 1980s rock, and the finest work Mick Jagger had done that decade, but it still bombed. Mick's single, "Let's Work," didn't make the Top Forty. It seemed obvious that the Stones' loyal army of fans wasn't interested in Mick Jagger's solo act.

Privately Keith sort of enjoyed Mick's album, but felt duty-bound to smear it in public, especially since the record contained a song, called "Shoot Off Your Mouth," aimed right between Keith's eyes. Keith accused Mick of having a Peter Pan complex about not wanting to grow up. He was quoted on Jagger's isolation and his lack of friends, but later in 1987 his comments were more sad than barbed. "The fact is that I wanted to keep the Stones together and he didn't," Keith told a reporter. "He has to justify it one way or the other, but the guy just wasn't there. It was very frustrating. I love him and he's my friend, but I don't really feel he's mine. And there's no way I can express my friendship if someone doesn't accept it . . . But I'm not going to give up easily. I'm trying to keep a great band together, and I figure that any day maybe he'll come around—you know, male menopause, whatever—and the next week it'll be all right."

Keith had been in Montreal since August, recording a solo album with his band. Bobby Keys was now on board, and Keith hired L.A. session guitarist Waddy Wachtel to fill out the group he was calling the X-Pensive Winos after he found them passing a bottle of Château Lafite during a break one night.

Mick rehearsed with Jeff Beck for about a month to take *Primitive Cool* on the road, but the chemistry between the two rock stars didn't work. Beck didn't like playing old Stones songs and finally walked out when Mick insulted him with a low offer for the tour. "Mick's problem is that he's a meanie," Beck told the *Sun*. "He's no better than a glorified accountant. I'd love to go on tour with the old geezer, but I can't believe how tight he is."

The idea of Mick touring by himself embittered the other Stones, especially when they heard he would play Japan first, a lucrative market the Stones had never penetrated because of past drug problems. Charlie Watts told a London paper that "Mick's decision virtually folded up twenty-five years of the band." Keith took it very hard, and his public comments grew harsh as he called Mick a wimp and a back-stabbing cunt.

Needing to regroup, Mick retreated to his French chateau, where a team of English landscape designers was restoring the house's once-elegant parterre gardens. Ron Wood was touring clubs with Bo Diddley, and Bill Wyman was again seeing Mandy Smith, who at seventeen was no longer jailbait.

Talk Is Cheap

January 1988. It was Mick Jagger's turn at the Rock and Roll Hall of Fame inductions in New York. He introduced the Beatles, sang "Like A Rolling Stone" with their fellow inductee Bob Dylan, and finished off the obligatory superstar jam afterward with a torrid reading of "Satisfaction," with Jeff Beck on guitar.

As the Stones' feud continued to fester, people close to the band noticed a strange phenomenon: Mick and Keith began to take on subtle aspects of each other's personality. Keith became more fey and self-referential, more "camp," while Jagger was noticeably earthier and more human. Jerry Hall told friends that Mick was having trouble sleeping, seemed preoccupied, always had his nose in a book.

Mick toured Japan at the end of March, not without serious misgivings. Guitarists Joe Satriani and Jimmy Ripp replaced Jeff Beck in what Keith derisively called "Jagger's little jerk-off band" in a *Rolling Stone* interview. Simon Phillips and bassist Doug Wimbish anchored the group, with two black singers, Bernard Fowler and Lisa Fischer, adding a massive attack to Mick's vocals. They opened shows with "Honky Tonk Women" and deployed a Stones-heavy set with intense pyro effects and silly guitar-hero posing by the histrionic Satriani. The encores were

"Sympathy for the Devil" and "Satisfaction." In Tokyo one night, Tina Turner joined Mick to sing "Brown Sugar" and "It's Only Rock 'n' Roll."

Mick was jazzed and invigorated by the tour. Ron Wood was also playing in Japan, and when the two Stones met for a drink in Osaka, Ron told him he thought Keith would be eager to patch things up. So, after fighting off a $7-million plagiarism suit by a Jamaican singer against "Just Another Night" in New York in April, Mick asked for a Stones sit-down in London the following month.

They met at the Savoy Hotel on May 18, 1988. Mick said he wanted the Stones to tour in the fall, but Keith demurred, saying he was too busy with a solo album already in production and his own tour planned late in the year. But they finally agreed to make a new Stones album and tour in 1989. "We had a meeting to plan the tour," Mick said later, "and as far as I was concerned it was very easy. Everyone was asking, 'Wow, what was it like? What happened? How did it all work?' But it was a nonevent. What could have been a lot of name-calling, wasn't. I think everyone decided we'd done all that." The atmosphere of conciliation was helped by bulletins of the megamillions the Who had been guaranteed for an American tour that summer. If the Stones could get it together, they were looking at the biggest paychecks in history.

"Listen, darling," Keith acknowledged to Mick at the end of the day, "this thing is bigger than both of us."

————

Mick Jagger was forty-five years old that summer. He and Jerry weren't getting along because she wanted to marry and he didn't. A projected solo tour of the United States that autumn was canceled due to *Primitive Cool*'s low sales. Keith was still sniping away at Mick in the press, and the industry buzz on Keith's new album was that it was brilliant.

Keith and his African-American rhythm section ("I got three niggers and a Jew") had been working on his album all year, on and off. Engineer Rob Fraboni had given Keith a tape of pop music from the South African township of Soweto—guitar-crazy, jumping street jive with a sweet spirit.

It fascinated Keith to hear Africans throwing rock and roll back where it came from with twining guitars and a twist of Zulu funk, and it informed some of the touches Keith added when mixing his album that summer. When the record was ready for release that fall, Keith told friends that he was really scared to be putting out something he alone was responsible for.

Talk Is Cheap was released in October 1988 on Virgin Records, to positive reviews from critics relieved that something of the dormant Stones magic still existed, like a hot coal at the bottom of a cold campfire. Many of Keith's fans thought it was the best Rolling Stones album since *Exile on Main Street*, sixteen years earlier.

Mostly a collection of funk-style riffs (all written with Steve Jordon) overlaid with Keith's misterioso rasped vocals, *Talk* was the opposite of Mick Jagger's commercially generic solo style. Keith was after groove and feel, his lyrics little more than catchphrases. Free of Jagger's outré posturing, it was the record that Keith's fans needed to hear. "Keith wanted it to be antiformula, anticommercial," Waddy Wachtel said. "He wanted it to be art."

The album's masterpiece was "You Don't Move Me," Keith's desperate *J'accuse*. Starting as a dub-wise reggae track, it moved into a swampy, hypnotic song about alienation and lost friendship, a "Dear Mick" letter. Quoting old Stones riffs behind a keening, disconsolate chorus, with Keith singing in a minor, arabesque key, the song touched on many of Keith's public criticisms of Mick: the ambition, avarice, cruelty, and shallowness that Keith deplored in his old friend. "What makes you so greedy," Keith sang, "makes you so seedy. You don't *move* me anymore." Touring with Mick in Australia, singer Bernard Fowler noted that whenever anyone put on *Talk Is Cheap*, Mick immediately left the room.

"You Don't Move Me" was the last shot fired in World War III, the war between the Stones. Keith, in interviews, denied the song was about Mick, but nobody believed it. *Talk Is Cheap* wasn't the big success that Keith's camp had prayed for and that Mick Jagger had dreaded. It stayed on the charts for six months, got to no. 24, and sold about a million copies. Its success or failure seemed to mean little to Keith. He told interviewers that he felt guilty because he couldn't keep the Stones on track. At first, doing a solo record seemed like a defeat.

Keith: "And then I ask myself, 'What am I so scared about?' Was I trying to keep the Stones together because I was scared of being left out there on my own? What was really my reason for this desperate fight? Was it that I wanted to keep in the cocoon and not break out?" In the end, he admitted to Stanley Booth, the fact that he was forced out on his own had been a great thing for him.

Keith Richards and the X-Pensive Winos began a three-week tour on November 24, 1988, in Atlanta. "You wanna hear some good music?" Keith told the audience. "Here's some guys that wanna play it for you." Dressed as a Transylvanian count in a black jacket and white tuxedo shirt, smoking like a devil (an ashtray was bolted to his mike stand), Keith prowled the stage and used crouching body language to get his songs over. Unlike Mick's solo shows, Keith played his album instead of the Stones' catalog. But, halfway through, ex-Bluebelle Sarah Dash brought the house down with a churchy "Time Is on My Side." The first encore, after the obligatory "Happy," was a faithful rendition of "Connection," the first Stones song on which Keith sang the lead vocal.

Keith loved the Winos because they'd become his friends rather than a hired band. He loved what he called "this feeling of unity" and told people he was in awe of the cats in the band because they knew even more than he did. They got stronger as they crossed America that fall, and were at their zenith for a Los Angeles show taped and recorded on December 15. The last show was at the Brendan Byrne Arena in New Jersey on December 17, with Johnnie Johnson playing piano on a rough Wino version of "Run Rudolph Run." Afterward a party was held in the hall's bar to celebrate both a successful tour and Keith Richards's forty-fifth birthday. Patti and the girls were there, as well as a healthier Anita Pallenberg. Mick Jagger couldn't make it.

"*Talk Is Cheap* didn't just recharge my batteries," Keith said later. "It brought me back to life. I felt like I'd just got out of jail." For the X-Pensive

Winos, the atmosphere was bittersweet. They knew that the boss was going back to the Stones and that it would be years before they worked together again. Whatever happened, they had all been part of the process that allowed the Rolling Stones to regroup and attempt the most difficult trick in show business—the comeback.

ten:

Old Gods

The Steel Wheels *tour press conference, New York, 1989.*

I never intended to be a sex symbol. I thought of myself as

a serious musician. I didn't want to be a stripper. But then, in

the end, I turned out to be just another girl on the runway.

Mick Jagger

You never know what the sound's gonna be like in those stadiums.

You're relying on God, who joins the band every night in one

form or another.

Keith Richards

Speed of Light

The small private jet carrying Keith Richards dropped over the aquamarine Caribbean and landed on the green island of Barbados on January 12, 1989. He was on his way to meet with Mick Jagger at Blue Wave Studios to resuscitate the Rolling Stones, and the road was going to be rocky. For the long-absent and estranged Stones to come back, they had to not only recapture their own generation but also seduce young fans currently owned by post-punk bands like Guns 'N Roses—groups that had molded themselves on Keith's death's-door legend. The Stones were competing with their sons now.

Keith was unsure if he and Mick could work together again. He was pessimistic. Leaving his girls in Connecticut, Keith had told Patti that he'd be home in either two weeks or two days. Mick was already at work on new music when Keith arrived late in the afternoon.

"I drove up to the rehearsal place," Keith recalled, "and I heard him playing ["Hold On to Your Hat"]. I just sat in the car for five minutes and listened, and I said, 'Yeah, no problem, this year's *made.*'" It was almost that simple, mostly because they were so rushed. The Stones planned to tour in the fall as the biggest single-act rock extravaganza ever attempted, which demanded that a new Stones album be finished by May at the latest. Their schedule didn't give the Stones much time to kill each other.

Mick and Keith started right away in Barbados, playing guitars together. Keith had ideas left over from his solo album: "Almost Hear You Sigh" and "Slipping Away." Seizing the edgy vibe at Blue Wave by the throat, Keith found the tonally complex and evocative chords to "Mixed Emotions" the day after he arrived. "Rock and a Hard Place" was next, and "Can't Be Seen with You." After a few days, Patti got through to Keith on the phone. "Two weeks, then?" she asked. "Happily, yes," he replied.

They interrupted their work on January 16 to fly to New York. Back in the Waldorf ballroom, the Rolling Stones were inducted into the Hall of Fame by Peter Townshend. Ron Wood came in from England without Bill and Charlie, killing any hope the Stones would play. (Bill slagged the Hall of Fame honors as too little recognition too late, and even Mick and Keith were concerned lest the Stones now be perceived as museum relics rather than a fire-breathing rock band.) Mick Taylor, who was living in New York, helped accept the award from Townshend, who delivered an idolatrous induction tirade that ended: "Guys, whatever you do, don't try to grow old gracefully. It wouldn't suit you." In his turn, Mick spoke of Brian Jones and Ian Stewart, and nervously added that the Stones weren't quite ready to hang up their number yet.

Back to Barbados in February 1989. Mick and Keith jammed and trolled for songs on a hotel balcony, waves crashing below, with guitars, a keyboard, tape recorder, and bottle of vodka. Keith: "Once we cleared the air, something entirely different took over. I can't define it. It's what always happens. I just start banging out a little riff. He'll go, 'That's nice,' and he'll come up with a top line. Once Mick and I settle down to work, everything else goes out the window." At night, Mick dragged Keith out to nightclubs; Keith hated it, but Mick liked to go dancing and wanted Keith along, since Jerry Hall refused to return to Barbados.

Soon Prince Rupert Lowenstein joined them for a business meeting. The Stones would now pioneer a new way of presenting themselves that changed the concert business for the biggest acts in the world. They sold their whole tour—concerts, merchandising, TV and film rights—to their longtime Canadian promoter, Michael Cohl of Toronto's Concert Productions International, for about $70 million. Backed by big beer money (Budweiser would be the official tour sponsor), Cohl guaranteed the Stones their paychecks, assuming all financial risk in return for a share of the tour's profits. CPI paid out millions for stage design and construction, manufactured the T-shirts and tongue decals, handled promotion, and kept ticket prices down to a top of $31.50.

It was a landmark deal, one that almost killed Bill Graham. Graham had run the last Stones tour in '81–'82, and Mick had toured Australia under the aegis of his company, Bill Graham Presents. But Graham had missed some of Jagger's solo shows due to other commitments, and it may have cost him dearly. Mick was determined to make a change. The Stones' lawyers only told Graham about the CPI deal after the fact, and wouldn't let him bid on the tour. They offered him $500,000 to consult on the tour, which the volatile impresario took as an insult. He fought back, put his own deal together, made a counteroffer to Mick on a Concorde flight to London in early March. He told Mick that with his offer, the Stones would take home $16 million apiece. The Canadian deal would give them each $18 million. Pleading with Mick, trying to appeal to his sense of their long history together, Graham rhetorically asked him what—after all these twenty years in business together—was *really* the difference between $16 and $18 million.

Mick: "Two million dollars, Bill."

The other Stones flew to Barbados in March. Coproducer Chris Kimsey brought in a young English synthesizer whiz named Matt Clifford to sweeten and modernize the Stones' ambient sound for the new digital era. As they worked, some of the feuds and bitterness of the past resurfaced and spilled over into the sessions, fueling the vibe of "Mixed Emotions." Keith and Ron split into their own faction, while Mick paired with Matt Clifford. But by the end of the month, Mick and Keith had about twenty songs they liked, and after a break the sessions resumed at Beatles producer George Martin's AIR studios on the green, idyllic (and doomed) volcanic island of Montserrat.

They kicked Bill Wyman off the island for a week because he (fifty-three) had proposed to Mandy Smith (nineteen) by telephone from Barbados, and she had accepted. As London reporters began to descend, Bill was banished to Antigua to deal with them and keep the press away from the Stones' sessions. Ron Wood took over on bass, and the Stones cut their best tracks without Bill, including "Sad Sad Sad," "Hold On to Your Hat," and "Call Girl Blues" (which became "Break the Spell"). A killer version of the Impressions' 1958 "For Your Precious Love" would be left off the album, as would be the blues "Wish I'd Never Met You" and a mock-obscene song about underage girls called "So Young" (rumored to be about Mick's new friend, teenage model Carla Bruni). Time pressure kept things rushed, a crammed schedule less than satisfying to Keith. Mick was playing guitar and trying to run the band's traditionally long and slow instrumental sessions. Keith told friends that Mick hadn't the knack for either job.

Charlie Watts assumed a new role in the Stones as well, becoming an arbiter between Mick and Keith. If they couldn't agree on something, it was "Let's ask Charlie" now. During the five weeks the Stones banged out *Steel Wheels* in Montserrat, Charlie was often in the studio twelve hours a day. People familiar with the Stones felt that Charlie thought he had something to prove to Keith, who had dared to work with another drummer on his solo deal. Charlie drove Keith so hard that at the end of one of these fifteen-hour sessions Keith could hardly stand up. He'd be lying on the floor and Mick would say, "What's wrong with you? It's Charlie, man. I *know* it."

By May 1989, the Stones were back in London, mixing tracks at an old haunt, Olympic Studio. They were still working on Mick's trippy song "Continental Drift." Written in Barbados on a Korg synthesizer programmed by Matt Clifford, timed by an almost subliminal rhythm track of Keith playing the spokes of a bicycle wheel, the neo-Sufi love poem was missing the trance-inducing melodic hook it needed. Then, out of the blue and after a twenty-year silence, Mick Jagger received a letter from the Master Musicians of Jajouka in Morocco.

The Jajoukans were down on their luck. Many of the older musicians who had played for Brian Jones in 1968 had died or were retired, and their band was now led by Bachir Attar, the twenty-six-year-old son of the late chief. (Bachir was a dancing boy when Brian Jones had visited twenty years before.) Jajouka had never seen any money from Brian's album, which by then was generally described as the alpha recording of the world music movement. The Jajouka musicians were broke and themselves split into traditionalist and modernist factions. Bachir Attar was married to an American photographer, Cherie Nutting, who contacted the Stones on the tribe's behalf with the idea that both Jajouka and the Rolling Stones could breathe new life into each other.

Mick: "When I was writing ["Drift"], I said, 'Oh, this would be great if we could have someone like Jajouka on it.' And a week later I got a letter from them saying, 'Can we come and play on [the tour] that you're doing?' "

In mid-June, Mick, Keith, Ron, Matt Clifford, and a technical team arrived in Tangier. Bachir Attar brought a dozen musicians down from the mountains, and they spent a weekend recording their pipes and drums in the courtyard of the nineteenth-century casbah mansion known as Palais Ben Abou. Dressed in a silk caftan, Mick conducted the Jajoukans as a BBC crew filmed the sessions. Keith, Ron, and Jo watched from the shadows with Paul Bowles while the Moroccans sent waves of ethereal music into the North African air and the tapes rolled in a dark room off the sun-splashed tiled atrium.

The Glory, Darling

Summer 1989. The Stones were in London, annoyed at Bill Wyman for opening a memorabilia-filled burger joint called Sticky Fingers without asking for permission. They were also put off by having to attend, with their grumbling wives, Wyman's June wedding to Mandy Smith, a certified tabloid carnival.

Late in June, they put the final touches on *Steel Wheels,* a double-entendre title that referred both to locomotive power and to the wheelchairs of the aged and infirm. Mick had this album and tour pegged as emblematic of Industrial Age decline and the dawn of the Digital Age of megabytes, cyberpunks, and *Blade Runner*-style decay. His conceit was reflected in the stadium production designed by London architect Mark

Fisher for the Steel Wheels tour. An immense sculptured scaffold artwork with catwalks, chutes, and antennae suggested a closed steel mill, a redundant oil refinery, or a useless launching pad—all the obsolete detritus of a once-great but now-rusting civilization. With sixty-two American shows scheduled for the fall, the Stones ordered two of these stages built and hired a 350-man crew to hopscotch them around the country in a fleet of fifty tractor trailers. Total cost: $4 million. There was also a traveling retinue of about fifty managers, assistants, publicists, and security. Keith said it was like having four hundred guys in the band instead of five.

In July, the Rolling Stones gathered at a secluded girls' boarding school, Whykham Rise, near Keith's house in ex-urban Connecticut to regroup as a Vegas-style show band. Chuck Leavell was back on piano, with Matt Clifford working the samples, synthesizers, and orchestrations. Three singers were hired: Bernard Fowler, Lisa Fischer, and Cindy Mizell. The Uptown Horns, a busy New York quartet, came to play, but it didn't click. Keith: "A whole brass section had been hired—good guys. But something wasn't happening, so I call Bobby Keys: 'Not gettin' any answers, Bobby. So just come up to New York. Just come to rehearsals. Be there. I'll guarantee you.'" Keys took charge of the horn players, which added up to a touring band of fifteen musicians.

Amid rehearsals and business meetings projecting a $200-million gross, protected by security goons whose roadblock enraged the townspeople of sleepy Washington, Connecticut, Mick was jogging five miles a day through the green summer hills with an Olympic trainer. Keith, eager to verify the Baudelaire maxim concerning the systematic derangement of the senses, maintained a daily regimen of vodka, pills, hash, and cocaine. Over the next month, they built a show that began with the rush of "Start Me Up" and progressed through a mix of oldies and songs from *Wheels* in a theatrical pageant spanning almost thirty years. "Paint It, Black" got a new Anatolian/klezmer arrangement. "2000 Light Years from Home" was dusted off to be performed as a psychedelic nugget for the acid-house generation under a throbbing Frisco light show. "Little Red Rooster" got a new, lazy-slow arrangement featuring Ron Wood on slide guitar. With women onstage with the Stones for the first time, some flirtatious stage business was choreographed for Mick and sultry Lisa Fischer during "Miss You." The twenty-eight-song set tried to touch on every major era of the Stones since 1964, and seven weeks were spent working the singers and horns into the act.

———

Apropos of the railway theme, the Steel Wheels tour was announced at a press conference on July 11 at Grand Central Terminal in New York. The Stones arrived in an old caboose, debuted the new single "Mixed Emotions" on a little boom box (which gave Mick some trouble), and took the usual questions. *Are you doing this for the money?* Mick looked pained, since they obviously weren't doing it for their sanity. "What about love and fame and fortune?" he responded innocently. "Have you forgotten about all those things?" Keith leaned into the mike and croaked, "It's the glory, darling. The *glory.*" Everyone laughed except Bill Wyman, who collapsed a day later from food poisoning.

On August 12, the Rolling Stones ambushed Toad's Place, a three-hundred-seat club in New Haven, on a Saturday night. The regular band, Sons of Bob, didn't even know who the night's other group was until they saw the Stones' gear being loaded in. Without a word, Keith crashed into "Start Me Up" for a delirious bar crowd that saw a terse, fifty-minute show.

Steel Wheels was released on the eve of the tour in September, reaching no. 1 in America and no. 2 in England. "Mixed Emotions" was the (unsuccessful) first single, backed with "Fancyman Blues," a twelve-bar blues in the manner of Jimmy Reed (Mick tasty on harp), recorded in Montserrat.

"Sad Sad Sad" began the album with a hard rock blast and a corrosive message of trouble in the air, as if to reassure their fans that all was not well with the Rolling Stones. "Mixed Emotions" seconded that emotion with its demand to "Button your lip, baby" and honest ambivalence about staying together to work out deeply personal problems. The harmonizing chorus singing with Mick was a new format the Stones would use for the rest of the decade and beyond.

"Terrifying" was a Jagger/Clifford collaboration about the singer's "strange desires" and anxiety-provoking obsessions, delivered with cool detachment and synthetic washes of pop-jazz ambience. The punkish minimalism of "Hold On to Your Hat" was followed by "Hearts for Sale" with its loping vibe of serial infidelity. "Blinded by Love" was a country-politan history lesson with Professor Jagger recounting the romantic miseries of famous suckers for love—Marc Antony, Samson, the prince of Wales.

"Rock and a Hard Place" was the album's failed Big Statement. Its vague global concerns tried to echo the political tumult of 1989—velvet revolution, the fall of the Berlin Wall, the end of communism in Europe—but the moment was too big to be captured in a guitar-band anthem. "Can't Be Seen" was more to the point, as Keith led the Stones (without Mick) in a churning, passionate romance of pursuit and escape, a quest decorated with blazing guitars and the first real passion to appear on the album. Mick and his chorus sang the Richards/Jordon "Almost Hear You Sigh," which had some beautiful acoustic guitar fills by Keith.

"Continental Drift" announced itself as Serious Art in the first moments of sampled *rhaita* music from the Jajouka musicians. After lyrics inspired by Andalusian love poetry, "Drift" evolved into a complex, synthetic representation of the dance of Bou Jeloud under a full moon—an extended foray into mysticism, trance music, and the certain magic of repetition. It was the last Mellotronic echo of Brian Jones and his Panic obsessions on a Rolling Stones record. The long track ends in a mountain travelogue of cane flutes and a Sufic conference of the birds, in what appeared to be a nostalgic dreamscape of the misty 1960s.

"Break the Spell" brought the album back to earth with a blues shuffle; Ron Wood on dobro, Mick Jagger as Tom Waits. The finale was Keith's "Slipping Away," a rock ballad (cut without Mick) that limned the composer's existential philosophy of loss, impermanence, and detachment.

Steel Wheels was another Stones album made by two different factions within the band, with a lot of outside help on both sides. Critics and fans found the music cold and without much soul, an attitude mirrored in the gray, high-tech ripsaw design of the album package. It was as if the Rolling Stones saw no further point in trying to fool anyone about what was going on. Mick maintained his hard gloss of glamour and cynicism, while Keith fought in his corner as the beating heart of the band. If it was now all an act, it was at least well played.

––––––––

Any doubts about the marketplace viability of the Rolling Stones in 1989 were dispelled when 2 million fans tried to get tickets for the opening shows in Philadelphia. The Canadian promoters were so overwhelmed by demands for backstage passes from the self-entitled that they created a VIP pass that got the badge-holder into an empty room. On August 31, after black heavy metal band Living Colour opened the show, the Stones took the stage at JFK Stadium amid explosions and a hundred-yard wall of fire as Keith cuffed the chords to "Start Me Up." Outside, the ticketless were fighting with the cops, who made twenty-eight arrests as the Stones thundered through their set. All went well until halfway through "Shattered," when the Stones' eighty-ton, half-million-watt sound system went dead. After three minutes of horrible silence, the sound crew (supervised by Benji Lefevre of Led Zeppelin fame) fixed a faulty generator and the set resumed. The fabulous "Shattered," presumed jinxed, was dropped for the rest of the tour.

It was a new Rolling Stones in 1989, with new rules imposed by the magnitude of the business they were now in. Everyone had to be on time. No hard drugs backstage, sound checks before every show. The tour's in-surers had demanded physical checkups; Keith passed his, to the amaze-ment of all. No longer sequestered in drugdom, the band was virtually living at the gigs. "Backstage" now meant a mobile village of dressing rooms, dining areas, a meet-and-greet bar, tuning rooms, and a traveling lounge with comfy sofas, potted plants, and a pool table. In its enormity and almost military precision, Steel Wheels became the model for the road tours the Stones deployed from then on.

It took half a dozen concerts for the Stones to feel comfortable on their stage, which was longer than a football field. Charlie Watts could only see the heads and legs of the rest of the band, and when Mick was off on the ramps or Keith decided to take a walk, the drummer sometimes lost visual contact with them for twenty minutes. From the top rows of a stadium, the stage looked like a high-tech puppet theater, with tiny figures running around.

With its prerecorded samples and hundreds of cues for lights and pyrotechnics, there was little room for improvisation in the performances, and fans who attended multiple shows heard virtually the same set every night. During "It's Only Rock 'n' Roll," the big video screens on either side of the stage showed clips of rock heroes from Chuck Berry and Buddy Holly to Bowie and Zeppelin. Gargantuan inflatable bimbos (Angie and Ruby) ballooned voluptuously over the stage during "Honky Tonk Women" every night. The show's coup de théâtre would come when Mick vanished from the stage while being whisked eight floors to the top of the set by express elevator, appearing seconds later to sing "Sympathy for the Devil" amid a sulfurous curtain of smoke. The set ended in a finale of "Brown Sugar," "Jack Flash," and a rocking, soul-posturing "Satisfaction" before a Big Bang of fifty tons of fireworks and a pompous recording of Bizet's "March of the Toreadors" from *Carmen*.

On the road for the first time in seven years, everyone got along by doing his own thing. The after-show party was always in Keith's suite, with Otis Redding and obscure old reggae songs as background music. Although the Mick/Keith feud was supposedly history, Matt Clifford was deputized by Mick to keep him company after hours at dinner, a nightclub, or a movie. Clifford would get in trouble by trying to keep one foot in Mick's camp and one in Keith's.

Keith played almost every show on that tour with a pair of his wife's panties in his back pocket. Sellouts at Shea Stadium in New York, the Astrodome in Houston, the Gator Bowl and Orange Bowl in Florida, the Pontiac Silverdome, Montreal's Olympic Stadium. Rock monsters Guns 'N Roses opened four nights at the Los Angeles Coliseum, with Axl Rose in full skull costume in Keith's honor.

The American leg of the Steel Wheels tour ended in Atlantic City, New Jersey, a once-faded resort that had been successfully repositioned by legalized gambling as Las Vegas East. The final show at the Convention Center was simulcast over cable TV and FM radio networks. The Stones' special guests included seventy-two-year-old John Lee Hooker chanting his monochromatic boogie to the largest audience of his life; Eric Clapton painting a busy, pointillistic guitar solo on "Rooster"; and Axl Rose singing with Mick on "Salt of the Earth." The Stones' broadcast set a record for pay-per-view television in America. The tour itself, in which 3.4 million customers had seen the band in fifty-nine shows, was the biggest ever mounted at the time.

As they parted ways to spend the last Christmas of the 1980s with their families, the Stones were jubilant and unapologetic about the incredible success of their comeback. Only a year earlier, the band didn't exist and weren't even speaking.

Keith: "We asked ourselves, 'Why are we doing this? Do we really want to?' And the answer was that we *have* to. Not from the money viewpoint as from the fact that none of us was about to let the Stones drift away. We're still looking for the ultimate Rolling Stones. We're never going to find it, but it's like the Holy Grail. It's the quest that's important, not finding it."

Tanks Roll Out, Stones Roll In

In February 1990, after a month's rest, the Rolling Stones played their first-ever concerts in Japan. They flew in early without Bill, whose father was ill and whose young wife was convalescing from a severe intestinal disease. Arriving ten days early, they did a round of press conferences and receptions featuring samurai honor guards and barrels of sake, a traditional welcoming gift. After watching Buster Douglas win the world heavyweight boxing championship from Mike Tyson, the Stones played ten sold-out Steel Wheels shows at the Tokyo Dome, the immense covered stadium (called the Big Egg) usually used for baseball games. Japanese audiences took some getting used to: thunderous applause was followed by pin-drop silence as the immense crowds waited for the next number.

Architect Mark Fisher came to Tokyo to consult on a new set for the European leg of the tour that summer. The Steel Wheels rig was too big and expensive to trot around the continent, and the late European summer twilight made the intense Wheels lighting unnecessary. Fisher's new set was a lighter, summery curtain of colorful cloth scrims hung from the scaffolds. Instead of industrial apocalypse, the 1990 Urban Jungle tour would imply a derelict plantation amid tropical decay and wild beasts.

————

The Stones left Japan and took some time off. At the end of April, the band gathered at a chateau in Normandy to rehearse in its ballroom. "Street Fighting Man" was resurrected as a big production number during which four giant saber-toothed dog balloons would unfurl. The cartoonish rabid canines (equipped with hard-ons) became the Urban Jungle logo, inspired by "Terrifying," released as a European single to go with the tour.

The forty-five Urban Jungle shows began in Rotterdam's Olympic Stadium on June 2, 1990. "Blinded by Love" and "Terrifying" were added to the set, and Keith alternated "Can't Be Seen" with a skewed, cubist "Happy" in his solo spot. Mick prodded one of the four dog balloons (Top Dog, Kennel Dog, Skippy, and Shagger) in its balls with a long pole, and was eaten by Shagger at the end of "Street Fighting Man." The ancient Stones rave-up "I Just Want to Make Love to You" was rumbled out before seventy thousand on the first of three nights in Paris, sending older fans into paroxysms of nostalgia. The former outlaw blues band now found itself politically attractive. Jacques Chirac, then mayor of Paris, gave the Stones the keys to the city. In Madrid, Mick was received by Spanish premier Felipe González. Keith was drinking heavily and playing louder than bombs. At Berlin's Olympic Stadium on June 6, Mick made the mistake of telling Keith it would be the largest crowd the Rolling Stones had ever faced. Keith turned up the juice even higher, and Mick complained that his ears were bleeding.

The Urban Jungle stages could be built in six days instead of the ten required by Steel Wheels. This kept ticket prices down, but cash was tight for European kids that summer and many shows failed to sell out. In Rome at the end of July, an embarrassing three thousand customers were scattered around Stadio Flaminio for what had been billed as Mick's forty-seventh birthday party. It was also a wet summer, and many shows were performed in a downpour.

In August, the Urban Jungle careened through Scandinavia and, for the first time, East Germany and Czechoslovakia, dates added late to the schedule. In Prague, the Stones were received like a liberating army by the country's new president, Václav Havel, the dissident playwright often jailed by the communists who had relinquished power in November 1989. "Tanks are rolling out," the poster for the concert read, "and the Stones are rolling in!" The Czech government even let a giant yellow tongue logo be placed on a hill overlooking historic Prague, a spot where a giant statue of Stalin once stood. President Havel, a longtime rock fan, told the Stones over drinks in an Old Town bar how crucial their music had been for the postwar generation that had grown up behind the Iron Curtain. This seemed to validate one of Keith's most devoutly espoused theories. "It was rock and roll and blue jeans that took down that Iron Curtain in the long run," Keith insisted. "It wasn't all those atomic weapons, and facing them down, and all that big bullshit. What finally crumbled the wall was the fuckin' *music*, man. You cannot stop it. It is the *most* subversive thing . . . You can build a wall to stop people, but eventually the music—it'll get across that wall."

The Stones played at Prague's Strahov Stadium on August 19. Havel and 107,000 fans saw the band in the open air under a stunning downpour. A ticket to the concert served as a one-day passport so thousands of Hungarians and Poles could attend as well. The Stones' fee was donated to a children's charity run by Havel's celebrated wife, Olga.

The Stones flew back to London on the Czech president's plane, and the tour ended with two shows at Wembley Stadium on August 24 and 25. Since these shows were filmed with IMAX cameras (Julian Temple directed), the huge Steel Wheels set was re-created, minus the fireworks, which were banned by local authorities for safety reasons. Both shows sold out, and the Stones pulled out the stops for the London crowd, who got an extended, smoking Keith Richards blues guitar solo during Mick Taylor's old spot in "Sympathy for the Devil."

The last Wembley show was the 115th of the Steel Wheels/Urban Jungle cycle. The shows always ended with the whole ensemble taking their bows together in a line. Then the auxiliaries would fade off, leaving the five Rolling Stones standing alone as waves of cheering broke over them. (An old inside joke required that Charlie Watts always held a guitar at the final bow.) The nostalgic and affectionate Wembley crowd on that final night had no inkling that it was also Bill Wyman's last appearance with the Rolling Stones.

The band gave a party at the Kensington Roof Gardens later that night to thank the crew. Anita Pallenberg came, on her way back from years of addiction. After a cure finally stuck, she was working with a narcotics help line, going to the gym, riding her bicycle around London, about to go to college to study textile design. Marianne Faithfull, off heroin and recovering her beauty and her career, made a low-key appearance. The end-of-tour relief and fatigue were offset by high spirits. The whole venture was counted a big success: it reunited the Stones, generated a reported $200 million, and gave the rock music community a much-needed boost of glamour and grit. The Stones had pioneered a new standard with their dressed-up stadiums, raising the bar for all the big rock acts that tried to follow them.

————

September 1990, and the Stones scattered to their other lives: Keith to Jamaica, Charlie to England, Wood to Ireland. Mick took his family on a long Asian holiday. Surrendering to the romance of the South Pacific, Mick married Jerry Hall (without papers) in Bali, in a ceremony officiated by a Hindu priest and witnessed by their two children and Alan

Dunn. (Jerry reportedly signed a prenuptial agreement limiting a divorce settlement to $10 million. The British press looked into the legality of the wedding and decided it wasn't binding under Indonesian law.)

Bill Wyman published his memoirs, *Stone Alone*, that autumn. A compulsive diarist and collector, Bill also proclaimed himself sexual champion of the band, detailing his countless conquests around the world. Keith: "I could never understand this thing about counting women. I was there, and he's probably got the number right—I'd see nine or ten go in there, but they were only there for ten minutes. What are you gonna do with a chick in ten minutes, for Christ's sake? It takes them half that long to get their drawers down." By years end, Bill's marriage had broken down after seventeen months. The couple had never lived together. Mandy's weight was down to seventy pounds, and she had a religious awakening that left her husband out. "Everyone knew it was a terrible mistake," Keith said later, "but what could you say?"

Keith lay low in Jamaica until December, when he flew to England to begin mixing the concert tapes for a new live album. At a band meeting, Mick and Keith told the others they didn't want to work for a couple of years. Keith missed Mick and Jerry's London wedding celebration on December 7, going instead to New York, where he celebrated his forty-seventh birthday and third wedding anniversary at home in Connecticut. No rest for the wicked, though, as the Stones would find themselves back in the studio in early 1991 as England prepared to go to war.

Pay Us in Crude

With hostilities about to break out in the Persian Gulf states in the aftermath of Iraq's sack of Kuwait, the Rolling Stones interrupted work on their concert tapes in London during January 1991 to record a topical new single, "High Wire." Mick Jagger's deeply ambivalent lyrics about international oil politics and the arms trade ("You can pay us in crude," he sneers) was set to the "Honky Tonk Women" chords. "High Wire" was an antiwar song that still expressed sympathy for the allied pilots flying the bombing runs on Baghdad that began on January 16, the day the Stones recorded the track. Released on the day the Gulf War ended in February, "High Wire" ("We got no pride, don't care whose boots we lick") managed to provoke Tory demands in Parliament for a BBC radio ban. Working with producer Chris Kimsey, the Stones also cut "Sex Drive," a Jamesian funk chant set to a "Hot Stuff" lick, as the single's B side. "Sex Drive" was possibly the most self-explanatory lyric Mick ever wrote, a candid psychodrama of erotic compulsion.

These were Bill Wyman's last sessions as a Rolling Stone, and he subsequently refused to appear on the "High Wire" video.

Keith Richards kept working in 1991, playing on albums by Johnnie Johnson, John Lee Hooker, and Tom Waits. The three songs Keith recorded with Waits were the maximum allowed under the Stones' record contract. He owed Virgin Records another solo album and began working with Steve Jordon and Ivan Neville in New York that spring. Virgin's Richard Branson was eager to sign the Rolling Stones as well, since *Flashpoint*, the Wheels/Jungle concert album released that spring, was the last record of the old CBS deal. CBS had been sold to Sony, Walter Yetnikoff was gone, and Mick was very interested in a new deal with Virgin, even if industry gossip whispered that Branson was selling the label and only wanted the reigning heavyweight champions of rock to boost its value.

While Mick Jagger was filming his villain's role in the sci-fi movie *Freejack*, Charlie Watts promoted his jazz album *From One Charlie*, a tribute to Charlie Parker. Ron Wood had successful art shows in London and Japan, and built an art studio, a recording studio, and a pub at his Irish farm. Bill Wyman told friends he was never getting on an airplane again and was leaving the Stones, this time for real. Keith downplayed this, telling an interviewer that Bill was of a different generation and on his third menopause.

Mick Jagger moved his pregnant wife and family back to England that summer, buying a Georgian mansion called Downe House (mature gardens, Adam ceilings, views of the Thames, $4 million w/AGA) on Richmond Hill, near Rupert Lowenstein's house. His daughter Elizabeth was starting school, and Mick wanted his children properly brought up and educated in England.

In November 1991, the Rolling Stones signed with Virgin Records for a reported $45 million at a meeting at Prince Rupert's London office. The contract granted Virgin the distribution rights to the Rolling Stones Records catalog and guaranteed the label three new albums. Bill Wyman, now almost fifty-five, fearful of flying and bored with playing oldies in stadiums, refused to sign the Virgin contract. No one quite believed he would quit, and the terms of the deal gave him almost a year to think about it. Richard Branson took his new clients and their wives out to dinner, a liquid affair that broke up at dawn. Four months later, Branson sold Virgin Records to Thorn-EMI and used the proceeds to start an airline.

———

Word that Bill Wyman had left the Rolling Stones leaked out in January 1992. Keith speculated in public that Wyman had gone mad, but others thought that crafty old Bill had spotted a trend. By 1992, the rock music movement was almost finished. The beginnings of Brit-pop, the riff-banging of heroin-fueled Seattle grunge, and the radical murder music of the rappers took over a new generation that had never known a world without the Stones. The new audience was as far removed from the English rock stars of the 1960s as the Stones had been from the primal bluesmen of the 1930s. U2's *Achtung Baby* and Aerosmith's *Pump*, both released in 1990, can arguably be called the last great rock albums.

Jerry Hall had a baby girl in January 1992, named Georgia May. After a decent interval, Mick flew to Japan to promote the Stones' movie *At the Max*, then flew to a Thai resort where he was spotted with the model Carla Bruni, whom he'd been seeing for a couple of years. This assignation got into the press and there were big problems at Downe House. Jerry kicked Mick out, told the *Daily Mail* that a man oughta stick by his woman after she's just had a baby, and started talking divorce.

So Mick stayed on the road, developing a new solo album with guitarist Jimmy Ripp in Los Angeles. He jammed with the Red Devils blues band at a club in the Valley and did a studio session with them that covered Little Walter, Muddy, Wolf, Elmore, Slim Harpo, and Bukka White—as if Mick were trying to jump-start the old Terraplane. In June, he attended his daughter Karis's graduation from Yale. In July, the forty-nine-year-old pop star, who'd sworn in 1969 he'd never find himself singing "Satisfaction" at fifty, became a grandfather when Jade Jagger had a baby girl in London.

For the rest of 1992, Mick worked with the young hip-hop producer/tycoon Rick Rubin on *Wandering Spirit*. His two previous solo albums hadn't established a separate identity for Mick, and he didn't bother to try too hard on *Spirit*, notable mostly for its three soul covers and an Irish song. He patched it up with Jerry that summer while he recorded at his French chateau, then moved the sessions to Olympic in London that fall and rejoined his family, the diamond in his tooth sparkling again. "I've led a very strange life," Mick told a reporter as he cut a series of tracks about loneliness, loss, and aging. *Wandering Spirit* was completed that fall at Ocean Way, an inexpensive, retrofitted studio in a sleazy part of Hollywood. Billy Preston helped with the gospel-flavored "Out of Focus," while retro-rocker Lenny Kravitz duetted with Mick on the old Bill Withers song "Use Me." Mick and Rick Rubin listened to the playbacks and argued with each other in Rubin's mobile headquarters, an old Rolls-Royce parked in back of the studio.

———

Keith was recording his second solo album with the Winos, *Main Offender,* a spare riff and roll guitar-band album of ten songs written with the group and done quickly in the spring and summer. The highlight and first single was the love song "Eileen," a thrilling rocker sung by Keith with camel-voiced arabesques and trills. *Main Offender*'s October 1992 release was accompanied by an X-Pensive Winos world tour (playing mostly theaters) that extended well into 1993.

Main Offender barely made it into the Hot Hundred in America, but Keith didn't care and stayed on the road. In interviews, he remained philosophical about what was important in life. "I love my kids and my wife most of the time," he told *Guitar Player* late in '92. "Music I love *all* the time. It's the only constant joy in my life. You're never alone with a guitar. It's the one thing you can count on."

Doc's Office + Voodoo Lounge

In 1993, Keith Richards still wanted Bill Wyman to stay in the Rolling Stones, but they didn't speak. "I don't wanna change this lineup unless I really got to," Keith muttered. "Playing guitar is one thing; playing the other guys in the band is another." Keith put his spies out, talked to Bill's ex-girlfriends on the phone. Word came back that Bill was serious. He had settled about a million dollars on his divorced young wife, whom he had genuinely loved, and wanted to put his past behind him. Bill had a new American girlfriend, wanted to start another family, and was ready to retire from the Stones after thirty years.

Bill quit the Stones on live TV when he appeared on *London Tonight* on January 6, 1993. He said he just didn't want to do it anymore and was content with his fortune and his memories. "I don't think it will faze us that much," Mick Jagger told the press. "We'll miss Bill, but we'll get someone good. A good *dancer*." Bill told Charlie Watts he figured he only had twenty years left and didn't want to spend two of them with the Stones. "I could understand when Bill left," Ron Wood cracked. "He was two thousand years old."

February 1993. While Keith kept touring, Mick's solo album *Wandering Spirit* was released on Atlantic Records as part of a two-album deal with Ahmet Ertegun. A blue and introspective album from the usually glib singer, *Spirit* tried to break through the heavier grunge and rap rhythms on the radio. It was a surprise success: there had been no new

Stones album in four years, and it reached no. 11 in the United States. With no Mick Jagger solo tour, the album was promoted by a flurry of magazine covers and interviews (sample headline: "Have You Seen your Grandfather, Baby, Standing in the Shadows?"). The stories emphasized Mick's marital troubles, his social coldness and perceived isolation, his six homes in England, America, France, and Mustique. Mick handled it all like an old pro. "Either you're dead," he told *Esquire,* "or you move along."

Though Keith was obviously enjoying the creative space that the X-Pensive Winos gave, he was also ready to revive the Stones. He didn't relish the front-man role and said that the experience had given him new respect for Mick. Near the end of February, Keith visited Mick's house in New York to discuss the next record. Keith said he wanted to make a *Stones* record this time, a stripped-down modern sound, not operatic and baroque. Mick agreed that this time he wanted the oddball, offhand moments of genius left in this album. Keith: "We sat around Mick's kitchen and kicked ideas around. I said, 'I got stuff.' He says, 'Yeah, I got stuff.' I came out with one word—focus. We would have to get some grooves down . . . We'd all be looking down the same scope this time, we've got all the other ingredients, all we need to do is *focus.*"

They started focusing together in Barbados in April at Blue Wave studio, leaning on Winos-type rockabilly and Afro-Parisian grooves for inspiration. Keith wrote "The Worst" in the studio kitchen, then "Through and Through" in the studio at dawn after a night out with guitar tech Pierre de Beauport, who played guitar on it. Charlie Watts joined them ten days later, relieved to find the atmosphere friendly and relaxed. The drummer plunged into the sessions and seemed a changed man. Now an experienced bandleader and record producer, Watts began to assert himself more in the Stones' production. "Turn me up," he barked at the astonished engineers.

Keith always took over a corner of the studio as his territory. At Blue Wave in Barbados, it was designated by a hand-lettered sign: Doc's Office. One night Keith was running from his cottage to the studio in a thunderstorm when he found a soaked and bedraggled kitten. It was the runt of a big litter and had been rejected by its mother. So Keith tucked the kitten under the plastic sheet that was keeping him dry and brought it to the studio. "This cat's Voodoo," he announced, and the kitten moved into Doc's office and made itself at home. Someone amended Keith's sign to read: DOC'S OFFICE + VOODOO LOUNGE.

The three Stones worked until May 18, when Mick and Charlie returned to England. Keith flew home, and eventually his kitten made its way to Connecticut too. Soon she had three kittens of her own. In June, the Stones were back in New York, auditioning twenty bass players, all of them great. Each musician got about an hour in a room at S.I.R. studio, playing "Brown Sugar," "Miss You," then a jam to see how they meshed with Charlie. *"Next!"* Living Colour's Doug Wimbish was rumored to have the job for a while, but when the Stones gathered at Ron Wood's Irish farm to rehearse in July, both Wood and Keith were playing bass. Keith moved into the granny flat Wood had built for his mother, and taped his Voodoo Lounge sign in the window.

The whole band, including the recently remarried Bill Wyman, attended Mick's fiftieth-birthday party for three hundred at Walpole House, the Victorian manor across the river from Richmond. The theme of the party was the ancien régime and the French Revolution. Jerry Hall presided as Marie Antoinette.

They were back in Ireland in September, working at the farm, when Darryl Jones arrived. He was a funky, mesomorphic, black bassist from Chicago who had made his name playing in Miles Davis's 1980s electric band (Miles called him "the Munch"). Jones had also toured with Sting, Peter Gabriel, Eric Clapton, and Madonna; he knew how to rock a house or a stadium. He was friends with the Winos' rhythm section. He had never seen the Stones play, but when he heard the job might still be open, he called the Stones' office and asked to audition. The Miles Davis gig counted for a lot. Darryl Jones was hired for the album and tour on Charlie Watts's say-so. At thirty-one, he was twenty years younger than the rest of the band.

"It's a big deal to change your rhythm section after thirty years," Keith said later. "It was a hell of a deal. We tried all the best bass players in the world, and there's no basis to make up your mind because they're all so good. We used Charlie as an arbitrator and said, '*You* choose the rhythm section,' and he said, 'You're putting me on the hot seat.' C'mon, Charlie—only once in thirty years! He plumped for Darryl straight off, and he slotted right in. I'm still trying to figure him out."

Ron Wood had an alcohol problem and a licensing deal with Guinness that kept his private pub stocked with the thick black fluid. The atmosphere at the farm was summertime-loose, and Keith spent hours in the studio playing acoustic guitar and singing by himself. One night Keith and Wood were tending a bonfire when a shower of sparks burst out of the flames. "Incoming!" Keith yelled as inspiration hit, and he ran to the studio to demo "Sparks Will Fly" with Charlie. The two Stones tenderly nursed the track for months, allowing no one else to touch it until they got it right.

Six weeks later, they returned to Dublin and cut the basic tracks of *Voodoo Lounge* with Darryl Jones on bass and American producer Don Was. Was had helped Bonnie Raitt relaunch her career and had produced Bob Dylan's *Under the Red Sky*. He was known as a musical eccentric who worked fast and took it seriously. Don Was reminded Keith of Jimmy Miller because he was a producer who was also a musician. Was helped the Stones pare an avalanche of new songs down to a manageable two dozen. Longtime coproducer Chris Kimsey was given a rest, and he did a clever album of symphonic Stones arrangements. Matt Clifford wasn't invited back, because, according to insiders, he had tried to bridge the social gap in the band. Clifford was said to be crushed.

Mick Jagger formally announced in late November 1993 that Bill Wyman had left the Rolling Stones, which would continue with four principal members "and a cacophony of bass players." Around that time, Ron Wood was finally made a junior member of the Rolling Stones, with a percentage. He'd been on salary since 1976. "I didn't mind doing, like, a seventeen-year apprenticeship," Wood said. "But it's a hard nut to crack, the Stones' financial side. Luckily the *big* money only came when I got cut in." Mick was said to have opposed Wood's elevation, but was outvoted by Charlie and Keith. "He's not grown-up," Charlie said. "He's not at all sensible, Ronnie. It's not his role. He's a maniac. He has the attention span of a gnat."

Keith Richards celebrated his own fiftieth birthday in December with all his children, Bobby Keys, Eric Clapton, and 150 friends who took over a restaurant on Manhattan's West Side and jammed late into the night.

String Us Up.
We Still Won't Die

In January 1994, Mick Jagger and Keith Richards were in Los Angeles to complete *Voodoo Lounge*. Five years had passed since *Steel Wheels,* the longest silence ever for the Stones. With another megatour scheduled through 1995, the Stones needed a murderously good album to carry them through, and insiders thought they had it. The basic tapes from Dublin sounded like the real, authentic Stones of Ian Stewart and Elmo Lewis. They sounded "live" and very rocky, with an intimate, un-produced feel that suggested the X-Pensive Winos with Charlie Watts. Keith called it "recording the room."

This Irish ambience didn't survive a transplant to Los Angeles. Don Was had already steered the Stones away from the odd grooves and African licks they'd started with. Now, at his studio in L.A., he was giving the ballads and rockers they'd recorded in Ireland a retrofitting: vocals were buried down in the mix and the funk got filtered. Mick complained that Don Was was trying to reproduce *Exile on Main Street.* Meanwhile, Was won a Grammy Award for his production of Bonnie Raitt the previous year, which made him much harder to argue with.

No time for a rethink. When Virgin needed the album title quickly, Mick told them it was *Voodoo Lounge* because he was looking at Keith's shingle, which had followed the sessions across the oceans. The Stones' machine was kicking in. Mick called it "the virtual corporation." While overdubbing and mixing at A&M Studios, Mick and Charlie were supervising the design of the next $4-million stage to be paid for by a brewery. Borrowing technology developed for recent tours by U2, Pink Floyd, and Michael Jackson, Mark Fisher designed another concept stage. This time it was the Rolling Stones driving along the Information Highway to Wired City in all its gigabyte enormity, with a three-hundred-foot gridlike wall of light and an immense, unearthly Jumbotron video screen behind the band. Instead of stacks of amps, the music pushed out of slender columns on both sides of the stage. A ten-story tower shaped like a cobra loomed over the set, recalling the mythic nagas, giant serpents that protected Lord Buddha as he meditated. When exploding in barrages of pyro, Voodoo Lounge would look like a nuclear power plant melting down.

Keith finished the album at the end of April with Wood, Ivan Neville, and Bernard Fowler. This team completed "Love Is Strong" and Keith's "Through and Through," which ended the album. On May 3, 1994, from the deck of John Kennedy's old presidential yacht docked in the Hudson in New York, the Stones announced their tour: America through the rest of 1994, followed by the Pacific markets and Europe in 1995. Darryl Jones was announced as the new man on bass guitar.

The Munch gave the Stones a jolt when the band gathered in Toronto that June to begin rehearsals at the Crescent School, a boys' academy in the suburbs. (The school's cafeteria was transformed into a lounge with leather sofas, pinball machines, a snooker table, and a huge satellite-fed TV.) Mick had told Jones not to bother copying Bill Wyman's signature style. "Some of those classic bass lines aren't so classic anymore," Jones told an interviewer. "Since I joined the band, I've changed them around a lot." Chuck Leavell was back in the band with his arsenal of Korg, Kurzweil, Midi-B, and Yamaha keyboards. So were singers Lisa Fischer and Bernard Fowler. Bobby Keys led the New West Horns, a trio of New York musicians who had played on the album. For a month, this twelve-piece Rolling Stones relearned old songs by listening to the CD versions, then copying them. Mick relied on a dog-eared Stones songbook for the lyrics. The band developed fifty-four songs in

Toronto, for a basic two-and-a-half-hour show using twenty-two to twenty-five numbers.

————

Voodoo Lounge was released in July 1994 with a whiff of brimstone and Santeria iconography. In publicity photos, Keith wore the black top hat of the vodun god Baron Samedi, while Mick sported a pair of satanic-looking horns. Dancing skeletons and malign ectoplasms pervaded the album design, which cast the Stones as demonic entities risen from an Afro-Caribbean underworld to harrow the planet with Plutonian mischief. Even the Stones' once invitingly lascivious tongue logo was now armed with barbed thorns that promised pain, not pleasure, in the age of AIDS. Keith's carefully sharpened sound bites maintained the Undead pose. "String us up," he larfed. "We still won't die."

The album began with the hoodoo whisper of "Love Is Strong," with good bluesy harmonica by Mick. "You Got Me Rocking" was a banging war chant about dissipation and redemption. Keith's "Sparks Will Fly" was a seventies-style lust anthem (Mick: "I wanna fuck your sweet ass!"). Keith's "The Worst" featured Ron Wood on pedal steel guitar, Irish fiddler Frankie Galvin, and the composer's emotionally plangent lead vocal. Then three ballads by Mick: "New Faces" (with Lady Jane's harpsichord), "Moon Is Up," and "Out of Tears" with Mick on piano, backing his own maudlin and insincere vocal.

"I Go Wild" had a Keithian two-chord chug and meaningful lyrics from Mick: "waitresses with broken noses checkout girls in striking poses and politicians garish wives with alcoholic cunts like knives." "Brand New Car" was a funny, simmering reexamination of the auto-vaginal metaphor, with the obligatory horns. "Sweethearts Together" was a lovey-dovey Latin cha-cha, sung by Mick and Keith face-to-face in the studio, with an accordian solo by Tex-Mex legend Flaco Jimenez. "Suck on the Jugular" was a funk riff with some good guitar, followed by Mick's "Blinded by Rainbows," a Semtex-scented ballad about "the troubles" in Northern Ireland. It sounded like a leftover from *Wandering Spirit*.

Voodoo Lounge wound down with the Memphis rhythm of "Baby

Break It Down" and Keith's dark soul ballad "Through and Through," which painted a gloomy portrait of betrayal and discovery. This ended the vinyl and cassette release; the CD version had an extra track, "Mean Disposition," an old-school rockabilly hummer with a Chuck Berry tribute tagged onto its tail end. Extra tracks from the *Lounge* sessions (all written by Mick) used as B-sides on the four singles included "The Storm," inspired by the earthquake that rocked L.A. while they were mixing; "I'm Gonna Drive"; "So Young" (Mick resolves to "put my dick back on a leash"); and "Jump on Top of Me," a fast Stones shuffle that was also loaned out to director Robert Altman for his movie on the fashion industry, *Prêt-à-Porter.*

Voodoo Lounge wasn't a great Rolling Stones album, and everyone knew it. Reviews were niggling at best, and "Love Is Strong" didn't sell; but the album reached no. 1 in England and no. 2 in America. It eventually sold a respectable 5.2 million units during the year the band was on the road. Mick was stoic about the record as he prepared to tour. "The ballads are rather nice," he told *Rolling Stone* later, "and then the rock & roll numbers sound enthusiastic—like we're into it. I think it's a good time-and-place album of what the Stones were about during that time in Ireland in that year." He also complained that Don Was and engineer Don Smith were retro-sluts and that they'd "gone too far" trying to make the Stones sound stuck in 1972.

———

After a publicity and merchandising blitz that included a week of Stones videos on the cable channel VH-1 and a warm-up club gig in Toronto, the Stones nervously began the "Budweiser Voodoo Lounge 1994 Tour" on August 1 in RFK Stadium in Washington, D.C. Neo-ruralists Counting Crows opened, sounding like The Band, before the Stones played (poorly) in a ninety-degree steam bath. Pyro sparks landed on Charlie in the fiery climax and burned through his drumheads. The next night in D.C. went a bit better.

With tickets at $50, sales were initially slow and the Stones played to empty seats some nights. Young fans were distracted by new heroes—

Nirvana, Pearl Jam, Soul Asylum, Blind Melon. The Woodstock twenty-fifth-anniversary concerts broke a lot of rock budgets that summer. The Stones would be on the road for three months before the tour broke even.

The band sounded ragged, and Mick had to make excuses for the first few gigs. Charlie looked to Keith and Darryl to pace the Stones, and to Keith and Chuck for the song endings. Watts had the demeanor of a well-dressed, solid old man: "Lloyd Bentsen on drums," New York radio star Don Imus called him. Despite the teasing, Watts drove the Stones like a Porsche and invariably received the longest ovation of the night when the musicians were introduced.

In the middle of August in the middle of America, the Stones finally began to cook, at least on the old songs. An Olympian thunderstorm at Giants Stadium in New Jersey on August 14 drenched the band and provoked the best show of the year. Mick licked the raindrops off the tops of Lisa Fischer's heaving breasts. "God joins the band whenever we play outdoors," Keith said soon after this. "Suddenly there's this other guy in the band, and he shows up in the form of wind and rain. And we've got to be ready to play with him." The Stones' families were along with them for the first dates. Backstage the nomad village looked like a company picnic, with blond kids running around the portable dressing rooms and trailers. Bert Richards presided over a running domino tournament. A white tent—the actual Voodoo Lounge—served as the bar and reception suite. Ronnie's tipple was cranberry juice and vodka. Keith didn't bother with the cranberry juice. It was an ambience in which the regulars could gather round the piano in the tuning room at the end of the day, harmonize on a few songs together, and then go out and play them for sixty thousand customers on the other side of the scrim.

As the shows started, guests took their seats, the entourage took their places, and backstage became empty and quiet. The band met in the tent and walked to the stage together, up some metal stairs and through a tunnel, bantering with the crew along the way. The African drumming on the P.A. slowed to the Bo Diddley beat ("a war-dance fanfare of primal sexual libido and the life force itself"—Camille Paglia). Charlie sat down at the drums and Mick high-stepped to the front of the stage in a curious bopping lope and declaimed, "I'm gonna tell ya how it's gonna be," amid a colossal roar from the multitudes. It was lean and hungry Mick's big maracas number in 1963: now he was a mullet-headed grand-dad whippet in a shiny knee-length coat, the first of many costumes during the show.

Lisa Fischer became a major stage presence on this tour as she undulated beside dreadlocked Bernard Fowler. During the "Miss You" fore-play, she and Mick used their tongues. On sexy nights, she licked his nipples.

During "Honky Tonk Women," the Jumbotron flashed old porno strips intercut with live shots of girls near the stage. "Live with Me" became the hottest number of the night, sliding into a *Sticky Fingers* Latin jam with Bobby Keys. Mick performed "Sympathy" as a top-hatted Lucifer in a Victorian frocked coat. After two hours, the giant balloons came out (Elvis, Kali, and a hydrocephalic baby) for the Big Four: "Start Me Up," "It's Only Rock 'n' Roll," "Brown Sugar," and "Jumpin' Jack Flash." Thunderous fireworks split the evening into wild magnolias of fire as the band ran for their Dodge Ram getaway vans and headed back to the hotel or their custom 727 jet, with four staterooms for the band. As always, especially when their families finally left them alone after two weeks, the party was in Keith's room.

————

In September 1994, the Stones were staying at the Four Seasons Hotel in Boston when they learned that Nicky Hopkins had died of Crohn's disease in Nashville, aged fifty. Bobby Keys went for a long walk by himself on Boston Common, and the plane ride to North Carolina was very subdued.

Late that month, Jimmy Miller died of liver failure at fifty-two.

The Rolling Stones played Las Vegas for the first time in mid-October, two nights in the Big Room at the MGM Grand, as their old Rat Pack tormentor Dean Martin lay dying in Beverly Hills. Mick seemed subdued at the second show. A rumor circulated in Voodoo village that

Jerry Hall had intercepted a fax from Carla Bruni concerning a rendezvous with Mick at the MGM Grand.

Voodoo Lounge ended in America with a record-setting gross said to be $140 million, but the tour had taken a toll on the Rolling Stones legend and the group's self-esteem. Mick was upset that the *Voodoo Lounge* songs "really didn't quite stand up" on the tour. Highbrow critics compared the vulgar spectacle to decadent seventeenth-century court masques that had bankrupted kings and burned down the theaters. Pop pundits found new ways of calling the Stones irrelevant dinosaurs. The whole thing was courting ridicule, and Mick was determined to play down the Stones' gigantism on the rest of the tour. It led to the downsized, "Stripped" shows of 1995.

Keith Richards was unapologetic, as if every day the Stones kept rolling was a gift from the gods. "We're the only band to take it this far," he mused, "and if you see us trip and fall, you'll know that's how far it can be taken."

Working for Jah

The Rolling Stones took their Voodoo Lounge machine to South America in 1995, inspiring fan mania unseen in years. They did four nights in Mexico in January, followed by massive shows in Brazilian soccer stadiums. A February 4 broadcast from Rio over TV Globo was seen by an estimated 100 million people throughout the continent. While in Buenos Aires for five shows, the Stones were mobbed by wildly passionate Argentine kids determined to kiss the group. Several thousand bivouacked outside their hotel, skirmishing with nervous security squads, effectively holding the band prisoner. Argentina's "Dirty War" against its leftist youth had been especially brutal, and Mick made it a point to include "Undercover" during every show at River Plate Stadium.

The Stones spent most of March 1995 in Japan, playing shows in Tokyo and Fukuoka, before an April swing through Australia and New Zealand. They had hoped to play in Beijing, but were refused admittance to China by the communist government, who told the Stones they represented "cultural pollution."

In Japan, the Stones booked into Toshiba/EMI studios to retool some classic tracks for an *Unplugged*-style acoustic concert album instead of what Keith said he dreaded—*Voodoo Lounge Live at the Stadium.* Don Was came in to produce and help arrange the material. In Tokyo, they recorded new versions of "The Spider and the Fly," "I'm Free," "Wild Horses," "Love in Vain" (Ron Wood crying on slide guitar), "Shine a Light" (Don Was on Hammond B3 organ), "Black Limousine," and "Slipping Away." The Stones also cut Willie Dixon's "Little Baby," a revision of Little Walter's "My Babe" that had been recorded by Howlin' Wolf. The Tokyo rehearsals were also filmed for possible broadcast, but the tapes were rejected by the band. "The dullest TV I've ever seen," Mick said, "and boring without an audience." Deploring MTV's *Unplugged* format of old guys on stools, Mick decided to film a few semiacoustic club gigs in Europe that summer.

On May 25, at an auction in London, a thirteen-song tape of Little Boy Blue and the Blue Boys—Mick, Keith, and Dick Taylor playing a dozen rock and roll tunes in 1961—was sold to an anonymous buyer for 50,000 pounds. The tape had been found in an attic in Dartford. London papers revealed a few days later that the new owner of the old tape reel was Mick Jagger.

The Stones built their new club show during rehearsals in Amsterdam in early May by assiduously mining their past. Ron Wood made the group rehearse its first single, "Come On," and even got them to do the flip side ("I Want to Be Loved") as well. The crude mix of folk-blues crusade and electric mojo that was the original Rolling Stones had long been hidden in the repetitious, grandiose posturing of their stadium act. Almost in desperation, the Stones morphed into a hot, pounding rock band that still had something to prove. That summer's Euro tour evolved into a mobile taping party stretching from Holland through France into Portugal and enlivening the thirty-nine shows they performed to mostly sellout crowds.

The Stones recorded and filmed four nights without the horn section at the Paradiso, an Amsterdam cannabis café in an old synagogue, in early May. The Stones' printed set list described the Paradiso shows as "The Toe-Tappers and Wheel Shunters Club Gig." Richards and Wood brought eighty guitars between them. Playing to seven hundred fans, the Stones delivered a blistering acoustic/electric set that began with a jammy "Not Fade Away" and ended with the trio of "Respectable," "Rip This Joint," and "Street Fighting Man," driven by two ringing Martin guitars, as on the old record. "Gimme Shelter" was a stunning showpiece for Lisa Fischer, whose high note at the song's climax was a time portal to the era of *Performance*. Another song from that year, "Live with Me," was now a diamond-hard rap extended in a Sticky jam by Bobby Keys. They played "Connection" like the punk anthem from hell that it was. The apex of the show was introduced by Mick: "This is a song Bob Dylan wrote for us." They gave "Like A Rolling Stone" an almost reverential, anthemic reading, with Mick playing harp more like Little Walter than Dylan. The audience roared along with the chorus, so the Stones kept it in the show for the rest of the tour.

At the party after the last Paradiso gig, Keith said it was the best he could ever remember doing. Mick said, "We're reinforcing that part of our music by doing it in a small place like this. It's part of the band we always need to remember, so we can keep on drawing on it."

The Voodoo Lounge toured Europe through the summer of 1995. The German magazine *Der Spiegel*, noting that the timing of several shows seemed suspiciously identical, accused the Rolling Stones of miming to prerecorded tapes, prompting howling denials and legal threats (the magazine printed a retraction one year later). In early July, the Stones taped and filmed their acoustic show before a berserk and sweltering mob at L'Olympia in Paris, where Charlie Watts got a five-minute chanting ovation during the band introductions. In Paris, Mick gave a birthday party for Jerry attended by Jack Nicholson and many friends. Then on to England for their first shows at home in five years. The three shows at Wembley Stadium were sellouts and received unusually affectionate reviews in the press (which noted that playwright Tom Stoppard, a friend of Mick's, was the only person in the crowd not wiggling his bum). Bill Wyman walked out of one concert after Mick told the audience, "I know you're all worried about our new bass player, but this time we've got one that dances and smiles." Bill was hurt and began slagging the Stones in the press as an oldies group.

On July 19, the Stones deployed their club show at Brixton Academy, the most coveted ticket in London in many years. They kicked off with "Honky Tonk Women" and watched with surprise at how reserved the three thousand fans and friends were. But the emotional dam broke after "Live with Me" and the slide guitar explosion of "Black Limousine." Keith: "Well, you looked down and thought, 'This is like Richmond Station Hotel in '62 and '63.'" At Brixton, the Stones revived "Faraway Eyes" in honor of Jerry, to whom Mick blew kisses. They also plugged away at the old blues "Meet Me at the Bottom."

One of their guests in the balcony was Marianne Faithfull, whose just-published autobiography revealed that she'd had a secret affair with Keith just before she'd taken up with Mick, and that Keith was the best she'd ever had. ("I'm a *lover,*" Keith commented proudly. "I've been trying to tell people this for *years.*") Marianne had fought back her addictions and reemerged as an iconic tortured artist and cabaret star, interpreting the Brecht-Weil canon of Weimar torch songs. She had wanted to sing onstage with Mick in Brixton, but he turned down her request.

On July 27, at a Voodoo Lounge show at Montpelier in southern France, Bob Dylan was the opening act. Dylan was on another leg of his years-long "Never Ending Tour"; like the Stones, he was revisiting his old songs with a great new band and new arrangements.

Ron Wood was dispatched to ask Dylan to sing "Like A Rolling Stone" with them. Dylan, nervous about appearing with the Stones, asked how they handled the chorus. "We leave that to the audience," Wood laughed, and Dylan seemed reassured. "The man who wrote this song is here *in person,*" Mick announced. Dylan came out and stood behind Charlie's drum kit as the song started. Ronnie gently shoved him onstage, but the wise old owl seemed dazed by the lights and wasn't singing. Keith finally gestured him up to the mike, and Dylan managed to croak along with Mick in the chorus.

The tour ended in Rotterdam at the end of August. The numbers—126 shows to 8 million people grossing more than half a billion dollars—added up to the biggest tour ever. The Voodoo Lounge troupe had been together for more than a year, and the last show was emotional. During "Miss You," Mick blurted, "Lisa, I've got to kiss you good-bye," and the scantily clad but vocally formidable Ms. Fischer burst into tears during the band introductions. The tour's final act, before the gear was stored away, was a September 21 video shoot for a single release of "Like A Rolling Stone" at a studio in London's King's Cross, before an audience of two hundred friends.

———

Stripped was released that November, containing fourteen tracks from the Tokyo, Amsterdam, Paris, and Lisbon taping sessions. Reviewers called it the best of all the Stones' live albums, and it reached no. 9 in America. Veteran fans found it charming that the machine operator in "The Spider and the Fly" now looked about fifty, rather than about thirty. "Stop Breaking Down" was again credited to Mr. Traditional, rather than Robert Johnson. Compact disc singles of "Like A Rolling Stone" and "Wild Horses" were released, both with superb concert performances of classic songs. "Gimme Shelter" from the Paradiso, part of the "Wild Horses" CD, is possibly the single greatest live recording of the Stones' career.

Accompanying *Stripped* was a TV documentary about the unplugged Stones, and a *Voodoo Lounge* CD-ROM computer game that featured a "Blues Room" where the Stones paid tribute to their Delta/Chicago ancestors. There also appeared on the bootleg market two sets of boxed CDs that appeared to come from inside the Stones themselves. Both *Voodoo Brew* and *Voodoo Stew* offered console-quality rehearsals and alternative mixes of the *Voodoo Lounge* music. It was all better than the album. One bootlegger released a disc of what appeared to be a secretly recorded haggle with Mick Jagger over the price for some tapes Mick was selling.

When they had finished promoting *Stripped* for the Christmas market, the Stones scattered again. Charlie went back to his Arab horses and his collections in Devonshire, then took Shirley on an African safari. Mick went home to Richmond, then to Indonesia (where he and Jerry could walk around unrecognized) and then to Mustique for the holidays. There was a cancer scare for Ron Wood, who had some minor surgery. At home in Ireland, he had Bo Diddley in his studio and threw a New Year's Eve bash that consumed fourteen hundred pints of stout.

Keith Richards returned to Point of View, his house above Ocho Rios on the north coast of Jamaica. Soon the local Rastas from the village of Steertown came around, and it was, "Hey Bredda Keet—yu ready fe drum?"

Keith: "I went to Jamaica to kick back after the Lounge tour, and there they were, my Rasta friends, who I'd been jamming with since 1972, and they were ready to go. The guy that made some drums for me in 1975 told me they took twenty years to sound good, and he was right on the money, baby."

They spent five days recording a Rastafarian groundation— *Niyabinghi* praise songs accompanied by hand drums—on an eight-track recorder in Keith's living room, with one wall open to the sea. Working at night, they were joined by a jungle chorus of atmospheric tree toads and peepers. Keith worked with a guitar, barefoot and shirtless, and tuned the Rastas to piano keys so he could dub over the music later on. Keith and lead singer Justin Hines had been talking about doing this for many years, but even Keith was surprised by how soulful and fervent the old hymns and chants sounded. He called it "marrow music" and would spend the next year tinkering with his Jamaican tapes.

Platinum Teeth
for Everyone

While Keith developed his Rastafarian project in 1996, Charlie Watts made his fourth and best album of jazz standards, *Long Ago and Far Away,* with the now-ubiquitous Bernard Fowler's smooth and creamy vocals. Charlie toured America that summer and talked about some of his bad times back in the eighties. "They used to call me Dracula," he said. "I was drunk at my father's funeral, and I regret that." Charlie's mother had died earlier in the year, which gave his record a veil of melancholy and memory. Keith dropped in when the Charlie Watts Quintet gigged in New York, along with Marlon and his wife and Keith's two-month-old granddaughter, Ella Rose Richards. Another night, Keith and Patti went to see Marianne Faithfull's cabaret show. Marianne's cigarette lighter failed while she was doing "Smoke Gets in Your Eyes." Keith yelled, "I'll give you a light, baby." Marianne, sultry sandpaper voice and slight smile: "I'll give you a *smoke,* baby."

———

In May 1996, Donald Cammell shot himself at home in the Hollywood Hills. The auteur of *Performance* left behind a short trail of perverse films, music videos, and missed opportunities, having never again risen to the brilliance of his collaboration with Mick Jagger. Cammell was depressed that his last film, *The Wild Ride,* had been shelved by its producers. Perverse to the end, Cammell shot himself in a way that allowed him to bleed to death in a forty-five-minute necro-narcotic stupor. He watched himself die in a mirror. His last words to his wife were, "Do you see Borges?"

———

Around this time, singer Don Covay suffered a stroke that left him almost blind and in a wheelchair. Mick Jagger had patterned his falsetto style after Covay's and felt he owed him something. The Stones quietly bought Covay a custom-built van with a chair lift and various computer-assisted amenities. "Everyone knows the Stones are a great band," their old friend Bobby Womack said, "but I know them as some of the finest people I've ever met."

Mick Jagger was setting up his movie production company, Jagged Films, in 1996 and was spending a lot of time in Los Angeles. He got in trouble in October following an incident in which bodyguards pounded a photographer who had snapped Mick tonguing actress Uma Thurman at the Viper Room. A day later, he allegedly spent the night with a young Czech model at the Beverly Hills Hotel. This got into the British press and Jerry Hall hired Princess Diana's divorce lawyer. Mick flew home to put out the fire, and let it be known that he and Jerry would stay together for the sake of their children.

———

By autumn 1996, the Stones had been off the road for a year, and Keith and Ron were getting itchy feet. There wasn't much talk about the Stones doing a record, so Mick was writing for another solo album, working on "Saint of Me" and "Might as Well Get Juiced." In October, as Allen Klein was finally releasing the 1968 *Rolling Stones Rock & Roll Circus* as an album and video, the Stones gathered in New York for a meeting. Mick thought it too soon for the Stones to make another record, but Keith and Ron insisted. The five years between *Steel Wheels* and *Voodoo Lounge* had made it much harder to sustain the Stones' market position, according to the businesspeople. So Mick gave in, with the provision that they use multiple producers on the new record. Mick didn't want to re-make *Voodoo Lounge*. He wanted "his" tracks realized with hot young techno-producers—the very studio geeks Keith enjoyed deriding as tape doctors, knob turners, and loop gurus.

In early November, Keith and Mick got started at Dangerous Music, a little demo room in Greenwich Village. With Mick on drums and Keith on guitar, they worked on Keith's winding riff for "Lowdown" and three Mick tracks: "Already Over Me," "Always Suffering," and "Anybody Seen My Baby." To London in December and a succession of studios, where Keith's "Too Tight" was developed. As he noodled on a little Mozart or Otis Redding on the piano, Keith waited for new songs to come in. "I realized a long time ago that you don't write songs, you receive them," he said. "You Don't Have to Mean It" started out as a Buddy Holly rock and roll number. Mick cut a rumbling crotch-shot demo of "Might as Well Get Juiced" that was thought by studio insiders to be the best thing he'd ever done. Mick called the song "fake blues for the nineties."

Just before Christmas, a band spokesman announced that the Stones would tour again in 1997. There was critical speculation that doing another tour so soon after Voodoo Lounge meant that the Stones were only in it for the money, but nothing was further from the truth. The Stones and their huge entourage were like a family now, a nomad tribe that had to migrate to survive. "Nobody wants to get off the bus while it's still going, y'know," Keith growled. "It's very difficult. You hurt yourself getting off buses while they're moving."

The working title for the new Stones album was *Blessed Poison*. The ancient songwriting firm of Jagger/Richards met in Barbados in January 1997 for writing sessions. "You Don't Have to Mean It" was taking shape as a reggae groove, and they developed "Out of Control" from the bass line of "Papa Was A Rolling Stone."

In March, the Stones gathered in Los Angeles to record at Ocean Way Studios, where Mick had finished his last solo record. (Ocean Way's venerable Room One was the site of many classic sessions for Frank Sinatra, Phil Spector, and Quincy Jones, among many others.) Mick arrived first and started working with local producers. He cut five tracks with the Dust Brothers (Beck, Beastie Boys) in their studio in the Silver Lake neighborhood; hired hot producer Danny Saber (U2, Garbage) to work on various tracks; took "Already Over Me" to slick R&B producer Babyface for sweetening. Co-executive producer Don Was cranked Dr.

Dre's rap masterpiece *The Chronic* through Charlie Watts's headphones
and had him play along with the whole album, using the tapes as a loop-
ing source for the new songs.

When Keith arrived at the end of the month, he was madder than
hell. He heard what the Dust Brothers had done to the great "Juiced"
demo and went to Silver Lake to see for himself. "Keith hated the Dust
Brothers," according to one engineer. "They were two stoners; one had
the record collection and a bong, the other was the knob turner. They got
this little drum machine called an 808 that everyone used, and it's ticking
away back there. Keith couldn't believe these loop gurus were producing
Rolling Stones tracks. He went like out of his way to insult them in public." Keith met Kenny "Babyface" Edmunds and told him, "You cut with
Mick, your face is gonna look like *mine*. You may be Babyface now, but
you're gonna be *Fuckface* after you get out of the studio with that guy."
One night Keith came to work, found Danny Saber rattling a guitar overdub on a Stones track, and expelled him from the studio. Don Was had
to work with Keith and Mick in separate rooms after that. The first thing
Keith cut, "You Don't Have to Mean It," was done without Mick. Keith
didn't play on "Anybody Seen My Baby," "Saint of Me," and "Out of
Control."

Charlie Watts got through the chaotic and dysfunctional sessions by
having drummer Jim Keltner always at hand. Hot off his own album and
tour, Watts became the driving force in the all-night sessions, which generally lasted until Keith was exhausted at ten in the morning. The manic
energy of "Flip the Switch" (originally a twenty-five-minute jam) and the
percussive crunch of "Gunface" were Watts/Keltner collaborations. Keith
often crashed out in the studio. "Once in the studio, I become a mole," he
explained. "Avoid sunlight at all costs."

The sessions continued in L.A. through April, with Mick commuting between Hollywood and Silver Lake in his black Lincoln Continental.
Keith's mood improved when he settled down. For years, tax and immigration problems had forced the band to record on little islands. "All very
lovely," Keith said, "but you feel isolated, get no feedback, have to draw
on your own resources. In L.A., we had all kinds of great cats dropping

by to lend a hand, guys who *suggest* things." Keith's commandos included Waddy Wachtel, keyboard player Bernie Worrell (from Funkadelic), and Blondie Chaplin, a South Africa–born L.A. musician who had been in the late-period Beach Boys. Bernard Fowler was singing. Billy Preston arranged and played on "Saint of Me." Charlie Watts recruited jazz star Wayne Shorter to play sax. Meanwhile, Mick was already meeting with the designers about the Stones' new touring stage. He went to see U2's Pop Mart tour in San Diego at the end of April and was impressed by their acoustic set, performed on a raised platform in the middle of the stadium, reached by a catwalk extending from the main stage.

Mick ended up not getting along with Babyface after all, and remixed "Already Over Me" himself.

By the time they finished the album, their best in twenty years, the Stones weren't on speaking terms. The last working week was incredibly tense, with Mick boycotting sessions that were completed by Keith's crew and Don Was. Keith and Rob Fraboni had to steal and remix the tapes of "Thief in the Night," written by Keith and his guitar tech Pierre de Beauport. (There was gossip that this track related to problems in Keith's marriage. His wife was reportedly caught up in a Bible-thumping, charismatic Christian sect at home in Connecticut, much to the exasperation of her atheist husband.)

The last three tracks on the album—"Too Tight," "Thief," and "How Could I Stop"—were done without much input from Mick, who was sulking in his tent like Achilles. Mick hadn't wanted to do the record in the first place and had walked out. Keith now countered Jagger's techno-grooves by overdubbing upright bass (played by Jeff Sarli) on several key tracks for some extra-classic rockabilly bomp. "What about the *roll*?" Keith asked rhetorically. "I want the *roll*. Fuck the rock—I've had enough of it."

On the morning of the last session (for "How Could I Stop"), Charlie Watts and Wayne Shorter played a crashing, wailing crescendo to end the album once and for all. "Right!" shouted Ron Wood. "That's platinum teeth for everyone in the room!" A few hours later, Charlie caught the night flight to London Heathrow and home.

Keith and his crew only heard that Mick liked their tapes when the girlfriend of Fred Sessler's son reported that a friend of hers, who was sleeping with Mick, confided that Mick had played them for her and said, "Isn't this great?"

———

July 1997. Bob Dylan was staying with Ronnie in Ireland, working on the songs for his late-period masterpiece *Time Out of Mind.* Keith was at home at Redlands that summer, obsessively playing the tapes of the Stones' new album, now titled *Bridges To Babylon.* Late one afternoon, his daughter Angela and a friend were having their tea and listening to "Anybody Seen My Baby," which would be the first single, when they started singing along with different words. It turned out Mick had unconsciously appropriated the melody to k. d. lang's "Constant Craving." Keith made some quick calls and there was panic at the record company. The CD was already pressed, the video already shot in the New York subway. But k. d. lang said she was flattered and accepted a cowriting credit. Keith, who hadn't even played on the track, made Mick pay k.d. out of his pocket since it was Mick's mistake, one that Keith had long dreaded making himself.

Would You
Let Your Granny?

August 1997, and the Stones rolled into Toronto to rehearse for the Bridges to Babylon tour. Keith was in rough shape, trying to stay off dope against heavy odds. (Reportedly he was dabbling with heroin for the first time in years.) His old drummer friend Bongo Jackie (Vincent Ellis) had died in Jamaica while they were finishing the Rasta album, and Keith was very upset. Patti Hanson's sister died, a tragedy that staggered the whole family. Keith missed his grandfather and displayed a framed picture of Gus Dupree in his scarf-draped, incense-fumed rooms. His rented house was called Doom Villa by his minders and the tour crew.

Keith snapped like a guitar string one Saturday night while he stewed and paced alone in the rehearsal studio as Ron Wood led a raucous group watching a prizefight in the next room. Keith had to carry his sister-in-law's coffin the next day and had asked Wood to stay with him. But Wood had money on Julio Cesar Chavez. No one dissed the guv'nor like this, *no one.* When the clueless Wood finally staggered into the studio, Keith grabbed his neck and started to throttle him in a red-face fury until he was physically pried off him. Everyone was deeply shocked. "I made a mistake," Keith said later. "I wasn't compos mentis. But in a band, anyone got a problem, it's best to flash it out straightaway."

On August 18, the Stones were in New York, driving across the Brooklyn Bridge in a red '55 convertible, Mr. Jagger at the wheel. Cameras beamed their progress to two hundred journalists waiting at a site under the bridge, enduring speeches by the presidents of Virgin and the phone company Sprint, the tour sponsor. When Mick arrived, he mocked the scribes, announcing he'd always wanted to be a journalist. He jumped down among them and started the questions: "Rolling Stones—I have a question. Will this be your last tour?"

Keith: "Yes—and the next five."

The tour would start in Chicago in September. Darryl Jones was still in the band. Opening acts included the Dave Matthews Band, Sheryl Crow, Blues Traveler, Foo Fighters, and Smashing Pumpkins. The stage was another Mark Fisher environment, supposed to evoke a lost Sumerian city in the desert. An eye-shaped sixteen-hundred-square-foot Jumbotron screen, the most sophisticated yet built, presided over the set like an omnipotent, all-seeing deity. Naked forty-foot big-nippled Golden Amazons in chains were built by the balloon company, and Mick had ordered a telescoping bridge that would arc over the crowd and carry the Stones to the rising small stage in the middle of the stadiums where they would play their old-school club set. The sound, lights, video, and pyro were all controlled by backstage technicians using laptop computers.

Keith Richards explained the big-bridge metaphor to the French magazine *Rock et Folk:* "Babylon, you see, is the outside world. And our music is the bridge between that world and mine."

———————

The black and blue funk riff that opened "Anybody Seen My Baby" was a signal that the Stones were back with another radio-friendly rock ballad when the single was released at the end of August 1997. The song came out as Princess Diana was killed in a car wreck with Dodi al-Fayad, a London playboy who'd dated Jo Howard just before she met Woody. The idolatrous public mourning for the divorced princess annoyed Keith, and he lashed out in the press at Elton John, who had sung at her funeral, as an opportunist who "writes songs for dead blondes." Bitchy Elton shot back that Keith looked like a monkey with arthritis.

Bridges To Babylon came out in September as the Stones were playing warm-up gigs at small clubs in Toronto and Chicago. An often-superb collection of thirteen tracks, *Bridges* was about a third Mick's, a third Keith's, and a third a mix of the two. It was also an unexpected work of art, played with more fire and conviction than the Stones had deployed in years. The rearing Parthian lion that guarded the CD jewel box seemed emblematic of the fierce energy that inhabited the work. Surprised reviewers even compared *Bridges* to exalted *Exile on Main Street.*

In a long career of black albums, *Babylon* was an especially noir dream. "Flip the Switch" was manic hard rock from the death chamber and the fastest song they'd ever cut. "Anybody Seen My Baby" was stark urban isolation and dementia. Keith's "Lowdown" was a swaying threat display and a demand for the bitter truth in an ambiguous sexual situation. "Already Over Me" was drenched in regret. Danny Saber's torchy production of "Gunface" gave it a rusty edge of sexual rage, validated in Mick's comment that it was a song about a guy who wanted to kill his woman's lover.

The sun came out briefly for Keith's "You Don't Have to Mean It," the best reggae song the Stones ever cut. Then "Out of Control" and its turbulent descent into obsession and emotional dislocation. No song of Mick Jagger's, with its hothouse ambience of hotel sex with a stranger, had ever come so close to describing its writer's desires and compulsions as "Out of Control," and the Stones backed it up with a churning throb that approximated a wandering spirit in serious torment. "Might as Well Get Juiced" was now a dusted drama of techno-funk, tinged with alcoholic despair. "Always Suffering" was another Jagger Bakersfield-style country weeper. The burning open G rock and roll of Keith's "Too Tight" had ominous warnings and furious threats buried in the lyrics. His "Thief in the Night" was the dark, stalking rumination of a jealous husband in a brooding soul setting. "Yeah, it's a story," Keith later said. "Every guy's been there, been thrown out and tried to get back in again. That's what it's about." "Thief" faded into the gentler reconciliation of "How Could I Stop," Keith in his Hoagy Carmichael sentimental mode, with a soul chorus. The album ended with Wayne Shorter blowing a moonlight mile on sax, and Charlie's cymbals ringing like a Javanese gamelan—music for antique shadow puppets in the Digital Age.

———

September 1997. There was a big press campaign for the album and the tour (sample London headline: "Would You Let Your Granny Go with a Rolling Stone?"). In public, Keith preached peace in the valley. "Mick's my mate, the longest friendship I've ever had. There's no possibility of divorce—we have to take care of the baby." He also preached war, calling in print for all the gang-banging gansta rappers to finish each other off after Tupac Shakur and Notorious B.I.G. had been murdered. "We never had the Temptations killing the Four Tops," Keith dryly observed.

———

The Bridges tour opened in Chicago on September 18, 1997, with astonishing digital sound clarity but without a bridge, whose arrival was delayed until ten shows in. The ensemble was the same as on Voodoo Lounge, with the addition of Blondie Chaplin on vocals and percussion on Keith's songs. The shows were roughly divided by Mick into four acts. Act One started with the Stones' logo on the "Eye of the Lion"

Jumbotron, dissolving into a ghastly liquid gold tongue as Jurassic roars flooded the air. Explosions! Nothing less than a rogue comet burst in the Eye of the Lion as Keith strode up in a fake-tiger-fur jacket to start "Satisfaction" amid erupting fireworks. A sampling of oldies—"19th Nervous Breakdown," "Let's Spend the Night Together"—led into the new songs of Act Two: "Anybody Seen," "Saint of Me," and the showstopping "Out of Control." Act Three was a random song chosen nightly by absent friends on the Internet; this was so often "Under My Thumb" that they added it to the show. Then Keith's pair of songs: "All About You" and "Wanna Hold You" early in the tour; "Thief in the Night" and "You Got the Silver" later on. The Stones then traversed their bridge and became the B-stage Bar Band, which often featured "It's Only Rock 'n' Roll," "The Last Time" (provoking a shower of bras and knickers), and "Like A Rolling Stone." Act Three ended with the band walking the bridge back to the main stage while samba drums pounded on tape and Mick changed costume in the dark for "Sympathy." Act Four was the Warhorse Suite: "Dice," "Honky Tonk Women," "Start Me Up," "Jack Flash." The encores were often "You Can't Always Get What You Want" and "Brown Sugar" amid a stupefying barrage of explosive glitter and fireworks.

The tour gathered momentum as it lurched around America during a chilly autumn. Blues Traveler (from New Jersey) opened the early shows, and Mick broke their harp player's heart when he refused to allow him onstage with the Stones during their last opening gig in Philadelphia. Mick complained that John Popper played too many notes and ordered Wood to fuck off when he tried to intercede for Popper. Missouri rock chanteuse Sheryl Crow joined the tour as opening act in Boston in October, an arrangement more suitable to Keith and Wood, who liked hanging out with the thirty-something ingenue, who idolized them. Unsubstantiated romantic rumors about Keith and Crow were allowed to filter out from the tour.

The fall months were unseasonably cold that year, and Mick Jagger, freezing, was working in a coat and hat. His hands were often too cold to play guitar on "Miss You," now an obituary piece as the screen flashed images of revered dead musicians: Muddy, Duke, Brian. "I don't know how you do it," he told the rest of the shivering band in a backstage huddle before the bridge came out in frigid Nashville.

In Oklahoma the next day, Sheryl told Keith and Ron that she'd been cold onstage too. "I bet your nipples were fucking *huge*," Wood deadpanned. "They were as hard as—" Crow started, but Wood interrupted her. "I bet you could get *Radio Luxemburg* on them!" They were in the Baboon Cage, Keith's hotel suite (so-called after a reviewer described him as "an ageless, grinning baboon"), doing an interview for an English rock mag. Keith was rolling joints while Wood poured and planted smooches on good-natured Sheryl's cheek. Wood sent a minder up to his suite for a harmonica and then tried to teach Sheryl "Ain't Got You." Keith got annoyed, snatched the harp, and tried to throw it out the window.

Ronnie, loaded on vodka and cranberry juice, tried to tell the interviewer that he was working all the time when Keith erupted. "You do shit-all! Working all the time? *I'm* working all the time. You do fucking nil, asshole."

Wood: "Keith, man, I'm working with *you.* C'mon . . . just 'cause you covered my ass in Nashville . . ."

Keith: "*I'm* the fucking sucker who covers *your* fucking arse all the time, shithead." Dead quiet in the room.

Wood: "Well, just for the last couple of weeks."

They looked over at a dumbstruck Sheryl Crow amid shocked silence and started to laugh. Keith: "Sorry about that."

———

Keith's Jamaican album was released that autumn on his own new label, Mindless Records. *Wingless Angels* was an hour of Rastafarian passion and tree toads, a documentary of spirit, smoke and laughter. Keith took the Jamaican heartbeat rhythms and decorated them with airs from the Irish and English sea chanties and quadrilles that informed traditional Jamaican melody. He got the idea of adding a bass after hearing the old Wailers song "This Train." This soulful synthesis even impressed Justin Hinds, who loved the album—much to Keith's relief. *Wingless Angels* was the work of a scholar and a true connoisseur. Critics called it Keith Richards's Jajouka. Keith insisted that listening to the Wingless Angels was good for you. "These people understand the necessity for trance in one's life," he advised.

———

By the end of the year, with the tour settling in for a long haul, Mick introduced Ron Wood as "stark raving bonkers." (Other nights he called him "barking mad.") The heart of the show was "Out of Control." On the instrumental break the Stones cut loose and turned into a harp-driven, fire-breathing blues dragon presenting a tense, tightly organized blues movie, as cogent and vital as any in their career. Despite all the jokes about the Stones as leathery relics, the Rolling Stones were the kings of showbiz, the biggest act in the world. They had already grossed 90 million dollars. *Bridges To Babylon* sold about 4 million copies in its first year of release. They had nowhere to go but onward.

On December 12, Jerry Hall gave birth to Mick's second son, Gabriel Jagger. Soon Mick's romantic life would spin out of control, and change everything for the true king of rock and roll.

Cynical Nostalgia Merchants

January 1998. The Rolling Stones moved their Babylonian circus indoors in New York and ratcheted up their price: $300 got you a seat around the B-stage for one of three nights at sold-out Madison Square Garden. Indoors, the Stones and their video screen were a lurid, vivid visitation. "When the Whip Comes Down" and "Rip This Joint" were revived. A diaphanous cloud of expensive, freshly shed lingerie enveloped the band during the miniset of "Little Queenie," "Let It Bleed," and "Like A Rolling Stone." Mick hung the biggest bras and sexiest knickers as trophies on his mike stand. The Stones grossed $6.5 million from the shows. In February in Las Vegas, they charged $500 a night at the Hard Rock

Hotel with Sheryl Crow opening. "It's only money," Mick shrugged to *Rolling Stone*. Then Pepsi-Cola paid the band $3 million for a private concert for its employees at a beach resort in Hawaii after they'd spent a million to use "Brown Sugar" in a commercial. No one except the Stones seemed to recall that the song was named for potent Chinese heroin and a black dancer.

Meanwhile, Bill Wyman was touring Europe with a new R&B band, the Rhythm Kings, playing clubs and dumping on the Stones. He told interviewers that he left the Stones because their music annoyed him. Georgie Fame was in his band, and Eric Clapton sat in on some dates as well. "My life is more exciting now that I'm not a Rolling Stone," the luckiest man in the world said, at the age of sixty-one.

———

In Brazil, Mick met a twenty-year-old lingerie model named Luciana Morad at a party at a rich man's house. According to Luciana, she stayed on the road with Mick for several months. When she pursued him for child support later on, she sued him under the names Mick Jagger and David James, his *nom d'hôtel*.

While in Rio, Ron Wood and his family went for a boat ride. The cabin cruiser caught fire and Wood and Co. had to be rescued by the paparazzi who were following them in a chase boat. The rapacious photographers had gotten a lot of bad press when they were accused of causing the death of Diana Spencer the year before. Wood now had a different view. "Thank God for the paparazzi. Sometimes they save lives."

———

The Stones did thirty-six shows in rain-soaked Europe that summer. Early dates were postponed when Keith cracked some ribs in May, supposedly falling off a library ladder. (This provoked puzzlement among those who wondered why a rock star was reaching for a book in the first place.) Many of the shows were washouts, and Mick was fighting laryngitis. His voice went south in Spain, and there were canceled shows in Italy and France. At the immense Nuremburg Zeppelinfeld,

Keith began his part of the show by saying, "Great to be back. Great to be here. Great to be *anywhere*."

Five nights in the hash-hazed Amsterdam Arena were reviewed by the London critics. "His face looks like month-old cat litter," wrote one, "but Keith Richards still plays like a gifted yet disturbed child." One writer called them "cynical nostalgia merchants who rely on antique hits. Thank God." At the Dutch shows, the Stones' backup singers were joined by pretty blond Leah Wood, twenty. After she sang on "Thief," Keith brought her up, kissed her cheek, and introduced her: "She's not mine, she's one of Ronnie's."

In August, the Stones finally made it to Russia. They'd tried to play Moscow in 1967 but had been told *nyet* by the cultural commissars. Back then, Stones albums circulated on underground discs cut from used X-ray film on which the grooves of vinyl records could be stamped. (These were known as "bones" for the faintly visible X-ray images.) The Stones played in Luzhniki Stadium in a cold rain before fifty thousand mostly middle-aged Russians, who couldn't believe the Stones had come at last. "Better late than never," Mick announced. They chanted "Satisfaction" word for word with the band at the top of their lungs. "I was a communist in college," Mick said before the show. "But then things tend to fall away, and you become more pragmatic."

The Bridges To Babylon tour ended with a show in Istanbul, Turkey, in late August, done mostly as a favor to Ahmet Ertegun. Keith skipped the end-of-tour party. The Stones had played 107 shows to 4.75 million fans over two years, grossing almost $300 million. After thirty-six years, they were still the biggest band in the world.

After the last show, Mick took his family to the Turkish coast for a vacation, then slipped back into tax exile in a discreet Paris hotel, where he was joined by his Brazilian girlfriend. He gave an interview to the *Times* in which he said his life was like "being trapped in a soap opera." He revealed that his kids liked to ransack his stage clothes from the seventies. "Dad," they'd say, "how could you wear *that*?"

The record company wanted *Bridges To Babylon Live at the Stadium*, and that's what it got, except the ten-track live album was called *No Security* instead. Rather than duck the problem of gigantism, they attacked instead, recording the ambience of packed soccer stadium sing-alongs and windswept acoustics. Most of the tracks were taken from the Amsterdam shows. A sing-along "Saint of Me" and a dark, driven "Out of Control" were from Buenos Aires. Other tracks were from Nuremberg, St. Louis, and a 1997 MTV broadcast. Released in early November 1998, in time for the Christmas market, *No Security* promptly bombed. Ridiculed in the press, it became the first Stones album in years not to make the Top Ten, and sold only in the low six figures. Mick later claimed he listened to it only once.

The Stones decided to stay on the road to promote the album. On November 16, designer Tommy Hilfiger announced that his clothing company would sponsor the Stones' No Security arena tour beginning in January 1999. "How can we stop?" Keith asked a reporter. "*You* tell me. When you've got a band rocking under you like that, you can give up thinking and just let it flow. I don't make plans. Why should I stop?"

The end of 1998 was rough for Mick Jagger, and it would get worse. Luciana was four months gone and told Mick the baby was his. The papers in London got the story and reported she was being paid to keep her mouth shut. Jerry and Mick patched things up for the holidays, with the massive rift between them passed off as a spat over fourteen-year-old Elizabeth Jagger's modeling career.

In January 1999, as the Stones prepared to go back on the road in America, Jerry Hall filed for divorce. "Every day it was in the papers," she told an interviewer. "Public humiliation and private heartbreak. It's not easy for any woman, and it doesn't do a lot for your confidence." When her children began to be disrespectful and mocking to her, Jerry told Mick not to come home. "I realized I was setting a terrible example," she said. The whole year would be spent in a battle over divorce and money, but Jerry Hall never seemed to lose her esteem for the wayward father of her children. "Mick's a wonderful man," she said, "and a terrible husband."

Anita, Recalled to Life

By the end of the 1990s Anita Pallenberg had created a new
kind of legend for herself on the streets of London, where she could be
seen speeding by on her ten-speed bike. Sober for more than a decade,
she lived in an elegant flat by the river, a stone's throw from her old house
in Cheyne Walk. To those who knew her story, Anita was now seen as an
inspirational and still-beautiful symbol of recovery and the road back
from addiction and its harrowing half-life.

Anita: "After the [1977] Toronto bust, we were supposed to clean
up, but I never did. We did this electric ["black box"] treatment with Meg
Patterson, which didn't work because there was no input from us. I went
along, happy that I could do as much drugs as I wanted, by myself. Then
Keith and I got separated by the lawyers. I went on a deadly binge, scoring in [Manhattan's] Alphabet City, a nonstop party for years. If I ran out,
I'd drink—even more lethal.

"I bottomed out for about five years. I was depressed, didn't move
from the couch. We lived on Long Island after that kid shot himself in my
house, staying in various places because they used to throw us out. Sands
Point. Old Westbury. I had a neighbor who kept retired racehorses. She'd
take a bottle of beer and inject horse tranquilizers with a syringe and I
would drink it. Three days, no idea what I was doing. I'd wake up in New
York, didn't know how I'd got there.

"Then my son started to intervene, hide the bottles, hide the
money—some things a child shouldn't have to do. No friends over, lots
of arguments. I was accident-prone—falling down, emergency room,
straitjackets . . . Oh, man.

"I went to London [in the early 1980s] to renew my visa—I was still an Italian citizen—but started having visa trouble with the U.S. and decided to stay. I was drinking heavily, stumbling around. I tore my hip out of its socket falling out of bed. There was an operation, then pneumonia. I ended up in a famous alcoholic ward: horrible withdrawal from drink and drugs, mattresses on the wall, sweating, paralyzed. Nightmare NA [Narcotics Anonymous] meetings where everyone seemed stoned to me.

"After eight weeks, I had to leave the hospital. I managed to find a flat—Marlon was living with Keith's father and a friend—and I stayed clean for six months, then relapsed. I was able to detox at a clinic in Kent after that, then moved to a halfway house in Notting Hill Gate. It was on Portabello Road, the front lines of London drug addiction every day . . . *but it managed to stick*. I did a lot of service, worked on the telephone help line, did office work. I rode my bicycle every day, and gradually the drug obsession was replaced by something physical. I went to the gym. My bicycle was almost like a crutch to me. I rode everywhere, spoke at meetings, treatment centers. You know—'serve by example.' I went back to school at St. Martin's College and studied textile design for four years.

"I've stayed sober now for a long time. Now I feel I can do anything I want to, a great sense of freedom. Getting this back was the hardest thing I've ever done, also the most rewarding. But it still didn't change my role in society. I'm still an outsider in a world where everyone drinks and you don't. Now I'm looking for a niche, a place where I can fit in. I feel like I've got all the time in the world. My children and grandchildren are around me, and I'm clean. Keith and I are friends again. He's married, and I'm respectful of that. On New Year's, the whole family gets together in Jamaica and we all have a good time.

"Life is more graceful for me now, more dignified. I see Ringo and Eric and Elton—all the people who made it over—and it's fascinating.

"Don't ask me about the past anymore. It's just mythology anyway. I *do* believe that the rock heroes are part of mythology. The comparisons are almost bewildering. When you talk about the Stones, you might as well be talking about Cadmus, Mercury, Artemis. It's the same thing.

"I always had loads of imagination, but not much business sense.

This always made me feel like a failure, a weak link in the chain of the Stones. I felt like I was supposed to come across as something gigantic and marvelous. Now I'm happy doing what I'm doing."

––––––––

In September 1998, Anita and Keith's daughter Angela Richards married a carpenter in a London church. Raised in Dartford by Keith's mother, Angela was a young woman of twenty-six who loved horses and lived in a modest flat near where she'd grown up. With the whole Richards family present, she was escorted down the aisle by her proud father, to the strains of "Angie."

Gather No Moss

In January 1999, the Rolling Stones moved back indoors, starting the thirty-four show No Security tour at the Oakland Arena. This was a lite edition of their stadium show, crammed with jukebox hits and light on gimmicks. The stage was bare except for the black and yellow tailboard motif at the edges. Fabric covers on the stage monitors, visible only to the musicians, bore pictures of Bob Marley and Little Walter.

The show began with a video clip of the band walking through the bowels of an arena like gladiators or the last gang in town. "Jumpin' Jack Flash" was given a high-speed launch before the Stones settled into a two-hour routine that ignored recent songs except "Out of Control" and "Saint of Me," which had been a popular sing-along in Europe. In Oakland, the Stones gave the concert debuts of "Moonlight Mile" and "Some Girls." Mick singing about some girls giving him children—and he'd only made love to them once!—got a knowing cheer from the audience. Keith Richards, sporting doodads and ribbons in his spiky gray coiffure, played a miniset that included "You Got the Silver" and "Before They Make Me Run" to the delight of his fans.

The tour sold out through the West and Midwest that winter. The Stones, liberated from the artistic shackles of their operatic stage set, were mixing surprise oldies into the shows. Bobby Keys's horns punched in and out with show band discipline. The Stones were a well-oiled dynamo that year, master musicians who sometimes seemed like they really could play the stars from the sky.

Those close to Mick Jagger knew that his current intensity was related to the disintegration of his family in London. Jerry wanted a chunk of his estimated half-billion-dollar fortune. His lawyers responded to her divorce petition by claiming that their 1990 wedding in Bali was invalid. Even Mick's friends thought that effectively bastardizing his four children with Jerry was too much. The press let fly. "Was it ever cool to be despicable?" asked the *Daily Mail*. "Was it ever sexy to be penny pinching and selfish? Of course not!" The *Times* mocked Jagger as "a rather pathetic old roué, desperately trying to recapture his long vanished youth by pursuing girls as young as his two older daughters."

Mick refused comment, but later blamed his solicitors. His daughter Elizabeth kept him company while the Stones stayed on tour. In Rio, a pregnant Luciana Morad flaunted her belly on a Carnival float, as if she were carrying the child of some god. Jerry Hall declared war. She called Patti Hanson and warned her that Rupert Lowenstein might not be their friend, and they better find out where their money was. Then Patti got annoyed because Keith didn't seem to give a shit where his money was. "I don't talk to Mick about his love life," Keith said, "because it's like, 'Whoops—you've skidded on another banana skin.'" Keith remained stoic about his friend's *amourettes*. "I'm always sorry for Mick's women, because they end up crying on my shoulder. And I'm like, 'How do you think *I* feel? I'm *stuck* with him.'"

No Security opening acts included the GooGoo Dolls, the Corrs, and blues infant Johnnie Lang. Mick and Keith notched some serious blues cred by starring on three tracks of *Blues Blues Blues,* a tribute album by Chicago guitarist Jimmy Rogers. ("Don't Start Me to Talkin'," "Trouble No More," and "Goin' Away Baby" had been recorded at Ocean Way as a favor to Ahmet Ertegun.) The Stones reshuffled their show when the tour reached the Northeast in March and April. Keith was doing "Thief" and "You Don't Have to Mean It," with Leah Wood joining the singers for his set. Bobby Troupe died during the tour, so the Stones added "Route 66" to the B-stage set, along with "Cloud" and a spare, harp-driven "Midnight Rambler," now devoid of sadomasochist belt-whomping. "Respectable" was transcendent on some nights. Charlie Watts was incredible on a revived "Paint It, Black." Lisa Fischer pretended to chase Mick during "Brown Sugar," and the encore was usually "Sympathy for the Devil."

After some shows, Mick went on the prowl. He made a date with Andrea Corr, but she had the sense to show up with her brother and their manager. In Boston for two nights, Mick picked a pretty girl out of the crowd at the first show and shouted at her to come to the Four Seasons Hotel. She dutifully showed up and spent the night with "David James." She returned the next night as well, but was told Mr. James had checked out. He was really upstairs, partying with a new friend.

Johnnie Lang opened the last few No Security shows, joined onstage by Leah and, in her singing debut, Elizabeth Jagger. They sang with him again at a club show in Chicago with Mick looking on. (Lang wanted to hire the girls but was told to forget it.) The tour ended on April 20 in San Jose. "Good night! You've been great! God bless you!" Mick shouted as the band walked off. The cheering went on for so long that Keith finally came back, in his bathrobe, to wave a last good-bye.

————

May 1999. The Stones rehearsed in Amsterdam for eleven postponed Bridges To Babylon shows (with a No Security flavor) outdoors in Europe that spring. Sheryl Crow opened in Poland, France, Spain, and Italy, joining the Stones onstage to do "Honky Tonk Women" with Mick.

In London on June 8, they played a theater gig at the Shepherd's Bush Empire. With the balcony full of guests (Anita, Jerry, Marianne, Pete Townshend, Page and Plant, Aerosmith, a Spice Girl), the Stones erupted into "Shattered" and shook everyone up. There had been buzz in the press that Marianne wanted to sing "Sister Morphine" with Mick, but instead he joked that she was going to do a number with Charlie. Then the Stones slipped "All Down the Line" and "Melody" into the show, perhaps in tribute to Billy Preston, who was doing prison time in California for a drug conviction.

A few nights later, the Stones finally played the Wembley Stadium concerts they had notoriously postponed for tax reasons. Still recovering from Shepherd's Bush, the jaded troupers listlessly phoned the shows in—to many empty seats. Keith, garrulous and looking loaded as he dipped into the crowd for high fives, was laughed at for the jujus in his hair. Mick's performance resembled an aerobic workout. Ron Wood seemed distracted. Charlie's roll-collar shirt was described in the papers as unforgivable.

But it didn't really matter. When the tour ended in Cologne, Germany, late that June, it was reported that the Stones had grossed $300 million. In America, *Amusement Business* magazine calculated that the Rolling Stones had become the highest-earning band in history. It was all about folklore now, and the Stones could do no wrong.

The Stones then disappeared for years.

————

Mick Jagger settled a reported $8 million on Jerry Hall and reluctantly admitted paternity of Lucas Jagger, born in May 1999, after the boy passed a court-ordered blood test. Though divorced, Mick moved next to his former Richmond home to be near his kids, but the arrangement didn't work out because he was jealous of Jerry's (much younger) dates. Learning the film business, he spent four years coproducing the independent thriller *Enigma*, with a screenplay by his friend Tom Stoppard. He also started a company that broadcast cricket matches on the Internet.

Mick was present, with his mum, at his old school when Dartford Grammar opened the Mick Jagger Centre, a music facility he had helped pay for. On Mustique, Mick was elected chairman of the trust that oversaw the education of the island's children. In his late fifties, Mick was a complex multiple of personae and interests, a connoisseur of high culture and low life, a micromanager and horn dog who lived for his work and his fun. His famous face was now heavily lined, with a broad crease down his left cheek. A full head of hair dyed a youthful brunette was incongruous with his weathered skin and pallor.

When his mother died in the summer of 2000, friends said Mick took it very hard. Later that year, he had to rescue his daughter Jade, famous as a twenty-nine-year-old jewelry designer and party girl unhappy over a failed romance with the grandson of Harold Macmillan. When Jade and her two daughters, Assisi and Amba, were injured in a car wreck on Ibiza, where they lived, Mick evacuated them to London by private jet before the police could investigate. He also chaperoned Elizabeth, sixteen, while she modeled on the Manhattan catwalks during a week of fashion shows. Mick escorted Elizabeth and her friends to concerts and clubs, and none of the kids seemed to mind her old dad tagging along.

Charlie Watts released *The Charlie Watts/Jim Keltner Project,* a CD with a global village twist that fused world beat, techno, and jazz in tribute to the pair's favorite drummers, recorded mostly during the 1997 *Bridges* sessions. Bill Wyman toured Europe by bus with his low-key R&B group. In interviews, the sixty-something Bill (father of three young daughters by his second wife) spoke of his continuing relief at being retired from the Rolling Stones. Mick Taylor, still playing with his trademark melodic flow, was also touring with a good band of his own that mixed airy fusion jazz and hard rocking blues. Many fans still deeply regretted that Taylor had ever left the Rolling Stones.

Ron Wood kept his head down while the Stones were on hiatus. Finally in the money, appearing to enjoy a permanent alcoholic binge, he bred thoroughbreds on his award-winning Irish farm and also lived comfortably in Richmond. He was the main investor in London's newest private club, the Harrington, which served only organic food and closed at midnight. In June 2000, Ron Wood checked into the Priory clinic, Brian Jones's old haunt, for alcohol rehabilitation.

As for Brian, his fan club raised funds for a statue of the late Mr. Jones in Cheltenham by selling tiles from the swimming pool in which he had drowned. His white teardrop Vox guitar hung on a wall at the Hard Rock Cafe in Honolulu. A small but devoted cult remembered Brian Jones as a brilliant and troubled rebel and scapegoat, a reckless bastard angel who taught those who tried to follow him how a real rock star should live, and die.

Keith Richards, who enjoyed his vodka mixed with Sunkist orange soda, moved between his homes in Jamaica and Connecticut. In the ragged glory of his late fifties, Keith seemed to embody Victor Hugo's maxim: "He who is a legend in his own time is ruled by that legend." He worked on an all-star blues album with guitarist Hubert Sumlin and turned up at film screenings, prizefights, and the occasional party in New York. He took his teenage daughters to see the boy band 'N Sync. He spent time with his ailing father, who winked at Keith just before he died in 2000. A few months later, Keith told a friend he was still getting off on that wink. That summer, Keith rented a house on the resort island of Martha's Vineyard, off the New England coast. He brought along his own bottle of Stolichnaya when he went to hear reggae bands at the local nightclub, the Hot Tin Roof, and eyed the place as a potential tour rehearsal retreat for the Stones until his plans were derailed.

In 2001 the Rolling Stones wisely stayed off the road amid an uncertain atmosphere of economic recession and twenty-first century weirdness. Jack Nitszche died in Los Angeles, followed by John Phillips just as his 1978 album featuring the Stones—*Pay Pack and Follow*—was finally released. George Harrison died at the end of the year, a blow. He'd gotten the Rolling Stones their record deal. He liked to tease Keith about how the cops had waited for him to leave before raiding Redlands back in 1967.

Mick spent the year sketching out film projects and recording his fourth solo album. The songs on *Goddess in the Doorway*, described by

Mick as ranging "from slightly introverted mysticism to comedy love letters," featured cameo performances by Bono, Pete Townshend, Aerosmith's Joe Perry and Wyclef Jean. *Goddess* was a not-bad, emotional, old-school rock album that was unfortunately released by Virgin just as America was blasted into a new reality on September 11, 2001. (Prophetic lyric in *Goddess*'s "Too Far Gone": "What was once the tallest spire / Is just a building crumbling down.") A few weeks later, in October, Mick and Keith appeared at "The Concert for New York," a benefit for the survivors, and performed "Salt of the Earth" and a version of "Miss You" with some of the naughty bits left out.

Goddess in the Doorway was a disaster. The single "God Gave Me Everything" died with the Taliban. In England sales of the album were so embarrassingly slow that one newspaper launched a facetious new charity—"Mick-Aid." The paper offered anyone who bought the disc a badge that said, "I did my bit for the old git." Ridicule was just a kiss away for the aging rock stars. The BBC sitcom *Stella Street* had a running skit featuring Mick 'n' Keef as owners of a corner shop in Surbiton, on the outskirts of London.

To promote his record, Mick performed one set in a tiny L.A. club to an audience of young models who had been paid $100 each to mime having a great time. "This is the world tour for this album," Mick told his crowd. "You can say you were at every gig." The video of this show was spliced onto the end of "Being Mick," a self-produced hour-long TV show broadcast in America on Thanksgiving night. An artful attempt to reposition its subject as a dutiful family dad and portray Jerry Hall as a nagging harridan, "Being Mick" offered tantalizing glimpses of Mr. Jagger's houses and children, but nothing could save the goddess in the doorway from her fate.

In early 2002 the Rolling Stones overcame the half-hearted reluctance of their sixty-year-old master drummer and decided to tour later in the year, in what insiders saw as their final bow before Mick and Keith turned sixty themselves. A Stones box set went into production, with "a few" new songs developed in the basement studios of Keith's house in

Connecticut. Ron Wood was sent to Arizona for another attempt at rehab. In May 2002 the Stones stepped out of a yellow blimp with a tongue logo that had touched down in a Bronx park and announced what was then called "Rolling Stones on the Road: World Tour 2002/2003 Arena/Stadium/Club." Beginning in Boston in September 2002, the forty-year-old group would tour through four continents over the next year, playing three separate shows with different stagings and set lists in venues of all sizes. Mick: "Either we stay at home and become pillars of the community, or we go out and tour. And we couldn't find any communities that needed pillars." Darryl Jones was back on bass, as was Chuck Leavell on keyboards. Opening acts confirmed for the tour included blues guitarist Buddy Guy, Sheryl Crow, No Doubt, and Jonny Lang. Asked once again how long the Stones could keep it up, Keith cracked, "Until the undertaker pulls up to the door." Ticket prices would average about $75, prompting a reporter to ask why the Stones were charging more than Sir Paul McCartney, who was touring at the time. Keith just shrugged. "There's more of us," he said.

———

One night during this period, Keith and Patti went to a movie premiere at Carnegie Hall in New York. When they came out the back door, a waiting fan handed Keith a vintage Telecaster and asked him to autograph it. Without breaking stride, Keith jumped into his limo with the guitar and took off. The fan chased the limo down 56th Street, begging for his guitar back. When he caught up with the car, Keith's driver jumped out and snarled, "Go fuck yourself—buy another guitar." Mr. Keith Richards sped off into the night, possibly playing a Chuck Berry lick—"You Can't Catch Me"—on the latest addition to his famed guitar collection.

Around then an interviewer had the temerity to ask Keith if he would ever retire. "Why in the world would you stop doing what you like to do?" he replied. "If we ever do a tour and nobody turns up, then I go back to the top of the stairs where I started. I'll just play to myself."

Selected Sources

Ali, Tariq. *Street Fighting Years*. London: Collins, 1987.

Amis, Martin. "The Rolling Stones at Earls Court." In *Visiting Mrs. Nabokov*. New York: Harmony, 1993.

Anderson, Christopher. *Jagger*. New York: Dell, 1993.

Appleford, Steve. *The Rolling Stones: It's Only Rock 'n' Roll*. London: Carlton, 1997.

Aronowitz, Al. "A Night with Bob Dylan." *New York Herald Tribune*, December 12, 1965.

———. "Over His Dead Body." *New York Post*, July 6, 1969.

Bailey, David. "Coming of Age in Swinging London." In *The Sixties*. New York: Random House, 1977.

———. *David Bailey's Rock and Roll Heroes*. London: Thames & Hudson, 1997.

Berry, Chuck. *Chuck Berry: The Autobiography*. New York: Harmony, 1987.

Bockris, Victor. *Keith Richards: The Biography*. New York: Poseidon, 1992.

Bonanno, Massimo. *The Rolling Stones Chronicle*. London: Plexus, 1998.

Booth, Stanley. *Dance with the Devil*. New York: Random House, 1984.

———. *Keith*. New York: St. Martin's, 1995.

——. *The True Adventures of the Rolling Stones.* New York: Vintage, 1985.

Bowles, Paul. *Two Years Beside the Strait: Tangier Journal 1987–9.* London: Peter Owen, 1990.

Brown, Mick. "The Final Cut." *Daily Telegraph* (London), May 9, 1998. Donald Cammell profile.

Brunning, Bob. *Blues: The British Connection.* Poole, England: Blandford, 1986.

Bulgakov, Mikhail. *The Master and Margarita.* London: Harvill, 1967.

Buell, Bebe, with Victor Bockris. *Rebel Heart.* New York: St. Martin's, 2001.

Bungey, John. "Mick Taylor's Goodbye." *Mojo,* November 1997.

Burroughs, William. *APO-33: A Metabolic Regulator.* San Francisco: Beach Books, 1967.

——, and Daniel Odier. *The Job.* 2nd rev. ed. New York: Grove Press, 1974.

Cahoon, Keith. "Jagger Tour Rolls in Japan." *Rolling Stone,* May 5, 1988.

Cammell, Donald. *Performance.* Unpublished shooting script. London: Goodtimes Enterprises, 1968.

Carr, Roy. *The Rolling Stones: An Illustrated Record.* New York: Harmony Books, 1976.

——. "Keef: I've Only Fallen Over Twice in 15 Gigs!" *Creem,* December 1978.

——. "No Stones in '77 and No Sex Pistols in '78!" *Creem,* January 1979.

Chang, Kevin, and Wayne Chen. *Reggae Routes: The Story of Jamaican Music.* Philadelphia: Temple, 1998.

Chapman, Rob. "The Bittersweet Symphony." *Mojo,* July 1999.

Charone, Barbara. "Bruce and Taylor's Band of Misfits." *Rolling Stone,* July 17, 1975.

——. "I Want to Go out on a Limb." *Crawdaddy,* August 1976. Mick Jagger interview.

——. *Keith Richards.* New York: Dolphin, 1982.

——. "Mannish Boy Gets What He Needs." *Creem,* January 1978.

——. "Peter Tosh." *Creem,* March 1979.

Clark, Ossie. *The Ossie Clark Diaries.* London: Bloomsbury, 1999.

Cohen, Rich. "It's Show Time!" *Rolling Stone,* August 25, 1994.

——. "Tour de Force." *Rolling Stone,* November 2, 1994.

Connelly, Christopher. "Jagger Steps Out." *Rolling Stone,* February 14, 1985.

Cooper, Michael, and Terry Southern, et al. *The Early Stones.* New York: Hyperion, 1992.

Coral, Gus, and David Hinkley. *The Rolling Stones: Black and White Blues, 1963.* Atlanta: Turner, 1995.

Cott, Jonathan. "Back to a Shadow in the Night." *Rolling Stone,* September 11, 1975.

———. "Jean-Luc Godard." *Rolling Stone,* June 14, 1969.

———, and Sue Cox. "The Rolling Stone Interview: Mick Jagger." *Rolling Stone,* October 12, 1968.

Creswell, Toby. "Jagger Scores Down Under." *Rolling Stone,* November 17, 1988.

Cutler, Sam. "Old Scores." Unpublished memoir, 1996.

Dahan, Eric. "Rolling Stones: L'Eternel Retour." *Rock et Folk,* October 1997.

Dalton, David. "1968 A Very Good Year." Album notes. *The Rolling Stones Rock and Roll Circus.* ABKCO, 1995.

———. *The Rolling Stones.* London: Star, 1975.

———. "The Rolling Stones Circus." *Rolling Stone,* March 19, 1970.

———. *Rolling Stones.* New York: Amsco, 1972.

———. ed. *The Rolling Stones: The First Twenty Years.* New York: Knopf, 1981.

Davis, Stephen. "Cold Steel People Don't Like." *OUI,* March 1981. Keith Richards interview.

———. "A Conversation with Peter Tosh." *OUI,* November 1979.

———. *Jajouka Rolling Stone.* New York: Random House, 1993.

———. "The Recycled Stones: Oldies and Outtakes." *Rolling Stone,* August 14, 1975.

———. "Rolling Stones in Jamaica." *Rolling Stone,* January 18, 1973.

Denning, Penelope. "Gathering No Moss." *Irish Times,* October 1, 1998. Bill Wyman interview.

Des Barres, Pamela. *I'm with the Band.* New York: Beech Tree, 1987.

DiMartino, Dave. "Jimmy Miller." *Mojo,* December 1994.

diPerna, Alan. "Rock and Roll Babylon." *Guitar World,* October 1987.

Doeschuck, Robert. "Keith Richards." *Musician,* November 1997.

Donahue, Tom. *An Interview with Mick Jagger.* Promotional LP. Rolling Stones Records, 1971.

Doyle, Tom. "One Careful Owner." *Q,* April 1996. Stones mobile unit.

Dr. John [Mac Rebennack] with Jack Rummel. *Under a Hoodoo Moon.* New York: St. Martin's, 1994.

Dylan, Bob. Liner notes. *Another Side of Bob Dylan.* New York: Columbia Records, 1964.

———. *Writings and Drawings.* New York: Knopf, 1973.

Elliott, Martin. *The Rolling Stones Complete Recording Sessions 1963–1989.* London: Blandford, 1990.

Everett, Todd. "Rolling Stone Gathers Respect for the Man Who Made It All Possible." *Los Angeles Herald Examiner,* October 9, 1987.

Faithfull, Marianne, and David Dalton. *Faithfull.* Boston: Little, Brown, 1994.

Fielder, Hugh. "Restart Me Up." *Pulse!* March 1993. Mick Jagger interview.

Flanagan, Bill. "Mick Jagger." *Musician,* April 1985.

———. "Mick Jagger's New Licks." *Musician,* March 1993.

———. "Stones at the Crossroads." *Musician,* May 1986.

Flippo, Chet. "Keith Richards Meets the Mounties and Faces the Music." *Rolling Stone,* May 5, 1978.

———. "Nothing Lasts Forever." *Rolling Stone,* August 21, 1980.

———. *On the Road with the Rolling Stones.* New York: Dolphin, 1985.

———. "Shattered." *Rolling Stone,* September 7, 1978.

———. "The Stones Serve Keith's Sentence." *Rolling Stone,* May 31, 1979.

———. "Teenager Dies in Keith Richards' New York Home." *Rolling Stone,* September 6, 1979.

———. "World's Greatest Performing Band Bewilders the South." *Rolling Stone,* July 17, 1975.

Fong-Torres, Ben. "Cooder Played, Jagger Danced." *Rolling Stone,* October 29, 1970.

———. "That's the Way He Planned It." *Rolling Stone,* September 16, 1971. Billy Preston profile.

Frame, Pete. *Rock Family Trees of the Early Sixties.* London: Omnibus, 1997.

Fricke, David. "Dutch Treat." *Rolling Stone,* July 13, 1995.

———. "The Rhythm Twins." *Rolling Stone,* September 4, 1997.

———, and Robert Sandall. *Rolling Stones: Images of the World Tour 1989–1990.* New York: Fireside, 1990.

Gatten, Jeffrey N., ed. *The Rolling Stone Index.* Ann Arbor: Popular Culture, 1993.

German, Bill. "Boogie with Stu." *Beggar's Banquet,* vol. 1, nos. 20 and 21, 1981.

———. "Keith Richards: A Stone Unturned." *Spin,* October 1985.

Giuliano, Geoffrey. *The Rolling Stones Album.* New York: Viking, 1993.

Graff, Gary. "The Naked Truth." *Guitar World,* February 1996. Keith Richards interview.

Graham, Bill, and Robert Greenfield. *Bill Graham Presents.* New York: Doubleday, 1992.

Graves, Robert. *Collected Poems.* New York: Doubleday, 1961.

Greenfield, Robert. "Goodbye Great Britain: The Rolling Stones on Tour." *Rolling Stone,* April 15, 1971.

———. "The Rolling Stone Interview: Keith Richard." *Rolling Stone,* August 19, 1971.

———. *S.T.P.: A Journey Through America with the Rolling Stones.* New York: Dutton, 1974.

Grogan, Emmett, *Ringolevio.* Boston: Little, Brown, 1972.

Gysin, Brion. "Moroccan Mishaps with the Strolling Ruins." In *The Rolling Stones: The First Twenty Years,* edited by David Dalton. New York: Knopf, 1981.

———. "The Pipes of Pan." *Gnaoua,* Spring 1964.

Hall, Jerry, with Christopher Hemphill. *Jerry Hall's Tall Tales.* London: Elm Tree, 1985.

Hamilton, Richard. "Swingeing [sic] London 1967." Photolithograph poster. Milan: ED 912, 1968.

Harris, Sheldon. *Blues Who's Who.* New Rochelle, N.Y.: Arlington House, 1979.

Heath, Chris. "Babylon by Jet." *Rolling Stone,* March 5, 1998.

———. "Notes from the Babylon Bar." *Rolling Stone,* December 12, 1997.

Hector, James. *The Complete Guide to the Music of the Rolling Stones.* London: Omnibus Press, 1995.

Henderson, David. *Jimi Hendrix.* New York: Doubleday, 1978.

Hewat, Timothy. *Rolling Stones File.* London: Panther, 1967.

Hill, Doug, and Jeff Weingrad. *Saturday Night Live.* New York: Beech Tree/Morrow, 1986.

Hoffman, Bill. "Mick Jumped on Me." *New York Post,* March 5, 1999.

Hoskyns, Barney. "The Good Ol' Boy." *Mojo,* July 1998. Gram Parsons profile.

———. "Keith Richards." *Mojo,* November 1997.

Hotchner, A. E. *Blown Away.* New York: Simon & Schuster, 1990.

Ingham, John. "Say Goodnight Keith." *Blast,* October 1976.

Isaacs, James. "Watts Nu?" *Roogalator,* November 1969.

Jackson, Laura. *Golden Stone.* New York: St. Martin's, 1992.

———. *Heart of Stone.* London: Blake, 1997.

Jasper, Tony. *The Rolling Stones.* London: Octopus, 1976.

Jones, Brian. Liner notes. *Brian Jones Presents the Pipes of Pan at Joujouka.* Rolling Stones Records, 1971.

Jones, Peter. "The Stones on America." *The Rolling Stones Book #2.* July 1964.

Kent, Nick. "Back to Zero." *Spin,* August 1986.

———. *The Dark Stuff.* London: Penguin, 1994.

———. "Mick Jagger Hits Out at Everything in Sight." *New Musical Express,* October 15, 1977.

———. "Outcasts All Their Lives." *New Musical Express,* October 1973.

King, B. B., with David Ritz. *Blues All Around Me.* New York: Avon, 1996.

Kooper, Al. *Backstage Passes and Backstabbing Bastards.* New York: Billboard, 1998.

Kutina, Scott. "Keith Richard." *Guitar Player,* November 1977.

LeBlond, Philippe. "Mick Mac." *Rock et Folk,* March 1985.

Lipcik, Roman. "The Stones' Czech Invasion." *Rolling Stone,* October 4, 1990.

Loder, Kurt. "Mick Jagger." *Esquire,* April 1993.

———. "The Stones: Is It All Over Now?" *Rolling Stone,* May 5, 1987.

Lomax, Alan. *The Land Where the Blues Began.* New York: Pantheon, 1993.

MacCabe, Colin. *Performance.* London: British Film Institute, 1998.

Mailer, Norman. *Pontifications.* Boston: Little, Brown, 1982.

Manoeuvre, Philippe. "Le Nomade." *Rock et Folk,* March 1979. Keith Richards interview.

Marcus, Greil. "Let It Bleed." *Rolling Stone,* December 27, 1969.

Marsh, Dave. "I Call and Call and Call on Mick Jagger." *Rolling Stone,* September 11, 1975.

———. "Mick Jagger: I Can Get It Up, but I Can't Get It Down." *Creem,* August 1975.

———. "Rolling Stones Are Born Not Made." *Rolling Stone,* November 1, 1977.

McLagan, Ian. *All the Rage.* London: Sidgwick & Jackson, 1998.

Melly, George. *Revolt into Style.* London: Penguin, 1970.

Miles. "Mick Jagger: Interview." *International Times,* May 1968.

———. *The Rolling Stones: A Visual Documentary.* London: Omnibus Press, 1994.

Morley, Paul. "Not Fade Away (and Radiate)." *New Musical Express,* June 28, 1980.

Murray, Charles Shaar. "Too Rolled to Stone?" *Creem,* August 1976.

Nelson, Paul. "Nicky Hopkins—'Session Man.' " *Rolling Stone,* May 17, 1969.

Neville, Richard. *Play Power.* New York: Random House, 1970.

Nolan, Tom. "Taj Mahal." *Rolling Stone,* January 4, 1969.

Norman, Philip. *Symphony for the Devil.* New York: Simon & Schuster, 1984.

Obrecht, Jas. "Filthy, Filthy, Filthy!" *Guitar Player,* December 1992. Keith Richards interview.

———. "Inside the Voodoo Lounge." *Best of Guitar Player,* 1994.

Oldham, Andrew Loog. *Stoned.* London: Secker & Warburg, 2000.

Paglia, Camille. "The Stones." *Boston Phoenix,* September 1, 1994.

Palmer, Robert. *Deep Blues.* New York: Viking, 1981.

———. "Jagger Finishes First Solo Album." *New York Times,* January 28, 1985.

———. "Jajouka: Up the Mountain." *Rolling Stone,* October 14, 1971.

———. "Memphis Hosts Stones." *Rolling Stone,* August 14, 1975.

———. "More Hot Rocks." Album review. *Rolling Stone,* February 1, 1973.

———. *Rock and Roll: An Unruly History.* New York: Harmony, 1995.

———. *The Rolling Stones.* Garden City, N.Y.: Doubleday, 1983.

———. "The Rolling Stones Gather Strength." *New York Times,* June 29, 1980.

———. "What Makes the Rolling Stones the Greatest Rock and Roll Band in the World." *Rolling Stone,* December 10, 1981.

———. "Still the Stones?" *Rolling Stone,* December 5, 1985.

Peellaert, Guy, and Nik Cohn. *Rock Dreams.* New York: Popular Library, 1973.

Perry, John. *Exile on Main Street: The Rolling Stones.* New York: Schirmer, 1999.

Phillips, John. *Papa John.* New York: Doubleday, 1986.

Pidgeon, John. "The Back Line Gets Out Front." *Creem,* November 1978.

Pond, Steve. "It's Only Rock 'n' Roll." *Live!* October 1997.

Rawlings, Terry, and Keith Badman. *Good Times Bad Times.* London: Complete Music 1997.

Regan, Marilou. "Drumming Up Business with Charlie." *Stones People Magazine,* no. 7 (1987).

Richards, Keith. "Well, This Is It." Booklet notes. *Robert Johnson: The Complete Recordings.* Columbia Records, 1990.

Robinson, Lisa. "On the Road to Buffalo." *Creem,* December 1975.

———. "Mick Jagger." *Hit Parader,* December 1977.

———. "Mick Jagger." *Interview,* February 1985.

———. "Richards Still Rollin'." *New York Post,* October 8, 1987.

———. "Tax Exiles on Main Street." *Vanity Fair,* November 2000.

The Rolling Stones. *Cocksucker Blues.* Directed by Robert Frank, 1972. Unreleased video.

———. *Gimme Shelter.* Directed by Albert and David Maysles, 1970. ABKCO Video, 1991.

———. *Live at the Max.* Directed by Julian Temple. Polygram Video, 1991.

———. *The Rolling Stones Rock and Roll Circus.* Directed by Michael Lindsay-Hogg, 1968. ABKCO Video, 1995.

———. *Stripped.* London: UFO Music, 1995.

———. *Sympathy for the Devil.* Directed by Jean-Luc Godard, 1970. ABKCO Video, 1994.

———. *25 x 5: The Continuing Adventures of the Rolling Stones.* CMV Video, 1989.

———. *Video Rewind.* Directed by Julian Temple. Vestron Video, 1984.

———. *Voodoo Lounge.* Directed by David Mallet. Polygram Video, 1994.

———. *Voodoo Lounge CD/ROM.* Second Vision/GTE Entertainment, 1995.

———. *Voodoo Lounge World Tour 1994/95.* Toronto: Brockum, 1994.

———. with Pete Goodman. *Our Own Story.* London: Corgi, 1964.

———, with Jools Holland and Dora Leowenstein. *The Rolling Stones: A Life on the Road.* London: Virgin Books, 1998.

Roud, Richard. *Jean-Luc Godard.* 2nd ed. Bloomington: Indiana University Press, 1970.

Sanchez, Tony. *Up and Down with the Rolling Stones.* New York: William Morrow, 1979.

———, with John Blake. *Up and Down with the Rolling Stones.* 2nd ed. London: Blake, 1991.

Sandall, Robert. Booklet notes. *Jump Back: The Best of the Rolling Stones.* London: Virgin Records, 1993.

Sandford, Christopher. *Mick Jagger: Primitive Cool.* London: Gollancz, 1993.

Santoro, Gene. "Keith Richards." *Guitar World,* March 1986.

Scaduto, Tony. *Mick Jagger: Everybody's Lucifer.* New York: Berkley, 1975.

Schiff, Stephen. "Mick's Moves." *Vanity Fair,* February 1992.

Schneider, Karen S. "Love in Vain." *People,* February 1, 1999.

Sessums, Kevin. "Honky Tonk Women." *Vanity Fair,* September 1989.

Shapiro, Harvey, and Caesar Glebbeek. *Jimi Hendrix Electric Gypsy.* New York: St. Martin's, 1990.

Shrimpton, Jean, with Unity Hall. *Jean Shrimpton: An Autobiography.* London: Ebury Press, 1990.

Simmons, Sylvie, et al. "The Aristocrats." *Mojo,* January 2002.

Sinclair, David. "But What Can a Poor Boy Do?" *Mojo,* May 1999.

Smith, Patti. "Jag-ahr of the Jungle." *Creem,* 1976.

Solway, Diane. *Nureyev: His Life.* New York: Morrow, 1998.

Southern, Terry. *Now Dig This.* New York: Grove, 2001.

———. "Riding the Lapping Tongue." *Saturday Review,* January 1973.

———, et al. *The Rolling Stones on Tour.* Paris: Dragon's Dream, 1978.

Stein, Jean, with George Plimpton. *Edie.* New York: Knopf, 1982.

Stern, Sol. "Altamont." *Scanlan's,* March 1970.

Stewart, Ian. Album notes. *Rocket 88.* Atlantic Records, 1981.

Tarlé, Dominique. *Exile.* Guildford [UK]: Genesis, 2002.

Thackray, Jerry. "Rolling Stones and Sheryl Crow." *Vox,* January 1998.

Thompson, Thomas. "The Stones Blast Through the Land." *Life,* July 14, 1972.

Tooze, Sandra B. *Muddy Waters.* Toronto: ECW Press, 1997.

Tremlett, George. *The Rolling Stones.* London: Futura, 1974.

Trudeau, Margaret. *Beyond Reason.* New York: Paddington Press, 1979.

Turner, Tina, with Kurt Loder. *I, Tina.* New York: Morrow, 1986.

Udovitch, Mim. "Keith Richards." *Details,* December 1995.

Vyner, Harriet. *Groovy Bob: The Life and Times of Robert Fraser.* London: Faber, 1999.

Wallis, Dave. *Only Lovers Left Alive.* New York: Dutton, 1964.

Warhol, Andy. *The Andy Warhol Diaries.* Edited by Pat Hackett. New York: Warner Books, 1989.

———. "A Stones Tea." *Interview,* November 1977.

———, and Pat Hackett. *POPism: The Warhol '60s.* New York: Harcourt Brace Jovanovich, 1980.

Weitzman, Steve. "Keith Richards Interview 1977." *Gig,* October 1977.

Wenner, Jann. "Jagger Remembers." *Rolling Stone,* December 14, 1995.

———. "L.A. Friday Night." *Rolling Stone,* September 11, 1975.

———. *Lennon Remembers.* San Francisco: Straight Arrow, 1971.

Wheeler, Tom. "Keith Richards." *Guitar Player,* April 1983.

Wheen, Francis. *Tom Driberg.* London: Chatto & Windus, 1990.

White, George R. *Bo Diddley, Living Legend.* London: Castle, 1995.

Wild, David. "The Rolling Stones." Concert review. *Rolling Stone,* March 4, 1999.

Wilde, Jon. "The Gangster of Pop." *Independent Magazine,* April 10, 1993.

Williams, Hugo. "Freelance." *Times Literary Supplement.* March 12, 1999. Tara Browne profile.

Williamson, Nigel. "As Time Goes By." *(London) Times Magazine,* November 14, 1998. Mick Jagger interview.

Winner, Langdon. "Captain Beefheart." *Rolling Stone,* April 1, 1971. Ry Cooder interview.

Wohlin, Anna, and Christine Lindsjoo. *The Murder of Brian Jones.* London: Blake, 1999.

Wolfe, Tom. *The Kandy-Kolored Tangerine-Flake Streamline Baby.* New York: Farrar, Straus & Giroux, 1965.

Wolff, Daniel. *You Send Me.* New York: Morrow, 1995.

Woodward, Bob, *Wired.* New York: Pocket Books, 1984.

Wyman, Bill, with Ray Coleman. *Stone Alone.* New York: Viking, 1990.

Zwerin, Mike. "Life After the Stones." *International Herald Tribune,* October 1, 1996.

Acknowledgments

Robert Altman, Ben Arons, Bashir Attar, David Bieber, John Bionelli, Boston Athenaeum, Boston Public Library, Paul Bowles, British Library, Lev Bronstein, Bebe Buell, Donald Cammell, John Catta, Chilmark Free Public Library, George Chkiantz, Graham Coster, David Dalton, Jeanne d'Arc, Christopher B. Davis, Hana and Howard Davis, India Davis, Lily Davis, Graham Dawes, Pamela des Barres, Bo Diddley, Sly Dunbar, Ed Dwyer, Maria Evangelinellis, Mick Fleetwood, Rob Fraboni, Holly George-Warren, Christopher Gibbs, Ivry Gitlis, Bill Glasser, Jean-Luc Godard, Elizabeth Gorzelani, Alan Greenberg, Brion Gysin, Tom Hamilton, Levon Helm, Adrienne Irvine, James Isaacs, Michael Jackson, Jajouka, Nick Johnson, Al Kooper, Wendy Laister, Dominic Lamblin, Helene Lee, W. M. F. Magicel, Jim Marshall, Mario Medious, Herbie Miller, James Miller, "Minnie," *MOJO*, New York Public Library, Jack Nitzsche, Cherie Nutting, Michal Ochs Archives, Roy Pace, Anita Pallenberg, Robert Palmer, Randy Paulsen, Joe Perry, John Phillips, Billy Preston, Retna, Keith Richards, *Rolling Stone*, Joel Rubiner, Amelia

Salzman, Bill Shinker, David Silver, Peter Simon, Vivian Simon, Richard
Skidmore, Roger Steffens, Gary Stromberg, Hubert Sumlin, Peter Swales,
Mick Taylor, Peter Tosh, Rona Tuccillo, Steven Tyler, Mike Verge,
Wenner Media, Stu Werbin, David Winner, Meg Wolf, Ande Zellman, Joel
Zoss.

Thanks to the great crew at Broadway Books and Random House:
Kim Cacho, Maria Carella, Rebecca Cole, Charlie Conrad, Heather
Flaherty, Rebecca Holland, Gerald Howard, Mark Hurst, Lawrence
Krauser, Marni Lustberg, and Shauna Toh, who cut some sharp riffs of
her own.

Thanks to Susan Vermazen for her great eye.

Thanks to American Airlines, especially John Spano.

Special thanks to David Vigliano for being so cool.

*"It took the people from England to hip my people—
my* white *people—to what they had in their own backyard."*

Muddy Waters

Index

Photo Credits

Chapter Openings
Chapter 1: Michael Ochs Archives. Chapter 2: Graham Dawes. Chapter 3: Blue Hills Archive. Chapter 4: Michael Ochs Archives. Chapter 5: Blue Hills Archive. Chapter 6: Michael Ochs Archive. Chapter 7: © Jim Marshall®. Chapter 8: Peter Simon. Chapter 9: Michael Ochs Archives. Chapter 10: Gary Gershoff/Retna.

Photo Insert 1
Page 1: Graham Dawes Archive. Page 2: Michael Ochs Archive. Page 3: Blue Hills Archive. Page 4: Michael Ochs Archives. Page 5: David Redfern/Retna. Page 6: Mangold/Camera Press/Retna. Page 7: John Kelly/Retna. Page 8: Michael Ochs Archives.

Photo Insert 2
Page 1: Michael Ochs Archives. Page 2: Michael Ochs Archives. Page 3: Michael Ochs Archives. Page 4: © Robert Altman/altmanphoto.com. Page 5: © Robert Altman/altmanphoto.com. Page 6: Peter Simon. Page 7: Peter Simon. Page 8: Top, Peter Simon; bottom, Joel Rubiner.

Photo Insert 3
Page 1: Patrick Lichfield/Camera Press/Retna. Page 2: Photo by Robert Altman from *Rolling Stone*, August 19, 1971. © By Straight Arrow Publishers, Inc., 1971. All Rights Reserved. Reprinted by Permission. Page 3: TIMEPIX/© Jim Marshall®. Page 4: Michael Putland/Retna. Page 5: Charlyn Zlotnick/Michael Ochs Archives. Page 6, *top and bottom*: Michael Ochs Archives. Page 7: Michael Putland/Retna. Page 8, *top*: Peter Simon. Page 8, *bottom*: Charlyn Zlotnick/Michael Ochs Archives.

Photo Insert 4
Page 1: Alan Davidson/Camera Press. Pages 2 and 3: Cherie Nutting. Page 4: Duncan Raban/All Action/Retna. Page 5: Dave Hogan/All Action/Retna. Page 6: Dave Hogan/All Action/Retna. Page 7: Jan Bown/Camera Press/Retna. Page 8: Peter Simon.

Stephen Davis is a veteran journalist and the
author of many books, including the international bestsellers
Hammer of the Gods, Walk This Way, and *Bob Marley.*
He lives with his family in New England.